Japan's
Foreign Policy
After the Cold War
Coping with Change

T0386515

Studies of the East Asian Institute, Columbia University

THE EAST ASIAN INSTITUTE OF COLUMBIA UNIVERSITY

The East Asian Institute is Columbia University's center for research, publication, and teaching on modern East Asia. The Studies of the East Asian Institute were inaugurated in 1962 to bring to a wider public the results of significant new research on modern and contemporary East Asia.

Japan's Foreign Policy

Gerald L. Curtis, Editor

Michael Blaker

John Creighton Campbell

David A. Titus

Nathaniel B. Thayer

T. J. Pempel

Frances McCall Rosenbluth

Timothy J. Curran

Michael W. Donnelly

Norman D. Levin

Martin E. Weinstein

Susan J. Pharr

Byung-joon Ahn

Motohide Saito

Se Hee Yoo

Dennis T. Yasutomo

Yasuhiro Ueki

After the Cold War
Coping with Change

An East Gate Book

LONDON AND NEW YORK

An East Gate Book

First published 1993 by M.E. Sharpe

Published 2015 by Routledge
2 Park Square, Milton Park, Abingdon, Oxon OX14 4RN
711 Third Avenue, New York, NY 10017, USA

Routledge is an imprint of the Taylor & Francis Group, an informa business

Library of Congress Cataloging-in-Publication Data

Japan's foreign policy after the Cold War: coping with change /
Gerald L. Curtis, editor.
p. cm. —(Studies of the East Asian Institute)
"An East gate book."
Includes bibliographical references (p.) and index.
ISBN 1-56324-216-8 (cloth)
1-56324-217-6 (pbk.)
1. Japan—Foreign relation—1945–
2. Japan—Foreign economic relations.
I. Curtis, Gerald L.
II. Series.
JX1577.Z5   1993
327.52—dc20
93-9483
CIP

ISBN 13: 9781563242175 (pbk)

To James William Morley,
teacher, friend, and mentor

Contents

Contributors

Byung-joon Ahn is professor of political science at Yonsei University and author of numerous works on Korean-Japanese relations.

Michael Blaker is currently a visiting fellow and advanced research fellow at the Program on U.S.-Japan Relations, Harvard University. A specialist on Japan's domestic politics and foreign affairs, his published work includes *Japanese International Negotiating Style* (1977) and, as editor, *Japan at the Polls*, (1976).

John Creighton Campbell is professor of political science at the University of Michigan. He is the author of *Contemporary Japanese Budget Politics* (1977) and *How Policies Change: The Japanese Government and the Aging Society* (1992).

Timothy J. Curran is general manager, Office Automation Group, Panasonic Communication and Systems Company in Secaucus, New Jersey.

Gerald L. Curtis is professor of political science and past director of the East Asian Institute at Columbia University. He is author of *The Japanese Way of Politics* (1988), and numerous other works on Japanese politics and foreign policy and U.S.-Japan relations.

Michael W. Donnelly is associate dean, Faculty of Arts and Sciences, University of Toronto. He has written on a variety of topics regarding Japanese politics and is currently completing a study of Japan's nuclear power industry.

Norman D. Levin has been at The RAND Corporation, Santa Monica, California since 1979 except for the years 1984–87 when he was on the policy planning staff, U.S. Department of State. He has written on East Asian regional security issues, Japanese security policy, and U.S. policy in Asia including "Japan's Defense Policy: The Internal

Debate," in Harry Kendall and Clara Joewono, eds., *ASEAN, Japan and the United States* (1990).

T.J. Pempel is professor of political science, adjunct professor of business, and director of the Center for Comparative Politics at the University of Colorado, Boulder. From 1972 to 1991 he was on the faculty at Cornell University and from 1980–85 he was director of Cornell's East Asia program. Among his numerous books and articles are *Policy and Politics in Japan: Creative Conservatism* (1982), and "The Unbundling of 'Japan, Inc.'," *Journal of Japanese Studies* 13, no. 2 (1987).

Susan J. Pharr is the Edwin O. Reischauer Professor of Japanese Politics and director of the Program on U.S.-Japan Relations, Harvard University. She is also the chair of the department of government. She is author of numerous works on Japanese politics, foreign policy, and society including *Political Women in Japan* (1981) and *Losing Face: Status Politics in Japan* (1990).

Frances McCall Rosenbluth is an assistant professor of political science at UCLA. Her books include *Financial Politics in Contemporary Japan* (1989) and, with Mark Ramseyer, *Japan's Political Marketplace* (1993).

Motohide Saito is associate professor of international relations at Kyorin University in Tokyo. He is coauthor of *International Relations in the Cold War* (1987) and his many articles on Moscow-Tokyo relations include "The Evolution and Evaluation of Gorbachev's Japan Policy," *Keio University's Journal of Law, Politics and Sociology*, Vol 65, no. 2 (1992).

Nathaniel B. Thayer is director of Asian studies and holds the Yasuhiro Nakasone Chair in Japanese Studies at the Nitze School of Advanced International Studies at the Johns Hopkins University. He is author of *How the Conservatives Rule Japan* (1968), "Beyond Security: United States-Japanese Relations in the 1990s," *Journal of International Affairs* 43, no. 1 (1989), and numerous other works on Japanese politics and foreign policy.

David A. Titus is professor of government at Wesleyan University where he has taught since 1966. He is author of *Palace and Politics in Prewar Japan* (1974) and "The Making of 'Symbol Emperor System' in Postwar Japan," *Modern Asian Studies* 14, no. 4 (1980).

Yasuhiro Ueki is attaché and researcher in residence at the Permanent Mission of Japan to the UN. Formerly, he was information officer in the UN Secratariat. He is author of "Japan's Approach to UN Peacekeeping and Peacemaking," the Ralph Bunche Institute on the UN, CUNY, December 1992.

Martin E. Weinstein is director of the Mansfield Center at the University of Montana, Missoula and former professor of political science at the University of Illinois. He also has held the Japan Chair at the Center for Strategic and International Studies in Washington and served as special assistant to the United States ambassador in Tokyo from 1975–77. His publications include *Japan's Postwar Defense Policy, 1948–1967* (1970), *Northeast Asian Security After Vietnam* (1982) and *The Human Face of Japan's Leadership: Twelve Portraits* (1989).

Dennis T. Yasutomo is associate professor of government and director of the East Asian Studies Program at Smith College. His publications include *The Manner of Giving: Strategic Aid and Japanese Foreign Policy* (1986) and "Japan and the Asian Development Bank: Multilateral Aid Policy in Transition," in Bruce C. Koppel and Robert M. Orr, Jr., eds., *Japan's Foreign Aid: Power and Policy in a New Era* (1993).

Se Hee Yoo is professor of political science and director of the Institute for Sino-Soviet Studies of Hanyang University, Seoul, Korea. His writings on East Asian politics include "Korea's Domestic Politics and Korean-Soviet Relations," *Chung-So Yon'gu* 14, no. 2 and "International Context of U.S.-Korea Relations," in Robert Scalapino and Sungjoo Han, eds., *U.S.-Korea Relations* (1986).

Preface

This volume is the result of a collaborative effort among seventeen individuals who received their doctoral training under the guidance of James William Morley, professor of government at Columbia University from 1954 to 1991. We did not write it to "celebrate" Jim's retirement—none of us felt like celebrating the departure from the classroom of a truly great teacher—but to express our appreciation to him. Jim Morley did more than help us hone the skills we needed to be professional analysts of Japanese politics and foreign policy. He devoted an enormous amount of energy and caring to his students and inspired us with his enthusiasm for scholarship. He made each student feel that he or she had an important contribution to make. As a result, all of the contributors to this volume and many others of Jim Morley's students embraced careers that have kept them deeply involved with Japan and Asia. As can be seen, for example, in the profiles of the authors of this volume, the reach of these careers touches academic, government, and business institutions around the world.

In January 1991 those of us represented in this volume met for three days at a conference in the Cayman Islands to discuss the early drafts of papers that eventually became the chapters of this book. After the conference ended, the process of revising the papers and preparing them for publication began. It did so, however, in a year of extraordinary change, culminating with the resignation of Mikael Gorbachev as president of the Soviet Union in 1991 and the dissolution of the Soviet Union. It was evident, of course, earlier in the year that the Soviet Empire had crumbled and that the Cold War era was coming to a close. The authors included here focused, even in their original drafts, on analysis of how Japan would cope in a post-Cold War world. As the events of 1991 unfolded, however, the implications of the historic changes occuring in international political and economic relations for Japan and for Japanese-American relations became more apparent. The final revisions of the papers that appear in this book were undertaken with these global changes very much in mind. The result is the first comprehensive analysis of

Japanese foreign policy in the post-Cold War age. We hope our readers will find it useful and that it will be regarded as a fitting tribute to the career of Jim Morley.

Many people played important supporting roles in getting this book from conception to completion. Special thanks go to Robert Uriu, a Ph.D. student in political science at Columbia when this project began and an assistant professor of political science at Columbia now, for helping me organize the Cayman Island conference and for serving as its rapporteur. His extensive summaries of the discussions proved to be invaluable in the process of revising and editing the papers. Madge Huntington, the East Asian Institute's publications coordinator, handled all the complex issues involved with getting these conference papers ready for publication with extraordinary efficiency and competence. Thanks are also due for research and publication assistance to William Heinrich, Akitoshi Miyashita, and Mika Hirotsune. I also want to express the appreciation of all of us involved with this project to the East Asian Institute of Columbia University and its Toyota Research Program for generous support of the conference and for covering expenses involved in getting the volume ready for publication. The East Asian Institute has been the intellectual home at one time or another for everyone involved with this book. No one deserves more credit for giving the Institute the reputation it enjoys as one of the world's great centers of learning on Japan than its long time director, James Morley. Finally, I have to add a personal note of thanks to my wife, Midori, and to my daughters, Elissa and Jennifer, for their support and encouragement while I was involved with seeing this book move from conception to completion.

Gerald L. Curtis

Introduction

Gerald L. Curtis

This volume on Japan's foreign relations covers a wide variety of subject matter—diplomatic style, foreign economic policy, issues of national security, and Japan's role in multilateral organizations. The sixteen contributors come to the task of analyzing Japan's foreign policy with different perspectives and different views on how to evaluate Japan's diplomatic behavior or what future developments to expect. Some are impressed with Japan's ability to achieve its foreign policy goals; others are as impressed with its diplomatic shortcomings and failures.

Through all the analyses, however, run certain common themes. The most conspicuous is an emphasis on Japan's minimalist strategy in dealing with foreign policy issues. None of the writers would disagree that Japan has pursued a low-risk strategy throughout the postwar years. Michael Blaker captures the essence of this strategy with the term "coping." For Japan's foreign policy decision makers the challenge of foreign policy has been to cope effectively with situations created by other countries.

Opinion divides on how effective and successful this coping strategy has been. Blaker for one is critical, believing that Japan's policymakers have failed to achieve even the limited goals they have set for themselves, much less the far higher expectations that foreigners have embraced. A number of other contributors to this volume argue quite the contrary, that Japan has been remarkably successful in achieving its goals, limited as they have been. Together the papers provide a wealth of empirical data and analysis that readers can mine to draw their own conclusions.

A second theme that weaves its way through all the chapters is the primary importance of the American connection in Japanese foreign policy. Americans only recently fascinated with Japan's economic challenge may not appreciate fully the degree to which Japanese decision makers and the Japanese public at large view their nation's foreign policy through the prism of its relationship with the United States. This was strikingly illustrated in the 1991 Persian Gulf War. Rather than a belief that Iraq's invasion of Kuwait directly affected Japanese national interests, it was the Japanese concern about the U.S. relationship which led Japanese leaders to respond time after time to American requests for financial support. In the end, Japan spent $13 billion and funded 20 percent of the total cost of Desert Storm. Instead of winning applause from the United States, however, Japan became the target of intense criticism. For Japan, the Gulf conflict demonstrated clearly how much more difficult managing the U.S. relationship had become in the complex and fluid post–Cold War international environment.

A third theme is the challenge to Japanese foreign policy posed by the combination of Japan's rise to economic superpower status and the end of the Cold War. If the coping strategies of the past are no longer adequate to serve Japanese national interests in this new world, what kind of strategy is likely to replace it? Some of the writers here are pessimistic that Japan will be able to break out of its traditional diplomatic mold and design a new foreign policy despite these changes in world politics and the international economy. Others argue that Japan already is moving toward a new, more active role in international affairs. Dennis Yasutomo and Yasuhiro Ueki, in particular, emphasize multilateral settings as having significant potential for Japan to play a major world role.

The chapters are organized into five topical sections, the first of which concerns Japan's diplomatic style. How do the Japanese approach negotiations? What do they see as strategic imperatives? What measurements do they typically use to evaluate their own performance. How do they develop the instruments and mechanisms for managing trade and other contentious issues with the United States?

Although there is much written about Japanese foreign policy processes, there is relatively little about why Japan does what it does in its foreign relations; that is, about the intentions, motives, principles, ideas, and concepts behind Japan's pursuit of its national interests. These are the issues Blaker addresses in the first chapter of this section.

Blaker argues that there is nothing inscrutable about Japanese diplomacy. It results from heavily bureaucratized policy-making and from a core of widely shared Japanese beliefs—notably an uneasiness toward the outside world, an obsession with Japan's vulnerability, and an ultrasensitivity to foreign criticism.

These ingredients combine to form what Blaker calls a Japanese diplomatic style of "coping." This approach produces an identifiable pattern of cautiously appraising the external situation, methodically weighing and sorting every option, deferring action on contentious issues, crafting a domestic consensus on the situation faced, and adapting to a situation with minimal risk.

However, based on case studies of the protracted United Nations Law of the Sea Conference (1973–1980) and the Persian Gulf crisis of 1990–1991, Blaker concludes that Japan's coping strategy has been strikingly unsuccessful. Although a central goal of a coping strategy is freedom from foreign criticism, the sheer amount of criticism heaped on Japan in these two cases underscores in Blaker's view how much Tokyo officials misread the international environment, the degree of American decline and Japanese independence in new global circumstances, and the extent of foreign expectations of Japan.

The following chapter, by John Campbell, offers a contrasting picture to the one provided by Blaker. According to Campbell, much of the friction in U.S.-Japanese relations and much of the criticism leveled against Japan are part of a highly ritualized scenario of accusation, negotiation, threats, and resolution that constitute the U.S.-Japanese relations "game."

While widespread media reporting of Japan bashing leaves the impression of a Japanese-American alliance in grave disarray, the U.S.-Japanese relationship at the government-to-government level has been remarkably strong and stable. Economic interdependence has been deepening; there has been a high degree of cooperation, or at least parallelism, in the two countries' policies toward third countries; a pattern of close bilateral cooperation and coordination on security issues has been firmly established; and, even on the volatile trade issue, nothing disastrous enough has occurred to shake the relationship loose from its moorings.

Campbell contends this stability results from the two governments' commitment to handling the bulk of their affairs through a set of games with fairly well-defined rules. These games—in effect procedural solutions to chronic tensions between the two nations—emerged after major crises that threatened the relationship.

The crisis in the political sphere arose in the early 1950s; since then Japan has deferred to the United States on virtually all diplomatic issues. In the military field, since the security treaty crisis of 1960, the two governments have argued each year about how much Japan would undertake to raise its "burden-sharing" effort, within an overall framework of increasing bilateral cooperation. In trade, the crisis produced by the dispute over Japanese textile exports led to an American-demand and Japanese-response ritual which in subsequent years invariably has produced a "solution" with Japanese concessions insufficient to resolve fundamental problems but sufficient to allow the game itself to continue. In each area, political, military, and economic, the United States has been the side to initiate the interaction, set the agenda by specifying the problem and proposing a solution, and win in the sense that Japan ends up acceding at least partially to American demands. From Japan's perspective, this is what diplomatic "minimalism" is all about: defining its goals by the least concessions required to avoid provoking a crisis in its relations with the United States.

The third chapter in this section on diplomatic style treats an institution rarely discussed where issues of postwar Japanese foreign policy are concerned. As David Titus points out, however, despite their drastically reduced roles in Japanese policy compared to what they had been from 1868 to 1945, the emperor and members of the imperial family have been more active in international affairs since the Allied Occupation ended in 1952 than at any other time in Japanese history.

Titus argues that since 1868 the imperial institution has facilitated Japan's "internationalization" by putting the imprimatur of this most Japanese of Japanese institutions on the importation of the world's cultural and material resources. As a limited head of state, the emperor faces the world; as symbol of the unity of his people, he faces the Japanese. Thus the emperor is in a unique position to connect the outside world to the Japanese people, and his activities are managed by the government and the palace staff to maintain Japan as a unique community within the world.

The role of the emperor today is not without its ambiguity, controversy, and uncertainty. This was starkly revealed, as Titus discusses, in the 1990 enthronement ceremony, which highlighted Japan's problems in reconciling its sense of communal self and a unique culture with a more universal notion of civilization. Titus's analysis offers an illuminating perspective on the century-long struggle in Japan to define a collective Japanese identity that can resolve the tension between the pull of universality and the tug of cultural uniqueness and a preoccupation with what makes Japan different.

In the first section's final chapter, Nathaniel Thayer looks at the issue of political leadership in the conduct of Japanese foreign policy. One of the most strongly entrenched images of Japanese policy making is the image of a "leaderless" process. Bureaucratic dominance, consensus building, the absence of charismatic leaders, and a constitutional structure limiting the prime minister's authority and autonomy are widely regarded as producing a system marked by the absence of strong political leaders.

Yet at critical moments in postwar Japanese foreign policy, political leaders, not bureaucratic institutions or some amorphous consensus process, have been the driving force behind major policy decisions. Examples include Yoshida Shigeru's push for a security treaty with the United States, Hatoyama Ichiro's initiative to normalize relations with the Soviet Union, Sato Eisaku's determination to realize the reversion of Okinawa, Tanaka Kakuei's move to establish formal diplomatic relations with mainland China, and Nakasone Yasuhiro's efforts to carve a new security policy.

Thayer's chapter focuses on Nakasone, the most recent of these postwar Japan's activist prime ministers. Having known Nakasone personally for over thirty years, Thayer brings to his analysis unique insights into Nakasone's character and leadership style. Thayer's account not only describes how Nakasone moved the national debate on foreign policy forward, but of how he capitalized on his high-profile stance on foreign policy issues to strengthen his own domestic popular appeal which he then used to buttress his power in the Liberal Democratic party.

The second section focuses on a key dimension—some would argue the only dimension—of postwar Japan's foreign policy: its thrust for economic success. As anyone familiar with the debate over Japanese economic policy is aware, controversy swirls around the issue of how Japan has manipulated the levers of government power to secure benefits for Japanese industry.

In his chapter, T. J. Pempel discusses the fundamental reorientation of Japanese foreign economic policy from that of an exporter to that of an overseas investor, a process which began in the 1970s and accelerated in the 1980s. He pays particular attention to the links between foreign economic policy and domestic political and economic factors, and, he argues that Japanese policy in this arena is not simply a response to outside "pressure," but stems from shifting economic and political power relationships within Japan.

To illustrate the point, Pempel asserts that Japan's early postwar export-oriented policy was part of a system that regularly favored small businesses, farming families, and large manufacturing firms, while treating organized labor and consumers with political indifference or neglect. By the mid-1970s, however, Pempel identifies a number of factors in the international environment which pushed Japan toward greater internal economic openness and a much heavier level of overseas investment. There is a great deal of ambiguity and incompleteness in this shift, however, as Pempel stresses. Despite market liberalization, certain politically sensitive areas remain heavily protected, and foreign investment in Japan remains very low.

Pempel's analysis also underscores the importance of relating changes in foreign economic policy to changes in the structure of domestic political power. He describes the relative shift of power from the central bureaucracy to politicians and big business. To LDP politicians, Pempel maintains, small business interests and farmers are less significant than before, while the white-collar and even some of the blue-collar work force wield more influence than in earlier years. The political challenge to the LDP as suggested in Pempel's analysis, is figuring out how to adjust its base of electoral support to reflect the impact of foreign economic policy on the shifting fortunes of different constituencies within Japan.

In chapter 6, Frances Rosenbluth examines Japan's political handling of the issue of yen appreciation. In particular, she discusses how the political leadership sought to balance demands from the international community to strengthen the yen against demands from small- and medium-sized business to protect them from adverse consequences of yen appreciation. Despite the politicians' rhetoric pledging to help small business survive this challenge to their competitiveness, and despite the ruling LDP's heavy dependence on these companies for electoral support, the LDP did very little to assist this sector.

The decision to let small business fend for itself cannot be explained by conventional models of Japanese policy making. As her essay makes clear, explanations of this issue based on bureaucratic power, foreign pressure, or economic expediency are not satisfactory. Rather, she argues, the LDP leadership acted according to its view of what was necessary to serve the collective interests of LDP Diet members. Her argument is that the LDP is more than the sum of its Diet members or its factions and that Diet members have delegated to the party's leadership authority to make policy choices based on calculations of the electoral consequences of those choices.

Rosenbluth notes that LDP leaders are moving away from electoral dependence on the country's economically noncompetitive sectors and toward reliance on groups having a stake in policies of freer trade. This process, as she acknowledges, is messy and incomplete, because the party must balance many competing interests, including individual Diet members' interests in getting themselves reelected. Rosenbluth's study reveals how international factors and domestic politics interact to produce policy change and organizational adaptation. Her analysis suggests, too, that any discussion of Japanese foreign policy which neglects domestic politics will fail to capture the dynamics of the policy process.

Timothy Curran's chapter on the role of Japanese multinational corporations in U.S.-Japanese relations is the only essay in this collection which addresses nongovernmental actors in Japan's external relations. The chapter is important precisely because it focuses on the globalizing Japanese company, the engine of Japan's integration into the world economy.

Curran argues that Japanese multinational firms in the United States, particularly those in the automotive and electronics industries are moving beyond setting up "screwdriver" assembly line factories toward establishing fully integrated businesses including product design, value engineering, and other value-added aspects of the manufacturing process. The consequent transfer of skills and technologies to the United States and the creation of new jobs suggest that Japan's multinationals are likely to evolve along lines quite similar to the experiences of the Swiss, Americans, and globalizing companies of other countries.

While Japanese industry will be a stiff competitor against America in key industrial sectors, Curran asserts that the pattern of growth of Japanese multinational corporations will likely create powerful constituencies in the United States that will work in favor of a strong and stable U.S.-Japanese relationship. Further, Curran anticipates that growing ties between Japanese U.S.-based multinationals and their local American suppliers will alter and open up the much criticized *keiretsu* and that the interests of Japanese business will contribute to breaking up the "iron triangles" of bureaucrats, LDP politicians, and local businessmen that often act as an effective nontariff barrier.

In chapter 8, Michael Donnelly uses the issue of nuclear power to challenge some of the most popular stereotypes of Japanese foreign economic policy. Of today's industrial democracies, Japan has the most ambitious plans for significantly enlarging its nuclear power capacity. This Japanese nuclear energy quest, Donnelly contends, has had little to do with foreign pressure, Japan's "minimalist" foreign policy, or a reactive policy to deal with international events. Nor, Donnelly argues, can Japan's nuclear energy policy be understood by treating the state as a rational, unitary actor in foreign economic policy making. Rather, it is important to analyze the technocratic, institutional and political forces that help shape the nation's approach to the international world. In the case of nuclear energy, this leads Donnelly to a two-level analytical scheme focusing on the formulation of nuclear programs in Tokyo, on the one hand, and the management of nuclear programs in small villages across the countryside, on the other. Using this framework, Donnelly then describes the structure of Japan's nuclear energy industry and the long-term nuclear development strategy. The result is an unconventional and insightful treatment of Japan's political economy and foreign policy.

Section three deals with political and security issues. The focus is on how Japan has sought to provide for its security in the postwar years and how thinking about security is evolving in Japan now that the Cold War has ended and Japan has achieved economic power.

Norman Levin's chapter reviews postwar Japanese national security policy and explores some challenges to this policy posed by changes in Japan's international environment. While Japan's minimalist foreign policy is sometimes confused with a "passive" policy, Levin sees nothing passive about Japan's approach to security affairs. To Levin, Tokyo has followed a clear strategy throughout the postwar era. Two main elements explain the strategy: economic growth through an aggressive export policy, and national security through low military expenditures combined with dependence on the United States.

Levin argues that this basic strategy of the early postwar years has continued to provide the fundamental goals of Japanese foreign policy despite dramatic changes in the international situation. Japan's shift from its export-oriented economic policy has come only because of intense foreign, and especially American, pressure. Higher defense expenditures and greater burden sharing similarly, in Levin's view, have been adopted to accommodate American pressure and have not resulted from any fundamental reassessment of Japanese strategic goals.

In thinking about the future, Levin raises several basic questions. Will Japan be able to bring its policies more into line with its capabilities and the changing international order? Can Japan achieve a more balanced relationship with the United States, sharing greater responsibilities for pursuing common global interests? What if it fails to adapt its postwar strategy to the post–Cold War era? What if it confronts a more isolationist America and moves itself in a more independent, autonomous direction? As Levin concludes, there may not be a need to consider these troubling "what if" questions if the United States and Japan can manage their relationship effectively. However, with the end of the Cold War and heightened U.S.-Japanese tensions, they are questions that now have to be seriously considered.

Recent Japanese opinion on such issues provides the theme of Martin Weinstein's essay, chapter 10. By setting forth and evaluating the viewpoints of six influential Japanese writers, Weinstein manages to challenge the all too popular notion that there is a lack of intellectual debate within Japan about the country's foreign policy and future options. A debate does exist, as Weinstein's material shows. That debate, moreover, has turned increasingly vigorous with the disintegration of the Soviet Union and rising discord in Japanese-American relations.

Nonetheless, as Weinstein argues, despite the profoundly changed international environment for U.S.-Japanese relations in the past few years, Japanese still see the alliance with the United States as the best vehicle for serving their national interests. Such thinking explains the emphasis within the Japanese debate on how to modify, adjust, or reorient the goals of the alliance to fit the post–Cold War era, rather than on what alternative instruments to construct in its place.

In his concluding section, Weinstein considers a number of international scenarios that might compel Japan to alter its basic foreign policy. No scenario, he argues, that would bring Japan to fundamentally reformulate its policies and undertake large-scale rearmament would serve American interests. He concludes, therefore, that Americans have as high a stake in preserving the U.S.-Japanese alliance as Japanese do.

In chapter 11, Susan Pharr provides an analytic overview of the postwar history of Japanese security policy and of Japan's response to American demands for greater "burden sharing." Pharr stresses the activist qualities of Japan's "defensive" foreign policy. She argues that Japan has conducted its foreign policy as a good defensive driver navigates an automobile, seeking to minimize risk while exploiting every available opportunity to move forward.

Pharr's analysis underscores the Japanese risk-minimization and benefit-maximization style that is echoed in many of the other papers in this volume. She also sees certain advantages this policy has gained for Japan: providing security at low cost, contributing to regional stability, and pushing Japan's own burden-sharing contribution into nonmilitary areas. Pharr does not see this fundamental foreign policy approach being undermined either by the end of the Cold War or by Japan's new status as an economic superpower. To the contrary, she is convinced that Japan will continue to pursue an activist, relatively low-cost, low-risk defensive strategy, and that the United States, out of its own national interests, will support such a Japanese policy even as it continues to express dissatisfaction with the level of Japanese burden sharing.

For Japanese diplomacy, it seems the most difficult relationships have been with countries nearest to it. With two of these neighboring countries, China and Korea, Japan has been unable to put history to rest, to establish the kind of relationship that Germany has managed to establish with France after World War II. Further, unlike Germany, Japan has never fully faced up to the historical record of its aggression against its neighbors. Despite repeated apologies to both China and Korea for its actions before and during the Pacific War, many Japanese remain reluctant to confront the truth of their nation's past behavior or to see it conveyed to younger generations through school textbooks. Consequently, history hangs like a dark cloud over Japan's relations with its neighbors, official apologies notwithstanding.

Japan's difficult relations with Korea, China, and the former Soviet Union are addressed in a set of three essays in the fourth section. In the first of these, Byung-joon Ahn highlights the various difficulties Japan must face in its diplomacy with Korea. It has to overcome the legacy of its colonial past. It also has to shift its focus from treating Korea as an element in its relations with the United States to a country vital to Japan in its own right. Its efforts to strengthen relations with South Korea are complicated by its desire to normalize relations with North Korea. Some kind of a regional division of labor with the United States in East Asia also needs to be hammered out. Finally, constructing a new policy toward Korea requires building a new political consensus within Japan about Korea policy, an enormously difficult task given the tangle of issues and interests involved in the Korea issue in domestic Japanese politics.

Ahn is sensitive to these difficulties but he concludes on an optimistic note. The common interests among Japan, South Korea, and the United States, he argues, will push them toward cooperation, so long as there is adequate consultation and coordination. As is the case with other writers in this volume, Ahn sees no alternative to a close U.S.-Japanese relationship, nor does he see an option for South Korea other than a close U.S.-Korean relationship and a relationship of growing intimacy with Japan. Thus, in Ahn's view, it is entirely possible that both the Japanese and Korean quests for a more active foreign policy can be accommodated within the context of a productive Japan-Korea-U.S. relationship.

Motohide Saito's chapter addresses Japan's relations with the Soviet Union and developments in the period since the Soviet Union's demise. What is striking about Japanese-Soviet relations, and Japanese-Russian relations in the period since the end of the USSR, is the persistent distrust and the overarching importance of the northern islands issue as a stumbling block to improved relations between the two countries. Even with the end of the Cold War and the disintegration of the Soviet Union, the tensions and troubles in the relationship between Japan and its neighbor to the north remain virtually unchanged.

Saito recounts the history of the Soviet entrance into the war against Japan in the last days of World War II and its seizure and occupation of the Northern Territories. These Soviet actions instilled the deep distrust of Moscow that has shaped Japanese policy toward the Soviet Union ever since. Japan's heavy emphasis on close ties with the United States, he adds, in the context of the Cold War, only further exacerbated relations with the Soviet Union.

Nonetheless, Saito identifies three points at which conciliatory efforts have taken place. In each case, however, a breakthrough was stymied by deadlock on the Northern Territories issue. Although both countries stand to benefit by having this issue resolved, Saito's analysis provides little room for optimism that it will be resolved easily and therefore concludes that marked improvement in the relationship is unlikely.

Se Hee Yoo's essay on Japan's relations with China explores the perceptual foundations of this relationship. Yoo identifies and appraises the attitudes and factors most instrumental in molding Japanese decision makers' viewpoints, choices, and policies toward China.

He devotes particular attention to the long history of mutual distrust and rivalry that continue to shape the relationship. He portrays a China wary of excessive dependence on Japanese development aid and investment, anxious over a revival of Japanese militarism, and worried that its spectacular economic growth might lead Japan to seek a prominent regional political role.

Yoo presents Japanese opinion leaders as highly skeptical of China's officially stated commitment to economic reform as well as its officially stated disinterest in a dominant role in Asian regional politics. Japan is aware, he notes further, of how acutely its Asian neighbors dread the prospect of a heavily remilitarized Japan.

Yoo argues that such Chinese and Japanese perceptions suggest that Tokyo will be constrained in its foreign policy toward China, toward other major actors in the region, and toward the Asian region as a whole. He also argues that Japan's major future challenge will be to devise workable instruments for overcoming these perceptual obstacles. These and other steps Yoo regards as essential if Japan is to head off what seems to be a budding Sino-Japanese rivalry over such issues as unifying the Korean peninsular or framing the multilateral structures for political and economic cooperation in the Asia-Pacific area.

Japanese diplomacy at the multilateral level provides the focus for the final set of essays by two specialists on multilateral issues and organizations. Given the constraints on Japanese foreign policy that arise from its constitutional restrictions, strongly antimilitary public opinion, and the difficulties in its relations with its neighbors, the United Nations and other multilateral forums may provide an arena where Japan will play a significant international role. Moreover, in the post–Cold

War world collective efforts through multilateral organizations to deal with economic, financial, political, and security problems will be more pronounced.

Dennis Yasutomo's essay examines Japan's role in the Asian Development Bank and the European Bank for Reconstruction and Development to see if Japan is more active, assertive, and independent in the multilateral arena. He argues that multilateral institutions, especially the development banks that form his case studies, assist Japan in forging a new diplomacy. In particular, they serve as conduits for specific regional policies, legitimize controversial policies, allow Japan to fulfill international responsibilities as a nonmilitary power, supplement national resources, compensate for diplomatic shortcomings and inexperience, permit greater independence from the United States, and enhance national prestige. According to Yasutomo, the banks provide Japan with an opportunity to experiment with greater diplomatic activism and politicization necessary for an economically powerful Japan to pursue its national interests in the emerging world order.

While finding an unprecedented degree of Japanese active participation in these two banks, Yasutomo also cites certain problems and contradictions in Japan's policy toward both institutions. These include political activism without firm political principles, a chronic Asian bias in its approach toward the banks, and the continuing need to weigh its independence in these organizations against its relationship with the United States.

The final essay, by Yasuhiro Ueki, describes Japan's pursuit of a more activist role in the United Nations and the obstacles that stand in the way. Japan's search for a larger international role commensurate with its economic power has coincided with the passing of the Cold War and with a new degree of UN involvement in regional conflict resolution.

In this context, the Gulf War became a particularly severe test for Japan. The Japanese government used the appeal of the UN and the rhetoric of "UN-centrism" to try to loosen domestic resistance to a more activist role abroad. The attempt had only partial success so far. Despite wider domestic support for Japanese participation in UN peacekeeping operations, many Japanese, fearful of a revival of military power, oppose their country's participation in operations of a military nature, even if under UN auspices. Nonetheless, as Ueki clearly demonstrates, Japan's desire for greater activism is manifest in other areas: in its role in brokering a resolution of the Cambodian conflict, and its pursuit of permanent membership on the UN Security Council.

Taken together, the chapters in this volume provide a panoramic view of contemporary Japanese foreign policy. They reveal both the dynamism and the extraordinary continuity of Japanese diplomacy. The dynamism reflects a finely honed Japanese sensitivity to changes in the country's external environment. The mark of a successful coping strategy, of a skillful defensive driver on the treacherous highways and byways of international politics, is a keen awareness of potential obstacles and the search for the lowest-risk, lowest-cost approaches to achieving national goals.

As Japan's position in the world changes, its companies continue to globalize, its financial and commercial power expands, and its desire for international status grows, Japan will seek out new ways to play a more assertive role in international affairs. It would be a mistake, however, to expect that the key features of Japanese foreign policy discussed in this volume will be suddenly tossed aside in favor of a drastically new approach. The one event which might cause such a dramatic shift in Japan's diplomatic orientation would be a collapse of the U.S.-Japanese relationship. Conceivably, a resurgent American isolationism and determination to break the pattern of Japanese-American relations established after World War II could bring this about. At this juncture, however, the idea seems conjectural and would not serve American national interests.

Paradoxically, the end of the Cold War has not undermined Japan's basic diplomatic strategy of the Cold War era. Instead, Japanese leaders have redoubled their efforts to hold fast to that strategy—of continued alliance with the United States, closer ties with its neighbors in East and Southeast Asia, and greater influence and higher status in multilateral forums. Japan, in short, continues to pursue its time-tested strategy of coping with change.

Japan's Foreign Policy
After the Cold War
Coping with Change

I Japan's Diplomatic Style

Chapter 1
Evaluating Japanese Diplomatic Performance

Michael Blaker

The graver the situation,
the more thorough the required assessment.
—Count Makino Shinken

Among the many diplomatic challenges Japan has faced since gaining independence in 1952, two have arisen at particularly historic moments. At these two junctures, fundamental international structures and relationships among nations seemed to be undergoing profound change. At these moments no one had the benefit of historical precedent, proven models, established guidelines, or fixed rules. To those in charge of Japanese diplomacy, most comfortable with routinized decisions in a known diplomatic framework, these encounters were especially wrenching, for they seemed to involve Japan in issues, choices, and decisions that seemed likely to determine the nature of the international structure itself. Each would prove a formidable test of Japan's policy-making structures and its leaders' values, diplomatic skills, and grasp of world politics.

The first of these critical moments came as a crushing aftershock of the 1973 oil "shock"—itself arguably the Godzilla of all "shocks" to jolt Japan since the term was coined—and related to redefining the rules and creating the regime that would govern the regulation of the world's ocean resources. This epic drama followed a complicated, if improvised, script played out on a vast new multilateral diplomatic stage, the Third United Nations Law of the Sea Conference (UNCLOS III), against a backdrop of geopolitical dueling and dealing over the world's ocean space and resources, with Japan in its omnidirectional diplomatic debut at the multilateral level.

The second encounter concerns Japan's tortured reaction to the initial diplomatic test of the post–Cold War period at the dawn of the 1990s, the crisis stemming from Iraq's sudden seizure of Kuwait on August 2, 1990. In this Persian Gulf case, Japan faced an even more jarring ordeal, which probed the essence of its global commitments, the raison d'être of its military establishment, the crisis management abilities of its leaders and bureaucrats, the value of its UN centered diplomacy, and its ties to the United States.

This essay assesses how and how well Japan responded to the UNCLOS III challenge and to the crisis in the Persian Gulf. A core maxim of Japanese diplomatic thinking is that only a fundamental alteration in the nature of the international order can justify basic changes in national policy. Japanese writers are fond of portraying Japan as perpetually standing at a crossroads in its diplomacy. However abused the term may be, it aptly describes Japan's position during these two diplomatically seismic encounters.

While the topic certainly merits analysis, picking a suitable approach for assessing Japan's performance is more complicated. Little guidance is found in the literature on Japanese diplomacy, which largely consists of nuts-and-bolts "how" or process-type analyses. Few specialists have addressed "why"- type issues—the ideas, concepts, intentions, motives, and principles that lie behind the conduct of Japanese diplomacy.

This subject, which seems to arouse the most intense public interest, has largely been neglected by the few serious scholars of Japanese diplomacy. Perhaps this inattention explains why so many popular accounts on this central dimension of Japanese diplomacy are so impressionistic, biased, self-serving, jingoistic, or speculative. Whether ill-intended or merely ill-informed, such "analyses" are based on outsiders' values, terminology, concepts, and "objective" standards. These authors seem obsessed with fathoming some inner motive, sinister intention, or grand design, or applying some catchy slogan or label so as to provide a groove for grinding some stereotypical ax, whether or not the behavior or thinking reflects reality.[1] Such interpretations merely add to the existing confusion and make Japanese diplomacy unnecessarily inscrutable.

"Coping with Change in the International System"

Stripped of its nonessentials, Japan's approach to foreign policy is scrutable enough. It follows from highly bureaucratized policymaking in a highly pluralistic society. Viewed from outside, the system looks tightly cohesive, stable, and bound by consensus. But in fact, any significant foreign policy issue manages to rock the domestic political boat, with politicians and bureaucrats in charge of policy constantly in motion, scrambling about to put out fires, plug leaks, and paper over cracks just to keep the vessel afloat. The task is complicated, too, by certain perceptions, notably an ambivalence toward the outside world, a preoccupation with Japan's vulnerability, and hypersensitivity to any form of anti–Japanese sentiment abroad.

The foreign policy behavior that reflects these political and perceptual patterns is—in a word—"coping." Coping means carefully assessing the international situation, methodically weighing each alternative, sorting out various options to see what is really serious, waiting for the dust to settle on some contentious issue, piecing together a consensus view about the situation faced, and then performing the minimum adjustments needed to neutralize or overcome criticism and adapt to the existing situation with the fewest risks. If it is determined that a sufficiently major change has occurred in the environments or factors relevant to Japanese interests, then and only then are changes in Japan's own policies considered desirable. As Tokyo University international affairs theorist Kumon Shumpei has written, "Once one recognizes the current, one dares not swim against it."[2]

This describes Japan's "situational ethic" or "go-with-the-flow" style of diplomatic conduct. Some observers are inclined to label it pragmatic or realistic; others call it spineless or immoral. Coping is no calculated strategy. Rather, it is an automatic, knee-jerk, almost unconscious pattern in Japan's handling of its foreign affairs. It is also time-tested, an accepted response mechanism of survival that stems from little-changing Japanese perceptions of the world and the way Japan's diplomatic policies are formulated and implemented.

The architects of Japan's postwar diplomacy have been permitted the luxury of following this minimalist approach in part because they have strictly adhered to Yoshida Shigeru's sage advice: "If you like the shade, find yourself a big tree," with the tree having been the United States. Of the three officially sanctioned and much hallowed "pillars" of post–World War II Japanese diplomacy (UN centrism, Japan in Asia, and close ties to the United States), the American pillar dwarfs the others. Indeed, the evolution of postwar Japanese diplomacy can only be grasped if it is examined through the prism of the U.S.-Japanese relationship.

In any event, Japan's ideologically muted, low-profile style, when placed dispassionately against the backdrop of Japan's historical experience, is in many ways a sensible, pragmatic response to the international conditions it has faced. Not surprisingly, in light of its diplomatic experiences, Japanese leaders have not displayed a global outlook, a geopolitical mentality, or a Wilsonian vision of world order—with Japan occupying a central role. Without any grand design or, for that matter, any grand designers needed to shape its preferred future international order, and having never conceived, initiated, and orchestrated any international conference–level policy of consequence through to a successful conclusion, Japan typically has deferred to others on grand strategy, seeking refuge in minimum-risk, blandly nonpolitical policies, somewhere in the shade.

But if Japan's diplomatic behavior is scrutable and straightforward enough, evaluating it is complicated indeed. As Japan's economy has grown, its international presence and role have expanded. The ever-widening spheres of Japanese economic engagement have multiplied the number of friction points. Weighted down by internal and external constraints, and without a diplomatic agenda of its own, Japan seems handicapped by its coping approach of not responding unless a warning light flashes somewhere on the screen. Even when a signal is received, however, Tokyo does not seem to get the message. Japan's problem is that it never seems to think it has a problem.

But others do think Japan has a problem—which itself suggests that the minimalist, coping approach has become jarringly inappropriate to Japan's vastly expanded international presence today. It is small wonder that, to foreign observers at least, Japan's leaders and diplomatic representatives seem indecisive, vacillating, and timid; their malleability betraying an underlying absence of conviction, purpose, coherence, or clarity. Outsiders not appreciating either Japan's internal political and social constraints or the Japanese sense of vulnerability tend to perceive the behavior differently than do the Japanese themselves. Their expectations of what Japan ought to be doing also differ, according to their assessment of Japan's capabilities. And they have applied different standards to judge Japanese diplomatic efforts and effectiveness.

A unique sensitivity to the external environment has given outsiders' opinions considerable weight among Japanese and has encouraged foreign observers to lecture endlessly on Japan's foreign policy agenda and performance. For example, various observers have assailed Japan's performance in the marathon UN Law of the Sea negotiations as "inept," "dismal," or "pathetic." Appraisals of Japan's response to the Persian Gulf crisis have been even more stinging. Japan's efforts were branded a failure scarcely a month after the crisis began.

This essay reviews Japan's handling of the UNCLOS III and Persian Gulf cases by highlighting the record to see if the coping model fits, and by setting forth some of the difficulties in appraising Japanese diplomatic performance. The essay concludes by speculating as to why such a yawning abyss exists between the high expectations for Japanese diplomacy and the low ratings given to its actual diplomatic performance.

Japan and the Third United Nations Law of the Sea Conference

A distant fishing nation, Japan catches a quarter of the world's fish. With a sixth of the world's merchant shipping, it handles a fifth of the world's maritime freight. It is the world's largest importer of raw materials and is heavily dependent upon imports of the minerals to be found in abundance on the deep seabed. Japan is one of a handful of nations with the technology to reap the vast potential harvest of nodules containing copper, manganese, cobalt, nickel, and possibly other metals that lie on the ocean floor.

The sea is truly Japan's lifeline. The traditional international maritime order had protected that lifeline and Japanese maritime interests. Japan's post–World War II prosperity stemmed in large measure from unfettered commerce and shipping, assuring the resource-poor nation a stable flow of raw materials and supplies to fuel its industrial machine and access to overseas markets for its manufactured products. Japan has prospered, too, by limited or narrow territorial seas; freedom of the high seas; unimpeded freedom of fishing, navigation, and access to and use of the seas through straits; and the opportunity to use its highly advanced technology to exploit oceanic resources, including deep seabed minerals. To some extent, too, the sea is Japan's strategic shield, protecting it against potential threats to the home islands from the continent and, with its own Self-Defense Forces backed by U.S. naval deployments in the Pacific, against possible disruption of its sea lanes and lines of supply.

Japan thus had a vital stake in maintaining the existing maritime regime. One would think that Japan would have acted promptly and firmly to assert its interests, even if only to block moves to alter the status quo. Japanese officials repeatedly had declared their resolve to participate actively in multilateral diplomacy. UN-CLOS III seemed the perfect opportunity to be present at the creation, to participate in the establishment of an international regime governing an area of Japan's most vital interests.

But there were reasons for restraint as well. The blossoming of Japan's global economic role had been cut short by the OPEC cartel's controls. The oil "shock" brought an end to the cheap energy supplies thought essential to Japan's sustained economic prosperity, leaving the Japanese acutely aware of their nation's fragility, dependence, and resource vulnerability.

Another anxiety stemmed from the rising assertiveness and expected clout of the less-developed "revisionist" states bent on pushing a "new international economic order" through confrontationist diplomacy. Peru, Chile, Guatemala, and many other coastal states already had imposed unilateral restrictions on others' access to their adjacent waters. Further, the swelling wave of sensitivity to issues of the environment, resources, energy, pollution, and endangered species would affect Japan. In fact, Japan was being pilloried in the press for unprincipled, irresponsible plundering of the world's fishing areas, for its rapacious whaling practices, and for being the world's number one ocean polluter. Widespread public attention to these excesses, along with intensified competition for a total world catch down by half from 1965–1975,[3] made Tokyo officials squirm even more.

In addition to these woes, Japan was linked to a weakened America still bogged down in Vietnam. Japanese analysts saw the United States as a fading economic power, a "crumbling giant" whose "era was over." Japan's diminished faith in the advantages of having a U.S. protective shield and its lack of the capability of its own to defend sea lanes or to monitor and defend a widened coastal space magnified the seriousness of threats from the resource-rich states and lessened its estimation of its own bargaining clout.

Omnidirectional Diplomacy

To most Japanese, Japan seemed on the threshold of a new but precarious world order in which its position was grimly weak. Circumstances seemed to dictate one solution, the *happo yabure* or "defenseless from every side" diplomatic approach whose banner the renowned economist and later foreign minister Okita Saburō unfurled in *Foreign Affairs* in mid–1974. Okita wrote: "In order to make *happo yabure* an effective diplomatic policy, Japan must avoid becoming a danger to any country in the world." He explained that "'being friends with everyone' may be justified as the basic principle of Japan's diplomacy in the present and future decades." Tantamount to a white flag of surrender, Okita's "omnidirectional" standard would hang until the end of the decade, a listless symbol of Japan's diplomacy of compromise.[4]

Japan's view of the approaching sea law conference[5] mirrored this bleak assessment of an international deck stacked against Japan, of Japan's very economic survival being threatened by a band of radical third world governments bent on restructuring the world economic order.[6] In Japanese eyes, with Japan totally boxed in (*happo fusagari*), the impending sea law conference seemed a noose that would be fastened tightly around Japan's neck.

What an intimidating environment for Japan to demonstrate its defenseless *happo yabure* stance! The sheer magnitude of the diplomatic spectacle was impressive. Beginning with some 90 participating countries, its membership later swelled to over 150. Its topics were of enormous technical complexity, negotiated through informal consensus-building processes, by loosely structured coalitions among a great many groups of states. The conference managed to function somehow, through an ungainly structure of three huge committees whose members interacted via smaller clusters of states loosely arranged by area, special interests, political linkages, or physical attributes. As the negotiations progressed, these clusters would include the "Group of 77" (G-77), the fifty-three "landlocked and geographically disadvantaged" states, various regionally based groups, a "group of 21," the "distant fishing" countries, maritime states, merchant states, archipelago states, coastal states, Soviet-bloc states, third world states, developed states, plus an assortment of committees, caucusing groups, and ad hoc coalitions.

The conference dynamics demanded considerable diplomatic skills—at tradeoffs, flexibility, quickness in response, and expertise. Japan, as it is in the UN system, was in an anomalous position at the conference, having membership both in the "Asian group" and in the "Western Europe and Other group" of developed industrialized nations. Yet another challenge for Japan was linguistic. Japan's participation would have to be expressed in one of the six official UN languages, none of which is Japanese. Finally, Japan had a reputation as being relatively unskilled at parliamentary diplomacy of the UNCLOS III type.

In light of these formidable obstacles and the prevailing crisis mood in Japan, one wonders where the Japanese delegation found the courage to show up at all, much less to attempt to seize the moment as a unique opportunity to shape the environment in preferred ways. But Japan, the thinking went, had to respond, to participate despite the adversity of the situation, and to do something. To do otherwise, it was believed, would entail far graver risks for Japan, possibly diplomatic isolation or even being rebuffed by the world community as the "world's orphan."

UNCLOS III: The Early Stage

Thus, Japan's posture toward UNCLOS III would be vintage *happo yabure*. In the initial stage of the conference, before the many negotiatory groups had coalesced, the sharpest battle lines were drawn along North–South or developed–underdeveloped country cleavages, and issues such as seabed mining or offshore jurisdictional rights became inextricably bound to the wider New International Economic Order (NIEO) political agenda. This two-camp polarization appeared to Japanese to have trapped Japan in an either-or position. Oddly, Japanese officials seemed almost to relish their self-assigned "special case" role, of being somehow caught between the developed country and developing country camps, forced to search desperately for some escape from the dilemma of having to choose between the two.

Such perceptions notwithstanding, a disaster seemed in the works. Japan's low-profile approach seemed in many ways sensible enough, given its many handicaps and the difficulty of rallying support for its pro–status quo position against the swelling revisionist tide. But the stance Tokyo finally adopted was virtually no stance at all: "Our country will cope with the conference while watching the moves to be made."[7]

In an editorial, Japan's biggest-circulation daily newspaper, the *Asahi shimbun,* offered the clearest rationale for the consciously ambiguous and defensive posture being taken by Japan at the conference: "Our nation, as a maritime nation, shall bring about a stable and fair law of the sea, while considering our security, the demands of the times and of the developing states. . . Judging by the situation in which Japan is being placed, it cannot be helped that this kind of policy has been formulated. As the only path remaining for Japan, the Japanese delegation must work to establish contacts with both the developing and the advanced nations, exerting every possible effort to persuade them both inside and outside the conference, to protect Japan's interests to the utmost extent, without becoming isolated."[8]

By contrast, the small corps of Foreign Ministry officials, the indefatigable core of Japan's conference delegation, were the collective prophets of doom: "There will be little possibility our position on economic zones will be approved at the conference."[9] Their gloomy prognosis was on target. As the Caracas meeting opened, Japan was caught by surprise by the seriousness with which others viewed the subject and by how central the exclusive economic zone concept had become in shaping any new maritime order. The adamant refusal of the Fisheries Agency to "lower the flag before the war is over" served to counter and neutralize the Foreign Ministry's compromising position. Given this inflexibility, when the matter came to a vote at the conference, the isolation that Japan had dreaded had become reality. Of the 116 countries expressing views on the 200-mile economic zone issue at the Caracas meeting, Japan found itself alone. In the voting, seventy-seven nations were in favor, sixteen were conditionally in favor, eight were generally in favor, seven abstained, six were not clear, and just one country, Japan, voted against.[10] With its single wagon, "except one" Japan could not even form a circle. Defenseless on all sides, Japan not only had lost out in the voting but also would not be able to work effectively at the meetings or behind the scenes.

At Caracas, then, Japan quickly found itself at sea, floundering at a distinct disadvantage in seeking to adjust to the highly fluid negotiatory environment. Japan had allowed others to set and control the negotiatory framework. Where its sparse agenda was blank, Japan would go with the flow, so long as it did not work to Japan's disadvantage.

Japan's sudden, unexpected isolation had turned what many had expected to be largely an exploratory, information-gathering meeting into a foreign policy "crisis." Nevertheless, there was no thought of quitting the conference. Japan was not about to jump ship, even if its views were rebuffed. There would be no repeat performance of 1933 when a defiant Foreign Minister Matsuoka Yōsuke led his delegation from the League of Nations Assembly Hall following the council's rebuke of Japanese aggression in Manchuria. At the sea law meetings four decades later, the awareness that Japan "cannot be an international Don Quixote"[11] meant that Japan had come to stay.

This initial pattern—testing the waters, avoiding commitment, waiting for others to take the lead, then following in their wake while deferring concessions until circumstances forced some later adjustment, and only then taking a deep breath and going on—was to characterize Japan's style through each of the successive negotiating rounds of the conference.

Six months after the Caracas meeting ended, the proceedings reconvened, this time in Geneva. Through informal post-Caracas bilateral consultations with many countries, and with the Soviet Union having tilted toward backing the LDCs on the issue, Japan had come to accept the inevitability of a 200-mile exclusive economic zone. Further, it was willing to adopt a twelve-mile territorial sea, siding with the United States and the Soviet Union on the straits passage issue, but with the condition that ships passing through Japan's straits be required to respect Japan's "Three Nonnuclear Principles" (not to possess, manufacture, or allow nuclear weapons into Japan). Still, as they had before Caracas, Japanese officials would not reveal what stance Japan would adopt at the approaching session, or what conditions or qualifications Japan might be seeking to attach to the now established economic zone concept. As before, the official posture was a laid-back "follow the Conference flow" (*kaigi no taisei ni tomonau*).[12] Meeting reporters upon his arrival in Geneva, Japan's Ambassador Ogiso Moto was blunt: "I have no particular instructions; I'll watch the situation and ask Tokyo what to do."[13]

By midsession it was obvious that Japan's position favoring complete freedom of access to coastal waters would be rebuffed, and stiff regulations upon fishing would be imposed. Moreover, Japan's earlier opposition to an extension of territorial seas to twelve miles was in vain; the matter was now a fait accompli. Thus, even as Tokyo wished to continue to negotiate for greater fishing rights, the conference agenda at Geneva had shifted tracks to discussion of another major topic, deep seabed mineral exploitation. Japanese private-sector experts were invited to participate in the discussions but did not appear until subsequent sessions of the conference.

The 200-Mile Exclusive Fishing Zone Shock

When the "greatest diplomatic show on earth" reconvened in New York in March 1976 for its fourth round of deliberations, the "trend of the times" had turned overwhelmingly against Japan's position. The product of this session was to be a revised text, with Japan now "conditionally" accepting the 200-mile zone, thus completing a 180-degree turn from its initial position on the subject at Caracas. Its desired conditions, limiting coastal states' authority to impose fishing restrictions within the zone, seemed only a face-saving device. One astute commentator pointed out the irony in the fact that the landlocked and geographically disadvantaged states' position remained consistent while Japan, with its rich historic knowledge of the ocean and its vital interests so clearly at stake, was the country to reverse itself. He charged that Japan's sea law diplomacy had failed.[14] Further, Tokyo's position for freedom of passage through international straits had not prevailed. As before, Japan was forced to follow in the wake of the major conference players, trying to limit any damage to its interests that might result from actions taken, through attaching conditions, noting exceptions, and introducing qualifications to the by then established economic zone structure.

Quite likely Japan would have extended its territorial waters and established its own economic zone even if the conference deliberations had not taken the course they did. After all, without waiting for a multilateral solution, the United States had acted on its own. In April 1976, the U.S. Congress drafted and President Gerald Ford signed legislation creating a 200-mile fishing conservation and management zone, to go into effect the following March. Many others also had taken unilateral actions. Then the Soviet Union, reversing its previous stance against the zone, set up its own 200-nautical mile perimeter in March 1977.

When the 200-mile zones had become widely established and the extent of

Japan's multilateral isolation had become brutally clear, the 200-mile exclusive fishing zone idea was amplified to a "shock." In Japanese diplomatic parlance, only a shock-level crisis could justify resorting to *realpolitik*, a unilateral, assertive action based on cold calculation of national interest.

It was the American and Soviet actions, taken outside the multilateral environment, that aroused Tokyo to act, and to act quickly. Legislation establishing Japan's own exclusive zone, the world's seventh largest and ten times the size of Japan itself, was approved by the cabinet on April 21 and was passed unanimously by the Diet's lower chamber a week later. Further, roused into action by powerful domestic interests and ocean (specifically fishing industry) interest groups, the government in 1977 enacted a bill extending Japan's territorial waters from three to twelve miles.

Deep Seabed Resources

A similar pattern of Japanese behavior appeared on another subject, that of deep seabed resources, the pivotal issue addressed at the 1976 session and thereafter in the First Committee. The Sixth Conference Session centered on the work of the First Committee (and, later on, of Negotiating Group 1), which dealt with matters relating to deep seabed exploitation, jurisdiction, privileges, and authority.

In the mid-1970s, Japan was one of a tiny group of states technologically advanced enough to exploit the potential riches of the ocean's bottom, It was also one of just eight countries favoring unilateral mining of the seabed.[15] But Japan chose a low-profile position. The Japanese delegation submitted no comprehensive plan of its own on deep seabed issues; rather, it advanced only very specific measures and partial plans (e.g., a modest proposal to restrict the number of mining sites that a single state might exploit within the zone) to augment or qualify the substantive draft proposals sponsored by such major players as the G-77, the USSR, and the United States (the United States advocated a "parallel" system of seabed development with states and private firms participating on an equal basis). At the same time, Japan was acutely sensitive to the adverse economic impact that any extensive exploitation of seabed minerals would have on such mineral exporting states as Chile and Peru. Thus, in conference sessions from 1976 to 1978, Japan sought to place itself in a "special"—that is, a relatively low-profile middle—position between the less-developed mineral exporting countries and the small group of technologically advanced countries.

With legislation on deep seabed exploitation pending before the U.S. Congress, and with forecasts that Britain, West Germany, France, and others were prepared to follow suit in taking action unilaterally, Japan seemed to find itself in the same isolated spot as in previous conference sessions on other subjects.

Deeply interested in exploiting the nodules,[16] but fearful of antagonizing the LDCs and the G-77, Japan settled on a pragmatic, opportunistic solution that smacked more than slightly of omnidirectionalism. To resolve its perceived dilemma at the conference, the chosen strategy represented a quintessential "Japanese" package of multilateral diplomatic items—seek to soften the harsh line being taken by Washington to keep the conference from collapsing (which collapse would leave Japan, as an advanced state technologically, vulnerable to charges of having sabotaged the conference), work to break the deadlock in Tokyo between the ministries and agencies still at odds over conference-related issues, formulate a comprehensive, long-range plan for the future, and—no matter what might happen at the conference itself—proceed without delay to develop the technology to enable Japan to be part of the inevitable trend toward exploitation of seabed nodules.[17]

Overall, Japan's alternatives on this key conference topic were structured in either-or fashion. The question the Japanese government sought to answer was the degree to which Japan maintain a balanced position as a technologically advanced country wanting to protect its private companies' interests against any unreasonable demands from less-developed countries while not aggravating resource-rich countries to the point of retaliation.

On issues of vital national interest, Japan eventually did choose sides, by acting in concert with the United States on the seabed mining issue from 1977 on, and even joining the United States at one point in denouncing the deep seabed mining provisions of the draft convention. Also, when Elliot Richardson was appointed to lead the U.S. delegation in January 1977, he traveled to Tokyo to meet with ranking Law of the Sea Office officials Kume Kunisada and Iguchi Takeo to obtain Japan's backing of the U.S.-sponsored "parallel" system for developing the deep seabed. Japan's response to these overtures ("okay, as long as it is not to Japan's disadvantage") seemed to fit Japan's low-key, supporter stance at the conference in 1977–1978.

Indeed, by the 1978 session, with the LDCs and the technologically advanced countries constantly at odds, Japan was growing disenchanted with the entire UNCLOS effort. Nor was Japan alone. As the conference progressed and the "new order" was turning into reality, the shrillness and ideological flavor of demands for the NIEO had transformed the conference deliberations into what noted sea law authority Ann Hollick has characterized as a "dialogue of the deaf."[18]

Japan sought to protect its private companies against the "unrealistic" demands of the mineral-producing states, on the ground that if Japan merely complained or failed to act, others would simply grab the nodules for themselves. Indeed, the degree of interest and responsiveness from the private entrepreneurial sector was quite high. Japanese fishing companies, correctly anticipating the coming enclosure of sea areas,[19] had moved to protect their business interests even before the conference diplomatic effort began. At the government level, too, Japan's complaints of its "difficult position" or "dilemma" over which path to take did not deter it from responding quite pragmatically when the need arose to act to guard Japanese vital national interests (e.g., freedom of passage for its vessels through straits, distant fishing, transportation, and the 200-mile limit).

Apart from its highly dramatic, volatile opening stage, the sea law conference was not a tension-filled diplomatic environment. In fact, the proceedings came to be fairly regularized, almost routine,[20] particularly when the format was restructured in 1978 to negotiate concrete details and hard-core issues in smaller working groups.

During the protracted talks, Japan had many chances to compensate for its initial handicaps, to adjust, to offer its own proposals and counterproposals. But for all practical purposes, the conference's critical stage for Japan terminated with the establishment of zones, although serious negotiations continued through the 1978 sessions in Geneva and New York on the seabed mining issue—after 1977 the key stumbling block to a treaty.

The mammoth UNCLOS III deliberations dragged on for a cumulative total of eighty-three weeks in ten sessions spanning seven years,[21] before ending inconclusively in 1982. Japan, which had originally seen the conference as a threat to its national survival, gradually lost interest as the process itself lost momentum. Toward the end, Japan's attitude seemed almost indifferent, merely a half-hearted "we really must respond, you know" attitude. Interestingly, the subject is not even mentioned in Japan's diplomatic blue books of 1980, 1981, or 1982.

Assessing Japan's Performance in the Sea Law Negotiations

Was the conference the disaster for Japan that so many Japanese observers expected? An objective assessment of Japan's handling of the negotiations, using the rough indicators below, does reveal a generally lackluster performance, particularly during the initial stages of the deliberations. The indicators applied here concern Japan's preparation, representation, output in statements and proposals, and impact on the proceedings and the text of the sea law convention itself.[22]

Representation. Japan's delegation ranked fourth in size behind the United States, the USSR, and Canada. Its impressive size was deceptive, however, for there was little continuity of representation from one meeting to the next or from start to finish. For example, while 83 percent of U.S. delegation members (67 of 81) at the Geneva session were present at the Caracas meeting, just 37 percent (14 of 37) of Japan's members had attended. Iguchi Takeo, counsellor to Japan's UN Mission and later deputy director of the Foreign Ministry's Sea Law Office, was the sole representative to attend every meeting. A small core of ten thoroughly overworked officials participated in at least five of the eight meetings examined here; but nearly two-thirds of the 163 Japanese participants attended just one meeting. The group was dominated in representation by the Foreign Ministry (74 of 163 participants), followed by the Transportation Ministry (15), the National Resources Agency (14), and more professors/advisers (8) than represented the Self-Defense Agency (7), the Fisheries Agency (6), or the Land Agency, the Justice Ministry, or the Education Ministry (5 each).[23] The delegation had three different chairmen; the key Law of the Sea Office in the Foreign Ministry had as many directors. The delegation boasted few experts in the initial stages of the conference, although some experts were added by the fourth session. Also, there were many observers, Diet members, and industry-related participants in attendance throughout the meetings.

Preparation. These impediments do not explain the disarray of Japan's delegation at the initial substantive discussions in Caracas in 1974. This was especially true since it had been clear for some time that the subjects on the agenda—ocean space boundaries, exclusive economic zones, territorial sea limits, and rules governing international straits—would be an integral part of any convention resulting from the deliberations. But Japan came out of the starting blocks late, having anticipated only a general debate at Caracas—certainly a fundamental misjudgment in the direction being taken in global ocean politics. A government planning group under the Foreign Ministry's direction was not formed until just before the opening Caracas meeting.[24]

Despite the considerable interest shown in Japan's position by other delegations, position papers had not been prepared in advance, the few maps available to the Japanese delegation were hand prepared and colored, and no funds had been allocated to reproduce them for distribution to others, even to delegation members themselves.[25] Most important, the views of the participating ministries (Foreign, Construction, Education, MITI, Transport, Justice) and agencies (Fisheries, Defense, Land, Natural Resources and Energy, Maritime Safety, Environment, Science and Technology) were at loggerheads on key issues. Each had responsibility for its own specialized area, with experts assigned according to topic, and positions were not reconciled adequately before the conference convened.[26]

During the ten-week Caracas meeting, there was much confusion and feuding among the ministries and agencies represented, over both information and authority. A strict compartmentalization of responsibility precluded any sort of free and open sharing of data within the Japanese delegation. Voluminous reports to Tokyo were filed separately by each organization. Literally swamped by data and requests for communications assistance, the Japanese Embassy staff in Caracas had to be recruited to assist with decoding and communication tasks that often lasted through the night.[27]

Not having top-ranking officials who were prepared to negotiate on their own authority diluted the impact of what the Japanese representatives had to say. At one unfortunately typical session, Japan's representative was forced to apologize for a lack of instructions from his government, several times for a "lack of expertise" on the subjects being negotiated by the committee, for his inability to present Japan's point of view, for lacking sufficient time to study the issue, and for repeating ground already covered by others. He then sought clarification on several trivial points in the text under consideration. Taken aback by this presentation, the Colombian representative snapped, "I think we came prepared for negotiations and don't need to ask for instructions from our governments." Indeed, it was ten days later, a full four days after the group had closed discussion on this article, when Japan's official position paper finally arrived and was distributed to the working group delegations to consider. Whatever persuasive influence Japan's delegates might have exerted behind the scenes, whatever chance Japan might have had to shape the debate in the conference room on the contents of the negotiating text—the purpose of the Conference session, after all—was surely lost in transit.

Output—Statements, Resolutions, Proposals. An idea of Japan's conference input is provided by the sixth session (May 23–July 15, 1977). In some fifty-six meetings over the first three weeks of that session, delegates addressed the seabed issue, by then the main work of the conference. During that period, Japanese representatives made just six statements and circulated one note (dealing with Canada's mining cost projections). Typically, the few statements of Japanese delegates were narrowly focused, nonideological, closely attentive to minor issues and textual details, and devoted to contrasting differences between existing drafts or raising rather inconsequential points about others' proposals, revisions, and drafts. The Japanese presentations were delivered in a flat, rambling, humorless style, punctuated by lengthy pauses.

In other committees, Japan offered occasional proposals, but on relatively minor subjects. Japan had been associated with an initiative proposing a 50-mile limitation on pollution restrictions by coastal states and, in Committee II, presented one of several plans relating to midoceanic ridges beyond the 200-mile boundary.[28] Japan submitted one of a handful of proposals on seabed exploitation at the 1975 Geneva session.

Leadership Positions. Japan did not chair any of the main or subsidiary committees of the Conference or head any of the seven negotiating groups. In the 1977 session a Japanese representative (Iguchi) served as chairman of the Asian group. Japan was a member of five committees. No Japanese participant was mentioned to me as having been a major player during the seven years of diplomatic negotiations at UNCLOS III.

Impact on the Convention Text. It is difficult to pinpoint where, if at all, Japan made an identifiable mark upon the text of the sea law treaty itself. A comparison of available draft texts to the final convention text does not suggest that Japan had any particular success in shaping the document. It did join with others on a few points relating to the marine environment.

Impact on Other Delegations. Again, this is a tricky factor to assess, but Japanese participants have not been mentioned as having played particularly prominent roles, at least according to analysts of UNCLOS III. At the sea law conference, Japan championed no significant causes, took no major initiatives, was not a key consensus-builder, and was not associated with any major formulation (such as the "Irish formula" for the continental margin, the "Kissinger package," the "Casteñada proposal," or the "Evensen compromise formula"). Japan did not seem particularly interested in making its mark on the conventional text. Nor was it an active intermediary, coalition-builder, or bridge-builder able to arrange some compromise solution, as was Canada with copper and nickel producers Peru, Chile, Zaire, Indonesia, and Cuba in the First Committee.

Japan's few proposals did not prove to be crucial to the negotiatory process. In statements by other delegates before the committee, Japan was rarely, if ever, mentioned. The scattered references to Japan that did appear tended to be toward the end of lists of members of working or caucusing groups.

Nor did other delegations seem to pay much attention to the occasional remarks that Japanese representatives made. At one point, when a member of the American delegation was observed to be concentrating intently while a Japanese representative was speaking, I asked him the reason for his intense interest. He replied, "Because he never fails to track me down afterwards to ask me what I thought of his speech." Others interviewed complained at great length about Japanese representatives' lackluster style, excessive formality (e.g., avoiding first names, using "Mr. Chairman" even in small, informal meetings) and lack of negotiatory authority, and the dominating presence in their delegation of "Foreign Office types."

Of course, inspired oratorical flourishes scarcely turned the tide in swaying national delegations at the conference. But personal flair can build a reputation and even get the attention of delegates. For instance, when U.S. representative Elliot Richardson, a man of considerable charisma, presented an American statement at one point in the deliberations—after more than enough prepared copies had been distributed in advance to all participants—all one could hear besides the speaker's voice was the sound of a hundred or so pages being turned simultaneously by a conference room full of attentive listeners. Another example: Late one night after a particularly tedious, inconclusive debate in the seabed committee, the British representative argued passionately for staying the course in the negotiations. Ending with a flourish, he exclaimed, "It's a Long, Long Way to Tipperary." It was a nice touch.

While behind-the-scenes, informal negotiations are critical, of course, and one offers such data with sagging conviction as to their cosmic significance, it is a fact confirmed by personal observation that of the forty total conference room personal exchanges or interactions between Japanese and American representatives and/or deputies in First Committee matters, thirty-nine were initiated by the Americans. Only once did the Japanese representative leave his seat to approach the U.S. delegation. Conference room conversations during proceedings between Japanese representatives and other delegates were rare. Overall, nothing at the sea law meetings would contradict the common "silence, smiling, and sleeping" characterization of Japanese international conference representatives.

The Persian Gulf Crisis and Japan

Toward the end of the 1970s, as the sea law conference was inching ponderously toward a conclusion, the Japanese government undertook a fundamental reappraisal of Japan's foreign relations. The result of this assessment was a reformulation of Japanese diplomacy toward a far more open, meaningful, and comprehensive alliance relationship with the United States. The following remarks by Prime Minister Suzuki Zenkō before the Diet in early 1982 illustrate just how radically Japanese thinking on security had shifted:

> Japan's diplomacy is no longer based on the principle of "omni-directional diplomacy" followed under the Fukuda administration. In response to an international environment changed since Afghanistan and Poland, Japan has had to align itself more closely with the United States and the European allies.
>
> We cannot accept such Soviet moves according to an unprincipled attitude of "looking pretty for everyone." Instead, we must pursue a diplomatic course that takes into full account the harsh realities of the international situation.[29]

The contradiction inherent in Japan's 1970s diplomacy—its mutually exclusive precepts of equidistance and military/security alliance with one superpower— seemed removed at last. Indeed, Japan had made a fundamental choice, deciding to haul down Okita's white flag of "omnidirectional" diplomacy to head in a single direction.

Four factors seem to explain this basic shift in policy: the Soviet invasion of Afghanistan, projecting the Soviet Union's strategic presence into Asia at the same time its Far East naval deployments were being increased; the American economic decline following the Vietnam debacle; the proven barrenness of Japan's resource diversification policies; and the realization that Japan's continued economic prosperity would depend upon open access to the U.S. market for high value-added Japanese manufactured products.

Aside from modest annual increases in Japan's own defense contributions, however, even the U.S. - Japanese strategic bonding process that would evolve in the 1980s did not require Japan to expand its own military contribution substantially. Of course, Japan became willing to permit a more elastic interpretation of existing bilateral agreements to allow the United States to do more, through deployments and operations outside the Pacific under the "Far East" clause of the mutual security treaty—with Japan paying a slowly rising share of the costs of U.S. forces based in Japan.

Thus, despite the inflated rhetoric of "alliance" and the vastly larger sums being allocated to a variety of global institutions and programs, Japan's relevant security environment and its defense role remained tightly circumscribed to a thousand nautical mile sea lane defense perimeter, by the Asian regional environment, and by calculations based more on money than missions with defense spending levels politically held under an arbitrary "1 percent of GNP" ceiling. Economic concerns remained at the core of Japan's foreign relations, beyond which only a calculation of yearly defense expenditures expressed Japan's direct participation in protecting its own national security.

Japan's meteoric rise in global economic affairs, culminating in its becoming the world's top creditor nation in 1985, thus had no parallel whatsoever in the defense and security areas. This nearly unidimensional Japanese security perspective was obscured further by topics commanding priority in Washington during the Reagan years: the deficit-ridden U.S. economy, a preoccupation with intensely politicized bilateral trade and economic matters, beefing up American military capabilities, and the pace and scale of Japan's economic ascendance, which had catapulted Japan to what some claimed would be "joint hegemon" status with the United States in global affairs. In Japanese eyes, as in the mid-1970s when the American era seemed at an end, the United States was looking very much like an over-the-hill hegemon whose national spirit and pocketbook were spent.

Japan's "Motivated" Diplomacy

The historic collapse of socialist regimes in 1990 seemed to bolster Japan's prospects for unshackling itself from its narrow diplomacy of the past to become a major world actor. At this extraordinary juncture, it seemed Japan might be able to win recognition as a leading global player, enhance its prestige, gain greater independence (less pressure from an America in decline combined with a diminished Soviet threat never related to Japan's force structure anyway), and separate politics from economics at last by elevating economic above military strength without having to deal seriously with the defense/security limits upon its diplomacy.

Certainly the Japanese prime minister seemed eager to step forward. But in what in retrospect seems a masterstroke of unfortunate timing, Prime Minister Kaifu Toshiki chose *Foreign Policy* magazine in which to proclaim "motivated" diplomacy as Japan's formula to deal with the emerging post–Cold War order. Based on the premise that "dialogue and cooperation now replacing missiles and tanks as the tools for achieving order," and that "the role of military might in the balance of power is diminishing and the importance of dialogue and cooperation is growing," the prime minister declared it Japan's "chance and duty" to marshal its "economic and technological strength, along with its store of experience and its conceptual ability" in facing the challenges of the new order.[30]

Whoops! Iraq's seizure of Kuwait on the second of August abruptly punctured this ascending balloon and brought it swiftly back to earth. The Iraqi attack would immediately test the motivation and conceptual ability of Japan's decision makers in figuring out what concrete actions would demonstrate convincingly their stated commitment to share in the process of building a new international relations structure.

Given this precrisis mentality, Japanese leaders would not be prepared for the sort of can-do operational role the crisis in the gulf would require from Japan. Indeed, as the Japanese symposia set was debating the prospects of a Japanese-American "pax consortis," or "post-pax Americana," or "The Japan that can say 'No,'" the Persian Gulf crisis struck. The crisis was to shatter any illusions of an easy transition to a new post–Cold War international order.

Early Calm. At the outset, there was no sign of panic in Tokyo. Nor was there much anxiety in Karuizawa where the vacationing prime minister assured reporters the invasion would have little impact on Japan.[31] In its beginning moments, the Persian Gulf situation did not seem to be a crisis, or at least not Japan's crisis. Ending his vacation a day early, Kaifu returned to Tokyo where he first conferred with his energy advisers. Tokyo's initial response was to figure out the domestic economic impact of cutoffs. That problem seemed manageable enough. After all, while Japan was the world's second-ranking oil importer, dependent on Middle East oil for over 70 percent of its oil supply, it was only marginally dependent on Iraq (5.8 percent dependency) and Kuwait (5.9 percent) during the first half of 1990.[32] Even though the 1973 oil shock had induced an intensive drive to lessen dependency, that attempt had failed.[33] Fifteen years later, Japan remained heavily reliant on imported, specifically Middle East, oil. But Tokyo had done far better in those energy policy areas it could control. Japan's energy conservation campaign and programs to build up its petroleum reserves had worked. Japan's fifty-eight-day stockpile in 1973 had grown to a 142-day reserve in 1990. Moreover, the promotion of alternative energy industries had reduced Japan's percentage of imported oil as a share of its total energy needs, lessening its vulnerability by 15 percentage points, from 88 percent in 1965 to slightly over 72 percent in 1990.[34] Simply by juggling energy supply sources, it seemed only a matter of days before Japan would be able to compensate for the anticipated shortfall in oil imports from Iraq and Kuwait and to avoid any immediate damage to the domestic economy.

Japan's initial package of economic sanctions, including a first-ever embargo on imported oil, was hurriedly approved in merely six hours, without waiting for passage of a UN Security Council resolution regarding the imposition of sanctions against Iraq. The Japanese government's uncharacteristic haste in reaching the decision stemmed primarily from an early morning telephonic prod from George Bush on August 4 and the European Community's announcement of stiff economic sanctions that evening. Prompted by the other Western allies' actions and Bush's personal urging, along with reportedly personally favored sanctions, Kaifu rushed through the four-point package which was announced the evening of August 5 and formally approved by the cabinet two days later. Pressures arising from Japan's enlarged global role, officials realized, ultimately left the country "no other choice"[35] but to go along.

So far so good. At this point, the situation seemed under control. Having handled the slow pitches coming his way, Kaifu must have been bursting with confidence. The months ahead would show, however, that as of that juncture, a bare five days into the crisis, his own political performance already had peaked. In the tortuous weeks to follow, Kaifu and other Japanese leaders would learn how little relevance the lessons learned from the 1970s would have to the dynamic political pluralism emerging at the dawn of the 1990s, particularly when "alliance" was expected to mean playing U.S.-Japanese security cooperation hardball at the global level.

Whatever opportunity the Japanese leadership might have had in the Persian Gulf case to seize the moment, to assert Japan's stated global interests in a fashion related to the situation—to demonstrate its heavy stake in Middle East stability and the depth of commitment to the U.S. alliance—was lost at the outset. Instead, the Kaifu Administration fibrillated. After much hesitation and Hamlet-like waffling (*Chuto: ikubeki ka, ikazarubeki ka* "The Middle East: Should I go? Should I not go?") over postponement of the Prime Minister's scheduled Middle East trip, the decision was made to call it off.[36] In Kaifu's place, Foreign Minister Nakayama Taro was selected to make the rounds of governments in the region, ascertain their views, and report back to Tokyo. Nakayama's trip was to consume considerable time. In the meantime, Tokyo officials tended to Japan's own interests, even to trying to get some of the Japanese detainees out, while awaiting any ideas Nakayama might bring back from his Middle East visit.

"Hai" Anxiety

Since Japan's original interest in the dispute had been limited, and with the foreign minister away seeking information, the Japanese leadership in Tokyo seemed to be open to advice. Not surprisingly, the Bush Administration was even more prepared to provide it.

But the situation changed abruptly when these other players raised the stakes. In a dramatic illustration of how intensely politicized, personalized, and pressurized the U.S.-Japanese bilateral relationship has become, even before Japan's sanctions had been announced,[37] over thirty (later all 100) U.S. Senators had signed and delivered through the Japanese Embassy in Washington a formal note for the prime minister urging Japan to take assertive action. Never before had Japan's buttons been pushed so quickly, by so many, with such telling effect. Japan was suddenly the target of a relentless barrage of proposals, demands, requests, advice, and recommendations, both sweeping and specific in content, through unofficial and official channels, from officials and private citizens alike, in virtually every major newspaper and magazine—all prodding Japan to act. Among the proposals were dispatching minesweepers, using Japan's airlift capabilities, transporting food and supplies for the U.S.-led multinational force being assembled in the gulf, providing economic assistance, making sizable purchases by cost sharing of U.S.-made weapons, expanding Japan's cooperation on sea-lane defense, and raising the sums paid to support American military forces in Japan.[38] Even Japanese corporations, which were to play a very low-profile role in the crisis, were asked to assist.

For Japan, the line was crossed into "crisis" only after a mid-August full-court press by Bush administration officials, including several phone calls from President Bush, an unusually intense personal appeal from Defense Secretary Dick Cheney to Self-Defense Agency Director General Ishikawa Yozo, and several requests from Ambassador Michael Armacost to Vice Foreign Minister Kuriyama Takakazu. Kuriyama was one of several key players in an inner circle task force of thirty or so officials, assembled to oversee the Middle East policy-making effort. Unfortunately, the group was not set up until two weeks after the Iraqi attack on Kuwait. This intensive arm-twisting transformed Japan's response into what was in effect a test of Japan's commitment to the U.S.-Japanese alliance.[39]

In any case, American blandishments underscored the urgency of doing more, quickly. Reportedly, the possibility of dispatching military forces was raised virtually from the start. Just as it had at the sea law conference, the Japanese government claimed Japan to be a "special case," as it searched about to find alternative avenues of participation beyond its initial sanctions package, to discover an appropriate contribution that others could accept from "economic not military superpower" Japan playing its role in a "world division of labor."

Thus, as at the sea law conference, Japan found itself on the defensive virtually from the beginning, guided only by self-styled notions of commitment, some empty set phrases and slogans. Above all else, there was the compelling wish to "avoid international isolation" (*kokusai koritsu kaihi*), no matter what.

Nonparticipation (saying "no") was simply not an option. Japan, it was felt, had to act. Government officials acknowledged the need for Japan to act. Moreover, Kaifu and other officials willingly stated their readiness to do their utmost—to do what must be done—to enable Japan to undertake a more prominent, responsible role. If "we can't, but we must" accurately expressed the thinking in Tokyo, certainly one very good reason for such thinking was that the U.S. Congress was scheduled to convene on September 5.

Thus, Kaifu's government already seemed locked into a no-win situation as it attempted to execute both a real and an anticipated agenda, both of which had been imposed from outside. Any sort of Japanese initiative seemed quite out of the question,[40] without first securing American approval or at least carefully weighing any possibly negative U.S. reactions.

Japan, it was agreed, "must do something more," but the action to be taken was not clear.[41] Outside criticism was expected if Japan's contribution was restricted to the economic sanctions. Potential reactions from Asian countries, notably China, certainly posed a key constraint to any suggestion of a Japanese military role.[42] Notwithstanding the urgency of Prime Minister Kaifu's need to provide some visible proof of commitment and his pledge to contribute more than money, just what was Japan supposed to offer, with a military role ruled out?

Among the options being discussed by mid-August were financial contributions, sending nonmilitary support personnel for the U.S.-led multinational force being deployed in the gulf, a communications and logistical support contribution, and even the possibility of some manpower being assigned in an unspecified noncombatant role. But at this juncture, with Japan already locked into a defensive position, the criteria for evaluating its performance in the crisis had shifted as well, to those governing Japan's ability to placate Washington, in the context of the U.S.-Japanese relationship. From early September on, discussion of Japan's potential contribution to the gulf crisis related to items on Washington's agenda. Henceforth, in short, Japan's "success"—or diplomatic performance—would be judged by how well it measured up to "good ally" tests.

From the outset, Tokyo seemed bereft of ideas, beyond "checkbook diplomacy" that would satisfy American and other foreign critics. Inasmuch as reacting to external pressure is reputedly Japan's strong suit in foreign relations, one might have imagined a superbly coordinated policy response. Alas, however, despite their oft-stated resolve to act decisively, Japanese officials could not, so long as appeasing the United States was the real objective. Even satisfying Washington proved an elusive, shifting target to track and bring down.

This was because what Japan was being requested to do was not only extraordinarily challenging but also extraordinarily vague. Partly as a result, Japan's responses likewise seemed hesitant, tentative, without purpose or direction. For instance, the Japanese government unwrapped its second package of gulf-related contributions on August 29. Again, as with the initial August 5 package, it was beribboned with official reaffirmation of Japanese commitment and concern. To wit: "We can't afford to be seen not doing anything about a problem which threatens our own national interests."[43]

But if placating the United States was the true objective underlying Japanese policy, how did this second offering measure up? Unfortunately, the package provided for 100 medical volunteers, to be dispatched quickly to the area, the chartering of two ships and two planes to provide supplies to allied forces in the gulf, and equipment to guard the troops against heat. The target had been missed, by a wide margin. At this historic moment, with its alliance commitment on the line, the Japanese government had come up virtually empty. The predictable, and predicted, U.S. response to this "doing our best" second package was to demand more.

If Tokyo's overall commitment level fell much below U.S. expectations, its level of performance in carrying out its pledges was even more disappointing, both in absolute amounts and with regard to the many delays, evasiveness, and procedural obstacles that emerged to thwart the effort. Regarding the promised dispatch of medical personnel, for example, only a few volunteered.[44] While far short of expected targets (to be exact, 83 short of the stated 100-volunteer goal), a seventeen-person contingent, five doctors, five technicians, four nurses, and three Foreign Ministry bureaucrats, was hurriedly assembled and dispatched gulfward. Always upbeat, Kaifu promised to send the full 100-member group later on.[45] It should be noted that the dispatch of medical personnel was viewed as the only way Japan could contribute with manpower, even though the medical team had not been requested, was not deemed necessary, and the group finally sent was not qualified to perform its duties in a region of conflict.

Further, Japan's follow-through on the delivery of promised equipment and logistical support became snarled in a bureaucratic and communication tangle. Delivery of a shipload of jeeps (some 800 four-wheel drive vehicles) stalled for two days in mid-September because no document formally requesting a ship to carry the cargo had been submitted. Moreover, lacking official confirmation that the cargo was unrelated to Japan's Middle East contribution, the All-Japan Seamen's Union refused to load the vessel and the crew refused to depart.[46] Similarly, the first chartered ship with food and supplies originally scheduled to sail twenty days earlier did not leave until September 25.

On a separate option path, any chance of sending minesweepers was discarded, at least according to one account, by this reasoning: "A minesweeper cannot operate alone. Two or three minesweeping vessels would be needed, plus a mother ship which, in turn, would require a supply ship as well. And an escort vessel would have to accompany them for protection. All in all, one would have a flotilla—clearly a military unit—whose dispatch would be unconstitutional."[47] Finally, regarding Japan's pledges of financial assistance, the earliest U.S. cost estimates quickly escalated far beyond Japan's calculations. Thus, the exact amount had not been okayed with the American side prior to Kaifu's unveiling of the second package on August 29.

During this "middle" phase—implementation of initial commitments with contemplation of additional, more substantial, and riskier steps with military implications—Tokyo still was addressing the Persian Gulf question along the familiar, albeit bumpy, road of U.S.-Japanese relations. As it had done throughout the tumultuous 1980s, Tokyo was probing for Washington's immovable bottom-line position among the barrage of incoming preachments, requests, and demands, euphemistically labeled "international expectations." Only indirectly, through Washington's perspectives and policies, was Japan at all concerned with the fundamental issue of resolving the first major crisis of the incipient post–Cold War era. Indeed, in their offices a world away from the gulf and the gut issue of expelling Iraqi forces from Kuwait, policy-makers in Tokyo might well have thought it business as usual as they scrambled about to conjure up a package which would satisfy the United States.

Only when implementation of its pledged contribution had bogged down completely by delays in sending equipment and supplies and providing even the modest types and amounts of medical assistance seemed in doubt did Japan begin in earnest to pursue other possible choices, more ambitious alternatives, with more far-reaching political repercussions.

Throughout the post–World War II era, the task of balancing U.S. demands and domestic Japanese constraints has become perhaps the thorniest task facing any Japanese prime minister. Whether accurately or not, Prime Minister Kaifu and his advisers had determined that Washington would not be satisfied with a Japanese gulf crisis package that failed to contain some direct commitment of Self-Defense Force manpower. But the harsh reality of Japanese domestic politics seemed to rule out any such direct role. Interestingly, public opinion seemed forgiving, at least early on, with one poll awarding the Kaifu administration a 60 percent approval rating.[48] Another survey, however, exposed Japan's gulf effort as a potential hitch to his popularity, by finding far more Japanese (nearly two-thirds of those surveyed) to be worried about sending Japanese personnel overseas than about any impact the crisis might have on the Japanese economy (51.2 percent) or even about the prospect of war itself (43.3 percent).[49] Further, in Kaifu's inner circle of policy advisers the Foreign Ministry was in charge; its officials had sought to block Self-Defense Agency involvement in Middle East decisions from the beginning, and Kaifu himself quite scrupulously had excluded the agency's director from top-level deliberations.

In addition, with his leadership abilities being savaged for having caved in to Bush's relentless arm-bending, Kaifu was clearly facing a domestic political limit to the extent to which he could take orders from Washington. For Kaifu, what had been external suddenly had become internal because of daily reports detailing the bureaucratic bumbling in the implementation of Japan's earlier pledges. Rivals within his own Liberal Democratic party (LDP) began to grumble out loud. Looking about for someone to blame, they looked first in Kaifu's direction. From his hospital bed, former foreign minister Abe Shintaro complained about the tardiness of Japan's response. Party elder Fukuda Takeo faulted the government's timing and lack of consensus. Ex-prime minister and party kingpin Takeshita Noboru cited insufficient preparation and inadequate consultations inside and outside Japan. And political "weather-vane" Nakasone Yasuhiro urged caution. Among the opposition, only the Democratic Socialist party (DSP) was generally supportive, initially favoring sending noncombatant personnel and financial aid while opposing the dispatch of minesweepers or surveillance vessels.

Under attack at home for having knuckled under to American pressure and for snafus in carrying out Japan's duly stated commitments, Kaifu was again blind-sided from Washington. Just as Japan had decided to raise its financial contribution to the multinational effort to $4 billion, the House of Representatives, by a 370–53 vote, passed a resolution favoring withdrawing U.S. troops from Japan, unless Tokyo consented to fund the entire annual cost of supporting them in Japan.

It seemed a good time for Kaifu to get out of town. Making the previously postponed trip to the gulf seemed a perfectly timed political move. Before leaving, however, he announced a plan. Throughout the gulf controversy, officials in Tokyo had been groping for some justifying standard, a plausible and workable rationale on which to hang Japan's Middle East contributions. Could it be "UN-centrism"? How about Japan as a "Good Ally"? Would "Financial Underwriter" play in Pittsburgh? Kaifu desperately needed some visible sign of Japan's commitment that could placate the United States, provide a face-saving cover, and finesse the politically explosive subject of a possible combat role for Self-Defense Force personnel. He finally hit upon the idea of dispatching uniformed—but unarmed and volunteer—Self-Defense Force support personnel to the gulf.

The plan was to frame Japan's participation as part of a UN peacekeeping task force. Given the popular appeal of United Nations slogans and the strong public support of UN Security Council resolutions already passed to address the gulf situation, any discussion of the plan was expected to have a positive, internationalist flavor.

A new plateau had been reached in Japan's handling of the gulf issue; a loftier multilateral and United Nations dimension had been added to the debate. But there were added options and complications in an already complex situation. But Japan now faced yet more tests, even vaguer standards, and equally elusive targets as before.

The "Middle East Diet"

The beleaguered Japanese prime minister, hoping to mollify both his Washington and his domestic critics at a single stroke, thus decided to introduce legislation before the Diet embodying a "new interpretation" of the Japanese Constitution to permit the dispatch of Self-Defense Force personnel outside Japan. The ensuing month was sheer political pandemonium.

During the latter half of October, in what could have been a truly enlightened and historic debate in the Diet, as that body celebrated its centennial, the discussion on the Middle East crisis instead dissolved into a stormy, bitter, and unproductive confrontation. From the Diet's opening on October 16 to month's end, over fifty hours were devoted in heated exchanges in both Diet chambers on the nature and permissible limits of Japan's military contribution to the Persian Gulf crisis.

This marathon Diet session was convened ostensibly to consider the government's proposed "UN Peace Cooperation Law" to permit noncombatant Self-Defense Force personnel to be sent to the gulf. The idea, which the Kaifu cabinet previously had ruled out, envisaged Japanese participation in a government "peace" organization that would cooperate with the United Nations, presumably under UN Security Council resolutions in peacekeeping operations sanctioned under Chapter VII of the Charter of the United Nations.[50] The presumption was that structuring Japan's role in this fashion would sanctify it with the multilateral international community, appease the United States, and deflect opposition party and media critics' accusations that Bush was the ventriloquist and Kaifu the dummy in dealing with the Persian Gulf situation.

Why Bush and his top aides deliberately acted to pressure and ultimately to embarrass a politically weak but pro–American prime minister on an obviously controversial subject in a crisis setting is not a question to be addressed here. As it happened, during the course of the debate, Kaifu repeatedly was required to listen and respond to opposition charges that he was an American lackey obsequiously carrying out commands from Washington to send Japanese troops. Still, it is clear that the debate itself would never have taken place had the United States not urged Japan to send troops to participate in the American-led multinational force.

Reminiscent of tempestuous exchanges in the Diet in past years touching on military/security questions, much of October's Diet discussion dealt less with issues than with bureaucratic procedures, semantic distinctions, petty legalisms, and trivial pursuits. The flavor of the discussion is suggested by just a few examples of questions raised. Would UN Peace Cooperation Task Force members be permitted to carry sidearms or other weapons for self-defense without authorization through a UN resolution? How could Japanese support for the U.S.-led multinational force be allowed under UN auspices in the absence of UN Security Council sanctioning of a peacekeeping force? How could one distinguish actions taken for "collective self-defense," which are barred for a victim of aggression and the victim's allies by Article 9 of Japan's Constitution, from actions taken for reasons of "collective security," which are permitted by virtue of being sanctioned by the international community and would fit the UN Peace Cooperation Task Force even while not being mandated by the United Nations? Would not *haken* (the dispatch of noncombatant personnel) under the bill in fact be indistinguishable from the unconstitutional *hahei* (dispatching soldiers abroad to threaten or use military force)?

Even the ominous subject of constitutional revision was raised. Further, the debate exposed the emptiness of such incantations as *heiwashugi* (peace-ism), *kokuren chushinshugi* (UN centrism), and other symbolic catch phrases with definite references for domestic politics but without much meaning for diplomacy.

At the same time, the debate did underline the firmness of political restrictions that continue to block Japanese military deployments abroad. The bill's "new" interpretation sparked a firestorm of opposition from all sides. The Japan Socialist party (JSP) hastily patched together a vaguely phrased counterdraft. For its part, the DSP reversed its original position of generally backing the LDP. Opposition to the bill from the Sokagakkai-backed Komeito then stiffened, presumably because of the party's concern over an upcoming election in Aichi to fill a key vacancy in the upper house whose approval was essential to the bill's passage. At each step, Japanese government proposals on the UN Peace Cooperation Force, particularly the idea of sending Japanese manpower to the gulf, were met by indifference, foot-dragging, and staunch resistance.

By early November, with opposition resistance having hardened, clear limits on Japan's possible contribution had been set. With his administration in disarray and faced with the impossibility of gaining upper house approval, an exasperated Kaifu had to abandon the proposed bill. The option of a substantially enlarged Japanese contribution, beyond the previous role of financial donor and partial underwriter of the larger allied gulf effort, now was out of the question.

The debate seemed to die by a thousand needles. The deliberations ended as they had begun, amidst Kaifu's declarations that Japan "cannot be a bystander," "will never become a military power," and "must contribute positively to the construction of a new world order."[51] Indisputably the final sign of failure, however, was a recommendation to organize a semi-official study group whose purpose would be to deliberate—at great length and in much detail—upon the nature and implications of a restructured international society for Japan's diplomatic role in the future.

Discussion

In the law of the sea and Persian Gulf episodes, Japan—the perpetual outsider, the latecomer who joins international structures already in place—was offered two chances to share in historic regime-building processes at the global level. In the first instance, in a period of severe economic upheaval, Japan clearly had a heavy stake in participating in the process of formulating rules to govern a new international maritime regime. In the second instance, in a time of grave political uncertainty, Japan had vital economic interests in building Middle East stability and shoring up its alliance bonds with the United States. These obvious concerns were duly acknowledged and in fact were underlined passionately in both cases by Japanese officials' declarations of their firm resolve to participate actively.

Once the initial hoopla was over, however, a starkly different behavioral portrait emerged. Despite the breathtaking diplomatic opportunities each encounter seemed to present Japan, its officials were unable to seize the moment, transcend narrow parochial attitudes and interests, and demonstrate that their rhetorical declarations of interest in regime building and their diplomatic catchphrases and slogans had meaningful roots. In the sea law case, when the polycentric, multipolar arena proved beyond the capabilities of its omnidirectional diplomatic instruments, Japan turned defensive and produced a multilateral mouse. In the gulf case, when its freshly minted "motivated" diplomacy and much-revered principles like "UN centrism" fizzled out against the harsh realities of alliance politics in the post–Cold War era, Japan turned defensive and produced a military/security mouse.

The gap between Japan's diplomatic wind-up and its diplomatic delivery is huge. Notwithstanding the possibility that it has the ability to play the enlarged international role others expect and Japanese idealize and promote, Japan seems to lack the will to execute its professed diplomatic goals. The application of performance-based criteria to Japanese behavior in both cases, moreover, reveals a Japan relatively unconcerned with the multilateral regime or the bilateral alliance regime.

Japan's diplomacy in both cases seems to fit the coping or minimalist model described at the beginning of this essay—a typically passive, watch-and-wait, damage-limiting approach. Whether viewed from a multilateral (UNCLOS III) or a U.S.-Japanese alliance (Persian Gulf) perspective, this Japanese coping style was not global, long-range, or regime-oriented.

Tokyo did not set out to play a major role at the Law of the Sea Conference. Rhetoric aside, Tokyo acted as though the sea law meetings were something of a curiosity, a diplomatic sideshow with only marginal relevance to Japan's own interests. Its behavior reflects interest in the status-enhancing benefits to be gained through participation, the significance attached to exhibiting a vague "internationalist" posture, to gathering information relevant to securing its own interests, and adapting to changing circumstances without external or internal political costs, particularly diplomatic isolation. In the Persian Gulf example, Japanese behavior— the initial Japanese focus on its own energy supplies, its snail-paced response to gulf coalition requirements, and the substance of the October Diet debate—seemed to reaffirm what has been a bedrock article of faith among many long-time outside observers of Japan. In the crunch, these realists contend, Japan will never risk its economic interests or the lives of its citizens on behalf of some principle or cause, another country or ally in need, or the international community.

Against this perspective, perhaps Japan's diplomatic "performance" ought to be assessed differently. From a Japanese perspective, results-based measuring rods seem to be of little use in gauging "success." For instance, toting up the number of Japanese diplomatic initiatives taken, speeches given, or committee meetings attended would be rather pointless if the Japanese government and its representatives had not sought the limelight or, as seems close to reality, even had sought to avoid center stage entirely, choosing instead to speak up only when pressured by others to do so.

In light of Japan's own impoverished "coping" agenda, what criteria can one apply to appraise its diplomatic performance in these two cases? Without clearly stated goals, particularly in fluid multilateral or crisis-type situations, one must infer performance standards from repeatedly consistent behavior. While the limitations of this formulation are recognized, the following three standards seem characteristically Japanese: (1) accurate assessment of the situation; (2) smooth adjustment to situational changes; and (3) protection of vital national interests.

Test 1: Accurate Assessment of the Situation. The external orientation of its diplomacy means that Japan's "success" requires accurately gauging the outside environment, reading the signals about and grasping the essence of external conditions so that its initial response, if any, can be framed appropriately, tailored to fit the expected requirements of a particular context. Japan's level of interest is therefore high in information gathering, in being briefed on developments, to obtain the clearest possible reading of the environment.

According to this first standard, Japan performed poorly. In both cases, Tokyo officials exaggerated the degree both of American decline and of Japanese independence in the "new" global order. Further, officials underestimated both how seriously other countries would pursue the topics and what they would expect from Japan. Throughout the gulf case in particular, Tokyo failed to grasp the Bush administration's perception of the crisis as a test of the American alliance structure's ability to handle a major threat and of allied willingness to respond positively. Japan did not assess the preconference environment accurately in the sea law case. During the early conference stage, Japan overestimated the political clout of the less-developed countries, underestimated the importance of the sea law effort to the United States and others, and misjudged how swiftly the national enclosure of ocean space would proceed.

In both the sea law and gulf cases, Japan's first response reflected its preoccupation with its own narrow economic interests (i.e., at UNCLOS III the impact of the economic zones and fishing limits, and in the gulf case the oil import supply and Japanese detainee issues) rather than as an opportunity to play an active role in a new international maritime or a post–Cold War framework. This short-sighted perspective explains why both episodes escalated to the "crisis" plateau when unexpected events "shocked" officials into realizing they had misread the situation (e.g., Japan's unexpected isolation at Caracas and the unprecedented intensity of direct U.S. pressure just after the Iraqi attack), and some unexpected decision/action would be required beyond the accepted perimeters of diplomatic action. This seems to be the reaction to Japanese-style failure.

Test 2: Smooth Adaptation to the Situation. A second "Japanese" test of diplomatic performance emphasizes smoothly responding to changes in external and internal contexts, particularly by anticipating, deflecting, or containing criticism. Japan did not react quickly or adequately within the multilateral diplomatic context at the sea law conference, nor in the alliance context in the Persian Gulf case. Even though it was recognized that a new order was emerging as each encounter began, in neither instance was Japan's own role linked purposefully to that process as later events unfolded. Interestingly, the original reactive pattern was to be repeated at each successive fallback adjustment sequence in each encounter (at UNCLOS III when adjustment levels changed on different conference topics, and in the gulf case when American dissatisfaction with Japanese responses forced reappraisal).

Smooth adjustment was impaired in both cases by private and bureaucratic interests unwilling to budge (such as the fishing industry at UNCLOS III or the Transportation Ministry in the Persian Gulf case). Japan's flawed adjustment during the gulf case can scarcely be attributed to having convened too few meetings; officials were huddled in virtually constant deliberations from mid-August to September's end. Nor did Japan's disarray stem from having too few options to consider; if anything there were too many alternatives.

Bureaucratic infighting and miscalculation seriously impaired the process of adjusting Japan's responses. While Washington's criticism had dwelt upon Japan's dilatoriness during the initial stages of the gulf crisis, as did some Japanese as well, most in Japan criticized the Kaifu cabinet for acting prematurely, with "insufficient preparations"—meaning insensitivity to adjustment and consolidation of view— points within the ruling Liberal Democratic party. But there had been little time for this: In volatile multilateral or crisis situations, faced with unpredictable shifts in others' goals and policies, any chance of quick, smooth adjustment via the ritual *nemawashi* process—testing the waters by a methodical canvassing of opinions to determine acceptable action—was virtually nil.

When the sea law conference began, many nations, including the United States, were undecided on their positions. Japan was not alone in that regard, but proceeded to isolate itself by resisting previously determined faits accomplis. No matter how commendable it may be to stick to your guns, it may not be such a hot idea if your goal is avoiding isolation.

Japan's use of the available multilateral diplomatic instruments—speeches, sponsorship of proposals, coalition-building, gaining and exercising influence in leadership positions—suggests that a low priority was assigned to the overall effort. Even when attempts were made, Japan's potential impact was lessened understandably enough by linguistic handicaps, and a stiffly formal diplomatic style that interlocutors often found frustrating and unattractive. Further, any possibility of reacting smoothly was thwarted by interbureaucratic feuding, government indecision, and the virtual veto power wielded by certain private interests.

The coping approach seemed to rule out initiatives. When Japanese concessions were made at the conference, they came late, were out of phase with the process itself, and failed to gain any negotiatory advantage for Japan.

In the Persian Gulf case, Japan's uncoordinated, haphazard implementation of even its limited goals is strikingly evident. In both cases examined, Japan struggled painfully from one compromise level to the next, only to find itself still one step behind, with the party over each time it arrived.

Test 3: Protecting Japanese National Interests. In both cases there was much evidence of soul searching, hand wringing, and head scratching. Despite official lamentations of Japan's "painful predicament" and like expressions of the notorious Japanese victim's mentality, in the end Japan did not jeopardize its own interests but acted methodically, pragmatically, and, when necessary, opportunistically to secure and protect those interests. Japan's critical decisions—those unilaterally reached outside the multilateral framework at UNCLOS III and those ultimately rejecting the military option and restricting both financing and manpower support in the gulf case—illustrate vividly the paramount significance Japan attaches to certain basic national interests. In fact, when the initial panic clouds cleared, Japan did move swiftly to secure its own interests, and the constraints suddenly did not appear so overwhelming after all. Despite its initial misreading of the situation, and the subsequent rough process of adjustment context, Japan did act to protect its own interests.

In the Persian Gulf example, Japan's response has not been based on Iraq's act of aggression in annexing Kuwait. Nor did Japan's approach reflect moral outrage over Saddam Hussein's actions or identification with the larger purposes of the exercise. Throughout the sea law meetings, Japan's diplomacy reflected little identification with the purposes of the UNCLOS process itself. Not being especially concerned with the common effort or the convention being negotiated, Japan did not compromise for the sake of contributing to the conference's overall success. Rather, the idea was that no matter whether the conference succeeded or failed, Japan would have to act on its own to develop the technology necessary to exploit the nodules when the time arrived. Similarly narrow thinking dominated the Japanese approach to the Persian Gulf case as well. In the latter case, the attitude was that, no matter what the outcome, Japan's task would be to place priority on setting up a crisis management organization—which, if carried out, would represent a significant departure from past institutional arrangements in Japanese diplomacy.

Despite the attractions to Japan of independent, looser associations, in the crunch it sided with the United States in both cases. Although no special U.S.-Japanese relationship was demonstrated during the initial stage of the sea law conference, and although Japan ultimately ratified the treaty that the United States thus far has failed to approve, the two countries' national interests converged compatibly on seeking unrestricted ocean space. Later, when Japan tilted toward the United States and advanced industrial countries on seabed exploitation, eventually backing the American proposals, it seemed a fitting prelude to Japan's rejection of omnidirectionalism and shift toward a U.S. alliance–centered diplomacy at the end of the 1970s.

It should be noted that the context-specific constraints Japan had to overcome at the sea law conference may be overstated, in particular the degree to which Japan was pressured to take action. Further, the inconclusive nature of the proceedings themselves tended to reduce the negative impact that Japan's misjudgments and inaction might have had otherwise.

Indeed, Japan's initial reading of a situation, for instance, may lead to a decision not to become involved. Along with its preparation of endless wish lists and soul searching, Japan has enjoyed the luxury of lengthy discussions of nonaction, about whether or not to become involved. For one thing, this has permitted Japan to conserve tremendous effort by not chasing every passing rabbit to places others later discover to be culs-de-sac. After all, by not pursuing a leading role in the sea law conference effort, Japan, the much maligned diplomatic "bystander," did manage to save the immense amount of time, energy, manpower, and money the United States and others poured into an ultimately nonproductive venture.

A Void at the Core?

There is an obvious discrepancy between performance-based, goal-oriented tests and these narrower "Japanese" criteria. Even according to its own standards, however, Japan's "coping" performance would be given a low rating. Certainly that evaluation is lowered further by calibrating a policy's "success" with the level of foreign hostility, criticism, and resentment it generates. The test of successful coping, presumably, is the level of flak, friction, or criticism Japan's diplomacy receives. A perfectly "successful" policy, an "A-plus in coping" report card, would be clear of critical marks or, better still, no card would even exist in the files.

After all, Japan's diplomatic performance has been judged by the application of externally determined criteria, standards, tests, principles, and values. Foreign critics regularly list the attitudes, principles, goals, policies, and methods Japan should follow in its diplomacy.

These external judgments are critically relevant because they seem to be incorporated indirectly into the Japanese view. External opinion has shaped not only the diplomatic agenda but the process and the standards of performance as well. Japan's reliance on outsiders' expectations and judgments extends beyond diplomatic goals to include process norms and values (e.g., acting quickly, spontaneously, voluntarily, on one's own initiative, generously, with a proper, give-and-take spirit). One may argue that Japan's recurring diplomatic woes may well stem from seeming to rely on anticipated external, particularly American, advice and standards to set its foreign policy environment, to frame its options and actions, as well as to appraise its own diplomatic performance.

Accordingly, no matter what the solution favored, the fundamental test of "success," the underlying motivation, for hawks and doves, for hard-liners and soft-liners alike, has been its anticipated impact on others—on allies, on key Asian countries, on resource suppliers. This bedrock concern, moreover, is reflected in arguments of both advocate and opponent on how well an option would sit with foreigners. The following randomly selected examples taken from the Japanese domestic debate on the gulf situation illustrate the point:[52]

> Doi Takako (JSP, Chairman): "Even if revised, the heart of the bill would remain sending the Self-Defense Forces abroad. To do that would be to *deceive the peoples of the world.*"
> Miyazawa Kiichi (LDP): "Even if we undertake the task of revising the bill and then fail to approve it, that will not be enough to *meet the minimum expectations of the world.*"
> Ozawa Ichirō (LDP, Takeshita faction): "If Japan does not send troops and American soldiers are killed, then *U.S. opinion will turn against Japan. We must act to avoid that.*"
> Suzuki Eizo (chairman, Nikkeiren): "Our emotional debate and legalistic interpretations like 'don't send our children to war' or 'it's no good' or 'we can't' will mean that *Japan in foreign eyes will become a wolf, an orphan, a friend to no one* in some future crisis."

But meeting outsiders' elevated expectations of Japan's performance has proved a difficult task indeed. Ironically, even though Japan has been wholly occupied with external opinions, standards, and tests, its diplomacy by these outside, performance-based standards has been weighed and found wanting. An evaluation of Japan's performance at the Law of the Sea Conference, using the preparation, representation, output, and impact criteria used in this essay, lends credence to the pithy though somewhat facetious appraisal of Japan's performance by one leading sea law authority, who ranked Japan's job at the conference at "the level of Chad." Except for the comparison with such a small country, perhaps, one suspects a minimalist Japanese diplomat might almost regard it a compliment to be graded on the "Chad" level. His response might well be, "As inconspicuous as Chad? Why, thank you very much!"

Nor has Japan's response to the Persian Gulf crisis exactly been its finest diplomatic moment, when viewed from outside. Far from it. Barely seven weeks into the crisis, *The Economist* became the first publication to label Japan's strained and meager efforts a "failure."[53] Except for a few thank-yous from front-line states in the gulf, Japan received very little credit for its efforts. And as the Persian Gulf crisis unfolded, each successive Japanese response—both in content and in process—was found wanting by others' standards, although Tokyo officials had expected such a negative reaction beforehand.[54]

One of the sternest judgments came in mid-November, when House Armed Services Committee Chairman Les Aspin announced the results of his in-depth examination of the responses of nineteen countries to the gulf crisis, measuring levels of military participation, financial outlays, compliance with UN sanctions, political support, reaction time, and "special factors" involving national ability to contribute.[55] Aspin's findings, released in "report card" format, gave Japan a letter grade of "C"—just one notch above Libya.

How on earth could such a low mark have been given to the diplomatic performance of "Japan as Number One," the architect of the emergent "Pax Nipponica," the "ascendant hegemon" purportedly champing at the bit to charge gloriously into the maelstrom of post–Cold War world politics?

This essay suggests that one reason was that Japan was being asked to undertake direct commitments and actions that exceeded the previously accepted and politically sustainable boundaries of Japan's foreign policy consensus. Possibly another among many plausible reasons stems from what some Japanese see as a lack of moral values in Japan, "a void at the core," to borrow Diet member and popular novelist Ishihara Shintaro's memorable phrase.[56] Interestingly, even as he bewailed Japan's vacuum of "moral principles," Ishihara nonetheless measured Japanese progress toward reaching morality against the yardstick of winning "international respect and trust."

Still another source of the gap between Japanese and foreign judgments about Japan's diplomatic motives, goals, and beliefs may be the result of countless interactions between Japanese representatives, government officials, businessmen, or private citizens and those non-Japanese who ask over and over again why Japan does not behave in some manner other than it does.

In the cases examined here, examples of such queries might be: "Why didn't Japan seek to play a leading role in parliamentary diplomacy at the Law of the Sea Conference?" or "Why didn't Japan contribute more meaningfully to the allied gulf effort?"

To pursue the matter a bit further, listed below are some of the statements of Japanese officials and commentators during the two cases analyzed. They can be regarded as typically "Japanese" replies to the two hypothetical questions above. All replies were made in the context of actual or anticipated criticism of Japanese performance or behavior. To understand the list, each typical "response" should be preceded with some positive statement regarding the Japanese action questioned (i.e., Japan's Persian Gulf contribution), then followed by an "if only" phrase before an item is chosen from the list. Thus, the reply would be: "Japan would have sought to contribute troops to the allied gulf effort if only [insert one or more items from the list]"

other countries gave Japan more time to reach decisions.
Japan knew how Asian countries would react.
other countries sent clearer signals of their intentions.
Japan was not so plagued by factionalism.
Japanese public opinion would go along.
the opposition parties would agree.

the prime minister had convened the Diet earlier.
Japan's officials had collected better information.
Japan had more experience in diplomacy.

Japan had a system of crisis management.
Japan's Constitution would permit it.
Japan had a permanent seat on the Security Council.
the problem was not multilateral in nature.
the problem was not bilateral in nature.

Japan was not so vulnerable.
Japan was not so dependent on foreign markets and resources.
Japan was not placed in such a terrible predicament.
Japan did not suffer from the legacy of World War II.

These are merely samples, drawn from a mountain of possible examples. At first glance, such responses may appear harmless enough excuses, apologetics, and rationalizations—the accumulated detritus of a half-century or more of defensive diplomacy.

But the numbing regularity of these comments suggests some deeper meaning. The responses seem to assume, first, that Japan is making an effort and, second, that Japan would have performed better "if only" it did not have to run the intimidating gauntlet of geographical disadvantages, parochial attitudes, sociocultural obstacles, constitutional constraints, bureaucratic hurdles, or linguistic stumbling blocks. These handicaps in and of themselves, the thinking goes, restrict Japan's options and rule out choices.

Having advanced to this point, one can carry the logic one step further, because such "if only" statements usually are followed by a reference to some positive result to take place. Thus, according to this "If only X, then Y" brand of logic, "Y" refers to a Japan able to be assertive, take initiatives, play a leading role, articulate its policies clearly, link the issues, undertake major commitments, react to fast-changing international developments, shoulder a larger defense/security burden (or take in more refugees, import foreign rice, correct the trade imbalance, whatever) swiftly, flexibly, and forthrightly. Finally, there is the wistful hope that Japan—at last freed from outside pressure, ridicule, criticism, and distrust—would be respected and admired, occupy an honored place in the international community, and have a diplomacy universally hailed as, well, a "success."

These statements are discussed here because they tend to distort the nature of discussion on Japanese diplomacy. To some extent, to be sure, they are of the "wouldn't it be nice if Japan were New Zealand, then we wouldn't have to worry about . . ." sort of wishful thinking. But, by sheer repetition, over a long period of time, such comments gradually come to acquire legitimacy as being Japan's own preferences, goals, and standards.

Most important, such statements impart an impression of common concern, of shared purpose, of genuine sincerity in wanting to achieve these same ends. While Japan may be successful in gaining prestige and assessing and adjusting to situational requirements, its visible behavior seems inappropriate to the context, whether it be measured against "good multilateral player" or "good alliance member" indicators. Japan's foreign audience, out of impatience or eagerness or both, is more than receptive to the impression of common values, goals, principles, and beliefs that is implied in such language. Japan's inability or unwillingness to voice its goals and standards straightforwardly, beyond mouthing such slogans as "peace diplomacy," "UN centrism," and the like, merely magnifies its dependence and deepens doubts about its intentions, values, and abilities.

The static generated by such ambiguous messages skews the analysis of Japanese diplomacy into pointless areas. One example is the endless, mindless speculation about when Japan is going to cross some arbitrary boundary (e.g., the "1 percent of GNP for defense" barrier, the FSX fighter issue, the LDP's 304-seat landslide election victory in 1986, even the buying of Pebble Beach) and metamorphose into whatever ghastly beast happens to inhabit a particular writer's Nintendo world of fantasized reality. Such messages help to form hopelessly vague, even contradictory stereotypical images of Japanese behavior. Thus: "The Japanese hate surprises" versus "The Japanese love change"; "The Japanese are preoccupied with domestic affairs" versus "The Japanese are totally other-oriented"; "The Japanese disagree but, when a consensus is reached, they pull together like a well-drilled army corps"; "The Japanese only respond to threats" versus "Threats don't work with the Japanese but just cause them to fly off in some crazy direction"; or "The Japanese have a blueprint, a long-range vision" versus "The Japanese are reactive, short-sighted, without long-range goals, and do just what the situation requires."

In this confusion, observers are left to guess at Japan's underlying motives. And they have tended to presume the worst. Naturally enough, a silent, passive Japan is viewed as an "unprincipled bystander," a "masterful procrastinator," a "reluctant ally," an "irresponsible partner," or an "unfair trader."

Some Costs of Minimalist Diplomacy

Despite its economic globalization, Japan has yet to connect its own interests effectively with the wider arenas in which it participates. Japan's narrowly defined, system-reactive but not system-centered brand of diplomacy of not challenging the existing order may work passably in routine, bureaucratized areas, although it has not proved "successful" even according to "Japanese" yardsticks of enhancing prestige, minimal-risk adjustment, and protection of national economic self-interest.

But the minimalist Japanese diplomatic approach may well exact a heavy, long-run price, by permitting Japan to be drawn into unwanted directions. The subject is significant, too, because Japan's global economic penetration inevitably will be accompanied by closer scrutiny and judgment of its performance. And, if the recent past is any guide, it will be judged more harshly.

What costs stem from Japan's minimalist style of diplomacy? The principal cost stems from Tokyo's inability or unwillingness to articulate its goals clearly and to relate those of others to the instruments being applied. This leaves its diplomatic goals obscured and the means determined by others and by the flow of events. Ultimately, judgments on Japan's role are made almost exclusively by outside measurements, with Japan finding itself seeking to satisfy others as it proceeds in unwanted situations.

Unappreciated Efforts. Not surprisingly, given the heavy weight Japan assigns to others' standards, goals, and approval, it rarely associates its own success with that of the conference, the alliance, or the organization. Japan's participation is seen as the cross Japan must bear; its commitment to carrying out those goals is lukewarm, even to the point of jeopardizing the success of the larger endeavors to which its own success is so intimately linked. Ironically, Japan, whose driving motive is placating or accommodating others—notably the United States—ends up pleasing no one and, in fact, being assailed as a half-hearted, free-riding, unprincipled ally.

Communication Static. From Japan's viewpoint, without articulating its foreign policy objectives clearly, it squanders much energy just to gauge what others want it to want or not want. In seeking to ascertain, clarify, and confirm others' policies, motives, and meanings, Japan unduly complicates its diplomacy with moving targets and sliding scales and, as in both cases discussed in this essay, ends up one step, one issue behind.

Distrust and Resentment. It is ironic, too, that Japan's understandably half-hearted effort to execute an externally prescribed agenda merely attracts the criticism it wishes to avoid. Acquiescing with "Okay, we will try, but . . ." when the motive is to placate or deter criticism only backfires as the process later exposes an evident disinterest. There is irony too in that the media saturation of Japan's diplomacy in the United States had its origins in Japanese desires to ease friction through information and exchange. Instead, it seems to have been hoisted by its own public-relations petard.

Official statements often strike others as excuses calculated to appease. Japanese officials often seek recognition for their contribution toward some development assistance program, multilateral agency, or issue (e.g., whaling, refugees, trade with South Africa) even though that "contribution" has been wrung from a reluctant Japan kicking and screaming every inch of the way. Then Japan turns resentful when its efforts are unacknowledged or unappreciated. In the Persian Gulf case one is likely to hear: "We made great efforts to do everything the United States wanted, but we can never do enough to satisfy them."

"Alice in Wonderland" Domestic Debate. What passes as Japan's domestic debate on foreign policy reinforces these misconceptions in that key policy issues are so radically altered when discussed in Japan's political arena, leaving outside observers often baffled. As in past controversies (e.g., whether the Soviet "threat" to Japan is "indirect" or "direct," what "1 percent of GNP" for defense really means, the third of the "Nonnuclear Principles," distinguishing "offensive" from "defensive" weaponry, defining "alliance" with the United States), the gulf crisis spawned similar bickering along peripheral factional, opposition, bureaucratic, and ideological battle lines, rather than a serious debate on the merits.

Japan's Future Left to Others. Minimalist diplomacy leaves others in charge of more than the grade sheets. By deferring to others, Japan lacks reciprocity in monitoring the monitors (e.g., Kaifu's valiant but vain attempt to pressure the United States during the Structural Impediments Initiative negotiations in 1989–1990) and, ultimately, lets control over its own future slip away. The gap between Japan's contributions and clout remains, on defense, foreign aid, and in multilateral organizations.

This assessment of Japan's performance suggests that Japan has its distinctive measuring rods of diplomatic performance. Against these "Japanese" standards as well as against "objective" standards, Japan's performance was lackluster. In both cases reviewed here, Japan allowed the game, the rules, and the scoring to be handled by others. Japan had neither an ocean policy nor a Middle East policy. Japan may have guarded its own interests but failed to project its interests in a wider multilateral or military/security context.

If Japan's minimum success standards are met, it can be a satisfied power, not a source of instability. But for that to happen, its own national policy goals must be articulated, even if they seem unduly modest or constrained, rather than leaving it to outside observers to imagine, intuit, or second guess Japanese objectives. Until then, Japan's motives must be inferred, as has been done in this essay.

This minimalist style doubtless will go on, despite external pressures and episodic Japanese vows to express its "leadership" or "global vision." Neither rhetoric nor wishing will make it happen. Japan's response to the mid-1970s' energy crisis did not prepare it to meet the gulf crisis. As this is written, not surprisingly, Tokyo is contemplating the enactment of laws to deal with a future situation similar to the gulf crisis. On this track, preparing for the last crisis, Japan inevitably will arrive at the station one crisis too late. But given the historical continuity of its diplomatic approach, even in such situations of perceived gravity as the two encounters this essay examines, one can merely wish for—and not expect very soon—a major change in behavior.

Notes

1. Examples: Karel G. van Wolferen, in " The Japan Problem," *Foreign Affairs*, 65, 2 (Winter 1986–87), pp. 288-303, jousts with a fantasized Japan; and Peter F. Drucker, in "Japan's Choices," *Foreign Affairs*, 65, 5 (Summer 1987): 923–941, reifies and then attacks Tokyo's "outflanking" strategy.

2. Kumon Shumpei, "Dilemma of a New Phase: Can Japan Meet the Challenge?" *The Trade Crisis: How Will Japan Respond?* (Seattle: Society for Japanese Studies, 1987), pp. 230–231.

3. Nihon keizai kenkyu senta, "200-kairi jidai no shokuryo mondai," no. 281 (October 1976): 46.

4. Okita Saburō, "Natural Resource Dependency and Japanese Foreign Policy," *Foreign Affairs*, 52, 4 (July 1974): 723–724.

5. Japan's ocean policies and approach to the sea law conference are examined carefully in Tsuneo Akaha, *Japan in Global Ocean Politics* (Honolulu: University of Hawaii Press and the Law of the Sea Institute, 1985), and in essays in Robert L. Friedheim et al., *Japan and the New Ocean Regime* (Boulder: Westview Press, 1984), especially Haruhiro Fukui, "How Japan Handled UNCLOS Issues," pp. 21–74; Tsuneo Akaha, "A Cybernetic Analysis of Japan's Fishery Policy Process," pp. 173–226, giving an incrementalist interpretation of Japanese decisional processes; and Robert L. Friedheim, "Japan's Ocean Policy: An Assessment," pp. 353–371.

6. Kei Wakaizumi, "Japan's Dilemma: To Act or Not to Act," *Foreign Policy*, 16 (Fall 1974): 30–47, sets forth the notion of U.S.-Japanese relations in a global context. The crisis mood was reflected in newspaper accounts. For example, the *Asahi shimbun* editorialized dramatically on March 1, 1975: "Japan, which has no resources at home, has no alternative but to repeat its earnest appeal to other nations for the survival of its 110 million people. The more hastily and harshly other nations try to force Japan to accept their demands, the stronger Japan will react, in order to survive."

7. *Nihon keizai shimbun*, June 19, 1974. Compare U.S. statements in 94th Congress, 1st session, *The Third United Nations Law of the Sea Conference*, Report to the Senate, June–August 1974.

8. *Asahi shimbun*, June 20, 1974.

9. *Nihon keizai shimbun*, June 19, 1974.

10. *Asahi shimbun,* May 23, 1974.

11. *Asahi shimbun,* March 1, 1975.

12. *Asahi shimbun,* March 3, 1975. Statement by Foreign Minister Miyazawa Kiichi.

13. *Asahi shimbun,* March 17, 1975.

14. Sumi Kazumi, "Umi kara shimedareru Nihon," *Asahi jyanaru,* 18, 3 (August 13, 1976): 28–32.

15. The others were the United States, France, West Germany, Italy, the Netherlands, Britain, and Belgium. The financial costs of the "Authority"—the organ expected to oversee deep seabed exploitation—and the contractual means of financing its activities are contained in Revised Single Negotiating Text (RSNT), A/CONF.62/WP8/Rev.1.

16. For the Sixth Session, New York, May 23–July 15, 1977, First Committee: Part XI of Informal Composite Negotiating Text (ICNT), p. 373; convention articles and annexes, A/CONF.62/WP.10 and Add.1; A/CONF.62/C.1/L.19.

17. *Asahi shimbun,* September 18, 1978.

18. Ann L. Hollick, *U. S. Foreign Policy and the Law of the Sea* (Princeton: Princeton University Press, 1981), p. 292.

19. Gene Gregory, "Japan and the Law of the Sea: Uncertainties of the New Order," *Asian Perspective,* 2, 1 (Spring 1978): 55.

20. Robert L. Friedheim, *Negotiating the New Ocean Regime* (forthcoming), p. 23, stresses how few turning points arose during the long negotiations.

21. Hollick, *U. S. Foreign Policy and the Law of the Sea,* p. 285.

22. Unless otherwise noted, specific references and examples cited here are from the deliberations on deep seabed mining issues before the First Committee and its Working Group during the Fourth, Fifth, Sixth, and Seventh (resumed) sessions during 1976–1978. The author attended these meetings through the auspices of the World Federation of United Nations Associations (WFUNA) in conjunction with Columbia University's East Asian Institute-sponsored Project on U.S.-Japan Relations in Multilateral Diplomacy.

23. From UNCLOS III official documents: A/CONF.62/INF.1 and Add. 1; A/CONF.62/INF.3/Rev.2; A/CONF.62/INF.4/Rev.1; A/CONF.62/INF.5/Rev.1; A/CONF.62/INF.6/Rev.7 and Corr.1; A/CONF.62/INF.8.

24. In May 1974, then Foreign Minister Ohira Masayoshi declared before the Diet that Japan could accept the 200-mile zone proposal on a "conditional" or "reservations attached" basis. Following Ohira's remarks, protests from fishing interest groups, plus intra-LDP anxiousness about the upcoming House of Councillors election, convinced the government to back off on the issue. See *Asahi shimbun,* May 30, 1974.

25. *Asahi shimbun,* December 2, 1975.

26. Ibid.

27. Ibid.

28. Hollick, *U. S. Foreign Policy and the Law of the Sea,* p. 345. Similarly critical views of Japan's behavior in other multilateral contexts are recounted in former diplomat Kawai Shunzo's anecdotal "Nihonjin no kokusai kankaku: kaigi ni najimanu kanryo tachi," *Gekkan ekonomisuto* (May 1976): 96–104.

29. *Asahi shimbun,* February 10, 1982.

30. Toshiki Kaifu, "Japan's Vision, " *Foreign Policy,* 80 (Fall 1990): 31,38.

31. *Yomiuri shimbun,* August 4, 1990.

32. Ibid., interview with Natural Resources and Energy Agency head Ogata Kenjiro. Also *Yomiuri shimbun,* August 7 and 11, 1990.

33. In 1978, MITI had projected Japan's 1985 oil dependency at 63 percent and its 1990 level at 50 percent. MITI, *White Paper,* 1978; and MITI, *Japan's New Energy Policy,* 1976, p. 21.

34. *Yomiuri shimbun,* August 11 and 12, 1990.

35. *Yomiuri shimbun,* August 7, 1990. Japan's near-total ban on exports to Iran in 1979 did nothing to block the aggressive Japanese purchases of Iranian oil that struck many enraged Americans as showing callous insensitivity to the plight of U.S. hostages.

36. *Yomiuri shimbun,* August 13, 1990.

37. Magami Hiroshi, "Kasumigaseki: meiso no hibi," *Shokun* (November 1990): 78–79.

38. *Yomiuri shimbun,* August 12, 1990, mentions early U.S. signals. Among these, according to later reports, was a formal and direct request on August 15 by Ambassador Armacost for Japanese support in three areas: (1) military aid, including minesweepers and support vessels; (2) personnel, supplies and financial and administrative assistance for the U.S.-led multinational force; and (3) aid for the front-line states in the Gulf. *Yomiuri shimbun,* October 24, 1990.

39. *Yomiuri shimbun,* October 24, 1990.

40. *Los Angeles Times,* August 19, 1990. This account, by the *Times'* Sam Jameson, includes this quote from Foreign Minister Nakayama: "Japan must absolutely not take any initiative that raises suspicions that it still clings to the thinking of the past."

41. *Yomiuri shimbun,* August 12, 1990.

42. Among these reactions, China's stern warning in August of a revival of Japanese militarism seems of paramount concern. *Yomiuri shimbun,* August 23, 1990.

43. For example, *Yomiuri shimbun*, August 17, 1990.

44. Magami, "Kasumigaseki," 86, quotes one Japanese hospital administrator's cold response to the notion of sending doctors: "It's tough to leave work. Maybe the Gaimusho has medical doctors abroad that it can send."

45. *Yomiuri shimbun*, September 18, 1990.

46. *Yomiuri shimbun*, September 7, 1990.

47. Magami, "Kasumigaseki," 87. Interministerial bickering extended to the detainee issue, regarding who would pay for the return flight to Japan of Japanese citizens stranded in Iraq. On the ground that it lacked a "precedent" for paying for stranded Japanese in politically sensitive scenes of conflict, the Foreign Ministry opposed government payment. It later yielded to Transport Ministry pressure in mildly embarrassing early crisis-stage flap. *Yomiuri shimbun*, September 2, 1990.

48. *Yomiuri shimbun*, October 2, 1990.

49. *Yomiuri shimbun*, September 30, 1990. National poll of 3,000 voting adults (55 percent women, 45 percent men), multiple answers, conducted September 22–23. Asked why they were concerned with the Persian Gulf crisis, respondents also mentioned: "Soviet-U.S. role in shaping Middle East peace" (19.6 percent); "harm global detente" (16.3 percent); "harm Japan's ties to other countries in region" (15.7 percent); "unconcerned" (3 percent); and "no answer" and "other" (2.3 percent).

50. The issue is reminiscent of a 1961 incident over UN Ambassador Matsudaira Tsuneo's statement that "It does not make sense absolutely not to send troops [to the Congo], for this forms the basis of UN cooperation." At that time, strong JSP and DSP reactions forced then Prime Minister Kishi Nobusuke to clarify the "statement" by ruling out the dispatch of SDF troops. Kato Shunsaku, "Kokuren to Nihon no ampohosho," *Kokusai seiji*, 1 (1963):33; *Asahi shimbun*, February 25, 1961.

51. *Yomiuri shimbun*, September 30, 1990; October 16 and 30, 1990.

52. Doi and Miyazawa quotes from *Yomiuri shimbun*, October 30, 1990; Ozawa quote from *Yomiuri shimbun*, October 24, 1990; and Suzuki quote from *Yomiuri shimbun*, November 1, 1990. Italics added.

53. *The Economist*, September 22, 1990. Article translated and published in *Yomiuri shimbun*, October 8, 1990.

54. *Asahi shimbun*, October 16, 1990, reported that President Bush had pressed Japan to send noncombat forces. Also *Yomiuri shimbun*, October 24, 1990.

55. Rep. Les Aspin (D-Wis.), "Burdensharing Report Card on the Persian Gulf Crisis," November 14, 1990, pp. 16–17. Aspin concluded: "The Japanese clearly have a great deal of homework to do before responsibly joining the post–Cold War world." Further, the report stated that the Japanese "are way below the curve in doing their fair share" compared to the "international community," which "has had to respond by putting

people and money on the line for common security" interests.

Some observers regarded Japan's mediocre "C" in Aspin's "A" to"F" grading scale as unduly harsh as it placed the country only slightly above Iran, Yemen, Sudan, and Libya. Japan's "C" grade was reported quickly in the Japanese press; *Yomiuri shimbun,* November 17, 1990.

56.   From Ishihara Shintaro, "A Void at the Core," *The New York Times,* May 22, 1974, op-ed page. His interesting rationale: "I am certain that only when we have been able to fill that void [of moral emptiness] will it be possible for Japan to gain international respect and trust."

Chapter 2
Japan and the United States: Games That Work

John Creighton Campbell

The relationship between the United States and Japan has been massively transformed in the postwar era. That transformation has generated great tensions; in particular, Japan's economic expansion has threatened the prosperity of many sectors of American society. The perception that the United States is slipping from its position as Number One, with Japanese success as the most visible symbol of that decline, generates psychological pressures as well.

The remarkable point is that in the midst of all this change and its accompanying resentments, the relationship between the governments of the United States and Japan has remained so stable. That is an important fact. As Stephen Krasner observes, "A breakdown or alteration in the pattern of interaction between these two countries would have consequences for the world system as a whole."[1] Krasner ably reviews a variety of domestic and international factors that appear to favor or undermine stability, but he does not much discuss what seems to me to be a key, that is the development of a political process, or a set of games, that has succeeded in avoiding crisis.

The word "crisis" is thrown around quite loosely in U.S.-Japanese relations. Casual newspaper reading leaves the impression that we are perpetually in critical condition, since journalists typically find threats and apocalyptic predictions the only aspects of the relationship worth reporting—no news is good news because any news is bad news. But crisis implies change, or at least likely impending change.[2] By that definition, there would seem to have been only two or three crisis points in postwar U.S.-Japanese relations, the most recent around 1970. Since then there have been plenty of conflicts, but the nature of those conflicts has been quite stable, and they have been managed skillfully enough to avoid breakdown. The purpose of this paper is to outline these crisis-management games and consider why they apparently work so well.

Functions of Games

"Game" is a metaphor for characterizing a relationship between individuals, organizations, or countries. It implies players with at least somewhat differing interests who compete for real stakes, governed (if imperfectly) by a set of rules—norms about what behavior is appropriate and expectations about how other players will react to various actions. If only because these U.S.-Japanese games have gone on for so long, we may assume that despite differences of interest, the players all benefit from maintaining the relationship rather than severing ties. This use of "game" is somewhat similar to the idea of "regime" in international politics, but it is less associated with formal organizations, and it focuses on bilateral rather than multilateral relationships.[3]

Where might the rules come from? At one extreme, the case of limited, arm's-length contracts, all norms and expectations are explicitly defined in advance, with sanctions for violations spelled out. At the other, rules evolve over time, modified consciously or unconsciously in response to a series of positive or negative experiences. In between, a fairly durable pattern may result from a traumatic event that impresses participants with the danger of not following rules. The "lessons" of that trauma soon become institutionalized into a durable set of norms and expectations with enough inertia to persist even when conditions change.

Without too much simplification, we can identify three such defining traumas in postwar U.S.-Japanese relations. They took place in the three conventional arenas of international relations: diplomatic, national security, and economic. These were the end of the occupation in the early 1950s, the revision of the Security Treaty in 1960, and the textile dispute around 1970.

None of the three was a "turning point" in the sense of an abrupt shift in how the two nations behaved toward each other. However, they **could** have been turning points, in both contemporary and retrospective judgment—all three cases seem to have had much more potential for a breakdown or major change in the relationship than any other events in the postwar period, certainly more so than the alleged crises of recent years. Moreover, each crystallized a set of rules that defined the games the United States and Japan have played with each for many years.

The Diplomatic Game

Diplomacy refers to the grand affairs of world politics, the fundamentals of foreign policy, and the relationships of friendship or enmity among nations. For postwar Japan, the most crucial element of foreign policy has been to maintain its relationship with the United States. Tokyo keeps that in mind in conducting all its other relationships; it nearly always follows a simple set of behavioral rules resulting from a tacit understanding with Washington that evolved in the first half of the 1950s.

The First Crisis

During the Occupation period and immediately afterward, when Japan was regaining its sovereignty in foreign as well as domestic affairs, there was considerable controversy in both Washington and Tokyo about where Japan would stand in the postwar world. Among the key questions were the following: To what extent should Japan subordinate itself to American policy? How much of a military was needed? Could friendly relations be established with the Soviet Union? What about China, and then Taiwan?

These and other issues were subjects of policy arguments in Washington and political fights in Tokyo, punctuated by intermittent hard bargaining between the two governments. Many of the rules of the game had been fairly well agreed upon by the time of independence in 1952, but some aspects remained ambiguous or controversial. In political affairs per se, the relationship can be seen as having settled down with the end of Hatoyama's push for a more autonomous foreign policy in the mid-1950s.

The Rules

The framework of rules that developed from this early period can be summarized as follows. Japan will verbally support U.S. foreign policy on any issue seen as important by Washington, and it will not criticize American views of the world. The United States will constantly reaffirm the alliance and the importance of Japan. At the behavioral level, Japan is expected to participate in passive American strategies (e.g., boycotts) but not necessarily in active ones (e.g., military action). Washington is expected to consult with Tokyo on issues vital to Japan, though not necessarily to do more than listen to its views. China is the sole exception: here, Japan is expected to be markedly more positive than the United States although still not directly challenging the American-defined framework of policy.

These rules have been well understood throughout the postwar period. A notable example is the similarity in intent and process of China policy in different eras: Japan's attempts to build quasi-private economic ties in the 1950s and 1960s, and its quick restitution of economic aid after Tiananmen. The Japanese government's support for American military policies in Vietnam and in the Persian Gulf, despite a general belief that both were wrongheaded, was also quite similar (as was Washington's toleration of what many Americans saw as inadequate direct participation in both cases).

Conflict

Binational conflict is not built into this game. The rather rare episodes of political tension occur mainly when the rules are violated. The two chief examples both occurred in the early 1970s: President Nixon's failure to consult about the American switch in China policy in 1971, and the Tanaka cabinet's verbal tilt toward the Arabs in 1973. These incidents brought openly expressed shock and bitterness in the other capital, although they had no important lasting effects. Usually, so long as the rules are observed, political differences between the countries either can be ignored or will be negotiated out in a relatively friendly, behind-the-scenes way: Okinawa reversion and the retraction of the American proposal to withdraw troops from Korea are examples of settlements favoring Japanese interests, while Japan has modified many foreign policy ideas in reaction to (or anticipation of) American positions.

The U.S.-Japanese political game has persisted partly from inertia—ingrained expectations about appropriate behavior—but mainly because both sides have benefitted. Certainly the United States enjoys the support from Japan that seems so automatic compared with more fractious European allies (who have been known to attack American policy or even act on their own). Japan has been spared the worry and dangers of making its own decisions.

The Military Game

Conceptually, diplomatic and military policy blur into one another, and several examples above blend both. In U.S.-Japanese relations, however, a relatively narrow and well-insulated game is played that concentrates on the Japanese defense effort and cooperation with the American military, without much reference to broader strategic (much less political) issues.

The Second Crisis

The crucial event that shaped this game was the security treaty controversy that culminated in 1960. Prior to that year, despite the overall settlement about Japan's political role described above, expectations about Japan's own defense capability and how it would relate to the American military were uncertain and divergent, within and between Washington and Tokyo. Since then, policy has been decided within a consensus produced by shock—massive demonstrations, resignation of a prime minister, cancellation of an American president's visit. Both sides were suddenly brought to realize that public emotions on this issue threatened to explode, and that preservation of the alliance framework was much more important than the details.

The Rules

The defense relationship came to be governed by a fairly stable and extremely prescriptive set of rules. First, similarly to the political game, Tokyo accepts American conceptions of security policy without criticism or suggestion, while the American government goes along with the constraints on Japanese military activity associated with the constitution, public opinion, and vulnerability to opposition party attacks. Second, Japan continually if incrementally expands both its defense budget and its cooperation with American military programs—joint planning and maneuvers, provision of technology, and so forth.

Conflict

The chief difference with the political arena is that the defense game includes binational conflict within its rules, rather than conflict occurring only when these are violated. That is, it is assumed that Washington and Tokyo disagree over how much Japan will do in a military way, and that these disagreements will be openly expressed as American pressure and Japanese resistance—though both are expressed rather gently. This conflict became highly ritualized through the 1960s and 1970s in the annual debate on defense budget growth rates, which was substantively trivial (what does it matter whether defense spending goes up 6 or 7 percent in a given year?) but symbolically important as a demonstration of both the disagreement and the underlying agreement on defense.

This conflict ritual had become so institutionalized that when the Reagan Administration decided it really wanted Japan to do more, it sensibly and quite deliberately changed the game. The Americans stopped talking about defense budgets and started talking about missions (1,000-kilometer sea-lane defense and so forth); moreover, they took much of the discussion behind the scenes. This new strategy, along with the coincidental arrival of a hawkish prime minister, did bring more explicit change in defense policy (if not necessarily defense practice) than had been seen in years. The arena soon returned to normal. The continued appeal of the old game, however, became evident later in the 1980s, when "burden sharing" came to dominate the binational defense agenda, with an annual fight over the even narrower issue of how much Japanese support for American basing costs would go up in a given year.

The defense game illustrates how conflict can be functional for maintenance of a stable relationship. Each government is able to respond to discontent within its own country by opposing the other. Congressional and public opinion in the United States resents Japan's "free ride," so Washington presses for a greater effort; the Japanese public and opposition parties worry about remilitarization, so Tokyo stands up to those pressures. The game is very simple when the score is kept in dollars (points of budget growth or percent of basing costs covered), and a bit more complicated when in military missions, but in either case the Japanese prime minister can tailor the response to his perception of the political situation in Washington and Tokyo.

It is important that this game is played frequently and regularly, for the same reasons that the annual budget cycle—itself an enormous conflict ritual—is the main mechanism to produce relative stability amidst the intense conflicts of interests among agencies and groups in all complex governments. The many binational meetings to discuss cooperation at various levels of the national security hierarchy are also helpful in providing flexibility of details within underlying stability. While this game is not the cause of U.S.-Japanese defense cooperation, which fundamentally depends on compatibility of interests, it helps it work by allowing efficient management of the built-in conflicts.

All this looks very positive for one who values "cooperation" above all else, but less so for the policy-minded. The incremental expansion of Japanese defense budgets, a basic component of the game, draws fire from those on both the right and the left who think that Japanese defense policy should actually stand for something. More fundamentally, security policy making in Japan is so dominated by gaming (binational and domestic) that it is responsive only to changes encompassed by the rules (i.e., new demands or more pressure from participants), not to shifts in what is supposed to be the security environment. The past three decades have seen major changes in the level of conflict and threat within Asia; the birth, death, and resurrection of U.S.-Soviet detente; and several explicit or implicit shifts in American-East Asia security policy. These events have provoked lively debates in the magazines about Japanese security (all, of course, mentioning the "taboo" on discussing military matters) but little change in actual policy.[4]

The Trade Game

A good introduction to the most contentious game, the trade game, is provided by excerpts from an insightful memorandum on "Executive Branch Attitudes toward Trade." It reports the Washington view that "Japan's trade policies are consistent neither with its current economic strength nor with the ground rules of reciprocity," that "Japan's idea of liberal trade is assuring open markets for its exports," and "that U.S. grievances against Japan are sufficiently numerous and justifiable (as evidenced by the current U.S.-Japan trade balance) to make it very difficult to forestall indefinitely hard line trade policies." Commerce Department officials have "lost faith in further talk" and are calling for direct action to spur "measures which have long and unsuccessfully been sought by this country."

This memorandum is cited by Stephen Cohen as a good portrayal of American views in 1982.[5] It is interesting how well it still applies after a turbulent decade. It is even more interesting that this memorandum was written by Cohen himself, when he was chief economist for the U.S.-Japan Trade Council, in the spring of 1970. Twenty-two years is a long time for the same argument; no wonder observers of US-Japan trade politics like Clyde Prestowitz point to "the constant repetition of the negotiating cycle with minimal results," or "deja vu all over again."[6]

Why do we keep doing the same thing over and over? Because, at some level, it works. The great number of issues that flow into the economic arena, and their high salience to various interest groups in both countries, have meant that a much more elaborate conflict ritual than in the defense case has evolved. It can be called

"U.S.-Japan-style negotiations." As indicated by the 1970 quotations above, elements of this game can be found in the 1960s or even earlier, but it appears to have become institutionalized as a result of the textiles debacle of the early 1970s.[7]

The Third Crisis

It will be recalled that in 1969, President Nixon pressed a political commitment given to southern textile interests on Prime Minister Satō, who rashly promised to arrange a voluntary export restraint. Satō could not deliver; Nixon would not back off; the conflict was aggravated by bureaucratic, interest-group, and legislative politics on both sides; and the negotiations themselves were studded with misjudgments and fumbles. All this occurred despite the fact that textile exports were a rather trivial economic matter for Japan, and Japanese imports were not at the time a major cause of the American industry's problems. The result was that by 1971, a poisonous atmosphere pervaded the entire U.S.-Japanese relationship, with a real prospect that the American Congress would invoke the Trading with the Enemy Act and hold up legislation for Okinawa reversion.

The Americans won the textile fight, in that they got pretty much what they demanded. One "lesson" they learned was that Japan can be moved (perhaps only can be moved) by intense pressure. The Japanese side learned several lessons: Do not say "yes" too quickly, but do not say "no" if at all possible; negotiate any demand, slowly, and give in as much as seems necessary at the end. Most important, those in charge of trade matters in both countries looked back on 1970 with the same shudder that security officials looked back on 1960. Both sides learned to fight hard, particularly in their rhetoric, but also to keep the conflict enough under control to avoid real disruption. Both sides also learned **how** to fight.

Rules

The operating assumption of the economics game since 1970 is that Japan is the problem. I say "operating" assumption because most Japanese and many Americans do not accept the proposition intellectually—today few experts would deny that the American savings–investment imbalance is the main cause of the trade deficit with the world, and thus of the imbalance with Japan. Nonetheless, nearly all binational economic conflicts have been based on the presupposition that it is some Japanese behavior that causes trouble. It is thus up to the U.S. to identify the problem and propose solutions, and up to Japan to react—the first rule of the game.

How does the American government select appropriate problems to negotiate with Japan? The vast and expanding number of U.S.-Japanese economic transactions produces many potential issues, enough to require a sorting process akin to triage in a hospital. Although I know of no research on how and why certain problems reach this agenda while others do not, it is likely that several factors come into play: perceived overall effect on the American economy (or some economically important subsector), political push, anticipated extent of Japanese resistance, chance, habit, and whether some solution is available and reasonably attractive.

Similarly, the attractiveness of one or another solution may have little to do with whether it is likely to solve any particular problem, and in fact many adopted solutions have had no impact at all. Just as important may be characteristics like low cost, ideological compatibility, straightforward logic, lack of opposition, and not being associated with any recent failure. Some problem–solution combinations seem to be chosen because they are relatively easy to deal with, such as the choice of artificial satellites, wood products, and supercomputers rather than a variety of much tougher issues as subjects of the first "Super 301" negotiations in 1989. [8]

It seems likely that in some cases the Japanese government has a direct, though certainly informal and behind-the-scenes, voice in determining which problems the United States will identify for attention or which solutions it will propose. Perhaps more often, the Americans in charge will be able to anticipate Japanese reactions and take those into account. It is common for Japan to respond to an initial American probe by denying there is a real problem, but that is not really an effort to control the agenda since eventually it will agree to negotiate anyway—a shy turning away is actually the first step in the dance.

In any case, once negotiations start, rhetoric flows back and forth along accustomed channels. The United States will castigate the Japanese behavior as unfair and as symbolic of Japan's overall neomercantilist policy. Japan will explain why things must be done that way and anyway it has done all it can, and complain about scapegoating, while dragging its feet through the negotiating sessions. Eventually, perhaps after a year, the Americans will seem to get angry and threaten dire consequences, usually a protectionist rampage in Congress. Japan will then give in and accept at least half of the American demands, pleading overwhelming pressure, *gaiatsu*. After initial congratulations that might include proclamations of "breakthrough" and a "new era in U.S.-Japanese relations," the United States would soon find another problem and the cycle would begin again.

Since the mid-1970s, U.S.–Japan-style negotiations that followed this scenario fairly closely have been carried out over many issues, several appearing more than once. The subjects of negotiations have changed along several dimensions. First, the level of sophistication of the industries in dispute has risen progressively—textiles to televisions and automobiles to semiconductors and artificial satellites. Second, there has been something of a shift of attention from Japan's exports toward its import barriers.[9] Third, the list of Japanese behaviors identified as unfair and as significant causes of trouble has been narrowed as various theories about what causes problems became discredited or simply less popular (e.g., that Japanese export subsidies or indirect taxation was a key, or that Japan was deliberately supporting an undervalued yen) and as various barriers were dismantled. Keeping the game going requires a good supply of new or plausibly recycled problems, one reason why the Structural Impediment Talks in 1989–1990 dealt with *keiretsu* and so forth.

Despite these changes, it is the stability of the basic U.S.–Japan-style negotiations game that is most impressive. The issues, the sequence of moves, the rhetoric about unfairness, the threats, the sky-is-falling media campaigns, the last-minute deals—all have become quite ritualized. My view, again, is that the two countries persist in replaying basically the same negotiations again and again not because they keep failing, but because they have been quite successful. Of course, that success has not been in correcting the trade imbalance or restoring American competitiveness—an impossible task for binational negotiations in any case. Rather, the function of this game is to avoid crisis by channeling and managing conflict, and that it does very well.

Conflict

Several studies by I. M. Destler and his associates suggest why the conflict management process takes this particular form.[10] Economic conflicts of interest are inevitable between two large countries that are so interconnected, and among various groups within the countries as well. In each, a coalition of top officials perceives the importance of maintaining the binational relationship as outweighing any particularistic interests. In the United States, these officials (USTR, State, the president, perhaps the Pentagon) must deal with interest groups and congresspeople favoring protection and tough action, as well as with popular attitudes hostile to Japan; in Japan, their counterparts (Foreign Ministry, MITI, the prime minister, perhaps Finance) worry about vested political, bureaucratic, and group interests opposed to change and, again, public opinion ready to see them as wimpy. In the resulting two-level game, the top officials have enough in common to engender surreptitious cross-national alliances, but they also must worry about maintaining their legitimacy at home.

For that reason, the officials need a constant flow of issues, and negotiations that stretch out for a long time, so they can demonstrate that they are taking the problems seriously and are working hard on solutions. All the arguments about fair behavior and the attribution of blame to the other country ("scapegoating" and *gaiatsu*) play to audience prejudices and provide reassuring explanations for uncomfortable changes. An atmosphere of crisis followed by the catharsis of agreement reaffirms the importance of both the problem and the relationship. Under the surface, because of all the repetitions, insiders on both sides know the script and can predict the outcome fairly well, so real anxiety, while never absent, may be minimized.

Lest anyone think that it is all done with mirrors, another key factor in the success of these negotiations as a conflict-management device is that they have provided a flow of substantive payoffs. The U.S.-Japan-style negotiations game requires Japan to accept at least in part nearly every direct demand from the United States, and even with some slippage in implementation it is clear that Japanese behavior has been substantially modified. Concrete results include the dismembering of many specific governmental trade barriers, to the point that in a formal sense Japan has one of the least-protected economies in the world; several export restraints aimed at limiting damage to American industries, some of which have seen substantial recovery; increased U.S. sales in Japan of many products; and the enormous surge of direct investment in manufacturing and other sectors—sharply criticized around 1990, but actually a long-held American goal. If American interests were not satisfied regularly, albeit with micro and perhaps short-term benefits, the game would not long persist.

Note, however, that this observation about the overall process need not apply to any specific instance. In a particular case, Japan may or may not implement its promises; the problem addressed may or may not get better; and the United States may or may not pay much attention to actual results. Usually, the question of whether the deal has a substantive impact is not much related to its effectiveness as a conflict-management mechanism in the short run.

Game-like Ploys

Incidentally, what I have called "U.S.-Japan-style negotiations" have not been the only mechanisms employed in attempting to manage bilateral conflict. Three other techniques may be mentioned. First, from the late 1970s until the mid-1980s, Japan responded to American pressures on tariffs, import procedures, and various licensing and quality standards with a series of seven unilateral import-liberalization "packages" containing as many as one-hundred items each. These packages, often announced before some high-level leadership meeting, were aimed at preempting U.S.-Japan-style negotiations and their accompanying "crises." Several did gain a measure of appreciation from Washington, but they soon came to be a joke, particularly when the same "problem" was "solved" again in successive packages with no impact on actual imports. In general, resisting and then acceding to specific American demands proved to be a more effective mechanism for conflict-management than anticipation and preemption (at least half-hearted preemption), and so the package strategy was abandoned while the U.S.-Japan-style negotiations game continued to be quite popular.

A second mechanism used throughout the period is the establishment of numerous bilateral groups aimed at talking over problems and solutions in a more-or-less friendly way. These may be governmental or private, they may or may not issue formal reports, and they range from groups of relatively low-level people discussing quite specific topics (e.g., the Ad Hoc Group on Petrochemicals) up to highly publicized exchanges between heavyweights about very broad topics (e.g., the "wisemen group" of 1979–1981).[11] In a sense the frequent top-level summit meetings with all the publicity about the "Ron-Yasu" or "George-Toshiki" relationship are similar; the main function is symbolic reassurance, although sometimes specific problems are dealt with as well.

The third mechanism is the effort to build cooperative relationships outside the areas of binational conflict. Establishment of the Japan Foundation and major grants by the Japanese government to American universities in the 1970s are early examples. The late 1980s saw an emphasis on corporate philanthropy by Japanese firms in the United States at the microlevel, and various notions of "global partnership" in dealing with world problems (third-world debt, global environment, etc.) at the macrolevel. Japanese financing of trade insurance for American exports is a recent example. A naive but widely held hope is that enough friendly ties will eliminate conflict or that feelings of gratitude will outweigh resentment; perhaps a more realistic expectation is that a few positive actions will balance the constant flow of negative news to some extent.

The continued popularity of at least the second two of these three techniques indicates that authorities on both sides of the Pacific find them helpful. However, they cannot substitute for U.S.–Japan-style negotiations as a mechanism for managing the relationship precisely because they are nonconflictive. Expanding interactions, mutual dependence, and the relative rise of Japan generate real conflicts of interest. These cannot be bottled up for long without risking a real explosion. U.S.–Japan-style negotiations allow resentments to be expressed and addressed, and they often lead to enough adjustment of interests, short of complete satisfaction, that at least keep the players in the game for another round.

Nongames

Is that enough? That is, have U.S.–Japan-style trade negotiations been adequate for the job of preserving the relationship in a shape that benefits both sides? Clearly not. Some issues come up that are too risky to fool around with, so important economically or so explosive politically that they need to be settled quickly and without all the publicity and apparent conflict of "U.S.–Japan-style negotiations."

Examples are the automobile voluntary restraint agreement of 1981, yen revaluation in 1985, and the FSX contract revision of 1989. For autos, the conflict about what to do inside the American government took many months to resolve, but the negotiation with Japan (essentially just about how many cars could be exported) was settled with little delay. The Plaza Accord was reached quietly and quickly; mutual recriminations about whose fault it was that the yen was so overvalued had largely been muted by the previous year. In the FSX case, well aware of American emotions, Tokyo reacted quickly and rather quietly to Washington's demand for renegotiation, despite the widespread bitter resentment at the Americans reneging on a deal they had pushed on Japan in the first place.

There is, then, a "fast track" available for the United States and Japan to make deals behind the scenes and without explicit conflict, when that seems necessary to maintain the relationship. Why is it not taken more often? One reason is that without evoking a genuine sense of danger, domestic opponents will not go along so easily, and if people get used to fictional cries of "wolf," disaster is likely when a real one appears. Another is that quick and quiet solutions do not fulfill the function of U.S.–Japan-style negotiations in regulating binational conflict through the expression and then adjustment of resentment and differing interests.

Is it Unique?

To summarize, the postwar U.S.-Japanese relationship has been managed in large part through a small set of institutionalized though informal games, in which the various players know their roles well and usually—not always—have good reason to follow the rules. In diplomacy, the rules say that Japan will defer to the United States with some accepted exceptions, so there is no room for conflict within the game. In defense, most of the relationship is similarly cooperative and hierarchical, but a routinized, cyclical conflict over a relatively trivial point is built in as a surrogate for deeper and more emotional (albeit quite ambiguous) disagreements about policy. In trade, there are many more disputes over a wider variety of more substantial issues, but the sequence of events and even the arguments used have become highly stylized (to the point that the most important and difficult issues must be handled with different rules). In all three arenas, nearly always it is the United States that initiates the interaction, that sets the agenda by specifying the problem and proposing a solution, and that "wins" in the sense that Japan winds up acceding to American demands at least in part.

How unusual is this relationship? On the one hand, any bilateral relationship no doubt develops repetitive patterns, if only because most interactions are handled by the same people, who get used to dealing with each other and who will favor the methods proved to work best. Such patterns are more likely to become institutionalized to the extent that the interactions are frequent and complex, and involve both differences of interest and mutual benefits from cooperation. These conditions increase the utility of establishing some predictable rules that permit but control conflict, especially for those responsible for maintaining and managing the relationship (i.e., the "level I negotiator" in a two-level game). When one side is more powerful than the other, an element of deference or subordination will be built into the rules.

The preceding paragraph avoids use of the word "nation," and in fact we would expect to find similar patterns not only in the international arena, but whenever two organizations are in analogous situations. In fact, U.S.-Japanese relations often do resemble the routinized and often ritualized conflicts in, for example, labor–management negotiations, contracts between manufacturers and subcontractors, deals between majority and minority parties in a legislature, and the governmental budget process. Such relationships can be found in many countries. The implication is that the basic structural features and even much of the style of the U.S.-Japanese relationship can be explained by such "objective" factors.

Still, it is interesting that according to various writers those labor–management, subcontracting, partisan, and budgetary conflict–cooperation relationships seem to take a distinctive form in Japan, perhaps because of culture.[12] Cultural explanations are so common in interpreting all aspects of Japan, including its foreign relations, that they warrant a brief examination.

Is It Japanese?

Several Japanese cultural traits appear conducive to my characterization of the U.S.-Japanese relationship. For example, Japanese think in terms of moving back and forth between formal and "real" (*tatemae* and *honne*) or front-stage and backstage (*omote* and *ura*), quite helpful in playing a two-level game. Similarly, they are skillful at manipulating a sense of inside–outside or we–they (*uchi* and *soto*)—Prestowitz repeatedly found himself and other American negotiators being drawn into an alliance with the Japanese government, against the American Congress.[13]

Still more fundamental is the famous "situational ethic," or the lack of principles so often derided in the Japan-bashing literature.[14] American negotiators have long been infuriated by the Japanese refusal to talk about general rules and insistence on getting a list of specific demands before beginning a negotiation. The same Americans perhaps insufficiently appreciate the Japanese willingness to talk about practically anything at the specific level without, for example, getting their backs up about principles like "no interference in internal affairs" (as in SII) or even "agreed-upon contracts cannot be reopened" (as in FSX).[15] Abstract arguments about principles can get in the way of making a deal right away, and an accepted principle becomes a precedent that constrains what can be negotiated in the future.[16] The Japanese instinct is to take each situation as it comes.

The clash between "principles" and the "situational ethic" shows up most clearly in differing conceptions of "fairness." Americans constantly are irritated at Japan for behaving unfairly in the sense of violating some purportedly universal norm. Japanese are often irritated in turn when the United States seems to come up with a different moral principle in every different case— GATT rules here, national treatment there, reciprocity somewhere else; free trade here, fair trade there, "look at the results" somewhere else; "please understand our special situation" when nothing else applies. Actually, fairness in terms of results—making a deal that does not hurt any participant too much and takes special problems into account, while certainly favoring the more powerful player—is the more legitimate conception in Japan, and most U.S.–

Japan-style negotiations are finally settled that way despite all the rhetoric.

Looking back over twenty years of U.S.–Japan-style trade negotiations, and indeed at the still longer-running political and security games outlined above, one cannot escape the impression that Americans have been drawn into a very Japanese sort of relationship. It is, of course, impossible to prove, but I would guess that if the United States had interactions of similar magnitude and difficulty with another Western nation, it would rely more on treaties and other specific agreements and on permanent structures for adjudicating conflicts, instead of so many highly situational negotiations going on at once. Conventional wisdom holds that the former is preferable, but the latter pattern can also work well.[17]

The most Japanese characteristic of the relationship is that it has retained so much of its patron–client or senior–junior flavor from an era when the United States was far more powerful than Japan and Japan was far more dependent on the United States. Of course the relationship is still objectively asymmetrical, in that a breakdown would hurt Japan more than United States (at least in the short run), but the two countries are closer to being equal and are much more interdependent than when these games took shape. The rules nonetheless still dictate that the United States establishes the conceptual framework and makes the demands, and that Japan resists and asks indulgence but always gives in, at least symbolically. To a cynic, it looks like a fair exchange: the Japanese might make all the money, but the Americans get all that reassurance that they are still Number One.

Stability

There may be a substantial cultural component in the way these games are played, in their style, but it bears repeating that the U.S.-Japanese relationship rests fundamentally on the compatability of interests and goals of the two nations and on the environment of postwar international relations. Substantial changes in national interests or in the environment would of course change the way the two countries deal with each other. Assessing such factors is beyond the scope of this essay.[18] We should, however, address the narrower questions of whether the games outlined above will continue to be a mechanism for stability, and of their capacity for managing new forms of conflict.

With regard to the first question, the view of Destler and his colleagues tends to be gloomy. They stress the role of trade negotiations in channeling and dampening conflict by leading to deals that both sides can live with in the short run. Unfortunately, in the long run the negotiations tend to have the opposite effect. It is not only American and Japanese officials playing their cards badly, although that happens often enough; rather, the structure of the game itself functions to amplify tensions.

Their chief example is that intense external pressure (*gaiatsu*) is seen as necessary to get Japan to move, and indeed is often invited by Japanese participants favoring change. Over time, American credibility will be diminished as threats are not carried out, and negative stereotypes will be reinforced in both countries. In general, much about the way negotiations are conducted breeds unrealistic expectations and therefore disappointment among Americans, and increasing resentment among Japanese.[19]

With all these difficulties, no wonder Destler and Sato were surprised to observe, after analyzing the several economic conflicts of 1977–1981, that "in the end, things seemed to work themselves out." In fact, they judged that at various junctures "a major political blow-up seemed at least possible," à la textiles, and they warned that unless the conflict-provoking factors in the conduct of U.S.-Japanese relations could be improved (they offered many suggestions), tensions would build to the point of a real explosion in economic relations or a serious spillover into political or security affairs.[20]

Destler's process-oriented approach thus had much in common with the arguments of those more concerned with substance (that is, with what they see as Japanese exploitation of the United States or vice versa). In both lines of analysis, the U.S.-Japanese relationship is viewed not only as precarious, but as containing the seeds of its own destruction—full of contradictions, in the old Marxist sense. Breakdown impends unless one or both governments shift strategies, either to be more careful about causing tension and resentment according to Destler, or conversely to get tough enough to force real change according to the revisionists (on either side of the Pacific).

However, the evidence of the 1980s supports neither proposition. That is, the number and intensity of trade conflicts in the 1980s was much greater than earlier, and from revisionist points of view the results were much worse in that the trade deficit reached previously unimaginable heights, or that the gap between Japan's capability and the way it is treated in negotiations became still wider. Incidentally, it is ironic that the development that observers in the 1970s had assumed would improve the relationship—increased Japanese direct investment in the United States—turned out to be the single biggest irritant at the popular level in the late 1980s.

As for process, there was little indication that the two governments had improved their negotiating techniques enough to be able to handle all this new pressure. The main concern of Destler and his colleagues had been that the attacks, complaints and exaggerated expectations that are inherent in U.S.–Japan-style negotiations would snowball and poison the atmosphere with emotional hostility; certainly that is exactly what happened in the 1980s. Across the entire decade there was not a single year, and even not very many months, in which a "crisis" in U.S.-Japanese relations was not being proclaimed, with warnings of a massive breakdown unless things were soon changed.

Still, the game went on, and with only marginally more dire outcomes than usual. Congress passed a trade bill, but it was not that tough; sanctions were imposed here and there, but they were not that extensive. Even in 1989, a set of negotiations that looked much like earlier ones wound up in congratulations and talk of a "new beginning" for the relationship. American officials were still selecting and shaping issues to fit them into the U.S.–Japan-style negotiations framework. When truly difficult issues arose, such as FSX, the games were bypassed and quick resolutions found.

These events suggest that the games are quite robust, capable of handling substantial amounts of conflict and of withstanding (if often by not directly confronting) tough new issues. Clearly, the key is the executive authorities on both sides of the Pacific, those who deal with both levels of the two-level game. They have been committed to maintaining the relationship, they have been skillful in devising strategies to deal with contingencies, and they have been powerful enough to maneuver effectively amid domestic pressures (though of course not enough to get their own way all the time).

Change in any of those factors might threaten the equilibrium, as indeed has occurred from time to time. In the early 1970s the Nixon–Kissinger administration's obvious lack of interest in maintaining the relationship, plus a lack of skill on both sides, nearly led to a breakdown in binational ties. And when President Bush took some bad advice from the Commerce Department and converted his early 1992 visit to Japan from the "global partnership" style to trade bashing—in effect behaving like a congressman—it seemed to threaten a new crisis. Remarkable, however, was how quickly first the vice president and then the president himself tried to restore the balance by touting partnership and consciously avoiding criticism in subsequent high-level meetings. By summer 1992 things were back to normal.

There is no denying, of course, that under some set of circumstance pressures could get too intense to handle and the binational relationship would be blown apart. That would be more likely to the extent that the two nations lose their capacity to manage conflict, due perhaps to a loss of regard for the benefits of the relationship by the American or Japanese executive, perhaps because these would come to appear less valuable with the end of the cold war.

In my view, however, the mechanisms described here are not as fragile as would be suggested by a view that they are simply devices adopted to serve a single purpose. They may have been that at first, in the aftermath of some crisis, but with time and repeatedly effective use they became more and more normal. These U.S.-Japanese games are now an institutionalized system based as much on established relationships and mutual expectations as on short-run cost-benefit analysis. They will not be abandoned quickly.

Assessment

Unsurprisingly, the conduct of U.S.-Japanese relations is widely criticized. Anyone who sees Japan as either the main cause or the best solution for the American economic plight, and who thinks that the United States should have the power to get Japan to behave more conveniently, will obviously see these mechanisms as ineffectual at best. Japanese vexed by continued subordination have similar views. Moreover, anyone with a low toleration for angry speeches and seemingly perpetual crisis will find this style of interaction actually perverse, as making matters worse. And people with a strong belief in such transcendental values as rationality, equality or fairness, from either an American or Japanese perspective, can hardly be happy with the trimming and making-do of U.S. Japanese negotiations.

For that matter, no one is actively happy. Those who manage U.S.–Japanese relations generally get complimented only when they seem to break through the usual patterns. The direct beneficiaries of the trouble-avoidance style are the businessmen and others in both countries who have gained from the constant expansion of cooperation—not a very vocal audience. Keeping public dissatisfaction and criticism within manageable limits is the best that can be expected. Political scientists should be quite pleased, however; the maintenance of the U.S.-Japanese relationship despite so much conflict of interest and nagging irritation should be seen as a triumph of diplomatic technique.

Notes

1. Stephen D. Krasner, "Japan and the United States: Prospects for Stability," in Takashi Inoguchi and Daniel I. Okimoto, eds., *The Changing International Context. The Political Economy of Japan*, vol. 2 (Stanford: Stanford University Press, 1988), p. 381.

2. The first two definitions in the American Heritage Dictionary: "A crucial or decisive point or situation; turning point," and "an unstable condition in political, economic or international affairs in which an abrupt or decisive change is impending." 2d college edition, 1985.

3. The U.S.-Japanese relationship could well be treated as an iterated prisoners' dilemma in which a heavy shadow of the future brings substantial cooperation: Robert Axelrod, *The Evolution of Cooperation* (New York: Basic Books, 1983). More specifically, the politics of the interactions described here (particularly trade negotiations) are well captured by Robert D. Putnam, "Diplomacy and Domestic Politics: The Logic of Two-Level Games," *International Organization* 42:3 (Summer 1988): 427–60. Since I am emphasizing rules rather than strategies and outcomes, however, the use of the term "game" here does not overlap much with game-theoretic analysis.

4. Not only has the total defense budget grown at an even pace, the shares of that budget going to the individual services remained remarkably constant—a clear indication of a lack of policy change.

5. Stephen D. Cohen, *Uneasy Partnership: Competition and Conflict in U.S.-Japanese Trade Relations* (Cambridge, Mass.: Ballinger, 1985), p. 123.

6. Clyde V. Prestowitz, Jr., *Trading Places: How We Allowed Japan to Take the Lead* (New York: Basic Books, 1988), pp. 299, 302. In fact, the "revisionist" critics see this endless negotiating as not only useless but counterproductive, in that it diverts

attention from confronting the real issues; the officials in charge are thus accused of playing into Japanese hands.

7. Actually, many economic conflicts of the 1950s and 1960s, mainly about Japanese exports but also about market or investment access, were generally similar to those after 1970, but the volume was lower and the rules-of-the-game less well established (Japan often just gave in quickly). The textile dispute in effect codified the rules by testing their limits. Taken together with the three "Nixon shocks" (China, the dollar devaluation and import surcharge, and the soybean embargo) plus tensions associated with the Arab-Israeli war and the oil shock, this incident marks the early 1970s as the low point in postwar U.S.-Japanese relations.

8. A functional categorization of problems (e.g., import penetration, access for exports, third-country issues, macroeconomics, and "structure"; or, overall vs. specific, government-private, etc.) and of solutions (e.g., dismantling barriers, voluntary restraints, market-share promises, strengthening enforcement, deregulation, public spending) is quite possible but not needed for the analysis here. See e.g. Ellis Krauss and Simon Reich, "Ideology, Interests, and the American Executive: Toward a Theory of Foreign Competition and Manufacturing Trade Policy," *International Organization* 46:4 (Autumn, 1992) 857-97.

9. This is partly due to the strength of the free-trade ideology in the United States. Even on issues where the main problem is damage to American producers by rapidly increasing Japanese exports, such as auto parts, the tendency is to conceptualize the problem as one of market access, and the solution as getting Japanese companies (in Japan or the United States) to buy more American products.

10. The well-titled books are (with Hideo Sato) *Coping with U.S.-Japan Economic Conflicts* (Lexington, Mass.: Heath, 1982); (with Sato and Haruhiro Fukui) *The Textile Wrangle: Conflict in Japanese-American Relations, 1969–1971* (Ithaca: Cornell University Press, 1979); and (with Sato, Fukui, and Priscilla Clapp) *Managing an Alliance: The Politics of U.S.-Japanese Relations* (Washington, D.C.: Brookings, 1976).

11. Cohen mentions fifteen such bilateral groups operating around 1980: *Uneasy Partnership*, pp. 119-20.

12. See, respectively, Eyal Ben-Ari, "Ritual Strikes, Ceremonial Shutdowns: Some Thoughts on the Management of Conflict in Large Japanese Enterprises," in S. N. Eisenstadt and Eyal Ben-Ari, eds., *Japanese Models of Conflict Resolution* (London: Kegan Paul International, 1990), pp. 94-124; Ronald P. Dore, *Flexible Rigidities: Industrial Policy and Structural Adjustment in the Japanese Economy, 1970–80* (Stanford : Stanford University Press, 1986); Ellis S. Krauss, "Conflict in the Diet: Toward Conflict Management in Parliamentary Politics," in Ellis S. Krauss, Thomas P. Rohlen, and Patricia G. Steinhoff, eds., *Conflict in Japan* (Honolulu: University of Hawaii Press, 1984), pp. 243-93; John Creighton Campbell, *Contemporary Japanese Budget Politics* (Berkeley: University of California Press, 1977), esp. chap. 11.

13. See Prestowitz, *Trading Places*, chap. 10, and for these concepts, Takeshi Ishida, "Conflict and Its Accommodation: Omote-Ura and Uchi-Soto Relations," in Krauss, Rohlen, and Steinhoff, eds., *Conflict in Japan*, pp. 16-23.

14. It is the main theme in Karel van Wolferen's *The Enigma of Japanese Power*, (London:

Macmillan, 1989), which despite disclaimers is essentially a culturalist interpretation of Japan.

15.   In 1991 some Japanese auto executives (if not the government) were even receptive to the new demand coming from the American industry that a cap be placed on all Japanese cars, those produced in North America (even in joint ventures) as well as imports. *Wall Street Journal*, January 14, 1991. Given that getting the Japanese to make cars in the United States was the major American demand of the early 1980s, this new effort would seem to violate not only widely accepted principles, but an explicit bargain.

16.   Studies of legal and status conflict in Japan are congruent with this point: see Frank K. Upham, *Law and Social Change in Japan* (Cambridge, MA.: Harvard University Press, 1987), and Susan J. Pharr, *Losing Face: Status Politics in Japan* (Berkeley: University of California Press, 1990).

17.   Cf. Krasner: "The absence of any clear regime in automobiles, as opposed to textiles, may have made it easier to adopt relatively liberal short-term quotas rather than long-term quasi-permanent restrictions. When technology, interests, and actors are rapidly changing, it may be better to cut specific deals than to attempt to find some appropriate general rules." "Stability," p. 405.

18.   Krasner, "Stability," does exactly that.

19.   See Destler and Sato, *Coping*, chap. 7.

20.   Their suggestions for improvement as of 1982 are worth noting. The United States should try to avoid highly visible pressure, find leverage on individual issues rather than making broad attacks, avoid intrusion into Japanese domestic decision making, seek reciprocity in fact and appearance, resist using Congress as the "heavy," avoid scapegoating, be specific rather than vague in demands and responses, and not expect too much of MITI's power over business. Japanese negotiators should speak up more, respond earlier to softer signals, find other support for change besides *gaiatsu*, not be hypersensitive to U.S. criticism, and make better use of country specialists in the policy process. Both sides should establish strong policy leadership and coordination, not exaggerate the utility of numeric targets, not link issues to summit meetings without sufficient preparation, utilize analytic dialogues between experts, and strive for reciprocal political sensitivity. These suggestions are all listed in ibid., though not in this order; few if any were followed seriously in the 1980s.

Chapter 3
Accessing the World: Palace and Foreign Policy in Post-Occupation Japan

David A. Titus

From the late nineteenth century on, Japan's imperial institution has been used to access the world, to make the world accessible to Japan and to make what is accessed part of Japanese culture, society, and politics. Though it no longer enjoys the centrality it had from 1868 to 1945, the imperial institution today is still organized and staffed to promote Japan's "internationalization." Ironically, in fact, the emperor and imperial family have been more active in international affairs since the Allied Occupation ended in 1952 than at any other time in Japanese history, despite a drastically reduced palace staff and a drastically reduced role for the emperor in the Japanese polity.

Central to the palace's capacity to make the world and "civilization" part of Japan and Japanese "culture" today is the Board of Rituals of the Imperial Household Agency. An unofficial palace organ financed from the emperor's privy purse and not directly from state funds, the board conducts Shinto rites as the "private" or "personal" religion of the emperor and members of the imperial family. Since the Meiji Restoration and subsequent creation of State Shinto, Shinto and the imperial institution have been inseparable. Although Shinto is certainly not as salient as it was in prewar Japan (State Shinto was dismantled during the Occupation), the presence of Shinto rites in the palace serves to enhance the imperial institution's symbolic role as quintessentially and unquestionably Japanese. Its extensive international activities thereby make what is accessed in the world more legitimately Japanese. The imperial institution facilitates Japan's internationalization by putting the imprimatur of this most Japanese of Japanese institutions on the ingestion of the world's cultural and material resources. It provides an important psychological, though by no means uncontroversial, vehicle for the internationalization of the Japanese, by the Japanese, and for the Japanese.

After the Restoration of 1868 the imperial institution was made central in Japan's efforts to secure a place in the world while retaining its sense of being a uniquely Japanese polity. Since then the imperial institution has assisted in creating the *context* within which Japan has conducted its foreign policies. Today, for example, "if the head of state is defined as a person who is the symbol of the state and is empowered to represent the country in foreign relations, the Emperor can be called the head of state of Japan, because under the present Constitution the Emperor is the symbol of the state and represents the country in a very limited way by performing certain affairs of state." Neither he, the imperial family, nor the palace makes foreign policy or conducts concrete negotiations. Therefore, "if the head of state is defined as a person who has the administrative power and represents the country in all aspects of domestic affairs and international relations, as the Emperor did under the previous [Meiji] Constitution, the Emperor under the present Constitution cannot be regarded as the head of state."[1] As such a limited head of state, the emperor faces the world. As symbol of the unity of the people, the emperor faces his people as the expression of their unique community. Like Janus, these two faces are conjoined, working together to maintain Japan as a community within the world, though not without ambiguity, controversy, and uncertainty, as we shall see.

The Unprecedented Pace of Imperial House Activities

The 1965 official manual of the Imperial Household Agency records that the late Showa Emperor attested 1,390 documents submitted by the cabinet in 1965. Fifty-four involved diplomatic appointments, forty-six international documents, and twenty-six credentials from foreign diplomats. That year he also sent thirty-eight personal letters and 395 telegrams to foreign heads of state.[2] More importantly, "the international relations conducted by the Imperial House involve receiving foreign monarchs, members of royal families, presidents and others visiting Japan as distinguished guests, as well as welcoming other visitors such as foreign notables and diplomats; they also involve visits by members of the Imperial Family to foreign countries for the sake of international good will."[3] From April 1963 to May 1964 eighteen distinguished guests visited Japan, ten of whom were members of royal families. When the king and queen of Thailand visited Japan in May 1963 the emperor and empress greeted them at Tokyo International Airport. After lavish receptions, entertainment, and sightseeing they were personally seen off at the Tokyo International Airport by the emperor and empress.[4] That was one of 220 visits to Japan by royalty and heads of state from seventy-five countries up until the spring of 1988 that first began in December 1955 with the visit of Prince Sihanouk, prime minister of Cambodia.[5]

The first visit abroad by a member of Japan's imperial family in postwar Japan was Crown Prince Akihito's visit to Great Britain as his father's representative to the coronation of Queen Elizabeth II in June 1953. That trip took over six months and included a visit to the United States. From 1953 through August 1988 members of the imperial family made or were scheduled to make 106 visits abroad to fifty-three countries and two cities (Hong Kong and Berlin). Every member of the imperial family has been abroad since 1953, including all three of the present emperor's children. The Shōwa Emperor was the first reigning emperor in Japanese history to go abroad. He and the empress visited Belgium, Britain, Denmark, the Federal Republic of Germany, France, and Holland in September–October 1971; from late September to early October 1975 they visited the United States.[6] Prior to these visits, the Shōwa Emperor had been abroad only once: as the first crown prince to leave Japan's sacred shores, he had toured Great Britain and a few other European nations in 1921. In an interview with *Newsweek*'s Bernard Krisher on the eve of his 1975 visit to the United States the Shōwa Emperor stated: "My happiest memories are of my visit to Europe fifty years ago and again with the Empress there a few years ago. Now my happiest expectation is looking forward to our trip to the United States."[7]

On the other hand, Emperor Akihito as crown prince had been abroad, singly or with Princess Michiko, twenty-three times from 1953 to October 1987, when he and Princess Michiko visited the United States at the invitation of President and Mrs. Reagan, and had visited thirty-eight countries, twenty-eight as official representative of his father and ten in his own right as crown prince.[8] In terms of actual experience abroad, Emperor Akihito is the most internationalized of any emperor in Japanese history. And so are his offspring. His eldest son and now crown prince, Prince Naruhito, has been abroad eight times; his second son, Prince Akishino, seven times; and his daughter, Princess Sayako, twice. Both sons did graduate work at Oxford for two years.[9]

The number of visits abroad by members of the imperial family since the end of the Occupation in 1952 (almost three a year) and the number of visits by foreign royalty and heads of state (6.5 a year—a figure that does not include imperial audiences with other categories of foreign notables) reveal a level of international activity on the part of Japan's imperial house unprecedented in Japan's history.

In the fall of 1988 the Shōwa Emperor fell critically ill, one year after undergoing pancreas bypass surgery. But the pace of his international activities and those performed in his stead remained much the same as in 1965. There were 1,250 attestations of cabinet documents, 383 of which were acted upon by the crown prince. There were some fifty ceremonies involving the accrediting or relieving of ambassadors plenipotentiary conducted in the palace "with due solemnity," eighteen of which were conducted by the crown prince. Some twenty-four lectures were delivered to the emperor on foreign affairs and related matters.[10]

But what does all this international activity mean? Concluding a far-ranging and incisive roundtable discussion on "the emperor in Japanese history," Professor Yano Tōru of Kyoto University's Southeast Asian Research Center stated:

> The emperor system must grow out of its shell and become internationally open. The point is that as of now the international responsibilities of the imperial house go no further than receiving guests of state or maintaining friendly relations with nations that are monarchic in form. I wonder if there isn't some way to go beyond this. . . . [If] that is not done there will be no filling of the moral vacuum vis-à-vis Asia prior to 1945. After all is said and done, the most distinctive, the most decisive problem of the emperor system from ancient times to 1945 has been its lack of responsibility toward the outside world.[11]

The imperial house most certainly maintains "friendly relations with nations that are monarchic in form." Of the 220 royalty and heads of state from seventy-five countries, 123 visits were by royalty from twenty-three countries that are, were, or became monarchies. Monarchies, less than one-third of the nations, accounted for more than half of the top-level visits to Japan. Of the 106 visits abroad by members of the imperial family to fifty-three countries and two cities, forty-five were visits to sixteen monarchies. Twenty-two of those visits were to England (as opposed to thirteen to the United States). Members of the English royal family, including Queen Elizabeth and Prince Philip, visited Japan fourteen times. Of all the nations sending royalty or heads of state to Japan, Great Britain has had the most (fourteen); of all the nations visited by members of the imperial family, Great Britain has been visited most frequently (twenty-two).[12] It is only natural that England should be the most visited country by members of the imperial family. Even before the war, Britain's royal house had been the model for constitutional monarchy in Japan.[13]

Japan is a monarchy, and it is therefore not unnatural that its royal family should reinforce ties with monarchies around the world. Moreover, once a country ceased to be a monarchy, "imperial house diplomacy" all but ceased. After the Iranian revolution in 1979, for example, no member of the imperial family visited Iran; there had been two visits prior to the revolution. Visits to Japan from Iran also ceased; there had been eight visits by Iran's royal family prior to 1979. Likewise, a nation that became a monarchy established relations with Japan's imperial house: Juan Carlos of Spain visited Japan in 1972 prior to becoming king and then again in 1980—the only visits to the imperial house by royalty or heads of state from Spain as of April 1988.[14]

On the other hand, members of the imperial family have visited nations on every continent of the world, whether or not those nations were monarchies. The second most visited country has been the United States. Crown Prince Akihito and Princess Michiko had even visited Bulgaria and Rumania, although those were the only two Communist nations to have been visited by members of the imperial family. Heads of state from the Communist nations of Yugoslavia, Czechoslovakia, Romania, Bulgaria, the People's Republic of China, East Germany, and Poland had been received by the emperor as of April 1988.[15] The symbolic bias of imperial house diplomacy is fairly clear from the visits to and from the imperial house: monarchies; the nations of the "free world" other than monarchies; the nations of Africa, South and Latin America, the Middle East, South and Southeast Asia; and finally, the nations of the "Communist bloc." But it should be emphasized that this is a justifiable bias, not exclusivity: it fits Japan's perceptions of itself as a monarchy, member of the "free world," and trading partner with many nations of the world.

Moreover, "the moral vacuum vis-à-vis Asia" up until 1945 has, in fact, been "filled" by imperial house diplomacy. As of August 1988, members of the imperial family had visited the Philippines twice, Thailand six times, Malaysia three times, Singapore three times, the Republic of Korea twice, Indonesia once, and Hong Kong once—a total of eighteen visits to countries and cities in East and Southeast Asia invaded and/or occupied by Japan in the twentieth century. Members of the imperial family have also visited Ceylon (Sri Lanka) twice, India twice, Nepal five times, and Pakistan twice, for a total of eleven visits to South Asia. Of the 106 trips abroad by members of the imperial family, 17 percent have been to East and Southeast Asia and 10 percent have been to South Asia. Visits to Japan's imperial house by royalty and heads of state from Asian nations have been equally frequent. From 1955 to the spring of 1988 there were forty-three such visits: Indonesia thirteen, Thailand twelve, Philippines seven, Laos four, Malaysia three, Cambodia two, the People's Republic of China one, and the Republic of Korea one. There were seventeen visits to the imperial house from the nations of South Asia: Nepal nine, Bangladesh four, Pakistan two, India one, and Sri Lanka one.[16] Of the 220 visits to Japan by foreign royalty or heads of state who were received by the emperor, almost 20 percent were from East and Southeast Asia, and almost 8 percent were from South Asia.

Whether moral or not, the pre-1945 vacuum in Asia no longer exists as far as the imperial house is concerned. Imperial house diplomacy has extended widely into Asia with reciprocal visits. The imperial house of Japan is doing as much as or more than other royal houses in terms of interaction with the other nations and peoples of the world as well. In marked contrast to Japan's prewar imperial house, and in even more contrast to the imperial house prior to the Restoration of 1868, the Japanese imperial house since 1952 has reached out to the world, and a key feature of such energetic imperial house diplomacy since 1952 has been its reciprocity.

Since succeeding to the throne in January 1989, Emperor Akihito has continued imperial house diplomacy in a more outspoken and energetic manner than his father. When Premier Li Peng of the People's Republic of China visited Japan in April 1989, Emperor Akihito personally apologized for Japan's wartime role in China. On May 24, 1990, he expressed his "deepest regret" over Japan's colonial rule in Korea to South Korea's President Roh Tae Woo during President Roh's state visit to Japan.[17]

Emperor Akihito's apology to President Roh caused a furor in Japan and aroused strong emotions in both countries. South Korean officials were dissatisfied with the Shōwa Emperor's apology to President Chun Doo Hwan when Chun visited Japan on September 6, 1984. The late emperor said: "It is indeed regrettable that there was an unfortunate past between us for a period in this century and I believe that it should not be repeated again." This was criticized by South Korean officials as being vague about who was responsible for the "unfortunate past."[18] Before coming to Japan, President Roh had asked that the emperor make a clear apology for Japan's misdeeds in Korea, which was not well received in Japan. Prime Minister Kaifu said that he wished to apologize, honestly and in his own words, when President Roh visited Japan, but the South Korean government wanted the apology to come from the emperor. Many members of the LDP protested: the constitution did not allow the emperor to make such "political statements." Doi Takako, head of the Japan Socialist party, also objected. At a press conference she too argued that the emperor's acts in matters of state stipulated in the constitution do not permit him to make political statements. Both LDP dissidents and the JSP pointed out that the Korean request for an apology was politically motivated, an effort to strengthen President Roh's position in Korea.[19]

Amidst this emotionally charged atmosphere in both Korea and Japan there were several objective causes for confusion over whether Emperor Akihito should make such an apology—a second imperial apology as far as many Japanese were concerned. First, it was argued that public statements by the emperor are not included among the acts in matters of state set forth in Article 7 of the constitution, nor can statements by the emperor be construed as personal matters since they are public acts pertaining to his role as symbol. Second, it is open to question whether public statements by the emperor are political or not. Third, there is deep ambiguity over the meaning of his role as symbol as far as foreign affairs are concerned. Who in fact is Japan's head of state? The emperor? The prime minister? No one?[20]

In any event, Emperor Akihito went through with the apology at a state banquet for President Roh on May 24, making clear who was responsible for the "unfortunate past": "I think of the sufferings your people underwent during this unfortunate period, which was brought about by my country, and cannot but feel the greatest regret."[21] Surely Emperor Akihito's apology was a major effort to fill the "moral vacuum" that existed between Japan's imperial institution and the rest of Asia. That apology and the unprecedented pace of "imperial house diplomacy" since 1952 also indicate how "internationally open" the "emperor system" has become, and how open to controversy.

The Emperor's Two Faces

Professor Sugihara Yasuo of Hitotsubashi University argues that the emperor is head of state toward the outside world and symbol of Japanese unity for the Japanese.[22] The controversy over the emperor's apology to President Roh illustrates the interconnected nature of these two imperial "faces": The emperor's role as head of state is intimately tied to his role as symbol of Japan and the Japanese people, and because the emperor's international activities have domestic repercussions, the relation between the two is ambiguous and problematic.

Despite the ambiguity, foreign nations regard the emperor of Japan as head of state, in however limited a capacity. Foreign emissaries present their credentials to the emperor. Article 7 of the constitution stipulates that he is to receive foreign ambassadors and ministers. Although that role is a topic of debate among the Japanese, as noted above, more and more Japanese now accept the emperor's role as head of state in foreign affairs. In 1963 the Prime Minister's Office polled the public on whether "the constitution should make it clear that the emperor represents Japan in foreign affairs." Thirty-five percent said yes, 21 percent no.[23] In 1967 the Prime Minister's Office asked: "Who do you think should represent the Japanese nation in relations with foreign countries—the emperor or the prime minister?" Forty-three percent of those responding said the emperor, 35 percent the prime minister.[24] "These PMO polls lead to the conclusion that most Japanese were satisfied with the emperor as a symbol of state. They did not want to see his powers strengthened. A possible exception might be in the area of foreign affairs since in two polls, taken in 1963 and 1967, 35 percent of the respondents thought the emperor should represent Japan in its dealings with other countries."[25] After the emperor and empress visited the United States in 1975, the Kyodo News Service conducted a poll in which a "large majority, 69 percent, thought well of the emperor's visit to the United States; 6 percent did not." "Should the emperor undertake a more active diplomatic role? Whereas 19 percent said that they would encourage such an initiative and 11 percent said they would discourage it, 61 percent thought that what the emperor was currently doing was about right."[26]

The notion that the emperor is head of state in international affairs only took hold after the 1868 imperial restoration. When all political authority, but not political power, was vested in the emperor by the 1889 Meiji Constitution, that authority included the emperor's acting as head of state in foreign relations. But that role was a greatly constricted one, and nonexistent in the preceding Tokugawa period from 1603 to 1867. Only since 1952 has the imperial house emerged as a truly energetic actor in international affairs.

But how do the emperor's roles as symbol of the Japanese community and as head of state relate to each other? Yano Tōru made a fascinating observation about the emperor's two faces in Japanese history:

> . . .the emperor system would seem to have eternal life. Even in the Shōwa era, in which Japan has become so civilized, so modernized, it seems to me that, counterintuitively, the more Japan adopts civilization the more in fact the entity called emperor is sought after.
>
> This was previously pointed out in *Japan the Theater Country*. "Theater country" means that the more Japan takes in civilizing influ-

> ences from the outside, and the more it borrows the format of state
> administration from the outside, the stronger the emperor system has
> had to be made in actuality: this paradoxical state of affairs is what is
> taken to be a theater country. At the heart of the Japanese people,
> therefore, there is something like a vacuum chamber, and I cannot help
> but sense that it is the emperor system that fills it.[27]

Ueyama Shumpei agreed, citing Rousseau to the effect that religion is essential in creating a state, that religion is the centripetal force in that extensive human grouping called the state. It was in the eighth century, when so much of Chinese civilization was systematically introduced into Japan, that the myth of Japan as a divine land was created. The Meiji period witnessed powerful centrifugal forces, but Japan was able to go back to the precedent of the eighth century.[28] The suggestion here, of course, is that the religious centrality of the emperor becomes important in proportion to the degree to which Japan adopts the trappings of civilization: state forms of administration, laws, learning, even formal religions such as Buddhism or Christianity. This was especially true of Japan from the sixth through the end of the eighth century, when Chinese "civilization" revolutionized Japanese society and politics. At the same time, the Japanese emperor was made the center of the divine land and qualitatively different from the Chinese emperor. The very name "emperor" (tennō) was created for that purpose, coined for the first time during the time of Shōtoku Taishi (572–622). And it was in response to such pervasive Chinese influence that Japan's emperor system acquired its distinctiveness.[29] If all Japan was a vacuum chamber, an empty space to be filled with the props of civilization, the imperial institution was the stage itself, the religious space where the props could be placed.

Earlier Yano had suggested a distinction between "civilization" (*bummei*) and "culture" (*bunka*) in discussing the central role of the emperor and imperial institution in the modernization of Japan after 1868. From the Meiji Restoration to 1945, the emperor system had functioned both as the axis of civilization and as the axis of a national polity in which the military and its allies ultimately held sway. Yano then equated the national polity with Japanese culture, implying that civilization is universal while culture is particular to a given ethnos. Although the emperor system was to fulfill both cultural and civilizing functions, the problem with Japan from 1868 to 1945 was that Japanese culture eventually overwhelmed civilization. In response, Ueyama pointed out that although civilization has many meanings it has more sweep than culture, transcending national boundaries. From the sixth to eighth century, for example, Japanese culture fell within the sphere of Chinese civilization.[30] Yano remarked that civilization seeks after universal values, while culture affirms the identity of human beings as a specific people or ethnos (*minzoku*).[31]

Here, I would suggest, are the two roles of the emperor system: accessing civilization and sustaining Japanese cultural identity. The former, in all its historical manifestations, has been the international face of the emperor system; the latter its domestic face. The more Japan has been involved with civilization, the more the need for national identity. To extend Yano's logic one step further, the unprecedented international activities of the imperial house since 1952 are a reflection of the unprecedented interdependence of Japan and the world.

How does the emperor fulfill both roles? Ueyama, Umehara, and Yano agreed that the emperor system, in contrast to the Chinese model imported in the seventh and eighth centuries, had never been one of direct rule by the emperor but had always been a "system of delegation" or a "structure leaving matters to others" *(makaseru kōzō)* as far as politics was concerned, despite attempts by individual emperors to assert themselves, despite the Shōwa Emperor's acceptance of the Allied terms of surrender in 1945 when Prime Minister Suzuki Kantarō asked the emperor to break the deadlock among the key cabinet ministers. Umehara likened the emperor to the pole star or the god of Daoism, who rules by being there and "doing nothing" *(wu wei)*. From its very inception the emperor system was religious in nature, and today the emperor has no political functions. Throughout Japan's history it was a calamity when the emperor asserted himself or herself.[32] Ideally, both the emperor's faces are "selfless": he affirms Japan's adoption of civilization without defining it; he affirms Japan's identity without defining it.[33] As the central living presence in Shinto, the "way of the gods," the emperor facilitates the ability of "the Japanese to devour various alien cultures without any particular sign of indigestion and to make them, in some fashion or other, their own." This is because the way of the gods, in which the emperor is the key figure, "seems consistently to have extolled the principle of no principle and the value of no value."[34] In this idealized sense, the emperor and imperial institution facilitate both culture and civilization, joining a unified Japan to the world—or more properly, joining the world to a distinctly Japanese community. Both his faces are, after all, Japanese. How those two faces are joined depends on how they are managed in light of the "trends of the times." As seen in the controversy surrounding the apology to President Roh Tae Woo, and as will be seen see below, those two faces do not always function as the mirror images of themselves that the idealized version would have them be.

The Managers of the Emperor's Two Faces

The immediate managers of the emperor and imperial family are the officials of the Imperial Household Agency, an office under the direction of the prime minister. Although court and palace officials have always been gatekeepers of the imperial will, their importance has varied greatly over the centuries in accordance with the salience of imperial authority, the configuration of power outside the palace gates, and the "trends of the times" within and outside Japan. With the Restoration of 1868 the authority of the imperial institution was made even more central and salient than it had been in the ritsu-ryō system of the eighth century: arguably, the impact of "civilization" on Japan from the mid-nineteenth century was even greater than it had been in the sixth through eighth centuries. After 1868 a bureaucracy of over six thousand officials manned the palace, led by prominent civilian and military officials who were to end their careers "at the emperor's side." Their role was to coordinate as best they could the emperor's two faces in the modernization of Japan.[35]

The 1947 Constitution of Japan divested the emperor of all "powers related to government" (Article 3). He was hereafter to be "the symbol of the State and of the unity of the people, deriving his position from the will of the people with whom resides sovereign power" (Article 1). Gone was the theory of imperial prerogative on which the emperor's authority had been based in the 1889 Meiji Constitution; in 1947 the emperor's political authority was reduced to "such acts in matters of state as are provided for in this Constitution" for which the "advice and approval of the Cabinet shall be required" and "the Cabinet shall be responsible" (Article 3). A coherent and democratic cabinet system gave coherence to political decision making, and neither the necessity nor the justification for palace intervention in politics existed, as it had in prewar Japan. Although reduced in authority and salience, however, the emperor still remains legally central as symbol of the state and of the unity of the people, and he retains a role that the palace officialdom coordinates with government officials. But the altered and reduced role of the emperor since 1947 called for a reduction in the palace bureaucracy from some 6,200 in the early 1940s to 1,500 in 1947.[36] In 1949 the number of agency officials was reduced again, to around 960. In 1988 the official roster of agency officials was 1,128.[37]

The structure of the postwar Imperial Household Agency, however, retained significant components of its prewar counterpart, the Imperial Household Ministry, which in turn retained significant components of the sinicized model of 701. The two faces of the emperor have been retained covertly and overtly. The overt aspects concern the formal palace officialdom as managers of the emperor's roles in both domestic and foreign affairs. The covert aspect involves the presence and functions of Shinto ritualists in the palace, even though there no longer exists a department of Shinto rituals in the palace's formal organization as there had been in the Meiji imperial system.

Although Shinto has been disestablished as a state religion, and there is no Board of Rituals in the agency's formal organization, Shinto ritualists (classified as "inner court officials" along with laboratory assistants and other miscellaneous types) conduct Shinto rites at the three Shinto sanctuaries in the palace. These "officials" are evidently paid from the inner court account, which is considered "money in hand" (*otemotokin*) and not public funds for which the agency is accountable. Moreover, the ritualists are not listed in the government's *Shokuin roku* (official roster). Even without enjoying the public visibility and importance they had in prewar times, Shinto rites are still a part of palace life. In 1965 there were twenty-five Shinto ceremonies in the palace; twenty of these were precisely the same as in prewar times (as of 1942), two closely resembled prewar rites, and three were added because of special circumstances.[38] In 1988 there were twenty-four rites conducted by the court ritualists and the imperial family, of which nine were major rites conducted by the emperor in person, eight were lesser rites conducted by the chief ritualist, and seven were undesignated but appear to have been rites and ceremonies conducted by the emperor, members of the imperial family, and/or chief ritualist. In addition there were rites conducted on the first, eleventh, and twenty-first days of each month; as a general rule the emperor performed the rites on the first day of each month. A deputy chief ritualist, ritualists, and inner court ritualists function under the direction of the chief ritualist. None of these functionaries appears in the imperial Household Agency's official roster.[39]

Shinto rites, therefore, continue to play a central role in the symbolic functioning of the imperial institution, though one that is not publicly prominent or publicized by the palace and the media. Because of the new constitution, the old Board of Rituals had to be "separated from the Imperial Household Agency, which is an organ of state."[40] But some have argued that, also because of the new constitution, the emperor and members of the imperial family enjoy freedom of religion and therefore can perform Shinto rites "as individuals." Thus the imperial institution's role as the embodiment of the "divine land" has been covertly preserved.

Who manages the emperor's overt roles, both domestic and international? As in prewar Japan, and indeed throughout most all of Japan's recorded history, the emperor's roles have been managed for him. In prewar and postwar Japan, the emperor's activities have been coordinated by palace officials in cooperation with the government of the day. The prewar palace officials may have had more autonomy in managing the emperor and imperial family because the Imperial Household Ministry was structurally, legally, and fiscally independent of the government. Today's Imperial Household Agency is under the direction of the prime minister.

But it would be misleading to stress the discontinuities between the prewar and postwar managers of the emperor's two faces. Even though the symbolic content of the imperial institution, as expressed in the popular weeklies and mass media generally, is "human," "popular," "democratic," "modern," and "peaceful," the internal structures and functions of the palace today still bear a strong resemblance to those of the prewar palace. This means that the palace has a wide range of cultural, traditional, moral, religious, and even political elements that can be used as resources to rearrange the symbolic content of the imperial institution in accordance with the changing conditions outside the palace gates. The humanized symbol emperor system of today has *superseded* the authoritarian and "transcendental" emperor system of the Meiji Constitution, but it has by no means eliminated the various components of the imperial symbol acquired throughout history. The accretions of time and circumstance have been absorbed into the palace, giving it a breadth and depth of resources that will allow it to adjust to almost any conceivable swing in the trends of the times. Although those trends today indicate further popularization, the internal resources of the imperial institution are such that they could easily be made to adjust to conservative or progressive changes in external conditions. But it is quite inconceivable that anything approaching the "emperor system fascism" of prewar days would be resurrected by external conditions, or that a progressive swing of the pendulum would bring on a revolution that would abolish the imperial institution.

In 1943, 68.7 percent of the eighty-three Imperial Household officials of section chief rank and above came from "the outside"—they were officials who had at least one year's experience outside the palace before coming into the imperial household. Of these eighty-three, thirty-six (43.4 percent) had started out in the civil government bureaucracy, twelve (14.5 percent) had come from the military, and nine (10.8 percent) came into the palace from other careers such as teaching. Only twenty-six of the eighty-three (31.3 percent) were strictly court officials in career. Fully 18.1 percent of the eighty-three leading palace officers had had experience or careers in the home ministry—the bureaucratic component of imperial prerogative that had managed the civil police, local politics, and shrines and temples in prewar Japan.[41]

The palace bureaucrats in 1962 had marked similarities to their 1943 predecessors. Of the forty-seven Imperial Household Agency officials of section chief rank and above in 1962, thirty-two (68.1 percent) had come into the palace from the outside, and only fifteen (31.9 percent) were purely court careerists. These percentages are almost exactly the same as those of 1943. In 1962, twenty-two of the forty-seven (46.8 percent) came from the civil government, four (8.5 percent) came from the military (although only one of the four was a graduate of the military academies), and six (12.7 percent) came from other careers, such as business, teaching, and medicine. As in 1943, those with prior careers in local government, the police and other components of the home ministry or its postwar equivalent were the most numerous of the outside officials, numbering twelve (25.5 percent) of the forty-seven leading palace officers in 1962. Again, as in 1943, none of the 1962 leading palace officials had served in elective office (the Diet, Prefectural Assemblies, etc.). Finally, 59.0 percent of the leading officials in 1943 had graduated from Tokyo University, as had 66.0 percent of their 1962 successors.[42]

What accounts for this remarkable similarity between the palace personnel of 1943 and those of 1962? As Prince Saionji Kimmochi remarked in 1932, "It's by having the Minister and Vice Minister brought in from the outside that the Imperial Household Ministry gets its raison d'être as an 'Imperial Household Ministry in line with the times' in the first place."[43] The same reasoning seems to be operative in the case of the postwar palace leadership as well. By bringing in officials from the outside, the Imperial Household Agency, like its predecessor, is able to bring the emperor "in line with the times." However altered the conditions outside the palace gates, the imperial institution has and is to have the internal resources to respond to those external conditions. Management of those resources by officials brought into the palace from the outside would best insure the responsiveness of the imperial institution to the trends of the times.

This is nowhere more apparent than in the top leadership of the palace bureaucracy. From 1927 to 1945 all four of the top palace leaders (imperial household minister, grand chamberlain, privy seal, and chief aide) had come into the palace from distinguished careers on the outside, most notably the Home Ministry, Foreign Ministry, Navy, and Army. Today's Imperial Household Agency is also led by prominent officials brought in from the outside, though by no means as prominent as the prewar palace's "big four." Although there are others listed in the top category of "special officials" (the deputy grand chamberlain and secretary to the director), the Household Agency's leading officers today might be listed as follows: the director, grand chamberlain, grand steward to the crown prince, and grand master of the ceremonies. The deputy director, though merely a "general official" like most other palace officers, might also be added to the top leadership group.[44]

In 1962 the director of the Imperial Household Agency was Usami Takeshi. Born in 1903, Usami graduated from Tokyo Imperial University in political science (1928). After twenty-two years in various local government and Home Ministry posts, Usami entered the palace in 1950 as deputy director. Becoming director in 1953, he served in that capacity until his mid-seventies. In May 1978 he was succeeded by Tomita Tomohiko, likewise a Tokyo University graduate (law) and a career Home Ministry bureaucrat (police) who had served as deputy director of the agency from 1974. Retiring at the age of sixty-seven, he continued to serve as an adviser to the Agency when he was succeeded by Fujimori Shōichi in June 1988. Born in 1926, Fujimori graduated from Tokyo University (political science) in 1950. Unlike his predecessors, Fujimori became a civil servant in the Welfare Ministry, serving off and on as a councillor to the cabinet (1966–68, 1973–79), becoming a bureau chief in the Environmental Agency and then its vice-minister in 1981. Serving as deputy cabinet secretary in 1982 and then consultant to the cabinet Secretariat in 1987, he became deputy director of the Imperial Household Agency in April 1988, two months before becoming director.

Fujimori's appointment appears to be something of a break with tradition. He was not a Home Ministry bureaucrat but a civil servant in the Welfare Ministry and then the Environmental Agency, with extensive service in the cabinet as secretary and consultant. Many members of the imperial house, including the present emperor and his late father, have or had a deep and abiding interest in nature and biology, and the environment has been of major concern to the Japanese government since the 1970s.[45] Second, his liaison and secretarial experience would appear to equip him to be an effective coordinator between palace and government. In any event, all agency directors since 1953 have come from careers in the domestic bureaucracy, emphasizing that the agency's chief function has been to manage the emperor's role as symbol of the unity of the people, or the emperor's inward-looking face.

The grand chamberlain in 1962 was Mitani Takanobu (b. 1892). After graduating from Tokyo University in German law (1917), he went briefly into the Home Ministry before transferring to the Foreign Ministry. Having served as minister to Switzerland (1940) and then France (1942), Mitani became grand chamberlain in 1948. In 1962 he was succeeded by Inada Shūichi, a Tokyo University graduate (German law) and career Home Ministry bureaucrat. He had served as Deputy grand chamberlain in 1946 and again in 1950. Thereafter the grand chamberlains have been former aristocrats and career palace officials, Irie Sukemasa from 1968 to 1985 and Tokugawa Yoshihiro from 1985 to 1988, and a career Home Ministry official, Yamamoto Satoru, 1988–. The salience of the emperor's domestic role was also symbolized by the fact that the grand stewards to the crown prince from 1952 to 1989 had been a professor at the Peers School (Nomura Kōichi), a Home Ministry bureaucrat (Suzuki Kikuo), and an official of the Ministry of Education (Yasujima Hisashi) before entering the palace.

The grand master of the ceremonies in 1962 was Harada Ken, also a graduate of Tokyo University (German law, 1918). His predecessor, Matsudaira Yasumasa, had been chief secretary to Privy Seal Kido Kōichi and then director of peerage affairs in the palace until that office was abolished in 1947; serving as grand master from 1947 to 1957, when he died in office, Matsudaira was the only Grand Master not to have been a career diplomat. Grand master from 1957 to 1968, Harada Ken was born in 1892 and graduated from Tokyo University (German law) in 1918. He was the son of the chancellor of Dōshisha University and a Christian. An official with the League of Nations from 1918 to 1938, he served as special emissary to the Vatican from 1942 to 1946. In 1952 he was ambassador to Italy. In 1968 Harada was succeeded by Shima Shigenobu, also a graduate in law from Tokyo University. A career diplomat, he became vice-minister in the Foreign Ministry in 1963 and ambassador to Great Britain in 1964. His successor in 1973 was Yukawa Morio, yet another graduate in law from Tokyo University. He entered the Foreign Ministry, serving as ambassador to the Philippines (1957), Belgium (1963), and Great Britain (1968). Like Harada, and probably Shima as well, Yukawa was a Christian. The present grand master is Abe Isao, who succeeded Yukawa in 1979. A graduate of Tokyo University (political science), Abe was a diplomat who had served as Japan's ambassador to the United Nations in 1965, ambassador to

Belgium in 1971, and chief of delegation to the United Nations in 1976. The distinguished diplomatic careers of the four grand masters since 1957 make it abundantly clear that the grand master of the ceremonies is the chief manager of the emperor's international role, his outward-looking face. Their diplomatic careers counterbalance the domestic civil service careers of the other leading palace officials. In cooperation with the Foreign Ministry they have been highly qualified to manage the emperor as head of state in international affairs.

As in the case of the prewar palace leaders, all leading officials in the postwar Imperial Household Agency were expected to end their public careers "at the side of the emperor." I know of no postwar palace leader who left the palace for other public office. In 1975 the director was seventy, the grand chamberlain sixty-nine, the grand steward to the crown prince sixty-eight and the grand master sixty-seven. In 1988 they were, respectively, sixty-one, sixty-two, sixty-six, and seventy-four. All of them ended, or will end, their careers as palace officials, many of them dying in office (Irie Sukemasa, Matsudaira Yasumasa, Nomura Kōichi). The postwar palace, like the prewar palace, continues to be led by officials with no further public or political aspirations so that they might be objective evaluators of the trends of the times outside the palace gates and relate them to the emperor's domestic and international roles in cooperation with the government of the day.

Managing the Emperor's Two Faces: The 1990 Enthronement

The unprecedented international activities of Japan's imperial house since 1952 occurred in parallel with the enormous growth of Japan's importance in the world and Japan's deep interdependence with the world. The Shōwa Emperor's death on January 7, 1989, the long awaited "x day" in Japan, drew press coverage around the world. His funeral on February 24 was attended by some ten thousand people, including heads of states and representatives from 164 countries, the European community, and twenty-seven international organizations, making it "one of the greatest events in Japan's recent diplomatic history."[46]

The two grand enthronement ceremonies of November 1990 were if anything even more significant in terms of Japan's efforts to affirm itself as a community as well as situate itself in the world. This was the first enthronement since the Kyoto enthronement of the Shōwa Emperor in November 1928. And it was the first enthronement under Japan's new 1947 Constitution, a constitution drafted by the largely American occupiers of a defeated and prostrate Japan.

Each of the emperor's two faces was revealed in the two enthronement ceremonies. The first, the Accession Ceremony (*Sokui no rei seiden no gi*), was performed on November 12. In March 1990 Japan had sent invitations to 166 countries and several international organizations.[47] Representatives of over 150 countries were among the 500 foreign dignitaries in attendance.[48] As in 1928, the Accession

Ceremony of 1990 was based on the 1909 Enthronement Ordinance, which was in turn a significant modification of the traditional Accession Ceremony institutionalized in the eighth century under the powerful influence of Chinese civilization. While retaining its Chinese format, that ceremony was modified in 1909 to accord with Japan's new world status. Elements derived from Western coronation ceremonies were incorporated. Provision was made for a cannon salute. The empress was to take part, evidently for the first time in Japanese history. Foreign guests were to be invited, also for the first time in Japanese history. The Chinese-style then Chinese-cum-Western-style Accession Ceremony was and is a public event to proclaim and confirm the new emperor to the public—to the Japanese and, after 1909, to the world.[49]

Foreign dignitaries were to attend only the Accession Ceremony. The second grand ceremony, the Great Food Offering Rite (*Daijōsai*), was an exclusively Japanese affair performed from the evening of November 22 into the predawn of November 23. Having its origins in the harvest festival, which certainly predates the Chinese-style Accession Ceremony, it is said to derive from the Yayoi period (circa 200 B.C. to circa A. D. 300) when rice cultivation was introduced to Japan. A Shinto rite, the harvest festival (*niinamesai*) is still performed by the emperor annually in the palace.[50] As a grand ceremony to be celebrated once in an emperor's lifetime, the Great Food Offering Rite took form in the seventh and eighth centuries as a "psychological balance" to the Chinese-style Accession Ceremony introduced then as part of the massive adoption of Chinese political forms (the ritsuo-ryō system). That rite can also be viewed as a submission ceremony incorporating the powerful provincial clans, as a ceremony politically motivated to help consolidate the political authority of the emperor and his court in a newly centralized legal order by using a "traditional" Japanese sacred ritual:[51] a case of the emperor and court eating their *mochi* and having it too.

The codification of the Great Food Offering Rite was thus a nativist response to the enormous influence exerted on Japanese culture by Chinese civilization and was used politically to enhance the very system that it was designed to balance "psychologically." That codification occurred

> . . . in a time of rapid transition, [when] it was necessary to encapsule the power of the past. . .in the heart of a very different culture, and thereby unify the two.
>
> The next stage after the mythical was precipitated almost too rapidly by the stabilization of agricultural society, the influx of continental culture [or "civilization," to use Yano's term], and the effective unification of the state. At once Japan had to discover itself as historical, that is, as living in a present obviously different from a concretely remembered, non-mythological past. Yet the situation had to be interpreted religiously in order to preserve its obvious continuity with the theocratic past.[52]

That "theocratic past" centered on the emperor's "priestly rather than political function, which explains the continuity of the dynasty."[53] The influx of Chinese civilization amounted to "a 'patriarchal' transformation." "Neither the Confucian state nor the Buddhist church could abide the archaic experience that. . .genuine power could center in female sexuality."[54] In the Great Food Offering Rite, therefore, the sun goddess Amaterasu Ōmikami, progenitrix of the imperial line, "blesses the present heaven-descended patriarchy while preserving the memory of a sovereign queen."[55] The Great Food Offering Rite is also "the most pivotal celebration of Shinto," and "in the richness and variety of its origins, and the uniqueness of the religious vision it has come to represent, Shinto excellently reflects the genius of the Japanese people for combining assimilation with preservation of the past and conservation of the special spirit of culture."[56] What exactly transpires during that nocturnal rite is a matter of mystery and controversy. It may be a rite of death and rebirth, a sacred marriage, a simple communion with the gods, or all three.[57] In any event, "Japanese emperors are believed to begin life as wholly human entities to whom the imperial spirit later attaches itself and in whom it indwells; this, in turn, creates a new divine personage who stands midway between the traditional functions of the priest and the shaman, partaking of both roles but belonging wholly to neither."[58]

With the Meiji Restoration the Great Food Offering Rite was to acquire a centrality well beyond that of the seventh and eighth centuries. It was revived and enhanced in the 1909 Enthronement Ordinance, based on the Engi Codes of 927. From the twelfth century onward, the prestige of the imperial court declined as Japanese feudalism increased its sway over the land. Enthronement ceremonies were simplified, postponed, even discontinued. After Gotsuchimikado's enthronement in 1465, the Great Food Offering Rite lapsed entirely for over two centuries. With the 1868 Restoration, ironically a restoration of the Chinese model of direct imperial rule set forth in the 701 Taihō Institutes, the Great Food Offering Rite was fully resuscitated; it was performed by Emperor Meiji in 1871. The 1909 Enthronement Ordinance made it the core ritual in the enthronement, divesting it of all religious elements and trappings except for Shinto, which was nurtured, transformed, and expanded by the state.[59]

After 1868 the revived Chinese-style monarchy was to be transformed and bolstered by Western theories of imperial prerogative set forth in the Meiji Constitution of 1889, the first constitution enacted by a non-Western nation. At the same time, the imperial institution was also to be made the essence of Japanese spirituality, of Japan's cultural uniqueness. Once again foreign "civilization" was to be "psychologically balanced" by the assertion of that which is uniquely Japanese: the imperial institution. The 1909 ordinance emphasized the Great Food Offering Rite as the essence of the enthronement. Under the Meiji political system it was a secret ceremony deemed to transform the human emperor into a god manifest, a shaman-priest whose role was to communicate with the imperial ancestors and gods of the land and thereby facilitate the communal solidarity of the Japanese people.[60]

The 1990 enthronement involved a modified Accession Ceremony, but the Great Food Offering Rite followed the 1909 ordinance to the letter. Whereas the November 12 Accession Ceremony publicly affirmed Japan's communal space in the world, the November 22–23 Great Food Offering Rite affirmed the sacred distinctiveness of the Japanese community and was off limits to foreign guests, who were to be the guests of the Japanese government from November 11 to November 14.[61]

Combined, the two enthronement ceremonies suggest that Japan is in but not of this world, and that was one source of controversy that surrounded the 1990 enthronement. As mentioned earlier, the enthronement was the first under the "MacArthur" Constitution of 1947. To some Japanese that constitution represents a violation of Japan's sacred community. To others it represents an opportunity to free themselves of the primitive mythology surrounding the emperor and embodied in the enthronement ceremonies, a mythology that both inhibits freedom at home and prevents the Japanese from accepting human beings around the world as their fellow human beings. To this latter group, largely progressives and radicals, Christian believers, liberals, and cosmopolitans with extensive experience abroad, the enthronement ceremonies are not only primitive; they glorify Japanese particularism and undermine universal standards of human dignity and equality. For some Japanese Christians and other citizens, the Great Food Offering Rite in particular violates the distinction between religion and politics, or church and state. By funding that ceremony from the public purse, the so-called court budget as opposed to the imperial house privy purse, the government, which acknowledges the deeply religious nature of that rite, is concretely supporting religious activities. In September 1990 a group of about one thousand citizens filed a lawsuit with the Osaka District Court against the government's allocation of funds for both the Accession Ceremony and the Great Food Offering Rite, alleging a constitutional violation of the separation of religion and state.[62]

The opposition was not limited to Christians or Japanese influenced by only Western ways and thinking. In its October house organ called "Shinshū ," the Ōtani branch of the Jōdo Shinshū sect of Buddhism headquartered at the Higashi Honganji in Kyoto called for the abolition of the Great Food Offering Rite. Kodama Gōyō pointed out that the Great Food Offering originated in primitive folk religion based on divine myths that were repudiated when the emperor declared that he was a human being on January 1, 1946. He argued further that the view of Japan and the emperor in those myths was confined to Japan alone, making Japan "unique," and was therefore incompatible with securing an international position for Japan in the world.[63]

Though not particularly strident, opposition existed throughout Japan among many different groups. The opposition was mainly concerned that public funds were being used to support a ceremony that in effect transformed the emperor into a god manifest. This not only violated the distinction between religion and state; it was a regressive effort to restore the prewar oppression of State Shinto based on a deified emperor. Doi Takako, head of the Japan Socialist party, and other members of her party participated in the Accession Ceremony because religious elements as well as offensive mythological and militaristic symbolism had been removed from that ceremony. But she and her party had no part of the Great Food Offering Rite. The Japan Socialist party and other opposition groups were also concerned that the Accession Ceremony, extravagantly supported by public funds, would be an effort to throw Japan's weight around, to show off Japan's economic power and success to the world.[64]

Those supporting the enthronement ceremonies, on the other hand, have argued that those ceremonies merely maintain an ancient tradition that affirms a sense of community. They suggest that Shinto rituals are not religious but traditional rites of community. They imply that all viable communities rest on such affirmative rituals and symbols.[65] Moreover, by facilitating a self-confident sense of identity, such community rituals allow that community and its members to participate in an international society of equals who are different. Only a confident community of people self-conscious of their own cultural identity can recognize the same in other peoples and their communities and engage in healthy mutual respect and interaction.

Japan's prewar legacy of chauvinism and militarism, the disaster of World War II, the unprecedented occupation of Japan's sacred soil, a constitution drafted by Americans, the massive transformation of Japanese society since 1868 and even more so since 1945, the remarkable success of that transformation, and Japan's increasingly prominent international role made last year's enthronement a matter of deep ambiguity, producing fragmented opposition as well as fragmented support. At the extremes were violence, mostly by left-wing "guerrillas," as the Japanese press and the police termed them, but also on the part of right-wing true believers. Occupying a large part of the middle ground was public apathy, or "benign indifference" as Steven Weisman of the *New York Times* called it.[66] On January 20, 1990, the *Asahi shimbun* reported that public opinion was not stirred up over the enthronement one way or the other. That same newspaper reported on October 21 that general interest in the enthronement was low, that the organization of celebrations backed by business in cooperation with Shinto shrine offices was getting off to a slow start. People were "tired" of the whole business of the emperor. Low-key confusion reigned. Japan has not come up with new terms and concepts to deal with a relaxed and open "symbol emperor system" in an age of prosperity, the *Asahi* claimed. Denunciation of the prewar emperor system and fears of its revival are irrelevant and inapt, and people do not really know what the modern emperor and imperial institution *mean* today. Big business was concerned about how foreign nations would view the ceremony and has been reluctant to participate enthusiastically in the rounds of celebration that were to take place throughout the country. In short, the *Asahi* suggests, the enthronement ceremonies may very well bring to the fore a chaotic Japanese view of their imperial institution and what it means for a modern, cosmopolitan, and sophisticated Japan. Far from affirming community solidarity via the confident manipulation of the ancient rites and traditions of the Japanese imperial institution, the enthronement may very well highlight the weakening of community, a cacophony of voices both affirmative and critical, negative and positive, and above all uncertain and bored.

Placed squarely in the middle of this controversy, uncertainty, and apathy were the government, which was responsible for arranging the Accession Ceremony, and the Imperial Household Agency, which was responsible for the Great Food Offering Rite and assisting (or fighting with) the government over the procedures for the Accession Ceremony. The Enthronement Committee headed by Prime Minister Kaifu met three times—January 8, January 19, September 19—to set the format and procedures of the Accession Ceremony. In late 1989, an Enthronement Ceremony Preparatory Committee chaired by Chief Cabinet Secretary Moriyama Mayumi recommended that the Accession Ceremony should be an act of state, as set forth in the Imperial House Law, and that the Great Food Offering Rite, with its deep religious tone, should be an imperial house event. It was decided that the Government Enthronement Committee set the agenda for the Accession Ceremony, and the Imperial Household Agency set the agenda for the Great Food Offering Rite. While the director of the Imperial Household Agency sat on the Enthronement Committee, no government official apparently sat on the Imperial Household Agency committee, also created on January 8, to deal with the Great Food Offering Rite. This arrangement was evidently made in accordance with the separation of politics (Accession Ceremony) and religion (Great Food Offering Rite). The relation between the government committee, with the Director of the Cabinet Legislation Bureau as its leader, and the Imperial Household Agency committee was like a traditional three-legged race: two people running together, the leg of one tied to that of the other. Running together, they struggled over what was to be retained as tradition in the Accession Ceremony and what was to be altered to accord with the new constitution, modern Japanese life, and Japan's international role. The Great Food Offering Rite, however, was left entirely up to the Imperial Household Agency committee.

The date for the Accession Ceremony was first set at November 10, the date of the 1928 Accession Ceremony, then changed to November 12 at the January 19 meeting of the Enthronement Committee. No explanation was given for the change, but we may speculate why. November 10 was a Saturday; the 12th was a Monday and would give many Japanese a three-day weekend.

At the January 8 meeting the date for Great Food Offering Rite was set for November 22–23. That date remained unchanged. The announcement of November 12 and November 22–23 for these two key enthronement ceremonies was made by the emperor in person at the three shrines at the palace, first at the Imperial Sanctuary (Kashiko dokoro) where the sun goddess Amaterasu Omikami is worshipped, then at the shrine to the spirits of the departed emperors and the shrine to the gods of the land. This announcement ceremony, of course, was one of the close to sixty ceremonies involved in the enthronement. Those ceremonies formally closed with Emperor Akihito's "audiences" at the tomb of the legendary first emperor, Emperor Jimmu, and the tombs of the four immediately preceding emperors, Kōmei, Meiji, Taishō, and Shōwa, between December 2 and December 5, and with his audiences at the three palace shrines on December 6.[67]

The planning for the enthronement ceremonies by the government and Imperial Household Agency reflected the controversies among the public at large, though of course on a more limited scale. Compromises were painstakingly worked out. Changes were made in the procedures and symbols of the Accession Ceremony to make it appropriate to the new times. Yet those changes did not disturb the basic format of the 1909 Enthronement Ordinance. No changes were apparently made in the Great Food Offering Rite, a carbon copy of that stipulated in the 1909 ordinance.

Some five-hundred foreign and two-thousand Japanese dignitaries attended the Accession Ceremony at the Imperial Palace in Tokyo, that being a public ceremony for public consumption. The prime minister led a modified banzai cheer after he presented his felicitations to the emperor on behalf of the people. He did not dress in ancient court costume, as was the case in 1928, but wore a Western swallow-tailed coat and formal attire. He did not retreat to the courtyard below the throne platform to deliver the three banzais, as Prime Minister Tanaka Giichi had done in 1928. Prime Minister Kaifu led the banzai cheer from the throne platform about 1.3 meters below the throne out of consideration for popular sovereignty and his status as representative of the sovereign people. And he did not simply shout banzai, as was the case in 1928, because that would have called to mind the military banzais of prewar Japan: he shouted "Felicitations to Your Majesty on your accession to the Throne, banzai"—three times.[68]

Seated on the ancient but modified Chinese-style throne, the emperor was flanked by two small stands on which were placed the sword and jewels, two of the three emblems signifying his legitimacy as emperor and which he had received when he succeeded his father in January 1989. Added to these were the Great Seal of State and the Emperor's Privy Seal. Apparently the Cabinet Legislation Bureau was concerned that the sword and jewels had religious significance and wanted them removed from the ceremony. But the Imperial Household Agency insisted on "tradition." So the Cabinet Legislation Bureau compromised by having the two seals placed on the stand as secular emblems of the emperor's true functions under the new constitution, along with the sword and the jewels. Moreover, the brocade banners in the courtyard were embroidered with a chrysanthemum motif in place of motifs representing the legendary Emperor Jimmu's legendary military expedition that allegedly unified Japan in 660 B. C. Gone also were motifs representing Empress Jingu's Korean expedition, said to have been mounted in the third century. Although the authorities gave euphemistic explanations about these banner changes, the *Yomiuri shimbun* commented that they were made in order to dilute Japanese mythology and to erase military symbolism from the enthronement, out of concern for public censure and out of consideration for Japan's relations with Korea.[69]

Because so many high foreign dignitaries were present, unlike the representation from abroad in 1928, foreign guests took their place in the Grand Hall across the courtyard from the State Hall where the emperor and empress were seated upon their thrones. Foreign guests were not to be at a lower, inferior position. And they did not need to join in the banzai cheer.

Otherwise, the Accession Ceremony was conducted largely as prescribed in the 1909 Enthronement Ordinance. There were seventy-four retainers in ancient court dress lined up in the courtyard. Twenty were guards armed with bows and arrows. Another forty guards were outfitted with bows, swords, crossbows, halberds, and shields, in groups of eight, respectively. There were fourteen court musicians.[70]

The Accession Ceremony was followed by a series of banquets, after which foreign guests returned to their countries. Foreign guests were not to be near the Great Food Offering Shrine compound during the Great Food Offering Rite, as they had been in 1928. The Great Food Offering Rite was strictly for the Japanese, so that they could reaffirm, if that were possible, their distinctive and sacred community.

Accessing the World

For many Japanese today, however, that very ritualization of Japan's sacred community is incompatible with modern community life in Japan, with the nature of the modern Japanese individual, and above all with Japan's international position and role. To them, Japan must be both in and of this world, and the enthronement represents a notion of a unique sacred community that needs to be overcome, not reinforced.[71]

By separating a public Accession Ceremony so clearly from a sacred Great Food Offering Rite, the Japanese government and palace authorities attempted to have the best of both worlds, to keep the sacred we and link it to the profane they. This is a Japanese version of a universal human dilemma, the problem of creating a sense of community solidarity yet one that contains some notion of a universal humanity. Given the distinctive nature of Japan's imperial institution, and the sacred renewal of its distinctive community through the enthronement ceremonies, there is justifiable doubt among the Japanese themselves as to whether Japan has or will ever overcome this dilemma. But the ambiguity, controversy, apathy, and uncertainty of the 1990 enthronement ceremonies do indicate that the attitudes of the Japanese people were indeed diverse and in a state of flux as the authorities attempted to regroup the nation around its ancient symbol of community and continuity. And the government did so with no small degree of uncertainty on its part as well. The tradition of the manipulation of tradition that the imperial institution has embodied throughout its history, going back to its primordial origins, was employed in an attempt to accommodate a transformed Japan and a new emperor who just might not be willing to remain the shaman-priest prisoner of a unique and sacred Japanese community.

It is the Great Food Offering Rite above all else that is designed to imprison the emperor as the ritual center of the Japanese nation, a nation that now embraces a remarkable diversity of values and points of view, particularly regarding Japan's place in the world. In the words of Richard Madsen, "Ritual brings many different levels of meaning together to form a resonant unity . . . ritual—when it works— unifies people around a complex of meaning."[72] Given the public controversy and apathy surrounding the 1990 enthronement, and the style, personality, and convictions of the emperor himself, imperial rituals based on Shinto rites may no longer fuse "many different levels of meaning together to form a resonant unity."

Emperor Akihito has consistently and publicly vowed to uphold Japan's made-in-America Constitution. He did so immediately after becoming emperor in January 1989: "His words must have come as a great shock to the right-wing extremists."[73] And he did so from the throne during the Accession Ceremony.[74] The emperor's pronouncements and behavior indicate that he wishes to be an emperor "with the people," a modern monarch along the lines of his fellow monarchs, particularly in Western Europe. He projects a style that is utterly incongruous with the prewar emperor system, and with the ancient rituals of communing with the gods that he undertook in the Great Food Offering Rite—and indeed with the Shinto rites he has performed and will continue to perform in the inner sanctum of the palace.[75]

Also problematic is the emperor's international role. His projection into the international arena via "imperial house diplomacy" as a human, relaxed, modern personality may enhance Japan's image in the world as well. "If the emperor as symbol can be humanized, he can be used as a symbol of Japan to open the entire society [to the world]."[76] This is only problematic if the government and palace do not allow the kind of "imperial house diplomacy" that has taken place since 1952 to continue and expand, if, in the judgment of those concerned, Japanese community solidarity and "internationalization" come into conflict. More problematic is what the emperor can actually do as the "humanized" symbol of a "humanized" Japan. To many Japanese, for example, Emperor Akihito's apology to President Roh Tae Woo of South Korea went beyond the permissible role of the emperor as a limited head of state. It went beyond his constitutionally specified duties, it amounted to "politically" using the emperor, and, it might be suggested, for some it posed a threat to Japan's sense of self-esteem as a community.

Despite problems of reconciling Japan's sense of its communal self with a universal notion of humankind, culture with civilization, Japan and the world— seen poignantly in the enthronement ceremonies, Japan's imperial house will most certainly maintain or increase the unprecedented international activities it has been engaged in since 1952. However successfully, Japan's imperial house symbolizes an internationally dependent Japan, and it will continue to access the world for a Japan that has greatly changed over the course of the twentieth century, and that is struggling to be both in and of this world on its own terms.

Notes

This essay would not have been possible without the indispensable assistance of Arima Yoshiko, who supplied much of the material on the organization, personnel, and functions of the palace, articles in the Japanese media, official documents on Emperor Akihito, and extensive official and media material on the Enthronement Ceremony. Anthony Chambers also sent me materials from the Japanese press on the Enthronement. I also thank my colleagues at the January 16–20, 1991, conference on postwar Japanese foreign policy for their helpful suggestions and comments.

1. "Reference Materials: 1. The Imperial Family and Imperial System, 2. Questions and Answers, 3.Glossary" (Tokyo: Foreign Press Center Japan, November 1990), p.14.

2. Kunaichō, *Kunaichō yōran* (Tokyo: Kunaichō, 1965), p. 28.

3. Ibid., p. 19.

4. Ibid., pp. 20–21.

5. Kunaichō, *Kunaichō yōran* (Tokyo: Kunaichō, 1965), pp. 31–38.

6. Ibid., pp. 39–45.

7. *Newsweek: The International Newsmagazine*, September 29, 1975, p. 7.

8. Kunaichō, 1988, pp. 39-45; "Reference Materials," pp. 2, 4–5.

9. Ibid., pp. 41–45; "Reference Materials," pp. 7–9.

10. Ibid., pp. 15–16. Such lectures to the emperor on foreign and domestic affairs as well

as scholarly subjects were first inaugurated in the Meiji period. "Nihonshi no naka no tennō," *Chūo korōn*, (November 1988): 69.

11. "Nihonshi no naka no tennō," p. 79. All graduates of Kyoto University, the participants in the roundtable discussions in addition to Yano were Ueyama Shumpei, professor emeritus of Kyoto University and curator of the Kyoto National Museum, and Umehara Takeshi, director of the Center for the Study of Japanese Culture.

12. Kunaichō, 1988, pp. 31–45.

13. "Nihonshi no naka no tennō," p. 67.

14. Ibid.

15. Kunaichō, 1988, pp. 31–45.

16. Ibid.

17. *Japan Times Weekly, International Edition,* November 12–18, 1990, p. 9.

18. Ibid., May 21–27, 1990, p. 4.

19. "'Okotoba' to iu meikyū" (The mystery of 'His Majesty's Words'), *Asahi Journal*, June 1, 1990, pp. 104–5.

20. Ibid., p. 105. The complexity of the issues—legally, generationally, politically, and in terms of Japan's resident population of 700,000 Koreans—and the widely divergent views of the Japanese over the apology are taken up in a somewhat helter-skelter roundtable discussion among Professor Watanabe Shoichi of Jōchi University, non-fiction writer Inose Naoki, and novelist Nosaka Akiyuki in *Bungei shunju* (July 1990): 124–32. Watanabe was strongly opposed to making the apology, arguing that matters between Korea and Japan had already been settled by the 1965 treaty of normalization between the Republic of Korea and Japan. He considers the anti-American feeling in South Korea as an indication that Koreans are ingrates for the sacrifices Americans had made for the sake of the Republic of Korea. And he suggested that if North and South Korea were ever united, a united Korea would demand yet another apology from Japan. Representing the younger generation, Inose was far more sympathetic to Korean grievances. Nosaka, who grew up amidst a large Korean population in Kobe before and during the war, took the middle ground between Watanabe and Inose.

21. *The Japan Times Weekly*, International Edition, June 4–10, 1990, p. 5.

22. "'Okotoba' to iu meikyū," p. 105.

23. Nishihira Shigeki and Nathaniel B. Thayer, "The Japanese Emperor in Perspective: A Summation of Postwar Opinion Polls," *Journal of Northeast Asian Studies* (Summer 1986): 78.

24. Ibid., p. 79.

25. Ibid.

26. Ibid., p. 83.

27. "Nihonshi no naka no tennō", p. 74.

28. Ibid.

29. Ibid., p. 67.

30. Ibid., pp. 66–67.

31. Ibid., p. 79.

32. Ibid., pp. 66–67, 70. For a brief discussion of how the emperor's role in ending the war and his "war responsibility" have been handled in the popular press, see my "The Making of the 'Symbol Emperor System' in Postwar Japan," *Modern Asian Studies* 14, 4 (October 1980): 558–61.

33. For an idealized and romanticized discussion of the origins of the emperor's selfless ritual functions in setting the stage for a Japanese collective will, while grafting on the accoutrements of civilization, see Watsuji Tetsurō, *Sonnō shisō to sono dentō* (Tokyo: Iwanami Shoten, 1943), Chaps. 1–3.

34. Doi Takeo, *The Anatomy of Dependence* (Tokyo:Kodansha International, 1982), p. 78.

35. For the role of the emperor and his managers in prewar Japan, see my *Palace and Politics in Prewar Japan* (New York: Columbia University Press, 1974), Chaps. 1–4; for the meaning of the emperor in mid and late Meiji, see Carol Gluck, *Japan's Modern Myths: Ideology in the Late Meiji Period* (Princeton: Princeton University Press, 1985), Chap. 4.

36. "The Making of the 'Symbol Emperor System' in Postwar Japan," p. 565. See pp. 530–64 for a discussion of the changed role of the emperor in postwar Japan and pp. 565–75 for a discussion of the restructuring of the palace bureaucracy.

37. Kunaichō, 1988, p. 56, and chart following p. 58.

38. Kunaichō, 1965, pp. 42, 13, 30–31.

39. Kunaichō, 1988, pp. 52–54, chart following p. 58.

40. Ibid., pp. 30–31.

41. *Palace and Politics in Prewar Japan*, p. 87.

42. Data on palace personnel have been compiled from various editions of *Shokuin roku, Nihon shinshi roku*, and *Jinji kōshin roku*.

43. Harada Kumao, *Saionji-ko to Seikyoku*, 9 vols. (Tokyo: Iwanami Shoten, 1950–56), 2: 397.

44. Kunaichō, 1965, p. 41; Kunaichō, 1988, chart following p. 58.

45. "Reference Materials," pp. 2–3, 8, 9.

46. Kunio Nishimura, "The Curtain Rises," *Look Japan* 35, 398 (May 1989): 4.

47. *Japan Times*, September 10, 1990, p. 2.

48. *New York Times*, November 30, 1990, p. A7.

49. Togashi Junji, *Kōshitsu jiten* (Tokyo: Mainichi Shimbunsha, 1965), p. 20; "90 nen aki, kamigami wa fukken suru" (In the fall of '90, the gods will be reinstated), *Asahi Journal*, October 19, 1990, pp. 88–89.

50. Kunaichō, 1965, p. 32; Kunaichō, 1988, p. 54.

51. "90 nen aki kamigami wa fukken suru," p. 89.

52. Robert S. Ellwood, *The Feast of Kingship: Accession Ceremonies in Ancient Japan* (Tokyo: Sophia University Press, 1973), p. 79.

53. Ibid., p. 81.

54.   Ibid., p. 79.

55.   Ibid., pp. 80-81.

56.   Ibid., pp. vii, 37.

57.   "90 nen aki, kami wa fukken suru," pp. 90–91. Carmen Blacker, "The *Shinza* or God-seat in the Daijōsai–Throne, Bed, or Incubation Couch?" *Japanese Journal of Religious Studies* 17, 2–3 (June–September 1990): 179–97.

58.   Peter Nosco, summarizing the views of Sasaki Kōkan, *Japanese Journal of Religious Studies*, p. 100.

59.   "90 nen aki, kami wa fukken suru," pp. 91–93. For a rather one-sided account of Shinto in modern Japan, see Helen Hardacre, *Shintō and the State, 1868–1988* (Princeton: Princeton University Press, 1989).

60.   "90 nen aki, kami wa fukken suru," pp. 91–92. See also Nojiri Ichirō, *Koshitsu gisei to keigo* (Tokyo: Shinkokaku, 1942), pp. 4–8, and Ihara Yoriaki, *Koshitsu Jiten* (Tokyo: Fuzambō, 1942), pp. 9–14.

61.   Foreign Ministry Circular, GO No. 41/MPL.

62.   *Asahi shimbun*, January 20, 1990, p. 3; September 21, 1990, p. 2; *The Japan Times*, October 16, 1990, p. 4; *Asahi shimbun*, October 21, 1990, p. 1.

63.   *Asahi shimbun*, November 7, 1990, p. 3.

64.   *The Japan Times*, October 7, 1990, p. 2.

65.   Kenichi Kohyama, "Why It's Still Important," *Look Japan* (October 1990): 40–42.

66.   *The New York Times International*, November 11, 1990.

67.   *The Japan Times*, January 9, 1990, p. 2; *Asahi shimbun*, January 8, 1990, p. 1; January 20, 1990, p. 3; September 4, 1990, p. 1; *Yomiuri shimbun*, September 20, 1990, p. 1; *Sankei shimbun*, September 20, 1990, p. 1.

68.   *Yomiuri shimbun*, September 20, 1990, p. 1.

69.   Ibid.

70.   Ibid.; *Sankei shimbun*, September 20, 1990, p. 1.

71.   Flora Lewis wrote from Kyoto four years earlier that Japan "requires acknowledging a new kind of responsibility, quite simply to others, as self-fulfillment," Japan "has entered the world. That isn't enough, for itself or for others. It should join." *New York Times*, September 12, 1986, p. A27. The 1990 enthronement did precious little to address this problem, or rather quite the opposite. I am indebted to Michael Blaker for calling the Lewis piece to my attention.

72.   Richard Madsen, *Morality and Power in a Chinese Village* (Berkeley: University of California Press, 1984), p. 9.

73.   Nishimura, "The Curtain Rises," p. 5.

74.   *Japan Times Weekly International Edition*, November 19–25, 1990, p. 6. At the January 1991 Cayman Islands conference, Nathaniel Thayer argued that one might call Emperor Akihito "the first left-wing emperor." "One of the many things he has done has been to sink the right-wing movement in Japan, . . . since he will have nothing to do with the right wing." Conference transcript, p. 72. While the emperor is a truly

modern monarch and a strong personality, however, he is not completely his own man. His role will be managed in large part for him, as it was for his father and predecessors, by the government and palace officials in charge of judging the "trends of the times" inside and outside Japan.

75. Emperor Akihito "is the first emperor to have a foreign tutor [a Quaker, Mrs. Elizabeth Vining], to marry a 'commoner' and to raise his own children as a family." *The Japan Times Weekly International Edition*, November 12–18, 1990, p. 9. His informal, "popular" style has caused palace and Foreign Ministry officials considerable difficulty, and he seems bent on making himself a "monarch of the people" in a modern, middle-class, and internationalized Japan. "Tennō no Hyōban," *Shukan asahi*, November 23, 1990, pp. 20–29.

76. Comment by Susan Pharr, Cayman Islands conference. Conference transcript, p. 72.

Chapter 4
Japanese Foreign Policy in the Nakasone Years

Nathaniel B. Thayer

On November 26, 1982, Nakasone Yasuhiro became prime minister of Japan. Three elections brought him to this position. First was a party primary: It made him one of two candidates to lead the ruling party, the Liberal Democratic party. Next was a runoff: It made him the *sosai* (top leader). Third was a vote in the national assembly, the Diet: In its chambers, the LDP Dietmen transformed their *sosai* into the prime minister.

In the party primary, Nakasone got 56 percent of over a million votes. Reporters could have considered this victory as a popular mandate. They did not. Dietmembers dominate the second and third elections. Factions divide the Dietmembers. They vote as their faction leader instructs them. Tanaka Kakuei was the leader of the largest faction. His voice was determining. He had chosen the previous two prime ministers. He was saying publicly that Nakasone's time had come. And what would be the relationship between Nakasone and Tanaka? Tanaka spelled that out privately to his faction followers, though they leaked it to the newspapers.

"Nakasone is the jockey," said Tanaka. "I own the horse."

Reporters also said that Nakasone would be transitional. They meant that Nakasone would not complete his term of two years. Tanaka was under indictment for malfeasance while he was prime minister. Allegedly, he had accepted money from the Lockheed corporation and had his transportation minister direct the purchase of its airplanes for a national airline. Doubtless, the judges would find him guilty. The constitution specified an election for the upper house by summer of the following year. The public would use it to show its disgust. Far fewer LDP Dietmembers would return to office. Nakasone would have to take responsibility for the bad showing: He would have to resign.

How prescient were the reporters? The judges found Tanaka guilty. But Nakasone did not have to resign. By the following summer, Nakasone was well along on his climb to power. He went on to serve almost five years, a record matched by few prime ministers in the century Japan has had prime ministers.

What gave Nakasone his political strength? I argue that Nakasone found in foreign affairs a source of popular, political authority.

All prime ministers have spoken about the centrality of foreign affairs to the well-being of the Japanese nation. Specified in the constitution is the power of the Japanese prime minister to manage foreign affairs. Yet most prime ministers have been cautious in the exercise of this authority. Why? Because failure in its exercise has most often furnished the reason a prime minister has had to leave office.[1] Only Nakasone Yasuhiro, whose story I tell below, was able to turn the management of foreign affairs into enhanced authority and extended rule.

I

The highest calling in prewar Japanese society was to become an imperial official. That was the goal that the father, Nakasone Matsugorō, set for his son, Nakasone Yasuhiro. The son proved equal to the challenge. He competed for and won admission to Tokyo University, the school which most imperial officials attended. While still a college junior, he took his upper civil service examination, did well, and entered into the Interior Ministry, where he served until he joined the Imperial Navy.

Upon discharge at the end of the war, he found that the Occupation authorities had dismembered the Interior Ministry. Too powerful, they said. In the new government, power is divided, checked, balanced. Not clear what he wanted to do, Nakasone accepted a post in a remnant division as an inspector of police. It promised a comfortable, mildly challenging, and prestigious life. Within the year, he realized that he was giving little to the remaking of Japan. Politics was his calling. Winning elections was the only door to such a career. He returned to his birthplace, where he declared his candidacy for a seat in the Diet. The year was 1947. The election was the second postwar election. Nakasone won 65,484 votes, the highest amount among the four winners in his electoral district. Twenty-eight years old, he became the youngest member of the Diet.

Transcripts of Nakasone's campaign speeches for this election are extant. I quote several sentences from one of them:

> The new Japan must put aside the self-serving nationalism and the narrow prejudice seen in prewar Japan. We must adopt principles common to the world. We must also maintain our dignity. We must restore Japan's prestige. I firmly believe dignity and prestige are important if we are to live in international society. People who do not have pride and love for their own country will neither respect the people of other nations nor will the people of other nations respect them. People who have lost their pride will be unable to fulfill their responsibilities as respected members of international society.

Nakasone still makes these points in his speeches today.

II

In 1946 the American Occupation authorities rewrote the Japanese Constitution. They made explicit who should exercise what powers by what means. In article 73, they gave the power to manage foreign affairs to the prime minister and his cabinet. In article 9, they restricted the prime minister and his cabinet to peaceful means since, in that clause, the Japanese people renounce the sovereign right to wage war and the right to maintain armed forces for that purpose.

Japanese conservatives have found article 9 unrealistic. They have said they intend to rewrite the constitution. Though the conservatives occupy a majority of the seats in the Diet, which gives them the authority to rule Japan, they do not occupy two-thirds of the seats, which would permit them to start a constitutional amendment. Furthermore, the voters must also support this amendment. Every public opinion poll taken since 1946 has shown strong public support for article 9.

Article 9 came into being before relations with the Soviet Union turned into a Cold War. With its onset came the question: Who would protect Japan?

Some Japanese believed that Japan needed protection only from itself. After all, its military forces brought war to the Pacific. These Japanese were adamant that Japan should *not* rearm. Often men of the left, they saw the Soviet Union and Mao Zedong's China as peace-loving nations. They preached a policy of unarmed neutrality.

Yoshida Shigeru, a prewar diplomat and a postwar prime minister, came forward with the formula that became national policy: Japan would ally itself with the United States. It would defend Japan. That would allow Japan to focus its efforts on economic recovery and growth. In return, Japan would accept American leadership in its foreign policy.

Nakasone spoke out against the Yoshida formula. It justified the continuation of the Occupation under a new guise. Japan's principal task was the restoration of its national élan. It could not do that if it gave to another nation the task of defending Japan. The United States had its own interests, which might or might not coincide with Japanese interests. Japan should hold on to the right to decide its own destiny.

Such sentiment stimulated Japanese of the left to identify Nakasone as a person of the right. Nakasone did little to dispel this identification. The Occupation authorities frowned on displays of national sentiment; Nakasone installed a flag pole outside his home. Every morning, he sallied forth to raise the *hinomaru*, the national flag, and sing the *kimigayo*, the national anthem. American authorities dispatched military police to intimidate him; Nakasone welcomed them. They showed other Japanese that American authorities took him and his philosophy seriously.

Nakasone did a lot of America-baiting. He sent General Douglas MacArthur, the supreme commander of the allied powers (SCAP), a memorial rating the

Occupation. He invited the general to leave. He urged the United States to serve its own interest in offering a generous peace. Nakasone also sent the memorial to several key United States senators so the general could not ignore it. Nakasone took to wearing a black necktie, which he vowed not to remove until the Occupation was over. Less conspicuously, he maintained friendships with American scholars serving within the American command, who taught him English and American politics. He was a good student.

III

Nakasone entered a churning political world. The Occupation authorities had ordered to leave public office those leaders who had been active in the prewar government. This purge affected even Hatoyama Ichirō. He had organized a political party, enough of whose members won Diet seats in the first postwar election to make him the prime minister. Hatoyama offered the chair of the prime minister to Yoshida Shigeru. Although a prewar ambassador, he openly opposed the militarists' rule of Japan. The militarists responded by throwing Yoshida in jail for a few months in last year of the war. That exempted him from the purge.

Yoshida accepted Hatoyama's offer to become prime minister. Yoshida also promised to return the seat when the Occupation authorities lifted the purge. At least, that is what Hatoyama claimed; Yoshida did not recall that part of the agreement. Eventually, Hatoyama took the prime minister's chair away from Yoshida. That was after Yoshida had been prime minister twice, ruling for a total of eighty-six months.

The purge determined the thrust of politics. The new politicians were inexperienced. They clustered around the few experienced politicians whom the purge had spared. These experienced politicians met with one another, forming parties and counterparties, casting about for a coalition strong and coherent enough to take over the country. In the first decade after the war, sixteen conservative political parties occupied the national scene.

Yoshida had never been an elected official. Initially, he depended on Hatoyama's party. With time, he came to realize that he needed his own following. He reached into the ministries to pluck out talented officials whom he appointed to his cabinets. Such appointments made them famous enough to win elections. All told, Yoshida formed five cabinets to which he made 194 appointments. These Yoshida lieutenants set a distinct political style.

Opposing the Yoshida lieutenants and other former bureaucrats were "party politicians." Their origins varied. Many were sons in locally powerful families. The most common designation used in official biographies was "self-employed." They were also fiercely independent. Unlike the former bureaucrats who used the government to broadcast their name among the electorate, the party politicians won office through their own efforts.

The former bureaucrats gave priority to running a government and spent their time in administration. The party politicians wanted to make a nation and spent their energies in Diet debate. The former bureaucrats were at ease working under an American hegemony. The party politicians wanted no less than total freedom. The former bureaucrats were cautious and prudent. Prime ministers drawn from their ranks lasted a long time. Party politicians were outspoken and emotional. Prime ministers drawn from their ranks had short tenure.

To which group did Nakasone belong? He was the son of a locally powerful family. He also had the credentials to join with the former bureaucrats but he chose to identify with the party politicians. Nakasone was the politician who introduced the vote of nonconfidece that forced Yoshida from office.

IV

By 1955, the sixteen conservative parties had come together into a single conservative party, the Liberal Democratic party (LDP). Challenging it to rule was a unified left-wing party, the Japan Socialist party. It did not stay unified for long. By the 1958 elections, each splinter could not run enough candidates to take over the government were all its candidates to win. Struggle to rule, then, stopped being a struggle between the parties. Struggle to rule took place within the LDP.

On the remnants of the sixteen political parties, men who wanted to become prime minister built factions. At least every three years, sometimes more often, the factions would coalesce into alliances competing to choose a *sosai* of the party, who would become prime minister. An election tested the soundness of the alliances. Thus, the faction leaders were under constant pressure to increase the size and unity of their factions. The maneuvering and building of the factions was the sum and substance of Japanese politics.

Nakasone chose to join the faction of Kōno Ichirō, a party politician. Kōno was ruthless toward enemies, prickly about Americans, scornful of business, soft toward the farmer, always ready for a political fight. Some polls of the day show that Kōno was the most popular politician in the country. He was also the most feared, particularly by the businessmen. He demanded funds of them. They dared not refuse him. So they also financed his rivals. Somehow the rivals got better financed. Kōno never sat in the prime minister's chair.

These years were good to Nakasone. The faction backed him in doing what he did best: oppose. Mostly, he opposed the ideas of the Yoshida lieutenants. One idea he put forward was the direct election of the prime minister. That idea received great support from the populace, none from the former bureaucrats.

Kōno died. Nakasone moved to take over the faction. Another Kōno lieutenant, Mori Kiyoshi, challenged him. The faction split. Nakasone announced that his faction would no longer be a "strategic faction" (interested in money and posts); rather, it would be a "policy faction" (interested in political ideals and how to achieve them).

Expecting praise, he got none. "Learn to drink muddy water," said a critic.

In time, Nakasone learned about the care and feeding of factions. He gained new members, mostly through running his own men in elections. Sometimes he recruited former Kōno men who had become disenchanted with Mori Kiyoshi. Nakasone's support for other potential prime ministers became a sought-after prize. Nakasone himself never got talked about as a potential prime minister. Why?

He was too hard-charging. Even Kōno had said he could never relax in a hot tub with Nakasone. That frightened the businessmen. He was too brilliant, too excoriating in his opposition. That frightened the bureaucrats. Though he often talked politics through the night into the morning, he didn't drink much. And he didn't play around. That dismayed the politicians. "Join a cabinet," advised a confidante. "Everyone must learn that you can run a government."

Nakasone took this advice. He became minister of transportation. The cabinet he joined, though, was that of Prime Minister Satō Eisaku, who had been a Yoshida lieutenant, a perfervid Yoshida lieutenant. Politicians had seen Nakasone as Satō's nemesis; now he was Satō's subordinate. Someone called him a cock on a political weather vane (*kazami dori*). Nakasone said that he could be such a cock because his feet didn't move. Reporters ridiculed the argument.

Time passed. Nakasone joined other cabinets and eventually came to head major ministries. He was doing what he set out to do: Show that he could cooperate in running a government. Secretly opposing him were Japan's professional diplomats. They never let the Yoshida lieutenants forget that the foreign policy that Nakasone urged was fundamentally at odds with the foreign policy that they had hammered out with Yoshida. Nakasone never got offered the post he wanted most —the Foreign Ministry.

Satō Eisaku announced he would leave the prime minister's chair. His faction split, one group accepting the leadership of Tanaka Kakuei. Nakasone aligned his faction with Tanaka Kakuei, who became the next prime minister. Tanaka owed Nakasone. When and how would he repay him?

Tanaka and Nakasone differed in interest and personality, though reporters identified both men as party politicians. Foreign policy attracted Nakasone. Domestic affairs attracted Tanaka. Policy making and debate were Nakasone's metier. Tanaka dealt with people. Many politicians out-foxed Nakasone. Nobody got around Tanaka. And he never forgot a slight.

Japan was equipping itself with the legal framework to be a welfare state. Tanaka knew the laws; he could figure out ways to make the government pay his political costs. Using the public record, an investigative reporter laid out the many Tanaka deals. None were illegal, but many were questionable. Tanaka tried to wait out the resulting storm. It did not subside. He said he was sick and resigned from office. Six months later, authorities charged him with accepting money from the Lockheed corporation for an illegal purpose.

Recognizing that his absolution could only come from the political world, Tanaka saw the need to maintain a powerful political presence. He continued to build his faction. In time, it became a third larger than anyone else's faction. Other faction leaders found allying with Tanaka easier than allying to oppose Tanaka. He became known as the prime ministerial king-maker.

Tanaka's practice was never to select as a candidate for prime minister anyone from within his own faction. That would encourage rivalry among his lieutenants. Instead, Tanaka picked a leader of another faction. Tanaka's faction and the picked prime minister's faction provided almost enough votes to win the *sosai* election. Tanaka never had difficulty picking up the remaining votes.

Tanaka had first backed Ohira Masayoshi, an old friend and a demonstrated leader. Ohira died. Tanaka then backed a politician named Suzuki Zenkō, a member of the Ohira faction. The choice was surprising, since Suzuki had not been a faction leader, and had been known only for his backstage maneuvering. Still Tanaka pulled his selection off. As a prime minister, Suzuki was inept. Nobody recognized that more than Suzuki, and he announced his intention to retire during his second year in office. Tanaka then turned to Nakasone.

Cynicism greeted his choice. "Who would be the new prime minister?" asked a wit. He answered his own question: "Tanakasone." Reporters repeated the elision endlessly in their columns.

Nakasone needed to get Tanaka off his back, out of his name. He needed a strategy; he needed new allies. The strategy was to bring Japan into active participation in world affairs. His new allies were to be, initially, the Foreign Ministry and, eventually, Ronald Reagan and the summits.

V

Nakasone soon set about this strategy. To his foreign minister, his finance minister, and his chief cabinet secretary upon closing his first cabinet meeting on November 30, 1982, he said,

"I'd like to start by bettering relations with South Korea."[2]

No problem looked less promising than bettering relations with South Korea. Agreeing to exchange embassies had taken fourteen rancorous years—an exchange made possible only when a Japanese-trained general, Pak Chung-hui, seized power and made himself president of the Republic of Korea.

Relations degenerated with the accession of his successor, General Chun Doo Hwan, who described himself as a member of the Hangul (Korean language) generation. General Chun spoke no Japanese, distrusted those Koreans who did. He fostered the purge of Japanese-trained Koreans from business and politics.

General Chun sentenced to death, then commuted to twenty years imprisonment, Kim Dae Jung, a Korean politician whom the KCIA had kidnapped from a

Tokyo hotel. He demanded of Japan six billion dollars to support Korea's new five-year-plan. "Japan owed the Republic of Korea at least that much," he said, "because the Republic of Korea defended Japan." He demanded the rewriting of Japanese textbooks when he discovered they described the March First Uprising of Koreans in 1919 as a mob riot instead of a popular revolt. On August 15, Korean Independence Day, he delivered a speech in which he held that Japan had raped Korea.

Japanese were equally harsh in their view of Koreans. Starting in 1936, Japanese authorities drafted and brought Korean farmers to work in Japan to perform the tasks in the Japanese economy that Japanese would no longer do. These farmers were often illiterate, and certainly not prepared to make a living in an industrial society. They formed an underclass easily roused to violence, often associated with the water trades, certainly not in harmony with the goals of Japanese society. For the Japanese, what these Koreans did in Japan formed the image of Koreans everywhere.

Mutual antipathy faced Nakasone. He sent a Japanese trading company official to secretly negotiate Japanese support for the Korean five-year-plan. That stopped posturing on both sides. He persuaded the Korean authorities that Kim Dae Jung was sick enough to send to the United States for treatment. That removed him as a source of contention between the two countries. He instructed the Education Ministry to review Japan's textbook policies. Through a reporter, Nakasone let it be known that he was rehearsing a speech in Korean. Two months later, on January 11, 1983, he stood on the tarmac at Kimpo Airport, the first Japanese prime minister to pay a formal visit to the Republic of Korea. Over the next two days, President Chun and Prime Minister Nakasone spoke often of friendship. That was a word not heretofore used to describe the relationship.

How had Nakasone resolved such contention so quickly? Some Japanese thought that Nakasone had not negotiated but given in to Korean demands. They said so loudly. Polls showed that the most Japanese supported Nakasone. They wanted better relations with the Republic of Korea.

My explanation starts with the few sentences I quoted earlier, the sentences that came from Nakasone's 1946 campaign speech. They show he is preternatural in sensitivity toward issues of national identity. Compare Nakasone's speech with Chun Doo Hwan's Independence Day speech:

> We celebrate this day with profound emotion because the ordeal
> of subjugation has left such deep scars on our psyche. Punctuated by
> blood and tears, anguished sorrow and tortured laments, the pain can-
> not possibly be understood by anyone who had not experienced such
> an ordeal.[3]

Chun Doo Hwan found in Nakasone shared values.

"Apprehensive," said a high-ranking diplomat to describe the mood within the

Foreign Ministry when Nakasone became prime minister. Some diplomats went so far to suggest limited cooperation with Nakasone to slow down his foreign activities and hasten his departure from office. The Korean experience arrested these thoughts. The diplomats found impressive the ease with which Nakasone had surmounted the colonial disdain toward Korea held by so many Japanese. Nakasone was a man who could help the foreign ministry. He could lead. He could engender excitement and support. The Foreign Ministry needed those attributes in a prime minister.

VI

Japanese law does not prohibit media empires. Newspapers, magazines, journals, books, and radio and television networks can cohabit in a single company. Dominant, though, are the newspapers, particularly in covering government and politics. Other media in a media empire rely on the print reporters for guidance.

Attached to each ministry and to the political parties is a press club. These clubs exclude everyone but reporters from commercial newspapers. Officials and politicians talk first, sometimes only, to the reporters in the clubs covering them.

Membership in the clubs changes slowly. Every two years, the political news editor of each newspaper will move his reporters around. He might send a reporter in the Kasumigaseki club, which covers the foreign ministry, to the Hirakawa club, which covers the prime minister's residence. Within a newspaper, though, once assigned to the political section, a reporters stays with the political section for the first twenty years of his newspaper career.

While revolving slowly through the clubs, the reporter hastens to establish ties with the LDP factions. There is the "dawn attack (*asagake*)": A reporter stands silently outside a faction leader's home, morning after morning, until the faction leader invites him into his car for a talk during the ride to his office. There is the "evening strike (*yo-uchi*)": Reporters gather in the informal dining room of the faction leader to eat and drink and question him when he returns from the banquet circuit. In time, the faction leader comes to trust the reporter, expects him to gather intelligence for him, may use him to carry messages to the other factions. Ultimately, he may solicit advice from the reporter.

The reporter, the official, and the politician grow up together. Do they come to empathize with each other? Critics level that charge. Are Japanese news articles inherently unbalanced? To the contrary, they are scrupulously balanced. No article has a single author. Every view is considered and pertinent views given a few sentences. How does the political editor maintain objectivity? No article has a single author.

Reporters, then, are integral to politics. They not only report ideas, they develop ideas. Some politicians come to rely upon them. Not Nakasone.

To the right of the portico covering the main entrance to the prime minister's residence sits a starkly modern cement building. It houses the press. To the left of the entrance hall is the room in which the prime minister holds press conferences. Along a long side of the room is a dais on which is a brocade-covered table, overburdened with microphones. Behind them sits the prime minister. Arrayed in rows in front of the table are seats for the reporters. And behind the seats, on another built-up section, are the television cameras.

Reporters do not rise or wave their hands seeking the prime minister's eye. Rather, the reporters have met earlier, pooled their questions. One of their number poses them to the prime minister.

Nakasone announced that he wished to change this system. The reporters should expect him to speak before answering questions. He didn't need the brocade-covered table. He said that he would stand. A single hang mike would replace the cluster of microphones. While he would try to honor the tradition of giving hard news first to the reporters in his press club, he intended to appear, perhaps weekly, on television. These appearances might also produce news.

The reporters objected. They could see Nakasone slipping from their grasp. The fight was silent—not a word about it appeared in the newspapers. After a few months, Nakasone agreed that he should appear on television perhaps every two weeks. That was the reporters' victory. Nakasone had won freedom from the press's interlocution. He could speak about what he wanted to speak about directly to the people. That was Nakasone's victory.

VII

Most Japanese prime ministers arrange to visit Washington soon after assuming office. During the Occupation, Prime Minister Yoshida was one of the few Japanese allowed to talk with General MacArthur. Since the Japanese public saw the general as the ultimate authority in Japan, those visits gave Yoshida immense political authority. Though the Occupation ended, the Japanese continued to see the United States as having great influence over their lives. They transferred their interest to the American president. Post-Yoshida prime ministers sought to visit him.

The trick, of course, was to create instant personal ties between the president and the prime minister. To that end, the diplomats of the two countries labored mightily. Prime Minister Kishi Nobusuke, for example, came to the United States to sign a security treaty with the United States. Despite its importance, Japanese diplomats directed press attention to a round of golf Kishi played with the senior American officials. The next prime minister, Ikeda Hayato, had a twos-only meeting with President John Kennedy on board the presidential yacht, the *Sequoia*. The only real friendship that budded was between President Jimmy Carter and Prime Minister Ohira Masayoshi. That ended with Ohira's heart attack and death. President Carter attended the funeral.

In truth, no American president particularly welcomed the visit of a Japanese prime minister. Though Japanese and American diplomats always prepared a long agenda, discussions did not lead to important decisions. On no occasion did the diplomats have to change the communiqué that they had written before the meeting. The short biographies of Japanese leaders in the American briefing books were colorless. They offered no thoughts that a president could use to penetrate the politeness enshrouding each prime minister. Only one prime minister (Ohira) spoke English. Most prime ministers limited their remarks to short, set speeches, which the Japanese diplomats corrected as well as translated.

Why did the Japanese prime minister get in to see the American president? Japan was an ally. A treaty of mutual security and cooperation tied the two nations together.

Even the treaty was in question after the visit of Prime Minister Suzuki Zenkō. He had come to Washington, sat in the Oval Office, let his diplomats speak for him. His toasts at the banquet were perfunctory. He showed no interest in the picture taking with the president that, for other prime ministers, was the high point of the trip. The diplomats issued a communiqué, which said the United States and Japan were allies. Earlier communiqués had also called the United States and Japan allies but this one said it differently enough to start a clamor in the Japanese press. Had the Americans persuaded Prime Minister Suzuki to shoulder greater military responsibilities? Prime Minister Suzuki denied that the alliance even had a military aspect. His foreign minister resigned.

Not too much later, Prime Minister Suzuki resigned as well. Nakasone succeeded him. When Japanese diplomats in Washington asked for a meeting for Nakasone with the president, the White House officials remembered Suzuki's visit. They gave the Japanese diplomats a brusque response. Usually, the president met with the head of a government twice, one meeting to discuss bilateral affairs, the other to discuss world affairs. "Unfortunately, the president's schedule would permit only one meeting," the White House officials said. Further, that meeting would span a luncheon. The president's schedule would not permit him to host the customary banquet. That would be done by the vice-president. Oh, yes. Japan was an ally. Would its new leader wish to reaffirm that alliance?

The Japanese ambassador in Washington recommended that Nakasone delay his trip. With time, he felt sure that he could persuade Washington to be more hospitable. Nakasone did not accept this advice. He would come at the earliest time. That proved to be January 18 and 19.

Nakasone arrived in Washington with his wife Tsutako and his younger daughter Mieko on January 17. He met for breakfast the following morning with the editorial staff of the *Washington Post*. The staff asked for permission to tape his remarks. He gave it—and proceeded to speak more freely than any previous prime minister on a visit to Washington.

Much of the talk was on military matters. "Japan is a big aircraft carrier," Nakasone said. Further, he would strengthen defenses. He noted that Japanese territory abutted the four straits through one of which the Russian Navy would have to pass to get from Vladivostok to the open sea. Finally, Japan intended to mount air defenses to counter Russian Backfire bombers. The *Washington Post* carried a story reporting the conversation. A Japanese diplomat denied to Japanese newspaper reporters that Nakasone had ever made such statements. Not wishing to discredit his diplomat, Nakasone said nothing while in Washington. On the way home, he told the Japanese press precisely what he had said.

Nakasone met President Ronald Reagan at 11:25 A.M. in the Oval Office. No aides attended. President Reagan took from his pocket three-by-five cards. "I want to talk about beef and oranges," he is remembered as saying. At the time, Japan was blocking the import of these agricultural products. "Let's leave that discussion to the experts," replied Nakasone, "I wish to talk about global issues." Reagan said once more that he wished to talk about beef and oranges. Nakasone said once more that he wanted to talk on global issues. Reagan repocketed his cards. The two men talked about global issues.

Nakasone reaffirmed the vitality of the alliance between Japan and the United States. He went further. "Japan and the United States are two nations with a single destiny (*unmei kyodotai*)." He repeated that sentence several times in Washington, many more times when he returned to Tokyo. To some Japanese, the phrase was ominous. It supposedly revealed Nakasone's latent military tendencies since it came from a strand of German philosophy that was popular in Japan in the 1930s. Ominous or not, many Japanese felt the phrase expressed too intimate a tie between Japan and the United States.

The conversation between the two heads of government broadened to include the foreign minister, the secretary of state, the secretary of defense, and economic officials. The subject of oranges and beef did get raised again, as did China, Korea, and the Soviet Union and foreign aid. Some actions Nakasone said flatly he could not take. For other actions, he said, he would have to pay a political price. Supplying the United States with weapons technology, increasing the defense budget, opening the agricultural market were such actions. Nevertheless, he would do them. "I take mutual trust seriously," he said repeatedly. Nakasone left the White House in the early afternoon. He had with him an invitation to bring his wife and daughter back for breakfast with Nancy and the president the next morning. At the president's suggestion, the two men agreed to call each other by their first names, Ron and Yasu.

Nakasone continued with his description of the U.S.-Japanese relationship. To the Japan-America Society of Washington he said, "World peace is secure so long as Japan and the United States remain together." In his toast at Vice-President George Bush's dinner he said, "Japan and the United States used to be 'independent' allies. Now they are 'mutually interdependent' allies."

Nakasone got his lumps when he returned to Tokyo. A Foreign Ministry official said dryly that *unmei kyodotai* was not a condition recognized in international law. A Finance Ministry official said that funding Nakasone's ideas was out of the question (*muri*). A member of the delegation said, "Nakasone was speech making, not policy making." Everybody worried that Nakasone had whetted the American appetite for action. They particularly worried about his military talk. What would the United States make of that? Nakasone had already learned that a prime minister must measure the value of what he does against the time it takes to do it. He had to spend long hours defending himself in the Diet. Yet he saw his visit as a success. He had the relationship he wanted with Washington.

VIII

Summits are a new international institution. Started as a one-time gathering of heads of state to discuss the world economy, they have become yearly exchanges and highly political. National staffs work full-time to prepare for them. Membership started with the Atlantic democracies, then broadened to include Japan. Befitting a newcomer, Japanese prime ministers were decorous, spoke diffidently. Sometimes, they spoke not at all when the talks turned political. For the 1983 meeting, the United States was the host. It set the site and the date: Williamsburg, Virginia, late May.

In their first meeting, Reagan had invited Nakasone to talk with him before the May summit meeting. That invitation was not unusual. The heads of the other governments met with the American president before the formal summit sessions. What was unusual was a letter that Reagan sent Nakasone in March. He asked for Nakasone's support for the American position. Upcoming were talks with the Russians and the Europeans on intermediate nuclear missiles. Reagan wanted to limit warheads to three hundred and missile sites to one hundred in Western Europe. Nakasone responded that he thought the Russians should limit their missile sites worldwide. Nevertheless, he would back the president. By early April, Reagan and Nakasone had agreed to meet to discuss a common strategic position.

That meeting took place on May 27 in the White House. Since Nakasone and Reagan had last met, economic issues had dominated the public dialogue between Japan and the United States. In his opening sentence, Reagan recognized that Nakasone had worked to further their resolution. "I wish to thank Japan for the progress it has made on each of the issues since our meeting in January," he said. Still, problems in the relationship remained. Secretary of State Schultz warned Nakasone not to sell militarily useful technology to the Russians. Secretary of Commerce Baldridge advised Nakasone that members of Congress still complained angrily about Japan's industrial policy.

Nakasone took up the reins of the conversation; his talk was political. He said that the ASEAN nations feared that the United States was losing interest in Southeast Asia. He said that China wished to improve relations with the United States. No American challenged his presumption to represent Asia.

"The president had important conversations to carry on with the Russians over the INF," continued Nakasone. Europeans, Japanese, and Americans had to unite on this issue. He was ready to guarantee Japanese cooperation. He would work to ensure European support.

"The president is the pitcher. I am the catcher," said Nakasone.

"The pitcher waits for the catcher's signal," said Reagan.

The following evening, Reagan sizzled his fast ball across the plate(s) at the banquet for the seven heads of government gathered at Williamsburg. Reagan was the host; he could not deliver the keynote address. He asked Nakasone to do so. Nakasone was clever. He spoke mostly of the need for economic solidarity. Inter alia, he identified Japanese's interests as Western interests. Before the summit was over, the participants decided to issue a "political statement." All powers stood behind the United States in the INF negotiations. Further, they urged the consideration of weapons reduction in a global context. The Soviet Union could not satisfy G-7 interests by moving its SS20s out of Europe to deploy them in Asia.

France objected to Japan becoming part of the INF negotiations. One Japanese writer said that Nakasone was nothing more than Reagan's *ichiban te* (first line of attack). Another Japanese writer said Nakasone was playing sumo with a borrowed sash. For sure, no summiteer had asked Nakasone to make clear his degree of interest in European security. When he returned to Tokyo, he had to listen to people tell him that the constitution prevented Japan from doing anything about European security. Everyone was critical of Nakasone's performance. Even so, Nakasone had done something that no other Japanese prime minister had done: He had been a principal in a world drama.

During his five years as prime minister, Nakasone would meet with Reagan twelve times. Six meetings were for summits; two other meetings were to prepare for summits. The Williamsburg meeting provided the script from which they worked. First there was the new idea; then there was the accommodation of the new idea to both nations' interests; finally there was the selling of the idea to the world community. That last step took place at a summit. Japanese newspapers gave heavy coverage to the summits. The summits portrayed Japan as a leading nation respected by other leading nations.

IX

Forty-eight men have served as Japan's prime minister since the office came into existence in 1890. The average time in office is 499 days. While Nakasone was prime minister, the LDP rule was that no person could serve as *sosai* (prime minister) more than two consecutive two-year terms (four years). Nakasone won a national election for the LDP in his fourth year in office, giving it seats in the Diet that it had not held for decades. The LDP Dietmembers believed he should be rewarded with another year in office for his victory. That gave him a total of 1,806 days in office, one of five men to have served so long.

Scholars are now evaluating Nakasone's days in office. A retired professor of the Defense Institute, and a secretary of Nakasone's in the sixties, is one of them. He writes, "After having done over thirty interviews with people related to Nakasone's administration, in political, bureaucratic, business, and journalistic communities, I [have come to] understand that one of his strengths was undoubtedly his outstanding ability showed in domestic decision-making. In particular, his skill in maneuvering and handling bureaucrats as well as other people surrounding Nagatacho was exquisite. He earned his popularity among the general public with his foreign policy performance and among professionals with his political talent. The former was visible. The latter proceeded behind the scene."[4]

The understanding of foreign affairs, then, is just one of several Nakasone virtues. What were his beliefs about foreign affairs? A foreign occupation, no matter how high-minded in goal, was extraordinary. It could not, should not last. Japan, in turn, could not exercise leadership in Asia if nations such as Korea, saw vestiges of colonialism in such leadership. The skills of diplomacy are important to the conduct of a successful foreign policy. Direct, political leadership is also important. The Japanese nation can derive pride from contributing to a world order. These thoughts dominate Nakasone's thinking. They also occupy the imagination of his successors.

Notes

1. In the twenty-seven years between 1955, the year when the LDP took over control of the Diet, and 1982, the year when Nakasone became prime minister, Japan had thirteen prime ministers. Of the thirteen, four left for different reasons, four left because their health turned bad, and four left because they failed in foreign policy.
2. Takahama Tatoo, *Nakasone Gaiseiron* (Tokyo: PHP, 1984), p. 70.
3. The speech is translated in Paul Huen Chan, "From Colony to Neighbor: Relations Between Japan and South Korea, 1945–1985," Ph.D. dissertation, The Johns Hopkins University, 1988, pp. 298–300. I have also relied on this dissertation for my narrative of events.
4. Kobayashi Katsumi, letter, May 12, 1992. Nagatachō is the name for the small village which used to occupy the land where now sits the Diet building, various political party headquarters, other government buildings.

II The Thrust for Economic Success

Chapter 5
From Exporter to Investor:
Japanese Foreign Economic Policy

T. J. Pempel

On the surface, Japanese foreign economic policy in the 1990s bears little resemblance to that pursued during the first two and a half decades or so following World War II. In broadbrush terms, the earlier policy was marked by protection from most imports and capital investments, by restrictions against the outflow of capital from Japan, by a high reliance on technology purchases from other advanced economies, by tight control over foreign entry into the labor market, and by a foreign aid policy designed to develop Asian markets for Japanese manufacturing firms. Economics took clear priority over security considerations, and low levels of defense spending freed up investment capital for use in industrial development. Few foreigners lived or worked in Japan, and most Japanese citizens had little direct experience abroad, since foreign travel was economically difficult and was impeded by government restrictions and a weak yen. [1]

In the period since the late 1970s, Japan's formal trade barriers have been drastically reduced; its currency flows have become far more internationalized; Japanese banks float company debt warrants in Europe with minimal oversight from the Bank of Japan or the Ministry of Finance; Japanese companies, once subject to heavy MITI and MOF directions to ensure conformity with particular government industrial plans, are now largely liberated from the club of capital controls. Their capability to raise capital through the domestic equity markets, through overseas warrants, and through international currency swaps has left them far freer to pursue individual company strategies rather than government directives.

Illegal foreign workers have become a new problem for the Ministry of Justice. Technology-transfer agreements leap across national boundaries with nary a governmental signature. Japan's foreign aid has expanded rapidly and Japan is now the largest single donor of economic assistance. Furthermore, aid is no longer so geographically concentrated in Asia nor so tied to market development. While the end of the Cold War has led the rest of the world's industrial powers to cut military and defense expenditures, Japan stands alone in moving toward greater military spending. Finally, Japanese travelers have joined both the Americans and the Germans in the competition for the label of world's "ugliest" tourists as middle and lower middle-class tour groups lurch feverishly through the luxury shopping streets of Paris or Los Angeles, the beaches of Waikiki or the Costa del Sol, the museums of Florence or Madrid, the game parks of the Masai Mara or Yellowstone, and the erotic zones of Amsterdam or Bangkok, cameras, yen and cultural insensitivity equally at hand. As with trade, capital, and technology, the doorman of the state finds it difficult to monitor much more than their visa status as they go forth and return. [2]

These changes are not always fully recognized, particularly by Western companies facing intense competition with Japanese counterparts both in Japan and in their home markets. Many continue to perceive the Japan of the 1990s as not significantly more open than that described by the cliched phrase "Japan, Inc." Similarly, Japan's trading partners, and particularly the United States, often mesmerized by the continued macrolevel success of Japan's economy in comparative terms, have been slow to recognize the character and extent of the changes. Instead they have devoted the bulk of their public-relations attention to the still-closed features of the Japanese economy and to criticisms of Japanese governmental efforts to liberalize trade, capital movements, and foreign aid. Do the formal changes hammered out in Japan's foreign economic policy represent a fundamentally different direction? Or do current policies represent simply the old wine of mercantilism in the new bottle of internationalism? Certainly, the rise within the Western world of the so-called Japan bashers [3] makes it even more necessary than normal to establish some of the basic facts concerning the character of Japanese foreign economic policy.

Any nation's foreign economic policy reflects an interaction between domestic and international pressures—both political and economic.[4] The particularities of these interactions differ from one country to another, from one time period to another, and in accord with endogenous changes in either the domestic or the international arena. But almost without exception, foreign economic policy will be incomprehensible without an understanding of that policy's domestic roots and domestic consequences. [5]

This is certainly the case with regard to Japan. The foreign economic policies of the 1950s, 1960s, and early 1970s rested fundamentally on a specific set of domestic political and economic structures, without which the policies would have been impossible to pursue and sustain. Just as important, current policies, particularly insofar as they are different from those earlier policies, are embedded in a rather different set of structures and institutions. Yet the socioeconomic bases of foreign economic policy in Japan are by no means totally different from those of a decade or two ago. This is particularly so in that the country has continued to be ruled by the same Liberal Democratic party since 1955. As a consequence, policy today retains many of the underlying motivations of earlier policies, even if certain goals and the specific mechanisms for advancing them have changed.

The principal argument of the paper is that Japanese foreign economic policy operates out of a set of identifiable domestic bases in politics and economics. During the 1950s, 1960s, and early 1970s these domestic bases were of a specific nature giving a particular coherence and internal clarity to Japanese foreign economic policy during these years. The overall thrust of this policy was export-oriented growth. Yet as international and domestic conditions changed in the early 1970s, in some cases abruptly and radically, a new and often strikingly different direction has been given to Japanese foreign economic policy. [6] This new direction has been rooted in a different set of domestic political and structural conditions in support of these new foreign economic policy positions. The new policies center around overseas investment. In this sense, not only is Japanese foreign economic policy not what it was two decades ago, Japanese domestic economic policy and domestic politics have also been altered. Nonetheless, with certain core components of domestic politics still in place, there remain many continuities with the foreign economic policies of the past. This paper attempts to outline these changes and continuities and the linkages between them.

The next section provides a brief overview of the linkages and interactions between Japanese foreign economic policy and domestic Japanese politics and economics until the early 1970s. The following section outlines the major changes that have taken place in Japanese foreign economic policy since then, focusing on the ways in which one relatively coordinated and interactive set of policies has been replaced by a set of policies rather at odds with its predecessor policies. The third section points out the ways in which certain aspects of current policies, while different on the surface, retain important continuities with past policies. The final section concentrates on the political and economic changes that have accompanied these continuities and changes in foreign economic policy. It focuses on the extent to which the new policies, emerging in response largely to changing world economic conditions and to Japan's place within them, have necessitated moves toward a drastically altered domestic politics and economics but in ways that retain some important continuities with past power distributions.

Japanese Foreign Economic Policy and Its Domestic Bases: 1950-1973

For the first two decades or so following the loss of World War II, despite many important twists and turns, there was a high degree of congruence between Japanese domestic politics and economics, on the one hand, and the nation's foreign economic policy, on the other. Despite the electoral success of the left-of-center opposition in the 1947 elections and the opposition's ability to form the only (albeit short-lived) nonconservative government in Japan's modern history, electoral conservatism prevailed through the 1950s and into the early 1970s. Especially since the unification of the Liberals and Democrats on November 15, 1955, into the Liberal Democratic party (LDP), Japan's conservatives have had a single and eminently successful electoral vehicle by which to exert unprecedented control over the national (and, with the exception of the mid-1970s, local) government. [7]

Japan's dominant conservative coalition rested on the fusion of two key social sectors: business and agriculture—an alliance of iron and rice. Electorally, the alliance rested on small, medium-sized, and larger business firms, while the agricultural segment did not consist principally of major landlords, but of numerous small plot holders held together through the Association of Agricultural Cooperatives (Nokyo). This social coalition was capable of exerting a coherent electoral voice through a single political party, the LDP. In contrast, white-and-blue collar workers, urbanites as a group, intellectuals, and the ideologically left-of-center citizenry found their electoral voices fragmented among several minor and competing niche parties. [8]

Continual electoral success was fostered by the coalition's close allegiance to the state bureaucracy, while in turn the continued electoral dominance of the coalition ensured that bureaucrats anxious to advance their careers would adhere to, and advance, the conservative policy agenda.

Continued electoral success for the LDP rested heavily on the extraordinary success of Japan's domestic and foreign economic policies. [9] A sequence of industrial policies sought to improve the domestic infrastructure and international competitiveness of certain targeted Japanese industries, particularly in machinery, chemicals, and steel, by allowing oligopolistic reorganization of companies, selective imports of foreign technologies, lower than market-interest capital loans, R&D cartels, and a host of cognate policies, all in the interest of increasing Japan's international competitiveness and maximizing economic growth rates.[10] During the 1960s, upwards of five-hundred major and minor mergers occurred each year; by the end of the 1960s and the beginning of the 1970s these were taking place at the rate of more than one thousand annually. [11]

At the same time, Japan remained then, as it remains today, an economy "teeming with small-scale family enterprises, more so than any other advanced industrial country."[12] From then to now, Japan's has been an economy of giants striding above these many pygmies, the latter often linked to the former through extensive subcontract arrangements.

Several dozen of Japan's largest companies were truly world players with offices throughout the world and with total sales and employed personnel figures comparable to other companies in Fortune's International 500. This was especially true of Japan's major manufacturing firms, the biggest and best of which were rapidly approaching, if not already surpassing, their Western counterparts in industrial productivity, introduction of technology, wage rates, total sales, and market penetration. For example, Japan had no meaningful automobile manufacturing capability as late as the end of the 1950s; by 1972, it was producing four million units per year, of which nearly one-half were destined for export.[13] Japan also moved from manufacturing approximately one-tenth of the world's ships in 1950 to producing one-half in 1972.[14] As late as the mid-1960s, Japan's companies were barely coming to grips with the most simple computer chip; by the end of the 1970s, they controlled about 40 percent of the world market in 16K ram chips. Although the statistics differ in specifics, the picture is similar in 35 mm cameras, home electronics equipment, watches, calculators, small trucks, machine tools, and dozens of other products.

Success in the external market was paralleled by a domestic market that remained relatively closed and protectionist. The American Occupation had initially and theoretically committed itself to an antimonopoly policy. Yet under the Export and Import Trading Act of August 1952, virtually coterminous with the end of the Occupation, the Japanese government explicitly permitted exporters to enter cartel agreements on price, quality, design, or other matters connected to the export of their products.

The government also controlled the access of Japanese firms to foreign technology and to large quantities of raw materials. Formally until 1961 and informally for a long period thereafter, the government maintained strict controls over Japanese imports. Consumer products were tightly restricted, through both tariffs and import quotas; in contrast, raw materials and the machinery needed to fuel the domestic transformation were encouraged. However, the raw materials that were imported were subjected to strict government controls to ensure that they were distributed in conjunction with governmental economic and sectoral priorities. Only in 1962 did the government replace its short list of items that *could* be imported by a list of items that were explicitly prohibited without specific governmental permission.

All technologies brought into the country until 1968 were screened by the government on a case-by-case basis, even though such screenings were by then difficult to justify on the basis of the original balance-of-payments claims. Japan remained the only OECD nation to maintain such restrictions at that late date.[15]

Indeed, until 1974 restrictions were maintained on numerous specific technology imports. Furthermore, the government exercised strict controls over the companies allowed access to key technologies, typically insisting that no single domestic company be allowed to enter into monopoly use agreements with holders of foreign technologies.[16] As a result of aggressive searches for appropriate foreign technologies, between 1950 and 1970 Japan spent about $3 billion in foreign technology acquisition.[17]

Extensive restrictions on the import of most manufacturing goods and the high degree of manufactured exports from Japan left it a country with one of the most skewed import-export balances in the industrial world.[18]

Financial policy, too, was enlisted in the support of Japan's overall domestic and foreign economic policies. Both MITI and the Ministry of Finance provided financial assistance to targeted firms and sectors through low-interest government loans, aid in securing private loans, accelerated depreciation, and tax-free reserves. Even more important for the overall direction of economic policy, the Ministry of Finance managed to maintain overbalanced budgets until 1965. In effect the balanced budget principle prevented the government from borrowing from the Bank of Japan and from issuing marketable bonds to fund its programs.[19] Regardless of the theoretical economic benefits of such measures, this policy allowed for exceptionally low-cost government and—once the economy began to grow at double-digit rates, increasing government revenues automatically—frequent and politically popular, tax cuts.

Even more fundamental to monetary policy was the maintenance of an undervalued yen. From the time of the Dodge Mission to Japan in 1949 until the end of the Bretton-Woods System in 1971, the Ministry of Finance maintained a yen closely linked to the U.S. dollar at a rate that rarely deviated more than a yen or two from Y360 to $1. As the Japanese economy grew in strength, the yen became an ever more undervalued currency. This in turn provided both a catalyst to Japan's exports and a barrier to foreign imports and investments.

A weak domestic position in foreign exchange originally made it essential for the government to discourage direct overseas investments by Japanese companies in all areas except direct extraction of raw materials. In 1949, concerned about this balance-of-payments problem, the government enacted a Foreign Exchange and Control Law that remained in effect until 1980. Initially, foreign investment by Japanese firms was permitted only if it would promote exports from Japan or develop natural resources unavailable or scarce in Japan. The Export-Import Bank also helped to restrict unwanted overseas investments by selective use of its financial support. Thus, from 1951 until 1971, total Japanese direct foreign investment totaled just slightly over $4 billion, with nearly 60 percent of that total coming in the last three years of that period.[20] Through fiscal 1972, nearly three-quarters of Japan's limited overseas investments were in nonmanufactured items. In effect,

Japan was not much of an overseas investor.

Meanwhile, foreign direct investment in Japan was also strongly discouraged through the same Foreign Exchange and Control Law. Initially, balance of payments considerations provided the principal rationale for restricting such investment. Subsequently, investment was allowed only if it did not unduly challenge small enterprises, seriously disturb industrial order, or severely impede the advancement of Japanese technology.[21] A series of liberalizations took place in 1963 when Japan joined the OECD. Subsequent liberalizations followed in July 1967, March 1969, September 1970, and August 1971. But the burden of proof remained on the potential investor to prove to almost invariably dubious Japanese officials that the proposed investment would not be detrimental to the Japanese economy as a whole. With few major exceptions, into the early 1970s Japan was a country almost devoid of significant foreign direct investment.[22]

In a most fundamental way, this restriction of capital investment allowed Japanese foreign and domestic economic policies to be fused in the creation of industries at home that were deemed critical to Japan's overall economic success without having to confront, as did many European countries at the same time, the problems associated with foreign or multinational penetration and internal market competition. Indeed, by securing foreign technologies through government-assisted purchases and simultaneously restricting opportunities for foreign direct investment, Japanese policy succeeded in attracting needed technologies without the accompanying problems of foreign management and control.

A relatively abundant supply of domestic labor, much of it the result of the large migration from rural to urban areas, helped initially to keep down labor costs. It also functioned to dampen any desire by government or employers to search abroad for lower-cost labor.

In the area of "foreign aid," the close linkages between domestic commercial and financial interests and foreign economic policy are even more explicit. Japan's aid effort began with reparations payments to several Southeast Asian countries in the early 1950s, the specifics of which were typically developed at the initiative of Japanese businesses, involving export credits, tied loans, plant exports, and long-term investment projects relying on Japanese capital. Until 1972 Japanese aid was typically tied to the purchase of Japanese goods and actual Development Assistance Committee (DAC) recognized official aid from the Japanese government was exceptionally low by comparative statistics.

One final element critical to foreign economic policy was Japan's relatively low commitment to the security and military aspects of foreign policy. A close security alliance with the United States and a low posture in international affairs left the Japanese government free to hold down the military share of the national budget. During the period from the 1950s to the early 1970s, the United States devoted between 7 and 9 percent of its GNP to military expenditures, and most major

Western European countries were spending at least 4–5 percent of theirs in the same way. In contrast, after 1956 Japan's military budget rarely consumed more than 1–1.3 percent of that country's GNP and, as is well known, for most of the period the figure has been maintained as a matter of policy below 1 percent of GNP.[23]

Even more striking is the fact that as a proportion of the national budget, Japanese defense expenditures during the 1955–70 period typically consumed 7–8 percent of the budget, declining gradually throughout the period, while in the United States the figure was dramatically higher at 40–60 percent.[24] Patrick and Rosovsky have concluded that this lower level of military spending played a major role in Japanese capital formation, and that defense expenditures on the order of 6–7 percent of GNP during the period 1954–74 would have reduced the size of the 1974 economy by about 30 percent.[25] Without question such a reduction would have made for a profoundly different, and substantially less prosperous, Japan.

As has been widely catalogued, this combination of domestic and foreign economic policies was instrumental in improving macrolevel economic conditions in Japan. Far more important politically, it also provided the basis for holding the conservative coalition together. Japanese businesses profited tremendously under these policies. For example, by the end of 1960 Japan's net fixed capital stock was ¥14,353 billion (in 1965 yen) and by the end of 1971 that had grown to ¥46,880 billion—a real growth of 327 percent.[26] Moreover, because the government kept at bay the competition from the outside world's often more competitive products and more capital-rich, technologically and managerially sophisticated firms, Japanese products came to dominate the expanding domestic market and were able to create an industrial structure that could eventually withstand foreign competition at home and then ultimately could compete effectively with it abroad.

In a similar vein, the successful economy, plus its specific policies designed to provide a protective fortress for agriculture and small businesses, as well as a continued stream of direct subsidies, tax incentives, pork barrel projects, land-use policies, and side payments went a long way toward ensuring the continued collaboration of these two key sectors with the conservative coalition. Agricultural expenditures as a proportion of total government spending were typically four times greater in Japan as late as the early 1970s than in France, Britain, the United States or West Germany.[27] At the same time, farm incomes remained as high as those in urban and manufacturing areas, and regional disparities in incomes were kept extremely low. Conservative policies continued to make farming economically attractive in Japan. Farm subsidies were so extensive that, as Donnelly phrased it, "rice farmers and agricultural cooperatives had become political wards of the state."[28] Only high growth allowed such economic inefficiency.

Much the same could be added for small business owners who benefited from direct assistance programs but also from a politically driven laxity in the enforcement of labor, environmental, and tax laws.[29] Furthermore, as the economy soared, so did individual incomes and living standards, again with highly positive results for the electoral fortunes of the LDP.

If economic growth policies were essential to the domestic and the international success of this conservative coalition, so was the maintenance of close ties to the United States. Anxious to see the creation and adaptation of a developmental model that mixed capitalism and democracy in Asia, and anxious to develop a worldwide system of "free trade," "free currency movements," and alliances among the "free world," the United States fostered a succession of international organizations into which Japan's participation was welcomed. This included the United Nations, the OECD, the General Agreement on Tariffs and Trade (GATT), the International Monetary Fund (IMF), and others. More fundamentally for Japanese foreign economic policy, until at least the early 1970s, U.S. aims were principally strategic and military in character. As a result, the U.S. government was typically quite willing to underwrite much of Japan's foreign economic success, even when that meant substantial economic cost to its domestic manufacturers and financial institutions.

If organized agriculture and organized business formed the socioeconomic core of Japan's foreign economic policies, the national bureaucracy provided the major engine for its implementation. Thus, MITI served as the principal advocate and agent of the country's widespread industrial policy. Sectoral cartelization and oligopolization in the interests of international competitive efficiency were central to the MITI strategy. The Ministry of Finance, directly and through the Bank of Japan, exercised strict control over capital allocations, and through a policy of overloan all but forced monies onto targeted industrial sectors and individual firms, providing them with cheap capital to modernize, engage in extensive R&D, and develop export markets. The MOF also exercised tight control over international exchange rates policy, keeping the yen pegged at the importantly undervalued ¥360 to the U.S. dollar, an undervaluation that implicitly subsidized and certainly stimulated Japanese exports.

At the same time that government policies were important to Japanese foreign economic policies, it is worth noting that policies, while not driven by "the market," were normally market-compatible. Firms that benefited from government assistance were most often in capital intensive, technologically sophisticated, and higher value added areas of the economy, sectors, in short, that were in "sunrise" rather than "sunset" sectors of the economy. Competitors and competitiveness fueled Japan's high growth. Japanese industrial policy created no parallel to the single French "national champions." Export success depended heavily on the creation of products that could compete effectively on grounds of price, quality, and after-care service.[30]

The overall portrait that emerges from this brief sketch is of a foreign economic policy that relied heavily on a relatively closed market at home, and extensive barriers to the import of both manufactured and consumer products as well as the import of foreign direct investment. It also depended greatly on a strong governmental bureaucracy capable of ensuring private compliance with the main objectives of the government's foreign economic policy goals. This included the government's filtering of imported technology for use by private-sector Japanese firms. Meanwhile, foreign aid and export policies were also developed with the interests of Japanese businesses principally in mind.

The political bases of these policies at home were quite clear. They were held together by interlinked policies that permitted the key elements in Japan's conservative coalition to engage in mutually profitable backscratching. Most businesses, but especially large businesses, benefited tremendously from foreign economic policies during this time; they, in turn, rewarded conservative politicians with both their public and their often unpublicized financial contributions. Agriculture and smaller businesses benefited from the mixture of state subsidies and protection from foreign competition. The tradeoff was extensive electoral support for the LDP.

With powers derived from an extensive tool kit of laws and ordinances, most governmental agencies also profited from the policies, even if it meant having to be formally under the supervision of politicians from the LDP. Their regulatory powers grew as did their budgets, and careers in the national bureaucracy continued to be among the most attractive goals for graduates of elite universities. Furthermore, those bureaucrats who worked closely with the private business or financial firms could look forward to profitable and rewarding jobs in those firms upon retirement.

Certainly, the LDP benefited from high levels of electoral support at home, support from the United States in most international matters, and support from the talented policy-making efforts of the national bureaucracy. In the fortuitous phrase of Yamamura Kōzō, during this period the Japanese foreign economic policies and policy-making machinery worked like a "marriage made in heaven."[31]

This heaven-made marriage, like many earthly marriages, regularly showed signs of tension. But two major shocks jolted it out of its previous bliss: the breakdown of the Bretton-Woods system (i.e., the sudden and forced revaluation of the Japanese yen) and the quadrupling of world oil prices as a result of OPEC policies in 1973–74. Following these two events, Japanese foreign economic policy could never again be the same. Nor could the domestic coalition on which those policies had rested. Yet as a major irony, even though policy changed, the ruling party and the dominant coalition remained the same.

Foreign Economic Policy after the Shocks

The principal thrust of foreign economic policy through the 1960s was overseas exports from a protected home market. In the early 1970s that basic thrust shifted to greater integration of the Japanese and world markets, led principally by overseas investment.

One of the main props of early foreign economic policy in Japan was destroyed by the breakdown of the Bretton-Woods system and the consequent strengthening of the Japanese yen. This change drastically altered the economic incentive structures for Japanese companies, and to a lesser extent for the Japanese government's economic agencies. The incentives for Japanese companies to continue manufacturing at home diminished as the costs of investing abroad dropped dramatically and as the implicit subsidization of Japanese-based manufactures was eroded. Similarly, once the Ministry of Finance could no longer control exchange rates, the economic incentives for Japanese firms to borrow only in yen were drastically reduced. The rising yen also altered the relative land, labor, and asset costs in Japan and abroad. Foreign labor, land, and factories all became much cheaper when paid for in the newly appreciated yen.

Meanwhile, as the price of oil soared (and not at all incidentally as concerns about the environmental impact of many of Japan's manufacturing firms increased), policies predicated on cheap energy and cheap international transportation costs were also undercut. Instead, there were strong incentives to move many energy-consuming, and manufacturing, plants to sites abroad.

These two changes in exchange rates and the prices of energy were accompanied by strong Western pressures for Japan to reduce the quantity of its exports and also to open its home markets to Western products and capital investments. As Watanabe notes, these pressures began as frictions over specific sectors such as textiles, steel, and automobiles starting in 1965, but they soon took the form of broader bilateral clashes with the first of the so-called Nixon shocks in the form of yen-dollar currency realignments.[32]

Finally, Third World countries began to pressure Japan for more capital and technology investment and for more foreign aid as Japan's capabilities to do so became undeniable. These pressures eventually came to accord well with government concerns about how best to recycle Japan's immense foreign economic surpluses as well as with Japanese companies and financial institutions' desire to expand into new potential markets.

These combined external pressures were paralleled by significant changes in Japan's domestic economy. Its once abundant labor force became scarce. Full employment was the norm. The transformation to an industrialized economy was more or less completed. The capacity for continued high growth declined. All of these changed the political calculations for Japan's conservative government, pressing it to strike out in several new directions to deal with the new economic conditions, to placate powerful critics from abroad, and, most important politically, to do so in a manner that would not threaten its continued dominance within Japan. Just as the incentive structure for the Japanese government had changed, so had the incentives for private Japanese businesses. In short, the entire incentive structure for key players in the conservative coalition was no longer what it had been. Many key conservative actors had to play both the domestic politics and the international politics games simultaneously, with a very different matrix than had existed during the 1950s and 1960s.[33]

One of the first changes involved a governmental liberalization of the conditions for foreign direct investment by Japanese firms starting once the country began to witness a large current accounts surplus in 1971–72 (although these were temporarily tightened with the oil shock and long-term capital outflows in 1974). As government constraints were lifted, Japanese firms responded with alacrity to their new opportunities to invest abroad.

A drastic expansion in capital outflow and overseas investment ensued. Thus, the total investment for the four years 1973–76 was nearly double that for the preceding twenty years.[34] This expansion has continued throughout subsequent years with ever-escalating proportions. For example, some $4.7 billion was invested in 1980; in 1985 the figure was $12.2 billion, and in 1988 the figure had rocketed to $47 billion, some ten times that of eight years earlier.[35]

These foreign investments occurred in virtually all sectors of business, including huge automobile plants in Ohio, Tennessee, and Newcastle; semiconductor plants in Dublin, the north of England, Germany, and California; and textile plants throughout much of Southeast Asian and Latin America. In a simple area like glass manufacturing, for example, one company, Asahi Glass, alone has at least thirty overseas manufacturing operations.[36] Japanese companies also began to export turn-key operations ranging from the gargantuan and problematic Bandar Khomeini oil-refining plant in Iran to the smaller and more successful IHI LPG plant in Algeria or its cement plant in North Yemen.[37] New Japanese investments also included resort complexes such as Seibu Railways' $315 million Westin Mauna Kea Hotel in Hawaii, and banking, shopping center, office building, and trading operations from Sydney to Singapore and Tijuana to Dusseldorf, not to mention massive equity, bond, and government note holdings in Europe and the United States. Not only Japan's larger financial, commercial, and manufacturing institutions moved abroad; large numbers of subcontractors and other small firms have been relocating overseas since the late 1970s.

The government also eased access to its home market by a substantial program of tariff reductions. Accelerating the tariff liberalizations of the Tokyo Round, the Japanese government had by 1983 reduced Japanese tariff levels from a 6.9 percent average to a 4.9 percent level, and then to an average of 2.5 percent by the early 1990s. This level, as the government has been diligent in reporting in virtually every one of its official publications, was by the 1990s below the 2.7 percent level for the European Community, 3.5 percent for the United States, and 4.2 percent for Canada.

Residual import restriction also dropped rapidly. In the 1960s Japan had restrictions on some 490 product categories. This figure was reduced to 120 in April 1968 (fifty-four in manufacturing and sixty-eight in agriculture) and to twenty-nine in February 1975 (seven in manufacturing and twenty-two in agriculture).[38] By early 1981 the twenty-two agricultural restrictions remained, but there were restrictions on only one manufacturing item. (Scheduled agricultural liberalizations will reduce the twenty-two to thirteen by 1992). In contrast, there were forty-six such restrictions in France and forty-one in Italy, while industrial restrictions posed an even sharper contrast, with the United States, France, Britain, Italy, and Canada all having more products under restrictions than did Japan.[39]

In short, the formal barriers that had been such strong impediments to the sale of foreign goods in Japan were rapidly swept away and Japan's market became, at least on paper, one of the most open in the industrialized world.

Japanese governmental assistance also underwent substantial readjustments. As an international consensus coalesced against the export-promotion basis of Japan's earlier aid efforts, Japan began providing increased levels of untied aid. In 1972 Japan extended its first untied loan, and in 1978 it declared its support for the principle of untying most development loans.[40] A dramatic expansion began in 1977, and by 1989 Japan had advanced to being the world's largest single aid donor.

Opportunities for foreign capital to move into Japan were also liberalized, most fundamentally with the scrapping of the Foreign Exchange and Control Law in 1980. Further, the Ministry of International Trade and Industry, once the principal promoter of Japanese exports, reversed its official course of action to promote imports. It retooled its Japan External Trade Organization (JETRO) offices to make it a more active promotor of imports; it created the Manufacturers Imports Promotion Organization (MIPRO) to aid foreign firms anxious to get into the Japanese markets and it created a trade ombudsman's office to deal with specific complaints by foreign companies against Japanese governmental agencies. At the cabinet level, a joint ministerial committee was put together to encourage liberalization efforts in each individual government agency.

Direct investment jumped as a result. Some $299 million was invested in 1980; by 1983 this had nearly tripled, and by 1988 it was up nearly tenfold to $2.6 billion.[41] During the mid-1980s, some 3,000–3,500 investments were made annually, and Japanese government and quasigovernmental publications tout with self-satisfaction the success stories of Western firms that had set up successful ventures within the country.[42]

A less welcome foreign addition, at least from the standpoint of the government, was the influx of illegal foreign immigrants. The rise of the yen has also led to pressures from workers outside Japan anxious to take advantage of the potential disparity in earning power between their own countries and Japan. This pressure has been exacerbated by domestic Japanese employers, typically producing for the domestic market and often in subcontracting positions, which have made them even more cost conscious since the yen's upward revaluation. Discarding longstanding appeals of Japan's presumed racial harmony, they have tacitly welcomed any increase in the low-cost labor supply. So too do organizations such as the Japan Food Service Association, which in May 1990 urged the government to import as many as 600,000 foreign workers each year on two- or three-year contracts. [43]

Since 1985 the number of foreign illegal workers has risen from virtually nil to somewhere in the neighborhood of 100,000–150,000. In part this is due to increasing numbers of syndicates between foreign employee brokers and Japanese job brokers, not a small number of which are linked to organized crime. Though the number of illegal foreign immigrants is miniscule by comparison to most Western European countries or to the United States, illegal immigration is a component of Japan's foreign economic policy that was not present a decade or two earlier, and it is one that is likely to loom even larger in the future.

Finally, Japan's relationships with the United States and its own defense and security spending have also changed substantially. The United States was once the tolerant "big brother" providing large quantities of what Japan needed, from a nuclear umbrella and a defense shield to cheap technology and a wide open market. That is the case no longer. Indeed, it is hard not to conclude that the United States has been the occasion of more foreign policy, and foreign economic policy, controversies than all of Japan's potential enemies combined.[44]

Japan's defense and military spending have subsequently shifted considerably—largely in the direction of greater defense planning and higher shares of the national budget. Much of this expanded budget is clearly linked to the increasingly blurred lines between "military" and "civilian" uses of much high technology. As a consequence, and in a radical break with past policies, the Japanese government in 1986 entered into an agreement with the United States that allowed Japan to export military-related technologies.[45]

In all of these ways, and many more, Japan's foreign economic policies have a distinctly more international character than the mercantilist caste they carried in the first two decades or so after the war. The basic bias of foreign economic policy has been the move from exporter to investor. At the same time, it is an open question just how much has "really" changed, and participants in the policy process—with differing agendas and goals—reach quite different conclusions when they concentrate on alternative aspects of current Japanese foreign economic policy.

Plus Ça Change. . .?

There is no question but that Japanese foreign economic policy has become substantially more liberal and international since the early 1970s. Yet, a good deal suggests that the continuities with the past outweigh the changes.

Thus, if Japanese firms have become investors, they have by no means ceased to be formidable exporters. Japan continues to enjoy a favorable balance of trade with virtually all major regions of the world, and certainly with most of the industrialized democracies. Without question, while many Japanese firms have moved their operations abroad, Japan's domestic economy remains an exporting juggernaut. Japan's trade policy remains biased in many ways. Accusations have variously been made against a still undervalued yen, overseas dumping, an ever-changing list of nontariff barriers, internal collusion among Japanese industries, public-sector purchasing policies, a systematic disregard for Japanese consumers, underhanded government assistance, and the like.[46] Without question, many of these elements reflect continuities with earlier policies.

Former Prime Minister Nakasone once argued that Japan should become "an import superpower." Indeed, Japanese manufacturing imports have expanded greatly, albeit from a small base. But two major areas of import liberality remain: manufactured goods and agriculture. Although Japanese government officials (correctly) note that Japanese shares of manufactured imports are expanding at one of the most rapid rates in the world, for a country with its industrial structure, Japan maintains an inordinately low ratio of manufactured imports.[47]

Furthermore, Japan imports very few "intraindustry" manufactured items. In effect, Japan rarely imports items in industries where it exports; to date its manufactured imports have been largely in areas not competitive with its own export industries. At the same time, with the rise in regional integration among many Asian firms, often around core Japanese firms, even this pattern is beginning to change. But at the same time, such imports come heavily from Japanese-owned plants in these areas rather than being indigenously owned products.

In agriculture as well, Japanese policy represents at best a mixed picture of moves toward greater internationalization. On the one hand, Japan is one of the industrial world's largest importers of various agricultural products. Some 15 percent of its total annual imports are made up of food and agricultural products. Certainly, Japan is by far the best market for U.S. agricultural exports, taking a total value greater than that of America's number two, three, and four markets combined. In the late 1980s Japan also agreed to the liberalization of once highly sensitive items including beef, citrus fruits, processed cheese, canned pineapple, and orange juice, most of which either were implemented by 1990 or were scheduled for liberalization by 1992.[48]

Nevertheless, on the singular issue of rice, Japan has remained steadfastly opposed to the liberalization of imports demanded in particular by the United States. Although there is some support within Japan for backing the prevailing policy of "not one single grain of rice," it is quite probable that some gradual liberalization of the Japanese rice market will take place as a result of the Uruguay Round of Trade negotiations.

In focusing on trade, however, it is essential to note that trade is increasingly influenced by the changes in foreign direct investment (FDI) throughout the world. Thus, due to FDI, governments must now compete for competitive tax rates, infrastructure, and the like so as to hold down capital and entrepreneurial flight. Consequently, a country's trade balance no longer reflects how well that country's businesses are doing.[49] The United States for example, is a heavy overseas investor. Putting the currently huge U.S. trade balance on an ownership basis would force a drastic revision in the thinking of those worried about America's economic decline. Julius, for example, estimates that about one-third of U.S. exports were bought by American-owned companies abroad, and about one-fifth of U.S. imports were bought by foreign-owned companies in the United States receiving goods from their own countries. On an ownership basis, the U.S. trade deficit of $144 billion in 1986 becomes a trade surplus of $57 billion.[50] From this view, a focus on the bilateral U.S.-Japanese trade balance seems meaningless.

Further, while Japanese trade policies have formally changed from export promotion to investment promotion, it is not at all clear that this distinction alone makes a great deal of difference in assessing the changing or unchanging character of Japan's trade balances. Far more critical is the overall strength of its corporations, many of which are benefiting more from their moves overseas than they would have if protectionist trade and investment policies had been sustained at home. Certainly, few of Japan's major firms have suffered as a result of moving abroad.

Japan has also become far more open to capital investment since the revision of the Foreign Exchange and Control Law, and the country has witnessed numerous foreign economic success stories, from the long-term Japanese giants like IBM-Japan, Coca-Cola, and Nestle, to newer and/or smaller-scale companies ranging from Mercedes Benz and BMW to Wella and Fox Bagels. Needless to add, the Japanese economy has hardly become dominated by foreign control.

According to one comparative study, in 1986 only 1 percent of Japan's assets were owned by foreign-controlled firms, and just 0.4 percent of its workers were employed by them. In the United States, by way of contrast, foreign-controlled firms owned 9 percent of the assets, employed 4 percent of the workers, and accounted for one-tenth of all sales. And even the United States looked autarkic in comparison with the major Western European countries. In Britain, 14 percent of its assets, one-seventh of its workers, and one-fifth of the nation's sales were accounted for by foreign-controlled firms. In West Germany, foreign-owned companies held 17 percent of assets and accounted for 19 percent of sales, while in France, foreign dominance was greater still.[51]

Without question, Japan is a highly profitable market for foreign firms that actually succeed in gaining entry. Moreover, because market forces, including technology and information, are increasingly important within the domestic Japanese market, some vital areas at the core of Japanese finance and manufacturing have come under incredible pressure from foreign firms. For example, there has been great success by Western ventures in the Japanese stock and warrant markets.

The Japanese securities market was dominated for the bulk of the postwar period by an oligopoly of four giant brokerages—Nomura, Yamaichi, Daiwa, and Nikko—and appeared impenetrable to foreign competition. Yet the best American and British firms, including Morgan Stanley, Salomon Brothers, S.G. Warburg, and Goldman Sachs, now have more profitable activities in Tokyo than in New York or London. The reasons are the much greater efficiencies in capital, technology, and information that these firms can bring to bear in the otherwise rather inefficient Tokyo market.

For example, in the rising stock market of the early to mid-1980s, the Big Four enjoyed a highly profitable business by sitting on equity warrants and then selling them through their retail branches in Japan (earning perhaps $2 billion in the six months prior to September 1989).[52] But such profitability left them too disinterested to sell and trade the warrants for institutions, a market that fell quickly to such foreign firms as Baring Security and Jardine Fleming. Meanwhile, in Tokyo, these Western firms also made markets for Japanese institutional buyers. Key to the success of the Western firms has been their edge in information and technology (not to mention the use of the English language) to allow rapid movements of positions between the Tokyo and London markets. As one manager at Salomon Brother's Tokyo office put it, "It's free money." [53]

In the early 1980s, Nomura, Daiwa, Nikkō, and Yamaichi together handled three-fifths of the turnover of the Tokyo Stock Exchange. In December 1989, the four were down to just 34 percent and falling fast. Unlike Wall Street firms, the Big Four continue to earn the bulk of their profits from commissions. While in 1950 approximately 60 percent of all Japanese shares were owned by private individuals, today the figure is closer to 20 percent. Yet the Big Four have continued to rely heavily on private clients for the bulk of their business, resulting in a vacuum in more profitable transactions for Western firms able to deal in more sophisticated products.

A similar opening for foreign firms as a result of domestic oligarchy-monopoly control has existed in commercial aviation. ANA's manager of international relations, Kumugi Yoshio, indicates that the airline may be forced to relocate its base from Narita before 1995. Yet in looking to the regional airports available in Japan, ANA has found that foreign carriers already have the jump on them in the international charter business. [54]

Western computer companies, too, have made major inroads into the private marketplace. There, concerns for competitiveness, speed, and price have begun to outweigh *keiretsu* ties and nationalism.

From all of this it is clear that the areas of foreign penetration of the Japanese economy are by no means limited to fast foods and franchising as is frequently alleged. Yet success in the Japanese market is by no means a simple matter of market competitiveness, as the major Western brokerages engaged in arbitrage found out.

Following their success in the early 1990 downswing of the Nikkei Dow, there was a highly politicized finger pointing at such firms for the decline in the stock market itself. Subway graffiti in Tokyo urged Japanese consumers not to buy their shares from Goldman Sachs. Even more important from a political standpoint, as the Nikkei tumbled, foreign program traders were quickly brought before Ministry of Finance officials and forced to promise to restrict arbitrage to purchases only when the futures market moves to a premium, rather than a discount, that is, when the arbitrage would involve buying rather than selling the underlying equities. Thus, there remains in Japan a curious by-play between "free markets" and "competition," on the one hand, and a governmental bureaucracy that is hardly neutral toward such forces, on the other.

One question posed by the surge in foreign investment will be whether foreign-owned firms can become accepted players in the Japanese economy. As Japanese companies and, more important the "industrial groups" themselves become more international the incentives to allow them to do so will appreciate geometrically. At an extreme the question is whether Western firms could enter established Japanese *keiretsu*. Firms like IBM-Japan and Motorola have moved in that direction. Another major indication of this potential, suggests Yamaguchi Toshio, a top-ranking LDP member of the party's Committee for Economic Adjustment, lies in the summer 1990 summit of leaders of Mitsubishi and West Germany's Daimler-Benz aimed at broad-scale cooperation between these two international giants. [55]

The essential question is the extent to which the changes in Japanese foreign economic policy will offer new opportunities to foreign firms in their competition with Japanese firms versus the extent to which such policies will continue to privilege Japanese-owned firms regardless of whether their operations are located in Japan or elsewhere in the world. Is Japanese internationalization for real?

Changes are made, the criticisms go, but always after foot dragging and an eleventh-hour deal. Thus, Japan is castigated as the willing beneficiary of the free-trade system when it comes to taking advantage of the open markets of other countries; it is a reluctant participant, however, in terms of opening its own domestic market to foreign competition. A similar picture is painted with regard to investment. Japanese property companies, manufacturers, banks, insurance firms, and general trading companies avariciously gobble up choice properties and assets around the world while hiding behind protectionist walls maintained by government practices and a host of ingenious, corporately created nontariff barriers to prevent foreign companies from doing likewise on Japanese terrain.

These elements crystalize into a reactive pattern of "too little, too late," requiring in turn forceful actions by other states, especially the United States, to force Japan to live up to international expectations, through pressures for trade and investment liberalizations generally, and for more specific actions in individual fields.

Japanese officials have openly embraced the phrase "internationalization" at least at the rhetorical level, and in many cases at the practical level as well. In many instances, real moves are being made to change Japanese foreign economic policy in more international directions. Nevertheless, such internationalization is normally that which is clearly congruent with Japanese corporate, financial, and governmental interests, that is, with the interests of core elements in the conservative coalition. And certainly, such internationalization as has taken place is clearly not contradictory to the perceived self-interest of these key sectors. As they would define it, Japan's national interests lie in the direction of increased internationalization; as skeptics might rephrase it, core members of the conservative coalition would identify Japan's national interests as identical with their own narrower self-interest. Regardless, both would appear to lie in the direction of greater (albeit occasionally highly selective) openness at home and investment abroad.

To assess the politics underlying both the continuities and changes in Japanese foreign economic policy over the past three decades, it is essential to understand not only the foreign pressures to which Japan has been subjected, but also the changes in the domestic power alignment that have been occurring simultaneously. Only in this way will it be possible to appreciate and perhaps measure both the real changes and the unremitting continuities.

The Politics of Foreign Economic Policy: Shifts in the Dominant Domestic Coalition

Current debate over change and continuity in Japanese foreign economic policy is marked by an irrelevantly bimodal pattern. Those who focus on continuities downplay recent changes as little more than clever tactics and cosmetic alterations designed to obscure the fundamentally unchanging and self-serving character of Japanese policy. In contrast, those who stress changes typically ignore the important residuals of the past. These latter, it is often argued, will soon be gone since the trajectory of change toward greater internationalization has taken on a life of its own. As Fallows has characterized this position, "Japan. . .used to be xenophobic, but is now internationalist. It used to have closed markets, but now it has opened up. It threw the GATT talks onto the shoals last year by refusing even to discuss the opening of its rice market, but eventually its policy will change. The key is patience and 'understanding' from the outside world."[56]

A more accurate weighting of the tension between change and continuity requires an examination of Japanese domestic politics. As was noted above, Japanese foreign economic policy is not only the consequence of international pressures and opportunities, but also deeply rooted in the balance of political power within the country. This internal balance has without a doubt been altered in certain fundamental (although by no means total) ways. And this mixture of changes and continuities, in turn, will have a profound effect on the extent to which the various changes and continuities in foreign economic policy will in fact be so deeply rooted as to become permanent.

For the entire period since its formation in 1955, the Liberal Democratic party has held virtually 2:1 majorities over the next largest party in the nation's lower house of parliament. For the bulk of that period, the LDP enjoyed a fundamentally synergistic relationship with the state bureaucracy, most of whose senior members held their posts only after passing political muster with the party hierarchy. The party was the electoral link holding together the social coalition described above.

Until at least the early 1970s, as noted earlier, the conservative regime in Japan was built around two major policy pillars: close strategic alliance (and cultural affinity) with the United States, plus high economic growth policies that rested heavily on protectionism at home and export-led growth in the international marketplace.[57] On the first of these issues, there was a high degree of controversy from a countercoalition built around organized labor and formulated politically by the Japan Socialist party (JSP) and the Japan Communist party (JCP) and occasionally by other minor parties. On economic policy, there was strong opposition, less to the tactics and policies of high growth than to the purportedly uneven distribution of the benefits of these policies. Despite such controversy, however, these two policy positions became well engrained in the national agenda and took on the aura of unquestioned givens by the mid-1960s. On the overall policy agenda of the nation, the conservative coalition enjoyed a hegemony unseen in almost any other major industrialized democracy.

Although the conservative regime confronted several electoral challenges during the thirty-five odd years of its reign, including the loss of Upper House control in 1989, on balance elections per se posed little serious challenge to the regime.[58] For all of these reasons, it would seem safe to conclude that the domestic basis for Japanese foreign economic policy would have been relatively consistent over the entire thirty-five plus years of LDP hegemony. In turn, it would also seem safe to conclude that whatever changes have occurred in elements of foreign economic policy have been reflections of external pressures, consistently resisted for domestic political reasons.

Yet the conservative coalition, and the LDP, in the early 1990s are substantially different in several key ways from what they were two or more decades earlier. A number of serious challenges to the base of the conservative coalition have come in the form of sociodemographic changes.

One of the most substantial challenges demographically was the decline in the agricultural population. While nearly 50 percent of Japan's population were farmers at the end of World War II, the figure today is below 10 percent, with a large proportion of these being part-time farmers, the bulk of whom are over age sixty. Clearly, even with the extensive gerrymandering that exists in the Japanese electoral system, this is hardly an electoral constituency on which to rest the LDP's long-term future. Major budgetary and public policy efforts directed at sustaining the life-styles and economies of an ever-diminishing number of farmers may have been possible during the high-growth period of the 1960s; it has been far less feasible during the slower-growth years of the 1980s and 1990s. Internationalization of foreign economic policy clearly threatened agricultural interests, but these agricultural interests were of decreasing electoral value within the conservative coalition.

Self-employed and small-business people continue to constitute a comparatively high 29 percent of the work force in Japan, and their support for the LDP and for the conservative coalition has been more problematic. But few would benefit from greater liberalization of imports or direct investment. Indeed, many clearly have vested interests at odds with even Japanese-owned larger businesses, as has been seen in the debates over possible revision of the so-called large-sized retail store law.[59]

Meanwhile, Japan has seen the rise of what Murakami has called "Japan's new middle mass," reasonably affluent, white-collar workers living in urban or suburban settings.[60] Political demands from this group have been inchoate at best, but clearly most favor cleaner environments, lower taxes, increased varieties of consumer goods, continued ability to travel abroad, more social benefits, and so forth. For this group at large, "internationalization" in foreign economic policy was generally seen as a plus, and attracting them to the LDP camp has necessitated far greater receptivity to internationalization by the party.[61]

In addition to these changes, there has been a metamorphosis in the character of organized (principally blue-collar) labor in Japan. In the mid- to late-1950s, organized labor was highly ideological and committed to variations of a "nationalist" or "socialist" economy. More important, it was highly militant on the shop floor in numerous sectors of the economy, including autos, mining, shipbuilding, and transportation. Strike rates in Japan during that period were high by international standards, [62] and, more important for conservative hegemony, they were potentially quite disruptive of government and big business efforts to modernize production and to hold down labor costs.

In a series of coordinated actions, the government and the major employers' federation, Nikkeiren, broke the backs of the most militant unions through lockouts, layoffs, the use of police, and the recognition of competitive, less militant unions. There was also a strong reliance by business on (generally nonunionized) subcontract and part-time labor, as well as on company bonuses, all of which reduced union bargaining power and increased management's flexibility in controlling labor costs.

The cumulative effect of these efforts was the overall pacification of Japanese private-sector labor.[63] Throughout most of the 1960s and 1970s, strike rates fell sharply and while the union movement attempted to bargain hard on the economic front, for the most part, private sector unions came to identify their particular economic interests less with the working class and far more with the bottom-line balance sheet of productivity and profits within their specific companies.

With the externally induced inflation of 1973–74, due largely to the quadrupling of world oil prices, labor once again had the economic potential to present a formidable challenge to the conservative coalition, this time in the form of demands for large wage hikes to offset the domestic costs of externally-induced inflation. Sustained economic growth in manufacturing was challenged by the potential that high labor costs would reduce the price competitiveness of Japanese goods, particularly in overseas markets. Quickly, a three way "de facto incomes policy" was created. Under its terms, private-sector labor agreed to moderate future wage demands in exchange for business guarantees of continued job security and job retraining programs, along with government guarantees of low taxes, anti-inflationary policies, and financial support for worker retraining and industrial reorganization. As a consequence of this arrangement, Japan was the first of the industrial countries to put a halt to wage-price inflation, and there was barely a glitch in its overall economic growth. In short, the combination of government resources and managerial concessions provided the main ingredients in warding off what might have been a severe challenge to the underlying economic growth policies advocated by the conservatives.

As a subsidiary consequence of the arrangement, even closer ties were forged between unionized blue-collar workers and management in the large private firms. Furthermore, the private-sector union movement as a whole has become far more politically and economically moderate, reorganizing in 1986 into a single peak federation with a largely nonpolitical, nongovernmental, economic agenda. [64] And finally there is early evidence that the electoral orientations of blue-collar workers have shifted as well, with evidence that significant proportions have begun to vote for the LDP.[65]

As a consequence of these varied demographic changes, the conservative coalition in Japan faces a problem: how to restructure the electoral and socio-economic support base of the party in the face of increasingly competitive international economic pressures.

While this issue is far from resolved, substantial evidence suggests that the conservatives are once again moving to reshape their coalition, at an extreme, leaving farmers and, to a lesser extent, small business people to the mercies of greater international competition, while attempting to replace their votes with those from urbanites and the blue-collar workers noted above. Thus, the food-control system has been dismantled, rice subsidies have been reduced drastically, imports of meat and citrus fruits have been greatly liberalized, and an active land-diversification program has begun under government supervision designed to move farmers off the land or into nonrice crops.[66] The influence of the farm lobby, most specifically Nokyo (Association of Agricultural Cooperatives) and Zenchu (Central Union of Agricultural Cooperatives), has been in decline as a result of both foreign pressures on the rice import question and a decline in electoral strength. In the February 1990 elections, several leaders of the LDP's farm lobby failed to gain reelection. At the same time, while the LDP has a macrolevel electoral interest in breaking with the farmers, the party also has numerous members who would find this counter to their microlevel interests. In effect, because of the importance of even small numbers of well-organized constituents under the Japanese electoral system, rural LDP representatives in numerous districts will continue to find it difficult explicitly to oppose Nokyo demands for continued protection.

In an ironic twist of ideologies, Nokyo now finds its anti-import stance closely akin to that of the JCP. Though weak in the rural areas, the JCP has close ties to unions organizing the thirteen thousand officials who work for the government's Food Agency, which in turn administers the rice wholesaling system. Import liberalization would undoubtedly cost many of them their jobs.

Meanwhile, the problems of the small shopkeeper have been less centrally addressed and are currently still under widespread debate, but there is strong evidence that at least one route might provide a partial and less painful solution than forcing all small shopkeepers to compete with large and often international shops. The solution has become franchising. Japan's government has actively encouraged such foreign franchising firms as Colonel Sanders, 7-11, Shakey's Pizza, Haagen Daas, and others to enter Japan where a ready consumer market awaits them. But so too do lots of "mom and pop merchants" willing to get out of the noodle or sake business and into the pizza or hamburger business. They may still depend on intensive labor and high-quality service, but they will be doing so under the aegis of a corporation offering international brand-name recognition and market organization.[67]

One of the more noteworthy changes in the conservative coalition is the fact that it has become far less corporatist and far more pluralistic in terms of the interest groups it is willing to work with. Particularly after the shredding of labor's muscle in the early 1960s, there has been a distinguishable rise in the number of free-floating interest groups in Japan. Moreover, most of them, including those not initially disposed ideologically to consider themselves "conservative," have begun to expand their ties to the conservative camp. In most instances they have little choice, given the relatively permanent hegemony exercised by the LDP. Overall, this has meant an increased strength in appeal of the conservative message, but at the same time it has also meant a diluting of that message and a blurring of the boundaries between "government" and "opposition" support groups. This has confounded the clarity of the foreign economic policy, since many of these newer groups come to the LDP with mixed agendas on issues of protection, import liberalization, tax reform, illegal immigration, foreign aid, and so forth.[68]

As there have been changes in the socioeconomic bases of Japan's conservative coalition, so too have there been changes in the character of the government agencies charged with carrying out those policies. As noted, for example, MITI has gone through important restructurings to position itself to deal effectively with the new pressures for greater foreign direct investment and imports. While it has lost many of its powers concerning industrial restructuring, it has acquired others as compensation. Among other things, it is now the primary agency for carrying out the terms of the so-called voluntary export restraints entered into by various Japanese industrial sectors and foreign governments. But MITI has also retained important coordinating influence in the setting of broad national industrial priorities, particularly with regard to high-tech industries, and also with regard to "visions for the future."

With the success of the tax-base shift, an end to deficit-financed budgets, and the growing recognition of a need for regulation of both the stock market and land prices, the Ministry of Finance has also regained a strong component of its past influence. [69]

Similarly, many would argue that because of the overall appeal of internationalization in so many aspects of foreign economic policy, the Ministry of Foreign Affairs, a perennial advocate of that trend, has also gained new influence.

Conversely, agencies with close ties to politically sensitive groups that are likely to be negatively affected by greater liberalization have also witnessed certain increases in their powers. This has been particularly true when they can simultaneously meet the protectionist needs of their constituency groups and the electoral needs of the LDP. This would include the Ministry of Posts and Telecommunications, Agriculture, Forestry and Fisheries, the Police, Construction, and the National Land Agency, among others.[70]

At the same time, with internationalization and complexity of issues, the specific spheres of influence of the major ministries have become blurred at least at the edges. It becomes harder and harder for any single bureaucratic agency to claim exclusive authority in most areas of foreign economic policy. But ironically, this often leads to greater opportunities for greater change. Thus, in the recent SII talks, the government was able to make certain concessions to the U.S. position largely because many of the issues raised by the Americans straddled the territories of the traditional ministries.

This might suggest that trends within the bureaucracy would be favorable to openness and internationalization. However, bureaucratic power has declined as well in response to the increased strength and autonomy and internal channels of mobility within the Liberal Democratic party. The rise of technical specialists within the LDP, the sharp dropoff in the recruitment of top bureaucrats for posts in the LDP, the greater role of pork barrel as a proportion of the total budget, and so on have all reduced the influence of "the bureaucracy" as a whole, even as it has opened up opportunities for different segments of specific agencies to forge de facto coalitions with LDP politicians and interest group leaders around specific issues. Ex-bureaucrats were typically important advocates of more cosmopolitanism in the LDP. As their power has diminished, electorally driven parochialism in the LDP has grown.

Perhaps the most strengthened segment of the conservative coalition has been big business and finance, most of which has been favorable to greater internationalization, openness, and cross-national integration. Changes within the conservative coalition in Japan have been reflected in a number of important policy changes, some of them related to foreign economic policy, some of them not tied in directly.

The recent consumption, or value-added, tax, for example, has as one of its most important consequences a reduction in the tax burden on larger businesses, a key need in a situation in which businesses can move their operations and assets worldwide. The prevention of long-term capital flight out of Japan will clearly be helped by the new tax, even if in at least the short term it threatened to alienate large numbers of potential LDP voters. In addition, the manner in which the government has framed the new tax allows one of its most important constituent groups, small businesses, to all but escape payment of the tax through a simplified system of write-offs.

In short, just as the external pressures for changes in Japanese foreign economic policy have mounted since 1971–73, so the domestic bases of foreign economic policy have been changing, largely in response to changed political needs and to altered political and economic calculations. Certain important actors in Japan's conservative pantheon are pressing for greater liberalization and internationalization; others are pressing in precisely the opposite direction. The result is a contemporary foreign economic policy which shows a mixture of both.

Clearly, therefore, many of the changes in foreign economic policy that Japan has seen in the past two decades are deeply rooted in changes taking place within Japan as well as being responses to pressures from abroad. The Japanese state has not been afraid to slaughter certain sacred cows in steel and shipbuilding, for example. At the same time, the government has been far more reluctant to rush in and liquidate interests of high political sensitivity to the ruling conservative coalition. Most especially this has been true of the protectionist farm lobby and the overwhelmingly inefficient distribution system. As Richard Samuels has effectively argued, the Japanese political economy is biased in favor of producers, not consumers.[71] Many of the less-internationalist components of contemporary foreign economic policy are also deeply rooted in the deeply entrenched powers of domestic groups that remain essential to the political continuity of conservative rule in Japan. Changes are unlikely to come willingly from conservative politicians if those changes are going to put them out of office.

The overall conclusion that emerges from the Japanese case is that of cohesive and intermeshing efforts of most segments of the conservative coalition to maintain the longstanding conservative regime. The ways in which the conservatives have confronted threats from outside forces, from demographic changes, and from economic challenge have involved important alterations in the powers and priorities of party, bureaucracy, and business. The tactics have included outflanking and coopting potential opponents, and these in turn have required changes in laws, expanded government subsidies, side payments for possible losers, and even harsh demands to bear adjustment costs by longstanding members of the conservative regime. That the LDP has held such a strong monopoly on electoral power has been a major asset; vast state resources have been available to cope with potential threats. In this way, too, Japan is reforming its regime from within by using the powers made available to the conservative party by virtue of its continual success in electoral competition.

Key changes have taken place in Japanese foreign economic policy, represented by the unmistakable transition from "exporter" to "investor." At the same time, the changes that have taken place are by no means as sweeping and unidirectional as any such bifurcation might imply. Japanese foreign economic policy remains deeply rooted in the nation's domestic politics, a politics that is inherently "messy." The power of many protectionist members of the conservative coalition remains strong, although that of organized agriculture is undoubtedly on the wane. That of small business seems destined for a similar reduction in power. Conversely, forces that have more to gain from increased openness and internationalization, such as big business and finance, private-sector blue-collar labor, and urban consumers, have been gaining in their relative power over public policies. But on the specific subissues that make up the nation's overall foreign economic policy, many internecine battles remain to be fought within the conservative coalition. At the end of a decade or two, the general direction of greater openness seems confidentally predictable as does the predominance of more "investor" driven policies. Yet, in the interim, policy is far more likely to be the outgrowth of politically driven zigs and zags than of any adoption of universalistic principles and the unidirectional embrace of either continuity or change.

Notes

1.   This portrait is consistent with the views expressed in Andrea Boltho, *Japan: An Economic Survey, 1953–1973* (London: Oxford University Press, 1975); Haruhiro Fukui, "Economic Planning in Postwar Japan; A Case Study," *Asian Survey* 12 (April, 1972): 327–48; Iida Seietsuro, "Nihon keizai no kiko to kodo seicho no shikumi," in Ienaga Saburo et al., eds., *Showa no sengoshi IV* (Tokyo: Sekibunsha, 1976); Chalmers Johnson, *MITI and the Japanese Miracle* (Stanford: Stanford University Press, 1982); Eugene Kaplan, *Japan: The Government–Business Relationship* (Washington, D.C.: U.S. Department of Commerce, 1972); Yutaka Kosai and Yoshitaro

Ogino, *The Contemporary Japanese Economy* (Armonk, N.Y.: M. E. Sharpe, 1984); Edward Lincoln, *Japan's Industrial Policies* (Washington, D.C.: Japan Economic Institute, 1984); Ira C. Magaziner and Thomas H. Hout, *Japanese Industrial Policy* (London: Policy Studies Institute, 1980); Hugh T. Patrick and Henry Rosovsky, eds., *Asia's New Giant* (Washington, D.C.: The Brookings Institution, 1976); T. J. Pempel, "Japanese Foreign Economic Policy: The Domestic Bases of International Behavior," in Peter J. Katzenstein, ed., *Between Power and Plenty* (Madison: University of Wisconsin Press, 1978); Ezra Vogel, *Japan as Number 1* (Cambridge: Harvard University Press, 1979); Kozo Yamamura, "Structure is Behavior: An Appraisal of Japanese Economic Behavior, 1960 to 1972," in Isiah Frank, ed., *The Japanese Economy in International Perspective* (Baltimore: Johns Hopkins University Press, 1975); John Zysman, *Governments, Markets and Growth: Financial Systems and the Politics of Industrial Change* (Ithaca: Cornell University Press, 1984), among others.

2. This perspective is less fully developed than that of the earlier contrastive period, but it can be found to a greater or less extent in works such as Ronald Dore, *Flexible Rigidities* (Stanford: Stanford University Press, 1986); David Friedman, *The Misunderstood Miracle: Industrial Development and Political Change in Japan* (Ithaca: Cornell University Press, 1988); James Horne, *Japan's Financial Markets: Conflict and Consensus in Policymaking* (Sydney: Allen and Unwin, 1985); Inoguchi Takashi, *Gendai nihon seiji keizai no kozu* (Tokyo: Tokyo Daigaku Shuppan, 1983); Daniel Okimoto, *Between MITI and the Market* (Stanford: Stanford University Press, 1989); Otake Hideo, *Gendai nihon no seiji kenryoku keizai kenryoku* (Tokyo: Sanichi Shobo, 1979); T. J. Pempel, "The Unbundling of 'Japan, Inc.': The Changing Dynamics of Japanese Policy Formation," *Journal of Japanese Studies* 13, 2 (Summer 1987); Frances Rosenbluth, *Financial Politics in Contemporary Japan* (Ithaca: Cornell University Press, 1989); Kozo Yamamura and Yasukichi Yasuba, eds., *The Political Economy of Japan*, vol. 1: The Domestic Transformation (Stanford: Stanford University Press, 1987).

3. This term is of salience mostly within the United States and refers to a diverse group, some of whose members welcome membership, others of whom decry the label. Major works in the Japan-bashing school include Karel van Wolferen, *The Enigma of Japanese Power* (New York: Knopf, 1989); Clyde Prestowitz, *Trading Places: How We Allowed Japan to Take the Lead* (New York: Basic, 1988); James Fallows, "Containing Japan," *The Atlantic Monthly* (May 1989); Pat Choate, *Agents of Influence* (New York: Knopf, 1990).

4. Robert D. Putnam, "Diplomacy and Domestic Politics: The Logic of Two-Level Games," *International Organization* 42, 3 (Summer 1988): 427–60.

5. Peter J. Katzenstein, *Between Power and Plenty* (Madison: University of Wisconsin Press, 1978); Peter Gourevitch, *Politics in Hard Times: Comparative Responses to International Economic Crises* (Ithaca: Cornell University Press, 1986); Peter Hall, *Governing the Economy* (Oxford: Oxford University Press, 1986); Francis G. Castles, *The Comparative History of Public Policy* (London: Polity, 1989).

6. This perspective draws heavily on the notion of "punctuated equilibrium" originally developed by Stephen Gould and others in the field of biology. But it has been made explicit in the area of political economy by Stephen Krasner, "Sovereignty: An

Institutional Perspective," in James A. Caporaso, ed., *The Elusive State: International and Comparative Perspectives* (Newbury Park: Sage, 1989).

7. An effort to understand the character of the LDP's dominance in comparative terms is found in T. J. Pempel, ed., *Uncommon Democracies: The One Party Dominant Regimes* (Ithaca: Cornell University Press, 1990).

8. On the party system and its support bases, see Miyake Ichiro, *Seito shiji no bunseki* (Tokyo: Sobunsha, 1985); Gerald L. Curtis, *The Japanese Way of Politics* (New York: Columbia University Press, 1988).

9. An excellent treatment of this relationship for a slightly later period is Takashi Inoguchi, "The Political Economy of Conservative Resurgence under Recession: Public Policies and Political Support in Japan, 1977–1983," in Pempel, *Uncommon Democracies.*

10. See, for example, Kozo Yamamura, "Caveat Emptor: The Industrial Policy of Japan," in Paul R. Krugman, ed., *Trade Policy and the New International Economics* (Cambridge: MIT Press, 1986).

11. Kosei Torihiki Iinkai, *Kosei torihiki iinkai nenji hokoku* (Tokyo: Okurasho In-satsukyoku, 1975), p. 177.

12. Hugh T. Patrick and Thomas P. Rohlen, "Small-Scale Family Enterprises," in Yamamura and Yasuba, eds. *The Political Economy of Japan,* vol. 1: *The Domestic Transformation,* p. 332.

13. Nihon Kokusei Zue, *Suji de miru: Nihon no hyakunen* (Tokyo: Kokusei Zue, 1981), p. 167.

14. Ibid., p. 169.

15. Robert S. Ozaki, *The Control of Imports and Foreign Capital in Japan* (New York: Praeger, 1972), p. 94.

16. This point was particularly interesting in the case of Texas Instruments which concluded an agreement on licensing technology for semiconductors. In conjunction with Japan's electronics trade associations, MITI insisted that no single Japanese firm be able to monopolize the technology and ensured that the major Japanese electronics firms would be granted roughly equal access. See *Business Week,* January 27, 1968, p. 132.

17. G. R. Hall and R. E. Johnson, "Transfers of United States Aerospace Technology to Japan," in Raymond Vernon, ed., *The Technology Factor in International Trade* (New York: Columbia University Press, 1970), p. 87.

18. See Kokusei Zue annual for specific figures. But while most of the major industrial countries had imports made up of approximately 50–65 percent manufactured goods, Japan in the mid-1970s had only 30 percent. No other country came close to Japan's 95 percent manufacturing exports.

19. Gardner Ackley and Hiromitsu Ishi, "Fiscal, Monetary, and Related Policies," in Hugh Patrick and Henry Rosovsky, eds. *Asia's New Giant* (Washington, D.C.: The Brookings Institution, 1976), p. 212.

20. This figure is interesting in that the $4 billion for the twenty years, 1951–71, was equal to the figure for most single years in the early to mid-1970s once foreign direct

investment was actively encouraged by the government. Slightly different figures and calculations, but with the same thrust, are given in Lawrence B. Krause, "Evolution of Foreign Direct Investment: The United States and Japan," in Jerome Cohen, ed., *Pacific Partnership; United States-Japan Trade—Prospects and Recommendations for the Seventies* (New York: Japan Society and Lexington Books, 1972), pp. 166–68.

21. Krause, "Evolution of Foreign Direct Investment," p. 164.

22. The exceptions most worth noting were the yen-based companies that invested early even though profits could not be repatriated to the home country.

23. Figures on Japanese defense spending are somewhat controversial and the 1 percent of GNP figure is based on official Japanese calculations that are different from, and biased toward, lower percentages, calculations done by NATO. Nonetheless, even by the NATO calculations, Japanese figures are still only about 1.5 percent of GNP. As a specific matter of policy Prime Minister Miki in 1976 established the policy of limiting defense expenditures to 1 percent of GNP. On the politics surrounding subsequent military expenditures, see Joseph Keddell, Jr. "Defense as a Budgetary Problem: The Minimization of Conflict in Japanese Defense Policymaking, 1976-1987," Ph.D. dissertation, University of Wisconsin-Madison, 1990.

24. Figures drawn from Kar-yiu Wong, "National Defense and Foreign Trade: The Sweet and Sour Relationship between the United States and Japan," in John H. Makin and Donald C. Hellmann, eds. *Sharing World Leadership? A New Era for American and Japan* (Washington, D.C.: American Enterprise Institute, 1989, pp. 94–95.

25. Hugh Patrick and Henry Rosovsky, "Japan's Economic Performance: An Overview," in Patrick and Rosovsky, *Asia's New Giant*, p. 45. A different and much more conservative set of calculations for the period 1970–1985 suggests that capital stock would have decreased by about 17 percent at the end of the period had Japan devoted 3 percent of its GNP to defense, leaving total GNP down about 3 percent after the fifteen year period. Wong, "National Defense and Foreign Trade," pp. 108–09. At the same time, South Korea and Taiwan have spent considerably larger budget shares on the military, and their growth rates have remained high.

26. Robert Dekle, "The Relationship between Defense Spending and Economic Performance in Japan," in Makin and Hellmann, eds., *Sharing World Leadership?* p. 139.

27. Kent Calder, *Crisis and Compensation: Public Policy and Political Stability in Japan, 1949–1986* (Princeton: Princeton University Press, 1988), pp. 234–35.

28. Michael W. Donnelly, "Conflict Over Government Authority and Markets: Japan's Rice Economy," in Ellis Krauss et al., eds., *Conflict in Japan* (Honolulu: University of Hawaii Press, 1984), p. 336.

29. Patrick and Rohlen, for example, suggest an implicit political exchange between the LDP and the small family enterprises: "Support us and we won't tax you." In "Small-Scale Family Enterprises," p. 367. At the same time, it is useful to recognize that small firms became even more central targets of governmental policies in the early to mid-1970s, with numerous expansions in subsidies, loan guarantees, and the like. See also Calder, *Crisis and Compensation*, chap. 7.

30.   These points are well made in Daniel Okimoto, *Between MITI and the Market* (Stanford: Stanford University Press, 1986), and Richard Samuels, *The Business of the Japanese State* (Ithaca: Cornell University Press, 1986), inter alia.

31.   Kozo Yamamura, "The Cost of Rapid Growth and Capitalist Democracy in Japan," in Leon Lindberg and Charles Maier, eds., *The Politics of Inflation and Economic Stagnation* (Washington, D.C.: The Brookings Institution, 1985), p. 468.

32.   Watanabe Akio, *Sengo Nihon no taigai seisaku* (Tokyo: Yuhikaku, 1985), p. 258.

33.   It is important to realize that this articulation is quite different from notions that treat Japan as purely a "reactive state" or that argue that Japan only moves in response to pressures from abroad (the *gaiatsu* argument). Without a doubt, foreign pressures on Japan are not unfelt; but Japan does not move as a billiard ball when struck by these outside pressures. Rather, there is a highly differentiated set of responses, some governmental, some private, and with many pushing and pulling in different directions. All of these responses, the above perspective argues, are the result of changes in the decision options and payoff structures for Japanese domestic political actors. This point is well made in George Tsebelis, *Nested Games* (Berkeley: University of California Press, 1990).

34.   Keizai Koho Center, *Japan 1987: An International Comparison* (Tokyo: Japan Institute for Social and Economic Affairs, 1987), p. 56.

35.   Ministry of Finance figures as presented in *Japan, 1990*, p. 56. The jump would be less monumental but still impressive if denominated in yen.

36.   Charles Smith, "Overseas Focus: Asahi Launches Expansion Drive in Asia," *Far Eastern Economic Review,* September 28, 1989, p. 149.

37.   See Thomas L. Ilgen and T. J. Pempel, *Trading Technology: Europe and Japan in the Middle East* (New York: Praeger, 1987), esp. pp. 130–31.

38.   Economic Affairs Bureau, Ministry of Foreign Affairs, *Statistical Survey of Japan's Economy, 1975* (Tokyo: Ministry of Foreign Affairs, 1975), p. 53.

39.   These figures are from GATT and JETRO as presented in *Japan, 1990*, p. 44. Alternative figures presenting somewhat the same picture are in Watanabe Akio, *Sengo Nihon no taigai seisaku* (Tokyo: Yuhikaku, 1985), p. 258. Watanabe cites Japan as maintaining twenty-seven categories, including five in manufacturing. This latter figure accords also with Leon Hollerman, *Japan, Disincorporated: The Economic Liberalization Process* (Stanford: Hoover Institution, 1988), p. 44.

40.   Junichi Hasegawa, "Japan's Official Development Assistance and an Analysis of the Macroeconomic Effects of Aid," USJP Occasional Paper 89-06 (Cambridge: Program on U.S.-Japan Relations, Harvard University, 1989), p. 4.

41.   *Japan, 1990*, p. 58.

42.   See, for example, the regular publication from Look Japan, *Taking on Japan*. In these pamphlets, typically ten to twelve Western CEOs discuss how their particular firm managed to do well in Japan.

43.   *Far Eastern Economic Review,* June 21, 1990, p. 62

44.   The literature on this point is so voluminous that it makes little sense to spell out details; its simple assertion should be self-evident to followers of Japanese politics and U.S.-Japanese relations.

45. See T. J. Pempel, "From Trade to Technology: Japan's Reassessment of Military Policies," *Jerusalem Journal of International Relations* (December, 1990 forthcoming).

46. Prestowitz, *Trading Places*, chap. 3, summarizes many of these viewpoints.

47. Edward Lincoln, *Japan's Unequal Trade* (Washington, D.C.: Brookings Institution, 1990), pp. 18-25.

48. Kusano Atsushi, *Nichi-Bei Boeki no Massatsu* (Tokyo: Iwanami, 1984) inter alia.

49. An excellent treatment of this problem is Robert B. Reich, *The Work of Nations: Preparing Ourselves for 21st Century Capitalism*, (New York: Knopf, 1991). Also see T. J. Pempel, "The Trade Imbalance Isn't the Problem," *Cornell International Law Journal* 22, 3 (1989).

50. As reported in *The Economist*, June 23, 1990, p. 67.

51. DeAnne Julius, *Global Companies and Public Policy* (RIIA/Pinter nd) as noted in *The Economist*, June 23, 1990, p. 67.

52. *The Economist*, "Capital Markets," July 21, 1990, p. 17.

53. Ibid., p. 18.

54. *Far Eastern Economic Review*, June 21, 1990, p. 61.

55. See, e.g. *New York Times*, March 7, 1990; September 20, 1990, inter alia.

56. James Fallows, "Is Japan the Enemy?" *New York Review of Books*, May 30, 1991, p. 34.

57. As a corollary to these policies, and perhaps deserving of note as a third pillar, was the strong commitment to small government and to low levels of spending for social welfare.

58. This point would by no means be universally accepted among students of Japan. Journalists have long predicted the demise of the LDP in particular elections; the party's secretary general is constantly expressing fears about whatever electoral campaign is in the offing; there was a steady decline in the proportion of the total vote won by the LDP over most of the 1960s and 1970s; the loss of the Upper House in 1989 would also suggest that the LDP has hardly enjoyed electoral invulnerability.

59. This last law is quite similar to the Royer law in France in the early 1960s. See Suzanne D. Berger. "Regime and Interest Representation: The French Traditional Middle Classes," in Berger, ed., *Organizing Interests in Western Europe* (Cambridge: Cambridge University Press, 1981), p. 94.

60. Murakami Yasusuke, *Shinchukan taishu no jidai* (Tokyo: Chuo Koronsha, 1984).

61. A good example of this shift and the resultant electoral impact can be found in Takashi Inoguchi, "The Political Economy of Conservative Resurgence under Recession: Public Policies and Political Support in Japan, 1977–1983, " in Pempel, ed., *Uncommon Democracies*.

62. Korpi and Shalev, for example, found that Japan ranked sixth of eighteen industrialized countries in strike involvement from 1946 to 1976; the ranking would almost certainly have been even higher had the data been through the mid-1960s. Walter Korpi and Michael Shalev, "Strikes, Power and Politics in the Western Nations, 1900–1976," in Maurice Zeitlin, ed., *Political Power and Social Theory*, vol. 1 (Greenwich: JAI Press, 1980), p. 301.

63. Public-sector labor, particularly in transportation, teaching, communications, and white-collar work, tended on balance to be a mainstay of labor militance even into the mid-1980s.

64. Tsujinaka Yutaka, "Rodokai no Saihen to Hachijurokunen Taisei no Imi" ("The significance of the reorganization of labor relations and the 1986 system") *Leviathan* 1 (1987): 47–72.

65. Sato Seizaburo and Matsuzaki Tetsuhisa, *Jiminto-seiken* (LDP power) (Tokyo: Chuo Koronsha, 1986); Miyake Ichiro, ed., *Seito Shiji no bunseki* (Tokyo: Sokobunsha, 1985).

66. This problem is analyzed further in T. J. Pempel, "The Unbundling of 'Japan, Inc.': The Changing Dynamics of Japanese Policy Formation," *Journal of Japanese Studies* 13, 2 (Summer 1987): 287–88. See also Michael Donnelly, "Conflict over Government Authority and Markets: Japan's Rice Economy," in Ellis Krauss et al., eds. *Conflict in Japan* (Honolulu: University of Hawaii Press, 1984).

67. As Robert Cox has noted, franchising has provided an important mechanism for defusing potential intrabusiness cleavage in the United States particularly since 1973. Robert W. Cox, *Production, Power, and World Order: Social Forces in the Making of History* (New York: Columbia University Press, 1987), pp. 362–63.

68. The expansion of interest groups can be seen in Muramatsu Michio et al. *Sengo Nihon no Atsuryoku Dantai* (Tokyo: Toyo Keizai Shimposha, 1986), chap. 2.

69. Cf. Yamaguchi Jiro, *Okura kanryoshihai no shuen* (The death of bureaucratic rule by the Ministry of Finance) (Tokyo: Iwanami Shoten, 1987).

70. This point is advanced in more detail in Pempel, "The Unbundling of 'Japan, Inc.'" pp. 289–91.

71. Richard J. Samuels, "Consuming for Production: Japan," *International Organization* 43, 4 (Autumn 1989): 625–46.

Chapter 6
Japan's Response to the Strong Yen: Party Leadership and the Market for Political Favors

Frances McCall Rosenbluth

Between February 1985 and December 1988 the yen appreciated sharply, hurting many small manufacturers in Japan. The appreciation in the 1980s was roughly twice as large as that in 1971–73, when the Nixon administration forced the yen off its fixed rate of 360 to the dollar, and also larger than that in 1977–78 when the yen recovered from the first oil crisis.[1] While many large firms flourished under the strengthening yen because of their ownership of foreign assets, small exporting and import-competing firms had little to offset the squeeze on their profits. Small firms had to settle for cutting prices severely or selling at a price disadvantage against goods produced in countries that did not undergo a currency appreciation.

Despite the blow of the strong yen, however, government budget allocations to small business actually declined during this period and have continued to do so. Japan's political leaders made a lot of noise about helping small businesses that were particularly hard hit by the stronger yen, and in fact they came up with some money from government coffers. But this did not amount to more than political "leaning against the wind," and no great sums of money were doled out. The Japanese government's response to the plight of small manufacturers presents a puzzle. The Liberal Democratic party's postwar protection of the small-business sector has been recounted elsewhere and is well known.[2] If ever there were a time when an observer familiar with the historical record would expect lavish government aid to small business, it would surely have been during the "yen shock" of the mid-1980s.

One might suggest a number of reasons for the LDP's less-than-generous treatment of the small-business sector. One is that competent bureaucrats bypassed irresponsible and constituency-minded politicians in formulating and implementing this policy to increase Japan's economic efficiency. But there is compelling evidence that politicians were key policy makers in handling this issue. A second reason might be that public opinion had forced LDP politicians to reconsider their protection of small manufacturers in the interests of allowing domestic consumers to enjoy cheaper imported goods. But the pass through of windfall gains from a stronger yen to small consumers was only gradual and partial. In fact, benefits from a stronger yen seem to have accrued disproportionately to certain segments of the big-business sector. A third possible explanation for the LDP's change of heart is that foreign pressure on Japan to open its markets was finally too strong to resist. But foreign pressure alone is rarely an adequate explanation for any policy shift, since the LDP typically has a range of choices in placating Japan's important trading partners. Foreign demands must filter through the domestic configuration of interests, meeting with more or less success depending on the relative political influence of the potentially affected groups. The LDP could undoubtedly have found a way to compensate small manufacturers more thoroughly had it chosen to do so.

Although each of the factors enumerated above are part of an explanation of LDP policy, none is completely satisfactory. The bureaucracy assisted the LDP in "holding the line," but there is no evidence that the impetus for restraint emanated from MITI or other parties of the bureaucracy; on the contrary, the impetus for restraint clearly was political. The LDP may have been concerned about a public backlash if it went too far in compensating small business, but public opinion was hardly an articulate, organized force on this issue. And though Japan is widely regarded as unusually responsive to American pressure, it is not possible to draw a direct line between that pressure and the government's restraint in compensating small business.

The argument advanced here is that the LDP leadership, acting in the *collective* interests of the LDP Diet members, has decided to reduce gradually protection of small business. An LDP that comprised only self-directed back benchers with no effective party leadership would have been incapable of limiting its protection of the small-firm sector, which is represented in every electoral district in Japan. But given Japan's demographic shifts, the growing divergence of interests between the smallest and largest corporations, and unabating foreign pressure, the LDP's traditional solicitousness of small business increasingly endangers the LDP's longer-term electoral prospects. It is for their own electoral survival that individual LDP Diet members have delegated to the leadership the task of calculating the electoral consequences of alternative policy choices, as well as the authority to enforce those choices within the party.

Reduction of budgetary allocations to small business is only one indication of an across-the-board LDP policy shift away from coddling its traditional, often economically inefficient, bases of electoral support. Another example is in the consumer credit market. The Ministry of Finance will soon permit bank subsidiaries to offer revolving credit to consumers for the first time in postwar history. The ban had been aimed at protecting small credit companies as well as small retail stores that didn't handle credit cards. The combination of U.S. pressure and pressure from large Japanese banks has resulted in the overturn of this longstanding protection. In exchange for their loss of protection, small credit companies and larger credit card companies will gain access to bank ATMs, but this is a modest concession.

A second example is the gradually decreasing subsidization of agriculture. The process is painful to all concerned: the 12 percent or so of Japanese who farm are loathe to see their income diminish, though all but about 5 percent of the population are only part-time farmers who hold on to their agriculture land for the generous tax breaks. And for major corporations that are on the front line in dealings with an impatient U.S. Congress, the reduction in protection is painfully slow. Consumers are the silent bystanders, torn because of family ties to the countryside and low per capita stakes in the issue, and in any case unorganized. But even if an aroused electorate is not the reason, the LDP leadership is moving slowly toward agriculture liberalization.

Even the implementation of the consumption tax, with all of its loopholes, demonstrated the ability of the LDP leadership to move the party away gradually from small-business concerns. Particularly since the U.S. and British corporate tax cuts of the early 1980s, large Japanese corporations had pressed for a broadened tax base so their corporate taxes could be reduced. Japan's aging population and consequent shrinking of personal income taxes in future years is cited as further reason to shift the tax system away from overwhelming dependence on income taxation. After more than ten years of attempting to introduce a broad-based indirect tax, the LDP finally succeeded in 1987. The concessions to small businesses—exemption for the smallest firms, delayed payment for taxes that provided time to invest the money in the meantime, and a simplified accounting rule that allowed small firms to count an unduly large percentage of sales as costs—have gradually been reduced.[3]

As all of these cases show, LDP leaders are inclined to move away, if gradually, from electoral dependence on the country's uncompetitive sectors. The costs to the LDP of protection have become too great. The LDP's half-hearted policy toward small business in the face of yen appreciation is but one instance. If the yen's appreciation represented one step forward for the broader interests of the LDP's electoral base, the compensatory schemes to losers amounted to only a half-step back. The net half-step forward suggests that the political leadership is capable of moving, if slowly, in the direction of freer trade if that is what electoral survival requires.

The Landscape of Japan's Political Economy

Japan's Small Businesses

The definition of small firms in Japan depends on the sector. A small manufacturing firm is defined as having capital of 100 million yen or less and 1,000 or fewer employees; in the retail and service sector, a small firm has capital of 10 million or less and 50 or fewer employees; in the wholesale sector, a small firm is defined as having capital of 30 million or less and 100 or fewer employees. As of mid-1990 Japan had 1,640,000 small firms, which accounted for 99.3 percent of all Japanese firms and employed approximately 80 percent of Japan's nonagricultural work force.

However, the number of small firms has declined by 100,000 since 1984. Almost all of the decline was among small producers of finished goods as opposed to subcontractors and parts suppliers. It is these independent manufacturers, many of which lost their price competitiveness under a strong yen, that the LDP leadership found less useful to protect.[4]

Although it is difficult to find reliable statistics that divide small manufacturers into independent producers of finished goods and subcontractors, it is estimated that small finished-goods producers account for between 15 percent and 20 percent of Japan's manufacturing output.[5] Of all the types of small firms in Japan, it was these manufacturers without strong ties to a larger company that were most hurt by the yen's appreciation, and whose standardized products tend to be price-elastic.

These small-firm products—typically light manufactured goods such as processed foods, toys, buttons, cigarette lighters, pottery, stainless steelware, and even some lower-end electronics—compete directly with goods from the newly industrializing economies (NIES) more than with U.S. goods. Although the Taiwan NT and the Korean won also increased in value against the dollar during this same period, the rate of appreciation was not nearly as sharp as the yen's. Consequently, since Japan's small finished-goods manufacturers produce rather standardized products, neither brand-name appeal nor significant product differentiation was available to buffer them from the increased direct price competition of the NIES. Large Japanese firms, on the other hand, even though they were competing head-on against dollar-denominated U.S. products, were able to rely on brand-name appeal as well as an ability to transfer some of the burden of yen appreciation to their subcontractors to offset a potentially severe price disadvantage.[6]

Subcontractors are a second group of small manufacturers that are forced, by dint of domestic competition among suppliers for large firm business, to be more efficient producers. These firms are quasi-independent parts of a group of companies that make parts for a larger company at the center. Industrial organization scholars have pointed out that, while subcontracting is found in every economy, it is used more extensively in Japan than in other industrialized economies.[7] Many large Japanese corporations prefer long-term buying relationships with subcontractors to in-house production or to spot purchasing from outsiders (domestic or foreign).[8]

In understanding why the propensity for long-term contracting rather than vertical integration should be stronger in Japan than elsewhere if the costs and benefits of such choices are similar across countries, it is important to remember that the LDP has made the independent existence of small subcontractors feasible with special tax treatment in exchange for a supply of votes. Large firms therefore have an incentive not to take over the ownership of these suppliers but rather to take indirect advantage of this special treatment of their suppliers.[9]

Small and medium-sized subcontractors account for roughly 55 percent of all manufacturing output in Japan. As a percentage of the number of small businesses in the manufacturing sector, subcontractors represented 55.9 percent in 1987. The importance of subcontracting in total production of small and medium-sized manufacturers varies by product market. In transportation equipment, the figure in 1987 was 79.9 percent. Subcontractor production as a percentage of total small and medium sized firm production was 80.1 percent in electronics; 79.4 percent in textiles; 74.8 percent in general machinery; 71.0 percent in metal products; 70.4 percent in precision machinery; 42.0 percent in publishing; 41.3 percent in paper products; 38.5 percent in furniture; 22.0 percent in chemicals; 21.7 percent in wood products; 18.4 percent in oil products; 8.2 percent in food products. As a general rule, those industries in which subcontractors have accounted for a growing proportion of the industry's production grew faster between 1976 and 1987.[10]

Subcontractors have been hurt by the trend of large firms to increase their production in foreign markets, though 80 percent of Japanese firms producing abroad import at least some parts from Japan. Recognizing the pressure on Japanese producers abroad to secure more of their inputs from local suppliers, Japanese subcontractors have responded by locating abroad themselves near their parent firms, as well as by diversifying their parent companies.[11]

The distribution sector employs the largest number of workers among small and medium-sized firms and in fact employed 27.8 percent of Japan's entire nonagricultural work force in 1986.[12] However, the distribution sector was not hurt directly by the strong yen since their profits are from turnover rather than from exports. The oligopolistic big retailers did benefit by pocketing much of the windfall from cheaper imports rather than passing lower prices on to consumers. The Economic Planning Agency estimated that 30 percent of savings in import prices from the strong yen was absorbed by the distribution sector. But small retailers do not handle as large a proportion of imported goods of their total sales as large stores do, presumably because there are economies of scale in importing, and because many of the smallest stores are exclusive distributors for domestic producers.[13] Therefore, retailers profited from yen appreciation only to the extent that they handled imported goods and were in a restrictive sales arrangement with an importer that allowed them to share the windfall, which is true for a small percentage of retailers and wholesalers.[14]

The Political Organization of the Small Business Sector

Small businesses in Japan are well organized, both by industry and across industries. Small firms within a given industry band together in organizations with national headquarters, such as the Nihon senmonten rengokai, an association of small retail shops. Small firms of all industries are members of the local chapters of the Japan Chamber of Commerce, represented nationally by an office in Tokyo. The Japan Chamber of Commerce (*Nihon shōkō kaigi sho*) is the only one of the "big four" business organizations in Japan—the others being the Keidanren, Keizai Doyukai, and Nikkeiren—to represent small businesses.[15]

Although the Chamber of Commerce is legally required to maintain political neutrality because its operations are subsidized by the Ministry of International Trade and Industry, the pro-LDP stance of Chamber of Commerce officers is no secret. Moreover, a large subset of Chamber of Commerce members are also members of the Japan Commerce League (*Nihon shōkō renmei*), a parallel organization with the explicitly political function of supporting and lobbying LDP representatives. Officers of the Nihon shōkō renmei's local chapters by and large hold simultaneous positions in the Chamber of Commerce.[16]

Small Business and Japan's Political Leadership

Japan has an electoral system that places a premium on locally organized groups of voters. In electoral districts ranging from two to six seats, each voter has a single, nontransferrable vote. This means that for the LDP to maintain a majority of seats in the Diet, several LDP candidates must run against each other in most districts. These LDP candidates cannot campaign on the basis of a party platform since this would not provide a way to divide the votes among themselves. Instead, LDP candidates concentrate their energy and resources on building up personal bases of support, or *koenkai,* to develop identification and loyalty to themselves as individuals.[17]

Small businesses are important sources of LDP electoral support. Unlike workers in large firms who are at least nominally members of pro-JSP or pro-DSP unions, workers in small firms are more likely to vote for the LDP.[18] Despite the importance of the small-business vote and the small-business sector's impressive organization, however, there is little evidence that the Chamber of Commerce or even the Nihon shōkō renmei is able to allocate votes for different LDP candidates among small businesses. It is the efforts of individual LDP candidates that lead to some degree of specialization along industry and geographic lines.[19]

This candidate-specific electoral strategy requires more facilitation services to individuals and groups of constituents than if candidates were able to campaign on the basis of a broad set of party policies as in Britain and Germany. For the unorganized general voters, personal ties with and small favors from their representative reduce the salience of issues in their electoral choices. This positions well-organized groups such as small business and agriculture to translate their collective action advantage into influence on individual LDP Diet members since political competition from the opposition on the basis of issues—small-business protection or food prices, for example—is necessarily less effective.

If the LDP were composed only of back benchers, the LDP would be hard pressed to adjust to demographic shifts and other changing circumstances. Particularly for LDP politicians elected from rural constituencies, their personal support bases are adequate to insure their reelection despite fundamental demographic changes in the rest of the country. To put some limits on the opportunistic behavior of individual legislators in the interests of the broader, longer-term prospects of the party, the LDP's leadership intervenes to solve what might be thought of as the collective-action problem of the party's Diet members.[20] While each individual Diet member is motivated to provide local constituents with favors to maintain their personal support bases, the party's leadership balances these motivations with other concerns. It has to ensure that overspending does not hurt the sources of financial support for the party, including the big-business sector, which provides large donations to the LDP, and Japan's economic performance generally, which produces the tax revenues that support the government budget. The leadership also knows that poor economic performance due to the LDP's profligacy would jeopardize votes, particularly those from the general public who are not part of the network of LDP personal support groups.

The enormous effort and large sums of money each LDP Diet candidate must spend to cultivate personal support groups creates a powerful restraint on the party leaders' ability to act decisively in the party's longer-term, broader interests. This would seem to be the case in Japan more so than in countries in which party-centered campaigns are more the norm, whether in the single-member constituency system of Great Britain, or the mixed single-member and proportional representation system employed in Germany. To the extent that short-term interests are pressing for the individual Diet members in the LDP, they are by extension pressing for the party leaders as well, who must ensure the election of a Diet majority to retain control of the government. A key institutional feature of the LDP, however, is that the Diet members in each of the intraparty factions come from every kind of district and represent the full range of intraparty policy groups. As a result, the faction leaders in the LDP, who are also the party's leaders, share the broad interests of the entire party's constituency.

The LDP leadership is capable of acting in concert on issues of electoral importance, but it is constrained by the short-run need to ensure the election of a Diet majority. Even though the LDP leaders can enforce voting discipline, party leaders must stop short of mandating policy stances that will endanger a majority of LDP Diet members from being elected.

During the decades of Japan's rapid economic expansion, the LDP could content itself with distributing resources to the electorate from an ever-growing pie while at the same time keeping its business supporters happy. The interests of the leadership and back benchers were therefore consistent insofar as a growing government budget continued to support generous public works with little inflation.[21]

Three changes have led to a greater divergence of the leadership's long-term strategy and the back benchers' short-term concerns. The first is demographic change. Over the past two decades the proportion of the urban salaried workers has increased relative to the farm and small independent manufacturer population. The problem for the LDP is that urban "floating voters" are more difficult to reach through services. They are typically better educated, more mobile, and harder to enlist in the LDP candidates' traditional personal support groups. These are the voters who are more likely to vote on the basis of the economy's overall health and its impact on their level of income.[22]

Second, the big-business sector is worried about the government deficit that began to expand after 1965, first gradually, then explosively after the recession of 1975. Its concern is less with the deficit per se than with its potential tax burden. Even before the Reagan and Thatcher administrations were able to reduce corporate taxes in their respective countries, the Japanese business sector pushed for a restructuring of the tax structure away from its heavy dependence on (corporate) income tax to more revenue from indirect, value-added taxes that the LDP began with the introduction of the sales tax in 1987. The following year, as a result of the Structural Impediments Initiative talks with the United States, the Japanese government decided to spend 430 trillion yen in public works between 1990 and 2000. But it will no doubt try to minimize the burden on the government budget by doling out as much of this money as possible in the form of loans rather than outright grants.

Third, U.S. pressure on Japanese business makes protectionism less tenable. Competitive corporations are willing to compete domestically and internationally with less government help but have to bear the brunt of U.S. ire for the coddling of less efficient sectors such as agriculture and certain segments of the small-business community. Since the LDP leadership has relatively closer ties to the big-business sector than does the typical Diet member, this is a considerable source of tension within the party.

How the political market redistributes income after economic forces wreak their initial havoc tells us a great deal about the internal contours of a political system.

The LDP's decision to let small business swing in the wind generated by the yen's appreciation is an example of the LDP's capacity to make choices in the party's broader interests. On the basis of intense discussions in the party, the LDP determined that it could compensate only nominally small independent manufacturers without jeopardizing the LDP's Diet majority in the short term.

The Plaza Accord

Beginning in 1981 the United States adopted a mix of loose fiscal and tight monetary policy that succeeded in halting inflation but resulted in a seriously overvalued dollar. Inflation dropped from 12.4 percent in 1980 to 3.8 percent in 1982, but real interest rates remained high because of heavy government borrowing to finance the U.S. government deficit and continued tight monetary policy.[23] Popular lore notwithstanding, it was not so much that Reagan and his advisers wanted a strong dollar, but that they did not want to divert macroeconomic policy tools to target the dollar at a lower level. Martin Feldstein, chairman of the Council of Economic Advisors, assumed that the U.S. budget deficit was temporary and felt that capital inflows due to the strong dollar were preferable to increased exports at the cost of reduced investment with a low dollar.[24]

Between February 1985 and December 1988 the yen appreciated 93 percent against the U.S. dollar. Japanese manufacturing firms faced either severe price cuts or a 93 percent price disadvantage in the U.S. market.

The consequence of the strong dollar/weak yen was a surge in American imports, provided cheerfully by Japanese and other foreign producers. Increases of external demand (export growth less import growth) accounted for 35 percent of Japan's GNP growth between 1980 and 1985. Japan's current account surplus surged from $4.77 billion in 1981 to $20.8 billion two years later and $85.8 billion in 1986. The American share of Japan's growing exports—which had declined from one-third in the 1960s to one-quarter in 1980—increased to 38.5 percent by 1986.[25]

This worsening of the U.S. current account deficit with Japan (and the rest of the world) fueled concern in U.S. business circles about the value of the dollar. In 1983 Lee Morgan, chairman of Catapillar as well as of the Business Roundtable in Washington, commissioned the so-called Solomon-Murchison Report, a paper written by a Stanford professor and Washington lawyer that concluded that the government should adopt measures to lower the value of the dollar against the yen. The subsequent "Yen-Dollar Talks" between the United States and Japan beginning in 1984 focused on ways to increase the demand for yen by making yen-denominated financial instruments more attractive to hold for investment.[26] Congress also began to blame the strong dollar for America's trade problems. Senator Danforth (R-MO) stated on the Senate floor in the summer of 1985 that "Resolving the exchange rate problem is the *sine qua non* of effective trade policy."[27] Later that summer, Senators Bradley (D-NJ), Moynihan (D-NY), and Baucus (D-MT) submitted bills making foreign-exchange intervention mandatory when the United States was running large current account deficits.[28]

By the summer of 1985, however, without direct government intervention, the market tide already began to turn against the dollar. Market players seemed to have gotten a signal of policy change when Chief of Staff James Baker and Secretary of the Treasury Donald Regan switched jobs in January 1985. More importantly, U.S. interest rates began to drop in response to an easing of monetary policy. By February the dollar was beginning to depreciate as investors found lower interest rates less attractive.

As in the Nixon administration's decision in 1971 to take the U.S. dollar off the gold exchange standard to force the Japanese yen to appreciate, the Reagan administration hoped in 1985 that more appreciation of the yen would increase the competitiveness of American exports. The Japanese were also aware that the some $80 billion current account surplus with the United States in 1984 was politically untenable and hoped that their cooperation in exchange rate policy would assuage growing protectionism in Congress. The Japanese government's support for the Plaza Accord stood in sharp contrast to its recalcitrance fourteen years earlier.

Many big businesses in Japan welcomed a stronger yen, at least somewhere in the range of 200 to 220 rather than in the 260s.[29] In a March 1, 1985, U.S.-Japan satellite talk show, Fuji Bank Chairman Matsuzawa Takuji told Commerce Secretary Baldridge that the United States should get its interest rates and the value of the dollar down to lower levels.[30] Inayama Yoshihiro, chairman of the big business federation, the Keidanren, stated in a meeting with Osaka business leaders that "a strong yen is necessary to keep U.S. markets open."[31]

The Finance Minister at the time, Takeshita Noboru, actually claims credit for broaching the idea that key currency countries try to bring the value of the dollar down with coordinated intervention. The idea was also floating around in Congress, but irrespective of who first suggested the joint measures, the point is that Takeshita was not opposed to trying to raise the value of the yen despite potential political difficulty at home as a result.[32] One Japanese newspaper reported about two weeks before the Plaza Accord that the LDP was considering a currency summit to the chagrin of the MOF, which was concerned about the use of fiscal and monetary policy for foreign policy ends. But the LDP leadership saw currency adjustment as the best alternative, since outright trade liberalization would be politically even more difficult, and business opposed aggressively expansionist domestic spending as well as capital export controls. The calculation seems to have been that if the yen were to rise by 10 percent, the $40 billion trade deficit would go down by $4 billion.[33]

Not wanting to attract the attention of the foreign-exchange market in order to give the joint statement maximum impact, Finance Minister Takeshita staged a secret departure from Narita on September 21. After playing a few holes of golf with Yamamura Shinjirō, one of his faction members from the Narita electoral district, Takeshita slipped undetected onto an airplane bound for New York with Bank of Japan Governor Sumita, MOF Vice Minister for International Affairs Ōba Tomomitsu, and MOF International Finance Bureau Director General Gyohten Toyoo.[34]

Takeshita was soon dubbed the "Strong Yen Minister."[35] Takeshita was pleased with the yen's jump of twenty yen in a few days, but when the yen kept rising with no sign of peaking, he ran into static in local areas with a high concentration of small independent exporters. At a public speech in December in the town of Tajimi in Gifu Prefecture, known for small-scale production of pottery and flatware, a disgruntled man in the audience shouted, "You'd better be prepared to be a singer because you won't be a politician much longer!"[36]

Takeshita was replaced by Miyazawa Kiichi as minister of finance in the summer of 1986. It was not that Prime Minister Nakasone was displeased with Takeshita's performance in managing the foreign-exchange issue or any other issue. But Nakasone was concerned that Miyazawa was calling for fiscal expansion despite the Nakasone administration's explicit policy of fiscal austerity, and Nakasone calculated that Miyazawa would be forced to take a more fiscally conservative stance if responsible for the finance portfolio in the cabinet.[37]

The yen continued to rise, and more rapidly than most Japanese firms had anticipated.[38] Some industries in the heavy-industry sector, such as steel, were faced with fierce competition from Korea and Taiwan and were concerned about their ability to adjust if the yen were to appreciate too fast, too far.[39] At the meeting of the G-5 finance ministers in Louvre in February 1987, Finance Minister Miyazawa attempted to get support for the existing rate of 153 yen to the dollar, within a band of 140 to 160.[40] But the response of the other countries' representatives was lukewarm, and the market continued to buoy the yen upward. In April 1987 the yen hit the 140 level, and by December 1987 the yen was in the 120 yen range.

Most large businesses were not particularly hurt by the strong yen, however. Many Japanese industries had healthy margins, they could hedge their foreign exchange risks, the stronger yen boosted their assets with which to invest in more foreign assets, and to the extent that they imported foreign inputs, their costs were reduced. Nonetheless, firms used the rhetoric of pain and suffering as a good opportunity to press employees for wage restraint and subcontractors for rationalization.

Other industries, as noted, actually benefited considerably from the stronger yen. Japanese banks were catapulted to the top of all cross-national comparative tables that ranked banks by size.[41] The windfall to direct users of imported fuel were huge. Tokyo Electric Power gained four billion yen in windfall profits for every yen increased against the dollar. Gas companies also benefited enormously, particularly because the yen's rise happened to coincide with a general decline in the world's price of oil.[42]

LDP members of the PARC's Commerce Division and Small Business Research Committee began to look into the possibility of forcing oil refineries and utilities companies to pass windfall profits on to small firms.[43] MITI also set up a study group to examine pass through of utilities' windfall profits.[44] But Prime Minister Nakasone, at a cabinet meeting in November 1985, argued that no policy regarding windfall profits should be taken for about a year until the level of the yen and world fuel prices became clearer. There is no point, he said, in forcing utilities and refineries to pass through windfall profits "the size of sparrows' tears," since that would have no effect on the economy.[45] Party leader Kanemaru Shin echoed this sentiment at a Tanaka faction meeting, stating it would be preferable to allow electric utilities companies to keep the windfall for investment in new equipment than to give 300–400 yen to each citizen.[46] The general ranks of the LDP's Diet members favored legislation to pass through some of the windfall profits of the oil refineries and utilities companies to small-business end users. But the party's leaders resisted such pressure for two reasons. First, most front-line big-business firms could already compete globally with existing rates and were more worried about steady supply of utilities down the road.[47] Second, utilities firms are big financial contributors to the LDP.[48] Tokyo gas and the other big three gas companies in fact did cut prices somewhat for biggest users, and they were stopped by MITI from raising prices for smallest users.[49] A Small and Medium-Sized Enterprise Agency (SMEA) survey showed that big firms received more raw materials windfall than small firms, presumably because they import themselves whereas small firms buy from big firms after some degree of processing, and also because big users typically have more ability to switch among types of energy and are therefore in a stronger market position to affect prices.[50]

Consumer prices did not drop in the wake of the stronger yen.[51] The consumer price gap between Tokyo and New York actually widened with yen appreciation, suggesting at least a lag before cheaper goods were imported. Purchasing power parity with the United States put the dollar at 218 yen according to OECD calculations, food at 294 yen, recreation at 291, transportation and communication at 280 yen. The Economic Planning Agency admitted in a white paper that a large price discrepancy may suggest some rigidities in the Japanese economy.[52]

Small Firms and Yen Appreciation

Press reports were in agreement that the rise of the yen had the biggest impact on small independent manufacturers. This strikes one at first as somewhat puzzling since large firms, in fact, have a higher dependence on trade than do small firms. Large firms' average dependence on exports as a percentage of total sales revenue is 32 percent whereas for small firms it is about 6.5 percent, or 17 percent when including sales of parts to large firms for final assembly and export.

There are a number of reasons, however, why small firms are more vulnerable to the impact of a stronger yen. First, big firms are also more dependent on imports in addition to exports so they receive more benefits from a stronger yen—27 percent of purchases are imports compared to 17 percent for small firms.[53] Second, small firms' export products and markets were less diversified than those of large firms. Small firms tend to be highly specialized in their product lines and have more focused marketing strategies.[54] Third, small firms were less able to hedge their exchange-rate exposure with forward contracts, and they had fewer foreign direct investments to offset the losses in their exports. Finally, small firms had smaller profit margins than oligopolistic large producers with which to absorb the brunt of the stronger yen.

Possibly because small firms had less room to cut costs, they passed along over 60 percent in 1986 (70 percent in 1987) of the exchange-rate effect to foreign purchasers, whereas big firms passed along only 45 percent (53 percent in 1987) of the cost increase.[55] This resulted in a larger drop in the exports of small businesses than of big firms as their goods rather dramatically lost their price competitiveness. In 1986, compared to 1985, small manufacturers' exports were down by 2.3799 trillion yen; another 2.3767 when include indirect exports (exports of parent company) are included. Big firms lost 4.2341 trillion yen in sales, 4.5147 indirectly by virtue of loss in direct sales. Small firms' drop in exports of 4.7566 trillion yen represented a fall-off of 7.8 percent, whereas large manufacturers' loss of 8.7488 trillion yen in exports was for them a mere 0.7 percent drop. Even domestic-demand-oriented small firms experienced a serious slump in 1986–87 because of less business with exporting firms.

By 1987 small-firm exports were down by 6.2147 trillion yen since 1985, which includes a 3.118 trillion loss in exports and a 3.967 trillion drop in sales to large exporting firms. This compares to a decline in the value of total big business exports of 10.7 trillion yen, of which 5.4 trillion was loss of exports and 5.2 trillion was from a fall off in sales to exporters.[56] Large-firm export volume also dropped sharply from the end of 1985 to the beginning of 1986, but resumed growth. Small firms' export performance continued to languish through the beginning of 1988.[57] But before extrapolating too much from this broad sketch, we need to outline the contours of the varied small-business sector in Japan and see how this sector's status is changing politically.

The LDP's Response to the Strengthening Yen

Government budget outlays for small business actually peaked in 1982, and even the outcry over the strong yen did not elicit government help to match funding of earlier years.[58] But small businesses are still politically well organized and typically hold important positions in the personal support groups of LDP Diet members.

Not surprisingly, the feeling among the LDPs Diet members was overwhelmingly in favor of helping small firms liberally.

The least costly and hence most lavish response by LDP politicians was rhetorical. In response to a MITI/SMEA survey showing that 10 percent of firms were cutting orders from subcontractors (which was hardly surprising or unreasonable), Tamura Hajime, the minister of MITI, publicly urged big firms not to pass the burden of a strong yen disproportionately on to suppliers. In February 1986 MITI set up a Subcontractor and Other Small and Medium-Sized Business Policy Team (*Shitauke nado chūsō kigyō taisaku suishin honbu*) to "monitor" the behavior of large firms towards their suppliers. The head of this task force was Takashi Tawara, the LDP's parliamentary vice-minister of MITI in charge of small business. Other members of the task force included the director of the SMEA and directors of sixteen departments in MITI's various bureaus. But no sanctions were ever imposed on large firms.[59]

Within two months of the Plaza Accord, when the yen had reached the 230 level, the Japanese government began providing low-interest loans to small businesses through government financial institutions, primarily the People's Finance Corporation (*Kokumin kinyū kōko*), Small Business Finance Corporation (*Chūshō kigyō kinyū kōko*), and the Central Cooperative Bank for Commerce and Industry (*Shōkō chūkin*).[60] Prime Minister Nakasone, in a speech before a small-business organization, stressed the LDP's commitment to helping small firms deal with the stronger yen through the provision of "international adjustment loans," though in fact the terms were not as generous as the LDP's Commerce Division called for.[61] The LDP's leaders viewed yen appreciation as a positive development for trade relations and for stifling inflation, but they recognized that some measures were necessary to mollify the small businesses that were hurt and the LDP Diet members who rely on their votes.

The Small and Medium-Sized Enterprise Agency designated fifty industries for the special loans on the basis of the following criteria: exports must account for 20 percent or more of the industry's total sales value, and the industry had to have experienced a 10 percent drop in sales since September. The industries included, for example, makers of canned fish, canned mandarin oranges, frozen fish, textiles, and cigarette lighters.[62]

Very soon after the government financial institutions began to dispense subsidized small-business loans, the U.S. government expressed its concern that these were in fact disguised export subsidies. Deputy U.S. Trade Representative Mike Smith conveyed to his counterparts at MITI that the U.S. government would prefer that the Japanese government attempt to expand domestic demand rather than prop up existing inefficient exporters. MITI objected vociferously to the U.S. complaint, claiming that the funding for strong yen victims was in fact intended to help these small firms adjust to domestic sales, but that in any case the issue was an entirely domestic problem.[63]

As is often the case in Japan's trade relations, LDP party leaders intervened when the "tough cop" routine of MITI failed to produce results in discussions with the United States. Finance Minister Takeshita stopped in Washington on his way back from a London G-5 meeting to discuss with Treasury Secretary Baker Japan's loans to small exporters. Baker requested a reduction of what he termed tied aid and suggested that these subsidies artificially added to the export competitiveness of the target firms.[64] To placate the United States, MITI, at the LDPs prompting, inserted the words "business conversion" (*jigyō tenkan*) into the law authorizing the loans to emphasize the shift to domestic-oriented production.[65]

The United States was still not satisfied, and U.S. Trade Representative Clayton Yeutter stated to the House Foreign Affairs subcommittee that Japan's aid to small exporters violated GATT article 16 prohibiting export subsidies. Pressed by angry members of Congress, Yeutter stated that the U.S. government would be forced to consider applying 301 sanctions under the 1988 Omnibus Trade Act if GATT was unable to solve the problem. MITI continued bitterly to deny wrongdoing.[66]

To avert a trade disaster, the LDP's leaders intervened once again, and this time they guessed right about what would be necessary to dissuade the United States from taking Japan before the GATT. The LDP ordered the Small and Medium-Sized Enterprise Agency to make the loans contingent on their use for converting businesses to nonexport-based lines of production. The SMEA procured pledges from loan recipient companies not to use the funds to subsidize exports.[67] And although the LDP did not want to say it too loudly, it pointed out to the U.S. negotiators that the total amount of subsidized loans to small businesses would not increase, since the same money was merely placed under a different title. The United States finally agreed to the loans without further complaint. Indeed, loans from the three government financial institutions targeting small business totaled 3.48 trillion each of 1985 and 1986, down from 3.66 trillion in 1984. The loans grew only gradually in 1987 and 1988, more slowly than either GNP growth or the growth in the government budget.[68]

The LDP leadership also managed to hold the line on budget expenditures, despite back bencher pressure in anticipation of summer 1986 elections. An Upper House election was scheduled for summer 1986, and by late fall 1985 it appeared increasingly likely that the LDP would call simultaneous elections of the Upper and Lower houses. Rank-and-file members were worried about polls that showed 60 to 80 percent of small manufacturers felt hurt by the yen's appreciation and pushed for generous government spending in the face of the Nakasone administration's policy of limiting budget expenditures and reducing the budget deficit.[69]

After heated internal LDP discussions over the relative merits of fiscal laxity versus continued stringency, the party settled on a compromise closer to the fiscal restraint scenario. Some in the party had been stressing the need for more public spending and domestic demand expansion as a way, among other things, to placate the United States.[70] But Prime Minister Nakasone and Finance Minister Takeshita stressed the importance of not repeating the mistake of the post-yen-appreciation spending in 1971 and 1972 which led to spiraling inflation.[71] In October 1985 the government decided on a 2-trillion-yen package, much of which were loans and "reliance on private-sector dynamism." The supplementary budget for 1985 was actually only 723 billion yen, and none of that was allocated to small business.[72]

Most of the big-business sector, eager for the success of the government's "fiscal reconstruction plan" and the possibility of future tax cuts, was relieved that the LDP managed to restrain spending in the wake of the yen's appreciation.[73] But some in the LDP remained dissatisfied with the final package. An LDP "Strong Yen Project Team" had called for the issuance of more construction bonds that were left out of the plan altogether. Finance Minister Takeshita and his aides in the party worked hard putting out this fire, stressing (somewhat disingenuously) that the consensus of the G-5 countries was to cut government deficits.[74] In FY 1986 sales of NTT stocks brought a 6 trillion yen increase in revenue, which the government spent on tax cuts of 1.5 trillion and 4.5 trillion in public works. The government kept the budget increase for FY 1986 at 1.3 trillion over FY 1985. In 1986 the supplementary budget actually adjusted total expenditures downward, though small business was allocated an additional 20.4 billion yen; in 1987 the expenditure for small business was 40.5 billion out of a supplementary budget of 2.1 trillion, and in 1988 small business was allocated 62 billion out of a 5.2 trillion supplementary budget.[75]

Meanwhile, the government implemented a lax monetary policy for the entire economy, despite the Bank of Japan's protestations that the money supply was growing too rapidly. The Bank of Japan's Governor Sumita Satoshi opposed lowering interest rates to coordinate with lowering U.S. rates because interest rates were "already too low," but the BOJ lowered the official discount rate five times between 1985 and 1988, from 5 percent to 2.5 percent.[76] This loose monetary policy also pleased business, though it was probably maintained too long, fueling one of the most dramatic rises in the Tokyo Stock Exchange as well as Tokyo land prices in postwar history.

The Electoral Outcome

Despite the LDP's limited aid to small business following the "yen shock," the LDP won a landslide electoral victory in July 1986. One reason is the competition among LDP candidates for the same seats in each electoral district. When voters are unhappy with one LDP representative, they can vote for another LDP candidate who promises to serve their interests better within the party. Although the LDP won a total of 304 seats, fifty of those were won by first-time LDP candidates. Another twenty-eight LDP winners were previous LDP representatives who had been out of office for at least one term.[77]

The second reason for this and other LDP victories is that the opposition parties have been unable to present voters with an attractive enough alternative. While the opposition parties offer different ideological visions, the LDP candidates provide constituents with tangible material benefits.

Third, for small businesses that continued to be hurt by the strong yen or that were forced to choose other lines of business, the LDP could hide behind the "inevitability of change" in the face of foreign market and political pressure. Although the LDP could have accomplished the same diplomatic goal vis-à-vis the United States by imposing an export surcharge, the domestic political culpability would have been greater. Inefficient small businesses in Japan are not prepared to relinquish protection, but they seem to recognize that a certain reduction is inevitable.

Conclusion

The strong yen story is one of the LDP partially, but not completely, compensating inefficient groups that were disadvantaged by market forces. LDP leaders are inclined to move Japan towards greater global competitiveness, since many big businesses are already prepared to compete and because the international political costs of protection are increasing. The LDP leadership, considering the broader interests and longer-term prospects of the party, must weigh the costs of protection in terms of budgetary outlays, the impact of regulatory favors on other supporters and the rest of the economy, and on relations with important trading partners, including the United States. But individual Diet members of the LDP are first of all concerned about their chances of reelection, and they balk at any measures that leave their constituencies too unhappy. LDP leaders must also calculate the short-term electoral costs of policies, since they need a majority of Diet members to remain government leaders. The LDP leadership may therefore set the direction of policy choices, but the electoral needs of the rank and file determine the pace of change.

The LDP leadership almost never takes a step forward toward broader and longer-term goals without taking half a step backward toward the narrow and short-term worries of its individual Diet members. The question raised by this and similar cases is whether or not the party can take enough half-steps to avert a trade disaster with Japan's most important trade partner, the United States.

Past experience shows that it probably will, if just barely. Trade retaliation by the United States, after all, would clearly hurt the typical LDP Diet members' electoral prospects as well, since they all benefit from the LDP's public image of diplomatic competence. What the party members need, therefore, is a leadership that can calculate the collective electoral gains and losses that follow from alternative policy choices and, upon making a decision, is capable of enforcing it.

Enforcing party loyalty in Diet votes, and then ensuring faithful bureaucratic implementation of policy decisions, are the least of the LDP's problems. The party does both of those things rather well. The far more difficult task is the calculation of the costs and benefits, in electoral terms, of alternative policy decisions. Because Japan's current electoral system forces LDP Diet members to build large personal support networks, policy shifts are extremely difficult and potentially disastrous electorally. On the other hand, continuing demographic change and expected large costs of big business in the event of foreign retaliation make policy changes necessary. It is no wonder that the LDP is once again seriously considering electoral reform to reduce the party's electoral need for particularism. But in the meantime, the LDP leadership has to manage cross-cutting pressures with little margin for error. It is, paradoxically, the delegation of this authority to party leaders that has been LDP Diet members' best insurance against electoral defeat.

Notes

1.   Peter Petri, "Market Structure, Comparative Advantage, and Japanese Trade Under the Strong Yen," paper prepared for the Japan Economic Seminar, April 21, 1990, p. 1.

2.   See Kent Calder's excellent book on Japan's public policy, *Crisis and Compensation* (Princeton: Princeton University Press, 1989).

3.   "Shōhizei tokurei minaoshi hōkoku e," *Nikkei shimbun*, October 12, 1990, p. 7; *Nikkei shimbun*, April 26, 1991.

4.   It is important not to conflate small firms with inefficient firms. Many suppliers in particular have been extremely successful at niche market production and technological innovation. See David Friedman, *The Misunderstood Miracle* (Ithaca: Cornell University Press, 1989). But in 1981, value added per worker in large manufacturing firms (1,000 or more workers) was an average of 2.39 times that of a worker in small firms (4–99 workers), though the wage gap was narrower in part because of favorable tax treatment for small firms. See Hugh Patrick and Thomas Rohlen, "Small Scale Family Enterprises," in K. Yamamura and Y. Yasuba, eds., *The Political Economy of Japan: The Domestic Transformation* (Stanford: Stanford University Press, 1987), p. 340

5.   *1987 chūshō kigyō hakusho*, p. 141.

6.   Hideo Kobayashi, "Kinrin Ajia shokoku to nihon sangyō," in K. Kitada and K. Aida, *Endaka fukyōka no Nihon sangyō* (Tokyo: Ōtsuki shoten, 1987).

7.   See, for example, Masu Uekusa, "Industrial Organization, 1970s to the Present," in K. Yamamura and Y. Yasuba, *The Political Economy of Japan: The Domestic Transformation* (Stanford: Stanford University Press, 1987), pp. 499–501.

8.   Fully 35 percent of firms in Japan import only 5 percent of their parts from foreign suppliers. *1988 chūshō kigyō hakusho*.

9.   For the argument that big firms' preference for purchasing from their own subcontractors builds in an anti-import bias, see Peter Petri, "Market Structure, Comparative

Advantage, and Japanese Trade under the Strong Yen," paper presented at the Japan Economic Seminar, April 21, 1990.

10. *1987 chūshō kigyō hakusho*, pp. 140–43; "Shitauke kigyōsū no sūi," materials from the Chūsho kigyō chō, December 21, 1987.

11. Hideo Kobayashi, "Kinrin Ajia shokoku to Nihon sangyō," in Kitada and Aida, eds., *Endaka fukyōka no Nihon sangyō*.

12. 1989 *chūshō kigyō hakusho*.

13. While the involvement of small stores in importing is still small, it is slowly growing. In 1982, 60 percent of small wholesalers and retailers handled no imported goods; by 1987 that percentage had dropped to about 50 percent. About 37 percent of retailers and 31.5 percent of wholesalers handle about 20 percent imports; about 8 percent of retailers and 6.7 percent of wholesalers handle 40–60 percent imports. Thirty-five percent of those imported goods from the NICS, 23 percent from the United States and Europe. For an account of how domestic producers and large importers blocked small retailers from engaging in "parallel importing" to pass along more price cuts to consumers, see Hiroyuki Itami, *En ga yureru, kigyō wa ugoku* (Tokyo: NTT Shuppansha, 1990), pp. 95–98.

14. 1988 *chūshō kigyō hakusho, pp. 56–57*.

15. See Gerald L. Curtis, "Big Business and Political Influence," in Ezra Vogel, ed., *Modern Japanese Organization and Decision-Making* (Tokyo: Tuttle, 1975).

16. Interview with Nobuo Kamino, president of Chubu Gas and chairman of the Toyohashi Chamber of Commerce and Toyohashi Shōkō renmei, July 21, 1990.

17. For the classic work on LDP campaign strategies, see Gerald Curtis, *Election Campaigning Japanese Style* (New York: Columbia University Press, 1971).

18. LDP politician Yanagisawa Hakuo, for example, relies more on the votes of the employees of Yamaha subcontractors in his district than on the votes of the huge Yamaha plant's workers themselves, though the two categories of employees are roughly equal in number. Interview, July 25, 1990. As a more general confirmation of this personal story, NHK polls that proprietors and employees of small firms are more likely to vote for the LDP than are employees of large firms. See Arai Kunio, *Senkyo, jōhō, yoron*, (Tokyo: NHK Books, 1988).

19. Interviews with LDP politicians, summer 1990. Also see Curtis, *Election Campaigning Japanese Style* .

20. By "LDP leadership," I am referring to the ten or fifteen most senior members of the LDP who have distinguished themselves not only by managing to get reelected for many terms, but by being able to broker the various conflicting interests the party represents.

21. Since constituents and their Diet representatives compete over expanding pies as well as over contracting pies, the LDP leadership had to keep spending from going through the roof.

22. See, for example, T. Inoguchi, "Economic Attitudes and Voting Behavior," in J. Watanuki, I. Miyake, T. Inoguchi, and I. Kabashima, *Electoral Behavior in the 1983 Japanese Elections* (Tokyo: Sophia University Institute of International Relations, 1986).

23. I. M. Denning and C. Randall Henning, *Dollar Politics: Exchange Rate Policymaking in the United States* (Washington, D.C.:Institute for International Economics, 1990) p. 19; Hiroyuki Itami, *En ga yurerum kigyō wa ugoku* (Tokyo: NTT Shuppansha, 1990) pp. 49–51.

24. Destler and Henning, p. 27.

25. Hugh Patrick and Frances Rosenbluth, "Japan's Industrial Structure in Crisis: National Concerns and International Implications," Japan Society Public Affairs Series, 1988, p. 2.

26. Frances Rosenbluth, *Financial Politics in Contemporary Japan* (Ithaca: Cornell University Press, 1989), chap. 6; Destler and Henning, pp. 33–47.

27. Senator John Danforth, address to the National Press Club on United States Trade Policy, Washington, April 25, 1985, in Destler and Henning, p. 39.

28. Destler and Henning, p. 39.

29. "Kyōsōryoku shimpai no yushutsu gyōkai," *Asahi,* October 11, 1985; interview with Tomomitsu Ōba, then vice minister of the MOF for International Affairs, July 20, 1990.

30. "Josei ni yori endaka taisaku," *Tokyo shimbun,* November 21, 1985.

31. "Jiyū keizai no tame endaka gaman o," *Tokyo shimbun,* December 7, 1985.

32. Takeshita stated in an interview that "supporting a strong yen and taking responsibility for Recruit were the biggest, most difficult decisions of my life" (July 17, 1990). Nakasone apparently favored a stronger yen as early as 1982. Yoichi Funabashi, "Nakasone's Economic Credo,"*Asahi Evening News,* December 9, 1982), cited in Yoichi Funabashi, *Managing the Dollar: From the Plaza to the Louvre* (Washington, D.C.: Institute for International Economics, 1988).

33. "Tsuka sammitto ni ōkurashō konwaku," *Tokyo shimbun,* September 12, 1985; Also see "Nichibei shunō kaidan tsūka ga gidai ni," *Nkkei,* September 19, 1985, which reported that Prime Minister Nakasone was planning to visit the United States in late October for a UN meeting at which time he would discuss foreign exchange issues with President Reagan.

34. Takeshita claims that "the only time I ever lied to (then foreign minister) Abe Shintarō was in not telling him I had planned to agree to coordinated intervention to raise the value of the yen. This would have affected, possibly, the defense budget allocation that had just been decided by 6:30 a.m. on September 18, 1985, after all-night discussions," (July 17, 1990). But in fact the LDP leadership had already agreed to yen appreciation in principle, if not the exact timing. "Tsūka de kinkyū kaigi," *Nikkei,* September 22, 1985; "Doru daka zesei kyōgi," *Yomiuri,* September 22, 1985; "Sōba suijun teisei nerau,"*Nikkei,* September 24, 1985, "Tainichi shisei issō kyōkō ni," *Nikkei,* Septemner 25, 1985.

35. "Tsuka no Takeshita urikomi ni kekki," *Asahi,* October 2, 1985. Takeshita reminisced about President Carter approvingly dubbing him the "Strong Yen Minister" when he was finance minister in 1977–1978. The yen was 242 when he became minister but had risen to 219 when his term expired in 1978. "At this exchange rate (200+ in 1985), I couldn't graduate from the MOF because the yen

was still too weak."Interview, Noboru Takeshita, July 17, 1990.

36. Interview, Noboru Takeshita, July 17, 1990; interview, Tomomitsu Ōba, July 20, 1990.

37. There are, of course, some differences among LDP leaders at various times as to what the proper level of fiscal stimulation should be. But these differences are usually politically motivated. Nakasone Yasuhiro and Takeshita Noboru, for example, sided with big business in holding down the size of the budget. Miyazawa Kiichi and Toshio Kōmoto, who did not hold cabinet positions, favored a more expansionist fiscal policy; their support for fiscal expansion clearly was a political move against the Nakasone–Takeshita coalition within the LDP. If Miyazawa were to be minister of finance, he would have to adopt the cabinet's position. Interview with Hakuo Yanagisawa, former MOF bureaucrat and currently representative from Hamamatsu, in Shizuoka prefecture (July 1990).

38. "En 14% no kyūjōshō; kainyū mokuhyō hobo tassei ka," Nikkei, October 5, 1985.

39. "Kyōsōryoku shimpai no yushutsu gyōkai," Asahi , October 11, 1987.

40. "Rūburu gōi no kyōchō keizoku kurojikoku no sekinin towaremai," Asahi, September 22, 1987.

41. The same caveat noted earlier applies here: Japanese banks enjoyed increased business as a result of the stronger yen, but not larger profits.

42. Economic Planning Agency, Bukka repōto, (Tokyo: Economic Planning Agency, 1987), p. 29.

43. "Kyōsōryoku," Asahi, October 11, 1985; "Endaka saeki suiage," Asahi, November 26, 1985; "Endaka saeki o chusho kigyo taisakuni," Tokyo shimbun, December 4, 1985.

44. "Raigetsu ni kondankai," Nikkei, February 21, 1986.

45. "Raigetsu kara choreiri no chusho kigyo muke yushi o," Sankei, November 27, 1985.

46. "Endaka no saeki setsubi toshi ni," Yomiuri, February 14, 1986.

47. Interview with Jirō Ushio, chairman of Ushio Denki, July 16, 1990.

48. Interviews with LDP representativesi Yamashita Sōhe, June 28, 1990; Arai Shōkai, June 29, 1990; and Yosano Kaoru, July 5, 1990. Kamino Nobuo, president of Chubu Gas, said the gas industry gave up LDP contributions for a short time after the oil shock, saying they "couldn't afford political contributions without raising the price of gas substantially." They were permitted to raise their prices. Interview, July 21, 1990.

49. "Ōguchi yasuki, koguchi waridaka ni," Asahi, March 30, 1987; "Toshi gasu heikin 4% neage; kigyō chūshin, katei wa kohaba,"Sankei October 13, 1987.

50. 1988 chūshō kigyō hakusho, pp. 55–56.

51. Hiroyuki Itami, En ga yureru, kigyō wa ugoku (Tokyo: NTT shuppan, 1990), pp. 14–15.

52. Economic Planning Agency, Bukka repōto 1988 (Tokyo: EPA, 1988), pp. 31–34.

53. 1988 chūshō kigyō hakusho, p. 9.

54. William Rapp, "Firm Size and Japan's Export Structure," in Hugh Patrick, ed.,

Japanese Industrialization and Its Social Consequences (Berkeley: University of California Press, 1976).

55. In competitive markets, each firm should already be pricing at marginal costs and there should be no "room to cut costs." Only if large producers are able to price oligopolistically will they have this "room," but most industries in Japan seem to be quite competitive.

56. *1988 chūshō kigyō hakusho*, p. 33.

57. *1988 chūshō kigyō hakusho*, pp. 30–57.

58. *Kuni no yosan*, various years. Kent Calder, *Crisis and Compensation*, p. 348.

59. "Shitauke shimetsuke yameyō," *Nikkei*, December 6, 1985; "Shitauke ni shiwayose,"*Asahi*, December 17, 1985; "Shitauke ijime ni kugi,"*Nikkei*, December 17, 1985.

60. "Chūshō kigyō ni tokubetsu yūshi," *Tokyo shimbun*, November 7, 1985; the Democratic Socialist Party also submitted a bill to assist small firms, although of course this small party's bill did not pass the Diet. "Nennai ni mo jisshi,"*Nikkei*, November 10, 1985.

61. The LDP Commerce Division called for an immediate commitment to 100 billion yen in loans at 5 percent instead of the 7 percent decided upon. The long-term prime rate for top business borrowers from private financial institutions, by contrast, was 7.5 percent The special small-business rate was lowered only as the prime rate was reduced over the next year. "Yushutsu kanren 50 gyōshu shitei," *Asahi*, December 3, 1985. Nakasone's speech at the Zenkoku shōkōkai rengōkai was basically supportive of loans "depending on the need,"athough this small-business organization wanted a pledge of funding on more generous terms. "Hachikō no endaka kinkyūsaku o seifu ni yōsei,"*Yomiuri*, November 14, 1985.

62. "Chūsho no endaka taisakuhō kokaku katamaru," *Nikkei*, December 3, 1985.

63. "Bei seifu ga kenen hyōmei," *Nikkei*, December 1, 1985; one Asahi reporter agreed that the loans were intended as a bailout of LDP friends rather than as an effort to encourage domestic-oriented production. He cited the example of the stainless steel industry in Niigata using funds to help continue exporting. "Chūshō kigyō no endaka taisaku," *Asahi*, December 3, 1985. See also "Shōshi dokomade kantetsu?" *Nikkei*, December 4, 1985.

64. "Takeshita zōshō ni bei zeimu chōkan," *Sankei*, January 22, 1986; "Tsūsanshō Bēka hatsugen ni towaku," *Nikkei*, January 23, 1986. Sasaki Shuichi, vice-chairman of the Tokyo Chamber of Commerce, said the government should provide *more* assistance and ignore America's "unwelcome meddling." "Seifu taisakuhi no zōgaku o," *Nikkei*, December 15, 1985.

65. "Chūshō kigyō jigyō tenkan taisaku nado hōan," "Namae kaete, bei settoku e," *Nikkei*, January 28, 1986.

66. "Bei wa Gatto ihan teishō e," *Asahi*, February 21, 1986; MITI Minister Michio Watanabe blamed the United States for "complaining like a child." "Gatto ihan no beigawa kenkai," *Asahi*, February 25, 1986; "Bei chokusetsu settoku e keikan o ha'i," *Nikkei*, February 26, 1985. The Japanese government was prepared to appeal to GATT,

but preferred to persuade the United States to drop its charge. "Yushutsu hojokin de wa nai," *Nikkei*, February 26, 1986; Senator Danforth et al. continued talking about applying 301: "Tsūshōhō 301 jō no hatsudō taishō," *Asahi*, February 26, 1986.

67. "Bei no hihan ni hairyo," *Nikkei*, March 4, 1986; "Yahari ki ni naru ōbei no me," *Nikkei*, March 15, 1986; "Beigawa ga ryōshō kettchaku,"*Nikkei*, March 18, 1986.

68. *Kuni no yosan*, various years.

69. "Senkyo no fuatsu mo muryoku," *Yomiuri*, May 13, 1986.

70. "Kensetsu kokusai de naiju kakudai o," *Nikkei*, September 20, 1985; "Bei gikai nao hageshiii kūki," *Tokyo shimbun*, October 5, 1985; "Jiminnai ni sekkyoku yosanron ga kyūfujō," *Sankei*, September 21, 1985; "Kensetsu kokusai zōkatsu de jimin yonyaku ashinami," *Mainichi*, September 22, 1985; "Sekkyoku zaiseiron ga kyūfujō," *Asahi*, September 22, 1985; "Naiju kakudai ni bapponsaku," *Asahi*, September 25, 1985; "Yureru zaisei shijō shugi," *Nikkei*, October 1, 1985; "Kensetsu kokusai ya shotoku genzei," *Asahi*, October 2, 1985.

71. The FY 1973 budget jumped 24.6 percent from the previous year, which was an even larger percentage increase than the famous FY 1975 budget. *Kuni no yosan* (Tokyo: MOF, various volumes). Tadashi Ogawa, MOF Shingikan for the Tax Bureau, in 1985 an assistant (*hisshokan*) to MOF Takeshita, interview, July 18, 1990.

72. "Nichō en no naiju kakudai 15 nichi ni seifu kettei," *Yomiuri*, October 11, 1985; "Naiju kakudaisaiku 15 nichi kettei," *Nikkei*, October 4, 1985; "Naiju kakudai e genzei mo," *Nikkei*, October 9, 1985; "Shushō jūtaku genzei jisshi de," *Mainichi*, October 14, 1985; 1986 kuni no yosan.

73. "Naiju kakudai wa genzei de," *Sankei*, October 4, 1985; "Maimuri na kettei," *Tokyo shimbun*, October 16, 1985.

74. "Naiju kakudaisaku jimin ga fuman," *Nikkei*, October 16, 1985; "Miyazawashi naiju kakudai de kyocho,"*Asahi*, November 17, 1985; "Nihyakuokuen no tsuika yushi o," *Nikkei*, November 27, 1985; "Seikyoku karami de kappatsuka, *Asahi*, March 23, 1986; "Endaka de shushō hihan," *Nikkei*, May 8, 1986.

75. *Kuni no yosan*, volumes for 1985 and 1986.

76. "Nihon naiju kakudai mattanashi," *Nikkei*, September 26, 1985; "Tsūka kyōkyūryō sarani kosuijun ni," *Asahi*, October 9, 1985; "Chūshō kigyō ni teiri yūshi," *Nikkei*, November 26, 1985. Average bank loan rates, already down from 8.27 percent in 1980 when the official discount rate was 7.25 percent, dropped from 6.467 percent in 1985 to 4.93 percent in 1988. *1989 Toyo keizai tokei nenpo* (Tokyo: Tōyō keizai shimposha, 1989), p. 29.

77. *Seikan yōran* (Tokyo: Seisaku jihosha, 1987), pp. 290–306.

Chapter 7
Internationalization, Innovation, and the Role of Japanese Multinational Corporations in U.S.-Japan Relations

Timothy J. Curran

In Smyrna, Tennessee, a small town nestled in the foothills of the Appalachian Mountains, 240,000 cars and trucks a year roll off the assembly line at the Nissan Motor Manufacturing Corporation. The plant is the fourth largest Japanese-owned manufacturing facility in the United States, employing over 3,000 workers and revitalizing a rural and underdeveloped area. It is also a symbol of the growing impact of Japan's enormous wave of direct investment in the United States. Japanese-owned auto plants have sprung up in Flat Rock, Michigan; Georgetown, Kentucky; and Marysville, Ohio, the site of Honda America.

The trend is the same in other industries and communities as Japanese corporations respond to the high yen and the threat of protectionism with a flood of direct investment. According to the Department of Commerce figures, Japanese direct investment in the United States totaled $69.7 billion at the end of 1989. At the same time, Japanese corporate investors held a controlling interest in almost 1,000 manufacturing or assembly operations with an estimated employment base of over 400,000. Over forty American states have offices in Tokyo hoping to capture their share of the Japanese investment boom.[1]

A dream for some, a grave concern for others, Japanese investment in the United States has become a new source of tension, exacerbating an already tense economic relationship between these two trading partners. The surge of Japanese direct investment is creating concerns among American political and labor leaders who see Japan's growing presence in the United States as a threat to our economic vitality. Critics of Japanese direct investment in the United States argue that dependence on Japanese manufacturing investment for jobs and economic growth mortgages the American future. The Japanese, they say, establish manufacturing sites in the United States primarily to circumvent protectionist barriers. In addition, they argue that the manufacturing sites so far completed by the Japanese are no more than low-level assembly operations, or "screwdriver" shops, with little value-added work being performed. The long-term effect of this trend away from full-line production facilities, critics argue, will be to short-circuit the technology-development process in the United States.

American labor unions are fearful that their power will be significantly reduced or eliminated at Japanese-owned plants. And American business is afraid that the benefits of Japanese investment will elude them if they are unable to penetrate the tight web of Japanese corporate relations, which link manufacturers to an extended network of Japanese suppliers.

Americans who fear the increase of Japanese direct investment see it as the end of a process—the triumph of Japan and the conquest of U.S. industry. There is powerful evidence, however, that Japan's direct investment makes an important contribution to U.S. industrial renewal and that, in fact, the recent surge in Japanese investment is not the end of a process but the beginning of one. It is the beginning of the internationalization of Japanese companies. Japanese multinational corporations are undergoing a process of internationization in which they are transferring more of the production process and more value-added technology to their American subsidiaries. The result of this process will be to transform these subsidiaries into fully integrated companies—rather than "screwdriver shops"— capable of providing a full range of value-added jobs and new production methods to the U.S. economy.

The Pattern of Internationalization

Japanese multinational corporations in the United States, particularly those in assembly-intensive manufacturing businesses such as automobiles and electronics, are gradually building fully integrated businesses in their U.S. operations. They are moving away from primarily importing activities and simple assembly operations toward more complex product design, value engineering, and manufacturing. The result of this shift will be to produce companies that employ a full range of skills and technologies and that transfer these skills and technologies to their local work force.

To appreciate the change taking place, it is necesary to understand the production process and distribution system in assembly manufacturing industries such as automobiles or electronics, industries that the Japanese are eager to internationalize. Six key stages comprise the process: research and development, product engineering, manufacturing, marketing, distribution, and sales. If thought of as a sequential process, production begins with basic research and development of a technology—the transistor, for example, or the internal combustion engine. From there engineers work to design a product, taking the basic technology and applying other technologies to it to result in a coherent product concept. Manufacturing, which follows product design, is a complex process involving detailed negotiations and discussions with the various internal departments and outside vendors supplying the main product components, as well as the planning and implementation of the final assembly process. The management of this assembly process is key to successful manufacturing. It has often been said, for example, that Japan's great "manufacturers" are actually not in the manufacturing business, but in the business of assembling components manufactured by a network of subcontractors. The selection, management, and integration of these vendors into a total manufacturing system represents one of the great strengths and competitive advantages of many Japanese companies.

Subsequent business activities include marketing, which involves pricing, packaging, advertising, and positioning of the product, the selection and management of distribution channels, and finally the sales and ongoing servicing of the product.

It is useful to think of the business functions described as discrete functions in a sequential process beginning with research and development and ending with sales and service. In Japan, however, these business functions are thought of not as discrete functions but rather as the closely interwoven strands of an integrated product-development process. It is precisely because the elements of the process cannot be easily separated that internationalization presents so many difficulties for Japanese manufacturing companies.

Japanese companies are internationalizing by gradually moving backward along the business function process. Most automobile and electronics manufacturers began business activities in the United States by opening sales and service subsidiaries here. All of the other parts of the process, from R&D to marketing, were performed in Japan. Over time the companies have added more of the business functions to their local American subsidiaries (see figure 1).

Figure 1

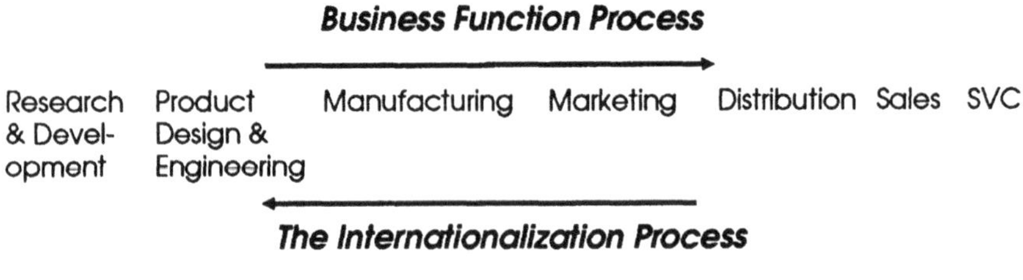

Business Function Process

→

Research & Development | Product Design & Engineering | Manufacturing | Marketing | Distribution | Sales | SVC

←

The Internationalization Process

For example, in the 1970s all of the major Japanese automobile companies had substantial sales, service, and marketing operations in the United States, but none had manufacturing, product design, or technology development. Today the situation is dramatically different. All of the major Japanese auto companies perform manufacturing assembly in the United States, and several also do product design and technology development in their American subsidiaries. With regard to manufacturing, the business function with perhaps the greatest impact on employment, the Japan Economic Institute estimates that at the end of 1989 there were 980 Japanese affiliated manufacturing companies in the United States operating over 800 manufacturing facilities. These plants employed approximately 260,000 workers. California led the list of states with 259 Japanese-affiliated plants, followed by Illinois (56), Ohio (51), New Jersey (41), and Georgia (40).[2] In some industries virtually every Japanese manufacturer has established U.S. manufacturing facilities. In the auto sector, for example, there are ten independent or jointly owned Japanese production facilities with yearly capacity of 2.3 million units and employment of over 30,000 workers. Every major Japanese automobile manufacturer is on this list.[3] The establishment of these main assembly facilities is now being followed by the creation of components facilities, either by the auto companies themselves or by their affiliated components suppliers. The most advanced of the Japanese auto companies, such as Honda, have moved from simple assembly of imported components to actual product engineering and design using locally sourced components.

To support the local manufacturing and engineering effort and to stay abreast of local technology, Japanese companies are also expanding their research and development activities in the United States. There are two approaches to domestic R&D: affiliations with American universities and research centers and the establishment of local R&D laboratories. For example, in 1987 Nippon Telephone and Telegraph and the Mitsubishi Corporation jointly established with the Battel Memorial Institute of Photonic Integration Research to explore the commercial production of optical integrated circuits.[4]

Major electronics manufacturers are establishing independent research centers in the United States. NEC has opened a lab in Princeton, New Jersey, that is expected to employ sixty researchers by 1992. NEC has ambitious goals, according to Dr. William Gear, vice president for computer science at NEC. Dr. Gear notes, "We would like to achieve the kind of reputation that IBM or Bell Labs has had." Matsushita, Mitsubishi, Ricoh, and Fijitsu have disclosed plans for similar R&D facilities.[5] Some observers see these attempts at foreign research centers as a mere attempt to imitate successful American multinational companies. Aoki Masahiko, for example, an economist at Kyoto University, believes that the key to IBM's global strength in computers "is its basic research laboratories in the United States, Switzerland, and Japan, plus 30-odd research divisions around the world."[6]

This progress from sales and service activities to local product development, manufacturing, and research is part of the changing configuration and internationalization of Japanese companies. The driving forces behind these changes have been the shifting economic and political environments in which Japanese multinational corporations must operate.

The Political and Economic Structure
Surrounding Japanese Multinationals

When Japan's automobile and electronics manufacturers began their overseas expansions in the 1960s and 1970s, the technological environment favored a strategy that emphasized centralized mass production of standardized products and export-based foreign sales. In the electronics industry, for example, the development of the transistor in 1947 coupled with the introduction of new production technologies such as printed circuit boards and integrated circuits, greatly increased mass production capabilities, and increased product quality. Consumer demand was for standarized, low-cost, quality merchandise.[7] Japanese electronics companies responded to these technological changes with an export strategy built around centralized mass production facilities for radios, televisions, and other electronic products.

Economic considerations also favored an export-based strategy. Until the early 1970s the yen/dollar exchange rate was fixed at ¥360 to $1, and ever after the adjustment and introduction of flexible exchange rates in 1972 the yen remained relatively low. In the trade area, the Kennedy Round of Multilateral Trade Negotiations in the early 1960s ushered in an era of declining tariffs and the dismantling of other barriers to trade in the United States and other countries.[8]

As a result of these factors, Japan's major automotive and electronics manufacturers pursued an overseas strategy that centralized all major product development, manufacturing, and marketing operations in Japan. This export-led strategy was reinforced by Japanese management systems that are heavily culture bound and favor a closed decision-making system based on intensive face-to-face interactions. Well-known features of the Japanese management system, such as *nemawashi* (consultation) and the *ringi* decision procedure are difficult to export, or at least difficult to open to non-Japanese, and so made Japanese companies unlikely candidates for internationalization.[9]

But in the last twenty years the political winds have changed. Growing protectionism in Japan's major foreign markets has necessitated the placement of manufacturing operations outside Japan. In 1977, the United States and Japan negotiated a voluntary export agreement on television sets. By the end of the decade every major Japanese television manufacturer was assembling television sets in the United States. Following the voluntary export restraint guidelines on Japanese automoblies begun in 1982, Toyota, Nissan, Mazda, and Mitsubishi began American production of their product.

New production technologies are also facilitating the move of manufacturing offshore. With the development of computer-aided design and computer-integrated manufacturing, the production volume needed for efficient operation has declined, enabling companies to establish multiple manufacturing sites. Consumers are demanding it, too, with a growing desire for customized and specialized models. At Matsushita, for example, the portable audio product range was increased from fifteen models in 1980 to thirty in 1985, thus reducing the benefits of centralized production.[10]

The increasingly important role played by software in many products has also stimulated a higher degree of local content in Japanese products sold in the United States. For example, production robots operate on American manufacturing lines in different ways than they do in Japan due to the different work habits, union rules, and skill levels of American workers. These differences are controlled by the robot's operating software. Japanese robot manufacturing companies that have tried to export robots and software to the American market have generally failed; the mechanics of the robots work well, but the software does not meet local needs. To succeed, these manufacturing companies are shifting the software design function, and in some cases the hardware manufacturing function, to the local American subsidiary.

The Fuji-Xerox Example

The process of internationalization can be illustrated by the case of Fuji-Xerox, the 50-50 joint venture between Rank Xerox and Fuji Film that has grown to become one of Japan's most successful copier companies. When Fuji-Xerox was established in Japan in 1962, its sole purpose was to market in Japan Xerox copiers manufactured in the United States. In the ensuing years, as Fuji-Xerox developed its own internal engineering and manufacturing capability, it gradually began to exert its independence by developing and manufacturing its own products in Japan. In the book *Xerox: American Samurai* author Gary Jacobsen describes the Fuji-Xerox subsidiary this way: "The history of Fuji-Xerox in a sentence: A marketing subsidiary that sold American made equipment in Japan becomes an expert design and manufacturing company that wants the unhindered ability to sell Japanese made equipment in the United States and around the world. . . . In two decades [Fuji-Xerox] has grown from a strictly sales organization into a completely self-sufficient high technology company with annual revenues exceeding $1.5 billion."[11]

For the first ten years of its existence, Fuji-Xerox took what the parent company, Xerox, had to offer and marketed those products in Japan. Sometimes the products were not completely appropriate for the Japanese market, as with the Xerox 7000, a large-volume copier. When the product was introduced in Japan, secretaries had to stand on a small box to operate it since it had been designed for generally taller Americans.[12] Fuji-Xerox gradually became frustrated with the products that did not fit its market needs, and it began to develop its own products. This effort became especially important as the low and more expensive end of the copier market boomed and the parent Xerox Corporation did not respond with a competitive product line. Starting with development of products for its own use in Japan, Fuji-Xerox expanded its activities to the point where today products it produces are sold by the Xerox organization worldwide.

A key figure in the emergence of Fuji-Xerox as a successful and fully integrated manufacturing company was Kobayashi Yōtarō "Tony", president of Fuji-Xerox. In 1976 Kobayashi led the "New Xerox" quality-control movement at Fuji-Xerox, which was instrumental in helping the company overcome the effects of the oil shock and establishing the foundations for growth. The first goal of the movement was to reduce by half the time and cost of developing a new copier. The FX-3500, a mid-range copier developed in 1976, achieved the goal. The 3500 development project was Fuji-Xerox's declaration of independence from Xerox. Xerox executives, seeing duplication in Fuji-Xerox's development of the 3500, asked Kobayashi to stop development of the product. Kobayashi refused. He said, "As long as I am running this company I can no longer be totally dependent on you for developing products. We are going to have to develop our own." [13]

Fuji-Xerox has devoted great efforts toward improving its total quality and manufacturing efficiency. In the early 1980s the company won the coveted Deming Prize, Japan's highest award for quality. Product development is now one of the company's strengths, together with training and engineering. Fuji-Xerox spends 8.5 percent of revenue on R&D, and in 1984 it completed a training center at the cost of $8 million, where roughly 6,000 workers per year are trained. Included is English-language training, which is required for anyone having contact with the parent corporation.[14]

American managers at the parent Xerox also played a role in the development of Fuji-Xerox. In 1971, for example, Xerox executives Peter McColough and Joe Wilson urged Fuji-Xerox to develop an independent manufacturing capability by taking over the Fuji Film manufacturing plants, which had previously been used for copier assembly. David Kearns, the current Xerox chairman, also encouraged the development of Xerox's foreign subsidiary. He recalls thinking in 1975 after his first visit to Fuji-Xerox in Japan, "How is Fuji-Xerox ever going to be successful? They were basically taking equipment designed in the United States and making changes to it for their market. What that did was bring the product to market later and at a higher cost against their competitors over there. . . . I encouraged them to begin to develop some products on their own, which they wanted to do."[15] At the same time Kearns was not involved in product development, and he notes that many of the Xerox executives who were directly involved in product planning and development did not share his enthusiasm for encouraging Fuji-Xerox's independence. In fact, many mid-level Xerox executives believed that the creation of an independent product-development capability at Fuji-Xerox represented as much a competitive threat to Xerox as did Canon or Ricoh.

Today Fuji-Xerox is accepted as a Japanese corporation, contributing a full range of manufacturing, engineering, and other jobs to the Japanese economy. It also contributes to the total global competitiveness of Xerox Corporation by providing competitive low- and mid-range copiers to the company's lineup. Other American companies in Japan, such as IBM Japan and Texas Instruments, that have made similar investments in Japan—establishing totally integrated subsidiaries—are equally accepted.

Japanese companies in the United States have not proceeded quite as far along the internationalization road as Fuji-Xerox, but some, such as Honda America, have made important progress and are emerging as fully integrated subsidiaries.

Honda America

The start of Honda's American strategy was in 1959 when Honda America was established in Los Angeles. Like other Japanese companies, Honda followed an export strategy for the introduction of its motorcycles into the U.S. market. From the beginning, however, Honda demonstrated a global outlook, particularly focused on success in the U.S. market. For example, when Honda began to look at its first export markets for motorcycles in the late 1950s, both European and Southeast Asian markets offered greater short-term possibilities due to the greater acceptance of motorcycles in those areas. According to Fujisawa Takeo, vice president of Honda at the time, "It was my long held contention that America was where Honda would be able to make its dreams come true. . . . I was convinced that a product that couldn't make it in America could never become an international product."[16] Honda America was started with a staff of ten, including five Japanese.

As early as 1974 Honda started to study the feasibility of local production of motorcycles and cars in the United States. Honda officials are quick to point out that this was well in advance of any trade friction in the transportation area. Sugiura Hideo, retired chairperson of Honda, has said, "I wish to emphasize that our decision to produce in the United States was not meant to circumvent trade restrictions."[17] Rather, the localization of production was already a central part of Honda's global strategy. According to Sugiura, "A corporation does not merely make profits by exporting completed products: it carries out production activities where major markets exist."[18] Honda began production of motorcycles in Marysville, Ohio, in 1979, and automobiles in 1982. Auto production at that plant is currently 360,000 units per year.

Honda engineers understood that having production and design capabilities close to the market helped them respond to the local market needs in much the same way that Fuji-Xerox tried to serve their local market with domestic machines. One of the first motorcycles Honda began producing in Ohio was the Gold Wing, a large bike designed in Japan. Honda engineers observed how the bike was being used in the United States and discovered that rather than becoming a "superbike" as the engineers in Japan had intended, the Gold Wing was being used for long-distance touring. Honda's American development team redesigned the bike, adding features better suited for touring. As the *Economist* noted, "The effect was to transform a Japanese product that was also built in America into an American product built only in America. The Gold Wing model is now made only in the United States and exported to fourteen other countries, including Japan."[19]

When production began at the Marysville plant in 1979, workers began by assembling parts supplied directly from Honda Japan or by Japanese suppliers. As Honda has built a local network of suppliers, and as the local work force has been trained in production techniques and the "Honda Way," more of the component production and design work has been shifted to the U.S. subsidiary. In 1987 Honda announced a five-part strategy that was intended to make the automobile manufacturing operation in Ohio "a fully integrated, self-reliant entity." [20] According to Sugiura, the plan was as follows:

- By 1991, 70,000 Ohio-built cars would be exported to various world markets, including Japan.
- The number of engineers engaged in research and development activities in North America would be increased to 500 by 1991, compared with 200 in 1989. Another 200 engineers would design and develop new production equipment and machinery.
- A new automobile production plant would soon start operating adjacent to the existing factory. It would ultimately produce 150,000 cars a year, bringing Honda's total car production capacity in Ohio to 510,000 units annually.
- The engine plant located in Anna, Ohio, would be expanded to produce half a million engines per year.
- The domestic content of the Ohio-built cars would reach 75 percent in the near future.

The first product to reflect this emphasis on local design and development is the new Honda Accord station wagon, which was designed by Americans at Honda facilities in Torrance, California, and built in the Ohio plant. According to *Fortune* magazine, "It is the most American car ever produced by the Japanese."[21] The Accord wagon is an American design, but one derived from an existing Honda model. Building the car "required Honda to teach its United States employees, most of whom are American, sophisticated engineering skills that in the past were not needed at Japanese plants in the United States, which imported many parts and simply assembled them." [22] Plant workers in Ohio are committed to developing their new skills by producing their own, original auto designs in the future, and Honda appears ready to support them. According to John Adams, who supervises 150 engineers at the Marysville complex, "Eventually we will be able to create full and original vehicle models here but we have to learn gradually the way Honda wants it done; you have to learn by doing."[23]

Matsushita

Matsushita is another Japanese firm that is seeking to expand aggressively its manufacturing and research activities in North America. Best known for its brand-name products, Panasonic, Technics, National, and Quasar, Matsushita is the world's largest consumer electronics company with revenues of over $40 billion. Spurred by the same political and economic pressures that moved Honda and other Japanese companies, Matsushita has also been driven by the philosophy of its founder, Matsushita Kōnosuke, which holds that for a company to be successful it must give back to society a return on the assets it has borrowed, such as land, people, and resources.

Compared to other Japanese electronics companies, such as Sony, Matsushita has traditionally been more focused on the domestic Japanese market where it holds a commanding market share based on a network of over 20,000 "National Shops" that sell Matsushita products in virtually every village and neighborhood in Japan. By the late 1980s, however, the company has focused on the international expansion of its manufacturing, resulting in over fifty overseas manufacturing companies in twenty-six countries. [24]

In North America Matsushita began manufacturing in 1965 with a clock radio assembly operation in Puerto Rico. Between 1986 and 1991, twelve factories were added bringing the total number of manufacturing facilities to nineteen. Matsushita now has more than 11,000 employees in North America with over 50 percent employed in some aspect of manufacturing.

Matsushita is moving aggressively to expand its network of local suppliers, to cultivate internal engineering talent, and to develop an organizational system that allows U.S. subsidiary executives to participate in product development and other discussions with headquarters.

Matsushita's target is to have 50 percent of the products it sells in North America manufactured there. The goal is also to establish a network of over 1,000 local suppliers who can provide 70 percent local content of the products manufactured in North America. As part of the internationalization effort, Matsushita encourages the exchange of personnel between Japan and the United States. These extend from routine product-planning meetings where Japanese and Amercian engineers and marketing personnel jointly plan new products, to sophisticated seminars conducted in Japan for American and other overseas executives in which the total global strategy of the company is analyzed and discussed.

The process of internationalization of Japanese companies in the United States has advanced to the point where Honda, Matsushita, and other Japanese companies are beginning to do a significant amount of manufacturing and even design work in their local subsidiaries. As this process continues there are three important areas that will help determine the continued success of the internationalization process.

The Need for Critical Mass

When Fuji-Xerox sought to develop its own copier in Japan, in opposition to Rochester's wishes, it was critical that Fuji-Xerox management have available to it a well-established manufacturing base, a group of engineers skilled in all aspects of the copier development process, and a network of local suppliers of key copier components who were themselves intimately familiar with Fuji's product line and product needs. Honda America's ability to create the Accord wagon a derivative of a best-selling model, is a result of Honda's previous efforts to staff and train its team of engineers, the construction of full-scale assembly and component-production facilities, and the creation of a local network of Japanese and American component suppliers.

In short, the continued ability of Japanese companies in the United States to move beyond the assembly manufacturing stage to become fully integrated manufacturing companies will depend on the creation of a critical mass of skills such as manufacturing, engineering, marketing, and organization, and the development of a manufacturing and supply infrastructure.

A critical mass of skills and capabilities is especially important because of the unique nature of the innovation process in Japanese companies. Nonaka Ikujirō of Hitotsubashi University has argued that Japanese organizations use a "redundant, overlapping" approach to information processing and innovation, in contrast to western organizations that employ a more sequential, "problem-solving" approach.[25] In the West this process begins with market research, which determines what kind of products to produce at what price and in what quantity. American firms traditionally use an orderly, sequential approach to development, breaking the development process into discrete parts and then solving them in a sequential fashion. According to Nonaka, "Japanese organizations, in contrast to this sequential approach, employ an aggregated or overlapping approach where the multiple parts of the innovation process overlap and there is intensive sharing of information."[26]

This process can be seen at work at Fuji-Xerox in the development of the FX-3500, the pathbreaking copier that signaled Fuji-Xerox's independent product development capability. Fuji-Xerox calls their approach to product development the "Sashimi System," because it resembles the slices of sashimi overlapping on a plate.

> The Sashimi System requires extensive interaction not only among project members but also with suppliers. The FX-3500 team invited [suppliers] to join the project at the very start. [They eventually produced 90 percent of the parts for the model.] Each side regularly visited the other's plants and kept information channels open at all times. This kind of exchange and openness—both within the project team and with suppliers—increases speed and flexibility. Fuji-Xerox shortened the

development time from 38 months for an earlier model to 29 months for the FX-3500. [27]

In this way Fuji-Xerox has created a tight, interactive network among the members of its internal project team and its outside network of suppliers. The internal product development team at Fuji-Xerox, moreover, consisted of specialists from marketing, design, production, and product planning who had each had multiple previous job responsibilities. Because of their diverse backgrounds, Nonaka notes, "They not only bore information pertaining to their specific functions, but bore information pertaining to other functions as well."[28]

Will Japanese multinationals be able to transfer this product innovation process to their overseas subsidiaries? The process will require a critical mass of skills among the local staff of these companies, and the development of a network of loyal and committed local suppliers. It will require patience on the part of local staff as they learn the necessary product knowledge and organizational skills, and perseverance on the part of local suppliers who try to become part of a Japanese company's local supply network.

The Need for an Open System

Despite progress in transferring multiple business functions to overseas subsidiaries, many Japanese companies have yet to allow their subsidiaries to act as integrated or unified units. Instead the individual functional units report directly back to their functional counterpart in Japan; marketing in the United States reports to marketing in Japan, manufacturing to manufacturing, and so forth. Honda America, for example, is set up as five separate organizations in the United States: Honda Sales, Honda Manufacturing, Honda Service, and so on. Each of these functional units has strong ties back to Japan and close daily interaction with Japanese management in the corporate functional counterpart, with correspondingly less control over the subsidiary by local top management. This organizational structure inhibits the development of a unified identity within the subsidiary and constrains its ability for innovative action. [29]

In a recent report analyzing the organization and performance of Japanese subsidiaries in the United States, the Boston Consulting Group recommended "that the U.S. subsidiaries have a single country head with full responsibility for the plans performance of the subsidiary; divisions within the subsidiary should be organized around customer segments rather than functional lines and report to the country head rather than their functional counterpart in Japan; the U.S. subsidiary should be empowered to develop its own business strategies." [30]

The development of fully integrated subsidiaries that are also able to participate in the parent company's global strategy will require that headquarters open its decision-making process to foreign participation. As noted above, Japanese corporations have a closed, culturally bound decision-making system that stresses intensive face-to-face interaction. According to Bartlett and Yoshihara, "The very nature of the system makes it virtually impenetrable to non-Japanese multinationals except at the periphery."[31] The challenge for Japanese multinationals is not necessarily to change this system, but rather to open it to foreign participation. Many companies are beginning to do this by developing the ability of local American management to understand how the decision process works and to participate in it. Local management is taken on frequent trips to Japan where they are encouraged to develop their own network of contacts within headquarters. Language classes are offered for those wishing to learn Japanese. In many companies all meetings in the local subsidiary are conducted in English in order to permit local management participation.

One step Japanese companies must take to ensure the long-term development of their American subsidiaries is to create a deeper local management team. A recent MITI survey indicated that in this respect Japanese multinationals lag behind foreign multinationals. According to the MITI survey 45.4 percent of the managing directors of Japanese companies overseas are Japanese transferred from their head offices. At foreign companies in Japan the comparable number is 17.3 percent.[32] One Japanese researcher asked a group of Japanese businessmen whether a Japanese or non-Japanese would be best suited to head the Japanese subsidiary of a foreign company. The majority responded that a Japanese would be best for the following reasons: only a Japanese can understand Japan; without Japanese language it is impossible to work in Japan; it is easy for Japanese middle management to work if the president is Japanese; it is easier to hire good people coming out of college if the president is Japanese. Conversely, when this group was asked why non-Japanese were not made the heads of Japanese subsidiaries overseas, they could not give a clear reason.[33]

The decision-making system *can* work, and local management *can* effectively participate in it by taking the time to understand the system and by sticking to business fundamentals: by mastering the details of a particular business function, understanding the overall corporate goals, developing a personal information and influence network, and openly communicating with local and headquarters Japanese staff. Undoubtedly the system is difficult to penetrate. However, many Japanese companies in the United States have a stated policy and desire to internationalize their companies and open their decision making to trusted foreign employees; they know they must gain local input to succeed in foreign markets. Local management staff that takes the time to understand the system and build a personal network of supporters can successfully operate within it.

The Need for Leadership

Several men played important leadership roles in the development of Fuji-Xerox from a sales and marketing subsidiary to a fully integrated manufacturing and product development center. Tony Kobayashi was committed to the development of Fuji-Xerox as a *Japanese* company as well as a key part of the global Xerox network. He took the steps to improve quality, increase local manufacturing, and train a local work force. At Xerox headquarters Peter McColough and Joe Wilson strongly encouraged the subsidiary to strengthen its manufacturing capability, and David Kearns supported Kobayashi's desire for local Japanese product development, in spite of midlevel opposition.

The continued development of strong, integrated Japanese subsidiaries that contribute to the achievement of parent-company goals as well as to the growth of the U.S. economy will require leadership on both sides of the Pacific. In Japan management needs to recognize the inherent benefits to effective internationalization and also see the need to contribute to the real development of overseas economies. As Yoshihara Hideki of Kobe University argues, "In promoting multinationalization, it would be advisable to abandon the passive attitude held up to the present and in its place seek the inherent advantages possessed by the multinational company. That is a conversion from 'multinationalization under duress' to 'multinationalization in quest of advantages.'"[34]

Local American management of Japanese companies must also show leadership and initiative in developing the innovation capability of their subsidiaries. Although the senior management of Xerox in the United States broadly supported the development of Fuji-Xerox, it was strong initiative and vision by Kobayashi that drove the development of that subsidiary. Likewise, local American management of Japanese subsidiaries not only must be concerned with their personal fortunes and careers within Japanese companies, they must also work to make their companies fully integrated organizations, contributing value-added jobs and technology to the U.S. economy.

Japanese Multinationals and the Future of U.S.-Japanese Relations

In 1986 research scientists working in IBM's Zurich Research Laboratory announced the discovery of a new class of ceramic-copper oxides that become superconducting at higher transition temperatures. In 1987 these scientists were awarded the Nobel Prize in physics for their efforts. Twenty years after Jean-Jacques Servan-Schreiber published "The American Challenge" warning that an unfettered flood of American investment into the continent "would consign European industry to a subsidiary role and Europe herself to the position of a satellite," European scientists working in the European laboratory of an American corporation were awarded the Nobel Prize. In Europe, Japan, and other countries, IBM is accepted as a local company that provides real advantages to the local economy. This is partially the result of its strategic placement of research and production facilities in different countries and its use of local nationals in key executive

positions. Such accomplishments are not out of reach for the U.S. research
subsidiaries of Japanese companies.

Japan will always be a competitor of the United States in significant industrial sectors and to individual American companies within those sectors. However, to the extent that Japanese companies contribute jobs and technology to
the U.S. economy, it will create broad constituencies in the United States for a
strong and stable U.S.-Japanese relationship. These constituencies will include
the direct employees of Japanese enterprises, which could total as many as one
million within the decade, the employees of supplier firms that become part of
the Japanese components-supply network, and finally—the largest group—satisfied consumers of products made by Japanese companies in the United States.

The increased pace of overseas investment and internationalization by Japanese
multinationals will also have an impact on Japan, most notably on the structure of
Japanese companies, on the nature of relations within Japan's industrial groupings
or *keiretsu*, and on the relationship between the Japanese government and the
business community. Japanese companies will have an increasing percentage of
their total work force non-Japanese, and they will increasingly seek to internationalize their senior managements. As the chart below shows, among Japan's top
electronics makers 34 percent of their total work force are non-Japanese.[35] For
Sharp, Sanyo, and Alps, more than half the work force is non-Japanese (see table 1).

Table 1

Non-Japanese Employees as a Percentage of Total Work Force

Company	Percent	Company	Percent
Sharp	55	Canon	33
Alps	50	Mitsubishi	30
Sanyo	50	NEC	19
Sony	42	Fujitsu	12
Toshiba	38	Hitachi	8
Matsushita	37		

Source: Nikkei sangyo shimbun, in Electronic Business, July 24, 1989.

As the size and seniority of the foreign work force within Japanese companies
grows, it will create a strong internationalist constituency within those firms. As
local nationals assume the top management positions within Japanese subsidiaries,
they will be able to exercise influence within the highest levels of the corporate
structure. And it is not far-fetched to think that within the foreseeable future foreign
executives will be placed on the boards of directors of parent Japanese companies.

In addition to developing a strong and effective foreign constituency, many
Japanese companies will seek to internationalize the Japanese management and
work force. Canon, for example has begun teaching English to its blue-collar

Japanese production workers to enable them to work more effectively with workers overseas. Canon is also broadening the exposure of its management corps by increasing international training, and increasing the number of executives who serve overseas. According to Canon, those individuals on an executive career path will be expected to spend fifteen years overseas as part of their development process. In addition, other companies are internationalizing their operations by bringing foreign employees to corporate headquarters in Japan for extended assignments in an attempt to develop an elite corps of foreigners with a clear understanding of the parent company.[36] The purpose and result of these and other tactics will be to create a more internationalized work force and executive corps in many of Japan's most prominent and influential companies.

Japanese analysts have pointed out that the true test of Japan's internationalization should not be the number of tourists visiting Japan or the number of Japanese businessmen traveling abroad, but rather "the capacity of the domestic system to accommodate within itself alien activities—people, systems, experiences."[37] Japanese companies are significant and influential actors within Japanese society. As these companies accommodate larger and larger numbers of foreign workers, as they find meaningful and influential roles for foreign executives, and as their Japanese senior executives expand their international outlook, it will inject a powerful internationalist influence into Japanese society.

Increased internationalization will affect two other institutions of Japanese society: the *keiretsu* or industrial groupings of related firms, and the "iron triangle" or network of relations among the Japanese business community, government bureaucracy, and Liberal Democratic party (LDP). *Keiretsu* or industrial groupings is an important institutional feature of Japanese business that has had a major impact on the competitiveness of Japanese industry and, more recently, the difficulty of U.S.-Japanese trade relations. As noted earlier, the existence of close networks between manufacturers and suppliers is a key part of the innovation process in Japan. Because of the closeness of these relations it has also made it difficult for foreign firms to penetrate the Japanese market—even when these foreign firms marketed a competitive product. Japanese companies are willing to pay more for a component or service from a member of their suppliers network in order to preserve the integrity of the network.

One of the continuing problems of U.S.-Japanese trade relations is the tendency of these supplier firms to follow manufacturers overseas. For example, not only does Honda America displace sales by GM, Ford, and other domestic U.S. auto makers, the Japanese supplier firms that have followed Honda to the United States also displace domestic U.S. auto parts suppliers. As important as this problem is, the reverse can also be true. Increasingly, American firms are penetrating the supply networks of Japanese firms in the United States. Over time these American firms will build credibility and contacts within Japanese manufacturers that will enable them to protect their American business and, possibly, allow them to export to Japan. By becoming part of a *keiretsu* relationship in the United States, an astute and aggressive American firm can develop the relationships needed to do business in Japan.

Finally, the increased internationalization of Japanese business will have an impact on the structure of Japanese domestic politics, particularly business-government relations. Since the LDP has governed Japan for such a long time, business groupings, related government agencies, and interested conservative Diet members have formed close associations and worked together in a mutually supportive way. Professor Satō Seizaburō has noted that "this so-called iron triangle which permeates all administrative areas, constitutes a prerequisite for the smooth functioning of 'administrative guidance,' while at the same time it has also functioned as an effective non-tariff barrier with which to deny the entry of foreign enterprises into Japan."[38] Satō goes on to note that the pace of technological change and the increased internationalization of Japanese business "have exerted a relaxing influence on the unity of the sectoral associations and the cohesion of the 'iron triangle.' "[39]

As Japanese firms see more and more of their total business volume and manufacturing being conducted outside of Japan, and as international constituencies of workers and management develop, the interests of Japanese business will begin to diverge from the more narrowly focused domestic interests of the bureaucracy and politicians. Perhaps the most visible example of this is the increased pressure of Japanese business for agricultural liberalization in spite of resistance by the ruling party. From the point of view of U.S.-Japanese relations, however, the relaxation of the iron triangle will be a double-edged sword since it may weaken the foundation of the LDP's coalition and the party's current policy of close collaboration with the United States.

Notes

The opinions expressed in this paper are those of the author only and do not necessarily reflect those of his employer or other institutions.

1. Japan Economic Institute, *Japan's Expanding U. S. Manufacturing Presence: 1989 Update* (Washington, D.C., April 1991).
2. Ibid., p. 3.
3. *Business Week,* August 14, 1989.
4. *Japan Economic Journal,* December 31, 1988.
5. *New York Times,* November 11, 1990.
6. *Economist,* June 24, 1989.

7. Christopher Bartlett and Sumantra Ghoshal, *Managing Across Borders: The Transnational Solution* (Boston: Harvard Business School Press, 1989), pp. 26–29.

8. Ibid.

9. Christopher Bartlett and Hideki Yoshihara, "New Challenges for Japanese Multinationals: Is Organization Adaption Their Achilles Heel?" *Human Resources Management* (Spring 1988): 25.

10. Ibid., p. 23.

11. Gary Jacobsen, *Xerox: American Samurai* (New York: Macmillan, 1986), pp. 296-97.

12. Ibid., p. 303.

13. Ibid., p. 299.

14. Ibid., p. 312.

15. Ibid., p. 305.

16. The quote from Fujisawa's memoirs is cited in "A Case Study of Honda America," unpublished manuscript translated by Joe Greenholtz, p. 9.

17. Hideo Sugiura, "How Honda Localizes Its Global Strategy," *Sloan Management Review* (Fall 1990): 79.

18. Ibid., p. 78.

19. *Economist*, April 15, 1989, p. 79.

20. Sugiura, *How Honda Localizes its Global Strategy*, p. 80.

21. *Fortune*, September 10, 1990, p. 65.

22. *New York Times*, December 14, 1990.

23. *New York Times*, March 14, 1990.

24. Bartlett and Ghoshal, *Managing Across Borders*, p. 75.

25. Ikujiro Nonaka, "Redundant, Overlapping Organization: A Japanese Approach to Managing the Innovation Process," *California Management Review* (Spring 1990), 32, 3:27.

26. Ibid.

27. Hirotaka Takeuchi and Ikujiro Nonaka, "The New New Product Development Game," *Harvard Business Review* (January–February 1986): 141.

28. Nonaka, "Redundant, Overlapping Organization," *California Management Review*, p. 36.

29. William Taylor, "Managing Across Cultures: Human Resources Issues in Japanese Companies in the U.S.," *Japan Society*, 1989, p. 22.

30. Ibid.

31. Bartlett and Yoshihara, "New Challenge for Japanese Multinationals," p. 26.

32. *Japan Economic Journal*, December 31, 1988, p. 5.

33. Hideki Yoshihara, "Internationalization at the Top," *Management Japan* 20, 2(1987):8.

34. Ibid., p. 12.

35. Figures from *Nikkei sangyo shimbun*, cited in *Electronic Business*, July 24, 1989.

36. *Electronic Business*, July 24, 1989.

37. Alan Romberg, *The United States and Japan* (New York: Council on Foreign Relations, 1987), p. 14.

38. Satō Seizaburō, "Social Change in Japan and its Impact on U.S.-Japan Relations, in ibid., p. 44.

39. Ibid., p. 45.

Chapter 8
Japan's Nuclear Energy Quest

Michael W. Donnelly

The nuclear age was born in the embers and human horrors of Hiroshima and Nagasaki. Atomic bombs first dropped on Japanese soil mark a tragic turning point in this century. Since those demented days in August 1945 the world of the atom has haunted international politics, profoundly shaped the content of scientific and technological invention, and scarred our modern psyche. What happened in Japan has become a frightening scientific paradigm used by the rest of the world as one measure of the potential consequences of unchecked atomic power.[1]

Now the first nation to experience nuclear extinction is considered by atomic power advocates throughout the world as a rare example of a more positive sort: how a country can successfully meet the economic, political, and technological challenges of nuclear energy development.

For Japan, a country plagued by a lack of natural energy resources, the civilian use of nuclear power is central to the viability and direction of the nation's entire economic strategy. [2] As the largest importer of energy in the world, the government is realistically wary of unpredictable international energy markets. What can be properly characterized as a Nuclear Quest is underway, framed by bureaucratic, political, technocratic, financial, and corporate elites, to create a complete Japanese fuel cycle and thus virtual national independence in all aspects of nuclear power generation.[3]

Among democratic industrial countries, no country has in place such ambitious plans for a substantial increase in nuclear power capacity. Widespread doubt in the United States is part of a worldwide trend toward lowered nuclear expectations as national programs have been halted, slowed down, or crippled by one problem after another.[4]

Although achievement of national independence is a long way off and the national effort not without major uncertainties, Japan has become an international standard-bearer for the development of nuclear power.[5] Technological and engineering practices are studied very closely abroad. How Japan deals with nuclear power economics, long-term planning, the dangers of radiation, nonpoliferation agreements, reactor safety, management of radioactive waste, and domestic political disagreement all have profound international implications. Japan and France now provide new paradigms of "national success" for advocates, replacing as they have the United States.

Indeed, in recent years pronuclear forces in Japan have come to see their task of maintaining faith in nuclear power as extending well beyond national shores, recognizing that the country cannot pursue its Nuclear Quest in isolation, no matter how safe, reliable, and necessary the atom might be for their own nation's goals of security, independence, and economic prosperity. As a supplier of nuclear technology, equipment, and services, the nuclear industry in Japan is also positioned to become a formidable competitor in any future nuclear export markets.[6]

The Domestic Politics of National Ambitions

The central concern of this analysis is to suggest how best to understand the politics of nuclear power development in Japan. A good deal of commentary suggests that the country has succeeded in building a substantial civil nuclear program, in part, because there has been so little bitterness, open contention, and political disagreement. Politics hardly counts. Judged from the secondary literature, the Nuclear Quest is a kind of national exercise in applied engineering. It goes like this.[7]

A geological map shows that Japan lacks basic energy resources, making the nation dependent and vulnerable in dealing with unpredictable international markets. Economic rationality, a scarcity of options, and national self-interest all dictate that the country should develop nuclear power, given its comparative cost advantage, predictable and stable supply, and thus its potential for enhancing national self-sufficiency.

Domestic organizational structures, technological excellence, and managerial talent facilitate the venture. Government officials are able and powerful, institutional arrangements in both the private and public sectors centralize decision making, the Liberal Democratic party remains the dominant political party, and government is generously endowed with policy instruments necessary to achieve official objectives. Goals and policies can thus be formulated within "state-centered" policy networks. The Quest is made even easier because public participation in politics is passive, political opposition to the LDP government is weak, and the nation's courts are extremely reluctant to rule against government decisions.

As this study will show, this applied engineering model is certainly suggestive but incomplete, while the apolitical picture and emphasis only on Tokyo does not do justice to the underlying complexities. Nuclear energy is not a technical end in itself. It is also a means to achieve other values as well:

economic, political, social, ethical, and national. Thus ambitious goals for nuclear self-sufficiency have emerged out of politics: disagreements over priorities and judgments based on considerations that go beyond how to technically build a reliable power reactor. The exercise of power has been crucial in resolving these differences. The ability of the nuclear power advocates to achieve future goals will also depend on the exercise of political power and the nature of policy choices as much as it does on science, technological excellence, and rational engineering.

This view will not be surprising to participants in the Nuclear Quest. Even the most zealous technological enthusiast or the most fervent cost-benefit advocate will acknowledge that many nontechnological imponderables obstruct such a long-term, risky enterprise. A good deal of attention is thus given by pronuclear forces—at the apex of power—to maintaining a style of politics that permits constant monitoring and feedback about errors, successes, wrong interpretations, and changing circumstances. Ample opportunity is reserved for those considered most qualified to calibrate anew, adjust, and revise.

It is an approach to policy making that shows no blind faith in technology nor undue optimism about the capacity of humans to respect all the private and public interests involved or to do the job well. Research, sober analysis, permanent consultation, and careful but not excessively explicit planning are requisites to reconciling differences and reducing risk to the minimum. An atmosphere of steady progress also helps reassure an uncertain public. Basic assumptions and dissenting views, however, are not easily raised for open discussion in this style of bureaucratic, technocratic, yet ritual-infused politics.

Policy implementation greatly complicates the picture. A whole host of practical issues are added to what is already a world of uncertainty. Participants are different, too. Implementation is more decentralized while policy is more directly a part of the complex social context of human communities. Residents of small villages are asked to adapt to new technological forms. Farmers, fisherman, environmental groups, labor unions, citizen groups, antinuclear activists, local politicians, and many others who are not invited to participate in designing the Nuclear Quest are apt to express dissenting views, in a different rhetoric and style of politics.

Utilities and government officials in recent times have been forced to deal with the politics of open confrontation, the questioning of major premises, a critique of what is said to be a secretive, unreliable, risky, and arrogant style of centralized decision making. Advocates of the Nuclear Quest must win over people who see their communities, economic interests, and occupational aspirations threatened by technological expansion. A call to opposition joins people who believe themselves victims and who question both the feasibility and desirability of nuclear growth. Political tensions are exacerbated around competing claims of technology and bureaucracy against those of participation, local citizenship, and the fear of nuclear terror.

Moreover, since Chernobyl showed the size of the population that might be at risk in the event of a nuclear disaster, what has been an essentially localized antinuclear movement is developing into a national effort. Local protests are reported nationwide on television and analyzed at length in the written press. Members of the pronuclear community reluctantly participate in televised debates with their critics.

Different ideas about what values and interests should be considered with nuclear power, different styles, and codes of behavior—even different language—assure that there is less than perfect communication or mutual understanding. The clash helps determine what has become the two-layered character of nuclear power politics in Japan: formulating the Nuclear Quest and managing the Nuclear Quest.

Approaches to foreign economic policies that emphasis the nation-state as a rational, unitary actor in the international system are inadequate in this case. Nor can Japan's nuclear policies be simply derived from its resource endowments or position within the international structure of nations. Foreign policy is rooted in domestic politics and priorities. Thus far, nuclear advocates have the upper hand but there are signs of change.

The Nuclear Industry

As of January 1991 there were thirty-nine commercial reactors operating in Japan with an aggregate capacity of about 31.5 megawatts (MWe) supplying nearly 26 percent of Japan's total generated electricity power.[8] About 10 percent of the country's total energy now comes from nuclear power. All but one are light water reactors (LWR). In addition, the prototype advanced thermal reactor (ATR) called *Fugen* sells its output on a commercial basis. An additional eleven LWRs are under construction, and three more are officially in the planning stage.

At the time of the first oil crisis, nuclear power's share in the nation's electricity supply was only 2 percent. Now it is Japan's single most important source of electricity, exceeding slightly that provided by oil-powered thermal reactors. While Japan ranks third in the world in terms of installed generating capacity (following the United States, and France), other nations are more dependent on nuclear power. The United States produces only 20 percent of its total electrical power from nuclear power, while the figure for France is 75 percent.

Nuclear power reactors are nestled along the coastline, most of them bunched together at one site, in the following prefectures listed in table 1.

Table 1

Location of Nuclear Power Plants
(As of April, 1991)

Prefecture	Plants*	Sites
Hokkaido	2	1
Miyagi	2	1
Fukushima	10	2
Ibaraki	2	1
Niigata	8	2
Fukui	15	5
Shizuoka	4	1
Ehime	3	1
Shimane	2	1
Saga	4	1
Kagashima	2	1
Ishikawa	1	1

*Includes plants under construction or in formal planning stage; also FBR and ATR in Fukui Prefecture

Source: Japanese Government, Science and Technology Agency

The average operating rate for reactors was 71 percent in 1990, high by international standards but a drop from 79 percent in 1987, which was an all-time high.[9] It is widely assumed that if nuclear power is to become the mainstay of electricity supply, the higher figure, close to full capacity, must be sustained. Unplanned shutdowns per unit were easily the lowest in the world in 1990, despite an increase in the number of reactors in operation, helping to demonstrate the country's enviable operational history based as it is on careful construction, cautious operating procedures, and detailed maintenance programs. While two incidents in 1990 blemished the industry's reputation somewhat, government figures also show that the total dose equivalents of workers in radiation-control areas of commercial plants was a national all-time low.[10]

Approximately 765,000 drums (200-liter containers) of low-level waste had accumulated by March 1990. At the moment, low-level waste is buried on site. Total drum storage capacity at all plant sites is about 1,154,600. High-level waste is kept in a storage pool at the Tokai Mura processing plant.[11] The question of spent-fuel disposal remains a difficult technical and political challenge in Japan and elsewhere.

Japan's electricity industry is composed of ten regional power companies. Access to the industry is limited. Prices are publicly determined and territory is essentially fixed. [12] Most of the major utilities are among the most powerful companies in Japan. Tokyo Electric Power Company is the largest privately owned utility in the world. The company's electric power sales and revenues are almost one-third of the total for all Japan.

The size, financial health, technical capability, political influence, economic scope, and capacity for close collaboration among themselves are all reasons why the utilities must be judged among the most powerful groupings in Japan's. It is not an exaggeration to state that the Nuclear Quest is substantially arranged to suit the interests and needs of the utilities. At the same time, the utilities also receive the brunt of the attack from antinuclear forces.

The huge nuclear supply industry includes companies engaged in the design, manufacture, construction, and maintenance needs of nuclear power plants and associated fuel-cycle facilities.[13] The health of the industry is widely regarded not only as crucial to Japan's long-term energy security but also as a locomotive industry to help advance scientific and technical skills. At a minimum, activities of the industry affect consumers (residential, commercial, industrial), government regulators, stockholders, corporations assisting utilities in raising capital investment funds, government planning agencies, the research and technology community, local residents where facilities are located, and politicians. Since the nuclear supply industry is among the nation's biggest spenders for capital investment, any delays in construction of large power plants reduces private-sector capital spending and seriously hampers regional economies.[14]

The construction of a nuclear power plant is a composite project, involving approximately thirty million parts and pieces of equipment. The supply system is fairly integrated, horizontally and vertically. At the apex of the supply industry are the three manufacturers of LWRs who sign turn-key contracts with the utilities: Hitachi, Toshiba, and Mitsubishi. Within each industrial grouping the reactor manufacturer, with its financial and technological resources, is linked with affiliated component suppliers in a very close, if not exclusive, relationship.

The construction period is also a long one, requiring a large outlay of capital. Government energy policy is thus designed to stabilize investor expectations.[15] Technological development costs are high (and for the most part covered by government subsidies), safety and reliability demands are stringent, and nonproliferation considerations must be part of all engineering designs. A long-term business relation is maintained between the three plant manufacturers and the electric power companies to ensure safety, reliability, various forms of technical cooperation, and post-sales services. Architect-engineering work is carried out by the reactor manufacturer in close cooperation with the electric utility. Reactor types have also been limited to two LWR types: the pressurized water reactor (PWR) and the boiling water reactor (BWR).

The nuclear industry has essentially only one market: the domestic Nuclear Quest, including the research and development effort. What happens in this single market is thus extremely important, although the sales of nuclear equipment account for only a small percentage of overall sales for many firms. Construction investments have gone down in recent years, reflecting the difficulties utilities and the government are experiencing in finding new sites to build nuclear facilities. But operational maintenance business has gone up, along with an increase in operational facilities. Industry journals are filled with articles trying to understand why nuclear power is losing its appeal among the best university graduates.[16] At a time when Japan is expected to be a world leader in technology, the nuclear power community is concerned about financial viability, overcapacity, maintaining technological excellence, and the attractiveness of the industry among the young.

The Nuclear Quest

Official policy remains undaunted despite uncertainties of many kinds. The long-term strategy for nuclear development—the Nuclear Quest—has remained broadly unchanged during the past two decades or more: maximum autonomy in all aspects of nuclear power generation.[17] Targets, details, and emphasis have changed in judging how fast the journey will take, reflecting such macrofactors as fluctuations in economic growth, energy demand elasticities, price of fossil fuels, government budgetary allocations, availability of new reactors sites, and rates of technological progress.

The most comprehensive statement of the Science and Technology Agency (STA) is the most recent "Long-Term Program for the Development and Utilization of Nuclear Energy" announced by the Atomic Energy Commission in June 1987.[18] It is the seventh of its kind since 1956 and will be revised sometime in early 1992. In 1990 three Ministry of International Trade and Industry (MITI) advisory bodies submitted energy demand forecasts and conservation plans that included views on nuclear development. Such "programs" and "outlooks" must be frequently revised as projections prove to be off the mark or ill-conceived. Nonetheless, based on consultation and information exchanges with the private sector, indicative planning helps define the current conditions of the Nuclear Quest while sending signals to the policy community on relative priorities and policy intentions. STA and MITI are sometimes in disagreement.

The official "long-term outlook for the supply and demand of energy" issued irregularly by MITI form the outside parameters for specific nuclear power planning by the Atomic Energy Commission (AEC).[19] The most recent MITI outlook, announced in the summer of 1990, showed that the country's energy consumption is moving ahead of GNP growth rates at a time when the public environment is less friendly to nuclear power development.

MITI planners projected that the nation's power capacity should increase from 28.9 gigawatt (GW) in 1988 to 50.5 GW in fiscal 2000 and 72,500 GW in 2010. Consequently, the share of nuclear power in the total supply of energy would nearly double from 9 percent in 1988 to 16.7 percent in 2010. Nuclear power will thus account for roughly 43 percent of the nation's total electrical needs. This will require about forty additional plants to the existing thirty-nine. The role of oil is expected to decrease from 34 percent to 15 percent during the same period. The MITI advisory committee was careful to point out that projections could be easily upset by developments beyond the control of government, including a third oil crisis or resistance at home to nuclear power.

It is clear that despite growing doubts abroad, Japan continues to adhere to its ambitious development goals: more and improved LWRs, use of plutonium in LWRs, development of an intermediate ATR, and, in the twenty-first century, introduction of the fast breeder reactor (FBR) on a commercial scale. A prototype FBR (*Monju*), constructed at a cost of approximately Y60 billion, underwent preoperational testing in May 1991.

Japan is able to fabricate its own fuel needs but depends on overseas facilities for such critical processes as enrichment and reprocessing. To complete the entire fuel cycle in Japan, the Japan Fuel Service Company and the Japan Nuclear Fuel Industries will build a spent fuel reprocessing plant, an uranium enrichment plant, and a radioactive waste storage facility in Rokkasho Village, Aomori Prefecture. Plans are also on the drawing board for a storage engineering center at Horonobe Village, Hokkaido Prefecture, in which vitrified high-level waste will be stored while research and development on geological disposal technology is going on.

Formulating the Nuclear Quest

The ability to mobilize government, industry, and research organizations toward achievement of national goals is one of Japan's major strengths in areas of new technology.[20] As has been the case with other officially designated "national" priorities, the development of nuclear power has required a concentration of effort that has blurred the distinction between public and private, state and society, and between political and administrative processes.

Nonetheless, advocates in political science who proclaim the virtues of an "institutional approach" are on safe ground when they argue that formal organizations and legal arrangements—laws, detailed rules, ordinances, predictable bureaucratic procedures—are important in shaping the character of politics.[21]

Institutions form the supra-rules that institutionalize conflict, provide political resources, and impose constraints on individuals and groups. As in other industrial countries, institutional arrangements in Japan give advocates of nuclear power far greater access to decision places than what is available to doubters. The record shows that advocates of nuclear power in the 1950s created policy arrangements and institutions that would keep the atom distant from the obvious tug and pull of everyday politics.[22]

Institutional arrangements that have been adopted over the years to facilitate the Nuclear Quest include laws and administrative practices that define the agenda-setting arena as relatively hierarchical, narrow, and insulated from broad societal pressures; reporting and coordinating requirements that promote relative cohesion in decision-making structures; instruments available to pursue substantive goals; regulatory arrangements that allow significant control by nuclear authorities; relatively minor roles for civil and administrative courts; and minimal legal prerogatives available to local levels of government to oppose nuclear priorities.

A brief outline of the policy-making process, beginning with the legal foundations, helps demonstrate this point.

The road from research and development to commercial applications is a long and difficult one. It is also richly textured by a complex of laws, rules, regulations, and other legal requirements, making it perhaps the most regulated industrial activity in Japan.[23] The legal framework includes the Atomic Energy Basic law; laws setting up or mandating various government agencies; a number of regulations governing safety, licensing, and safety procedures; liability, compensation, and disaster-relief laws; laws to promote the use of atomic power; and laws regarding plant siting. Laws are used to help formalize decisions, legitimate policy choices, maintain the prerogatives of the national government, assure successful implementation of policy, and discourage partisan politics. But laws are not enough to assure acceptable decisions.

Ultimate authority for the nation's policies rests with the prime minister. Like the emperor under the Meiji Constitution, however, the prime minister has never acted on his own in any major way.

Figure 1 outlines the complex administrative and policy-making organizations within which formal nuclear energy programs are formulated.

The Atomic Energy Commission (Genshiryoku Iinkai, AEC), established under separate law to advise the prime minister, consists of a chairman who is director general of STA and four commissioners. The commissioners are appointed by the prime minister and serve for a three-year period. The appointment is renewable with approval of the nation's parliament. Representatives from the government, private sector, and academy are usually chosen for these positions. A number of advisory committees, drawn from the private and public sectors, assist the AEC.

While not an administrative body, the mandate of AEC is broad and all-encompassing. Among its various duties is responsibility for formulating the government's long-term program for development and utilization of nuclear energy. In doing so, AEC is expected to view the total landscape of nuclear power, impartially and comprehensively. The AEC law requires that the prime minister "fully respect" its recommendations.

A separate Nuclear Safety Commission (Genshiryoku Anzen Iinkai; NSC) advises the prime minister on safety issues for nuclear reactors. It too is composed of a chairman and four commissioners appointed by the prime minister and uses advisory committees in its work. Proposals for new international conventions on

Figure 1
Administrative System of Atomic Energy Development in Japan
Administrative Structure of Atomic Energy Development

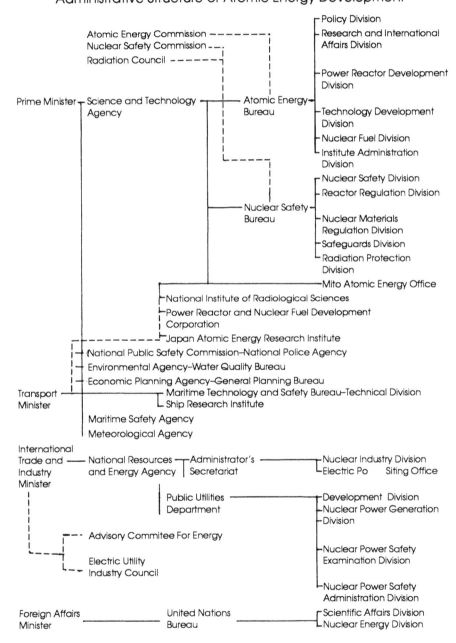

safety, including responses to the Three Mile Island and Chernobyl disasters, were dealt with by this commission.

STA is an extraministerial bureau of the prime minister's office. It is the most important government agency dealing with planning, formulation, and promotion of basic policies concerning the utilization of nuclear energy. Approximately 80 percent of the government's nuclear budget goes to STA and its constituent organizations. STA serves as secretariat for all advisory bodies on nuclear power to the prime minister. The Atomic Energy Bureau and the Nuclear Safety Bureau are the key units for nuclear policy within STA. Officials serving in the two bureaus are at the center of coordinating activities within the Japanese government.

The Japan Atomic Energy Research Institute (JAERI) undertakes research and development for atomic energy. Its main activities tend to be in basic, long-term areas such as development of advanced reactors, nuclear fusion research, and safety research. The Power Reactor and Nuclear Fuel Development Corporation (PNC) undertakes research and development on nuclear fuels and power reactors. Its responsibilities also include helping to develop the fast breeder reactor, nuclear fuel technology, fuel reprocessing, and the purchase and selling of nuclear materials and fuels.

MITI's role is the promotion of nuclear power and the nuclear fuel cycle at the more commercial and demonstration stage. Its responsibilities also include regulatory matters—licensing, site selection, plant inspection, public acceptance—and safety of commercial nuclear reactors, including physical protection of power stations. MITI has major responsibility for export and import controls and nonproliferation matters.

Most of the working responsibility in MITI for nuclear administration is allocated to the Agency for Natural Resources and Energy (ANRE). The Public Utilities Department and the Nuclear Industry Division are responsible in particular for the promotion of nuclear power. The minister is advised directly on nuclear matters as well by the advisory committee for energy and the Electricity Utility Industry Council. During licensing procedures MITI officials also consult with the Advisory Committee on Environmental Matters, the Technical Advisory Committee on Nuclear Power, and the Electric Power Resources Development Coordination Council.

Government institutions are clearly important because they are stable and deeply rooted, often as formal, legal, and codified powers. Yet rarely on their own can institutional arrangements explain concrete policies. Their impact is not automatic but depends rather on who uses laws, rules, and regular procedures and for what purposes. Moreover, laws and rules in Japan are often vague, sometimes ignored in the name of bureaucratic discretion, often in dispute among competing ministries, and, in any case, subject to change.[24] An excessive concern with institutions reduces political science to the study of mechanics, preventing the observer from appreciating how accepted practices are transformed in the course of political competition among individuals, agencies, and outside political groupings.

Nonetheless, research on Japan suggests that around state institutions will be formed a reasonably stable arena of nuclear policy in which most of the dynamics of important policy making will take place. The idea of policy community is a useful way to empirically trace the network of organizations that link government to society within the policy arena.[25] This is an especially plausible view given the organizational imperatives of a dangerous technology, the integrated features of the nuclear industry, and in light of the extraordinary efforts made by pronuclear forces to keep policy issues defined as technical and so best left to the informed judgments of a limited number of qualified experts.

Politicians in the parliament generally cooperate. Elected officials rarely make policy decisions issues for partisan discussion unless there is an accident, blunder, cover-up, or sudden threat to a favorite program. On the other hand, members of the LDP are kept informed, and many lend a hand in helping to persuade the public of the need for nuclear power.

A unified policy community, rooted in a strong institutional framework, assures that legitimate and acceptable decisions can be made by government. Definitive decisions, in turn, enhance the national ability to plan, widely assumed in the literature as an absolutely crucial requisite to any successful developmental program. Japan does this comparatively well, although policy advice is not the monopoly of any single interest or organization.

Agreement is facilitated because the broad goals of the Nuclear Quest have not changed since the early 1960s. A new consensus is not required each time a fresh vision or long-term outlook has to be designed, as long as proper clearance procedures are followed. Indeed, considerable effort is made to show the continuity of cautious, prudent, and responsible effort. Successive long-term programs are not plans so much as "future goals to be achieved through hard-effort" (*doryoku mokuhyo*).

Only in a limited way does the market provide any definitive cues for specific decisions. Instead, government statements and policies are expected to provide a stable economic environment within which private firms can make decisions about the future. The long-term energy supply-and-demand outlook put together by MITI provides many of the givens for considerations taken up by the AEC.

The community making these decisions is knit together through personal contacts, common background, intertwined careers, and a shared set of interests and ideas. In many ways, the character of the Nuclear Quest, the clearance procedures required before decisions can be made, and the distribution of power within the policy community make the process of decision reactive, slow, cautious, and incrementalist. Looked at in a different way, the decision to pursue the plutonium option more aggressively might show extreme daring or the extent to which policy is governed by momentum.

The esoteric nature of the technology, the fear of national vulnerability, and a highly instrumental attitude toward bureaucracy and politics in Japan have all enhanced the power of pronuclear forces at the stage of policy formulation, even as the participants can be divided among themselves on some important secondary issues or find themselves responding at times to issues and pressures framed outside the policy community. What, then, about implementation of the Nuclear Quest?

Implementing the Nuclear Quest

An institutional view of nuclear power development suggests that the Japanese government is blessed with all the instruments that can be technically deployed in the successful promotion of its policy objectives. Policy makers in a comparatively centralized and insulated policy community have a wide choice of policy instruments with which to empower the government with the capacity to match the vision of the Nuclear Quest with the daily challenge of getting the job done.

Among the most powerful tools are ability to influence utility investment decisions and profit rates; capacity to influence the allocation of investment capital; laws that can be used to control imports of oil and the domestic supply and demand of oil; powers of administrative guidance; generous budgetary allocations to help finance a major portion of research and development; site approval, construction permits, and operating licences all issued by the national government; subsidies that can be used along with payments by the utilities to persuade local villagers to sell or transfer some of their property rights; compensation programs to help persuade a local community to go along with nuclear power objectives; reliable knowledge, information, and human networks; managerial capacity to help deal with complexity, scale, and the complexities of private-public technological relations; lead agencies in the government to keep policy and programs related in a reasonably coherent manner.

In fact, in some important areas MITI and STA play only an indirect role in implementing policies. Most significant here is that the government does not have the legal capacity to claim local property rights protected as they are by law.[26] Negotiations are required between property holders and the utilities wishing to build a new facility. As suggested earlier, they have become a lot tougher than in the past, compensation levels have risen, and lead times have increased dramatically. A number of sites have been abandoned because of resistance. Some journalists and activists claim that there will never be enough sites for the government to achieve its present goals. Recent attempts to implement the Nuclear Quest have revealed a process that has become more permeable to a broader variety of interests than what is seen in the workings of the policy community.

The tradition of localism in Japanese politics and the structure of opportunity have tended to encourage antinuclear forces over the years to focus on particular sites. This political strategy continues to this day and has proven to be the most successful. Parallel with local protest is an attempt by other antinuclear forces to develop a regional and even national movement as well, demonstrating that the relative openness or closure of political institutions in Japan can change. Who are these people, and how are they caught up in the politics of protest? Although the antinuclear "movement" is somewhat inchoate, a few generalizations can be made.[27]

Dissenters do not act under the same organizational or ideological banner. The most important individuals are residents of the immediate community who have legal property rights: landowners, holders of fishing rights, those who can claim customary or traditional rights of access to land, water, and forest, and those who claim rights with respect to the environment. Parties without strict legal rights but who are members of the community can also be involved: immediate residents (*chonaikai, burakukai*), nearby residents, local chambers of commerce, agricultural cooperatives, local labor and fishing organizations, local chapters of political parties, newspapers, self-styled environmentalists.

The utility wishing to build a reactor will thus have to develop close links with "parties of influence" within the village. The support of the village mayor and assembly and the prefectural governor are essential since safety agreements must be signed with the utilities. A stubborn fishery cooperative can prevent agreement. In some villages outsiders advocating any position are not especially welcome, making it necessary for advocates and critics alike to move with considerable discretion.

Beyond the parties involved directly in a particular dispute, heterogeneity marks the plethora of organizations that bring together farmers and professionals, housewives and environmentalists. The "old-wave" organizations such as the Japan Democratic Socialist party (JDSP) and the Japan Communist party (JCP) along with their allied unions are still active, although with varying degrees of enthusiasm in different parts of the country. The JDSP and trade unions are especially strong in Hokkaido. Well over seventy-five citizen groups are also active in the prefecture, but their exact size and make-up is uncertain, even to prefectural organizers.

Uncertainty about numbers reflects the open, egalitarian and informal character of many environmental and citizen groups that weakens them politically at times.[28] Lawyers, scientists, and other professionals not associated with a particular political party are active at the local level. Consumer and agricultural cooperatives and women's groups involved in the movement have increased markedly since Chernobyl.[29]

A conspicuous development has been the "urbanization" of the antinuclear movement. The Citizens' Nuclear Information Center in Tokyo with ties and connections throughout the country serves as a national liaison office as well as provider of expert technical and political advice.[30] The Japan Lawyer Federation has been extremely active arguing cases in the courts, helping to organize support for a "denuclearization law," conducting studies of problems related to the nuclear fuel cycle facilities at Rokkasho-mura and Horonobe among many other activities. The national consumer cooperative movement has also become critical of the nation's Nuclear Quest. In an interview a member informed me that the real issue in Japanese politics these days is not ideology or class but rather food. In 1989 Nihon Seikatsu Kyodo Kumiai Rengokai had 625 affiliated organizations with 12.6 million members, making it potentially the largest antinuclear organization in the country.[31]

Individuals have also become important as critics of the Nuclear Quest. Hirose Takashi, a writer and lecturer, is credited by more than one nuclear advocate as the most threatening phenomenon in recent years because of his appealing speaking style and popularity among housewives and young people. [32]

Why has the movement grown in recent years? The immediate background is clear enough. Three Mile Island, Chernobyl, and a number of incidents and accidents in Japan continue to raise doubts about safety. With Chernobyl in particular, questions were raised in public about the relation of nuclear power to radiation poisoning, contaminated food, and genetic damage. As the Nuclear Quest expanded in Japan, doubts were also raised about policy processes and institutions that keep decisions about the atom seemingly apart from the public. The utilities have come in for their share of criticism about secrecy and misleading information.

The goals of such a diverse movement are as mixed as the people who participate: total rejection, a nuclear freeze, gradual reduction, shutdown of a particular reactor already in operation, assimilation of a broader range of people into the policy-making and regulatory process, transformation of the nation's overall energy strategy into new directions, or simply better financial terms before going along with a specific project.

Special effort is currently focused on sites where new types of facilities are planned or already underway: construction of the fast breeder reactor in Fukui prefecture, fuel-cycle facilities in Aomori Prefecture, the ATR also in Aomori Prefecture, and waste disposal facilities in Hokkaido. In these latter cases, the goal is total rejection of a major development in the Nuclear Quest: completion of the fuel cycle and an increased use of plutonium fuel. Some form of protest is currently underway at all nuclear sites.

Japanese antinuclear forces make the same kinds of political calculations seen in any democratic country by those who wish to challenge a major government commitment. How closed or open are political arrangements? Where are the most promising targets of opportunity? What are the major political and economic alignments in the country? How stable are these ties? Are there conflicts to be exploited within the policy community? How can widespread fear of nuclear power be exploited?

Political goals, structural opportunities, and resources are as much subjective perceptions as they are objective reality. Political activities thus span a broad range of political action: refusals to sell property rights; signature campaigns; sit-ins; recall movements; electoral politics, especially at the local and prefectural level; law suits; national and local rallies. A massive educational campaign has been underway since 1986: books, magazine articles, pamphlets, scientific studies, legal studies, study groups, visiting speakers, videos, and television debates. In one major bookstore in Tokyo there are ten long shelves of books related to nuclear power. Most have been published during the last five years and a majority are critical.

How do the Japanese people view this atomic quest? Public opinion polls suggest that a large number have considerable misgivings.[33] Nuclear advocates have a major public acceptance problem both nationally and, as the fuel-cycle facilities demonstrate, at various sites.

The Shimokita peninsula, located in northeastern Aomori Prefecture, is among the poorest in the nation.[34] It is also turning into what the antinuclear critics call a "nuclear peninsula." If planned projects are not completed in the region, the whole quest for national independence will be doomed. The greatest controversy centers on Rokkasho-mura, a small farming, dairy, and fishing community of 12,000 residents on the Pacific coast.

The tiny village was chosen by the nation's utilities in 1985 as the site for the country's first fuel-cycle facility. A federation of the country's nine major utilities, along with nuclear manufacturing firms and other financial interests, established the Japan Nuclear Fuel Industries and the Japan Nuclear Fuel Service Company to run the "national" project, the total cost of which will be over one trillion yen.

The site will include plants to enrich and reprocess nuclear fuel, which is now done overseas. Japan's power stations have sometimes been likened to "mansions without a toilet" because no solution has been found for their accumulating nuclear waste. The facility will also include an area for permanent disposal of low-level waste generated by all the country's nuclear plants and a temporary storage place for high-level waste.

The project has been controversial from the start, exacerbated in recent years by Chernobyl and kept in the news by the determined antinuclear movement headed in Tokyo. In December 1988 Rokkasho-mura's pronuclear mayor was defeated by Tsuchida Hiroshi, who during the campaign called for a "freeze" on plans to finish the facility. The utilities were shocked since they believed that villagers would never protest in such a manner.

An on-sight visit six months after the election indicated that the situation for the utilities and government was difficult, but not yet life-threatening. In interviews it was clear that the mayor is no firebrand about to use his office to stir up trouble.

The village had already received government subsidies, directly and indirectly, as a result of a previous decision to go along with national policy. Villagers were employed at construction sites, and long-term projects to improve village life were in the mayor's budget.

"Our village needs some more time" to consider the issue he explained, while voicing his trust that the utilities will do more to convince residents about safety. In the summer of 1990 opinion in the village was evenly divided, a local politician reported. "Let the people decide," he told us in an interview, "by expressing their views in opinion polls." As one fisherman noted, "He's simply an advocate of cautious planning."

The Tomari community comprises about one third of Rokkasho-mura. Some 80 percent of the adult population engage in fishing. "We think it's just a garbage dump," said one of the leaders of a group established six years ago to oppose the whole project. "We have an obligation to protect the sea from radiation," his colleague added. Although only a small number of Tomari residents publicly oppose the plant, I heard tales of bribes, deceit, job discrimination, law suits, sea battles, and social intimidation to keep doubters quiet.

Fishermen and their wives were not alone. Farmers are worried that their products will be boycotted by urban consumers at the slightest rumor about contamination. Labor unions, citizen groups, Socialist and Communist party politicians, environmentalists, consumer cooperatives, and various academic scientists have also visited the village in protest. Supporters of the project consider them as "outside agitators."

Prefectural, city, and village officials and politicians, meanwhile, generally continued to give guarded welcome to the facilities, saying that studies show that the new facilities will bring jobs for local residents and help to strengthen the local economy with new investments, subsidies, and property taxes. The site for the project is part of the unused land set aside for an industrial park launched in the 1960s by the national and prefectural governments to attract industry. In late 1990 only nuclear facilities, a few government offices and a crude oil stockpiling base occupied the three thousand hectares once seen as the economic future of the village.

In the spring of 1991 Governor Kitamaura Masaya, a strong advocate of the nuclear facility, was reelected. The other two candidates also expressed clear positions on the issue: One advocated a freeze while the jointly backed JDSP and JCP candidate called for cancellation of the project.

In many ways, all the forces that shape the politics of nuclear power in Japan are at work in Rokkasho-mura. Japanese utilities and manufacturers, along with their allies in government, have an awesome capacity to work smoothly together in planning and building projects of this sort. But the same tenacity of purpose and self-satisfaction encourages impatience with outsiders, a patronizing attitude toward local residents, quick dismissal of criticism, and heavy-handed practices such as holding a public hearing in the village on safety, widely regarded as a government ceremony, on the anniversary of Chernobyl.

Villages like Rokkasho-mura are chosen as nuclear sites partially because they are relatively distanced from population centers, poor, and have residents doubtful about their economic future. Until now, almost any kind of industrial activity has been welcome if it promised to create new employment. In the past local governments actively sought nuclear power plants. Now doubts about nuclear power have made it difficult for utilities to find additional power sites to fulfill the Nuclear Quest.

Among local officials there is a strong propensity to trust the central government regarding safety measures even though they do not participate in formulating the Nuclear Quest in Tokyo. In any case, prefectural and local governments have few resources to check national policy or even to confirm that they are being given all the facts. There are no referendums in Japanese politics to tap the public will. Nor are there strong-willed governors ready to question big decisions made in Tokyo, although the current JDSP governor of Hokkaido, with the backing of the prefectural assembly, opposes plans to build a nuclear waste facility in his prefecture. Following the election of the mayor in Rokkasho-mura the head of STA stated that no change will occur in the government's energy policy but that "we will do our best to assure the people's understanding and cooperation." This is a standard phrase when the Japanese power holder refuses to bend. The difficulty of open communication and the extreme reluctance by supporters to acknowledge that thoughtful people have misgivings are striking.

Conclusion

Basic analytic premises and empirical findings are at issue in contemporary debates about the foreign policies of Japan. In dispute are questions about how best to characterize and explain Japan's overseas activities. Certainly there is evidence in some of these chapters to suggest that the country most often simply moves with the flow, content to remain as a reactive economic giant, minimalist in its own diplomatic goals, deferential to the United States, disabled in any case by "constraints" and so forced to be "coping" in its external behavior. But empirical support can also be found for another interpretation that suggests that the country has clear, well-formulated goals, is pursuing them in a low-key but determined fashion, and has succeeded remarkably thus far in protecting the nation's vital national interests. Many of these "success" stories are in the area of foreign economic policy.

This debate is rooted partially in conflicting empirical findings. Analytical premises are also at issue, related as they are to questions of how best to construct explanations of Japanese foreign policy. Among the range of analytical and theoretical approaches often used, three are most promising: system-centered, domestic–political-centered, and state-centered.[35] Each of these perspectives, with qualifying additions, is well-represented in the general literature in political science including studies of Japan.

The arguments of this analysis draw attention to the need to explain foreign activities with reference especially to the shape of government institutions and the character of domestic politics.

The connection between politics and policy is hardly remarkable and should not be unexpected in the case of nuclear policies. Certainly, officials in Japan make considerable efforts to down-play politics, if not deny it altogether. This is not so much an attempt to mislead as it is a reflection of a deeper worry about what members of the policy community believe the public at large can understand and accept. When outsiders get involved in the debate, different questions are raised, issues that are not always acknowledged in a technocratic approach to policy.

To the world at large, the Japanese government has shown no disposition to abdicate the sole right to determine the scope and character of its own national development program. Yet the country is still constrained in its ambitions. No national program is independent of the need for international cooperation, including information exchange, safety research, joint technological ventures, and the sharing of accurate reports of operating experience. Japan's nuclear ties with the United States are numerous and long-standing. Tokyo has also assumed a more prominent role in various international arrangements, including the International Energy Agency (IEA). In recent years the government has been pushing IEA to adopt new guidelines encouraging nuclear power and curbing CO^2 emissions.

Japan also remains dependent on foreign sources of fuel, uranium enrichment, and spent fuel reprocessing. In some area of the fuel cycle, industry is still dependent on foreign technology. Advocates of nuclear power must necessarily be part of a worldwide network of individuals and organizations linking industries, corporations, utilities, governments, universities, research laboratories, international agencies, and public relations offices.

Nuclear ambitions in Japan reflect also the government's commitments to the world's "nonproliferation regime" or the loose collection of treaties, bilateral and multilateral agreements, voluntary guidelines, tacit understandings, and international institutions that are collectively intended to prevent the diversion of nuclear materials and technology from civilian to military uses. Tokyo is in line with a number of nations insisting that the North Korean government permit international inspection of its nuclear facilities. The Japanese are also firmly insisting that a new safety and technology pact include safeguards against any technology being used for military purposes.

Uncontrollable events abroad have also, in different ways, closed in around the nuclear power choices in Japan. Continuing political and economic uncertainties in the Persian Gulf area help reinforce persistent doubts in Japan about overseas oil supplies. On the other hand, major accidents like Three Mile Island and Chernobyl, reported in great detail by the media, have chilled enthusiasm for nuclear power and strengthened the movement against any further build-up.

All nations face a changing international environment that creates a complicated range of conditions—constraining, conflicting, threatening, interactive, and inviting—that will have some impact domestically. Decisions in Japan will also have consequences abroad. The important political question is who is advancing what kind of understanding of the international environment, especially as it pertains to how the nation should respond at home. Unlike trade and finance, international and domestic market signals are relatively weak. Resolution of policy differences is rarely an intellectual debate. Arguments win in politics because the individual or group has the power to persuade or impose a particular policy interpretation.

In a marginal way, critics at home have been influential: rejection at some sites, higher compensation and other rewards for going along, some procedural impact on the manner in which environmental studies or regulatory decisions are made. But to what extent a "movement" can be credited for these adjustments is unclear. It can't be demonstrated beyond doubt, but perhaps most important has been public pressure to help keep companies and government more honest, thorough, and careful.

Advocates of nuclear power in Japan have neither repressed the antinuclear movement at home nor given localities much in the way of new and significant political rights in the process of deciding the nation's atomic fate. Thus far, the government has not scaled down its nuclear program very much, nor has there been any substantial change in the overall shape of nuclear power ambitions. The economic and political power of established forces in the nuclear industry is formidable.

But the public is uneasy, and future implementation will not be automatic. A large-scale accident or series of minor mishaps would change the situation drastically. The outside world might also become more doubtful about Japan's plutonium ambitions, creating world interest in the nation's Nuclear Quest in a different way and thereby changing the variables most important for the analyst to take into account in understanding the country's policies toward the future.

Notes

1. See the fascinating study by Spencer R. Weart, *Nuclear Fear* (Cambridge: Harvard University Press, 1988); also Richard Rhodes, *The Making of the Atomic Bomb* (New York: Simon and Schuster, 1988); Robert Jay Lifton, *Death in Life: Survivors of Hiroshima* (New York: Simon and Schuster, 1967).

2. For an analysis of an earlier period see Laura E. Hein, *Fueling Growth: The Energy Revolution and Economic Policy in Postwar Japan* (Cambridge: Harvard University Press, 1990).

3. For a technical explanation of the fuel cycle see OECD, *Nuclear Energy and Its Fuel Cycle* (Paris: OECD, 1985); Japan Electric Power Information Center, *Nuclear Fuel Cycle in Japan* (Tokyo, 1987). The best historical study of nuclear development in Japan is Mori Kazuhisa, ed., *Genshiryoku wa, ima* (Tokyo: Nihon Genshiryoku Sangyo Kaigiin, 1986), 2 vols.

4. U.S. Government, *Nuclear Power in an Age of Uncertainty* (Washington, D. C.: U.S. Congress, Office of Technology Assessment, OTA E-216, February 1984); James M. Jasper, *Nuclear Politics* (Princeton: Princeton University Press, 1990); John L. Campbell, *Collapse of an Industry* (Ithaca: Cornell University Press, 1988); Joseph G. Morone and Edward J. Woodhouse, *The Demise of Nuclear Energy?* (New Haven: Yale University Press, 1989); Terrence Price, Political Electricity (New York: Oxford University Press, 1990).

5. A common conclusion in the literature on nuclear power, confirmed in various ways by studies cited in note 4.

6. See William C. Potter, *International Nuclear Trade and Nonproliferation* (Lexington, MA: D.C. Heath, 1990) especially Stephanie Sharron and Warren H. Donnelly, "Japan," pp. 199–220.

7. The most valuable single source of information and analysis in the English language, from the pronuclear point of view, is *Atoms in Japan*, published by the Japan Atomic Energy Forum. For an antinuclear perspective, see *Nuke Info Tokyo*, put out by the Citizen's Nuclear Information Center. *Genshiryoku hakusho* is the annual white paper on nuclear power assembled by the Science and Technology Agency.

8. Statistics on nuclear power in Japan are drawn from, MITI, Genshiryoku hakusho and *Genshiryoku nenkan.*

9. Figures from MITI.

10. Ibid.

11. See Japan Lawyer's Association, *Koreberu hoshasei haikibutsu mondai* (Tokyo, 1990), and *Genshiryoku hakusho* (1990).

12. Kobayashi Ryutaro, *Enerugi Gyokai* (Tokyo: Kyoikusha Shinsho, 1990).

13. The most reliable description of the nuclear supply industry is Nihon Genshiryoku Sangyo Kaigi, *Nihon no genshiryoku sangyo: Genjo to tenbo* (annual).

14. Kobayashi, *Enerugi.*

15. For support of this point as well as a number of other observations see the important work of S. Hayden Lesbirel, "Implementing Nuclear Energy Policy in Japan," *Energy Policy* 18, 3 (April 1990): 267–282. See also "The Political Economy of Substitution Policy: Japan's Response to Lower Oil Prices," *Pacific Affairs* 61, 2 (Summer 1988): 285–302.

16. See recent issues of *Enerugi Forum* and *Genshiryoku Kogyo.*

17. See Mori, *Genshiryoku.*

18. Atomic Energy Commission, *Long-Term Program for Development and Utilization of Nuclear Energy* (Tokyo, 1987).

19. MITI, irregular. AEC commissioners would not agree that MITI reports exercise such an influence on their long-term views.

20. The literature on this topic is vast. See Hugh Patrick, ed., *Japan's High Technology Industries: Lessons and Limitations of Industrial Policy* (Seattle: University of Washington Press, 1986); Daniel I. Okimoto, *Between MITI and the Market* (Stanford: Stanford University Press, 1989); Daniel I. Okimoto, Takuo Sugano, and Franklin Weinstein, eds., *Competitive Edge* (Stanford: Stanford University Press, 1984).

21. James G. March and Johan P. Olson, *Rediscovering Institutions* (New York: The Free Press, 1989); Peter B. Evans et al., *Bringing the State Back In* (New York: Cambridge University Press, 1985); Peter Gourevitch, *Politics in Hard Times* (Ithaca: Cornell University Press, 1986).

22. Mori, *Genshiryoku wa.*

23. MITI, *Genshiryoku jitsumu roppo*, various. See also Nihon Enerugiho Kenkyujo, *Nihon no genshiryoku hosei* (Tokyo, 1988).

24. Frank K. Upham, *Law and Social Change in Postwar Japan* (Cambridge: Harvard University Press, 1987).

25. John Campbell, "Bureaucratic Primacy: Japanese Policy Communities in an American Perspective," *Governance* 2, 1 (January 1989): 5–22. See also Daniel I. Okimoto, "Political Inclusivity: The Domestic Structure of Trade," in Takashki Inoguchi and Daniel I. Okimoto, eds., *The Political Economy of Japan: The Changing International Context* (Stanford: Stanford University Press, 1988): 305–344; William D. Coleman and Grace Skogstad, eds., *Policy Communities and Public Policy in Canada* (Toronto: Copp Clark Pitman Ltd., 1990); William D. Coleman, *Business and Politics* (Kingston and Montreal: McGill-Queen's University Press, 1988). There are a number of parallels with nuclear policymaking in France. See Frank R. Baumgartner "Independent and Politicized Policy Communities: Education and Nuclear Energy in France and in the United States," *Governance* 2, 1 (January 1989): 43–66.

26. Lesbirel, "Implementing."

27. Generalizations based on field research in Japan from June 1989 to August 1990.

28. An observation made in a rich account of the environmental movement in an earlier period by Margaret A. McKean, *Environmental Protest and Citizen Politics in Japan* (Berkeley: University of California Press, 1981).

29. Nihon Enerugi Keizai Kenkyujo, *Enerugi to genshiryoku o kangaeru* (Tokyo: NiKan Kogyo Shimbunsha, 1989).

30. Among their reports are *Genshiryoku shiryo johoshitsu tsushin* and *Hangenkpatsu shimbun.*

31. Nihon Genshiryoku Sangyo Kaigi, *Genshiryoku chosa jiho*, no. 56 (October 1989).

32. The most recent of his publications that has caused an unsettling stir among pronuclear groups is Hirose Takashi, *Kiken no hanashi* (Tokyo: Hachigatsu Shokan, 1987).

33. Science and Technology Agency, *Genshiryoku ni kansuru seron chosa*, 1990.

34. The following is based on two field trips during which some forty individuals, including the mayor of Rokkasho-mura, were interviewed. There is an enormous secondary literature on this little village and its dealings with nuclear power. For a

fairly technical but reliable account, see Nihon Bengoshi Rengokai, *Kakunenryo saikuru shisetsu mondai ni kansuru chosakenkyu hokokusho* (Tokyo, 1987).

35. For a theoretical discussion, see G. John Ikenberry, David A. Lake, and Michael Mastanduno, eds., *The State and American Foreign Economic Policy* (Ithaca: Cornell University Press, 1988).

III The Search for Security

Chapter 9
The Strategic Dimensions of
Japanese Foreign Policy

Norman D. Levin

Few people discuss Japanese foreign policy in "strategic" terms. Indeed, most observers characterize Japan's postwar policies as "passive," "reactive," excessively "deferential" to the United States, and lacking any articulation of "Japanese" interests—all characterizations that connote the absence of any strategic logic or rationale. This impression has been heightened recently by Western media attention to Japanese voices urging Japan to "say no," as well as by well-publicized criticisms of the Japanese government by former Japanese hostages in Kuwait and Iraq as lacking an "independent" policy. Indications of a Japanese search for expanded roles in world politics more broadly have reinforced the general characterization.

If "strategic" means a plan or stratagem for achieving some goal perceived as fundamental to a country's national interest, however, then Japanese postwar foreign policy can be said to have always had a "strategic" dimension. Indeed, the linkage between Japan's national strategy and foreign policy has been unusually direct. The question is what the implications are of the dramatic changes we have seen over the past couple of years—and the underlying global and regional trends more broadly—for Japan's basic orientation. This chapter addresses this question and raises some issues likely to confront Japanese policy makers in the 1990s.

Strategy and Foreign Policy in Postwar Japan

All nations have multiple objectives. The task of strategy is to prioritize these objectives and integrate them in a coherent set of policies. A successful strategy will keep the objectives in balance with both available resources and the environmental conditions that affect the ability of the state to achieve its objectives.

Among Japan's many national objectives, two have been overarching throughout the postwar period: promoting economic growth and prosperity, and ensuring national security. These objectives, of course, hardly make Japan unique. Almost all nations share these objectives. What does make Japan somewhat unique is the broad strategy its leaders adopted to achieve these objectives: to concentrate national energies on expanding foreign markets for Japanese exports while protecting Japanese industries against foreign competition and gaining control over high–value-added technologies critical to Japanese industrial competitiveness; and to minimize military expenditures while relying on the United States to provide Japan's external security.

This strategy has dictated *in general* a low-cost, low-risk set of foreign policies, with paramount importance—given the U.S. roles in facilitating access to both markets and technology and protecting against foreign intimidation or aggression —placed on maintaining close ties with the United States. As economic tensions mounted between the United States and Japan over the course of the 1970s and 1980s and American pressures for greater Japanese liberalization, internationalization, and "burden-sharing" increased, Japan modified its policies to palliate the United States and adjust to new environmental conditions. Japanese leaders did not, however, fundamentally alter Japan's basic orientation.

The viability of Japan's strategy hinged on three critical assumptions: that the global competition between the United States and Soviet Union would make Japan essential to U.S. global strategy, and hence that the United States could be counted on to help promote Japanese economic development; that the same competition would ensure a major U.S. military role in Japan's defense—as in maintaining regional and global security more broadly—and that hence Japan could make do with a relatively minimal defense effort; and that the world more broadly would "allow" Japan to concentrate on its own economic advancement, without requiring major reciprocal Japanese contributions to the common welfare. These assumptions, on the whole, have been well founded.

On the economic side, Japan parlayed its importance to U.S. global strategy into rapid reconstruction in the 1950s—benefitting in particular from large U.S. military procurement requirements during the Korean War—and a sustained high rate of economic growth throughout the 1960s (more than 12 percent in real terms annually). Under U.S. sponsorship, Japan joined international economic organizations like the GATT and OECD. It took advantage of the U.S. emphasis on maintaining a liberal trading system to gain broad access to the American and world markets, both for exports of manufactured goods and for imports of natural resources. And it exploited U.S. indulgence to prolong Japanese restrictions on imports and foreign investments, in what represented essentially a one-way Japanese definition of free trade. Japan even found ways to pursue its economic objectives when they collided with U.S. political interests, as reflected in its "separation of politics and economics" policy concerning trade with China in the 1960s.[1]

Beginning in the 1970s Japanese leaders modified their economic policies, largely to placate U.S. pressures for greater liberalization but also to adjust to broad macroeconomic changes reflected in the sudden move from high to low growth.[2] They gradually lowered tariffs and removed other trade barriers, for example, to the point where official levels today are generally below those for Western Europe and the United States. They liberalized Japan's financial system, allowing greater foreign access to Japanese capital markets. And they relaxed rules governing direct foreign investment, which, along with the dramatic appreciation of the yen, precipitated a major expansion in overseas investments. These changes contributed to making Tokyo one of the world's most important financial centers while transforming Japan into a more mature, industrial economy. They also helped precipitate a major growth in trade between and among the Asian countries and initiate a process of increasing *intra*regional economic interaction.

It is hard to argue, however, that they suggest any *fundamental* change in Japan's national strategy. While Japan liberalized its barriers to foreign imports, for example, it did so only grudgingly and incrementally, with key industries protected until they could compete internationally. In politically sensitive sectors like agriculture, Japan has limited itself to allowing increased levels of imports rather than agreeing to liberalization. Japan's decision in late 1990 to align itself with the European Community rather than support the U.S.-led effort to reduce agricultural trade barriers and subsidies—despite its awareness that EC opposition would doom the effort in any event—reinforced the perception that Japan is not a force for trade liberalization. This perception is born out by statistics: While the ratio of imports to GNP more than doubled for the United States between 1970 and 1988 (from 4 to 10 percent) and increased significantly for all of non-Communist Asia except Indonesia (which held steady at 11 percent), the ratio for Japan actually *declined* over this period from 9 to 7 percent.[3]

By the same token, although controls on capital were reduced over the course of the 1970s and 1980s, Japanese measures were both slow and piecemeal in nature. Even today, investment opportunities are far fewer in Japan than in the United States, and financial transactions remain considerably more restricted. A recent U.S. Treasury Department study, for example, found that in California alone Japanese banks now conduct more than 25 percent of the lending, whereas foreign banks' share of total lending in Japan was an anemic 1.7 percent at the end of 1990.[4]

Promises made in *both* merchandise trade and financial liberalization packages, moreover, have often either gone unmet—as had largely been the case until very recently with repeated Japanese pledges to stimulate domestic demand—or been realized only after additional U.S. prodding.[5] The Japanese pledge to open up fourteen large Japanese construction projects to foreign bidding, which Japan at a minimum appears slow to carry out, is a recent example. This performance, coupled with the extensive and highly visible wave of Japanese investments in the United States, has significantly intensified protectionist pressures in the United States and fueled rising resentment among Japan's trading partners more broadly.

Other chapters in this volume address this issue in greater detail. Here it is sufficient to note that the Japanese *strategic* objective of fostering economic growth and maintaining Japanese industrial competitiveness retains a critical influence on Japan's foreign policies. As a general statement, this objective dictates responsiveness to U.S. entreaties for greater trade and financial liberalization but in ways that minimize its domestic impact.

On the military side, Japan took advantage of the U.S. strategic interest in containing Soviet and Soviet-supported Communist expansion to lock the United States into a major role in providing for Japan's external security while ensuring that its own defense efforts would be both minimal and limited in nature. The original U.S.-Japan Security Treaty (1951) codified the U.S. commitment to defend Japan against external aggression, in exchange for the U.S. use of Japanese military bases for Japan's defense and the peace and security of the Far East.[6] Like Japan's approach to "free" trade, this approach was rather one-sided: although the United States committed itself to defend Japan, the Japanese assumed no obligation—even in the revised treaty of 1960 which inserted the word "mutual" into the treaty's title—to contribute to the defense of the United States.[7]

Although the United States pressed intensely throughout the 1950s for significantly increased Japanese defense responsibilities, including Japanese contributions to the "support of the defense...of the free world," Japan restricted its military efforts to a gradual and incremental buildup of its own indigenous defense capabilities. This buildup, moreover, had to be "in accord with national capability and the domestic situation" and "within the limits necessary for self-defense," a position formally codified as official Japanese policy in the 1957 Basic Policy for National Defense.[8] Together with the "Three Non-Nuclear Principles" and ban on arms exports, both adopted in 1967, and the 1976 "Basic Defense Program Outline," which lowered the formal target of Japan's defense buildup to the prevention of "limited and small-scale aggression," these policies completed Japan's basic security framework. This framework continues to govern Japanese defense policy today.

Japan's minimalist orientation was increasingly challenged over the course of the late 1970s and early 1980s by a series of international events, including the U.S. defeat in Vietnam, the Soviet military buildup in the Far East, and the combination of growing instability in the Mideast and increasing constraints on U.S. resources. As U.S. pressures mounted for greater Japanese self-defense and burden-sharing efforts, Japanese leaders began to modify, without formally revising, their defense policies. They utilized the provision in the 1976 National Defense Program Outline allowing for qualitative improvements in the Self-Defense Forces to improve significantly the SDF's capabilities, in terms of both the composition of units deployed and the kinds of weapons procured. They pushed out the perimeters of Japan's air and naval responsibilities from defense "at the water's edge" to extended (i.e., offshore) air and sea-lane defense. And they increased the resources allocated to defense, with real increases in defense spending of over 5 percent annually for most of the past decade.

At the same time, Japan significantly expanded its military interactions with the United States. It began to participate actively in expanded joint operational planning and military exercises, building on the 1978 "Guidelines on U.S.-Japan Defense Cooperation." It gradually increased financial support for the U.S. military presence in Japan—to the point where Japanese support now totals over $3 billion annually, the largest contribution ever made by a U.S. ally—while broadening its willingness to facilitate the operation of U.S. military forces in the region and beyond. And it agreed to make an "exception" to the government's longstanding ban on arms exports and allow the transfer of military technology to the United States. Although the formal agreement applies only to "military" technology, which Japan defines rather narrowly, the exchange of notes between the two countries suggests that "dual-use" technology transfers are also encouraged.[9]

These changes in traditional Japanese policies significantly improved Japan's military capabilities and made defense the happy part of the U.S.-Japanese relationship in the 1980s. But they should not be exaggerated. Japanese defense policies show a fundamental underlying continuity throughout the postwar period. The nonmilitary components of security continue to be emphasized. The basic security framework and host of policy restrictions laid down over the course of the 1950s and 1960s remain intact. And the Self-Defense Forces continue to be constrained by major resource, force structure, operational, technical, and political limitations.[10] Frequent allusions to Japan as the "third-ranking military power" in the world are doubly misleading: they overlook the effects of yen appreciation and confuse dollar value for military capability. When Japanese expenditures are calculated in terms of what they get for their yen, it turns out that Japan spends only a bit more today than Italy does on defense, and the actual *capabilities* of the Self-Defense Forces are roughly equivalent to those of a mid-level European power. Japan continues to lack both the ability and the will to play a regional military role. Indeed, it remains dependent on the United States for its own homeland defense, particularly in the areas of deterrence and offensive operations.

At the same time, thirty years after the word "mutual" was inserted into the title of the U.S.-Japan Security Treaty, Japan remains a reluctant partner. The response of Japanese leaders to U.S. requests in late 1990 and early 1991 that it assume responsibility for all yen-based costs for the maintenance of American forces in Japan, for example, was to haggle for months about the definition of the word "all."

In the end, Japan agreed to pay more of these costs (an increase of $600 million over five years to roughly 50 percent of the expenses) but refused to include expenses for such things as telephones and waste disposal.[11]

Finally, in terms of broader global contributions, Japan's assumptions were also well founded. The United States was aware of Asian sensitivities in the 1950s and 1960s and reluctant to exacerbate domestic political difficulties in Japan, particularly after the security treaty riots in 1960, and generally shied away from exerting much pressure. In any case, the United States was too preoccupied with pax Americana to pay much attention. No one else took Japan very seriously as a regional or global actor for more than two decades. This enabled Japan to focus almost singularly on the protection of its narrow economic interests. Given this opportunity, Japan behaved politically like the tall schoolboy who sits in the back of the class hoping no one will notice his presence.

Beginning in the early to mid-1970s, the Japanese began to modify their policies. This too was partly in response to U.S. pressures and partly a reaction to adverse international developments. Particularly important among the latter was the oil shock of 1973, which drove home Japan's vulnerability to events in distant places. In line with the new concept of "comprehensive" security and definition of Japan as a "member of the West," Japanese leaders began to broaden their horizons. They supported the Western allies on a string of international political issues including, among many others, the Iranian seizure of U.S. hostages, the Soviet invasion of Afghanistan, and the boycott of the Moscow Olympics. They endorsed allied statements on terrorism and arms control. And they resisted strong Soviet pressures and allowed Japanese firms to participate in the U.S. Strategic Defense Initiative. Most significantly, they began to increase substantially Japanese foreign economic assistance, to the point where today Japan is the world's largest donor of Official Development Assistance (ODA). As has frequently been emphasized by Washington, a growing share of this assistance has been targeted on countries—like Egypt, Pakistan, and Turkey—of strategic importance to the West.

These increased efforts fit in with Japan's historic desire to avoid international isolation. They also bolstered Japan's push for broader regional and global roles that emphasize nonmilitary factors. But here, too, the extent of change in Japanese policies should not be overstated. While Japanese ODA has risen rapidly, it still constitutes a tiny portion (0.3 percent) of GNP; it continues to emphasize project aid (much of which continues to be tied to Japanese purchases) rather than grant assistance; and it remains heavily concentrated in the region of the world where Japan's personal interests are greatest (Asia, which still gets roughly two-thirds of total Japanese assistance). Similarly, Japan's willingness to subordinate its interests indefinitely in favor of Western "solidarity" has clear limits, as seen recently on the question of loans to China.

Nor does Japan appear ready to broaden significantly its approach to "sharing" responsibilities for international security. The government will probably succeed ultimately in gaining legislative approval for Japanese participation in UN-led international peace-keeping operations. While symbolically important, however, this will be extremely limited; the number of forces is so small and their permissible operations are so constrained that their practical utility is questionable. It will be years before this embryonic group evolves into a normal, "after hostilities end" kind of peace-keeping organization, let alone be allowed to participate directly in collective security operations (such as Iraq) that require the use of force. While Japan clearly has come a long way, it equally clearly has a long way to go if it is to gain greater recognition from the international community for its contributions to regional and global security.

Globals Trends and National Strategy

Most observers agree that Japanese foreign policies—in terms of Japan's postwar strategic objectives—have been generally successful. From a country devastated by war, Japan has risen to the front ranks of the world's industrial and technological powers. Its personal-income levels are at least as high as those in the United States, and its economic impact is truly global in nature. Although Japan has not translated its economic capabilities into comparable military strength, and hence remains dependent on the United States as its ultimate security guarantor, it has managed to sustain an active U.S. involvement in Japan's defense while significantly improving its self-defense capabilities. If continued, the improvements made over the course of the 1980s should give Japan the capability to provide for its own immediate territorial defense in most conventional, non-Russian contingencies. They also will provide a fulsome foundation for expansion should international circumstances dictate. Japan coped well, on the whole, with the economic and military challenges of the 1970s and 1980s. Its successful adjustments bolstered national pride and self-confidence and generally reinforced the conviction that Japan's basic strategy is well founded.

The dramatic changes over the past couple of years and broader underlying trends, however, raise questions about the continued validity of the assumptions on which this strategy was originally predicated. Looking beyond the specific changes themselves, at least four broad megatrends call these assumptions into question.

The first is the global crisis of communism. This crisis, as is well known, stems from multiple sources: economic stagnation and decay, political disorganization, ethnic unrest, and rising nationalist aspirations. What makes it probably irreversible is the information revolution and increasing ability of both elites and masses within Communist societies to make comparative judgments.[12] One result of the Communist crisis is a general decline in the salience of ideology. Communism as an idea, let alone as a model for organizing and running a country, is simply bankrupt. Another result is a rise in the importance of performance as a basis for regime legitimacy. Governing elites can no longer rely on indoctrination to command popular support.

Both of these results have transformed internal Communist systems and dictated radical changes in foreign policies. In 1990 alone, the Ceaucescu regime in Romania was violently overthrown, East Germany disappeared, and even Albania opened itself to the rest of the world. Among the former members of Comecon, the Soviet-led trading group, Poland, Czechoslovakia, and Hungary have effectively rejoined Western Europe, propeled by the twin processes of democratization and economic transformation. Comecon itself has been disbanded. Most important, the Soviet Union has itself disintegrated. Whether the Commonwealth of Independent States holds together or not, the successor to the USSR will look very different. These developments have dramatically reduced the perception in the West of a threat from Soviet or Soviet-supported communism and fundamentally altered the structure of international relations. They also have occasioned a dramatic improvement in superpower relations, although the permanence of this improvement hinges critically on the future internal evolution of the former Soviet Union.

Although the changes have not been as dramatic in Communist Asia, they have been no less significant. There have been major policy departures (e.g., the Soviet decision to establish full diplomatic relations with South Korea, the initiation of talks between Vietnam and the United States, North Korea's proposal to open official ties with Japan) and new efforts to expand dialogue between traditional enemies (e.g., North and South Korea, China and Taiwan). The political and economic collapse of the USSR severely constrained the ability of any successor state to use military force in the region. Mongolia rejected Leninism entirely, opting for a rapid transition to democracy and a market-oriented economy. With the exception of North Korea, each of the remaining Asian Communist powers is trying to institute some measure of economic reform while insulating its political system from major changes. A process of gradual intraregional economic interaction is taking place more broadly, in which the Asian Communist countries themselves want to participate.

This clearly does not mean the dawning of a new age of peace and stability. The inherent inefficiencies of the Communist economic systems and magnitude of the problems they face make reform an extraordinarily complex undertaking. The decline of single-party states and widespread popular alienation foster serious political polarization, which further exacerbates the task of economic renewal. Together with rising ethnic tensions and competing nationalisms, the future of the states themselves is increasingly called into question. For these reasons, the Communist crisis is likely to be protracted and painful, with great uncertainty about its ultimate outcome.

However these situations play out, the exigencies of their internal situations and limited resources will probably limit the desire and capabilities of the major Communist countries—again, with the possible exception of North Korea—for foreign adventurism. Together with the irreversible collapse of the Soviet empire and the end of a *global* Communist challenge, this undermines support within the United States for a continuing heavy military burden.

The U.S. government has strongly emphasized the importance of U.S.-Japanese relations and publicly reaffirmed its commitment to the bilateral security alliance. U.S. regional military planning reinforces the central importance of Japan and the continuing U.S. defense commitment. But pressures are mounting in the United States for reexamination of this orientation. The strategy of forward deployment itself is increasingly being called into question. A continuation of present trends will almost surely lead to larger military drawdowns—globally and in the Asia/Pacific region—than anything yet anticipated.[13] Quite apart from the growing rancor in U.S.-Japanese relations, this could over time call into question Japan's strategic assumption of a continuing large-scale U.S. role in its defense.

A second historic trend is the relative shift of economic power to the Pacific. This shift has been in progress for some time. In 1960, for example, the combined national products of Japan, China, South Korea, and Taiwan were roughly half those of West Germany, France, and the United Kingdom (500 billion 1986 U.S. dollars versus 1 trillion); by 1980, they surpassed those of the three European powers. According to some estimates, the combined national products of the four Asian countries could exceed those of West Germany, France, and the United Kingdom by the year 2010 by as much as 120 percent (8.5 trillion 1986 U.S. dollars versus 3.9 trillion)—and could surpass the United States in combined GNP as early as the turn of the twenty-first century.[14] This transformation has resulted from sustained high rates of growth that, over the last two decades, far exceeded those for the United States and key Western European nations.

One well-known consequence of this power shift is the increased weight of the Asian-Pacific countries in global economic interactions. U.S. trade across the Pacific has surpassed that across the Atlantic for over a decade; in 1988, the former exceeded the latter by almost 50 percent, with East Asia now accounting for over one-third of total U.S. foreign commerce.[15] U.S.-Asian investment flows now total over $150 billion. The relative shift of economic power to the Pacific also has important political effects, bolstering the national self-confidence and self-esteem of the countries of the region and increasing their ability to play larger roles in regional politics.

In the United States, however, there are additional effects. For one thing, the shift of power further undermines political support for a leading U.S. role in regional defense. The argument is simply hard to make that such wealthy countries cannot do more to defend themselves. More important, perhaps, the shift exacerbates national anxieties over long-term American competitiveness and strengthens protectionist sentiment, particularly vis-à-vis Japan. Indeed, many polls suggest that Americans are increasingly coming to regard Japan's economic power as a "critical threat" to the United States.[16] As evident in the area of technology transfers, where the United States is becoming increasingly restrictive, this calls into question Japan's strategic assumption that the United States will continue to define ongoing Japanese economic development as in the U.S. interest.

A third broad trend is the increasing primacy of domestic considerations. This stems partly from the Communist crisis mentioned above: In the East, the crisis has unleashed previously suppressed nationalist and ethnic aspirations and intensified the preoccupation of Communist governments with their internal difficulties; in the West, both publics and elites have been freed to address long-neglected domestic problems as national security concerns abate. The emphasis on domestic consider-ations is also linked, however, to a growing struggle between nationalism and interdependence. Although the dominant economic trend is toward the latter, as the U.S.-Japanese talks on structural impediments so graphically symbolize, interde-pendence is a two-edged sword. While it bolsters the impetus toward cooperation, it also weakens national control over economies. As the decentralization of manu-facturing, globalization of major industries, and internationalization of capital flows have increasingly challenged national boundaries, popular pressures have mounted for a nationalist response. These pressures are particularly evident today in U.S.-Japanese relations, where a rising emotionalism on both sides strengthens insular tendencies and exacerbates the difficulty of containing economic ten-sions.[17]

Whatever its derivation, increasingly the interest of citizens is focused on local matters. This accounts for the heightened emphasis in much of the West on issues like crime, drugs, the environment, and inadequate or decaying domestic infrastruc-tures. The United States is no exception. One striking feature of the congressional debate on the Persian Gulf, for example, was the emphasis on the costs of foreign involvement in domestic terms (e.g., lives lost, scarce resources squandered) rather than on the foreign policy aspects of the crisis per se. This reflects the broader contemporary American preoccupation—not so much with problems of foreign policy but with disastrous public education, faltering living standards, and the rising challenge of foreign competition. In the process, economic competitiveness and quality of life are gradually replacing national security as the dominant concerns. In this sense, the Persian Gulf crisis may well turn out to have been mislabeled: not so much the "first crisis of the post–Cold War era" but the *last* crisis of the *postwar* era.

The trend toward increasing emphasis on domestic considerations, coupled with the collapse of the global Communist crisis and U.S. economic difficulties, has already fostered a political backlash in the United States against foreign aid and overseas spending. It also has bolstered pressures toward a less prominent regional military posture. While reaffirming longstanding treaties and defense commitments, the U.S. government is moving in response from a leading to a more "supportive" stance in the region. This involves a drawdown and restructuring of U.S. military forces deployed in the region and encouragement of greater balance and mutuality in U.S. relations with key allies. Although the force drawdowns to date have been minimal, further reductions are almost inevitable. Given U.S. budgetary problems and changing popular attitudes more broadly, efforts by U.S. allies to increase their support for the remaining American military presence will be essential. Broader efforts to contribute to regional and global security, through economic assistance, refugee aid, peacekeeping operations, and other international efforts, will also be emphasized. In the absence of such efforts, the United States could retreat from internationalization and make a major turn inward. Even short of this, Japan can no longer assume that it can focus on its own economic advancement without making significant reciprocal contributions to the common welfare.

A final megatrend is the proliferation of advanced technology and both nuclear and sophisticated conventional weapons. This trend is rooted in several developments: dramatic increases in the sales or transfers of military equipment to Third World countries as a result of the intensified superpower competition in the 1970s and early 1980s; a heightened ability of many Third World countries to demand top-of-the-line equipment as a result of increased competition among vendors for arms exports; and greater resources available to many of these countries as a result of increased oil prices and/or sustained high rates of economic growth.[18] These developments have enabled countries around the world to acquire sophisticated weaponry while developing domestic arms industries and becoming actors in the international arms market.

The developments have also fostered a quiet but significant arms buildup in Asia. This is probably not as surprising as it may at first appear: Asia has seven of the ten largest militaries in the world; the size and diversity of the region ensure the presence of numerous animosities, ethnic and religious tensions, and historic regional rivalries; and the successful growth and development of the region over the past decade have made new resources available for national military purposes. At the same time, growing population pressures, decreasing global reserves of petroleum, and increasing competition for food, water, and other natural resources have encouraged increased Asian attention to securing their territorial land and waters. The generally successful handling of domestic insurgencies—with the principal exception of the Philippines—has facilitated this shift in attention by enabling non-Communist Asian countries to focus greater attention on external threats to their security.

As a result, most are significantly expanding their military capabilities. This is reflected in Asian military spending. South Korea has been allocating roughly 5 percent of its GNP to defense for several years (with North Korea continuing to spend 20–25 percent of its GNP and in excess of 30 percent of its national budget). Thailand's defense budget increased 16 percent in 1989 to over $2 billion. Malaysia's budget expanded by 20 percent over the past two years. Singapore's defense budget now totals some $1.5 billion annually, which represents nearly a quarter of the total government budget and 5.5 percent of GNP. Including China, India, and Australia, regional military spending is now around $60 billion and is expected to more than double over the next decade.[19]

Much of this spending is going to power projection capabilities. South Korea, Singapore, and Indonesia all have F-16 fighter-bombers. India, Pakistan, China, Taiwan, and both North and South Korea have ballistic missiles either already in service or under development. Although domestic difficulties will make rapid development difficult, both China and India are intent on acquiring formidable blue-water navies. A number of the "have-not" states, including most ominously North Korea, are now developing nuclear weapons. Along with rising technological skills and organizational changes within the military services improving command and control, such acquisitions are significantly raising the military capabilities of many Asian countries. These capabilities are being formed, moreover, in an environment of rising regional anxieties about the long-term prospects for Japan—particularly in China and South Korea—and major potential political instabilities. These developments cut across Japan's strategic assumptions and underline the importance of the United States to both Japanese national interests and broader regional stability.

Global Trends and Foreign Policy in the 1990s
Few events symbolize the challenges for future Japanese foreign policy as do the Persian Gulf crisis and stalemate in the Uruguay Round of trade negotiations. The crisis in the gulf will have an impact on many aspects of international politics, first and foremost on the future of the Mideast, but a broad question will be how the outcome affects U.S. attitudes toward key allied nations. In light of the megatrends described above, a worst-case scenario is not required to envision a gradual U.S. retrenchment over the course of the 1990s and significantly altered U.S.-allied relations. Japan's response to the gulf crisis does not position it well to prevent adverse spillover. Already many in the United States have linked Japan's minimal efforts in the gulf (and those of other European allies more broadly) toward festering trade disputes and resentments, a particularly volatile linkage given the current American emphases on "fairness," "equity," and the "sharing" of international security "burdens."

The possible collapse of the GATT similarly strikes at longstanding, fundamental Japanese interests. Preservation and expansion of the liberal trading system over the postwar period has fostered an unprecedented period of global economic growth and prosperity. Japan, at least as much as most nations, has benefited from this system. At present, it is uncertain whether a collapse of the GATT will be averted. If not, the United States could move to unilateral measures that would significantly strain, and perhaps undermine, the U.S.-Japanese relationship. Even if collapse can be averted, however, a broader trend toward the development of regional trading groupings and different forms of managed trade is already well in progress. The European Community is on the verge of full economic integration, a North American (U.S.-Canada-Mexico) trading group is making rapid progress, and an Asian bloc led by Japan is in an incipient stage of development. Collapse of the GATT could significantly expedite this process and trigger a global turn toward protectionist measures. Even short of this, economic nationalism is rising in the United States. Japan could find its access to U.S. markets increasingly restricted and its opportunities to benefit from U.S. support of free trade abruptly curtailed.

Whatever the lasting impact of the Persian Gulf crisis and GATT negotiations, it is likely that the 1990s will present a less tolerant environment for Japan than that to which it has become accustomed. Projecting how Japan will respond is a difficult proposition. Two critical factors would need to be examined: how the United States responds to the broad trends and recent changes, and what will happen in Japanese domestic politics. Given the centrality of the United States to Japan's fundamental strategic orientation, its actions will be critical to Japan's direction. Indeed, if there is any single determinant of future Japanese policies, it is the United States and the state of U.S.-Japanese relations. At the same time, these policies will be heavily constrained and influenced by what happens inside Japan. There are elements of both change and continuity here that, depending on how they interact with the evolving international order, will help fashion Japanese responses. Without exploring these factors, it is difficult to project future Japanese policies, or even to identify real (as opposed to theoretical) policy options.

The purpose of this chapter is more modest: to initiate thinking about Japanese foreign policy in a broad, global context and stimulate discussion about the implications of international and regional trends for Japan's future orientation. Three broad questions seem particularly important, in this regard, for future Japanese policies.

The first question is whether Japan will be able to bring its policies more into line with its capabilities and the changing international order. There is no question that Japan's pursuit of its basic strategy has been very successful. By concentrating on economic development and minimizing both military and political efforts, the Japanese have been able to build a prosperous, advanced society while avoiding military conflict and foreign entanglements. There is also no question but that Japan has made important adjustments in its policies over the past two decades that have enabled it to adapt well to changes in the external environment, while continuing to meet its strategic objectives. These adjustments strengthened Japan and reinforced confidence in its basic orientation.

The dramatic global changes of the past couple of years and the underlying trends more broadly, however, are creating entirely new international and regional environments. In these environments, the continued validity of the assumptions underlying Japan's traditional strategy appear increasingly uncertain. For Japan to adhere to its basic strategy, it will need a more active and prominent international posture, one that draws on Japan's domestic strengths and is more commensurate with its economic, technological, and managerial capabilities. This also means continued progress on a troika of familiar policy imperatives: liberalization, internationalization, and burden sharing. How Japan addresses these imperatives will go a long way toward determining the durability of its traditional strategic orientation.

The second question is whether Japan can achieve a more balanced relationship with the United States. For reasons pertaining to Japan's increased status and capabilities, on the one hand, and U.S. budgetary difficulties and attitudinal changes, on the other, reducing asymmetries in the bilateral relationship is becoming increasingly urgent. Put simply, Japanese are tiring of being presented with faits accompli while being blamed for what they perceive as U.S. difficulties; Americans are tiring of the perceived one-sidedness of bilateral relations. Adjusting the relationship involves both substantive and procedural issues.

On the substantive side, the task will be to define and effectuate a relationship in which leadership is more equally shared. To the extent that Japan has thought about this issue, it has tended to see the United States assuming responsibility for the "guns" with Japan providing the "butter." If the analysis of the broad megatrends above is even roughly accurate, however, this definition is simply not adequate. The guns are going down, and the United States will not be long content with Japan getting fat off the butter. A more comprehensive conception involving integrated bilateral cooperation across the board will almost surely be necessary.

This will require in turn a greater sense of common purpose. Japan has benefited enormously from the U.S. preoccupation with the Soviet Union over the past four decades. The common interest in resisting Communist expansion has underpinned and cemented the bilateral relationship. Today there is an entirely new set of foreign policy issues: coping with the Communist crisis; managing ethnic tensions and regional disputes; containing proliferation; strengthening a free and open trading system; fostering the growth of democratic polities and human rights; and facilitating progress on a host of "new order" issues like drugs and environmental decay. At the same time, Asia is facing potentially dramatic change over the coming decade, including instability and possible systemic change in China and reunification—and/or an explosion—on the Korean peninsula. Whether Japan shares the U.S. perspective and definition of "global responsibilities" on these issues remains uncertain. A prerequisite for sharing responsibilities on these issues will be determining and affirming the two countries' common interests.

On the procedural side, the challenge will be to institute meaningful consultations at all stages of the planning process. The criticism is often made that the United States is unwilling to share decision-making authority with Japan, only to share the burdens that flow from unilateral U.S. decisions. While there is undoubtedly some truth to this criticism, there is also a question of whether Japan is willing to assume responsibility for making decisions that involve increased Japanese "burdens." Clearly, Japan has been trying for some time to expand bilateral consultations to exercise greater constraint over "unilateral" U.S. actions. This is understandable from a Japanese perspective. But absent greater Japanese willingness to accept responsibility for the decisions made, it is not clear why the United States would want to move in this direction.

The final question is "what happens if." We live, as the Chinese might say, in "interesting" times. If any single theme emerges from an analysis of recent global developments, it is one of uncertainty. What happens if the United States moves in more of an isolationist direction than is currently anticipated? Would Japan be more likely to become more insular itself or move in a more assertive, "independent" direction? To what extent is Japan planning for surprise? Its response to the Persian Gulf crisis does not suggest a very effective institutional capacity for responding to rapid changes. Most fundamentally, is there a strategic alternative to heavy reliance on the United States? What would this be, and how would it affect Japanese foreign policies? These questions may not have to be answered. But they are questions that thoughtful Japanese may want to begin considering.

Notes

The views expressed in this chapter are those of the author alone. They do not represent the positioning of RAND, the U.S. government, or any of its sponsors.

1. Mike Mochizuki, "Japan and the Strategic Quadrangle," in Seweryn Bialer and Michael Mandelbaum, eds., *The Politics of the Strategic Quadrangle: The United States, the Soviet Union, Japan and China in East Asia* (Boulder: Westview Press, 1990), p. 3.

2. Edward J. Lincoln, *Japan: Facing Economic Maturity* (Washington, D.C.: The Brookings Institution, 1988), pp. 14–129 and *passim*.

3. K. C. Yeh et al., *The Changing Asian Economic Environment and U.S.-Japan Trade Relations,* R- 3986-CUSJR (Santa Monica: The RAND Corporation, September 1990), p. 16.

4. *New York Times,* January 7, 1991.

5. Lincoln, *Japan,* pp. 238 and 288.

6. Although the United States pushed Japan for a security arrangement, the pact reflects

U.S. reluctance to make a major, long-term defense commitment. Noting that the United States would only "temporarily" station troops in Japan, it emphasized the U.S. "expectation" that "Japan will increasingly assume responsibility itself for its own defense against direct and indirect aggression."

7. The only element of "mutuality" in the defense commitments concerns "armed attacks against either Party in the territories under the administration of Japan" (article V).

8. For more details, see Norman D. Levin, *Japan's Changing Defense Posture*, N-2739-OSD (Santa Monica: The RAND Corporation, June 1988), pp. 2–3.

9. U.S. Department of Defense, *Japanese Military Technology: Procedures for Transfers to the United States,* February 1986.

10. Norman D. Levin et al., *The Wary Warriors: Future Directions in Japanese Security Policies* (forthcoming).

11. *New York Times*, December 21, 1990. This occurred in the midst of the U.S. deployment of 400,000 soldiers to the Persian Gulf, which, among other things, was meant to protect Japan's supply of oil.

12. Among many who make this point, see Albert Wohlstetter, "Towards a Coherent Framework for Cooperation and Competition," forthcoming, and Robert Scalapino, "Asia and the United States: The Challenges Ahead," *Foreign Affairs* (February 1990): 89–91.

13. Already U.S. defense expenditures have fallen to their lowest level as a share of federal spending in over fifty years (19.6 percent in FY 1992 vs. 27 percent as recently as 1987 and 39–57 percent over the 1950s and 1960s). The Pentagon's planned 25 percent ("base force") reductions increasingly appear a "best case" outcome.

14. Charles Wolf et al, *Long-Term Economic and Military Trends, 1950–2010,* N-2757-USDP (Santa Monica: The RAND Corporation, April 1989), p. 7.

15. Richard Solomon, "The Promise of Pacific Cooperation," *Current Policy*, no. 1208 (Washington, D.C.: U.S. Department of State, October 1989).

16. See, for example, Ed Reilly, *American Public Opinion and U. S. Foreign Policy in 1991* (Chicago: Chicago Council on Foreign Relations, 1991), p. 7.

17. Scalapino, "Asia and the United States" pp. 102–4.

18. Lewis Dunn and James Tomashoff, *New Technologies and the Changing Dimensions of Third World Military Conflict* (Center for National Security Negotiations, April 1990), pp. 3–7.

19. *The New York Times*, May 6, 1990.

Chapter 10
Japan's Foreign Policy Options: Implications for the United States

Martin E. Weinstein

There is very little evidence suggesting that fundamental or dramatic shifts in Japan's basic strategy and foreign policy are imminent or likely in the near future. Consequently, in looking at Japan's strategic and foreign policy options, I suggest that in addition to examining the recent and current foreign policy debate, we also attempt to peer into the next ten to twenty years, the late 1990s and the first decade of the twenty-first century. Given the rate and extent of change occurring in the international system, especially in the Soviet Union and Europe, and the Iraqi invasion of Kuwait, it is more likely than at any time since the late 1940s and early 1950s that fundamental changes in the international system will occur during the next decade or two, which could compel Japan to change its strategy and foreign policy.

Japan's strategy and foreign policy, including both its security policies and its foreign economic policies, have been highly successful and stable since the late 1940s and early 1950s, when they were formulated and defined. The success of these policies has generated enormous inertia and an enormous reluctance to depart from them, until and unless it becomes clear to the Japanese government and the voters that it is necessary to do so. Although the Persian Gulf crisis generated an unprecedented level of international criticism of Japan, and the Japanese are now much more aware of the need to enlarge their international role, it is still not clear what the nature and scope of their response will be.

Japanese Policy since World War II: The Yoshida Strategy
What are the defining characteristics of this highly successful policy? What is the baseline from which we begin our speculation about options and possible changes in the future?

Ever since the late 1940s, and indeed even back to the 1860s and 1870s when the Meiji oligarchs began Japan's industrialization, there has been a clear perception in the Japanese government that (1) the building of a viable and then a competitive industrial economy and a stable, effective political system has been the primary objective of national policy; (2) the achievement of these goals is very heavily contingent on foreign policy; and (3) the security and economic dimensions of foreign policy are inextricably linked. It has been clear to Japanese officials since early in the modernization process that, given its geographical position and resources, the success of Japan's industrialization would depend on access to overseas raw materials (and, in the twentieth century, especially energy) and to overseas markets. The particular lesson of World War II, which was engraved very deeply on the national psyche, is that Japan cannot achieve this necessary access to the world economy by the use of military force. The Japanese concluded, therefore, that they must avoid as much as possible any military role in international politics, and that they must rely on peaceful, nonmilitary means to build their economy and to make a decent life for themselves.

By the late 1940s and early 1950s, Japan's conservative foreign policy makers, especially Yoshida Shigeru, who served as prime minister from 1948 to 1954, had concluded that in the bipolar, U.S.-Soviet dominated international system, the best foreign policy for Japan was (1) to become an ally of the United States (not a military dependent), and (2) to base Japan's economic future on the relatively free, open international economic system that the United States was constructing—most especially on cooperative economic relations with the United States itself, which would be a major source of raw materials and a major market for Japanese manufactured products. It is worth noting forty years later that while Japan's reliance on American raw materials has declined somewhat since the 1950s, it still relies heavily on American farm products, timber, and coking coal, and in the 1980s, Japan's exports to the United States reached record levels, approaching 40 percent of total exports.

Prime Minister Yoshida's strategy was rooted in the belief that the alliance with the United States would protect Japan against the Communist, Soviet threat to its military security and political stability. Within the secure, stable strategic-political framework provided by the security treaty, and by the United States nuclear deterrent and naval and air preponderance in the Pacific and over the world ocean and trade routes, the Japanese would be able to concentrate their energies and organizational skills in the 1950s on the task of economic reconstruction, and then on the goal of becoming a highly efficient, competitive industrial economy.

Recent Events Shake the Premises of Success

As we know, this foreign policy was highly successful—perhaps too successful. By the end of the 1980s, however, the basic premises of the Yoshida policy were being called into question by two related developments in Japan's external environment. First, the Communist, Soviet threat appeared to be diminishing to the point where it could cease being the negative force binding the United States and

Japan into a security alliance. At the same time, Japan's successes in building a competitive, industrial economy were generating potentially dangerous levels of resentment, fear and antagonism toward Japan in the United States. As a consequence, Japan bashing became popular in the Congress and in the media, and the U. S. government began moving toward protectionist economic policies directed against Japan, such as the Super 301 provisions of the 1988 Trade Act. This mounting antagonism, and the creeping protectionism that accompanies it, threatened to undermine the GATT and the relatively open international systems of trade and finance upon which Japan's prosperity and security depends.

Obviously, these two related and, to some extent, mutually reinforcing international developments call into question the basic premises and elements of the foreign policy that has served Japan so well since the Korean War (1950–53). Equally significant has been the call from abroad that Japan take on a larger role in the international community to a level commensurate with its economic power. At no other time was this more clearly stated, and Japan's actions as closely monitored, as during the 1990–91 crisis and hostilities in the Persian Gulf.

Japan's apparently lethargic response in the gulf was in reality an abortive policy initiative encumbered by protracted legislative debate on issues of constitutionality, and exacerbated by the inability of a prime minister with a weak power base to win a timely consensus on either the allocation of funds or the dispatch of Self-Defense Forces (SDF) personnel overseas. The result was predictable: criticism from the international community, led by the United States, that Japan was shirking its international responsibility and reaping the benefits of the "allied" military action, to which Japan contributed money but not men.

The image of a Japan that reacts slowly and timidly only when forced to by an international crisis, or of an economic power that lacks geopolitical power, is indeed difficult to overcome, at home as well as abroad. "Tokyo would not have been criticized so harshly, if it had acted at the same time as Washington, or at least more promptly than it did," stated Professor Kitaoka Shin'ichi in the April 1991 issue of *Chuo koron*, "but because we were so slow, we always seem to be acting reluctantly in response to American pressure."[1] Following Japan's pledge on March 1, 1991, of an additional $9 billion to the gulf effort (beyond the $4 billion previously promised), an editorial in the *Nihon keizai shimbun*, Japan's leading financial daily, accurately concluded that because the Japanese government had moved so slowly, its willingness to pay for as much as 20 percent of the cost of the war "was not really appreciated,"[2] even though an earlier report in the same paper cited official American appreciation of Japan's generous and timely support, as expressed by Presidential Press Secretary Marlin Fitzwater.[3] Similarly, when a minesweeping group of six ships and approximately 500 Marine Self-Defense Forces personnel were dispatched to the gulf in April, 1991, the editors of the *Yomiuri shimbun* wondered in their headline "Will U.S. Dissatisfaction be Mitigated?"[4] while an article in the *Asahi shimbun* noted the low priority given Japan by Secretary of State Baker in his meetings with individual leaders of the allied nations foreign ministries.[5]

If nothing else, however, the events in the Persian Gulf may have heightened domestic awareness in Japan of the necessity of increasing its international role. In November 1990, before hostilities actually broke out in the gulf and before criticism of Japan reached its peak, an *Asahi shimbun* poll showed that public opinion ran very strongly against any Japanese involvement beyond economic support. As many as 78 percent of the respondents opposed the dispatch of SDF personnel to the Persian Gulf,[6] and 55 percent even rejected a plan for using SDF forces to transport Gulf War refugees.[7] By June 1991, however, only 13 percent of those polled in a survey conducted by the *Mainichi shimbun* were opposed to SDF participation in UN peace-keeping operations following the 1991 war,[8] and an *Asahi shimbun* poll showed that 64 percent had come around to the view that "it is now necessary for Japan to play a much more active role than before in settling international disputes."[9] Of course, one can argue that the Japanese public was more willing to consider SDF participation in a UN operation in June 1991, because the danger of imminent hostilities had passed. It is probably also true, however, that the protracted barrage of intense foreign criticism of Japan's policy of limiting its involvement in the Gulf to funding while avoiding the fighting also contributed to this shift in public opinion.[10]

The Current Foreign Policy Debate

The media in Japan is as open and free as any in the world, and the print media in particular is an extremely rich source in studying politics and foreign policy. Groups of journalists from each of the major national newspapers, organized into press clubs, have attached themselves to the prime minister, each of the powerful ministries, and the powerful faction leaders in the political parties, who serve in the National Diet. Politics and foreign policy are covered in extraordinary, generally accurate detail and with extensive analysis. Moreover, in Japan there are monthly intellectual journals, such as *Chuo koron, Bungei shunju,* and *Ushio,* in which foreign policy intellectuals of all political persuasions, from Marxists to right-wing nationalists, and everyone in-between, criticize policy and tell the government what it should be doing. Based on a study of several hundred newspaper articles and several dozen journal articles and books on foreign policy published between 1988 and 1991, and interviews with senior Japanese foreign policy officials, there appears to be virtually no evidence that Japan is planning to change fundamentally or even substantially its foreign policy. These materials do indicate, however, that there is widespread awareness in Japan that the alliance with the United States is in danger, that its future is less certain than ever before, and that substantial, even fundamental, changes in national and foreign policy may become unavoidable within the next decade or two.

One of the effects of the alliance's apparent vulnerability and uncertain future is that its Japanese critics have lowered their voices if not changed their minds. When, in the 1950s and 1960s, the United States had a position of unchallengeable economic and military strength, and when the reliability of its guarantee of Japan's security was hardly questioned, a slight majority of the Japanese voters consistently told pollsters that they did *not* support the security treaty. In those long ago days, there were many Japanese who believed that the Americans had too much military power, were excessively anti-Communist and trigger-happy, and that to keep the United States from behaving recklessly, it was wise not to support the security treaty. Most of those critics were actually content to have Japan protected by the United States, and polls indicated that approximately 80 percent of the Japanese then believed that the United States would come to Japan's defense if it were attacked or threatened with attack.

Following the rapprochement with China in 1972, the defeat of the United States in Vietnam in 1975, the apparent weakening of U. S. naval and air strength in the Pacific relative to that of the Soviet Union, and the increase in trade frictions, Japanese belief in the reliability of the American security guarantee dropped to about 20 percent in the 1980s. It is not surprising that under these changed conditions, many former critics of the security treaty decided it was now necessary to strengthen the credibility of the treaty by supporting it.

It should not be surprising, therefore, that during the last few years criticism against the U.S.-Japanese Security Treaty and the alliance has dropped to an all-time low. By the mid-1980s, a variety of opinion polls showed that between 70 and 80 percent of Japanese voters had become supporters or had a favorable view of the alliance. During the general election in the fall of 1989, Ms. Doi Takako, at the time the new, more pragmatic leader of the Japan Socialist Party (JSP) (the English version of its name since changed to Social Democratic party of Japan), bowed to public opinion by declaring that if the Socialists won the election and formed a government, they would *not* abrogate the security treaty. They would, instead, study the treaty and perhaps recommend some revisions. Since the JSP had been calling for abrogation of the treaty since the party was formed in 1954, Ms. Doi's change of line created dissension among her party cadres. A number of the more persistent, left-wing Socialists have publicly disagreed with the Doi position. Nevertheless, the effect of Ms. Doi's change was to sharply reduce and divide the harshest and most consistent critics of the alliance.

At the same time, on the center and right of the political spectrum there has been a lively debate about the future of the U. S.-Japanese alliance. The Toshiba Incident in the summer of 1987, the Trade Act of 1988, which led to the Super 301 actions of 1988–89, and the FSX controversy have been given much more coverage and attention in Japan than in the United States. Moreover, critics of Japan in the

Congress, such as Representative Richard Gephardt and Senators Lloyd Bentsen and John Danforth, and among intellectuals, such as Clyde Prestowitz and James Fallows, probably have a larger more attentive audience in Japan than they do at home. The natural and expected result is that many of the Japanese who have been publicly supporting and explaining the alliance for several decades have begun to wonder aloud about what has to be done to keep the alliance alive, or whether it can be saved at all. An examination of several representative writings indicates the variety of analyses and views in this new genre.

Save the Alliance Even at the Cost of Wrenching Economic and Social Changes in Japan

Sato Seizaburo, who recently retired as a professor of international relations at Tokyo University, is one of the leading and most outspoken advocates of preserving the alliance with the United States. In March 1990, Professor Sato published an article in *Chuo koron* in which he pulled together many of the ideas and arguments of those in and outside the Japanese government who believe that while the alliance has entered a period of instability and vulnerability, Japan has a vital stake in keeping it alive.[11] To preserve the alliance, Sato argued, Japan should make dramatic and substantial changes in its own foreign economic policies as well as in its domestic social and political structures.

Sato believes that there is a tendency in both Japan and the United States to act as though the Soviet threat has disappeared. In his view, while the Soviets are clearly in a period of confusion and decline, they still have enormous nuclear and conventional military forces, and depending on how their current crisis is resolved, these forces could once again become a serious threat to both Japan and the United States. He concludes therefore, that it is shortsighted and irresponsible to talk and act as though the U.S.-Japanese Security Treaty were obsolete.

Professor Sato then goes on to argue that even if the Soviet threat does, in the future, virtually disappear, the U. S. and Japanese economies have become intertwined and interdependent, and that the economic dimension of the alliance is fundamentally beneficial to both partners, and to the entire world economy. He believes that the economic costs of abrogating or abandoning the present high levels of economic interaction and cooperation would be staggering. If Japan and the United States start fighting trade wars and indulge in protectionism and techno-nationalism, Sato expects that not only the Pacific region but the entire global political economy would be dangerously destabilized.

Professor Sato's prescription for preserving the alliance is that Japan should take the lead in eliminating whatever restrictions remain on trade and investment. He advocates that Japan move quickly to reorganize its distribution system and business practices to make them more accessible and attractive to Americans. On the issue of technology, he urges Japanese to make available to the United States whatever superior technology it may have developed, especially if this technology has military applications. Sato urges Japan to "offer its best technology to America . . . and help Americans to build the best possible FSX fighter."[12] (The FSX is an advanced, experimental jet fighter based on the F-16, which is being jointly developed by General Dynamics and Mitsubishi Heavy Industry. It is to be manufactured in Japan for the Air Self-Defense Force in the late 1990s.)

Japanese (and Perhaps Americans) Underestimate the Danger of Their Economic Quarrels

Athough this is essentially a variant of the Sato approach, it is worth examining because it indicates the seriousness and depth of concern among Japanese conservatives over the future of their relationship with the United States. Okazaki Hisahiko has thoughtfully expounded this theme. He is a senior diplomat who has served as ambassador in Saudi Arabia and Bangkok and is well known in Japan for his many books and articles on foreign policy and strategy. In the January 1990 issue of *Bungei shunju*, Mr. Okazaki published an article entitled, "What Can Japan Learn From Holland?"[13] In this article Mr. Okazaki presented a scholarly analysis, drawing heavily on British sources, of the causes of the Anglo-Dutch wars of the late seventeenth century (First, 1652–54; Second, 1665–67; Third, 1672–78).

In these wars, Holland was defeated by Britain and lost much of its overseas holdings and influence, as well as suffering severe economic damage and dislocation. The main point that Okazaki makes is that the Dutch did not expect war and persisted in believing that Britain and Holland were basically friendly, compatible countries beset by economic frictions and quarrels, which would be peacefully resolved by mutual, enlightened self-interest. After all, Holland and England had fought together against Spain and the Habsburgs in the Thirty Years War. They were both Protestant states in a century when religion was as important as ideology was to be in the twentieth century. Both countries were proud of their commercial, trading, and manufacturing skills and viewed themselves as rational and enlightened rather than passionate and military. The Dutch firmly believed that even after the defeat of the Catholics and the decline of the Spanish threat, they and the English would continue as friendly trading partners, if not close allies.

Nevertheless, Okazaki draws on the writings of British historians to show that in the late seventeenth century, Holland's trade surpluses with England, together with its technological successes and its banking skills, generated such resentment and jealousy across the channel that enlightened English self-interest gave way to Holland bashing and protectionism that did as much damage to England as to Holland, and that finally led to war, which did much more damage to Holland.

Okazaki cautions that there are many differences between the Anglo-Dutch relationship in the seventeenth century and the current U.S.-Japanese relationship. But he concludes his article by asking:

Was there some way that Holland, itself a model economic superpower, could have avoided conflict with England while maintaining its
security interests and continuing its prosperity? If so, where did the
Dutch take a wrong turn? Did they have a plan to avoid this wrong turn?
Answers to these questions may provide Japan with vital information
by which to chart its course for the years ahead.[14]

Save the Alliance, but Only as an Equal Partnership

Ishihara Shintaro, a novelist and a Liberal Democratic member of the national Diet,
has gained a certain notoriety in the United States as a consequence of the
unauthorized translation and distribution in the summer of 1989 of a book of essays
he coauthored with Sony chairman Morita Akio, entitled *A Japan That Can Say
'No' to America.* The controversy surrounding the initial appearance of this book
seems to have led Mr. Morita to disassociate himself from it. However, an
authorized translation of five of Mr. Ishihara's original essays, together with six
additional pieces was published in early 1991 by Simon and Schuster, entitled *The
Japan That Can Say 'No'.* [15]

For several decades, Ishihara has run for political office on two foreign policy
planks. He has supported the U.S.-Japanese alliance, but he has wanted Japan to
stop being "subservient" to U.S. demands and "bullying." He has argued, long
before the revisionists and Japan bashers appeared in the United States, that unless
the growing economic and technological equality and interdependence of the two
countries is matched by more equal influence and control over alliance policy,
Japanese resentment and American arrogance are likely to destroy this highly
successful and mutually beneficial relationship. Several of Ishihara's older essays
in this vein appear in the new book, along with more recent pieces on the FSX
controversy.

In the FSX essays, he expressed great irritation at those congressmen and critics
in Washington who attacked U.S.-Japanese codevelopment of the FSX as a technological give-away to Japan, which would endanger the United States aerospace
industry. Ishihara wrote that Japan should have responded to those charges by
developing the FSX itself. Probably the most controversial and inflammatory point
he made was his contention that the Pentagon depends on Japanese chips to control
its strategic missiles, and that if Americans continue to bash and bully Japan,
Japanese should consider the possibility of selling their chip technology to the
Soviets as well as to Americans. This, he argued, would awaken Americans to the
reality of their technological dependence on Japan and get them to talk about power
sharing as well as burden sharing.

Ishihara's threat of selling chip technology to the Soviet Union faded quickly
as the Soviet Union slipped into deeper economic and political weakness during
1990–91. Whatever one thinks of Ishihara's approach, it should be noted that while

his arguments imply that the treaty is dispensable, he does not call for the abrogation of the security treaty, and he repeatedly states his support for the alliance as a partnership of equals. It seems to me that the greatest difficulty in Ishihara's approach is that it is not clear what he wants to do about the military inequality between Japan and the United States. Sometimes he seems to be calling for Japan to become a military as well as an economic superpower—a message that raises as much fear within Japan as it does outside.

On economic questions, Ishihara's views overlap with those of Sato. He urges that Japan drastically reform its distribution system and transform itself into a leading free-market, free-trading country. He believes that the Japanese consumer will benefit from such reforms, and he is confident that Japan is strong and competitive enough to thrive in this role. He contends, however, that unless the United States undertakes whatever reforms are necessary to regain its financial solvency, rebuild its industries, and educate its people, the American economy will continue to drift into ever greater difficulties, thus endangering the bilateral relationship with Japan and the entire world economy.

The Alliance Cannot Be Saved Because the United States Does Not Need It Anymore

In January 1990, Tahara Soichiro, a well-known writer on politics and foreign policy, published a brief article in *Ushio*, in which he summed up the views of pessimistic conservatives who are supporters of the alliance, but who believe its days are now numbered.[16] In this article, Tahara agreed with almost everything Professor Sato was to say in March, except that he was convinced that Americans had only put up with the U.S.-Japanese alliance because of the Soviet, Communist danger, and that Americans were prematurely concluding that the Russians were no longer a threat. Therefore, he wrote,

> . . . the United States needed Japan as an ally in the Cold War, and learned to tolerate us, even though our manufacturing success disrupted the American economy. But what will become of Japan if the Berlin Wall comes down, and if the Cold War disappears? The answer is obvious. Japan will become unnecessary. Unless Japan develops its own positive, acceptable strategy about what kind of a role it should play in the world . . . America and many other countries as well will turn more and more against us. [17]

Mr. Tahara's prescription for dealing with the postalliance world is not a foreign policy as such, but rather a proposal for Japan to become the model of a successful, industrial, urban country, which he believes will elicit the respect and admiration of the world, including the United States. For Mr. Tahara, the essence of Japan's foreign policy problems is not the existence of powerful and potentially hostile military states, or economic disputes and frictions, but that there is something about

Japan and the Japanese that makes them disliked and unpopular. He seems to believe that if Japan makes itself into a model industrialized, urban state, it will dispel suspicions and hostilities, will become universally respected and liked, and thus will have no need for alliances.

Japan as an Economic Hegemon

Although a number of non-Japanese writers have argued that Japan will overtake the United States as the world's leading economic power and will establish a Pax Nipponica early in the next century, it is not easy to find respected Japanese writers who take this position. It is, however, an option that bears examination. One of the more intriguing forecasts of Japanese economic hegemony has been written by Taira Kōji, a Japanese economist who is on the faculty of the University of Illinois. Professor Taira edited and contributed to the January 1991 volume of *The Annals of the American Academy of Political and Social Sciences*, entitled *Japan's External Economic Relations: Japanese Perspectives*.[18] His article—"Japan, an Imminent Hegemon?"—is the only one in the journal that focuses on the possibility of Japanese hegemony.

The first point to be noted is that Professor Taira expects that the post–Cold War world will be a relatively peaceful one, in which military politics will be almost entirely superseded by economic politics. In this world, he argues, Japan will achieve a hegemonic position based not on its capital surplus alone, which he believes will soon shrink, but on its unique organizational skills. He believes that it is organizational skills that have enabled Japan to attain the flexible, just-on-time manufacturing technology that has made it into the highest quality, most cost efficient manufacturer in the world. Professor Taira predicts that Japan will maintain its manufacturing lead well into the next century, and that Japanese manufacturing firms will continue to build plants worldwide. Japanese manufacturers, therefore, will assume leading positions in the American and European economies, as well as many other parts of the world. Since he also believes that there is and will continue to be a close, cooperative relationship between government and industry in Japan, he concludes that it is only natural that the Japanese government will use Japan's manufacturing and economic preponderance to serve Japan's political as well as economic interests. In Professor Taira's view (which he shares with writers such as Emanuel Wallerstein and Robert Gilpin), an economic hegemon is necessary to maintain a relatively open, orderly global economy, and Japan's economic hegemony will be benign and beneficial.

Professor Taira, in tune with Paul Kennedy's *The Rise and Fall of the Great Powers*, notes that Great Britain and the United States achieved their hegemonic positions partly as the result of lengthy, destructive wars that demonstrated their economic strength and staying power. He believes, however, that Japan will achieve hegemony in a peaceful environment without any dramatic confrontations. It will accomplish this feat by maintaining an unassuming, cooperative, nonthreatening posture in its foreign policy, while publicly continuing to treat the United States as the leading global superpower. According to Professor Taira, the *tatemae* (outward show) will be a U. S.-Japanese partnership with the United States as senior partner. The *honne* (hidden reality) will be quiet Japanese control and manipulation of this partnership behind the scenes. Taira believes the United States will be satisfied to appear to be in charge, while Japan will be satisfied to run things quietly.

My own view is that it is most unlikely, in view of the paranoia already demonstrated in the Congress and the media, that Americans will tolerate any form of Japanese hegemony, economic or otherwise. If the United States does not regain its economic vitality and self-confidence, I expect it will resort to protectionism and technonationalism, even though this will damage the U.S. economy and the entire international economic system.

Creating a Japan-United States-European Community Partnership to Shape and Maintain a New World Order

In Japan, Foreign Ministry bureaucrats are frequently criticized for being excessively conservative and unimaginative. Indeed, their harsher critics have characterized them as mere caretakers of the alliance with the United States. Although they are undoubtedly constrained by their official position in publicly expressing their views, the Foreign Ministry pitched into the public debate last May with a rather bold article in its house journal, *Gaiko Forum*, by its highest career official, Vice-Minister Kuriyama Takakazu.[19]

Mr. Kuriyama's sober view of the post–cold War world (published months before the gulf crisis and the stalled negotiations in the Uruguay round of trade talks) was that unless new global security and economic systems are soon created to replace the rapidly disappearing bipolar, American-Soviet structure and the GATT-IMF structure, the world was in grave danger of drifting into instability and violence, and/or destructive trade wars. He made the point several times that in the 1990s, the United States will not have the economic strength either to act as the world's policeman or to take the lead in promoting a system of global free trade and investment. Since the United States (GNP $5 trillion), the European Community (GNP $5 trillion) and Japan (GNP $3 trillion) together produce about two-thirds of the world's total goods and services ($20 trillion), he concluded that the best hope for the future lies in their forming a tripartite partnership that will make and implement the rules of a new international order.

Mr. Kuriyama was deeply aware of the antagonism developing against Japan in the United States, and his proposal for a global triumvirate was intended to help defuse the bilateral tension by transcending it. He also wrote that while Japan had reached a position of great wealth and influence in the 1980s, its economic achievements and prowess were frequently exaggerated in the United States and in Europe, as the 5-5-3 GNP ratio indicates. Nevertheless, he urged that Japan must now take an active role in the triumvirate.

Since Japan is constrained by its constitution and by public opinion from assuming any military responsibilities, he proposed that Japan make its contribution by becoming the world's leading free trader and importer—playing an indispensable economic role that the United States no longer seems willing or able to perform, and which Europe is not yet prepared to assume. Mr. Kuriyama points out that since it failed so disastrously in its efforts to play the role of a great power before World War II, it is crucial that Japan now allay any suspicions about its intentions by continuing to be peaceful, unassuming, and nonthreatening. Japan, he writes, should develop "the foreign policy of a great power without appearing to be a great power."[20]

Although Mr. Kuriyama indicates that "idiosyncratic nationalism" will become an increasingly serious threat to world political stability and peace in the 1990s, and that economic order and prosperity depend on political order and peace, it is not clear how the triumvirate would constitute a global security system, and what roles each of the partners would play, except that Japan could make no military contribution. The reader will have no doubt noticed that both Taira's "hegemon" and Kuriyama's "great power" bear a striking resemblance in their functions and disguises. The principal and crucial difference is that while Taira expects the post–Cold War world to be relatively peaceful and in no need of a military security system, Kuriyama sees a serious potential for political instability and violence but makes no clear proposal for coping with it.

In the historical context of this essay, and set against the climate of recent opinion in Japan reflected in the articles examined, it is easy to understand why the government of Prime Minister Kaifu Toshiki was unable to play any military role in the Gulf War, and limited itself to a monetary contribution of $13 billion, which was expected to cover about 20 percent of the cost of the war. As noted, critics within and outside Japan have argued that Prime Minister Kaifu's weak position in the ruling Liberal Democratic party, combined with his unassertive personality to prevent him from using the Gulf War as an opportunity to give Japan a more prominent, clearly defined foreign policy. I believe that it was most unlikely that any of the prime ministerial candidates would have made a significantly different policy. Moreover, among foreign policy officials and within the foreign policy community, views were sharply divided and ambivalent. Writers such as Satō Seizaburō spoke out strongly for Japan to be more supportive of the the United States in the gulf, and for Japan to play some kind of a military role within the framework of the United Nations. Tahara Soichirō argued that President George Bush had decided upon a war in the gulf without first consulting Japan, and that Japan's national interests in the flow of oil and political stability in the Middle East would have been better served by a policy of containing Saddam Hussein. Many

Japanese officials publicly took a position close to Professor Satō 's, while privately they leaned toward Tahara's views. There was a feeling among officials that Washington's idea of the New World Order was a system in which the United States makes the decisions and Japan pays the bills—and gets criticized for not doing more.

Before moving on to look at the possibility that changes in the international environment will compel Japan to change its foreign policy, it should be noted that within the government and among most foreign policy officials there is even more caution and uncertainty about future foreign policy than among the writers and publicists. Officials are working to preserve the alliance with the United States, and while they are aware of the strains and cracks in the relationship, they believe that for them to plan or speculate about alternative future foreign policies would undermine their work. Moreover, they believe that at this juncture in history the future is so murky and uncertain that contingency planning makes little sense. They are basically intent on shaping the future along the lines of Kuriyama Takakazu's US-EC-Japan concert system. They believe that while the end of the Cold War is not going to solve quickly and automatically all the world's problems, it is an opportunity for the United States to channel more of its attention and resources to economic revitalization, and for the advanced, industrialized nations to coordinate their efforts patiently and persistently to help the poorer nations, including perhaps the Soviet Union and former satellites, to build better lives for their people. As long as these goals seem attainable, they see no need to devise alternative policies.

Three Scenarios for the Future

The foreign policy debate in Japan indicates that there is a keen awareness of the factors that are threatening to make the Yoshida strategy inappropriate in the coming decade. There is a sense that Japanese foreign policy has to be more responsible and more active, but that responsibility and activity seem to be limited almost entirely to economics. Although the Japanese themselves do not appear to be planning and preparing to make a new security or defense policy, if during the next ten to twenty years the bipolar international security system continues to unravel, and if the global economic system breaks into regional blocs, Japan will have to adjust to the new environment. For purposes of discussion, let me suggest three future global futures and the impact they are likely to have on Japanese foreign policy, especially on the security component of foreign policy, which has been most resistant to change.

Scenario A

The Soviet threat continues to decline, the United States substantially reduces its conventional naval and air presence in East Asia and the Western Pacific, while U. S.-Japanese relations continue to be basically cooperative within the framework of the security alliance, despite the trade imbalance and economic frictions. The decline of the Soviet threat could take place in the context of economic development and peace in Russia and Eastern Europe, or it could occur in an economically distressed and violent regional environment. As long as the United States-Japan-NATO system holds, and the world economy remains intact, with high levels of trade and investment flowing between the United States, Japan, the European Community, and the rest of the world, the global outlook will be relatively good. Either the West will be able to assist in economic development in the former Soviet empire or it will be able to contain whatever threats might emanate from this region. This scenario assumes that the United States economy becomes sounder and more competitive, and that Japan and the European Community continue to move in the direction of open, freer trade, services, and investment.

In this case, Japan would probably have to assume responsibility for its own conventional defense, while the U.S. nuclear deterrent would continue to offer protection against Soviet or other nuclear threats. Assuming that the Soviet conventional threat in Asia will continue to diminish, Japan could assume responsibility for its conventional defense with gradual, moderate augmentations to its present force levels, especially its air, naval, and short-range missile forces, that would not be seen as threatening by its neighbors. This is basically a scenario for moderate, incremental change within a relatively stable, less threatening international environment.

Vice-Minister Kuriyama's proposal for Japan-United States-European cooperation would fit easily into this world. However, while the triumvirate would preclude wars among the great powers, it could not always prevent wars among the lesser states. The gulf crisis suggests that the effective control of local wars will be difficult and could disrupt the tripartite system, unless it becomes a military-security as well as an economic partnership. Although the Europeans and Japanese went along with American policy in the gulf, they have probably sent the message to the United States that they expect to be consulted in the next crisis, and not simply called upon for support after the key decisions have been taken in Washington.

Scenario B

The Soviet threat continues to decline as postulated in scenario A, but economic quarrels, protectionism, technonationalism, and trade wars lead to an end of effective U.S.-Japanese security cooperation as the United States withdraws from military positions in East Asia and the Western Pacific, including the Philippine bases. In this scenario it is likely that U.S. relations with the European Community will also deteriorate and that NATO will come apart. This would lead to the reemergence of a traditional, multilateral international system, with the United States, the Soviet Union or Russia, Japan, the European Community, and/or a unified Germany and China each operating on their own, outside the relatively cohesive alliances we have had since World War II. As long as none of these powers is perceived as militarily aggressive or threatening by the other major powers, this scenario could also lead to a relatively peaceful international security environment, albeit at lower levels of economic activity than in scenario A.

Japan would probably respond to this environment by attempting first to continue in its present nonnuclear, lightly armed posture, and then, if necessary, by building some kind of minimal, perhaps nonnuclear deterrent and augmenting its conventional air and naval forces, stopping short of an arms buildup that would cause military tensions with China, Russia, or the United States. Considering how difficult it would be to accomplish this buildup without generating tensions and instability, I believe scenario B to be possible but unstable and extremely difficult to maintain.

For this kind of international system to survive, and for Japan to pursue this kind of independent but nonthreatening security policy, the five powers would probably have to operate along the lines of the Concert system that prevented major wars in Europe from 1815 to 1914. They would all have to eschew ambitious foreign policies and be willing to negotiate and compromise whenever potentially disruptive disputes arose among themselves, and at the same time be prepared to cooperate on an *ad hoc* basis to intervene to keep conflicts among the lesser powers from disrupting the system. Again, the gulf crisis suggests how crucial and difficult this kind of cooperation would be. In fact, the twenty-first-century analog of the nineteenth-century European Concert system would probably have to be much more like scenario A.

It is important to understand that while the breakup of the global economy does not necessarily lead to political conflict and war, the economic and ecological costs of a system of uncoordinated, competing spheres of national influence or regional blocs will be very high, and the potential for conflict in scenario B is much greater than in scenario A. The European Concert system in the nineteenth century coincided with the early development of national manufacturing economies and was supported by the relatively free movement of international trade, investment, currency, and people. In the far more interdependent global economy of the 1990s, the breakup of the global trading and investment system would be likely to leave the Soviet Union, Eastern Europe, and the lesser developed economies of the world in desperate straits, which will tend to push all of us into scenario C.

Scenario C

The U.S.-Japanese alliance ends as a result of economic quarrels as postulated in scenario B, but after several years of economic decline and political disintegration there is a nationalistic, militaristic, authoritarian backlash in Russia. Russia has thousands of advanced nuclear weapons and is using its conventional forces to reconquer and impose its authority on the various national groups within the Soviet Union—rebuilding the Russian empire. It has no intention of reviving the Cold War with the United States but it is determined to prevent encroachments on its empire by a unified Germany, by China or Japan. It pursues detente with the United States, but takes advantage of the end of the United States-NATO-Japan coalition to assume a tough, truculent posture toward Japan, China, and/or Germany (perhaps allying with one of these against the others). In this anarchic, violent world, in which the global trading and financial systems have collapsed or badly deteriorated, it is likely that Korea would again find itself the cockpit for rivalry between Russia, China, and Japan.

In this kind of environment, Japan would probably see no alternative to protecting itself by becoming a major military power, both nuclear and conventional. This would be a dangerous, unstable world, and Japanese rearmament would aggravate the danger and instability.

Implications for the United States

It is difficult to conceive of a future international environment in which the United States would gain any substantial, lasting benefits by ending its alliance with Japan. If the Soviet threat does continue to diminish and we enter a relatively stable, less dangerous post–Cold War world, then the continuation of an effective U.S.-Japanese alliance enhances that stability and promotes higher levels of economic activity and cooperation. This is the most beneficial scenario for the United States as well as for Japan.

Scenario B suggests that minimal American security interests could be met in a relatively, peaceful post–Cold War world without an alliance or close cooperation with Japan, but the world of scenario B is less stable than in A, less prosperous, and less likely to deal effectively with international economic-ecological and political issues. If scenario B deteriorates into some variant of scenario C, and I think it will be prone to do so, then we will have exchanged the nasty old days of the Cold War for a nasty, new world that will be at least as dangerous.

Notes

1.   Masamichi Inoki and Kitaoka Shin'ichi, "Rekishiteki sokyo toshite no senso" (The Gulf War and pacifist Japan), *Chuo koron* (April 1991): 103.
2.   *Nihon keizai shimbun,* March 2, 1991, p. 2.
3.   Ibid., January 27, 1991, p. 12.
4.   *Yomiuri shimbun,* April 25, 1991, p. 2.
5.   *Asahi shimbun,* March 15, 1991, p. 2.
6.   Ibid., November 6, 1990, p. 3.
7.   Ibid., February 5, 1991, p. 3.
8.   *Mainichi shimbun,* June 23, 1991, p. 6.

9. *Asahi shimbun* , June 19, 1991, p. 15.

10. Ibid., May 9, 1991, p. 2.

11. Satō Seizaburō , "Jidaino henka ga yori kyokona domeio motomeru" (Changes in the times call for still stronger alliance), *Chūō kōron* (March 1990).

12. Ibid., p. 134.

13. Okazaki Hisahiko, "Oranda ni nihon ga mieru" (The Holland that can be seen in Japan), *Bungei shunju* (January 1990).

14. Ibid., p. 305.

15. Ishihara Shintaro, *The Japan That Can Say 'No'* (New York: Simon and Schuster), 1991.

16. Tahara Soichiro, "Nichibeianpojoyaku wa ippotekini haki sareru" (The U.S.-Japanese Security Treaty will be abrogated unilaterally) , *Ushio,* (January 1990).

17. Ibid., pp. 67–68.

18. Koji Taira, "Japan, an Imminent Hegemon?" *The Annals of the American Academy of Political and Social Sciences* (January 1991).

19. Kuriyama Takakazu, "Gekidono 90 nendai to nihongaiko no shintenkai" (The great upheaval of the nineties and the evolution of Japan's new diplomacy), *Gaiko forum,* (May 1990).

20. Ibid., pp. 15–17.

Chapter 11
Japan's Defensive Foreign Policy and the Politics of Burden Sharing

---

Susan J. Pharr

Japan's foreign policy is a major enigma of the 1990s. According to some, Japan is mired in "immobilisms," passive, adrift without goals—a "reactive state" lacking the will or capability to play a more assertive and active role in the world.[1] Indeed, so ineffective is its postwar foreign policy, according to one Japanese former defense official, that Japan cannot even be considered a sovereign state.[2]

Such a judgment is far from universal, however. Coming out of Asia, especially China and both Koreas, is a radically different view that sees a Japanese foreign policy, not passive but aggressive, not immobilist or goalless, but instead bent on regional dominance and operating from a grand design. In the same vein, recent American "revisionist" writers such as Morse and Tonelson portray a future Japan so assertive that any effort to contain it will ultimately fail.[3]

Between these extremes is still another view, regularly put forward by Japan's official spokesmen, which might be called a rising-state thesis. According to this view, Japan's postwar foreign policy may have been reactive and passive in the past when the country operated under the long shadow of the United States; but since the late 1970s, spurred by U.S. economic decline, its economic superpower status, world pressure, and by more assertive leaders like Prime Minister Nakasone Yasuhiro, Japan has been pursuing a more activist, independent, and assertive foreign policy. Those advancing such a view can point to increased defense spending and the rise of Japan in providing nonmilitary international public goods like aid and debt relief to the world as evidence that Japan has broken with its past and that it is moving forward steadily, if reluctantly, to develop goals and an activist orientation.[4]

Japan as a Defensive State
This chapter sees all three models as flawed. Focusing on Japan's response to burden-sharing pressure since the 1950s, it sees Japanese foreign policy as a low-cost, low-risk, benefit-maximizing strategy that has served Japan's national

self-interest extraordinarily well in the past, and that continues to do so today. The strategy is essentially defensive in character; yet to call it "reactive" misses the point, for what is impressive is the degree to which Japan, faced with a barrage of pressures from the United States and other industrial nations, has actively and successfully maneuvered to advantage among them while seeking to avoid risks of all kinds.

The analogy of defensive driving is apt, for driving defensively is neither aggressive nor passive, nor really "reactive" since the driver is hardly changing basic direction as he adjusts to obstacles before him. He is, after all, choosing a particular route even as he threads his way among the possible dangers before him. The defensive driving analogy, if it highlights the essential character of Japan's strategy, does not completely cover all points. For while the defensive-state strategy is essentially active rather than passive in character, it does not operate from a grand design—a single direction that was somehow "chosen" as Japan embarked on its postwar journey. Japan, like the defensive driver who picks his routes from those on the map before him, has worked within the options and possibilities available. Nor were the policies "made" in the sense intended by those who talk of a grand design operating behind the choices involved. Rather, they emerged out of debate, discussion, and the collective mood among successive generations of policy makers faced by pressures inside and outside Japan who shared a perception that the world was a dangerous place. Japan nevertheless has arrived at a destination today that is consistent with certain key aims dating back to the 1950s: regaining autonomy in the world order, achieving economic prosperity, minimizing risks, and pursuing its goals by nonmilitary means. Equally basic has been Japan's principle of containing the costs while maximizing the benefits of its foreign policy, independent of the issue of means.

To summarize, four characteristics of what might be called the "defensive-state strategy" stand out: (1) its activist character; (2) its aversion to risks; (3) its low cost, compared to what other major nations pay; and (4) continuity in the approach over the entire postwar era up to the present.

Burden Sharing in U.S.-Japanese Relations

To explore how the defensive-state strategy has operated, this chapter focuses on defense burden sharing in U.S.-Japanese relations. The relative economic decline of the United States and its emergence in the 1980s as the number one debtor nation, and the concomitant rise of Japan over the past two decades, added fire and fury to a bilateral debate over burden sharing that had been under way in a milder form since 1950, when the two countries embarked on discussions that resulted in the U.S.-Japan Mutual Security Treaty. The treaty, ostensibly an agreement to cooperate in containing communism in the Far East by allowing the United States rights to site bases on Japanese soil, set in motion a continuing conflict over military burden sharing, but at the same time it provided the institutional framework (or "regime") within which other collective action dilemmas over apportioning responsibility between the two countries could be debated. Group of Seven (G-7) summitry, which began in 1975, provided a broader framework for negotiations among the United States and its leading alliance partners, but the U.S.-Japanese dialogue continued unabated and indeed accelerated with the seemingly inexorable trans-Pacific shift in economic power that has been taking place.

In relations among the leading industrial countries, "burden sharing" in the pursuit of public goods has been a central issue, a major basis for agenda setting in the postwar era. The issues associated with burden sharing, of course, differ according to whose perspective is being adopted. For international relations theorists, the key questions are which country will take the lead, what kind of rewards and incentives are needed to win cooperation and to overcome the tendency of nations to free-ride, and how responsibility is to be apportioned in the first place.[5] For policy makers in the United States—a country already bearing a disproportionate share—the issue is how to keep power while shedding the burden.[6] For Japan—a country under pressure to pay more—the issue is how to gain maximum benefits while minimizing costs.

The central focus in debates over burden sharing is defense. Not only is military security the most costly of all international public goods to provide, and thus basic to the debate, but pulling and hauling over security has spilled out and influenced bilateral bargains over other public goods issues that have been subject to negotiation, such as Third World aid, debt relief, asylum for refugees, market-opening measures, financial liberalization, and aid to the former Soviet Union. Examining how Japan has managed burden-sharing pressure from the United States over the postwar era thus becomes a way to look at Japanese foreign policy in action, in order to see how the defensive-state strategy works, and to weigh the costs and benefits of the strategy from the standpoint of Japan and also the United States.

The Defensive Foreign Policy Takes Shape: 1950s

The origins of the defensive-state approach may be traced back to the darkest days of the Cold War. In his New Year's message in January 1951, General Douglas MacArthur launched what may be seen retrospectively as an early effort, following on the heels of attempts the previous June by John Foster Dulles, to bring Japan into a burden-sharing framework by calling on the Japanese to rearm to provide for their own self-defense. By July 1950 a National Police Reserve force (Kokka Keisatsu Yobitai) of 75,000 men had been created, laying the groundwork for establishing the Self-Defense Forces in 1954. In September 1951, on the same day it signed the San Francisco Treaty that formally brought the Occupation to a close, Japan also signed the U.S.-Japanese Security Treaty, setting in place the postwar framework for U.S.-Japanese relations. Over the period from 1950 to 1953, the

United States and Japan were embroiled in negotiations over a whole set of terms for Japan's participation in a Cold War collective security effort led by the United States. During the discussions, Japan agreed to build a 180,000 person force, keep U.S. troops in Japan indefinitely, reactivate dormant armaments factories to aid the United States in the Korean War effort, and recognize the Republic of China on Taiwan while helping to contain Communist China.

Japan met most of these requests, but during security negotiations before and after the treaty, American officials asked Japan to do far more. They pressed hard to involve Japanese troops actively in the U.S. regional scheme. At American insistence, the treaty preamble made clear the U.S. expectation that Japan would provide for its own defense, and U.S. officials sought to persuade Japan to embark on a large-scale, rapid rearmament program: indeed, Dulles sought a 350,000-person level for Japan's ground forces—well in excess of the number reached at any time in the postwar era.

Japan deflected these more extensive requests, however. Retrospectively, the agreement represented a lopsided U.S. pledge to defend Japan with no reciprocal agreement on Japan's part. The effort to involve Japan in regional security was dropped. Though Japan struggled in the 1950s to meet its security commitments under the terms of the treaty and the percentage of Japan's budget going for defense reached its highest level (almost 14 percent of the general account budget) of the entire post-Occupation era in 1954,[7] there can be little doubt that the burden-sharing agreement worked out by the two nations was highly advantageous for Japan. Why, we may ask, was this so? Why did the United States, operating from a position of astonishing military and economic strength in a nation emerging from an occupation, ask so little of Japan and make so many concessions? Japan, after all, was then a "vassal state" with little leverage.[8]

American goals provide an important part of the answer. In the country's Cold War strategy of the early 1950s, it was in the U.S. interest to stabilize the region and defend Japan. Pushing Japan to spend still more on defense also carried the risk of economically weakening a Japan that was perceived to be threatened by the possibility of domestic communist insurgency. Furthermore, the Korean War gave great urgency to U.S. efforts to establish base rights and enlist Japan's support logistically in the war effort. The Korean War, above all else, may have compelled the United States to offer a unilateral guarantee for Japan's defense.[9] Furthermore, once the United States developed deterrence capability, the cost of extending that strategic protection to Japan was virtually nil, especially at the time the security treaty was under discussion; it was not until the late 1950s, after Sputnik triggered the arms race, that the U.S. costs of providing deterrence rose significantly.[10] Finally, article 9 of Japan's Peace Constitution of 1947 (written by Americans) was politically embarrassing due to its popularity among a Japanese public that had had enough of war. Article 9, whereby Japan renounced war as a sovereign right of the nation and ostensibly was barred from maintaining troops even for defensive purposes, was a problem of America's own making that plagued American burdensharing negotiations from the early 1950s to the present. For American officials to renounce it was to admit an appalling mistake and to risk discrediting the United States at a time when both sides wanted to see the Occupation era end smoothly.

Why Japan did as well as it did, however, also rests on the skills and leverage that the Japanese brought to the discussions. Japan's greatest leverage derived from Prime Minister Yoshida Shigeru's belief that the type of full-scale, rapid rearmament sought by the Americans was excessive from the standpoint of guaranteeing Japan's security.[11] There is little doubt that Japanese policy makers saw the need for some level of protection; as early as 1946, Japan's bureaucrats were conducting studies of the country's strategic options, and indeed in May 1950 Prime Minister Yoshida had dispatched a secret mission to Washington proposing that U.S. forces remain in Japan to provide for Japan's defense and the security of Asia.[12] Although Yoshida was concerned with the internal threat posed by Japanese Communists with Soviet ties and with instability in nearby Korea, there is no evidence that he shared American fears at the time about an omnipresent external Communist menace. Even "military realists" in Japan hold that until the early 1980s Japan was little concerned about the global nuclear balance between the United States and the Soviet Union, partly because the American nuclear arsenal and overwhelming military superiority in the Far East provided a "safe haven" for Japan.[13]

Also working to Yoshida's advantage was another risk factor—the danger inherent in the treaty that Japan might be pulled into a conflict by virtue of its ties to the United States in the superpower confrontation. The thesis that the treaty meant inadvertent risk—referred to in Japan as the *makikomare-ron*—plagued Japanese leaders faced with selling the security treaty to the public. Long after the treaty won general approval, a significant minority of the public viewed it as making Japan susceptible to attack; indeed, more Japanese worried about the dangers to Japan arising from the treaty than about the insufficiency of Japan's defense power—the subject at the heart of burden-sharing negotiations.[14] But this risk factor also may have offered psychological leverage to Yoshida by reducing his stake in seeking the American security guarantee and his increasing determination to stay out of regional involvements that might result from full-scale rearmament.

The final factor was Japanese negotiators' skill in pursuing a low-cost, benefit-maximizing strategy at the bargaining table, exploiting the openings that the Americans gave them. On the crucial issues of troop levels and Japan's participation in regional security efforts, Yoshida marshalled rationales for why Japan could not meet American demands, focusing on public opposition to rearmament, fears on the part of Japan's Asian neighbors, and the need to use scarce Japanese resources for economic recovery rather defense. When pressed by Dulles in Tokyo in January 1957, he stonewalled and at one point withdrew to his seaside home in Oiso.[15] To give substance to the threat of domestic insurgency, Yoshida secretly sent word through relatives to both left-wing and right-wing Socialists urging them to demonstrate against remilitarization while Dulles was in Tokyo.[16] Partly as a result of his success with such tactics, he managed to hold down troop levels and sidestep a regional security commitment for Japan. In effect, operating from a weak bargaining position in an occupied nation, he successfully redefined comparative advantage and persuaded the Americans to include protection from domestic insurgency as part of Japan's contribution to the collective good—a cost-saving solution for Japan that shifted a larger share of the external security effort to the Americans.

For all the advantages to Japan of the security agreement reached, obviously there were disadvantages as well. As Yoshida's critics at home were to claim, the treaty cast Japan into a dependent role militarily and politically, with all the inherent dangers, as well as the political headaches, of being drawn toward policy positions (toward Israel, and South Africa, on terrorism and drugs, and aid to regions such as the Caribbean, as examples) in which the two countries' basic interests have been fundamentally different. The terms of the bilateral relationship embedded in the treaty gave the ruling party its single most volatile political issue in the 1950s, and they were to set back the political careers of numerous Japanese prime ministers by putting powerful ammunition in the hands of their domestic critics.[17] The containment policy to which Japan became a party also set constraints on Japan's relations within Asia, pressing Japan away from China and towards Taiwan.

Yet the treaty also brought an astonishing range of benefits. Japan got the U.S. bases it had sought, which in turn provided protection in the event that local conflict arose in the area around Japan. The treaty brought Japan, a pariah nation routinely blackballed in its efforts to join the United Nations until 1956, out of isolation and provided a basis for its reentry into the world of nation-states. The Cold War was a boon to Yoshida and Japan in that it transformed Japan from an enemy nation into an asset to be guarded.[18]

Meanwhile, the treaty and the conception of containment that gave rise to it left the economic domain rather free. In the name of strengthening the region to contain communism, Japan received license to rebuild its economic strength in Southeast Asia. Even in the case of China, as early as the Bandung Conference in April 1955, a Japanese representative was having breakfast with Zhou Enlai, and backstage economic relations were proceeding.[19]

Nor were direct economic benefits minimal. American expenditures in Japan to maintain its defense establishment were important to the struggling Japanese economy of the early to mid-1950s. The Korean War was an economic windfall for Japan; direct and indirect procurement made up 63 percent of Japan's exports at the height of the war.[20] A bilateral trade agreement in September 1955 threw open

American markets to Japanese manufactured goods while allowing the United States no comparable access to Japanese markets except for agricultural products, raw materials, and technology. Sponsorship into international organizations was not a cost-free activity for the United States; it offered trade concessions to several nations in exchange for their support for Japan's admission to the GATT, for example, and authorized Japanese whaling in Antarctica over the objections of other nations to help Japan increase its food supply.[21] For all the disadvantages of the treaty to Japan and the infinite political headaches it would bring to its conservative defenders beginning with Yoshida himself, the benefits were clearly abundant.

The alliance benefited the United States as well, it may be added. Japanese cooperation was crucial in the Korean War. Japanese laborers were unloading UN cargoes on the docks of Inchon, Hungnam, and Wonson, and Japanese crews manned almost a third of the ships used to support the Inchon amphibious landing. Ironically, given Japan's reluctance in 1987 to send minesweepers to the gulf, twenty Japanese minesweepers, under contract to UN forces, kept ports clear on both coasts of Korea.[22] Furthermore, the treaty virtually neutralized the possibility that Japan could challenge the United States militarily as long as it was in place.

Nor did the alliance relationship allow Japan to reap economic benefits at the U.S. expense. An economically revitalized Japan helped stabilize all of non-Communist East Asia, a major U.S. foreign policy objective. American surplus cotton and grain exported to Japan paved the way for highly lucrative agricultural trade, in which Japan was to emerge as the number one purchaser of U.S. agricultural products. American pressure to open world markets to Japanese textiles and shipbuilding was not especially harmful to U.S. interests at the time; such policies were far more costly to a Europe engaged in its own economic recovery effort. Despite the claims some people make today, evidence of American economic largess is hard to find. Indeed, scholar and later diplomat Edwin O. Reischauer took American officialdom to task in 1957 for miring Japan in what he then saw as a trade surplus hopelessly in America's favor:

> ... the extremely unfavorable balance of Japanese trade with us is
> and will continue to be a major economic problem. We are the chief
> source of Japanese purchases abroad but take relatively little in
> return. . . . Our actions . . . can only be explained by the peculiar
> sensitiveness of the American government to minority interests at the
> expense of the interests of the nation as a whole.[23]

The early burden-sharing negotiations between Japan and the United States show Japan's defensive-state strategy in action and reveal four key features.

1. *Risk minimization.* Partly due to the Janus-faced nature of the particular military alliance Japan entered, in which Japan was put at risk (as a result of the *makikomare* factor) even as it gained security, the centerpiece of the Japanese

approach has been an external policy aimed at reducing risk. This has been pursued through the years in several ways. The first has involved staying out of U.S. global strategy, as seen in Yoshida's resistance to major rearmament and to Japan's participation in regional security. Later the *seikei bunri* policy developed under Prime Minister Ikeda, which called for separating politics (*sei*) and economics (*kei*), would represent a way for Japan to duck American pressure to take foreign policy stances dictated by the U.S. goal of containing communism. A second route to risk minimization can be seen in Japan's efforts to neutralize the inflammatory potential of its tie to the United States by what amounts to a "politics of compensation"[24] used externally. Trade and cultural contact with the People's Republic of China prior to the restoration of relations in 1972 is one example of Japanese efforts to establish some level of relations with nations that were off-limits under the terms of containment; Japan's trickle of trade with North Vietnam through the war years, despite outward shows of support for the U.S. position, is another.[25] A third method can be seen in Japan's efforts to lock in the American commitment to the defense of Japan, as Japan did in offering base rights even before the treaty negotiation was under way. Later, even while resisting U.S. pressure to do more militarily, Japan often has sought reaffirmation of the U.S. commitment to the defense of Japan.

Finally, risk minimization involved measures aimed, in effect, at preventing provocative actions by the United States that increased the risk to Japan. Staying out of regional security and keeping Japanese troop levels down reduced the external resources available to the United States to pursue its foreign policy in Asia. More recent examples include Japan's lukewarm backing for U.S interventions in Vietnam and elsewhere, which have played a role in isolating the United States and thus in making such actions unilateral. G-7 summitry has provided numerous opportunities for Japan, through agreements with like-minded European countries, to attempt to constrain the United States.

While Japan has sought to reduce risk through its foreign policy, it also pursued a policy of self-containment at home. In effect, this involved erecting, brick by brick, a protective policy shield from U.S. pressure to do more militarily. Through article 9, the Americans provided the cornerstone of such a policy. Japan then added a succession of other barriers of its own: the *seikei bunri* policy of Ikeda in the early 1960s, which provided an out from taking provocative policy stances in support of U.S. political positions; the three "nonnuclear principles" that won the Nobel Prize for Prime Minister Satō Eisaku and set limits on what Japan's quid pro quo could be in any subsequent burden-sharing debate; the arms-export ban that, over the opposition of Japanese defense contractors, curtailed the possibility of providing arms to third parties should the U.S. seek Japan's help on behalf of other countries; and the "1 percent ceiling," put in place by Prime Minister Miki Takeo in 1976 and finally lifted by the Nakasone cabinet in 1987, by which Japanese spending was held to 1 percent of GNP, reducing U.S.-Japan defense negotiations to debates over budgetary shares.[26] Domestically each measure in Japan's self-containment policy represented compensation to key opposition groups that were at odds with the treaty, but collectively such measures encased the country in a protective shell from U.S. pressure.

2. *Skilled use of rationales.* As Paul Samuelson has said of parties to collective-action agreements "it is in the selfish interest of each person to give false signals, to pretend to have less interest in a given collective activity than he really has."[27] With this granted, Japan has marshalled an impressive range of arguments for why its own contribution to security in the U.S.-Japanese treaty should be limited. In the early 1950s, the main rationales for doing less centered on public opposition to rearmament, the restrictive nature of article 9, the setback to economic recovery were rearmament attempted, and the fears among Japan's Asian neighbors of Japanese remilitarization. By the 1960s, the public's "military allergy" became a mainstay, with the 1960 mass protest over the revised treaty as powerful evidence to back up the claim. After 1976, the 1 percent ceiling became a self-created barrier to greater Japanese burden sharing. Despite Japan's economic rise in the 1980s, Japan's determined efforts to deal with its budget deficit gave rise to a new economic argument for containing defense-spending increases. By the late 1980s, Japanese negotiators could hold that nationalism provoked by Japan bashing in the United States made burden sharing pressure risky.

3. *Substitution policy.* In the U.S.-Japanese dialogue over burden sharing, Japan has sought to gain ground in burden sharing by substituting contributions for nonmilitary public goods in the place of defense concessions. As early as 1954, for example, Yoshida sought U.S. support for a Marshall Plan for Southeast Asia to create a "new market integrating Japan, the United States, and Southeast Asia"; the plan, which would have been financed by the United States, in effect sought to redefine economic measures to fit them within the U.S. containment strategy.[28] The concept of "comprehensive security" launched by Japan in the late 1970s formalized the same type of repackaging effort by seeking to legitimize the substitution of development aid, strategic aid, and later debt relief for defense spending per se. Given the high costs of military spending and the lesser amounts involved in Japan's other public goods contributions, substitution has represented an effective way to keep Japan's foreign policy costs low.

4. *Ritualization of conflict.* A final feature of defensive state strategy, this time in cooperation with U.S. officials, is the ritualization of the continuing conflict over burden sharing in order to manage the complex, two-level game under way on both sides of the Pacific.[29] In bilateral negotiation, Japan—as occurred in the 1950s—regularly has entered commitments to burden share militarily, but at a level lower than that sought by the Americans. The backstage reality of level-one agreements often has been far more cooperative than things have appeared—witness Japan's permission, denied in public, to allow U.S. naval vessels with nuclear weapons to

use Japanese ports (thus violating the three nonnuclear principles) and the many forms of covert support for U.S. efforts in the Korean and Vietnam wars. To boost Japanese negotiators' efforts, U.S. officials have left the table publicly regretting Japan's unwillingness to do more; such a position not only helped the Japanese sell agreements domestically, but also helped U.S. negotiators explain results that fell short of public and congressional expectations. Meanwhile, Japanese officials back home found it in their interest to portray concessions as unavoidable steps to appease American demands.

1960s to Mid-1970s: Early Rumblings of U.S. Burden-Sharing Pressure

In the single most tumultuous foreign policy crisis in postwar Japan, a new Treaty of Mutual Cooperation between Japan and the United States was ratified in 1960 and passed into law to replace the agreement that Yoshida and Dulles had negotiated in 1951. The new treaty had been signed by Prime Minister Kishi Nobusuke in the East Room of the White House on January 19; so confident was he that the ratification process would go smoothly that President Dwight Eisenhower was slated to visit Japan thereafter to commemorate the new era in U.S.-Japanese relations. Six months later the visit had been cancelled, 500 policemen had forcibly removed opposition party members from the Lower House in May so that the ruling party could force through the ratification vote, 6.25 million workers had participated in a strike in June to protest its passage into law, and Kishi had resigned under pressure.[30] The anti-U.S.-Japan Mutual Security Treaty Struggle deeply colored U.S.-Japanese security relations well into the late 1970s and shaped, though it did not alter, the basic defensive state posture that Japan was developing.

The new treaty, negotiated over the 1957–60 period, involved several changes from the 1951 version. It upped the ante for Japan with article V, which committed Japan to "act to meet a common danger" in the event that U.S. facilities in Japan were attacked. But most of the gains in the renewal process were Japan's. The revised treaty strengthened the U.S. commitment to Japan by providing unequivocally that the United States would come to Japan's defense in the event of attack. From the Japanese standpoint, some of the demeaning features of the earlier agreement were rectified (by deletion of a provision that the United States could intervene in internal disorders and provision for prior consultation by the United States in major changes relating to U.S. troops stationed in Japan). Furthermore, the new treaty continued to represent a nonreciprocal agreement: there was no requirement that Japan participate in regional security or that it defend the United States outside Japan proper. At the time, given the upheaval that had accompanied the revision and ratification process, Washington officials could count themselves lucky that the revised treaty had been approved. With the benefit of hindsight, however, one could say that numerous efforts in the 1950s to get Japan to assume more of the burden for defense under a collective action agreement had come to relatively little, and indeed many of the strategies Japan would use later on to contain burden-sharing pressure had stood the test.

A number of factors help explain why the United States did not press harder for burden sharing in the 1960s and 1970s. The security treaty struggle of 1960 had given credence to Japanese claims that opposition to the security relationship itself was widespread and indeed, as the events of 1960 had suggested, were potentially destabilizing. The 1960 treaty was to be up for renewal in 1970, seriously constraining how far Washington could go in pressuring Japan publicly for a higher military profile. Another factor was the remarkable lag time before the United States—and indeed the world—began to comprehend the Japanese economic miracle that was taking place in the national income-doubling decade of the 1960s. By 1968, the centennial year of the Meiji Restoration that had set the nation on its development course, Japan had pushed past France, Britain, and West Germany to become, with a GNP of $133 billion, the number two nation among the capitalist countries. But recognition of Japan's rise was slow in coming. Zbigniew Brzezinski's *The Fragile Blossom* in 1972 mirrored the mood of skepticism in relation to Japan's economic success found among Washington's policy elite until the late1970s.[31] Doubting the long-term strength of Japan's economy, there was not yet a firm economic basis for policy makers to challenge the appropriateness of Japan's security contribution.

Finally, the importance of the nonmilitary role Japan played in the Vietnam War undoubtedly tempered U.S. pressure to redistribute the defense burden. In support of the war effort Japanese workers maintained U.S. planes, ships, trucks, and tanks, and the Transportation Ministry recruited civilians to staff cargo vessels in the war zone. According to one *Asahi* newspaper account, Japanese civilian crew members wearing U.S. uniforms operated twenty-eight cargo vessels carrying munitions and napalm along the South Vietnam coast in the early years of the war. Direct and indirect procurement did not exceed 7–8 percent of Japan's exports (as compared to the 63 percent reached during the Korean War), but the value of Japan as a staging and supplies center was obviously crucial to the United States.[32] Japan's political support for the war effort also won points for Japan. Despite public opposition in Japan to the war, Foreign Minister Shiina was prepared to call the U.S. bombings of North Vietnam begun in February 1965 "self-defense."[33] Prime Minister Satō was similarly willing to go out on a limb; reporting on a tour he had taken of the Asian region, he announced at the National Press Club in November 1967 that he had discovered "widespread support" in Asia for "free-world efforts to cope with Communist intervention and infiltration." The political mileage he gained was apparent two days later when President Lyndon Johnson told him that of the eighty-seven heads of government he had seen over the previous year, "none had been more direct or helpful than Satō himself."[34]

All these factors operated to constrain U.S. burden-sharing pressure on Japan. But Japan's defensive foreign policy can also be seen at work during these years.

For despite leadership's support for various U.S. policy positions, Japanese officials avoided wholehearted endorsement of the war effort per se and drew the line at weapons manufacture and sales. Japan similarly sought to avoid risk by pressing to keep international political issues off the multilateral agenda once G-7 summitry began in 1975.[35]

The 1960s and 1970s were also marked by "self-containment" initiatives. Once the security treaty crisis of 1960 ended, Prime Minister Ikeda Hayato formalized the *seikei bunri* foreign policy, as noted earlier. Such a policy allowed Japan to stand back from taking positions on controversial political issues, and to hover at the periphery of U.S. military interventions. Satō carried self-containment much further in leading Japan to adopt the "three nonnuclear principles" in December 1967 in the midst of the Vietnam War, whereby Japan pledged not to manufacture or transport nuclear weapons, or allow them to be brought into the country. Aimed, with the arms exports ban, at appeasing domestic critics who faulted Satō for Japan's support of the Vietnam War, the measures also served the very practical external purpose of containing Japan itself while setting limits on Japan's support role in U.S. military activities in the region. In 1976 Prime Minister Miki Takeo put in place yet another "self containment" measure when he set a 1 percent of GNP ceiling on defense expenditures to appease domestic critics of a new National Defense Program Outline Japan adopted under pressure from the Americans. The 1 percent ceiling, which became public in Diet interpellations over the NDPO, undercut the value of the plan from a burden-sharing perspective by limiting what could be spent to achieve it.[36] Japan's moves over these years, far from being the passive strategy of a reactive state, was a carefully calculated set of actions blending well-timed verbal endorsements of U.S. overall policy, disassociation from any overt role in U.S. interventions, lucrative back-stage support within carefully prescribed limits, and a variety of self-containment measures—a blend, in short, that minimized security risk-by-association with the United States while reaping maximum economic benefits.

Japan also sought to substitute nonmilitary public goods for defense efforts. The *seikei bunri* policy paved the way by legitimizing the development of an economics-centered foreign policy that involved, among other things, building the nation's economic ties within Asia. Once the Vietnam War was under way, it made sense for the United States to ask Japan for help in the region in ways that were consistent with Japanese foreign policy priorities. Thus, for example, in April 1965, at a speech at Johns Hopkins, Johnson sought and soon got Japanese participation in the Mekong River Basin development project. Over the war years, American requests for Japanese aid to Taiwan, South Korea, Indonesia, and the Southeast Asian region more generally, pulled aid giving into the burden-sharing framework; in effect, they signaled its willingness—which Tokyo welcomed—to see aid substitute for military spending commitments under the broad definition of security inherent in the notion of containment. Prime Minister Satō went out of his way, by visiting Seoul, Taipei, and Saigon, to stress that Japan's economic development interest jibed with an anti-Communist hard-line position. By the time the war ended, the pattern had become well established, as reflected in President Carter's request in February 1976 for increased Japanese aid to Southeast Asia if Japan were not prepared to increase its military spending.[37] Japan also became far more skilled than in the 1950s in getting side payments for its political support for U.S. containment policy. Satō moved closer to the United States on the Vietnam War issue to accelerate the return of the Ogasawaras to Japan in June 1968 and Okinawa in 1971; indeed, at the Satō-Johnson summit in 1967 at the height of the war, a bargain was apparently struck linking Japanese support for the war with the return of these islands.[38]

Through these years in which the United States was caught up in the Vietnam War, Japan was undergoing an astonishing economic transformation. The U.S.-Japanese textile wrangle, concluded in 1971, was the precursor of trade disputes to come as Japan's trade surplus with the United States and other industrial countries became endemic. The Nixon shocks in the same year—ending dollar convertibility, setting a 10 percent surcharge on imports, and announcing Nixon's visit to China, all without prior consultation with Japan—had the effect of opening up "space" in the U.S.-Japanese relationship. Meanwhile the 1973–74 oil crisis, in which Japan confronted the risks of a cut-off in oil as a result of its ties to Israel, brought home the risks of signing on to U.S. policy positions. Summitry, too, with its shifting policy alliances among the G-7 countries, offered Japan greater political maneuverability as a counterpoint to the bilateral relationship itself. Along with these developments was the growing Japanese awareness of American economic decline and the termination of clear U.S. supremacy.[39] All these developments opened up the possibility of a fundamental shift in Japan's foreign policy.

1980s: A Break with the Past or More of the Same?

Contemporary views of Japanese foreign policy have been deeply shaped by the events of the late 1970s and early 1980s. The era, some have claimed, brought about a "watershed" in Japanese diplomacy.[40] Press reports heralded Japan as a de facto member of the Western military system, and many foreign observers saw a convergence between Japan and Europe on security questions.[41] The distinguished *Asahi Janaru* had a special issue entitled "Dreams of Japan as a Great Power."[42] The view of Japan as a rising, more assertive power in search of a larger role—indeed, of a pax Nipponica to replace U.S. hegemony—became widespread in the 1980s.[43] If Japan had had a passive and reactive foreign policy in the past, the changes under way in the late 1970s and 1980s, in the view of many, supported a rising-state thesis.

The rising-state thesis saw that at least three factors were transforming Japan's defense profile: a worsening of Japan's security context due to the post–1976

Soviet military buildup in the Far East; the increase in pressure, or *gaiatsu*, from the United States and its allies on burden sharing; and the rise of Prime Minister Nakasone Yasahiro, the country's first prodefense prime minister of the postwar era.

Not only were the Soviets increasing their military capability in East Asia; they also demonstrated increased capacity and readiness to intervene in Third World conflicts (e.g., Afghanistan, Angola, and their aid to Ethiopia). In the Pacific there was the reality of Soviet backing of Vietnam (via the Soviet-Vietnamese Pact of November 1978), Soviet bases in the Northern Territories, SS-20 IRBMs in Siberia, and, in September 1983, the Korean Airlines incident. Soviet negotiators at the Geneva talks in 1983 asserted the country's right to transfer SS-20s from Europe to Asia as a way of achieving a reduction in tensions, raising the possibility of an even stronger future military posture in the Far East.[44]

Burden-sharing pressure was also mounting. Not long after his inauguration, President Ronald Reagan had declared burden sharing to be the "central thrust of [U.S.] defense policy towards allies" and had shifted the debate with Japan from a discussion of budgetary shares to one that focused on "roles and responsibilities." In 1985 both the Senate and House passed resolutions criticizing Japan's level of defense spending. The new pressure could be seen as part of a broader change that had brought defense-minded governments into power in Britain, Germany, and the United States in a way that was soon affecting summitry.[45]

Finally, changes in Japan itself were thought to undergird the new role. After the turbulent 1970s, which had seen LDP rule threatened, the 1980s were heralded as the age of conservative entrenchment, in which the ruling party could be less attentive to domestic voices opposing a stronger defense for Japan. There was much attention to the growing importance of the *zoku*, or policy tribes, made up of Diet member-experts, and in particular the defense *zoku*, and a broad consensus developed among analysts of Japanese politics that the LDP's power was rising in policy making at the expense of bureaucracy. In the 1980s, the LDP routinely intervened to secure budget increases in defense spending in the face of MOF opposition and indeed instituted a special budgetary framework for handling the defense budget in the early 1980s to facilitate that process.[46]

Many developments in the late 1970s and 1980s gave credence to the view that Japan's foreign policy was changing directions and that the country's defense profile was growing. Prime Minister Ohira Masayoshi in 1979 launched the concept of "comprehensive security," which brought defense, trade, aid, and other foreign policy activities into a common framework and at the same time called for a greater military defense role for Japan. In 1981 his successor Suzuki won praise in Washington for pledging that Japan would "strengthen [its] defense capability in order to defend several hundred miles of surrounding waters and the sea lanes to a distance of 1000 miles."[47] When Nakasone, long identified with a strong defense posture for Japan, took office in November 1982, he immediately called for a strengthening of Japan's military capability, and, soon after, his statement in Washington that Japan would serve as an "unsinkable aircraft carrier" in the Pacific was widely taken as a signal that Japan was making a break with the past on defense. In 1985, Nakasone took the same commitment to the Bonn summit, where he strongly backed a summit statement that the security interests of the G-7 countries were "indivisible."[48] In an era when Japan sought to reduce its budget deficit by putting a lid on almost all spending, Japan's annual 6.5 percent to 7.8 percent increases in military spending in the first half of the 1980s[49] offered yet more support for the rising-state thesis. Nakasone's move to lift the 1 percent of GNP ceiling on defense spending in 1987 was thought to be a crucial marker on the passage to a new era.

For all these indicators, however, evidence of a real change in Japan's defense posture and approach to foreign policy is lacking. The widespread popularity in Washington and other foreign capitals of a prodefense Nakasone created a great sense of movement, a watershed. In fact, however, his act of lifting the 1 percent ceiling in 1987 had not brought Japan above 1.013 percent of GNP for defense by 1990; and indeed, in 1990, Japan committed only 0.997 percent of GNP for defense—less than in 1955 or 1965.[50] A recent study concluded that despite all the rhetoric about a higher profile, militarily stronger Japan, Japan's defense establishment still lacks a strategy: the three services continue to acquire weapons haphazardly while keeping down budget items for maintenance, ammunition, and parts.[51]

All this raises questions as to how the objective situation of a rising Soviet threat was interpreted in Tokyo as opposed to Washington. Certainly the United States saw the Soviet Far East buildup as posing an immediate, broadscale threat to Japan; but, according to Sakanaka, Japan saw an increased threat only of a limited attack on Japan.[52] The distinguished diplomat Ushiba Nobuhiko stated candidly in 1983 that the Japanese were far less concerned about the Soviet threat than the Americans or Europeans. Indeed, Ushiba also voiced concerns that the Reagan military buildup would hurt American efforts at economic revitalization, suggesting that he shared such a view.[53] Nor did the rise of the Liberal Democratic party signal a shift in defense policy making, despite what many people assume. In 1980, the Ministry of Finance continued to have the upper hand in the budgetary process over defense.[54] In his comprehensive study of defense budget making, Joseph Keddell found that the ministry set the pace of military spending throughout the entire decade, and that the defense *zoku* actually lost power in the late 1980s.[55]

The foreign policy approach Japan used throughout the 1980s, far from representing a fundamental break with the past, was fully consistent with the defensive-state model. Japan continued to pursue a strategy of risk minimization, despite mounting foreign pressure to play a more active role in the world. In G-7 summitry, a multilateral context in many ways made it easier than in the past to take provocative political positions without provoking one's adversaries: It is harder to hear a single voice in a choir with seven members than in a U.S.-Japanese duet. Thus, for example, there were relatively few costs for Japan of joining in a G-7 condemnation of the Soviet invasion of Afghanistan at the 1980 Venice summit. The following year at the G-7 summit in Ottawa, Japan resisted pressure to sign on to a unified call for a major defense buildup in response to the Soviet threat, signaling the Japanese preference for a risk-minimization strategy.[56] Nakasone's move in 1983 at the summit to affirm the "indivisibility" of the security interests of the industrial countries was interpreted by some as a sign of a bolder Japan seeking a larger international role; but it also represented a way to stand shoulder to shoulder with Europeans at a time when the Soviets were threatening to shift SS-20s from Europe to Asia, and to signal Japanese objections to such a plan.[57]

In the 1980s, Japan's self-containment policies also continued. Its arms-export ban and the three nonnuclear principles stayed in place. The boldest break with containment policies was the move to lift the 1 percent of GNP ceiling on defense spending in 1987. But in 1990, the defense budget as a percentage of GNP had dropped to the 1985 level, and below the old ceiling.[58] The other area where the persistence of Japan's self-containment strategy could be questioned concerns defense technology cooperation. In 1980 the U.S.-Japan Systems Science and Technology Forum was established at the Pentagon's behest, ushering in numerous defense cooperation possibilities. Far from racing to the opportunities, however, Japan's response overall has been marked by ambivalence and fear of technology loss to the United States.[59] The country's decision to join with the United States in SDI research was motivated more by fears of losing commercial advantages (i.e., spin-off technologies) than by the chance to gain a leg up for rearming Japan.

Beginning with the emergence of comprehensive security as a concept in the late 1970s, substitution as a strategy came into its own in the 1980s. As noted earlier, "comprehensive security" formalized the notion that different types of international public goods contributed to security and held that all were interchangeable. Accordingly, contributions of aid and military spending should count equally in any burden-sharing formula. The architects of the concept sought "points," not only for what Japan was contributing in the aid area—which was a major consideration, given Japan's launching of its ODA-doubling plans after 1978 and growing U.S. pressure for strategic aid—but also for market opening and financial liberalization measures of the kind Japan was being forced to make by the G-7 countries. Strategic aid itself represented a way to respond to U.S. pressure to renegotiate the defense burden while carrying on Japan's aid program much as before.[60] The advantages of giving strategic aid can be seen in the Ottawa summit in 1981, in which Suzuki pledged a boost in aid to Turkey, Pakistan, and Thailand; as a result of this and other Japanese moves, the country avoided being singled out for criticism in the summit's summary report despite widespread pressure during the meeting itself.[61]

Generating rationales to justify Japan's contributions to burden sharing took on particular urgency in the 1980s as the United States slid into becoming the world's number one debtor nation and Japan surged into first place as the leading creditor. Furthermore, the Reagan defense buildup, which won firm backing from key G-7 allies, made Japan's own more limited contribution to burden sharing all the more glaring. As early as 1980, officials in Tokyo were struggling with rationales to counter a new round of U.S. claims that Japan was free-riding on defense.[62] Although Japan kept defense spending at or near 1 percent throughout the decade, each year it could point to big budgetary gains for defense relative to the previous year in a situation in which no other budgetary items (other than aid) were allowed to rise. Certain relatively new rationales gained major importance in the 1980s. The new phenomenon of "Japan bashing" gave rise to America bashing in Japan, and Japanese officials could argue that increased foreign pressure (*gaiatsu*) was producing a nationalism that could force the nation away from the U.S.-Japanese alliance altogether. Meanwhile, Japan was greatly aided in making its case by the growing American fear of Japan's rise, symbolized by *Atlantic* editor James Fallows' call to "contain Japan."[63] Uneasiness among Japan's Asian neighbors, particularly South Korea and the PRC, as the nation's military spending levels grew gave weight to Japan's arguments that constraint was essential. Citing various U.S. congressional reports, Japanese officials could claim that Japan contributed to security by *not* being a military power.[64] Finally, in the 1980s, Japan had gained the best rationale of all for limiting its defense profile: neither the United States nor the world at large wanted a rearmed Japan.[65]

Ritualization of conflict in U.S.-Japanese relations reached new heights in the 1980s. At front stage was a steady outpouring of criticism of Japan led by U.S. congressmen from both parties denouncing Japan as a free rider and demanding that Japan do more. The front-stage response from the Japanese side was equally predictable: limited concessions, countercharges directed at the U.S. budget deficit and other failings, and rationales for why Japan could not or should not do more. In the domestic debate in Japan, for example, the term strategic aid—routinely used in Washington and in the Western media—was anathema and was avoided wherever possible by Japanese officials.[66] The term "burden sharing" itself, widely used in the West, was generally skirted in Japan for a variety of euphemisms.

Backstage, however, were various forms of cooperation. Numerous leaders stumbled in the minefields of U.S.-Japanese relations, such as Foreign Minister Ito Masayoshi, who was forced to resign for the seemingly innocuous mistake of calling the relation an "alliance"—a term commonly used in the discourse in Washington.[67] Nor was the split between the public versus backstage aspects of the relationship merely a matter of nomenclature. "Strategic aid," as used by Washington, almost always referred to Japan's "aid to U.S. aid"—that is, Japanese aid given, upon a request from the United States, to countries or regions strategically important to the United States that the Americans saw as needing help. Such aid became a crucial Japanese substitute for military spending in the 1980s, legitimized under the rubric of comprehensive security, and one that the United States increasingly welcomed. Yet for Japanese officials to acknowledge publicly that aid was being given at America's behest and for security reasons brought forth storms of protest and criticism from outside and indeed within the ruling party back at home. Japanese officials thus found themselves trying to justify why Japan was suddenly giving aid to countries well outside the country's usual orbit of interest, with aid to Reagan's "Caribbean Initiative" in the early 1980s as one particularly awkward example. Should American officials slip and publicly thank the Japanese for strategic aid, they could inadvertently confer the metaphorical kiss of death on their Japanese counterparts. The importance of rituals in U.S.-Japanese relations was not new, but the hot glare of the media made it increasingly difficult for officials in both countries to play to different audiences at different times. The ritual nature of the relationship ran much deeper than has been discussed so far, however, for beneath the public trans-Pacific debate over Japan's "free ride" on defense was the tacit recognition that fundamental adjustments in the security responsibilities borne by Tokyo were not really sought in Washington, and that, correspondingly, most Japanese were still unwilling to endorse Japan's military participation in the U.S. global strategy.[68]

After the Gulf War: Burden Sharing in the Post–Cold War Era

Joyous multitudes of Germans celebrating the fall of the Berlin Wall in October 1989 marked the end of one era and the beginning of another in Washington and Tokyo as elsewhere. Euphoria soon turned to uncertainty and soul-searching in Japan, however, as Japanese officialdom watched American and European leaders race to embrace their former enemies while Japan, a long-standing alliance partner, observed from the sidelines, and while the Cold War continued in Asia. Japan's economic might, coupled with continuing friction over market opening and Japanese high-profile investments in the United States, gave rise to new rounds of Japan bashing. Indeed, a new issue that gained currency in the U.S.-Japanese dialogue was whether Japan, with the decline of Soviet power, was becoming for Americans the "substitute threat."

The Persian Gulf crisis became the first test of the post–Cold War era, and of how burden sharing in the face of a common problem would be negotiated. The United States quickly assumed leadership, and within weeks after Iraq's invasion of Kuwait in August 1990 Japan had pledged $4 billion to Operation Desert Shield. By late fall Japan was under attack in Washington for its slowness in making payments and in numerous support initiatives (in the dispatch of medical personnel, logistical support by commercial airlines, in the failed Gulf Cooperation Bill that would have dispatched Self-Defense Forces to the region in noncombat roles). In late September, *New York Times* columnist William Safire charged Japan with "national irresponsibility" for its low defense spending and lack of manpower commitment, and he urged that the country be pressured to spend 6 percent of GNP for "the poor and war ravaged" if it failed to contribute enough for the gulf effort.[69] A beleaguered Prime Minister Kaifu Toshiki moved quickly with a pledge for an additional $9 billion soon after the land war began in January 1991, but criticism of Japan's performance persisted in Washington. In a report on the allied effort issued after the war ended, the House Armed Services Committee credited Japan for its part in assuring that 75 percent of the U.S. costs of the war were covered by the allies, and was prepared to cede that Japan had paid its "fair share." But echoing the widespread view in Washington, it labeled Japan "a reluctant contributor despite its wealth."[70] Kaifu, a precarious choice for prime minister to begin with due to his weakness within the LDP, lost out on a possible bid for another term in October 1991 and became another casualty of U.S.-Japanese relations.

The first two years of the post–Cold War era in Japan have been marked by increased urgency in the debate over what Japan's world role should be. Projections of a drop in U.S. defense spending to 3.6 percent of GNP by 1995 spurred thinking on whether Japan could continue to rely on the United States for its own defense. Japan bashing and seeming American ingratitude for Japan's contribution during the gulf crisis led many in Japan to voice deep uncertainty about the relationship, and to ask whether the two nations, in the absence of a common threat, would turn inward and drift apart. Noting growing isolationist trends in both countries, for example, Eto Jun observed that "isolated nations may very likely hurt one another . . . and already, we can see trends in this direction."[71]

Nonetheless, for all this debate, Japan's conduct of foreign policy in the post-Cold War era so far has closely followed earlier trends. First and foremost, Japan's strategy has continued to be characterized by risk minimization. As in the past, Japan has resisted being swept up in U.S. global strategy. Before the gulf crisis, leading diplomat Owada Hisashi was heralding the demise of the era of U.S. "unilateral globalism."[72] In the gulf conflict itself, diplomat Hanabusa Masamichi publicly voiced a reluctance expressed privately by many Japanese opinion leaders to see the country involved in the conflict. Dismissing the U.S. argument that Japan was the prime beneficiary of allied action because of its resource dependence, he told a New York University audience that it made little difference who controlled Kuwait since experience had shown Japan that "whoever controls oil will be disposed to sell it."[73] As in previous wars in Korea and Vietnam, Japan avoided a direct role. Even if the Gulf Cooperation Bill had been approved by the Diet in October 1990, Japan's active support in men and materiel would have been less than what Japan provided to the United States indirectly in either previous war.

Japan's policy of minimizing risk by avoiding alienating anyone has surfaced repeatedly in the post–Cold War era. Japan backed the economic embargo on Iraq but assiduously avoided confrontational politics with that country during the war. In its China policy Japan once again sought to straddle the fence. After a Western hue and cry in the face of the June 4, 1989, crackdown in Tiananmen Square, it was four days before a public announcement was forthcoming from Prime Minister Uno, who said that "leveling guns at the people is serious."[74] Under pressure from the United States and other nations, Japan stopped its aid to the PRC, but by the summer of 1990 it had sought and won approval from the other G-7 countries for resuming it.

Japan pursued a strategy of risk minimization also through efforts to contain the United States. Foreign policy commentators in Japan pointed out the dangers in the post-Cold War era that the new U.S. security focus on low-level conflicts in Third World countries could pull Japan into such conflicts, especially if U.S. forces were dispatched from bases in Japan, and counseled consultation with the United States, presumably to constrain this potential "Vietnam problem."[75] Japan's 1991 aid policy initiative, by which Japan announced its intent of linking aid increases to levels of arms spending by recipient countries, serves as a valuable way to contain arms sales by U.S. suppliers and thus represents an indirect way of attempting to contain the United States.

Meanwhile, Japan's policy of self-containment continued, despite rhetorical calls by some for an enlarged military role for Japan. Its actual role in the gulf conflict, for all the talk of something more, broke little new ground. The dispatch of four mine-sweepers to the gulf following the conflict, and the plan to send Japanese troops to take part in UN peace-keeping operations, if approved, expands Japan's roles and missions, but on an exceedingly modest level.

The rationales for not doing more have had much consistency with the past. Japan's remarkable prosperity obviated the possibility of begging off from international public goods spending on economic grounds, but new types of economic arguments surfaced. The distinguished diplomat Kuriyama Takakazu, recalling the formula for naval balance set out in the Washington conference in 1922, urged that Japan share responsibility as part of a 5:5:3 structure, reflecting the relative GNP of the United States, European Community, and Japan.[76] While his intent was to urge Japan to do more, consigning Japan to the junior partner role in the tripartite arrangement mirrored earlier Japanese economic justifications for paying less. Scholar Iida Tsuneo, writing on the eve of the post–Cold War era, similarly found reasons why Japan should not seek a higher profile in its aid giving, or alter its policies: "By nature Japanese are not good at making clever speeches or making fanfare over our performance"; noting that economic prosperity had brought euphoria, he argued that the timing was poor for "embarking on something we're not good at."[77]

Adverse public opinion remained a crucial rationale for a more limited role. Japanese media reports of growing anti-Americanism carried the message that enough was enough when it came to pressuring Japan.

Burden Sharing and Beyond: Why Present Arrangements
Are in Japan's Interests

Stepping back from the defensive-state strategy still in place, there can be little doubt that from Japan's standpoint there are major disadvantages of pursuing it. On security grounds alone, there have been inherent dangers over the past forty years, acknowledged by everyone from defense planners to socialists, in being aligned with a superpower in a situation of military confrontation that was the Cold War. The consistency with which Japan has pursued a strategy of "three containments"—constraining not only the Soviet union, but the United States, and even Japan itself through an elaborate network of self restraints on military activity—suggests the degree to which Japan has perceived itself to be at risk. Furthermore, the basic mechanism of the relationship, in which Japan has actively steered its course among a barrage of U.S. demands, has left a foreign policy that is triggered in important ways by outside pressure, leading to a dependence on foreign pressure that, many writers note, is undesirable.[78] For practitioners—prime ministers and diplomats alike—the dynamics of burden-sharing negotiations, particularly their ritual aspects in which front-stage and back-stage positions radically diverge, make for no-win diplomacy in which the risks of a slip are high. One need only recall Kaifu's efforts to respond promptly to Bush's requests during the gulf crisis, while ducking charges from the public and from within his party of being another yes-man to the Americans, to appreciate the dilemma. The basic pattern of U.S.-Japanese relations and of burden sharing negotiations, as Curtis noted over a decade ago, is one that "leaves everyone dissatisfied and resentful."[79] For a nation like Japan, for which achieving status in the international order has been a prime goal of foreign policy for over a century, these terms clearly rankle.

But for all these costs of the present patterns of divvying up international public goods with the United States and its other alliance partners, Japan's present strategy has worked exceedingly well, serving both its short-term and long-term interests. First and foremost, it has represented a way to achieve security at low costs—lower in GNP terms than for any other major industrial nation. With only 1 percent of GNP going for defense, Japan could devote the other 99 percent to economic growth, the development of science and technology, and social welfare, as one recent writer put it.[80] In the East Asian region itself, the security relation overall must have been stabilizing; otherwise countries today would not be so eager to see the U.S. military presence remain, and thus the basic terms of Cold War security relations preserved. The foreign policy gains in terms of leverage have also been substantial. The burden-sharing relationship offered early postwar Japan a framework for recasting a foreign policy in a world hostile to Japan. The substitution policy that Japan has pursued in negotiations over burden sharing have legitimized, or won U.S. support for, initiatives such as Japan's foreign assistance program, the return of Okinawa, Japan's concerted and successful efforts to rebuild a zone of

Japanese influence and economic power in Asia, and other policies and goals. The need to cooperate with Japan in the name of exacting burden-sharing concessions meant less U.S. pressure and retaliation in the bilateral economic relations than might otherwise have been the case.

Nor are the costs to national sovereignty and independence of a responsive, risk-minimizing foreign policy carried out in the context of the U.S.-Japanese relationship as great as many critics claim. Though many Japanese nationalists through the years have deplored the subordinate status implied by Japan's military dependence on the United States, actual sovereignty has not been an issue since 1952. Meanwhile, there are numerous benefits to a nation from surrendering "operational sovereignty," such as gaining greater credibility because of constraints on oneself, and the ability to achieve goals that would be unobtainable on one's own.[81] From such a vantage point, Japan's foreign policy gains mentioned earlier, from the return of Okinawa to the rebuilding of its position in Asia, would have been virtually unachievable outside the regime set in place by the U.S.-Japan Mutual Security Treaty, and the burden sharing negotiations that grew out of it. Indeed, the constraints on Japanese defense efforts set by the relation and further advanced by Japan's "self-containment" and risk-minimization strategies reduced fears of Japanese militarism at home, gave Japan the credibility to reestablish itself in Asia, and helped it come to be perceived as a force for good in the Third World.

Even the rituals in the relationship, with the high demands they have placed on Japanese practitioners to maintain them, have had their uses. Decrying foreign pressure while quietly steering a foreign policy among demands placed on Japan has had practical political advantages, representing a way to deflect criticism from unpopular policies that, in the view of policy makers, were in Japan's interests. No issue in postwar Japanese politics has been more rancorous than security, and the burden-sharing framework, even if it has been a source of domestic tension, has also offered a way to manage it. For all these reasons, then, the burden-sharing framework that has grown up over the postwar era has advanced Japan's interests, and those of its political leadership, to a remarkable degree.

The U.S. Interest Satisfied

For all the dissatisfaction voiced in Washington and among the American public over Japan's foreign policy contribution, there is little to suggest that Japan's response to burden-sharing pressure is not in America's interest as well. Critics claiming that Japan does not pay its fair share of the costs in the burden-sharing relation ignore one of the most basic tenets of U.S. policy in the past and today, which has been to contain Japan. The types of "roles and responsibilities"—a euphemism of the Reagan years for encouraging increased U.S. military procurements, increased payment of base costs, and, in the Gulf conflict, "checkbook diplomacy"—the United States has sought have been fully consistent with the interests of the United States, for they have allowed the nation maximum gains with the smallest possible reductions in power and decision-making authority in security matters. The benefits of what Japan has provided cannot be overlooked. Given Japan's steadily increasing payments to maintain U.S. bases, it will soon be cheaper to operate American bases in Japan than in the United States, and Japan was the largest non-Arab contributor to the allied Gulf War effort. The concessions exacted from Japan in bilateral negotiations over trade, market opening, financial liberalization, and other issues often have been less than what was sought; but without the security treaty and its associated guarantees, the United States undoubtedly would have had far less leverage. The security relationship moreover has represented a way for the United States to exercise control over Japanese technology flows to nations under COCOM restrictions.

From a system perspective, it may be argued that Japan has paid less than it should in return for the security all capitalist nations enjoyed in the postwar era, but from a U.S. perspective, it is difficult to see any division of responsibility for providing international public goods with Japan that would have advanced American interests as effectively as the present arrangement. In the interchangeability that Japan has sought among public good, Japan has gained a position of leadership in the Third World, while the United States undoubtedly has lost ground; but America's declining role in Third World development and its loss of moral authority in that domain have stemmed more from the collective impact of U.S. private-sector decisions not to invest in the developing world than from Japanese gains in burden-sharing negotiations. Given the U.S. task today of keeping power while shedding its burden, the American conduct of its burden-sharing negotiations has been optimal. Finally, if one makes the case that the post–Cold War world may call for new approaches to foreign policy, one can argue that the U.S. conduct of the relation has served its own interests and that of other nations well; for by agreeing to a tacit division of labor in which Japan has been able to maneuver to advantage by exercising economic rather than military power, the United States has given Japan breathing room to establish a new kind of foreign policy—one that may offer a bridge t. the future in the emerging world order.

Notes

I am grateful to Oda Yukiko and Terry Kawashima for their valuable research assistance, and to Margot Chamberlain for her help in preparing the manuscript.

1. For the term "reactive state" applied to foreign economic policy making, see Kent E. Calder, "Japanese Foreign Economic Policy Formation: Explaining the Reactive State," *World Politics* 40, 4 (July 1988): 517–41. For a discussion of Japan's "immobilism" in key areas of domestic politics and foreign policy, see J. A. A. Stockwin et al., *Dynamic and Immobilist Politics in Japan* (Honolulu: University of Hawaii Press, 1988).

2. Sassa Atsuyuki, "Posuto Maruta ni okeru Nihon no chii" (Japan's status after the Malta summit), *Chuo koron* 106 (March 1991): 48-59. Sassa sees national sovereignty requiring that a state have a viable national security policy and foreign policy; lacking both, Japan is a half-nation (*han kokka*), according to him.

3. Alan Tonelson and Ronald Morse, "Outdated Alliance Strategies," in Clyde Prestowitz, Ronald Morse, and Alan Tonelson, eds., *Powernomics: Economics and Strategy After the Cold War* (Washington, D. C.: Economic Strategy Institute, 1991).

4. See Ezra Vogel, "Pax Nipponica," *Foreign Affairs* 64, 4 (Spring 1986), for one statement of the rising-state thesis.

5. See Nobuhiko Ushiba, Graham Allison, and Thierry de Montbrial, eds., *Sharing International Responsibilities among Trilateral Countries*, Report of the Trilateral Task Force on Sharing Global Responsibilities to the Trilateral Commission (New York: Trilateral Commission, 1983), for a summary of issues from such a perspective.

6. See Sadako Ogata, "Shifting Power Relations in Multilateral Development Banks," *Journal of International Studies* (Institute of International Relations, Sophia University, Tokyo), no. 22 (January 1989): 18, who defines the U.S. problem this way.

7. See Kent E. Calder, *Crisis and Compensation: Public Policy and Political Stability in Japan*, (Princeton: Princeton University Press, 1988), pp. 414-15. Japanese outlays as a percentage of budget declined thereafter, never to reach that level again.

8. Kamiya Fuji, "Nichibei shuno kaidan no kiseki" (The trail of Japan-U.S. summit), in Kamiya Fuji, ed., *Nihon to Amerika: Kyocho to tairitsu no kozo* (Japan and the U.S.: The structure of cooperation and conflict), (Tokyo: Nihon Keizai Shimbunsha, 1973), p. 177.

9. For a recent statement of this view by a Japanese security specialist, see Akira Kato, "Japan's Search for a New Security Relationship," *Occasional Paper Series*, Program on U.S.-Japan Relations, Harvard University, 1990, p. 2.

10. John H. Makin, "American Economic and Military Leadership in the Postwar Period," in John H. Makin and Donald C. Hellman, eds., *Sharing World Leadership?: A New Era for America & Japan* (Washington, D. C.: American Enterprise Institute for Public Policy Research, 1989).

11. Martin E. Weinstein, "Japan's Defense Policy and the May 1981 Summit," *Journal of Northeast Asian Studies* 1 (March 1982).

12. John W. Dower, *Empire and Aftermath: Yoshida Shigeru and the Japanese Experience, 1978–1954* (Cambridge: Harvard University Press, 1979), pp. 373–74. Also see Watanabe Akio, *Sengo Nihon no taigai seisaku* (Japan's foreign policy after World War II) (Tokyo: Yhikaku, 1985), p. 44.

13. Hisahiko Okazaki, "Far Eastern Strategic Balance," 1981, photocopy, pp. 7-8.

14. Prime Minister's Office, *Public Opinion Survey on Japan's Self Defense Force and Defense Problems* (Tokyo: Foreign Press Center, August 1985), p. 25.

15. John Welfield, *An Empire in Eclipse: Japan in the Postwar American Alliance System* (London: The Athlone Press, 1988), p. 51.

16. Dower, *Empire and Aftermath*, p. xxi.

17. Kishi fell after the ratification of the mutual security treaty struggle in 1960; Suzuki

shortened his life as prime minister with his trip to Washington in 1981; Nakasone, though he survived two terms in office, came under attack from Ishihara Shintaro and others as a yes-man to the Americans; and a similar charge helped limit Kaifu to a single two-year term.

18. Tetsuya Kataoka, *Waiting for a "Pearl Harbor": Japan Debates Defense* (Stanford: Stanford University, 1980), p. 12.

19. Shiro Saito, *Japan at the Summit: Its Role in the Western Alliance and in Asian Pacific Cooperation* (London: Routledge, 1990), p. 21.

20. Thomas R. Havens, *Fire Across the Sea: The Vietnam War and Japan 1965–1975* (Princeton: Princeton University Press, 1987), p. 96.

21. On the GATT, see Mike M. Mochizuki, "To Change or to Contain: Dilemmas of American Policy Towards Japan," in Kenneth A. Oye, Robert J. Lieber, and Donald Rothchild, eds., *Eagle in a New World: American Grand Strategy in the Post–Cold War Era* (New York: Harpers Collins, forthcoming), p. 338. On whaling concessions, see Frank Langdon, "Japan and North America," in Robert S. Ozaki and Walter Arnold, eds., *Japan's Foreign Relations: A Global Search for Economic Security,* (Boulder: Westview Press, 1985), p. 16.

22. Edward A. Olsen, *U.S.-Japan Strategic Reciprocity: A Neo-Internationalist View* (Stanford: Hoover Institution Press, 1985), pp. 75–76. Almost forty years later, Japanese officials fiercely debated whether the constitution permitted the use of minesweepers in the Persian Gulf and decided, at least in 1987, that it did not. The same debate in 1991 resulted in the dispatch of four minesweepers in the aftermath of the war.

23. Edwin O. Reischauer, *The United States and Japan*, 2d. ed. (Cambridge: Harvard University Press, 1957), p. 333.

24. Calder develops this concept in *Crisis and Compensation*, p. 438.

25. Saito, *Japan at the Summit*, pp. 28, 48.

26. See Joseph Patrick Keddell, Jr., "Defense as a Budgetary Problem: The Minimization of Conflict in Japanese Defense Policymaking, 1976–1987." Ph.D. dissertation, University of Wisconsin-Madison, 1990.

27. Paul Samuelson, "The Pure Theory of Public Expenditure," in *Review of Economics and Statistics* 36 (1951): 387-89.

28. Saito, *Japan at the Summit*, p. 19. The United States rebuffed the request at the time, but the same idea resurfaced later, leading to the establishment of the Asian Development Bank in 1965.

29. See Campbell elsewhere in this volume for an analysis that focuses on ritualization in U.S.-Japanese relations. On two-level games, see Robert N. Putnam, "Diplomacy and Domestic Politics: The Logic of Two-Level Games," *International Organization* (Summer 1988): 427–60.

30. See George R. Packard, *Protest in Tokyo: The Security Treaty Crisis of 1960* (Princeton: Princeton University Press, 1966), and Welfield, *Empire in Eclipse.*

31. Zbigniew Brzezinski, *The Fragile Blossom: Crisis and Change in Japan* (New York: Harper & Row, 1972).

32.   See Havens, *Fire Across the Sea*, pp. 89-96, for a discussion of Japan's role, including the *Asahi* account.

33.   Ibid. The Japanese public was deeply divided over the conflict. In a June 1966 survey, asked who was mainly at fault for the Vietnam situation, 31 percent of those questioned blamed the United States, while only 7 percent blamed the National Liberation Front. In a December 1967 Kyodo survey, 35 percent claimed to see danger that Japan would be involved in the war, with 37 percent disagreeing. (See p. 139.)

34.   Quoted in ibid., 138.

35.   Robert Putnam and Nicholas Bayne, *Hanging Together: The Seven-Power Summits* (Cambridge: Harvard University Press, 1984), p. 109.

36.   See Keddell, "Defense As a Budgetary Problem," and Calder, *Crisis and Compensation*, pp. 436-38.

37.   See Robert M. Orr, Jr., *The Emergence of Japan's Foreign Aid Power* (New York: Columbia University Press, 1990), pp. 109-10, for these and other examples of substitution efforts by Japan.

38.   Havens, *Fire Across the Sea*, p. 139; also see Miyasato Seigen, "Amerika no taigai enjo to Nihon no taiō" (U.S. foreign aid and Japan's response), in Hosoya Chihiro, ed., *Amerika gaiko: Nichibei kankei no bunmyaku no naka de* (U.S. diplomacy in the context of the Japan-U.S. relationship) (Tokyo: Nihon Kokusai Mondai Kenku, 1986) p. 160.

39.   For one authoritative statement of such awareness, see Yuichiro Nagatomi, ed., *Masayoshi Ohira's Proposal to Evolve the Global Society* (Tokyo: Foundation for Advanced Information and Research 1988), p. 224.

40.   Saito, *Japan at the Summit*, p. 6.

41.   Putnam and Bayne, *Hanging Together*, p. 191.

42.   *Asahi Janaru* (January 1979).

43.   Ezra Vogel, "Pax Nipponica," *Foreign Affairs*, 64, 4 (Spring 1986): 753–67.

44.   Putnam and Bayne, *Hanging Together*, p. 186.

45.   Ibid., p. 181.

46.   Keddell, "Defense as a Budgetary Problem," p. 267.

47.   Sakanaka, "Perception Gap," pp. 13-14. The comment came in reply to a question from a reporter after Suzuki's National Press Club speech in May 1981.

48.   Putnam and Bayne, *Hanging Together*, p. 191.

49.   Boeicho, *Boei Hakusho, Heisei gannendo ban* (White paper on national defense, 1989) (Tokyo: Okurasho Insatsukyoku, 1989), p. 331.

50.   Ibid., Ministry of Finance, *Financial Statistics of Japan* (Tokyo: Ministry of Finance, 1990), pp. 24 and 28.

51.   Keddell, "Defense as a Budgetary Problem," p. 176.

52.   Tomohisa Sakanaka, "Perception Gap between Japan and the United States on Defense Cooperation," paper presented at Conference on Japanese Comprehensive Security, SAIS, Washington, D. C., February 25, 1986, p. 9.

53.   Ushiba, *Sharing International Responsibilities*, p. 27.

54.   See Otake Hideo, "Bōeihi zōgaku o meguru Jimintō no tōnai rigigaku" (The inside

story of the power balance in the ldp on increasing defense spending), *Asahi Jānaru,* 23 (January 30, 1981): 12–15.

55. Keddell, "Defense as a Budgetary Problem," p. 273.

56. Saito, *Japan at the Summit, Financial Statistics,* p.72.

57. Putnam and Bayne, *Hanging Together,* p. 189.

58. Ministry of Finance, pp. 24 and 28.

59. Mike Mochizuki and Michael Nacht, "Modes of Defense Cooperation," in *U.S.-Japan Relations in the 1980s: Towards Burden Sharing,* pp. 129–37. Annual Report 1981–82, The Program on U.S.-Japan Relations, Center for International Affairs, Harvard University, pp. 134–35.

60. See Inada Juichi, "Nihon gaikō ni okeru enjo mondai no sho sokumen" (Various aspects of aid in Japanese foreign policy), *Kokusai mondai* (International Affairs) 326 (May 1987): 2-20. Inada holds that "strategic aid" could just as well apply to Japan's aid back in the 1960s, given the importance of the Western camp in earlier determinations of aid.

61. Saito, *Japan at the Summit,* p. 72.

62. Rifōmu Kurabu (Reform Club), "Nichibei sōgo anzen hoshō e no teigen" (A proposal for Japan-U.S. comprehensive national security). *Kikan Chūō Kōron Keiei Mondai* 19 (Fall 1980): 137–38. This article reports on the work of a study group made up of government officials, economists, and journalists.

63. James Fallows, "Containing Japan," *The Atlantic, Vol.* 263, 5 (May 1989): 40–54.

64. Rifōmu Kurabu, "Nichibei sōgo anzen hoshō e no teigen."

65. Ibid. Even in 1980 the authors of this proposal, citing U.S. congressional reports, noted U.S. claims that Japan sought increases in defense capability only within the limits of Japan's dependence on U.S. military power.

66. Inada, "Nihon gaikō," pp. 5–6.

67. Ito had been responsible for briefing Prime Minister Suzuki, who made the blunder. The term "alliance" connoted a close military relationship of a type that many people in Japan were unwilling to accept.

68. Mochizuki and Nacht, "Modes of Defense Cooperation," p. 130; Mike Mochizuki, "The United States and Japan: Conflict and Cooperation Under Mr. Reagan," in Kenneth A. Oye, Robert J. Lieber, and Donald Rothchild eds., *Eagle Resurgent?: The Reagan Era in American Foreign Policy* (Boston: Little, Brown, 1987), p. 335.

69. *New York Times,* September 27, 1991, p. A23.

70. Les Aspin, "Sharing the Burden of the Persian Gulf: Are the Allies Paying Their Fair Share?" Report of the House Armed Service Committee, (April 8, 1991), p. 4.

71. "Nihonjin wa naze Amerika ga kiraika," p. 109.

72. *Wall Street Journal,* August 27, 1991, p. A11.

73. John B. Judis, "Burden Shirking: A Free Ride for the Japanese in the Gulf," *The New Republic* 204 (March 4, 1991), p. 22.

74. Quoted in Uldis Kruze, "Sino Japanese Relations," *Current History* 90 (April 1991): 156-59.

75. Inoguchi Takashi, "Zen chikū anpo kyōryoku kaigi o teishō suru: Posuto reisen jidai no Nihon no ikikata" (Proposal for a conference on security and cooperation on earth: A way of living for Japan in the post–Cold War era), *Chūō kōron 106* (March 1991). Also see Igarashi Takeshi, "Seikimatsu Nihon no anzen hoshō seisaku" (Japan's security policy at the end of the century). *Sekai,* no. 543 (July 1990): 45–56.

76. Kuriyama Takakazu, "Gekidō no kyūjūnendai to Nihon gaikō no shin tenkai; Atarashii kokusai chitsujo kōchiku e no sekkyokuteki kōken no tame ni" (New directions for Japanese foreign policy in the changing world of the 1990s: Making active contributions to the creation of a new international order), *Gaikō Fō ramu,* no. 20 (May 1990): 12–13.

77. Iida Tsuneo, "Sekai senryaku o kataru nakare" (Don't talk about global strategy), *Voice* (May 1989).

78. Sasaki Takeshi, "Postwar Japanese Politics at a Turning Point," *The Japan Foundation Newsletter* 18 (May 1991): 6–7.

79. Gerald L. Curtis, "Japanese Security Policies and the United States," *Foreign Affairs* 59 (Spring 1981): 868.

80. Sassa Atsuyuki, "Posuto Maruta ni okeru Nihon no chii" (Japan's status after the Malta summit), *Chūō kōron* 106 (March 1991).

81. Robert Keohane, "Sovereignty, Interdependence and International Institutions," (Harvard University Working Paper Series no. 1, 1991), pp. 194–95.

IV Japan and Its Neighbors

Chapter 12
Japanese Policy Toward Korea

Byung-joon Ahn

Against the background of the ending of the Cold War and the emergence of Japan as an economic superpower, that country has been searching for a more independent and active foreign policy. Nowhere is this more apparent than in relations with Korea, where Japan's attempt to redefine its policy seems to be a testing ground for the search for a new role in Asia and throughout the world.

For Japan to develop a new Korea policy, however, it needs to tackle a number of thorny problems. It has to find a satisfactory way to liquidate the legacy of past colonial rule. It also needs to assert a relationship with South Korea separate from its security ties with the United States. Furthermore, to achieve a diplomatic breakthrough, it must normalize relations with North Korea without harming its traditional relations with South Korea. To successfully achieve these goals requires building a new consensus in its domestic politics. Finally, in making these efforts, Japan has to work out an appropriate division of roles with the United States since both Korea and Japan maintain security treaties with the United States.

The Search for a Greater Political Role in Korea

By addressing these problems, Japan has been seeking a greater political role in Korea. In the past, Japanese policy has been to reaffirm that peace and stability on the Korean peninsula is essential to peace and stability in Northeast Asia including Japan itself. This was the official stand that Prime Minister Miki expounded in 1975. In upholding this broad principle, Tokyo has regarded the development of friendly relations with Seoul as a priority task while maintaining only nonpolitical ties with Pyongyang in order to maintain some influence there. By undertaking formal negotiations for diplomatic normalization with Pyongyang, however, Tokyo is now moving toward establishment of a de jure two-Korea policy.

Clearly, Japan now is out to play a new political role not only in regard to Korea but in Asia as a whole in tune with the changing international environment and commensurate with its growing economic power. Indeed, Tokyo is projecting a new image just as Japan has entered the new Heisei era, inaugurated by the new Emperor, Akihito. In this attempt Korea and the Asian region have become a launching pad, as demonstrated by Prime Minister Kaifu's state visit to South Korea in January 1991 and then to Southeast Asian countries the following April. Emperor Akihito's visit to Southeast Asia in September 1991 was also designed to reinforce the image of a new Japan in Asia. Prime Minister Miyazawa's first foreign trip to South Korea in January 1992 reinforced this trend.

Five broad observations are in order to elaborate on Japanese policy. First, Japan has been making various efforts to liquidate the legacy of its past colonial rule in Korea by making apologies and by offering economic compensation. As a result, historical constraints on Japanese policy are being gradually reduced while its economic and political influence is being enhanced.

Second, faced with the end of the Cold War in East-West relations and the growing international status of South Korea, Japan perceives South Korea not only as being important as an ancillary element in to its relations with the United States but as being increasingly significant in its own right. South Korea is viewed by Tokyo not only as an economic and political partner but increasingly as a competitor as well, especially in developing access to China, the Soviet Union, and other Pacific countries.

Third, Japan is moving toward normalizing diplomatic relations with North Korea not merely to reduce tensions but more importantly to secure independent political influence vis-à-vis the Korean peninsula. This in turn has prompted South Korea and the United States to stress the importance of consultations on regional security and North-South Korean relations, especially in regard to nuclear issues.

Fourth, since the Korean question has been a divisive issue in domestic Japanese politics, Japan's Korea policy requires building a new consensus. Tokyo's initial moves to normalize relations with Pyongyang were made jointly by the Liberal Democratic party and the Japanese Socialist party. The actual negotiation and the process of normalization depend on forging a consensus involving not only these parties, however, but also other actors such as the bureaucracy, the press, and the public.

Fifth, insofar as leadership and regional roles are concerned, there is a discernible division of labor between Japan and the United States emerging with Japan assuming more economic and political roles while the United States continues to handle security measures. The overall trend is leading Japan to assume more and active political roles in Korea and the East Asian region as well, and for the United States to assume the role of a stabilizer and balancing force. Having said this, however, the precise roles Japan will play in Korea and Asia still remains to be seen.

Liquidating the Legacy of the Past

Japan has tried to liquidate the legacy of the past by providing economic compensation, making apologies, improving the legal status of Korean residents in Japan, and educating the postwar generation so that a new image of Japan, peaceful and remorseful, can be displayed to Korea. As a result, the constraints of past history are weakening, if not disappearing, and in their stead, the primacy of economics is exerting more influence on policy.

Japan and Korea are said to be close but at the same time far apart. Because of the historical legacy of Japanese rule over Korea in 1910–45, Koreans have harbored resentments and grievances about Japanese exploitation of their country and suppression of nationalist movements. Hence, it took fourteen years of negotiations before Japan and South Korea were able to sign a normalization treaty in 1965.[1] At that time the Satō government officially recognized the South Korean government under President Park as the "the sole legitimate government of Korea" and agreed to provide a grant of $300 million, another $200 million in long-term government credits, and $300 million in private credits. This was the first compensation that Japan paid to South Korea, and it helped South Korea generate sustained economic growth.

But that was hardly sufficient to relieve the profound sense of Korean resentment (called *han* in Korean and *urami* in Japanese). Such feelings were expressed in violent protests in Korea whenever Japanese were perceived to display insensitivity, as was the case with demonstrations in 1982 against "distortions" of facts in Japanese historical textbooks and in 1987 against Prime Minister Nakasone's visits to Yasukuni Shrine. Having witnessed these incidents, many Koreans felt that the Japanese had not changed their basic attitude toward Korea. This was why they expected that the late Emperor Hirohito would make a genuine apology to the Korean people when he welcomed President Chun in Tokyo in August 1984.

In fact, the kind of apology the emperor should have been expected to make became a contentious issue in Japanese-Korean relations. Then Prime Minister Nakasone did state that Japan indeed repented for its past wrongdoings and would rectify them in order to open a new chapter in its relations with Korea. But when the late emperor made his banquet remarks he only had this to say: "It is indeed regrettable that there was an unfortunate past between us for a period of this century, and I believe it should not be repeated."[2]

Even though President Chun took these words as an apology, most Koreans were far from satisfied with them. Once again, therefore, the politics of making apology faced both sides when President Roh hesitated to make his visit to Japan in May 1990 unless Tokyo would come up with a better statement. On this occasion Prime Minister Kaifu expressed "sincere remorse and honest apologies for the fact that there was a period in our history in which Japanese actions inflicted unbearable suffering and sorrow on the people of the Korean

peninsula." Moreover, the new emperor went further than his father by acknowledging for the first time who was responsible for the suffering when he said: "I
think of the suffering your people underwent during this unfortunate period, which
was brought about by my country, and cannot but feel the deepest regret."[3]
Responding to these words, President Roh said that it was time to forge a new era
of friendship and cooperation and to put "the mistakes of the past truly behind us."[4]
When he came to Seoul in January 1991, Prime Minister Kaifu laid a wreath at
Pagoda Park, the symbolic place where the March 1, 1919, independence declaration was made, in order "to have a correct recognition of history" and "to set an
example for the Japanese people."[5]

Another difficult issue derived from the past has been the legal status of about
700,000 Korean residents in Japan. Originally, most of these people or their parents
were forcibly taken to Japan for hard labor during World War II. Now they are
grouped into two organizations: some 500,000 belong to the pro–South Korean
Resident Union (*Mindan*) and about 200,000 belong to the pro–North Korean
General Association of Korean Residents (*Chosoren*). Adding to the many humil-
iations to which Koreans have been subjected, the requirements that they have their
fingerprints taken every five years and that they renew their alien registration every
year has created continuing controversies. Seoul has consistently called upon
Tokyo to do away with these violations of human rights.

Tokyo finally agreed at the foreign minister meeting in April 1990 to abolish
fingerprinting requirements and to enhance the legal status for third-generation
residents, the grandchildren of those who registered as residents as of 1971. At
Seoul's request, too, Tokyo promised at the fifteenth ministerial meeting held in
Seoul in November 1990 to suspend fingerprinting for first-and-second generation
residents as well. But it did not address Seoul's demands for granting voting rights
and job opportunities in the public sector. In January 1991 Tokyo agreed to stop
fingerprinting by the end of 1992 and to open some low-ranking teaching jobs to
Koreans.

Despite these efforts, many Japanese seem to be either ignorant or indifferent
toward Koreans. According to a survey conducted by the Japanese-Korean 21st
Century Committee, only 37.5 percent of Japanese people had some remorse about
the past, but 34.3 percent had no remorse at all.[6]

There is no doubt, however, that Tokyo has been making efforts to improve
relations with South Korea to pave the way for Emperor Akihito's planned visit to
South Korea, which in turn is part of Tokyo's effort to promote a new Japanese role
in Asia.

Autonomy in Its Partnership with South Korea

With the weakening of the historical legacy and the Cold War, Japan is beginning
to decouple its relationship with South Korea from its bilateral relationship with

the United States, thus displaying a new measure of autonomy in its policy toward Korea. Tokyo is recognizing the importance of South Korea as its second largest market and as an indispensable political partner for peace and stability in Northeast Asia. At the same time, South Korea, too, has sought to be treated as being vital to Japan itself.

During the 1960s and 1970s Japan tended to regard South Korea's importance mainly in the context of its relationship with the United States. In November 1969, for example, Prime Minister Satō told President Nixon: "The security of the Republic of Korea is essential to Japan's own security." However, Tokyo has never officially stated this position to Seoul. When President Chun asked Prime Minister Suzuki to grant $6 billion in credits on the ground that South Korea's enormous defense burden provides a shield for Japanese security, Suzuki refused to link economic cooperation to security in those terms.[7]

In January 1983, however, Prime Minister Nakasone came to Seoul and settled the economic assistance issue by agreeing to provide $4 billion in credits. While this decision was not officially linked to security issues, Nakasone made it clear to South Korean officials that it was motivated in part by Japanese appreciation for the contribution South Korean defense efforts were making for Japanese security. From this time on, Tokyo has been consistently stressing the need for friendly relations with South Korea. Prime Minister Takeshita, for example, made a personal trip in February 1988 to attend the inauguration of President Roh and went back in September for the opening ceremony of the Seoul Olympics. Kaifu's state visit in January 1991 also represented a deliberate policy to strengthen its relationship with the south before pursuing normalization of diplomatic relations with the north as did Miyazawa's visit in January 1992.

Japan's economic relations with South Korea have rapidly expanded and as a result, the two economies have become highly interdependent. However, the structural differences between a high-technology economic superpower like Japan and a middle-income NIC like Korea, coupled with Japan's perception of South Korea as a competitor, has produced a continuing trade surplus in Japan's favor. Between 1965 and 1989 South Korea suffered an aggregate trade deficit of $51 billion with Japan.

Japan has been the pivot for a triangular trading pattern involving South Korea, Japan, and the United States, with Japan serving as the primary exporter of intermediate goods and technology. Since the Plaza agreement on currency realignment in September 1985, Japan has increased its imports from South Korea. For a while this helped the latter's balance of trade, but yen appreciation since 1988 has again had an adverse impact on South Korea's exports. In 1991 South Korea suffered a deficit of $9 billion in its trade with Japan, the worst one-year deficit ever. Because of rising wage levels in South Korea, Japanese investments also are declining. As for Seoul's demands for technology transfer, Tokyo contends that technology transfer is being handled primarily by the private sector. Nevertheless, the Japanese side has agreed to cooperate on some scientific studies including nuclear energy and environmental protection.

Insofar as North-South Korea relations are concerned, in principle, Japan has lent support to South Korea's *Nordpolitik*. In practice, however, some areas of potential conflict and competition have emerged. Tokyo has endorsed high-level talks between the North and the South, and it vowed to consult with Seoul before making any new policy innovations toward Pyongyang. In November 1990, keenly concerned with Moscow's attempt to play Seoul against Tokyo in the hope that such a balancing act might attract more active Japanese interest in improving relations with the Soviet Union, Foreign Minister Nakayama asked the South Korean Foreign Minister to inform Tokyo about any new Soviet economic projects that Seoul planned to approve.[8] Seoul agreed to do so. Nonetheless, as suggested by Gorbachev's failure to obtain significant economic cooperation from Tokyo but his success in doing so when he met President Roh at Cheju Island on his way home from Tokyo in April 1991, there remain possibilities for friction between Tokyo and Seoul over their differing approaches to Moscow.

Although South Korea and Japan maintain no formal security relationship, Japan's strategic interests are the most important factor compelling it to overcome its differences with its neighbor. As long as North Korea remains a potential threat and as long as Japan and South Korea are linked to the United States as a strategic balance in the region, Japan needs to share common perspectives, intelligence, and even technology with South Korea.

As Washington is committed to undertaking adjustments in its forward deployment in Asia by gradually reducing troops in Korea and Japan, Tokyo has no choice but to cooperate with Seoul on security issues. And yet, Seoul is worried about Tokyo's increasing military potential as clearly expressed in its Defense White Paper for 1990. To alleviate this concern, Director General of the Self-Defense Agency Ishikawa Yozo carried out a three-day visit to Seoul in December 1990; in his talk with Ishikawa, Korean Defense Minister Jong-koo Lee proposed to establish a hotline to exchange information on coordinating air and naval activities around the peninsula.[9]

It should be clear that the contraction of the U.S. presence and the approach of North Korea have further increased Japan's autonomy in dealing with South Korea. Without necessarily referring its plans to the United States, Japan is now conducting its bilateral relations with South Korea with a sense of self-confidence. The challenge facing Tokyo, however, is how to cope with the North Korea problem to which we now turn.

Normalization of Diplomatic Relations with North Korea
Another dramatic move by Japan to grope for an independent foreign policy was

demonstrated by its decision to pursue negotiations with North Korea to establish diplomatic relations. The way in which Tokyo has approached Pyongyang reveals how serious Japan is about producing this diplomatic coup. All accounts thus far clearly indicate that Tokyo initially went it alone in this case without having prior consultation either with Seoul or Washington.

Before an LDP-JSP joint mission led by former Deputy Prime Minister Kanemaru Shin visited Pyongyang from September 24 through 28, 1990, Japanese relations with North Korea had been virtually frozen. Two key issues for Japan were Pyongyang's refusal to release two Japanese sailors from the Fujisan Maru held since 1983 and to pay interest on its debts outstanding to Japanese trading firms. During Kanemaru's visit, not only did Pyongyang free the two sailors, but, more important, it volunteered to negotiate diplomatic normalization. So unexpected was this offer that Kanemaru was said to have felt like crying!

Surprised at this unanticipated happening, the Kanemaru mission promised Pyongyang to lift travel bans on Japanese, to open satellite communications between the two countries, to pay compensation even before normalization and even for the "losses inflicted on the Korean people in the forty-five years following World War II," and to endorse the North Korean position that "Korea (chosen) is one."[10]

The last two items in particular clearly went beyond the official policy of the Japanese Foreign Ministry. Naturally, they caused an uproar in Seoul. Washington also conveyed some misgivings about the absence of Tokyo's concerns about Pyongyang's refusal to sign a nuclear safeguard agreement and to make substantive progress in the talks with Seoul. Kanemaru came to Seoul in October 1990 and tried to explain his case to President Roh, who pointed out that, above all else, Tokyo's normalization efforts should not undermine North-South Korean talks.

Although the Japanese government claimed that Kanemaru acted without the approval of the Foreign Ministry when he was in Pyongyang, the truth of the matter is that the Japanese Foreign Ministry had carefully carried out a series of secret negotiations with North Korean officials prior to Kanamaru's visit. Deputy Director-General of the Asian Bureau, Mr. Kawashima who accompanied Kanemaru to Pyongyang, for example, had a first meeting with North Koreans in Paris in March 1990. Japanese diplomats had a second meeting in Tokyo in early July and a third session in Kyoto in late July. Also of interest is the fact that Foreign Minister Nakayama stated in his speech to the UN on September 25 that Japan would respect the results of prime ministerial talks concerning the question of South Korea's admission into the United Nations, apparently complying with Pyongyang's request not to support Seoul's efforts for a simultaneous entry.[11] Only in January 1990 did Tokyo decide to support a simultaneous admission of North and South Korea into the United Nations.

Evidently, the Foreign Ministry succeeded in orchestrating the plan for normalization with the LDP, the JSP, and a study team on North Korea. Tokyo contends that such policy can contribute to reducing tension and building the international environment conducive to unification. Since Pyongyang had been under siege by diplomatic isolation and economic stagnation, it was more than willing to normalize relations with Tokyo for no other reason than to secure as much economic assistance as possible.

Evidently, a combination of several factors has prompted Japan to attempt improvements in its relations with North Korea. There is no doubt that Kanemaru was driven to grandstanding behavior by his personal ambition. Kaifu approved this in order to accomplish a diplomatic breakthrough and to sustain a conciliatory mood with the Socialist party. The Foreign Ministry probably welcomed these moves as part of Tokyo's broader efforts at enhancing political influence in Asia.

On the other hand, many South Koreans find signs of double talk and a dual attitude in Japanese behavior, for they see it as an attempt to play the North against the South to extract maximum benefit for themselves. There is a widely held perception in South Korea that Japanese do not favor Korean reunification for fear that a united Korea may pose either threats or competition to them.

Most important, they are seriously concerned with the negative impact that Japanese-North Korean normalization may cause for progress in North-South Korean dialogue. This is why President Roh asked Prime Minister Kaifu to observe five guidelines in January 1991 to which Kaifu agreed. Specifically, in negotiating with Pyongyang, Seoul expects Tokyo (1) to ask Pyongyang to sign a nuclear safeguard agreement, (2) to carry out prior consultation with Seoul, (3) to urge meaningful progress in inter-Korean dialogue, (4) not to pay any compensation before normalization, and (5) to encourage Pyongyang to come out of its self-imposed isolation. When Prime Minister Miyazawa met with President Roh in January 1992, he also reaffirmed these guidelines. As for Seoul's plan to enter the U.N. first, should Pyongyang continue to reject a simultaneous entry, Foreign Minister Nakayama promised to support Seoul's case when he met with Foreign Minister Lee Sang-ock in Tokyo in April 1991.

At a negotiating session in Beijing in May 1991, the head of the Japanese delegation, Ambassador Nakahira, made it clear that Japan would not establish diplomatic relations unless North Korea accepts international inspection of its nuclear facilities. Surprisingly, North Korean Vice-Minister Chon proposed that the two countries normalize relations before resolving other pending issues. When the Japanese side raised the issue of a Japanese woman reportedly abducted by North Korean agents, however, the North Korean side angrily broke up the session.

Whatever happens in these talks, one thing stands out clearly: Japan is serious about normalization. By normalizing relations, Japan is in a position of being cultivated by both the north and the south, which enhances the maneuverability for Japanese diplomacy.

Consensus Politics

Up until recently, Korea has been a most divisive issue in Japanese domestic politics. Any new departure with the existing policy, therefore, has to be reached through consensus-building processes.

Tokyo's search for normalization with Pyongyang began as a joint effort of the LDP and the JSP, but the actual conclusion of a treaty will involve more actors, including the Foreign Ministry, the press, and even the public.

It is interesting to note that Kanemaru formed a coalition with Japan Socialist party Vice-Chairman Tanabe Makoto in developing access to Pyongyang just after the LDP lost its majority in the House of Councilors. No less interesting is that Ozawa Ichirō secretary-general of the LDP, and Doi Takako, former chairperson of the Socialist Party, went together to Pyongyang in October 1990 to take the two sailors home, exhibiting a grandstanding gesture in national and patriotic spirit.

Mr. Kanemaru forwarded a personal letter of apology from Prime Minister Kaifu in September 1990 to Kim Il Sung for the hardships imposed on Koreans during Japanese colonial rule. Yet after the parties' mission issued a joint communiqué with the North Korean Workers party, the Foreign Ministry claimed that it had no official standing. Apparently, some Japanese diplomats objected to the idea of paying compensation for the postwar years and to the one-Korea doctrine on the agenda when a preparatory discussion with their counterparts was held in Beijing during November–December 1990. This was necessary perhaps to meet some of the criticisms made by South Korea and the Japanese press.[13]

On the other hand, the JSP also has moderated its criticism of the South Korean government. In fact, its representatives have been making increasing contacts with the ruling party and the government in Seoul in recent years. Some LDP members also have quietly worked to reconcile diverging views between Japan and South Korea on many pending issues. Even business leaders like Sejima Ryūzō also have served as mediators. Ultimately, a consensus has to be built through these intricate processes of interaction among many actors before Tokyo takes concrete action.

The conditions of normalization including the amount of compensation, therefore, are determined by such consensus-building processes. There is little evidence that Kaifu took leadership on this issue. Instead of the prime minister, Kanemaru as a king-maker seems to have taken decisive action in his approaches to both the JSP and Pyongyang. But even his power is being constrained by the bureaucracy, the press and public opinion once his action has gone beyond the boundaries of acceptable political norms in Japanese political culture.

In fact, Kanemaru was severely criticized for his abrasive action in Pyongyang.

More important, the Japanese public supported a more cautious approach. According to one poll, only 19.7 percent approved an early normalization, 18.9 percent thought that normalization was too early, and 51.9 percent said that normalization be preceeded by giving thorough consideration to the importance of South Korea over North Korea.[14]

Following the defeat of the LDP's candidate for the mayor of Tokyo, the power of Mr. Kanemaru and Mr. Ozawa has been on the decline. As a result, the Foreign Ministry's authority has been strengthened in carrying out negotiations. The public demands that Pyongyang allow Japanese wives to leave and provide a full account for the abduction of Taguchi Yaeko, the woman allegedly abducted by North Korean agents. Thus, without building a consensus it would be difficult for Tokyo to achieve normalization with Pyongyang.

A U.S.-Japanese Division of Roles

In conclusion, Japan's attitudes toward Korea show a more independent and active foreign policy instead of basically reactive responses to external pressures, as many observers have pointed out. But there seems to be certain limits beyond which Japan cannot go. These limits are in the security realm especially regarding nuclear weapons, for which the United States maintains hegemony. In exploring a new policy toward Korea, Japan has to share a division of roles in such a way that it can assume economic and political responsibilities while the United States retains its security roles.

Economically, many countries are indebted to Japan, as are both North and South Korea. As "a lender of last resort" and a center of technology, Japan can play a decisive swing role between the North and the South. By offering economic incentives, Japan is in a position to influence change in North Korean policy. In contrast to this economic clout, Japan has little military means to use for affecting such change. In response to Washington's demands, therefore, Tokyo began to raise the issue of a nuclear safeguard agreement in its negotiation with Pyongyang.

Moreover, both North and South Korea share one thing in common: their opposition to the rearmament of Japan. Many South Koreans hope that the United States will remain in Asia to leash Japanese military ambitions. Despite Pyongyang's persistent demands for withdrawal of American troops, only the United States can play the role of "a balancer, an honest broker, and the final guarantor of security" in Korea and throughout the region as a whole.[15]

The United States and Japan may not share hegemony in the form of "*bigemony*,"[16] but their collaboration is inevitable for ensuring peace and stability in Korea and East Asia. With a security treaty with the United States and with wide-ranging economic ties with Japan, South Korea can become a middleman in this "new special relationship" between the United States and Japan.[17]

In all probability, therefore, there are common interests and compatible values among Japan, South Korea, and the United States. As long as these interdependent allies carry out consultation and coordination on issues that directly affect their national interests, they can sustain a steady partnership for peace, prosperity, and democracy. It is against this background that Japanese foreign policy can be considered to have more in common with South Korea's quest for a more independent and inclusive foreign policy.[18]

Notes

1. Byung-joon Ahn, "The U.S. and Korean-Japanese Relations," in Gerald L. Curtis and Sung-joo Han, eds., *The U.S.-South Korean Alliance* (Lexington, Mass.: Lexington Books, 1983), pp. 134–37.

2. *Japan Times,* September 7, 1984, p. 1.

3. *International Herald Tribune,* May 25, 1990, p. 1.

4. Ibid.

5. *Mainichi Daily,* January 11, 1991, p. 2.

6. *Korean-Japanese Relations Toward the 21st Century* (in Korean), report of the Korean-Japanese 21st Century Committee, January1991, p. 5.

7. Byung-joon Ahn, "South Korea and Taiwan: Local Deterrence," in James W. Morley, ed., *Security Interdependence in the Asia Pacific Region* (Lexington, Mass.: Lexington Books, 1986), pp. 98–102.

8. *Korea Herald,* November 28, 1990, p. 1.

9. Ibid., December 8, 1990, p. 2.

10. Ibid., September 29, 1990, p. 1.

11. *Chosen il-bo,* December 5, 1990, p. 2.

12. *Korea Herald,* January 10, 1991, p. 1.

13. *International Herald Tribune,* October 4, 1990, p. 2.

14. *Nihon keizai shimbun,* October 15, 1990.

15. *Far Eastern Economic Review,* May 3, 1990, p. 10.

16. Takashi Inoguchi, "Four Japanese Scenarios for the Future," *International Affairs* 65, 1 (Winter 1988/89): 28.

17. Peter Tarnoff, "America's New Special Relationships," *Foreign Affairs*(Summer 1990), pp.67–80.

18. Byung-jung Ahn, "Foriegn Relations: An Expanded Diplomatic Agenda," in Chong-sik Lee, ed., *Korea Briefing* (New York: Asia Society, 1991), pp. 23–38.

Chapter 13
Japan's "Northward" Foreign Policy

Motohide Saito

The world witnessed an epoch-making change in the structure of international relations in 1989 and 1990. The socialist regimes in Eastern Europe disappeared one after another. The Berlin Wall, a symbol of the Cold War, was dismantled and German unification was achieved. A treaty of neighborliness and friendship was concluded between the Soviet Union and a unified Germany. Moreover, the tide of "new thinking" in diplomacy that had originated in Gorbachev's USSR was extended to Asia, resulting in the withdrawal of Soviet troops from Afghanistan, the reconciliation of Sino-Soviet relations, and the establishment of diplomatic ties between Seoul and Moscow.

In April 1991, with the Soviet Union in the midst of political turmoil, President Mikhail Gorbachev came to the "land of the rising sun." Despite being the first top Soviet leader ever to visit Japan, Gorbachev achieved little progress in Soviet-Japanese relations. No major breakthroughs were achieved, although the Soviet leader officially agreed for the first time to include in the joint statement a phrase indicating that the four islands off Hokkaido—Etorofu, Kunashiri, Shikotan, and the Habomai Islands—would be the subject of future bilateral negotiations over territorial demarcation. At the ill-timed Tokyo summit both sides apparently avoided making a major political decision concerning the northern territorial issue, the biggest obstacle to the signing of a peace treaty.

What is the guiding principle behind Japan's policy toward Moscow? What sort of priority has Japan given to its northern neighbor in the list of overall foreign policy objectives? How did Japan's Soviet policy evolve from the time of the signing of the San Francisco Peace Settlement of 1951 to Gorbachev's 1991 historic visit to Japan? How and to what degree did Gorbachev's policy of perestroika and the disintegration of the USSR change Tokyo's political stance toward Moscow? How is Japan's policy vis-à-vis Moscow formulated? What are the internal as well as the external constraints? What is the weight of each constraint? Among other things, why and to what extent does the U.S. factor influence Japan's policy toward Moscow? What are the new constraints on Japan's "northward" foreign policy that emerged in the Gorbachev's era? Finally, what direction will Japan's policy toward Moscow take after the December 1991 collapse of the USSR?

The Departure of Postwar Japan's "Northward" Foreign Policy and the Yoshida Doctrine

On August 9, 1945, with Japan on the verge of surrender, Stalin's Soviet Union abruptly declared war on Tokyo in violation of the Soviet-Japanese Neutrality Pact and swiftly took southern Sakhalin and the Kurile islands. Even after the termination of the war, the Soviets captured some 600,000 Japanese, both soldiers and civilians, and sent them to Siberian labor camps as prisoners of war in violation of the Potsdam Declaration, which had called for the speedy repatriation of Japanese after the war. Over 60,000 Japanese lost their lives in Siberia. The Soviet occupation of Japan's northern territories, together with the detention of Japanese in Siberia, fueled a deep-seated and widespread distrust of the Soviets among Japanese. This series of Soviet moves left the impression that the USSR was "a burglar at the fire," taking the territories illegally amid the confusion of the closing days of the Pacific War. Postwar Japan's policy toward Moscow reflects this strong sense of suspicion and mistrust.[1]

In September 1951, at the height of the Cold War in Asia, Prime Minister Yoshida Shigeru signed the San Francisco Peace Treaty. Flatly rejecting the idea of an overall peace as advocated by the Socialists, Communists, and progressive intellectuals, he choose to sign a peace treaty with forty-eight nations, led by the United States.

An initial draft of the peace treaty, which was prepared by foreign policy advisor to the State Department John Foster Dulles, explicitly acknowledged Soviet possession of southern Sakhalin and the Kurile islands in accordance with a confidential provision of the 1945 Yalta Agreement. But at the insistence of Yoshida, the final draft stipulated only Japan's unilateral abandonment of those territories and made no reference to Soviet possession.[2] As a result of Stalin's refusal to sign the San Francisco treaty, the initial chance to conclude a Soviet-Japanese peace treaty was missed. The legal state of war between the USSR and Japan continued and the dispute over the northern territories emerged. The Japanese government contends that the San Francisco Peace Treaty of 1951 provides no legal base for Soviet control over the northern territories since the USSR was not a signatory to the treaty.

The U.S.-Japanese Security Treaty was concluded on the same day as the San Francisco Peace Treaty. Thus, Japan was officially incorporated into the U.S.-initiated containment policy directed at the Soviet Union. In 1952 Japan joined the Coordinating Committee for Export Control (COCOM), which allowed the United States to influence Japan's trade with the communist bloc.

With the Yoshida Doctrine as its foreign policy guideline, Japan succeeded in rebuilding its economy in the midst of the East-West confrontation. Occasionally Tokyo played its "Soviet card" in order to obtain more aid from Washington, which was anxious to rebuild Japan as a bulwark against the spread of communism in Asia in the aftermath of the "loss of China."[3]

The "First Tide" and the Soviet-Japanese Normalization of Relations

As "distant neighbors," Tokyo and Moscow have been at odds with each other since the end of the Second World War; nonetheless, there have been three high points of relative relaxation in Tokyo–Moscow relations since the termination of the Second World War. Former Japanese ambassador to the USSR, Niizeki Kinya, refers to these as the "three tides" that reached Japan from the USSR, all of which involved efforts to improve relations.[4] These periods coincide with changes in the leadership in Moscow as well as the implementation of a Moscow-led policy aimed at the reduction of tensions with the West.

Conversely, the low points in Tokyo–Moscow relations were closely related to periods in which East-West tensions increased; Japan strengthened its security ties with the United States; and/or Moscow perceived that Tokyo was on the verge of an anti–Soviet entente with Beijing and Washington.

The signs of the "first tide" appeared immediately after Stalin's death. The major objective of the Soviet approach lay in the restoration of diplomatic relations with Japan, which had been suspended since the Soviet declaration of war on Japan in early August 1945.[5] The new Soviet approach was part of the diplomacy of peaceful coexistence pursued by the post–Stalin leadership that achieved the mormalization of relations with West Germany in 1955. Newly elected Premier Georgi Malenkov's speech before the Presidium of the Supreme Soviet in August 1953 and the 1954 Sino-Soviet Joint Communiqué issued in the Chinese capital are typical examples of the Soviet eagerness to reach a modus vivendi with the conservative government in Japan.

A series of Soviet signals indicating a desire for rapprochement with Japan, which were initially ignored by Prime Minister Yoshida, drew the attention of prime ministerial contender Hatoyama Ichiro.[6] Hatoyama was originally a liberal politician with a strong antipathy toward communism as well as the Soviet Union. Being a party politician, however, he was extremely sensitive to the growing sense of nationalism among Japanese who were frustrated with Yoshida's excessively pro–U.S. foreign policy orientation. Furthermore, the idea of restoration of official relations with the USSR appealed to Hatoyama, particularly because he was anxious to achieve a diplomatic victory comparable to Yoshida's San Francisco peace settlement. It was his wish to unseat his rival Yoshida that led Hatoyama to publicly call for the prompt normalization of Soviet-Japanese relations as part of an autonomous Japanese foreign policy.

It should be noted at this juncture that Hatoyama did not wish to precipitate a drastic shift in Japan's foreign policy orientation from Washington to Moscow, nor did he intend to neutralize Japan. In his view, the restoration of relations with the USSR would strengthen Tokyo's bargaining position vis-à-vis Washington, enabling Japan to have a more autonomous foreign policy orientation. Specifically, he contended that Japan should rigorously adhere to the existing 1951 U.S.-Japanese Security Treaty; were the Soviet Union to insist that the U.S.-Japanese security system be dismantled, he favored breaking off peace talks with Moscow. In short, Hatoyama had no intention whatsoever of fundamentally altering the Yoshida Doctrine.

In December 1954, Hatoyama became prime minister. Immediately afterward, Andrei Domnitsky, chief of the unrecognized Soviet mission in Tokyo, approached the Hatoyama cabinet. The new prime minister had initially planned for the rapid conclusion of a modus vivendi with the USSR, shelving the controversial northern territorial issue in order to realize (1) the repatriation of Japanese detained in the Soviet Union; (2) Japan's admission to the United Nations; and (3) agreement on measures to ensure the safety of Japanese fishermen operating in the North Pacific. Yet pro–U.S. forces—Foreign Minister Shigemitsu, the Foreign Ministry, Yoshida's Liberal party, and the big business community—bitterly opposed Hatoyama and insisted on the resolution of the northern territorial issue as a prerequisite for the restoration of official diplomatic ties. Due to his fragile political base as the head of a minority party government, Hatoyama, president of the Liberal Democratic party (LDP) was compelled to yield to the "go-slow" advocates and made a provisional agreement to open peace talks with the Soviets in such a fashion that Japan would open its door to the Soviet Union after the signing of a peace treaty.

The peace talks opened in London in June 1955, but soon reached a deadlock because of the northern territorial problem. Immediately following the Geneva Conference of the Big Four in August, however, Nikita Krushchev's Soviet Union unexpectedly made concessions to Japan, offering the return of the "Lesser Kuriles," that is, the Habomais and Shikotan, and agreeing to tolerate the U.S.-Japanese security arrangement. The Soviet side made these concessions with a view to promptly concluding a peace treaty with Japan, but the unexpected Soviet concession encouraged Japanese hard-liners.[7] As a result of Japan's rejection of Khrushchev's territorial concession, the peace talks again became deadlocked. Thus, the second chance to conclude a peace treaty in the postwar period was aborted in August 1955.

The conservative merger that created the Liberal Democratic party (LDP) in November 1955 severely constrained Prime Minister Hatoyama's Soviet policy, since large numbers of pro–U.S. Yoshida forces were brought into his own party. And they intensified their struggle both to block the establishment of diplomatic relations with the USSR and to force his resignation. Another difficult problem for Hatoyama was U.S. intervention. At the initial stage of the peace talks, the Eisenhower administration maintained a position of "interested by-stander," judging that Soviet-Japanese negotiations would either have only a slight chance of success or be greatly prolonged, in light of the disagreement over Soviet policy between the prime minister and the foreign minister, and in light of the territorial disputes. On August 19, 1956, however, U.S. Secretary of State Dulles intervened in the Soviet-Japanese normalization talks by warning that "if Japan gave better terms to Russia we could demand the same status by ourselves."[8] Implicit in this statement was a threat to annex Okinawa under article 26 of the San Francisco Peace Treaty if Japan accepted the full sovereignty of the USSR over Kunashiri and Etorofu. The announcement was apparently made to show American displeasure, and to halt imminent full-fledged Soviet-Japanese reconciliation.

Faced with the vigorous opposition of a mainstream faction in the Foreign Ministry, the business community, and the U.S. government, and in view of his fragile political position in the recently merged LDP, Prime Minister Hatoyama was determined to go to Moscow himself and press for Soviet-Japanese normalization without concluding a full peace treaty as his *hamamichi* (glorious way out) as prime minister. He visited Moscow in October 1956, accompanied by Minister of Agriculture and Forestry Kōno Ichirō, his right-hand man, and Matsumoto Shun'ichi, plenipotentiary at the London peace talks. The final negotiations began in Moscow on October 15, 1956. Following a series of intensive tête-à-têtes between Khrushchev and Kōno, the Soviet-Japanese Joint Declaration was signed on October 19.[9] Article 9 of the joint declaration reads:

> The Union of Soviet Socialist Republics and Japan agree to continue, after the restoration of normal diplomatic relations between the Union of Socialist Republics and Japan, negotiations for the conclusion of a Peace Treaty. In this connection, the Union of Soviet Socialist Republics, desiring to meet the wishes of Japan and taking into consideration the interests of the Japanese State, agrees to transfer the Habomai Islands and the island of Shikotan to Japan, the actual transfer of these islands to take place after the conclusion of a Peace Treaty between the Union of Soviet Socialist Republics and Japan.

The article does not explicitly state that the territorial question is to be part of the peace treaty negotiations. Had the Hatoyama delegation foreseen that the chances for the reversion of Okinawa by the United States were greater than those for the reversion of the northern territories by the Soviet Union, the wording of the joint declaration might have been substantially different and might have encompassed the phrase "inclusive of the territorial issue" after the passage "negotiation for the conclusion of a peace treaty."[10] Together with the signing of the joint declaration, the Matsumoto-Gromyko correspondence was made public. In it the USSR clearly acknowledged that it had no objection to the "continuation of negotiations on the conclusion of a peace treaty, inclusive of territorial problems, after the resumption of normal diplomatic relations between the two nations."[11] Along with the 1855 Treaty of Commerce, Navigation and Delimitation, the Matsumoto–Gromyko correspondence has served to legitimize Japan's claim for the restoration of the four islands off Hokkaido by supporting the position that the islands are part of its "inalienable territory." Since the normalization of diplomatic ties, Japan has been firm on winning recognition of its claim to four.

The 1956 Joint Declaration, which was officially ratified by the parliaments of both nations, is the most important document in the Moscow–Tokyo negotiations over the northern islands. With the conclusion of the joint declaration, the diplomatic channels were reopened, which was followed by Japan's admission into the United Nations and the repatriation of Japanese soldiers held captive by the Soviet Union. The Chinese government expressed its support for the resumption of diplomatic relations between Moscow and Tokyo. The former Soviet Mission in Tokyo was awarded the status of a formal embassy. In 1957, a treaty of trade and commerce was signed for the first time in the history of the two nations, granting most–favored-nation treatment to the USSR in advance of the United States. Consequently, bilateral trade started to increase, rising from $40 million in 1958 to $147 million in 1960. Following the conclusion of the Soviet-Japanese Joint Declaration, Tokyo's relations with Moscow steadily improved, aided by the relaxation of tensions between Washington and Moscow.

This "period of Soviet-Japanese friendship" ended with the the signing of the U.S.-Japanese Security Treaty on January 19, 1960. Claiming that the new security alliance was nothing but a military pact aimed at the USSR and China, the Soviet Union issued a memorandum on January 27 and unilaterally attached a new condition to the reversion of the two islands off Hokkaido. Known as the Gromyko Memorandum, it stated that unless *all foreign troops were withdrawn from Japanese territory* and a peace treaty was concluded between Japan and the Soviet Union, the Habomais and Shikotan were not to be handed over to Japan. According to Leonid Mlechin, the revision of the security treaty was "a pretext rather than a cause" of Soviet rejection of the reversion of the islands.[12]

The Kishi cabinet immediately protested, stating that at the time of the conclusion of the 1956 joint declaration the U.S.-Japanese Security Treaty was already in force, and asserting that the unilateral attempt to alter the provisions of the Joint Declaration not only ran counter to international fidelity (Pacta sunt servanda) but also aimed to drive a wedge between Tokyo and Washington. On February 6, U.S. Secretary of State Christian A. Herter voiced support for the Kishi administration and asserted that "the Gromyko Memorandum is an intervention in the domestic affairs of Japan." Thereafter, successive Japanese governments have denied the validity of the Gromyko Memorandum, whereas the leadership of the neighboring power including President Mikhail Gorbachev has refused to withdraw it. Later in 1961, Khrushchev further stiffened his stance on the controversial northern territorial problem, which was demonstrated by the letters he exchanged with Prime Minister Ikeda Hayato, a protégé of former Prime Minister Yoshida. These letters indicate that Khrushchev had shifted to the position that the territorial issue was already settled or that no territorial problem existed between the two nations. The Ikeda cabinet wasted no time in refuting the Soviets, stating that Japan would not be bound by the Yalta Agreement and that the territorial issue was still outstanding. It was against this background that the Ikeda cabinet made renewed efforts to strengthen the legitimacy of Japan's position for the reversion of the four islands.[13]

The new Soviet stance on the northern territorial issue was, in reality, closely related to the onset of the Sino-Soviet dispute. As demonstrated by First Deputy Premier Anastas Mikoyan's visit to Japan in 1961 and Chairman Mao Zedong's support for the Japanese position on the northern territorial issue in 1964, the 1960s was a period in which the deterioration of Sino-Soviet relations cast larger and larger shadows on the evolution of Soviet-Japanese relations. The territorial dispute became triangularized by China's entry in it.

The "Second Tide" and Tanaka's Visit to Moscow

The "second tide" of rapprochement in Moscow–Tokyo relations reached Japan in the early 1970s. This was the period in which General Secretary Leonid Brezhnev succeeded in consolidating his political power and began to commit himself to a policy of détente with the Western advanced industrial nations. It also coincided with the stunning announcement of U.S. President Richard M. Nixon in July 1971 that he would fly to Beijing early in the following year. Under the circumstances, that Brezhnev hurriedly dispatched Foreign Minister Andrei Gromyko to Tokyo in January 1972, prior to Nixon's visit to China, with a view to preventing the Sato cabinet from leaning toward the PRC. At the 15th Trade Union Congress in March, Brezhnev proclaimed of Soviet willingness "to establish and develop broad, mutually advantageous cooperation" with Japan in both the economic and political spheres.[14] It should be noted that Brezhnev's rapprochement policy put top priority on securing advanced technology and money from Japan for Siberian development projects.

In September 1972, newly elected Prime Minister Tanaka Kakuei quickly normalized relations with China in a *blitzkreig* fashion. Right after his visit to China, he began preparations for an official trip to Moscow, judging that improvement of ties with the USSR was especially important given the dramatic Sino-Japanese rapprochement.[15] Indeed, Tanaka's Soviet policy may be considered a harbinger of the "equidistance diplomacy" proclaimed by the Fukuda administration in the late 1970s.

In October 1973, Tanaka left for Moscow via three Western European nations. It was the first such visit by a Japanese prime minister since Hatoyama's trip to the USSR in 1956. Before the departure of Prime Minister Tanaka, Foreign Minister

Ohira Masayoshi declared that Japan would put top priority to the issue of the northern territorial question in Moscow.[16]

During the talks with Brezhnev, Prime Minister Tanaka repeatedly pressed for the return of "four dragon eyeballs" rather than two. Chinese Premier Zhou Enlai highly praised him for his aggressive stance on the reversion of the northern territories at the Moscow summit.[17] Contrary to the widespread interpretation in Japan, the top priority of Tanaka's Soviet trip was placed not on the territorial issue nor on the conclusion of a peace treaty but on the promotion of economic cooperation between the two nations.

In his note to Brezhnev dated March 8, 1973, Tanaka notified the Soviet government of Japan's policy to promote cooperative efforts to develop Siberian resources, thus modifying the Japanese strategy vis-à-vis the Soviets to link the northern territorial problem with the economic cooperation issue.[18] His note demonstrates that just prior to the Moscow summit he adopted the so-called "exit theory," hoping that Japan's economic cooperation toward the USSR would eventually lead to the solution of the controversial territorial question.

At the end of the three-day summit, Tanaka asked the Soviet leader to confirm that the northern territorial issue was included among "the yet unresolved problems remaining since the Second World War." Brezhnev, who refused to make direct reference to the issue in the final version of the joint communiqué, allegedly gave oral acknowledgment, but this was later denied by the Soviets.[19] In short, no substantial progress was made in terms of the territorial issue.

In contrast, progress was made on economic collaboration with the signing of an agreement on scientific and technological cooperation. Prime Minister Tanaka also agreed that Japan would participate in the development of natural resources in Siberia and the Soviet Far East, including the Tyumen oil project, the Yakutsuk natural gas project, and the Sakhalin oil and gas project. In April 1974, a group of Japanese banks led by the Export-Import Bank of Japan signed a protocol with the Soviet Foreign Trade Bank to provide large-scale Siberian development projects with Japanese yen loans, the first direct loans from Japan to the Communist bloc in the postwar era.

As demonstrated by its reactions to Japan's commitment to the Tyumen oil project, China was bitterly opposed to Japanese aid for Siberian development, largely out of fear that it would greatly enhance the military strength of the Soviet Union in the Far East. Additionally, doubts over the profitability of investment in the Soviet Union, coupled with Japan's success in dramatically reducing its oil consumption in the wake of the 1973 oil crisis, contributed to the cooling of Japanese enthusiasm for joint development of Siberia. In the words of Professor Kataoka Tetsuya of Tsukuba University, Siberia as a source of energy was attractive only to the extent that it enabled Japan to lessen its dangerous dependence on Persian Gulf sources.[20]

In the mid-1970s, negotiations began on the conclusion of the Sino-Japanese peace treaty and, as a consequence, Soviet-Japanese diplomatic relations began to cool off. The Chinese government insisted upon the inclusion of the "antihegemony clause" in the proposed treaty. This led the Kremlin to be preoccupied with the threat of an anti–Soviet Washington–Tokyo-Beijing axis. To prevent this, Brezhnev proposed signing a bilateral treaty of good-neighborliness and cooperation in February 1975, but could not reach agreement with Japan, which maintained that the solution of the territorial issue should come first. Then, in January 1976, Foreign Minister Gromyko came to Tokyo with a warning that the USSR would consider reviewing its ties with Japan in the event of the conclusion of a Sino-Japanese peace treaty.

In August 1978, as urged by U.S. national security advisor Zbigniew Brzezinski, the Fukuda cabinet concluded the Sino-Japanese Peace and Friendship Treaty over Soviet protests.[21] Although it made a concession to the PRC and included the disputed antihegemony clause in the peace treaty, Japan managed to insert an article stipulating that the treaty "shall not affect the position of either contracting party regarding its relations with third countries." According to then Foreign Minister Sunoda Sunao, this article was inserted lest Japan be dragged into the Sino-Soviet rivalry.[22] Admittedly, however, Japan's "equidistant diplomacy" was tilted—with U.S. consent—toward China rather than the Soviet Union.

The Soviet invasion of Afghanistan in 1979 and the imposition of martial law in Poland in 1982 further aggravated Soviet-Japanese relations. Protesting the Soviet invasion of Afghanistan, the Ohira cabinet implemented economic sanctions against the Soviet Union and boycotted the 1980 Olympic Games. Japan also strengthened its security cooperation with the United States. Thus, Soviet-Japanese relations reached their lowest point since the signing of the 1956 Joint Declaration.

Japan's Reactions to the "Third Tide" from Gorbachev's USSR

The "third tide" of rapprochement with Japan is closely related to Mikhail Gorbachev's rise to power in March 1985. To revitalize the Soviet economy, he radically altered Soviet conduct of foreign affairs and aggressively approached the Western industrial nations for technology, capital, and intellectual know-how. One of the distinctive features of the "third tide" is that it emerged at a time when the international structure of the Cold War was beginning to collapse, a process triggered by Gorbachev's "new thinking" in diplomacy. Another characteristic of the "third wave" is that the USSR was on the verge of disintegration due to the intensification of nationalist movements, whereas Japan had become the world's number two economic power. After 1988 the nationality problem in the Soviet Union, evidenced by the upsurge of secessionism in the Baltic states and the 1990 adoption of the declaration of sovereignty by the Russian Federation, came to cast an increasingly large shadow on the evolution of the Soviet-Japanese relations.

With the inauguration of General Secretary Gorbachev, the chilled atmosphere between Tokyo and Moscow began to warm, although few substantial changes were visible in Soviet policy toward Japan. Gorbachev's Soviet Union shifted away from the heavy-handed policies toward Tokyo pursued by the Brezhnev–Gromyko team and began to adopt a softer approach.

In March 1985, despite the opposition of the Foreign Ministry, Prime Minister Nakasone Yasuhiro flew to the Soviet Union for the funeral of General Secretary Konstantin Chernenko and held brief talks with the newly elected General Secretary Gorbachev, fifty-four years old, the youngest Soviet party leader since Stalin's rise to power in the 1920s. Nakasone visited the Kremlin with the belief that a change in leadership would be a favorable occasion on which to launch new diplomatic relations.[23] He returned home with a positive impression of the young, energetic, and talented Soviet leader.

Since taking office in November 1982, Prime Minister Nakasone had made every effort to strengthen the U.S.-Japanese relationship, which he referred to as "a community bound together by a common destiny." Nakasone supported Japanese participation in President Ronald Reagan's SDI program. At the same time, however, he was anxious to make a major breakthrough in Soviet-Japanese ties; he was in search of a "final solution" to postwar politics.

Needless to say, Nakasone welcomed the signs of change in Soviet policy toward Japan as seen in the visit of Foreign Minister Eduard Shevardnadze to Tokyo in January 1986. Shevardnadze, who had succeeded Gromyko in July 1985, was the first Soviet foreign minister to visit Tokyo since Gromyko in 1976. In return, his Japanese counterpart, Abe Shintaro, was dispatched to Moscow in May 1986 with a personal letter from Nakasone to Gorbachev inviting the Soviet leader to Japan. Out of these meetings, agreements were reached to hold foreign ministerial talks on a regular basis, and to resume the Soviet-Japanese Scientific and Technological Cooperation Committee, which had been suspended following the Soviet invasion of Afghanistan. Japanese no-visa visits to family graves on the northern islands, which had been suspended in 1975, were also reinstated. Thus, the channels of dialogue between Japan and the USSR were restored and gradually expanded.

In the spring of 1987, the violation of COCOM regulations by the Toshiba Machine Corporation was publicly disclosed and intensified Japan bashing in the United States. Under pressure from Washington, Tokyo drastically revised its COCOM procedures for controlling the export of strategic goods to Communist countries; one result was that Japanese regulations became the most stringent among COCOM members.[24] Interestingly, the Toshiba Machine Corporation incident had a most detrimental spillover effect on China, causing serious delays in technology transfer to the PRC. In any event, it is important to note that the governments of both the Soviet Union and Japan expended great efforts to minimize the damage of the incident, as was demonstrated by the holding of the Soviet-Japanese foreign ministerial talks that September, as scheduled.

Prime Minister Nakasone was anxious to arrange for state visits by top leaders of the USSR and Japan, which had been pending since the 1973 Tanaka–Brezhnev Joint Communiqué. Nakasone attempted to use the "Soviet card" as a means to prolong his days in office and at the same time to end his tenure on a positive note. In order to achieve his aim, he bypassed the Foreign Ministry and contacted with the Soviet Union through Sejima Ryūzō, a councilor of C. Itoh & Company, and Suetsugu Ichirō, the founder of the Council on Security Affairs, both of whom maintained their own personnel channels to Gorbachev's key aides.[25] Nakasone's goal for the summit with Gorbachev was to achieve agreement on reopening negotiations for the conclusion a peace treaty based on the 1956 Soviet-Japanese Joint Declaration.[26]

Nakasone was unable to attain his objective due to the following factors: (1) the rise of international tensions following the Reykjavik Summit in October 1986; (2) Gorbachev's difficulties in achieving domestic economic reform; and (3) the continuation of antagonism between Japan and the USSR over the northern territories. To fill the gap left by the cancellation of visits, Nakasone went to Eastern Europe in January 1987.

In spite of his well-known speeches in Vladivostok in July 1986 and in Krasnoyarsk in September 1988, in which Japan's economic power was given high regard, Gorbachev was unable to create a favorable impression with his policy toward Tokyo. As a mid-1988 roundtable discussion of Soviet diplomats and scholars on Japanese affairs indicates, three major obstacles prevented improvement in Soviet-Japanese relations: (1) the northern territorial issue; (2) Soviet threat; and (3) the U.S.-Japanese Security Treaty.[27]

Based upon the roundtable discussions, a new Soviet initiative was taken with Prime Minister Takeshita Noboru, who assumed office in November 1987. On his second visit to Tokyo in December 1988, Foreign Minister Shevardnadze proposed the establishment of a vice-foreign ministerial working group on the conclusion of a peace treaty. Moreover, the territorial issue, which for decades the USSR had refused to discuss, was put on the negotiation table. The working group held seven meetings prior to Gorbachev's visit to Japan in April 1991. And as former Japanese Ambassador Niizeki contends, the establishment of the working group may be considered a sign that the tide of Gorbachev's "new thinking" diplomacy had finally reached Japan.[28]

In Japan, however, newly elected Prime Minister Takeshita was not as interested in promoting the Soviet-Japanese relations as his predecessor. As a result, Foreign Ministry officials were released from the risk of "dual diplomacy" toward the

USSR that had occurred under Nakasone, who had maintained back-channel communications with the Soviet Union.

Takeshita's policy toward the USSR had two major features. First, he adopted a "strategy of 'internationalization' of the northern territorial issue."[29] Based on this strategy, the prime minister obtained a promise from U.S. Secretary of State George Schultz to make the northern territories an issue at the 1988 U.S.-Soviet summit. In addition, at his request the territorial issue was discussed at the summit meeting held in Toronto in June 1988.

As a top-ranking Foreign Ministry official remarked, the "strategy of internationalization" was adopted in order to make the Soviet Union realize that "the northern territorial issue stands in the way of Japanese aid for Soviet economic reform."[30] As was anticipated, the Soviet government bitterly criticized Takeshita's strategy, claiming that it would only complicate the settlement of what had originally been a bilateral matter.

The second feature was the concept of "expanded equilibrium" (*kakudai kinkoron*), which Takeshita introduced as a framework for dealing with Gorbachev's Soviet Union. Foreign Minister Uno Sosuke signaled this new approach at a meeting with Gorbachev in May 1989, just prior to the resignation of Takeshita as prime minister. Tōgō Kazuhiko, the head of the Soviet division of the Ministry of Foreign Affairs, reportedly coined the term.[31]

At the Soviet-Japanese foreign ministerial conference held in Paris in 1989, Shevardnadze bitterly criticized Japan's continuation of the policy of the inseparability of politics and economics (*seikei fukabun seisaku*). The prospect of Foreign Minister Uno's trip to the USSR, scheduled for May, seemed doomed to failure if Japan were unable to give the impression of a change in its policy toward Moscow.

The core of "expanded equilibrium" was that Japan would give humanitarian, technological, intellectual, and financial aid to Japan's northern neighbor in proportion to the degree of settlement reached on the northern territories issue.[32] This implied that Tokyo would not provide massive financial aid to Moscow unless some sort of agreement on the territorial dispute was reached.

Behind the new approach was recognition that Japan should, where appropriate and possible, give a helping hand to Gorbachev's USSR in order to promote democratization, freedom, and the shift to a market economy. Unquestionably this new concept was also introduced to avoid the impression that Japan was isolated from the international community, especially because European nations such as Germany and France that had begun to provide massive aid to the Soviet Union. The adoption of the "expanded equilibrium" approach marks the beginning of Japan's version of "new thinking" in diplomacy vis-à-vis the Soviet Union, although it should be added that Japan did not officially proclaim the abandonment of its *seikei fukabun seisaku* toward Moscow.

Significantly, during Uno's visit Foreign Minister Shevardnadze stated that the existing U.S.-Japanese security system would not hinder the signing of a Soviet-Japanese peace treaty.[33] Admittedly, the USSR had tolerated the U.S.-Japanese security alliance for years, as the mechanism (1) to keep Japan nonnuclear and (2) to stabilize the international situation in northeastern Asia. Yet the Soviet foreign minister's remarks were significant because it represented the first instance of official approval for the U.S.-Japanese security alignment. Another interesting feature of Uno's trip to Moscow is that General Secretary Gorbachev urged Japan to conclude a peace treaty under the "Senkaku Islands formula," by which the territorial issue would be shelved for future negotiations.[34] Gorbachev's position demonstrates that the formula may have been the ideal option for the Soviet Union.

Lastly, the Soviet policy of the Kaifu cabinet, which succeeded the short-lived Uno administration in August 1989, must be analyzed in depth. During talks in New York between the foreign ministers in September 1989, Schevardnadze abruptly announced to Foreign Minister Nakayama Taro that Gorbachev planned to visit Japan in 1991. *Izvestia* remarked that by announcing his plan to visit Japan in two years, Gorbachev made a terrific move to compel the Japanese to create a favorable atmosphere. Stunned by the announcement, the Foreign Ministry hurriedly set to the work to formulate Japan's policy for Prime Minister Kaifu, whose knowledge of the Soviet Union was minimal. The key figures engaged in the formulation of Japan's Soviet policy were Councilor Ōwada Hisashi and Director General Hyōdō Nagao of the European and Oceanic Affairs Bureau. Vice-Foreign Minister Kuriyami Shōicha and Head Tōgō Kazuhiko of the Soviet division were also involved.[35]

The following four pillars of Japan's policy toward the USSR gradually emerged: (1) the implementation of "expanded equilibrium" approach; (2) a switch from the simultaneous reversion to the staged restoration of the northern territories, i.e., Kunashiri, Etorofu, Shikotan, and the Habomais: (3) the rigid maintenance of the existing U.S.-Japanese security system; and (4) the discontinuance of publicly emphasizing the Soviet threat.

The "expanded equilibrium" approach was implemented by Japan in April 1990 when, after a heated argument among high-ranking officials, the Foreign Ministry decided to permit the entry of a perestroika research mission led by Anatoli Milyukov, deputy director general of the Social and Economic Affairs Department of the Communist party's Central Committee.[36] The purpose of the ten-member delegation was to conduct research on how the Japanese market economy functioned under administrative guidance. The acceptance of the Milyukov delegation, which came to Tokyo in mid-November 1990, reflects the judgment that Japan should take some measures to create a favorable atmosphere in Soviet-Japanese relations for Gorbachev's trip scheduled for 1991. As a result, the Kaifu Government decided to offer medical aid for victims of the Chernobyl nuclear power station disaster. The plan was revealed during the visit of Gorbachev aide Aleksandr

Yakovlev, who was in Japan to pave the way for the forthcoming visit of the Soviet leader.

In the following month, Japan announced a plan to extend emergency food and medical aid to the residents of the Soviet Far East through the Japanese Red Cross. In January 1991, MITI decided to dispatch a delegation to conduct research on the distribution system of the USSR, which seemed to be the major cause of a shortage of goods. Compared with that pledged from the United States and the European Community (EC), Japanese aid was far less. In late January 1991, both the United States and the EC temporarily suspended their aid to the Soviet Union, protesting the dispatch of Soviet troops to the Baltic states to suppress their independence movements. In contrast, the Kaifu cabinet continued to provide assistance, although it was confined to the technological, intellectual and humanitarian domains.

Another measure taken by the Kaifu cabinet to create a favorable atmosphere for the much-waited visit of Gorbachev was related to the security field. At the Houston summit in July 1990, Prime Minister Kaifu managed to insert a passage in the political communiqué, asserting that "we support the early resolution of the northern territorial issue as an essential step leading to the normalization of Soviet-Japanese Relations."[37] He thereby reminded the world that Gorbachev's "new-thinking diplomacy" had not yet extended to Japan. However, soon after returning home, Kaifu instructed the Defense Agency to delete the phrase referring to the "potential threat" of the Soviet forces stationed in the Far East from the 1990 edition of the White Paper on Defense. Previous editions had stressed the continuous Soviet military buildup in areas around Japan since 1980.[38]

As to the northern territories issue, the Kaifu cabinet continued to call for the reversion of the four islands as Japan's "inherent" territory. By January 1991, however, it had adopted the staged reversion formula, effectively abandoning the long-standing demand for the simultaneous return of the four islands.[39] The architect of the staged reversion formula was reportedly LDP Secretary General Ichiro Ozawa, the leading prime ministerial hopeful.

In March 1991, just prior to the scheduled visit of President Gorbachev to Japan, Ozawa flew to the USSR for informal talks with Gorbachev, who had been elected Soviet president in the spring of 1990. On this occasion, Ozawa informally sounded out the "Okinawa reversion formula" as a possible solution to the territorial issue.[40] The core of his idea was that following Soviet recognition of Japanese sovereignty over the four disputed islands, the two nations would conclude a peace treaty whereupon the Habomais and Shikotan would be returned to Japan. As to Kunashiri and Etorofu, the administrative rights would be returned to Japan ten years after the conclusion of the Soviet-Japanese peace treaty. Ozawa also revealed Japan's readiness to provide its aid package in case the Soviets accepted his proposal.[41] His proposal was similar to the "Okinawa reversion formula" in the sense that the rights of sovereignty and administration were separate. Contrary to the expectation of the ambitious Japanese political leader, however, the reaction of Gorbachev was cool. This was, in part, because the proposal was publicly disclosed by a Soviet newspaper and angered conservatives, who bitterly opposed any deal to exchange their land for money. The disclosure clearly narrowed Gorbachev's diplomatic options.

In early April, Prime Minister Kaifu flew to the United States to meet with President George Bush. A major purpose was to consult with Bush concerning Japan's stance on Gorbachev's four-day visit and inform him that settlement of the territorial issue was a prerequisite to the conclusion of a peace treaty and the establishment of genuinely friendly relations between Tokyo and Moscow.[42] He clearly had in mind the 1955–56 Soviet-Japanese peace talks, which had triggered U.S. intervention particularly because Minister Hatoyama had failed to keep Washington informed.

On April 16, 1991, President Gorbachev landed in Tokyo after making a stopover in Khabarovsk to pay his respects to the abandoned graves of Japanese POWs who had died in Siberian labor camps. He was the first Soviet leader to visit Japan in the history of Soviet-Japanese relations. But Japan was the last of the Western powers Gorbachev chose to visit after taking office in 1985. This was indicative of Japan's low ranking in Soviet diplomacy. Due to the territorial issue, Japan had long been regarded as a "neighbor to the East with whom discussions are difficult." During the four-day summit talks, most of the talks with Kaifu centered on the northern territorial dispute.

From the outset of the summit talks, Prime Minister Kaifu persistently pressed Gorbachev in an attempt to find a key to the reversion of the northern territories. Specifically, the Japanese prime minister tried to get agreement from the Soviet president that Japan's sovereignty extended to the four northern islands, judging that the 1956 Soviet-Japanese Joint Declaration promised the return of the Habomais and Shikotan.[43] Throughout the summit meeting, Kaifu kept in touch with the top-ranking Foreign Ministry officials, including Councillor Ōwada and Director-General Hyōdō, and with top LDP politicians.

After a marathon set of negotiations between the two leaders that "may become another entry in the *Guiness Book of Records*," a joint communiqué was issued and fifteen accords were signed.[44] It was the first Soviet-Japanese joint communiqué since the Tanaka–Brezhnev Joint Communiqué of 1973. In the 1991 Joint Declaration, the names of the four disputed islands were mentioned for the first time. However, the Soviet side adamantly refused to withdraw the 1960 Gromyko Memorandum. More important, the Soviet president declined to reconfirm the 1956 Soviet-Japanese Joint Declaration. In retaliation, Japan postponed financial aid to the USSR in accordance with the "expanded equilibrium" approach. Unlike Tanaka's visit to Moscow in 1973, Kaifu offered no commitment to Siberian development, nor was a long-term economic cooperation agreement concluded.

In the joint statement, both sides pledged to accelerate efforts to conclude a peace treaty by holding regular foreign ministerial consultations and through the regular exchange of high-level visits. Gorbachev's invitation to Prime Minister Kaifu to visit Moscow and the Soviet proposal for no-visa visits by Japanese to the northern islands were mentioned. Regarding security matters, at the last minute Gorbachev agreed to a partial withdrawal of the Soviet military forces on the islands—one 10,000-strong army division and 40 MIG-23 warplanes.

A Japanese newspaper carried a front-page article with a headline exclaiming "the Japanese-Soviet ties enter new stage." But because no logjam in relations between the two nations was broken at the Tokyo summit, such was not the case. As exemplified by the sudden resignation of Foreign Minister Shevardnadze in December 1990 due to the conservative backlash, Gorbachev's political clout severely weakened as the crisis of perestroika reform policies deepened. In the case of Kaifu, handicapped by his weak factional base within the LDP, he could hardly exercise strong leadership on the formation of Japan's Soviet policy. In this situation, as newly elected Vice President Gennady Yanayev remarked, Gorbachev could not afford to bring a "gift like Santa Claus." After all, "the negotiations conducted by the leaders whose footings are shaky," as former Prime Minister Nakasone stated immediately before the Tokyo talks, "can hardly warrant optimism."[45]

The Formation of Japan's "Northward" Foreign Policy

Thus far, an attempt has been made to explicate the major thrust of Japan's policy toward the Soviet Union from the 1945 termination of the Second World War to Gorbachev's historic visit to Japan in 1991. This chapter is especially concerned with the factors influencing the formulation of Japanese policy toward the Soviet Union.

The most important foreign policy decision maker in today's Japan is the prime minister, whose power was dramatically strengthened under the 1947 Constitution. In comparison with other political actors, from a legal point of view, he is assigned greater power in the formulation and management of foreign policy. All of the "highly crucial" foreign policy decisions in postwar Japan perceived to be watersheds by the decision makers and by observers have been made at the initiative of the prime minister.[46] In the case of postwar Soviet-Japanese ties, as has been noted, the restoration of diplomatic relations with the Soviet Union was achieved under the leadership of Prime Minister Hatoyama.

Following the 1956 resumption of relations, however, Japanese prime ministers have avoided risking their political lives to achieve a breakthrough on the issue of a Moscow–Tokyo peace treaty. When Prime Minister Tanaka flew to Moscow in 1973, he relied heavily on the manual drafted by the Foreign Ministry for his talks with Brezhnev and made a decision not to conclude a peace treaty.[47] Prime Minister

Kaifu also depended on documents prepared by Foreign Ministry officials during his summit meeting with Gorbachev.[48] Kaifu was in no hurry to conclude a peace treaty at the cost of his political career. He was of the opinion that a peace treaty should be signed within this century once the territorial issue has been settled.[49]

Why have successive prime ministers been hesitant to commit themselves to the conclusion of a peace treaty with Moscow? Two intimately related factors must be considered: (1) the existence of an outstanding territorial problem, which has proved terribly difficult to settle; and (2) factional politics within the ruling LDP. In other words, Japanese prime ministers have feared that, like Prime Minister Hatoyama, they too might be forced to step down from office due to the intensification of factional struggles if they were to push for the conclusion of a peace treaty with the USSR.

The Foreign Ministry is the institution given overall responsibility for Japan's conduct of foreign policy toward Moscow.[50] Russian experts in the ministry insist that policy toward Moscow should be left to experts like themselves.[51] They are earnest supporters of the "Yoshida Doctrine" and consider the maintenance of friendly relations with the United States to be essential for the national interests of Japan. They are basically hard-liners toward Moscow, and hold a deep-rooted mistrust against the Russians for declaring war against Japan in violation of the Neutrality Pact and for occupying the northern territories. In the view of the Foreign Ministry, the final goal of Soviet policy toward Japan was to drive a wedge between Japan and the United States and to bring about the demilitarization of Japan. Since the signing of the 1956 Soviet-Japanese Joint Declaration, the Foreign Ministry has maintained the position that reversion of the four islands illegally occupied by the Russians is a prerequisite to the conclusion of a peace treaty. Following the disclosure of the violation of COCOM by the Toshiba Machine Corporation, the voice of the Foreign Ministry in the field of Japan's trade with the Communist nations has increased.[52]

The Foreign Ministry is not the only governmental institution which takes a hard-line stance toward Japan's northern neighbor. Its closest ally is the Defense Agency (JDA), which entertains an equally skeptical view of Moscow's intentions. As mentioned above, under the instruction of Prime Minister Kaifu, JDA officials reluctantly agreed to remove the phrase "potential Soviet threat" from the 1990 edition of the White Paper on Defense. Although they admitted Soviet forces in the Far East had been reduced, they continued to argue that the Soviet Union possessed one-fourth to one-third of all its strategic forces deployed in the Far East and had been striving to improve their quality.[53] They maintain that the importance of the northern territories has not decreased, given the strategic value of the Sea of Okhotsk as the bastion of Soviet SSBM activities.[54] The Defense Agency shares with the Foreign Ministry a desire to maintain the U.S.-Japanese Security Treaty.

While the JDA has kept a relatively low profile on foreign policy issues, its influence behind the scenes should not be underestimated.[55]

Other governmental organizations are involved in the formulation of Japan's policy toward Moscow. The Ministry of Agriculture and Forestry and the Fisheries Agency, for example, are in charge of fishing in the northwestern Pacific. The influence of the Ministry of International Trade and Industry (MITI) in shaping Japan's Soviet policy remained limited by the relatively low level of trade relations with the USSR; trade with the Soviets had never amounted to much more than 2 percent of Japan's total foreign trade.[56] It should be noted that, unlike the foreign ministry, MITI tends to take a positive stance in promoting Japan's trade with Moscow. In 1978 MITI even approved the export of a 80,000-ton dry dock capable of servicing the *Minsk*, a Kiev-class aircraft carrier, to the Soviet Union. MITI, which favored giving a helping hand to perestroika, was reportedly in conflict with the Foreign Ministry concerning the trade with the USSR.[57] By October 1990 MITI had agreed to establish a Soviet version of the Japan Productivity Center to give advice on the economic reform of the USSR.[58] With the implementation of Japan's "expanded equibrium" policy, the role of the Ministry of Transportation and the Economic Planning Agency in the field of intellectual assistance will surely be enhanced. In contrast, the Ministry of Finance took a cautious approach, arguing that unless a comprehensive reform was effected in the Soviet Union, large-scale financial aid from Japan was meaningless.[59]

The predominant consensus within the ruling Liberal Democratic party (LDP) had been the conclusion of a peace treaty under the four-island formula, but by January 1991 it had shifted its position from simultaneous reversion to the staged restoration of the four islands. As mentioned, factional politics in the LDP has worked against the active involvement of the prime minister in Moscow–Tokyo relations. As a result, mainstream LDP politicians have largely refrained from making an active commitment to improving relations with the Russians since the 1956 Soviet-Japanese Joint Declaration.

Interestingly, with the advent of the Gorbachev era some of the more ambitious politicians in the ruling LDP began to show interest in achieving a breakthrough in relations with the Soviet Union. They included Nakasone Yasuhiro, the late Abe Shintaro, and Ozawa Ichirō, among others. After stepping down as prime minister, Nakasone went to the Soviet Union in July 1988 and January 1989, meeting with Gorbachev and calling for the reversion of the "four islands which were part of Hokkaido, taken by Premier Stalin by mistake."[60] The major purpose of the former prime minister was twofold: (1) to increase his political influence inside and outside of Japan by acting as an important intermediary; and (2) to find a way personally to force a breakthrough in the stalemated relations.

Abe Shintaro, former LDP secretary general and one-time foreign minister, led a delegation to the Soviet Union, where he met with Gorbachev in January 1990 and presented an eight-point proposal to dramatically improve ties with the USSR, putting aside the territorial issue.[61] Then LDP Secretary General Ozawa Ichirō flew to Moscow in late March of the following year, just prior to the Gorbachev–Kaifu summit in Tokyo, and proposed the "Okinawa Reversion Formula" to achieve the restoration of the northern territories. Both prime ministerial hopefuls strove to achieve an improvement in relations with the USSR, thereby enhancing their standing in the battle for the post–Kaifu prime ministership.[62] Yet Abe's serious illness and Ozawa's sudden resignation as LDP secretary general in early April 1991 following his mishandling of the Tokyo gubernatorial election severely reduced their influence. Abe subsequently died in May 1991.

The opposition parties did not have great influence in the formulation of Japan's policy toward Moscow. For years the opposition parties took a tougher stance than the LDP on the northern territories issue. The Socialist party continuously called for the restoration of the entire Kurile Island chain in addition to the abrogation of the U.S.-Japanese Security Treaty. Its firm demand for restoration of the northern territories was criticized by the USSR. Interestingly, the northern territorial issue functioned as a symbol of nationalism for the Socialists.[63] However, just prior to Gorbachev's long-awaited visit to Japan, the Socialist party, after heated discussion, shifted its support to the reversion of the four islands in view of an opinion survey conducted in March 1991 in which 80 percent of the Japanese called for the restoration of the four islands.[64]

The Clean Government party and the Democratic Socialist party, which had supported the simultaneous restoration of the four islands, also shifted their positions in late May 1991 to favor the LDP's proposal of a "staged reversion" of the four islands.[65] The only political party still calling for the reversion of all of the Kuriles and southern Sakhalin is the Japanese Communist party, which was very critical of Gorbachev's perestroika.[66] Ironically, the ultra–right-wing nationalists and the Communists are united in their tough, nationalistic territorial demand vis-à-vis the Russians.

The business community has not shown much interest in trade with the Moscow. During the peace talks in the 1950s, big business vehemently opposed the resumption of diplomatic relations with the Soviet Union out of fear that it might anger the United States and might adversely affect U.S.-Japanese relations. They also feared that the normalization of relations with the USSR would facilitate Communist penetration into Japan. It was the fishing companies engaged in operations in the disputed waters of the Northwest Pacific that pressed the Hatoyama cabinet for the prompt realization of official ties with the Soviet Union. At the time of Prime Minister Tanaka's China trip, the advocates of the promotion of Japan's economic cooperation with the Soviets were confined to the "resources school" of the *zaikai*, while the attitude of the mainstream of the business community remained detached.

Even in the post–Cold War era, the *zaikai*'s interest in the Soviet market remained minimal, although the Soviet Union had been stepping up its promotion of large-scale investment, especially in its Far Eastern region. Compared with the Chinese market, the Soviet market was much less appealing to Japan's business community.[67] The negative attitude was attributable to the following five factors: (1) the absence of infrastructure; (2) the inconvertibility of the ruble; (3) the delay in repayment and the inability to pay back; (4) the increased turmoil of authority and responsibility under perestroika regarding ownership of property; (5) the absence of an investment guarantee agreement between Japan and the Soviet Union; (5) the reluctance of the Japanese government to back development projects in Siberia and the Soviet Far East.[68] Most experts agree Japan's trade with the post–Soviet Union and Japanese investment in Russia is likely to be determined by more prospects of profits than by national honors.

Nongovernmental organizations work as liaisons behind the scenes in situations where formal channels do not function well. This has been the case in postwar Moscow–Tokyo relations. The National Council for the Restoration of Diplomatic Relations with China and the Soviet Union worked as the behind-the-scenes liaison between the unofficial Soviet mission in Tokyo and Prime Minister Hatoyama. Through the council, the controversial "Domnitsky note" proposing the initiation of peace talks was handed to Prime Minister Hatoyama, thus bypassing the Foreign Ministry, an opponent of the restoration of relations with the USSR.[69] In the case of Prime Minister Tanaka's trip to USSR in 1973, Chairman Matsumae Shigeyoshi of the Japan Cultural Association was one of those who paved the way for the summit. Before Gorbachev's 1991 visit to Japan, Suetsugu Ichirō, founder of the Council on the Security Affairs, actively worked behind the scenes.[70] As the organizer of the Soviet-Japanese specialists conference, Suetsugu maintained personal channels with Nakasone as well as Gorbachev's key aides, including the successive directors of the Institute of the World Economy and International relations (IMEMO), Aleksandr Yakovlev and Yevgeny Primakov. Suetsugu worked as intermediary for Nakasone's visit to the USSR in 1988 and for Yakovlev's trip to Japan in 1989.[71] Chairman Saito Rokurō of the All-Japan Former Internees Association was involved in the Siberian detainees problem and persistently urged the Gorbachev government to declassify and to make public a long-sought list of Japanese detainees who had died in the Siberian labor camps, bypassing the Ministry of Welfare, the Ministry of Foreign Affairs, and the Prime Minister's Office all of which had been reluctant to press the Soviet government on this issue. Eventually Saito prevailed in his attempts.[72]

As is true with other categories of policy making in Japan, the prevailing public mood set the parameters of Japanese policy toward Moscow. A deep-rooted anti–Soviet feeling facilitated the government's stance of maintaining close relations with the United States under the "Yoshida Doctrine" and rejecting a treaty of good neighborliness and friendship with the Soviet Union. With the advent of the Gorbachev regime, the popular perception in Japan vis-à-vis the USSR changed for the better. Yet even in the post–Cold War period, residual hostility remains. In a public opinion survey conducted by the Prime Minister's Office in 1990, 70.8 percent answered that they did not have friendly feelings toward the USSR, whereas only 23.3 percent responded that they had friendly feelings.[73]

The public demand for the reversion of the northern territories, moreover, has had a considerable influence on party positions. Currently, all the parties in Japan call for the reversion of the northern territories. It was the persistence of popular demand for the reversion of the four islands that prevented Prime Minister Hatoyama from concluding a peace treaty with the Soviet Union under the two-island formula proposed by Khrushchev in August 1955. In a *Nihon keizai shimbun* poll conducted just prior to Gorbachev's visit to Japan, slightly over 80 percent of those interviewed wanted all four islands returned, while only 4.7 percent supported the two-islands formula, with 5.1 percent approving the status quo. Among those who demanded the restoration of the four islands, 17.6 percent were in favor of simultaneous return, whereas 65 percent favored a staged restoration.[74] Had Kaifu concluded a peace treaty under the two-islands formula during the summit talks with Gorbachev, he was sure to have provoked bitter criticism from the general public as well as from within the LDP.

The External Factors

Of the external factors that influence the shaping of Japan's Soviet policy, the following four were particularly important: (1) East-West relations; (2) the United States; (3) China; and (4) Russia. It was often argued that Soviet-Japanese relations were simply a function of U.S.-Soviet relations. This argument is a slight exaggeration, but it is true that superpower rivalry exerted a strong influence on Japan's relations with Moscow. The northern territorial issue is a product of the Cold War. Without the East-West confrontation, the problem would not have arisen; the confidential territorial clause in the Yalta Agreement was to have been incorporated in the San Francisco Peace Treaty of 1951 without any modification. The Cold War also influenced Soviet-Japanese trade to a great extent, especially since Washington, which pursued a containment policy toward Moscow for decades and urged Tokyo to join COCOM, did not welcome any significant expansion of Japan's trade with the USSR.

Soviet-Japanese relations improved when the tensions between the superpowers lessened, whereas the bilateral relations deteriorated when East-West confrontation became tense. This is in part because Tokyo is closely connected with Washington through the mutual security treaty and in part because under the pragmatic "Yoshida Doctrine" Japan has avoided adopting a policy vis-à-vis Moscow that would anger the United States, its biggest trade partner. In the Cold War period, the United States did not welcome Soviet-Japanese rapprochement, although Washington itself maintained diplomatic relations with Moscow. At one crucial juncture, Washington even intervened in Soviet-Japanese peace talks to block full-fledged normalization as was clear from the aforementioned threat voiced by Secretary of State Dulles in August 1956. Subsequently, the United States made every effort to avoid giving an impression of direct intervention in Japan's policy toward Moscow so as not to provoke anti–American feelings in Japan.

Even in the post–Cold War era, the United States still appears to be concerned that Moscow–Tokyo rapprochement will occur at the expense of U.S.-Japanese relations, particularly in the security field. Prior to Gorbachev's visit to Tokyo, the Bush administration repeatedly stated that Japan should maintain close contacts with the U.S. government in conducting Soviet policy. Washington cautioned LDP Secretary General Ozawa in March 1991 that the improvement of Soviet-Japanese relations should be achieved within the framework of the existing U.S.-Japanese alliance system.[75] Assistant Secretary of State Richard Solomon remarked that Japan should be cautious about making investments in the USSR, adding that since the Soviet economy was near collapse, investing there would be like throwing away money.[76] It is true that Washington has been endorsing Japan's demand for the reversion of the four disputed islands since the mid-1950s. And it is also true that by the spring of 1992 the U.S. government has begun to urge Tokyo to shoulder more of the aid burden to Boris Yeltsin's Russia so as to facilitate the success of their experiments with democracy and market-oriented reforms. Nonetheless, Washington remains concerned lest Japan make major concessions to restore the northern territories in exchange for the acceptance of Moscow's Asian security proposal designed to achieve a drastic reduction in the U.S. naval presence in the Asia-Pacific region.[77]

With the sole exception of Prime Minister Hatoyama, successive Japanese governments have cautiously conducted policy toward the USSR, taking into account the possible repercussions in U.S.-Japanese relations to the extent that some argue that Tokyo has no independent Soviet policy. The U.S. factor will probably continue to play a major role in the formulation of Japan's Moscow policy and to work as a constraint, as long as the conservative government of Japan is prepared to avoid American displeasure that might engender intolerable conse-quences for trade with the United States.

Japan's Soviet policy was also influenced by the Chinese factor, although it was not as decisive as the U.S. factor. Especially in the years of the Sino-Soviet rift, the influence of the Chinese factor was not negligible. China persistently attempted to win Japan to its side and objected to Japan's cooperative efforts regarding Siberian development projects. Beijing even publicly endorsed Japan's claim for the rever-sion of the northern territory, although it had expressed unqualified approval of Soviet retention of all the Kuriles in 1950.[78] The Chinese objection compelled

Japan to scale down its economic cooperation with the USSR, whereas the PRC's territorial support drew Japan to the edge of the Sino-Soviet dispute and resulted in the stiffening of the Soviet stance on the issue. Presumably the Soviet refusal to return the northern territories arose partly out of the fear that it would fuel Chinese revanchism toward the USSR.

Following the May 1989 Sino-Soviet rapproachement, however, the Chinese government came to refrain from publicly supporting Japan's policy on the reversion of the northern territories, as exemplified by remarks made by Foreign Minister Qian Qichen in March 1990.[79] In May 1991 China signed a historic agreement with the Soviet Union concerning its eastern border, leaving the solution of the strategic Heixiazi Island issue for continued negotiations. As for the USSR, the post Sino-Soviet dispute era saw an end to Soviet criticism of the Sino-Japanese Peace and Friendship Treaty, which the Kremlin claimed was directed against the Soviet Union. It may be argued that since Gorbachev's May 1989 visit to Beijing, the Japanese government no longer has to pay so much attention to the Chinese factor in carrying out its policy with the Russians.

Finally, the Russian factor must be analyzed. One of the most distinct aspects of Soviet-Japanese relations in the Gorbachev era was that the USSR was in deep crisis and faced disintegration due to the intensification of nationalist movements within the federation. In June 1990, the Congress of the Russian Federation adopted a declaration of sovereignty, which stipulated that a change in its territory would not be recognized without 50 percent approval in a national referendum.[80] In accordance with a public survey conducted in the southern Kuriles in June 1990, an overwhelming majority (88 percent) of the respondents opposed the reversion of the islands to Japan, whereas only 8 percent approved it.[81] The vice-chairman of the Supreme Soviet and the foreign minister, both from the Russian Federation, accompanied Gorbachev on his historic trip to Japan.

These events suggest that the day had already passed when Japan's negotiating partner on the northern territories was the USSR. In 1990 the Russian Federation clearly emerged as a new constraint on the solution of the territorial dispute. Initially there were prospects that Russian diplomats would be more flexible on the territorial question, especially in light of the country's economic difficulties. When Foreign Minister Andrei Kozyrev visited the United States in November 1990, for instance, he privately suggested that Russia would abandon the islands in exchange for Japanese investment. [82] But conservatives and the military brought countervailing pressure on Gorbachev to retain possession of the territories. In addition to the opposition to reversion evidenced by the island residents themselves, strong criticisms of Russian diplomacy was voiced by Valentin Fedorov, who as governor of Sakhalin had direct administrative responsibility for the disputed islands. While promoting a free economic zone to integrate the Soviet Far East and northern Japan, Federov adamantly opposed reversion of the disputed territory and harshly criticized any attempt by Moscow to settle the issue without his input. This and other internal pressures effectively undermined President Gorbachev's ability to negotiate an agreement with Tokyo on the islands issue.

Conclusions and Prospects

Postwar Japan's Soviet policy was formulated under the influence of both external determinants (especially the East-West confrontation and the U.S. factor) and internal factors (especially public sentiment toward the USSR). With the upsurge of the nationalist movements, the Russian Federation and the Sakhalin Province emerged as additional constraints on Japan's Soviet policy making. Except for the Yoshida and the Hatoyama eras, in which the prime minister exercised initiative, the Foreign Ministry played a central role in the postwar formulation of Japan's Soviet policy in close collaboration with Washington, whose central interest in the Cold War years was to "keep Japan out of Russian hands."[83]

In Japan's foreign policy, achieving a breakthrough in the Moscow–Tokyo territorial stalemate has consistently been given low priority. Aside from rhetorical statements, no Japanese prime minister—including Hatoyama, Tanaka, and Kaifu—has considered the conclusion of a peace treaty with Moscow a pressing matter. In the Kaifu–Gorbachev Joint Communiqué of April 1991, the acceleration of negotiations on the conclusion of a peace treaty was pledged. In the foreseeable future, however, the prime minister is unlikely to risk a quick conclusion to a peace treaty by making a significant unilateral concession on the territorial issue. As analyzed in the previous section, pressure in Japan for the prompt signing of a peace treaty is by no means strong.

The continued Soviet refusal to give up the northern territory had certain political advantages for a conservative and pro–U.S.-Japanese government. The Soviet presence on the islands and the military buildup in and around the area served to maintain the salience of the Soviet threat to the Japanese public. This in turn helped to reduce public opposition to incremental increases in the defense budget. Increasing defense expenditures helped soften U.S. criticism that Japan was a security "free-rider," as well as helping to assuage U.S. demands for greater burden sharing. In addition, increased defense expenditures involving the purchase of large amounts of U.S. military hardware helped reduce the huge U.S. trade deficit with Japan. As Andrew Mark and Martin O'Hara argue in their coauthored article, "Moscow-Tokyo and the Northern Territories Dispute," an unresolved northern territorial issue thus had a positive function for the Japanese government in terms of both security and economic relations with the United States.[84]

In December 1991, the Soviet Union collapsed, leaving a smaller and economically devasted Russia struggling to survive. Most of the G-7 industrial nations have chosen to provide assistance to Moscow, rather than face the consequences of a destabilized Russia. Increasingly, Japan has found itself in conflict with Western industrial powers (including France, Germany, and the United States) over a policy toward Russia. Yet Japan has been withholding badly needed financial aid to Moscow until the northern territories issue is resolved. By early April 1992, out of fear that it might become isolated from the international community, Japan agreed to participate in a $24 billion economic aid package for Russia through the International Monetary Fund. But unless the Russian government decides to make substantial concessions to Japan with regard to the islands, Tokyo is unlikely to provide more than modest levels of assistance on a bilateral base. In early September 1992, President Yeltsin abruptly cancelled his Tokyo visit scheduled for September 13. Contributing to his decision was, first, that Japan was not prepared to offer much needed aid now and, second, Tokyo would probably refuse any compromise that fell short of recognizing Japanese sovereignty over all four islands.

For much of the world the Cold War is now largely a memory. But the issue of the northern territories, a remnant of the tensions between that once existed, remains caught in the Moscow–Tokyo ties. Questions of territory are often considered sacrosanct matters evoking patriotic and propriety emotions. Resolving this problem will require not only strong determination but also a diplomacy inspired by the art of possibility.

Notes

1. Tsuyoshi Hasegawa, "Japanese Perception of the Soviet Union: 1960–1985," *Acta Slavica Iaponica* (Sapporo: Hokkaido University), 5:37-70. For a recent opinion poll concerning Japanese perceptions of the USSR, see *Yomiuri shimbun,* April 7, 1991.

2. Miyazawa Kiichi, *Shakaito tono taiwa* (Tokyo: Kodansha, 1965), pp. 215–16. For Stalin's policy toward Japan from 1945 to 1951, see Saito Motohide, "Senryoki ni okeru soren no tainichi seisaku," *Soren kenkyu* (April 1988):126–49.

3. Yamamoto Mitsuru, *Nihon no keizai gaiko* (Tokyo: Nihonkeizai Shimbunsha, 1973), pp. 61–64.

4. Niizeki Kinya, *Nisso kosho no butai ura* (Tokyo: Nihon Hoso Shuppan Kyokai, 1989), pp. 227–30.

5. For a detailed analysis of Soviet policy of the normalization of diplomatic relations with Japan, see James W. Morley, *Soviet and Communist Chinese Policies toward Japan* (New York: Institute of Pacific Relations, 1958); Saito Motohide, "Khrushchev no tainichi kokko seijoka gaiko," 1 and 2, *Gaiko jiho* (April and May 1989):43–57 and 54–71, respectively.

6. For a detailed analysis of the decision-making process behind the normalization of diplomatic relations with the Soviet Union in the Hatoyama era, see Motohide Saito, "The 'Highly Crucial' Decision-Making Model and the 1956 Soviet-Japanese Normalization of Relations," *Acta Slavica Iaponica* (Sapporo-Hokkaido University), (1991), 9:146-59.

7. On Japan's initial policy toward the peace talks, see Kubota Masaaki, *Kremlin e no shisetsu* (Tokyo: Bungei Shunju, 1983), esp. pp. 32–34 and pp. 74–76. Sase Masamori, "Kokusai Seiji kara mita hoppo ryodo," in Kimura Hiroshi, ed., *Hoppo ryodo wo kangaeru* (Sapporo: Hokkaido Shimbunsha, 1981), esp. pp. 128–31. According to L. N. Kutakov, it was Malik's fault that the conciliatory scheme of returning two islands was presented too hastily. See NHK Nisso project, ed., *Kore ga soren no tainichi seisaku da* (Tokyo: Nihon Hoso Shuppan Kyokai, 1991), p. 133.

8. U.S. Department of State, *Foreign Relations of the United States, 1955–1957*, vol.23, part 1, pp. 202.

9. For the full text of the joint declaration, see Shigeta Hiroshi and Suezawa Shoji, eds., *Nisso kihon bunsho shiroyoshu* (Tokyo: Sekai no Ugokisha, 1988), pp. 151–53; *Pravda*, October 20, 1956.

10. Matsumoto Shun'ichi, *Mosukuwa ni kakeru niji* (Tokyo: Asahi Shimbunsha, 1966), pp. 148–49; Arai Shojiro, *Tsuranuke hoppo ryodo* (Tokyo: Nihon Kogyo Shimbunsha, 1973), pp. 176–77.

11. L.N. Kutakov, *Vneshiaia politika i diplomashiia iaponii* (Moskva: Izdatel'stvo mezhdunarodnye otnoshniia, 1964), p. 34. For the full text of the "Matsumoto–Gromyko Correspondence," see Matsumoto, *Mosukuwa ni kakeru niji*, 203–205.

12. *Novoe bremia*, 27 (1990), 13. For a detailed analysis of Soviet-Japanese relations around the revision of the security treaty, see Saito Motohide, "Sengo nisso kankei," in Okonogi Masao and Akagi Kanji, eds., *Reisenki no kokusai seiji* (Tokyo: Keio Tsushin, 1987), esp. pp. 323–26.

13. See Professor Wada Haruki's remarks at a round-table discussion, in NHK Sapporo Hosokyoku, ed., *Kosucha kara hoppo ryodo e* (Sapporo: Nakanishi Shuppan, 1991), pp. 217–18.

14. L.I. Brezhnev, *Prabda*, March 21, 1972.

15. Takayama Satoshi, *Tenkanki no nisso kankei* (Tokyo: Kyoikusha, 1986), p. 45.

16. *Asahi shimbun*, October 13,1973.

17. Ibid., October 11, 1973.

18. Gerald L. Curtis, "The Tyumen Oil Development Project and Japanese Foreign Policy Decision Making," in Robert A. Scalapino, ed., *The Foreign Policy of Modern Japan* (Berkeley: University of California, 1977), esp. pp. 164–66.

19. Young C. Kim, *Kremlin no tainichi senryaku* (Tokyo: TBS Britanica, 1983), pp. 127–34.

20. Tetsuya Kataoka, "Japan's Northern Threat," *Problems of Communism* (March–April, 1984): 14.

21. Zbigniew Brzezinski, *Power and Principle* (New York: Farrar, Strauss & Giroux, 1983), p. 218.

22. Furusawa Ken'ichi, *Nitchu heiwa joyaku* (Tokyo: Kodansha, 1988), p. 228.

23. *Asahi shimbun*, March 13, 1985. For an analysis of Gorbachev's policy toward Japan, see Saito Motohide, "Gorbachev no tainichi shin shiko gaiko no kiseki to hyoko," *Hogaku Kenkyu* (Tokyo: Keio University) vol. 65, no, 2: 207–227.

24. For an excellent analysis of the Toshiba incident, see Shioda Ushio, *Kantei ketsudan sezu* (Tokyo: Nihon Keizai Shimbunsha, 1991), pp. 185–251.

25. Tanihata Ryozo, "Nakasone to Mosukuwa wo kagede musubu 'misshi' tachi," *Seikai orai* (December 1986): 49–53; see also *Mainichi shimbun*, October 18, 1986.

26. Sugimori Koji, *Gorbachev no sekai seisaku to nisso kankei* (Tokyo: Tokai Daigaku Shuppankai, 1989), p. 125.

27. *Mezhdunarodnaia zhizni*, no. 7, 1988, pp. 140–55.

28. Interview with Kinya Niizeki, September 10, 1989.

29. Kimura Hiroshi, *Hoppo ryodo* (Tokyo: Jiji Tsushinsha, 1989), pp. 139–43.

30. *Asahi shimbun*, June 22, 1988.

31. *Mainichi shimbun*, August 11, 1990.

32. Gaimusho Gaimu Hodokan, ed., *Nihon to soren* (Tokyo:Sekai no Ugokisha, 1991), p.8.

33. *Asahi shimbun*, May 4, 1989.

34. Ibid., May 6, 1989.

35. *Yomiuri shimbun* (evening ed.), September 28, 1990; *Yomiuri shimbun*, November 26, 1990.

36. On the heated discussion in the Foreign Ministry over whether or not Japan should permit the entry of the Milykov mission, see *Asahi shimbun*, January 3, 1990.

37. Ibid., July 18, 1990.

38. Ibid., September 10, 1990.

39. *Yomiuri shimbun*, January 1, 1991.

40. *Nihon keizai shimbun*, March 24, 1991.

41. *Yomiuri shimbun*, March 24, 1991; for details, see also *The Daily Yomiuri*, March 25, 1991.

42. *Asahi shimbun* (evening ed.), April 5, 1991.

43. *Yomiuri shimbun*, April 17, 1991.

44. *International Herald Tribune*, April 19, 1991. For the text of the joint communiqué and agreements, see *Asashi shimbun*, April 19, 1991; *Izvestia*, April 19, 1991.

45. For Yanayev's remarks, see *Asahi shimbun*, December 28, 1990; for Nakasone's comment, see *Nihon keizai shimbun*, April 13, 1991.

46. See Saito, "The 'Highly Crucial' Decision-Making Model and the 1956 Soviet-Japanese Normalization of Relations," p. 147.

47. Hirano Minoru, *Gaiko kisha nikki* (Tokyo: Gyosei Tsushinsha, 1978), 2:144-45.

48. *Asahi shimbun*, April 21, 1991.

49. For Kaifu's remarks, see *Izvestia*, June 15, 1990.

50. Hiroshi Kimura. "Japanese-Soviet relations: On the Frontier," in Gregory Flynn, ed., *The West and the Soviet Union* (London: Macmillan, 1990), p.184.

51. Brian Bridges,"Japan: Waiting for Gorbachev," *The Pacific Review*, 4 (1991) 58; see also A.N. Panov, *Iaponskaia diplomaticheskaia slyzhba* (Moskva: Mezdunarodnye Otonosheniia, 1988), pp. 83–85.

52. Seki Tomoda, *Nyumon gendai Nihon gaiko* (Tokyo: Chuo Koronsha, 1988), pp. 164–65.

53. *Boei hakusho* (1990), pp. 44–59.

54. *Yomiuri shimbun*, January 6, 1991.

55. J.W.M. Chapman et al., eds., *Japan's Quest for Comprehensive Security* (London: Frances Pinter, 1983), p. 40.

56. Kimura, "Japanese-Soviet Relations," p. 184; Wolf Mendl, "Stuck in a Mould: The Relationship between Japan and the Soviet Union," in Kathleen Newland, ed., *The International Relations of Japan* (London: Macmillan, 1990), p. 191.

57. *Business Affairs,* November 23, 1989, p. 90.

58. *Nihon keizai shimbun,* October 4, 1990.

59. See, for instance, *Yomiuri shimbun*, March 28, 1991. However, following the failed August coup, the Ministry of Finance has become more positive toward Japan's aid to Moscow. *Asashi shimbun* , October 8, 1992.

60. *Asahi shimbun*, July 23, 1988; Kishimoto Kazuhiro, "Mata Gorbachev ni odorasareta Nakasone to shimbun," *Shokun* (October 1988): 26–38; Nakasone Yasuhiro, "Nakasone zenshusho Gorbachev kaidan wo kataru," *This is Yomiuri* (April 1989): 140–57.

61. *Yomiuri shimbun*, January 16, 1990; *Asahi shimbun*, October 7, 1990; *Nihon keizai shimbun,* October 8, 1990.

62. Bridges, "Japan," p. 59.

63. Iwanaga Ken'ichiro, *Sengo Nihon no seito to gaiko* (Tokyo: Tokyo Daigaku Shuppankai, 1985), pp. 72–73.

64. *Nihon keizai shimbun,* March 29, 1991; *Asahi shimbun,* April 11, 1991.

65. For the Clean Government party, see *Yomiuri shimbun*, March 21, 1991; for the Democratic Socialist party, see *Sankei shimbun*, March 26, 1991.

66. *Zen'ei* (December 1990): 26–88.

67. *Nihon keizai shimbun,* March 4, 1991.

68. *Yomiuri shimbun*, August 29, 1990; ibid., January 9, 1991.

69. See, for instance, Majima Kan, "Nisso kosho wa saikai sarete yuku, " *Chuo Koron* (March 1955):226ff.; Fujita Kazuo, "Domnitsky shokan shimatsuki," *Bungei Shunju* (April 1955):130–137.

70. *Asahi shimbun*, July 3, 1973.

71. For Yakovlev's visit, see *Sankei shimbun*, November 22, 1988; for Abe's trip,Gilbert Rozman, *Japan's Response to the Gorbachev Era, 1985–91* (New Jersey: Princeton University Press, 1992), p. 35.

72. Rokuro Saito, "Gorbachev no jindo gaiko wo miayamaru na," *Gekkan asahi* (February 1991): 97–103.

73. *Yomiuri shimbun*, April 7, 1991.

74. *Hokkaido shimbun*, January 1, 1991. Interestingly, according to a public opinion survey conducted in the northern territories in July 1992, prior to Yeltsin's cancelled visit to Tokyo, 79.6 percent of those interviewed supported the policy to transfer four

islands to Japan, in the case that (1)Tokyo bestowed the right of residence to those who wished to stay and guaranteed them living conditions equal to that of the Japanese, and (2) Tokyo provided appropriate compensation to those who desired to leave their land. For details, see *Yomiuri shimbun,* September 2, 1992.

75. *Yomiuri shimbun,* April 2, 1991.

76. Ibid., April 1, 1991.

77. See, for instance, *Mainichi shimbun,* April 5, 1991; *Yomiuri shimbun,* January 12, 1991.

78. John J. Stephan, "The Kurile Islands," *Pacific Community,* 7, 3 (1976): 328.

79. *Yomiuri shimbun,* March 24, 1991.

80. On Yeltsin's five-stage formula for the settlement of the northern territories issue, see *Novoe vremia* (February 6–12, 1990): 20–21.

81. *Mainichi shimbun,* June 27, 1990.

82. *Yomiuri shimbun* (evening ed.), November 29, 1990.

83. Thomas W. Robinson, "Japan and the Soviet Union," in Stephan P. Gilbert, ed., *Security in Northeast Asia* (Boulder: Westview Press, 1989).

84. Andrew Mark and Martin O'Hara, "Moscow–Tokyo and the Northern Territories Dispute," *Asian Survey* (April 1990): 387–88.

Chapter 14
Sino-Japanese Relations in a Changing East Asia

Se Hee Yoo

The expansion of economic relations under a banner of "friendship and coopera-tion" dominated Sino-Japanese affairs since 1972, when the two countries resumed formal diplomatic ties, until the Tiananmen incident of June 1989. Official "friend-ship and cooperation" notwithstanding, the two countries often have disagreed. China has objected to a bilateral trade gap widening in Japan's favor, to lagging technology transfers from Japan, to what Chinese see as a trend toward revived Japanese militarism,[1] to the way Japanese government-approved history textbooks interpret Japan's invasion of China in the 1930s, to Japan's position toward Taiwan, and, finally, to Japan's territorial claims to the Diaoyutai (or, in Japanese, Senkaku) islands.[2]

But with Japan being China's top loan source, its second-ranking trading partner (behind Hong Kong), and with neither country threatening the other militarily, the two countries had the ingredients for building a positive relationship. Moreover, Tokyo leaders believed China's post–1978 restructuring of the economic system would have a quite favorable impact on their mutual ties. Japan also supported Hu Yaobang and Zhao Ziyang in their attempts—however snail-paced—at domestic political reform.

Internal developments in post–Tiananmen China and changes in China's exter-nal environment, however, have planted seeds of possible future conflict in the otherwise pacific relationship between the two countries. The first of these: Chinese bitterness toward Japan when Tokyo reacted to Tiananmen by joining the Western industrialized democracies in imposing sanctions that Beijing rejected as interfer-ence in its internal affairs. Lessened to some degree when Japan subsequently reopened yen loans to China,[3] this Chinese resentment lingers.

A second potential source of trouble stems from the sharply different Chinese and Japanese responses to the number and accelerated pace of international developments in the aftermath of Tiananmen. The normalization of Sino-Soviet relations, the former Soviet Union's activist thrust toward Asia, the collapse of socialist regimes across Eastern Europe, and signs that European integration may follow German unification—all seemed to hint at the dawning of a new order in Asia as well.

Frustrated in its hopes for a breakthrough in its Soviet ties by the northern territorial controversy, Japan cannot give its wholehearted endorsement to Moscow's sudden surge of interest in Asia. But most of all China dreads any impact the disintegration of the Soviet Union and the collapse of socialist regimes in Eastern Europe might have on China. Chinese leaders understandably are cautious in their dealings with Japan, for Tokyo has applauded developments in Eastern Europe and the Soviet Union. These divergent Chinese and Japanese perspectives toward the international environment could widen to a point where the relatively pacific Sino-Japanese relationship of the recent past might take another, and far less favorable, path.

A third possible source of conflict stems from the series of hard-line economic and political measures the Chinese government has taken, while officially praising reform and openness. Even with Japan ending its sanctions against China, these regressive actions not only have returned China to its previous conservatism but also are bound to alter the future direction of Sino-Japanese relations.

Therefore, at least until these potential obstacles arising in the aftermath of Tiananmen can be resolved, Sino-Japanese relations are best regarded as in a transitional phase of particularly acute Chinese sensitivity to external developments. During this interim phase, as the period of restructuring the Asian regional and larger global political system approaches, it is useful to consider the type of relationship likely to emerge between these two Asian powers. In addressing this issue, three general topics are discussed here: Chinese and Japanese mutual perceptions, Chinese and Japanese views of the changing international setting, and several specific issues of urgent concern to both countries.

Mutual Perceptions: China and Japan

The task of analyzing how China and Japan perceive each other is complicated by their differing systems. Such is the Chinese system that free and open expression of opinion by the mass media or in publications is crippled by government curbs.

By contrast, the high degree of press freedom and wide diversity of opinions on China that exist in Japan make the analyst's thorniest problem one of determining which opinion most accurately reflects the views of decision makers. In many instances, after all, perceptions must be inferred from opinions expressed in the mass media, publications, or policy statements.

Of course, human beings are prisoners of past experience. Currently perceived "reality" originates in cognition of past events and is encumbered as well by cultural biases. Such factors help mold the mutual perceptions of China and Japan and seem particularly relevant to history-conscious and culture-proud China.

Chinese Views of Japan

In Chinese eyes, Japanese diplomacy rests on the "economics-first" principle with "separating economics from politics" motivating its policies toward China.[4] Accordingly, Japan's perceived reluctance to correct its lopsided trade imbalance with China and transfer essential technology to China merely follows its single-minded pursuit of economic interests. Further, the Chinese thinking goes, Japan's failure to shoulder such responsibilities as assisting the "have-nots" in the conflict between North and South demonstrates that Japan lacks the will befitting a true economic "power." In addition, Chinese are convinced that Japan's modest economic cooperation with China has no connection to any Japanese interest in the success of China's four modernizations but to bolster Japanese chances at exploiting the huge Chinese market.

The Chinese see three trends—escalating economic friction with the United States, a global economy fragmenting into regional blocs, and total European integration looming on the horizon—as leaving Japan with only one option: closer economic relations with China. The Chinese perceive Japan to be keeping step with the United States politically and militarily. At the same time, they see Tokyo warily but methodically seeking the military and political resources to play its "economic superpower" role in world affairs most effectively. They see "money politics" as adding as much punch to Japanese diplomacy as it does to influencing Japan's domestic politics.[5] By such sensitivity to Japan's overwhelming economic advantage, Chinese observers can appreciate the remarkable extent to which Japan already shapes international politics.

Nor do China's Japan watchers forget that Japan spends the world's third-highest amount for military purposes. At least to Chinese minds, a strain of chauvinistic militarism remains as potent in Japan as ever.[6] Among the signs Chinese cite to illustrate the point: the editing of government-approved history books that exalt and justify Japan's militarist past, former Prime Minister Nakasone Yasuhiro's epochal visit to pay homage to Japan's war dead at Yasukuni Shrine, and the seeming willingness of some Japanese leaders to dispatch Japanese Self-Defense Force personnel to the Persian Gulf during the 1990–91 crisis. Any remorse the Japanese might express for Japan's having invaded its neighbors in the past tend to strike Chinese observers as superficial and perfunctory, certainly not from the heart.[7]

To Chinese observers, Japanese diplomacy reflects a typically Janus-faced cultural trait which permits Japanese to blow hot and cold, depending on the situation. This aspect of the Japanese character, Chinese believe, lies behind Japan's much-vaunted realism. In foreign relations, it appears in the quite pragmatic "economics-first" or "separation of politics from economics" principles governing

Japanese diplomatic conduct. Specific examples given by Chinese analysts include Japan's hasty fence-mending campaign with China at the first hint of improvement in Sino-American relations, and Japan's contradicting its own official "one-China" stance by assiduously cultivating its relationship with Taiwan.

Japanese Views of China

To Japanese observers, China requires a peaceful international environment, without conflict of any sort with its neighbors, now that it has assigned top priority to the four modernizations program. Chinese authorities have so frequently affirmed their readiness to proceed with economic system reform and openness despite Tiananmen that Japanese take these statements as representing the true thinking of the Chinese leadership. A similar interpretation is given to frequent Chinese official statements favoring closer economic ties with various countries, and especially Japan.

Among the explanations Japanese give for the Chinese desire to continue and expand their economic relations with Japan after Tiananmen are Japan's economic might and the already substantial bilateral trade and investment level. At the same time, they suspect the real reason is Japan takes a rather passive posture and meddles very little in China's internal political affairs—as compared with the United States and other Western countries.[8] China is thus bidding to lure other Western countries into reopening economic relations with China by continuing and expanding economic relations with Japan.

To Japanese observers, China's leaders firm intention to maintain Chinese Communist party leadership means less chance of a quick collapse of the regime as happened in Eastern Europe. Simultaneously holding on to the socialist political structure while pursuing a policy of openness with the West is seen to suggest that Beijing has applied the "separation of economy from politics" approach to its own foreign relations. Nevertheless, these observers warn, the Chinese regime must consider carefully how reform and openness might affect Communist one-party rule. The Japanese expect the post–Tiananmen conservative shift in Chinese society to continue for the moment, with whatever future changes to develop at a glacial pace. Japanese observers thus stress how severely the maintenance of Communist party control constrains the economic reform and openness program.

Further, Japanese view China as desperately needing economic cooperation from Japan to overcome its present economic difficulties. China is acutely aware of its rivalry with Japan in Asia, amplified by its traditionally anti–Japan attitude and the intense pride characteristic of the Chinese people.[9] Such thinking, to Japanese observers, explains why China is so reluctant to accept the possibility of Japan becoming a political and military power. Japanese observers admit that China presently does not view Japan as its enemy in a military sense,[10] though it does wish to limit Japan's political influence in the region.

Japanese observers emphasize the significance of the principle of "let barbarians check barbarians" to Chinese diplomacy. Before Tiananmen, China was able to expand its influence in Asia by better relations with the United States while checking the Soviet Union. After Tiananmen, however, with the tumble of events in Eastern Europe, China is internationally isolated. Moreover, the recent improvement in Soviet-American relations has drastically diminished China's strategic significance to the United States.

At the same time, in Japanese eyes, normalization of Sino-Soviet relations after Gorbachev's 1989 Beijing visit slightly raised China's political leverage with the United States and Japan. Also, the flurry of recent Chinese diplomatic overtures toward Third World countries seems intended to bolster China's sagging international prestige and influence.

The Beijing government, however, preoccupied with issues of domestic political stability, economic reform, and Communist party control, simply lacks the solid base needed to launch an all-out diplomatic campaign to restore China's diplomatic standing.[11] China has long rejected any interest in seeking hegemonic status in its diplomacy. In fact, it has officially denounced the idea altogether. Nonetheless, Japanese observers have no doubt that China will assign heavy priority to attaining a prominent, high-status role in framing any new regional structure to emerge in Asia.

China and Japan View the International Environment

Chinese and Japanese opinions are similar in citing the transformation of the Soviet Union and Eastern European regimes as mainly responsible for the swift restructuring of the global system. Significant differences of opinion exist on the two sides, however, regarding what caused the transformation and what impact this sudden metamorphosis will have on Asia. As these differences surely will affect the two countries' foreign policies in different ways, it is useful to clarify their respective views before offering a prognosis of their bilateral relations and in an Asian regional context.

In the Japanese view, structural transformation in the Soviet Union and Eastern Europe stemmed from problems inherent to socialist regimes that rule out socialist systems in those regions. Under socialist regimes espousing economic equality— the ethical linchpin of socialist doctrine— productivity and efficiency fell drastically and inevitably led to the present level of economic backwardness in those societies. In China, the thinking goes, political corruption spawned by the Communist one-party bureaucratic system renders economic reform impossible. In addition, by devoting such a substantial proportion of its total resources to pursuit of the arms race with the United States, Moscow merely exacerbated its already serious economic woes. For the future, any hope of escaping the current economic predicament will require an avoidance of military confrontation with the United

States and introduction of free-market practices at home.

From a Japanese perspective, the fact that Gorbachev's perestroika and glasnost appeared at this time merely serves to emphasize the point. The former Soviet Union applied New Political Thinking to import from Western countries the capital and technology essential to domestic economic recovery. But that process of accommodation with the West brought about the socialist debacle in Eastern Europe.

For their part, Chinese officials recognize the need to open and reform the domestic economy through partial introduction of capitalist market elements. They acknowledge, further, that to be successful, these economic reforms must be accompanied by a certain degree of political reform as well.

But there is clearly a limit to political reforms possible. Chinese authorities flatly denounced the end of Communist party control in the Soviet Union. By relinquishing leadership of the Communist party, in the Chinese view, the Soviet Union evaded its responsibility to back other socialist countries and contributed to the meltdown of socialist regimes in Eastern Europe. Therefore, they insist the system of Communist one-party rule must remain intact in China under any future circumstances.[12]

Chinese opinion is that future economic development cannot occur unless the Communist party leadership remains in authority. The Chinese view apparently is that losing Communist party leadership will inevitably generate such grave political instability as to render impossible any degree of economic development whatsoever.

In Chinese eyes, therefore, it was Gorbachev's rashness, itself sparked by disillusionment at having lost the arms race with the United States, that spawned the transformation of the Soviet Union and Eastern Europe. Further, the Chinese thinking continues, intense military and economic pressure from the United States explains why Gorbachev came to have a defeatist attitude. In the past, they recall, Washington promised repeatedly to pull the roots from under the socialist system. The American policy of containment, in their view, had ravaged the Soviet economy just as promised. And today, to Chinese thinking, their country is the next target of American containment policy.

This belief is well expressed in China's interpretation of Tiananmen. The present ruling group believes that the Western bloc, particularly the United States, seizing the opportunity of China's economic openness and reform campaign, engineered the incident in order to execute a larger strategy of destroying the Chinese socialist system and bringing Chinese Communist one-party rule to an end.

The line of reasoning is that the United States has followed a policy of *"heping yanbian"* or "peaceful change of the Chinese system"[13] by manipulating an "impure force" behind the scenes in China. By this logic, Tiananmen erupted only when this domestic "minor current" or "impure force" of self-styled "democratic" elements protested in cooperation the "major current" outside China.

How will the collapse of socialist systems in Europe influence Asian socialist countries? Chinese claim an Eastern European-style chain of events is an impossibility in socialist countries of Asia, especially in China. Several distinctions are offered: First, the European socialist regimes were artificial entities, set in place when the Red Army marched into Eastern Europe after World War II while the Chinese regime, its roots solidly planted in Chinese politics and society, is an indigenous product of a long revolutionary struggle. Second, the geographical closeness that allowed the West to have such influence over East European countries does not apply to China, with its historic tradition of cultural independence. Finally, East European countries' military dependence on the Soviet Union scarcely compares to China, where the People's Liberation Army is fiercely loyal to the Communist party and, in fact, has been inseparably bound to the party since the revolutionary era of the 1930s.

Most Japanese specialists reacting to this Chinese self-appraisal would admit that certain inherent Chinese traits make the collapse of the Communist party less likely than was the case in Eastern Europe. At the same time, they see as inevitable a weaker, altered Chinese socialist system over time, so long as the government relies on the introduction of tools of the market economy and economic cooperation with the Western to build the domestic economy. The incumbent Chinese leadership is well aware of this issue, as demonstrated clearly by the sharpness of dissent expressed within the government over the scope and pace of economic reforms and market-opening measures.

China's dilemma is that economic development cannot happen without revamping the economic system and economic reform cannot occur without overhauling the political system. Moreover, political reforms will weaken the Communist one-party system and generate political instability, which retards economic development. Even keeping the existing system intact for dread of political instability will threaten economic development. On the other side, a stagnated domestic economy will imperil the socialist political structure itself.

At the moment the Chinese are seeking to resolve the dilemma by chasing two rabbits, one openness and economic reform, the other single-party Communist rule.[15] This approach will block the leadership from simply reverting to hard-line politics later on, once the Chinese people have tasted and wish to retain the benefits of a more productive and efficient economic system.

China and Japan share the view that Soviet-American detente heralds an end to the heretofore dominant bipolar system of world politics. Beyond that, the two countries disagree on the nature, linkages, and implications of several key elements: European political reform, Soviet foreign policy change, transformation of national political systems in East Europe, as well as on what specific shape the emerging political structure itself might have.

On whether or not the bipolar structure of global politics of the Cold War era will be replaced by a less tense and confrontational international system, Chinese thinking tends to be negative, even pessimistic. Japanese opinion, by contrast, tends to be positive, even optimistic.

The "Chinese" world view includes several elements.[16] First, military forces remain a key ingredient of national power, even as many countries assign greater importance to economic development and science and technology as sources of enlarged national power. Interdependence in the global economy acts as a deterrent to war, but economic blocs spur a few powers to guard their interests by military means. Concern with power politics and hegemony politics continue to dominate the foreign relations of several major countries.

A second aspect of the Chinese outlook is to see Soviet-American detente, the product of the recent transition in world politics, as having a destabilizing effect on the international political structure—by weakening military rivalry and upsetting the balance of power. Under these circumstances, the small and middle powers must expand their military capabilities, raising chances for regional conflict and conventional war.

Third, the advanced industrial countries—endowed with the sophisticated technology essential to mass produce up-to-date weaponry at a moment's notice—naturally can expand their military capabilities far more swiftly than those countries in dire economic straits. The temptation will inevitably exist for them to follow a military path. At this time Japan and Germany have the potential to become military superpowers. In fact, they will do so in the not too distant future.[17]

China and Japan stress the urgency of forming a new Asian order, in which all countries may prosper through reciprocity and equality. Neither clarifies its respective overall plan or role in preparation for the new order, however, for several reasons.

China and Japan concur that, aside from the Cambodian and Korean problems, particular features of the Asian political setting—cultural, racial and religious diversity, countries at widely divergent rungs on the ladder of economic development, and sharply clashing political ideologies—render Asia distinct from Europe. These characteristics also pose serious obstacles to any schemes to create "one Asia." Another point raised is that, just as in Europe, the Soviet initiatives provided the most direct stimuli to Asian regional political restructuring, not the countries in the region.

Both China and Japan, for different reasons relating to their domestic and foreign relations, have been reticent, unable to act forcefully to construct a new political order in Asia. China is unable to focus on external affairs because of its isolated diplomatic position after Tiananmen and its preoccupation with urgent domestic issues of political stability and economic development. Japan manages to ignore its twin advantages of facing no serious political crisis at home and the enviably robust economy to balk at launching initiatives of any kind, lest it should remind its Asian neighbors of past Japanese militarism and revive fears of another "Greater East Asia Co-prosperity Sphere."

Despite these reservations, Chinese and Japanese observers appreciate the mood of rising enthusiasm for a new Asian order. This awareness seems most evident on four issues directly related to the emergence of a new framework of Asian regional politics: first, the Asian diplomacy of the former Soviet Union; second, the U. S. role in Asia and its relations with China and Japan; third, the issue of Korea; and, fourth, multilateral economic cooperation in the Asian-Pacific area.

Key Issues: Japanese and Chinese Views

The Soviet Advance into Asia

The Soviet advance toward East Asian was first proposed in the "Asian Collective Security System" during the Brezhnev era. Asian countries gave the plan an indifferent reception. This was particularly so with China and Japan, both of which are geographical avenues to the region for the Soviet Union and both of which questioned the motives behind the plan. They ruled out potential benefits from any Soviet peace offensive so long as the Soviet Union continued to enlarge its military presence in the Far East. China and Japan, and most Asian countries, similarly opposed the "All-Asian Security Forum"—a revised version of the Helsinki-like "Asian Collective Security System, " which Gorbachev outlined for the region.

The two countries agree that Moscow must set up bilateral relations with Asian countries before proposing such grandiose schemes as the "Asian Collective Security System" or the "All-Asian Security Forum." For instance, from Beijing's standpoint, any improvement in Sino-Soviet relations depends on Moscow meeting three conditions: first, withdrawal of Soviet troops from Afghanistan; second, removal of Soviet troops and assault weapons deployed on the Sino-Soviet border and in Mongolia; and third, withdrawal of Vietnamese forces from Cambodia and terminating Soviet involvement in the Cambodian question. For its part, Japan has its own precondition for improved ties with Moscow: the return of all the disputed northern islands of Kunashiri, Etorofu, Shikotan, and the Habomais.

Recently, however, the two countries' thinking toward the Soviet Union has shifted markedly in response to Gorbachev's new political program of persistently seeking economic reform at home and military cutbacks abroad. With Moscow having removed all three of Beijing's requirements and no longer viewed as a security threat, China has normalized diplomatic relations with the Soviet Union.

The Chinese interpret the former Soviet's new Asian policy—as articulated formally in the Vladivostok Doctrine of July 1986 and the Krasnoyarsk Declaration of September 1988—as representing Moscow's readiness to abandon its policy of military expansionism, open economic ties with Asian countries, and enlarge its political influence in the region through peaceful initiatives.

In Chinese thinking, Moscow's most pressing need among the three bases of the new Asian policy is to fix its grave economic situation. Stated differently, the key element in the Chinese view of world political change is that the Soviet economic crisis rules out Soviet desire or ability to continue the arms race with the United States. Thus, Moscow finally has come to realize that economic cooperation with Asian countries and improvement of its political stature in the region can benefit its domestic economy.

The Chinese seem inclined to accept at least the broad outlines of the former Soviet Union's new peace-seeking policy. All evidence suggests China welcomes the change in Soviet policy: why else would China avoid criticism of Gorbachev's domestic actions spawning the multiparty system or his foreign policy decisions toward Eastern Europe that caused the downfall of socialist regimes in that area?

At the same time, the Chinese are opposed to any Russian-led movement for Asian peace, on grounds that Soviet initiatives to enlarge its regional political influence will be countered by the United States and Japan. Thus far, China has voiced neither support nor opposition to the Soviet-proposed plan that contains its concept of collective security for the Asian region.

Obviously aware of this Chinese thinking, Moscow refers to its peace plan as the "Asian equivalent of the Helsinki system" rather than the "All-Asian Security Forum." Moscow solicits Chinese support still further by associating the plan with "the spirit of Bandung"—the historic 1955 conference of Third World nations in which China played a leading role.[18]

The Japanese interpretation of Gorbachev's Asian policy differs little from the Chinese, save that Japan regards Soviet economic needs as the driving impetus for the changed line in Asian policy. But Japanese observers withhold judgment as to whether or not the Soviet Union has really abandoned its strategy of military expansionism in Asia. They refer pointedly to a strengthening, not a diminution, of Soviet military, particularly naval, forces in the Far East to support their contention that the Soviet Union remains a "threat" to Japanese national security.

This critical Japanese view is related directly to Moscow's continued unwillingness, while officially declaring its desire for improved relations, to accept Japan's main precondition for normalizing ties, namely, the return to Japanese sovereignty of the disputed islands north of Hokkaido. Moscow's stubbornness explains Japan's rather cold reaction to Soviet proposals for discussions on such matters as bilateral economic cooperation or the construction of a new peace structure for Asia.

Only Japan has the financial wherewithal to provide Russia enough money for costly Siberia development projects. And as long as Russians desire Japan's economic cooperation, Japanese analysts believe, eventually Moscow will return the disputed northern islands to Japan. Interestingly, Japan has reversed its usual approach, by following a "nonseparation of politics from economics" posture toward Moscow, employing economic power to pry loose a favorable outcome on the territorial issue. Finally, China's dissatisfaction with domestic political changes within the Soviet Union and its satisfaction with Moscow's new Asian policy line contrast sharply with the recent Japanese turnabout in its Soviet policy.

However, recent signs suggest a softening of the Japanese viewpoint. In particular, this is reflected in Japan's recent flexibility on the territorial question.[19] Japan was reportedly ready to negotiate a package deal on three issues—territory, economic cooperation, and an Asian-Pacific peace structure—when Gorbachev visited Tokyo in April 1991. This Japanese stance represented a significant break from the past Japanese stance of refusing even to sit at the same table with Soviet representatives until the territorial issue was settled.

There are several reasons why Japan decided to back off on the territorial issue. First, Japan came to accept that the territorial issue by its very nature could not be resolved at a stroke. Vice President Gennady Yanayev's statement in late December 1990 underscored that reality, that "return of the four islands is not a Christmas present that Gorbachev can just give to Japan when he visits the country."[20] Supposing Gorbachev were personally willing to agree to cede the territory to Japan, he must consider the domestic political climate in the Soviet Union, follow constitutional procedures, while paying attention to a deteriorating economy, pressures from ethnic minorities, and even independence movements by individual republics of the Soviet Union. Japanese came to believe that continued Japanese pressure on Moscow on the islands under these conditions would only undermine Gorbachev's domestic standing, which, in turn, would harm Japanese-Soviet relations and push the resolution of the territorial issue farther into the future. In the past, the Soviets intentionally avoided discussing the territorial problem by denying its existence in the first place. Moscow's stance changed radically toward the end of 1990, however, when Gorbachev acknowledged the existence of the jurisdictional issue over the islands when he declared, "It can be talked over."[21] This softening on the Soviet side led Japanese officials to conclude Japan stood to gain by extending the process of discussion and bargaining on the issue.

Second, Japanese economic calculations also played a part in softening Tokyo's harsh negotiating position.[22] Unlike Moscow, Tokyo has been less than energetic in its efforts to improve economic relations with the Soviet Union, largely because of the territorial issue. On the surface, lukewarm Japanese private sector interest stems from the unattractive investment environment in the former Soviet Union: an unstable political situation, the ruble's inconvertibility, an inadequate infrastructure and difficult physical conditions, along with the many yet unsettled matters of the law, structures, and customs that influence business. Despite these apparent obstacles, perhaps the real reason why Japanese business has chosen not to pursue economic cooperation with the Soviet Union is deference to Tokyo's policy.

With other countries' firms rushing into the Soviet market, Japanese business-men are having second thoughts about being patient. Many Japanese business executives interpreted the sudden improvement in Soviet relations with South Korea in 1990 as Gorbachev's playing of a South Korea card to pressure Japan into an earlier agreement on economic cooperation. No matter what motivated the Soviet side, the unexpected quickness of Soviet-South Korean normalization seemed to stun Japanese observers, who seemed most troubled by the possibility that South Korean firms would move swiftly to score an economic advantage in the Soviet Union.

A third factor leading Japan to bend on the territorial issue is political. The activist Soviet role played on a wide variety of fronts—the downfall of Eastern European Communist systems, the process of German reunification, the Paris Conference for Security and Cooperation in Europe, the Persian Gulf crisis, efforts to improve relations with Asian countries including South Korea—have trans-formed its old image into that of a peace-seeking country. Given that fact, it seems pointless for Japan to continue to brand the Soviet Union as posing a "military threat"—and, in fact, that explains why the phrase "the Soviet threat" was deleted in the communiqué announced at the end of the Houston summit of G-7 countries.

The latest Soviet regional plan is packaged positively as a design for a system of mutual security and peace for the Asian-Pacific region. There is no question that China has been more receptive than Japan to the latest Soviet peace initiatives. Given the very positive image the plan imparts, it will not be easy for Japan—which like China wants a major role in determining the shape of any future regional order in Asia— merely to sit idly by as the Soviet Union goes about the expansion of its political influence in the region.

Relations with the United States

Japan and China agree that the shape of any new Asian international order will depend largely upon the contents of whatever arms control agreement is ultimately negotiated between the two military superpowers. In contrast to the European peace process, the United States has yet to come up with a clear-cut alternative to Moscow's Asian peace initiative. Prolonged Soviet-American detente, however, will produce a gradual drawing down of American military deployments in Asia.

Japan and China expect to fill the political vacuum created by American withdrawal. At the same time, both recognize the risk that new problems will arise when the status quo comes to an end. Accordingly, both countries' planners are reflecting upon the type of relationship with the United States which would best serve their respective national interests during the ongoing period of reshaping international relationships in the Asian Pacific region.

As for China, its anxiety focuses on the following three among various effects that the changing international politics would have on U.S.-Chinese relations.

Beijing's main reason for pursuing amicable ties with Washington is to gain American help in meeting its economic development needs. This objective was relatively easier to accomplish during the Sino-American "honeymoon" of the 1980s. From today's perspective, that remarkably cordial relationship rested on the Japanese, Chinese, and American assumption that one country, the Soviet Union, represented a military threat. This rapprochement among the three countries made possible the flowering of cordial Sino-American relations during the decade.

China would have preferred to have the United States rather than Japan as its principal economic partner when Japan's relative weight in China's overall foreign economic affairs was rising continuously to a level of unbalanced Chinese dependence on Japan. No doubt the Sino-American economic relationship will continue, at least so long as the two countries' national interests are served. But, from China's standpoint, Soviet-American detente has reduced dramatically the need for political and military efforts that impair economic relations. On the other hand, China also must monitor any possibly antirevolutionary mood that economic relations with the United States might encourage.

A second concern among Beijing authorities is the impact a chill in Sino-American ties would have on the Taiwan and Hong Kong issues. Washington has backed Beijing's Taiwan policy to gain Chinese support to check Soviet expansion. Japan's support for the Chinese line mirrors this thinking. At the moment, however, with this rationale largely evaporated, it is highly doubtful the United States will continue its pro–Beijing stance unless it can be justified by improvement in the Sino-American relationship itself.

Significantly, demands for Taiwan's independence mounted after the Tiananmen crackdown. The harsh measures Beijing authorities imposed in crushing the prodemocracy demonstrators in Tiananmen Square sent shock waves to Hong Kong. Hong Kong citizens loudly oppose the mainland's rigid system, particularly its dismal record in political reform. Indeed, one cannot dismiss the possibility a Tiananmen-like scenario might happen in Hong Kong, sometime after the territory is returned to Chinese sovereignty in 1997. This scenario lends some credence to speculation that the ongoing East Shanghai Development Project is Beijing's way of providing a political and economic counterweight to Hong Kong, available to lessen the political and economic losses a major crackdown in Hong Kong might generate.

A third dimension of Chinese thinking is fear that Japan might rearm to fill the power vacuum left by withdrawal of American forces from East Asia.[23] This anxiety is part of a more general Chinese expectation that a sharp resurgence of nationalist sentiments throughout Asia will follow the breakup of the Cold War structure.

Primarily because their respective political systems differ so drastically, China and the United States are likely to encounter conflicts in their future relations. In

Japanese-American relations, however, there are far fewer sources of friction, aside from the chronically nettlesome trade issue, given the basically similar political and economic systems and extensive economic interdependency of the two countries. Moreover, both Japan and the United States remain wary of the Soviet Union.

The Issue of Korea

Until the Soviet Union normalized relations with South Korea on September 1990, China had the closest ties to both South and North Korea of the four powers surrounding the Korean peninsula (namely, the United States, the Soviet Union, Japan, and China). Having built a $3 billion-plus annual trade volume with South Korea while acting as North Korea's principal military and political supporter, China alone had the channels available to communicate with and to play a balancing role between both Koreas. At the same time, Beijing rarely neglected to stress pointedly how its purely economic links with South Korea posed no hindrance whatsoever to continued Chinese political and military backing of North Korea.

Indeed, on the surface Beijing acted precisely as its official statements suggested it would. For instance, China consistently had joined North Korea in urging the pullout of all American troops from Korean soil and in opposing such proposals as the Korean Federation, four-power cross-recognition of South and North Korea, and simultaneous admission of South and North Korea to the United Nations.[24] Despite China's consistently pro–North record, the constantly rising volume of bilateral trade and economic cooperation with South Korea, along with the substantial political progress thought likely for China during 1989 under Zhao Ziyang, made it reasonable enough to expect an imminent improvement in Chinese-South Korean ties.

But Tiananmen and the postincident development of closer Chinese links to North Korea have darkened prospects for improved Chinese political relations with South Korea. At the same time, there have been a few fragmentary signs of progress, such as an agreement permitting offices to be set up for each other's trade representatives in Seoul and Beijing.[25]

For its part, Japan, China's traditional rival for control of the Korean peninsula, faced many formidable barriers in seeking to expand its role in Korea following its devastating defeat in the Pacific War. In 1964 South Korea and Japan signed a treaty normalizing their relations. Although the agreement spurred closer bilateral economic ties, Japan remained a virtual bystander on issues involving the two Koreas, notably the unification question. The main reason Japan was kept at a distance was deep resentment among South and North Koreans alike over harsh treatment under Japan's thirty-five years of colonial rule. Moreover, Koreans on both sides believed that, while the United States and the Soviet Union had divided the peninsula,

Japanese colonial authorities bore ultimate responsibility by having encouraged divisive thinking between North and South and that, in any case, Japan was morally unfit to deal with the Korean unification issue. Finally, in the Korean view, inasmuch as Japan was not a party to the Cold War era military alliance structure of North or South Korea, it was unqualified to participate in the process of resolving the Korean question.

Only after Sino-Japanese relations were normalized, and particularly under Nakasone Yasuhiro's tenure as prime minister, Japan reached the plateau where it joined the United States, China, and the Soviet Union as a major player on the Korean issue. Nakasone sought a prominent Japanese role on resolving the Korean question as part of his wider attempt to raise Japan's clout in global politics to a level commensurate to its economic status. Nakasone is seen as having contributed substantially to resolving the Korean issue by supporting the Kissinger initiative to formalize the principle of cross-recognition of South and North Korea by the United States, China, the Soviet Union, and Japan. Notable, too, is that Japanese leaders, under intense pressure from South Korea to play an intermediary role in bettering Seoul's ties with Beijing, took advantage of every opportunity when visiting Chinese leaders to touch upon the subject of the Korean peninsula. Former Deputy Premier Kanemaru Shin's meeting with Kim Il-sung in Pyongyang at the end of September 1990 was a turning point, as Japan then began to move favorably in the direction of diplomatic relations with North Korea. Viewed against this backdrop, diplomatic ties between North Korea and Japan are likely to be established early in the 1990s.

Tokyo is less enthusiastic than Pyongyang about restoring bilateral ties at the moment. But what explains the relative modest degree of interest Japan does exhibit in normalizing relations with the North? In obvious contrast to economically vibrant South Korea and even to the Soviet Union and China—two problem-ridden countries Japanese have criticized loudly as poor economic partners, economically barren North Korea does not hold forth any potential economic gain that might justify Japan's current level of interest. In fact, Japan may have to provide economic compensation to North Korea—reparation for the Japanese colonialist period—before the relationship can be normalized.

Political motives lie behind Japan's positive interest in pursuing normalized relations with the North. In other words, Japan seems willing to pay a substantial economic price to become a top-level player in the political process of resolving the Korean issue in a changing Asian context. In view of China's already established influence on South and North Korea and sharply rising popularity of the Soviet Union in addressing the Korean question, Japan seems to have rejected its typically inferior political role of the past in favor of a higher profile role in the regional politics of Asia.

China formally supports improved relations between North Korea and Japan, apparently because the Chinese burden of providing economic support to Pyongyang would be eased thereby, and encourages the North to embark upon an economic open-door policy. Despite these official declarations, China, Japan's traditional arch rival over control of the Korean peninsula, may well have mixed emotions at the rapidly improving Japanese-North Korean relationship.

Multilateral Economic Cooperation in Asia

A fourth issue regarding the newly arising international order in Asia is the question of multilateral economic cooperation. Widely different political and economic systems as well as economic levels of development among countries in the region continue to be key features of Asian regional politics. This fundamental diversity in Asian regional affairs seems to leave little chance that a system of multilateral economic cooperation on the European Community model will be established in Asia for some time.

Given the modest possibility such multilateral approaches might succeed, it may be premature to discuss policy differences between Japan and China on the subject. But some fragmentary evidence— basically several quite self-serving maps the two countries have produced, appears to suggest rather clearly that a rivalry exists between them on the issue of multilateral economic cooperation in Asia.

Among various Chinese proposals, two stand out: "The Great Chinese Economic Sphere" and "The Northeast Asian Economic Sphere." Chen Yioun, director of the China Academy of Social Sciences' Taiwan Institute, presented the first of these proposals at a August 1988 seminar on the Chinese economy held at the University of California, Berkeley. Some two months before, the Taiwanese economist Zheng Shuyuan had offered his "Great Chinese Common Market" idea, which received widespread attention in China proper.[26] Membership in Chen's "Great Chinese Economic Sphere" reflects Chinese nationalist views, as Taiwan, Hong Kong, Macao, and Singapore along with China itself are included. According to one source, the "Great Chinese Economic Sphere" is China's counter to Japan's brainchild, the "East Asian Economic Community," composed of Japan, Korea, Taiwan, and Hong Kong.[27] Stated differently, when Japan included Taiwan and Hong Kong while excluding China proper in its Japan-led economic sphere scheme, China felt compelled to draft its own plan. Significantly, the resulting "Great Chinese Economic Sphere" proposal seems to accept the need to "separate economics from politics" to achieve Taiwan's economic integration into China, when the process of political integration falters.

The "Northeast Asian Economic Sphere" so widely discussed in Chinese circles recently has five member countries—China, the Soviet Union, North and South Korea, and Japan. The proposed arrangement generally corresponds to Japan's own plan for a "Japan Sea Rim Economic Sphere."[28] The two spheres differ in that the "Northeast Asian Economic Sphere" designates the area where three Northeastern

Provinces of China, the Far-Eastern region of the former Soviet Union, and North Korea converge—which is, therefore, China—as the hub of economic cooperation, with Japan and South Korea providing the necessary capital and technology.[29]

In addition to these five member countries, the "Japan Sea Rim Economic Sphere" will be enlarged later on to include Hong Kong and Taiwan, to form a Japan-led third economic bloc, modeled after the European Community and the North-South American Economic Sphere.

Conclusion

At this historic juncture, China and Japan, two powers with a long tradition of regional rivalry, must adapt to an international environment undergoing profound adjustments. Such dramatic developments as Soviet-American détente, the systemic reforms unfolding in the former Soviet Union, a European new order led by German unification, and the collapse of socialist regimes all across Eastern Europe will have repercussions on the ongoing process of transforming the regional political structure of Asia.

As such, they will require both and Chinese and a Japanese response. Heretofore, Sino-Japanese relations have been dominated by economic matters. However, the intrusion of political factors and demands of a changed international setting inevitably will complicate the relationship and increase the likelihood of conflict.

A new order is far less likely to emerge in Asia as in Europe. Still, the existing Asian regional political structure based on containing an expansionist Soviet Union has already begun to crumble, as Moscow continues to pursue an assertive, nonmilitarist diplomatic campaign in Asia. And already the region shows dramatic examples of change: normalized relations between China and the Soviet Union, South Korea and the Soviet Union, and good prospects for normalized ties between North Korea and Japan.

Backed by its prodigious and much-envied economic clout, Japan has persistently sought to elevate its political influence and status as well. Should Gorbachev's scheduled visit to Japan in April 1991 succeed in laying the groundwork for improved Soviet-Japanese relations, one can anticipate an intensified effort to enhance Japan's political position in both regional and global affairs. Japan can be expected to seek improved relations with the Soviet Union, despite the unresolved northern territorial dispute.

As for China, the highly activist role the country played in Asian politics during the 1980s seems unlikely to continue through the coming decade, for several reasons. These are: China's post–Tiananmen isolation, its diminished strategic significance under conditions of Soviet-American détente, and compelling pressures at home for political stability and economic progress.

At the global level, China will doubtless be dwarfed by Japan. Perhaps China will be overshadowed by Japan in regional influence as well. Certainly China's need for Japanese help in saving its domestic economy seems to require Chinese concessions to Japan outside the purely economic realm. Nevertheless, against the backdrop of enormous potential inherent in this vast territory and huge population, China will continue to seek the status of a major Asian power, forge amicable relations with its neighbors, and devote its resources to help resolve such thorny regional conflicts as Korea and Cambodia.

Notes

1. Shinta Kenzo, "Ajia beigun sakugen ni tomadou kakkoku (Chugoku)" (All nations [China] anxious over U.S. force reductions in Asia), *Sekai shuho*, December 18, 1990.

2. Sakai Shinnosuke, "Senkaku shoto jiken no hamon" (Impact of the Senkaku Island incident), *Sekai* (January 1991): 27.

3. Japanese loans thus far can be divided into three periods: the first, covering 1979–83, totaled ¥330 billion for four projects; the second, for 1984–89, totaled ¥470 billion for fifteen projects (disbursement for six of these was deferred to next period); and the third, covering 1990–95, was to total ¥810 billion (about U.S. $6 billion at $1 = ¥135 exchange rate) for forty-two projects. Shortly after Tiananmen, Japan suspended this entire third-period loan offer, in line with sanctions other Western industrial democracies were imposing against the Chinese regime. *Takungpao,* June 21, 1989. This six-year loan package was gradually unfrozen following the 1990 Houston summit.

    Japanese opinion is not unanimous on what impact Japan's loans to China will have on the bilateral relationship. For a detailed discussion, see Kojima Hoji, "Chugoku keizai to yen shakkan" (Yen loans and the Chinese economy), *Sekai shuho,* September 4, 1990.

4. While the principle continues to guide Japan's China policy, the "separating economics from politics" theme may be less applicable to other areas of Japanese diplomacy today. On foreign aid policy, for instance, see Dennis T. Yasutomo, "Why Aid?: Japan as an Aid Great Power," *Pacific Affairs* 62, No. 4, (Winter 1989–90): 490–503.

5. Ding Yongkang, "Riben huifu dui zhonggong daikuan de yingsiang" (Impact of Japan's reopening loans to China), *Zhongguo dalu yanjiu* (Mainland China studies) 33, 4, (October 1990): 62.

6. One prominent American commentator has urged China to end its criticism of Japanese domestic politics and its charges of Japanese "military reexpansionism." He argues that such Chinese attacks are unjustified, emotional, and rooted only in Chinese memories. According to his interpretation, the Chinese perception of chauvinistic Japanese militarism poses a cognitive obstacle to closer Sino-Japanese relations. See Harold C. Hinton, "China's Agenda in the 1990s," *The Journal of East Asian Affairs* 4, 2, (Summer/Fall 1990).

7. Just how little remorse, if any, many Japanese seem to have about their country's prewar conduct is clear in a statement made by Diet member Ishihara Shintaro denying

Japanese responsibility for the 1937 Nanking massacre. Just how keenly Chinese are aware of such attitudes is clear from their intensely hostile reaction to Ishihara's remarks. *Renmin ribao,* November 18, 1990.

8. In fact, Japan's interest in sanctions was lukewarm. Japan was the last country to join other Western democracies in imposing sanctions against China for Tiananmen. Just over a year later, at the July 1990 Houston summit of G-7 industrial nations, Japan strongly urged the reopening of World Bank loans to China.

9. Many Japanese scholars consider China to be the country most menacing to Japan. For example: Hideo Sato, "Maintaining Peace and Prosperity in East Asia after the Cold War and the US. Economic Hegemony: An Inquiry into the Role of Japan," paper presented for the 19th International Conference of the Korea Institute of International Studies, vol. 9, nos. 3-4, 1990; Hidenori Ijiri, "Tongbugaesoui t'alnaengchon chejeui tungchang—Ibonui sigak" (Crisis of the post-Cold War system in Northeast Asia— A Japanese view), *T'ongil munje yongu* (The Korean journal of unification affairs) 2, 3, (Fall 1990); Fred Charles Iklé) and Terumasa Nakanishi, "Japan's Grand Strategy," *Foreign Affairs* 69, 3, (Summer 1990):81–95.

10. Nakanishi Terumasa, "Asu e no Nihon no sekai senryaku" (Japan's future world strategy), *Chuo koron,* (July 1990): 92.

11. Many Japanese regard the current domestic political situation in China as extremely unstable. Among the variety of reasons mentioned are these: the government's questionable legitimacy to rule, popular distrust of the regime, an intra-Communist party schism of crisis proportions, stagnation of the domestic economy, local secessionist movements threatening central authority, and pressures from China's external environment. See Kojima Hoji, "Post–Deng Xiaoping no kuno" (Agony in the Post–Deng Xiaoping era), *Kaigai jijou,* (November 1990): 2–16.

12. Nakajima Mineo and Kakami Koko, "Chugoku wa kawari uru ka" (Can China change?), *Sekai,* (July 1990):133.

13. In the Chinese rendition, *"Heping yanbian"*—as conceived by Acheson and put in practice by Dulles—refers to the American psychological, cultural, and economic offensive against socialist regimes. The rationale for the concept: Once socialist leadership had three or four generations of contact with capitalist systems, they would decide to transform their own socialist societies into capitalist ones. *Renmin ribao,* July 26, 1989.

14. Party General Secretary Jiang Zemin articulated the "situations differ" concept when meeting with representatives of the Hong Kong press corps. The principle came to represent the official Chinese viewpoint on changes in the socialist world, particularly in Eastern Europe. *Takungpao,* December 22, 1989.

15. *Yomiuri shimbun,* December 31, 1990.

16. For additional Chinese perspectives on changes in world politics, see Tao Bingwei, "Jiushi niandai de yatai diqu jushi" (The Asian-Pacific situation in the 1990s), *Guoji wenti yanjiu,* (January 1990); Wang Lin, "Shijie jushi zhengzai fasheng juda de bianhua" (The world situation is only now undergoing major change), *Guoji wenti yanjiu,* (February 1990); Yao yun, "Zenyang kan dangjin shijie geju de biandong" (How to view the changes in the world situation), *Banyuetan,* (November 17, 1990);

Wan Guang, "Xifang yao jianji zenyang de 'shijie xinzhishi'" (What kind of "new world order" are Western countries seeking to establish?)," *Liaowang*, no. 37 (1990).

17. Shinta Kenzo, "Ajia beigun sakugen ni tomadou kakkoka."

18. In a press conference with *Asahi shimbun* press representatives on the topic of practical ways to achieve disarmament and build international trust in the Asian-Pacific region, Gorbachev stressed the importance of heeding the Bandung principles—ideals produced by Asian culture but reflecting the realities of world politics—rather than trying to transplant the Helsinki principles in Asian soil. *Hankook Ilbo*, December 31, 1990.

19. For Chinese observations on these moves, see Yang Bojiang, "Prospects for Japanese-Soviet Relations," *Beijing Review*, October 29, 1990, pp. 9–11.

20. Yanayev remarked that one should not expect President Gorbachev "to carry two islands in one pants pocket and two islands in the other pocket." He added, "Gorbachev isn't Santa Claus who gives everything away in a single visit." *Asahi shimbun*, December 28, 1990.

21. Yanayev recounted how Moscow had reversed itself on the Northern Territories issue—switching from a position denying the issue entirely, to a position of acknowledging its existence. *Yomiuri shimbun*, December 29, 1990.

22. Marubeni, Mitsui, and C. Itoh are among the Japanese corporations engaged in massive energy-related joint ventures in the Soviet Far East. These vast undertakings include production, refining, and export of natural gas, crude oil, and petrochemical goods. Among projects slated for a five-year plan beginning in 1991 are construction of a LNG factory on Sakhalin, and a repair facility plus a petroleum-refining factory in Khabarovsk. *Asahi shimbun*, December 29, 1990.

23. *Renmin ribao*, November 2, 1990.

24. *Renmin ribao*, September 29 and October 10, 1990.

25. China suddenly, unilaterally, and without satisfactory explanation, canceled the Shanghai-Seoul air route, opened in August 1989, which Korean Air Lines had used to provide once-a-week passenger service between the two cities. *Dong A Ilbo*, January 10, 1991, p. 19.

26. *Chungkuo shihpao*, January 4, 1989.

27. *Chosun Ilbo*, March 7, 1989.

28. *Yomiuri shimbun*, January 1, 1991.

29. Jin Taisiang, "Chugoku no Tohoku Ajia keizai kyoryoku koso" (China's plan for Northeast Asian economic cooperation), *Nitchu keizai kyokai kaiho* (The Journal of Japan-China Association on Economy and Trade) (November 1989): 25–31.

V Japan and the New Multilateralism

Chapter 15
The Politicization of Japan's "Post–Cold War"
Multilateral Diplomacy

Dennis T. Yasutomo

Japanese foreign policy has entered a transitional era, between the successful attainment of the national goals that led the nation to economic prosperity and international recognition and the painful search for new national goals that will lead the nation into the next century. Most observers find it easier to identify the road Japan has traveled in the post–World War II period to its current status as an economic and financial great power. Retroactively called the "Yoshida Doctrine," this policy emphasized economic reconstruction and growth, minimal defense efforts, and a reliance on the United States. This external policy was characterized by passivity and reactiveness regionally and globally, a near-obsession with economic and resource diplomacy, the avoidance of involvement in political and strategic issues, and strong dependence on a pax Americana international system. It was a neo-mercantilist, neo-isolationist, low-profile, low risk strategy—and one that basically worked, thus making it difficult for many Japanese to think about fixing what seemingly "ain't broke."

As many Japanese survey the road ahead, however, a realization is taking hold that a new course may be necessary to cope with the turmoil and uncertainty in the current post–Cold War era. Many Japanese are weighing the need to contribute actively to the agenda-setting imperatives of the new system-in-formation, which implies a conscious departure from the three pillars and behavioral pattern of Yoshida diplomacy.[1] Discussions at this stage seem to be coalescing around certain specific aspirations:

1. Japan aspires to an active rather than passive or reactive diplomacy;
2. This activism should take the form of involvement in the political-strategic and not just the economic arena.
3. This involvement should be global as well as regional.

4. But this political involvement should take the form of nonmilitary contributions since Japan is determined to avoid becoming a military great power.

5. This activism should be played out primarily in the form of multilateral diplomacy, rather than reliance only on unilateralism or bilateralism.

The aspirations are taking shape, but concrete policies that reflect these activist, politicized, globalized, nonmilitary, and multilateral themes remain ambiguous. We do see these themes increasingly at work, however, in one significant area of foreign policy in the 1980s and 1990s: Japan's policy toward multilateral institutions, especially multilateral development banks (MDB). It is in these forums that Japan is exhibiting greater activism, assertiveness, and independence, finally assuming what appears to be an international agenda-setting and rule-making role in the political as well as economic and financial arena. It is in these institutions that Japan seems best able to think beyond Asia to its international and global responsibilities. It is here that we especially see full-force the utilization of nonmilitary diplomatic tools (i.e., aid, trade, investment, technology transfer, human resources). These institutions also provide a collective diplomacy setting in which Japan has new opportunities to support or challenge American policy interests. Whether seeking increased vote shares or demanding managerial positions or establishing "Japan special funds," Japan's presence is increasingly felt and its behavior appears to be a departure from the passive nonpolitical approach of the past.

Therefore, by focusing on representative multilateral forums, we should be able to identify some of the emerging objectives, characteristics, and aspirations of an activist Japanese diplomacy. We should first be able to argue that Japan has, in fact, embarked in these forums on an activist diplomacy different from the past. We then need to explain why the Japanese favor multilateral institutions as the forum for this activism. Finally, we should be able to discern the underlying objectives of Japan's new politicized multilateral activism.

Multilateral Diplomacy: Cases

Throughout the 1960s and 1970s, Japan's MDB policies were low-key. Its financial contributions were respectable but not outstanding; professional staff members were few; and its presence in top management positions was negligible. By the 1990s, however, Japan has become a premier financial pillar for all MDBs. Japan's share of total contributions to MDBs, rose to either the number one or number two position in all MDBs. Japanese staffers and managers remain disproportionately low given the level of financial contributions, but there has been progress in this dimension as well.

Japan's activism has been visible especially in the World Bank Group. Ogata Sadako, herself an example of Japan's emerging presence in international organizations as the new UN high commissioner for refugees, contends that Japan shifted from a passive policy in the IBRD to redress the gap between Japan's substantial financial contribution increases and its vote share.[2] Japan had increased regular subscriptions, established a "Japan Special Fund" to deal with debt issues, and appointed a new vice president in 1989. In IDA, Japan's attempt to make contributions contingent on increased vote shares represents "a move that attests to the intensity of the desire to break the existing situation."[3] Voices are now suggesting the appointment of a Japanese to head the IMF, and Horiuchi, an analyst at the Japan Economic Research Center, contends that the IMF's problems can be traced to continued reliance on a declining United States and a failure to incorporate Japan more fully in IMF matters.[4] Japan achieved the number two status in all of these institutions during the 1980s.

Hirono, a former high-ranking official in the UN Development Program, asserts that MDBs serve as "an appropriate forum for Japan to express its views on the goals, instruments, and financial resources of the international community in an effort to promote world peace and development."[5] He even characterizes Japan's recent MDB, UN, and GATT activities as a "more aggressive" effort to attain a leadership role. Saito, a research analyst writing for a Japanese Foreign Ministry-funded institute, suggests that this new activism in the World Bank, IMF, and ADB represents a Japanese willingness to raise its "political voice" to begin sounding like "a soloist instead of a member of the chorus."[6]

These authors also assert or imply that Japan would be even more active were it not for the opposition of European and American MDB members, each concerned about their own status in these organizations in the face of a Japanese challenge. Each writer presumes that Japan has underlying diplomatic objectives beyond purely economic interests, and that these interests may entail differences with American interests, but none is especially clear about those objectives. Ogata cites Japan's desire for burden sharing; Saito emphasizes Japan's interest in private-sector development; Hirono writes of leadership, especially in the debt arena; and Horiuchi notes Japan's challenge to the American use of the IMF as a political tool. However, Japan's specific political agenda in MDBs remains unclear, especially the "big picture" that may underlie this politicized multilateral diplomacy.

These developments are visible not only in the World Bank but also in regional development banks. By looking at the Asian Development Bank and the European Bank for Reconstruction and Development, we can confirm the activism found in the World Bank and identify some of the underlying political themes in Japan's multilateral diplomacy. Both institutions are regional rather than global, but both welcome nonregional members, including a United States that carries considerable weight within these forums. And since the ADB Charter served as the model for the EBRD, both have similar articles of agreements and organizational structures.

The contrasts provide rich material for comparison: The ADB is approaching its twenty-fifth anniversary, while the EBRD has just opened its doors (May 1991). The ADB's mandate is nonpolitical, while the EBRD has an explicit political agenda. The ADB serves the Third World nations of Asia, while the EBRD will focus on former members of the Second World (East Europe and the new states of the former Soviet Union). Japan has been a key actor in the ADB's founding and subsequent management and operations, while Tokyo's involvement in the EBRD's establishment has been peripheral, and its presence in management and operations expected to be light. The ADB is Asia-centric, while the EBRD tests Japan's willingness to fulfill global responsibilities.

These two forums reflect many of the startling changes in a new post–Cold War world following the collapse of the Communist world in Europe, the political, and social and upheaval in the Soviet Union, and the resurgence of political instability and hard-line domestic policies in China. They touch upon Asia-related and global issues in an increasingly interdependent world in search of a new world order. They offer Japan a chance to participate in the shaping of a new international order, and there is some evidence in these forums that Japan is taking a step toward the kind of political activism avoided in the past.

The Asian Development Bank

The Asian Development Bank, founded in 1966 and located in Manila, represents the most intimate of Japan's relationship with any international body. Japan was a founding member, helped shape its by-laws, supplied all five of its presidents, dispatches a large number of professional staff members, and serves as its principal financial pillar.

Throughout the first two decades of the bank's operations, the Japanese maintained a high-profile status and a low-profile policy approach.[7] Tokyo's high profile was unavoidable, given its prominence in top management, its financial contributions, its presence on the staff, and its large share of project procurement. Japan's low-key policy was deliberate and consciously nonpolitical, befitting its general belief in the maintenance of the political neutrality of multilateral banks. Until the mid-1980s, Japan's main policy line focused on keeping the bank operating smoothly by propping it up financially and supporting its management, and by maintaining a close working partnership with the United States, symbolized by the equal shares held by Tokyo and Washington.

In the last half of the 1980s, Japan moved away from its low-key approach toward greater activism and preeminence within the bank.[8] Four main factors spurred Japan's efforts: the development of a clearer conception of the ADB as a foreign policy tool in a new debt strategy; the desire for an increased vote share, reflecting Japan's burgeoning financial support for the institution; the utility of the ADB for Japan's Asia policy; and concern over the impact of a new American policy toward the bank.

From 1986 to 1989, Japan engaged in a kind of accumulated debt diplomacy, centered on multilateral development banks. Japan pledged a total of $65 billion for debt relief, including a $10 billion package exclusively for MDBs, a $20 billion recycling plan with a substantial portion for MDBs, and a $35 billion supplemental package intended primarily for MDBs.[9] In addition, Finance Minister Miyazawa Kiichi proposed a debt reduction plan in 1988 that foresaw a critical role for private flows and MDBs. Although much of the multilateral portion of these plans was slated for the World Bank/IMF (since the debt problem is relatively less severe in Asia than other regions), the ADB was included in these plans. The ADB attained a new importance in Japan's debt diplomacy, including the establishment of a new Japan Special Fund in 1989 to serve as a conduit for surplus recycling in Asia.[10]

The Japanese became more adamant about achieving a balance between financial contributions and voting share as their contributions increased. Japan's total contributions to the Ordinary Capital Resources totalled $3.24 billion, or 15 percent of total contributions, at the end of 1988. Tokyo's share increased to 16.4 percent as a result of the 1988 Special Capital Increase. Japan supplied $6.99 billion to the Asian Development Fund, the soft loan window, or 37 percent of total contributions. Contributions to the Technical Assistance Fund totalled $47.7 million, or 56.9 percent of total subscriptions. In addition, Japan pledged about $100 million to the Japan Special Fund and established a $700,000 ADB-Japan Scholarship Program for postgraduate training throughout the Asian region.[11] Japan's total contribution to the bank consistently outstripped by far all other member nations.

In a move that reflected Japanese efforts in the World Bank and the IMF, Japan initiated a campaign in the mid-1980s to increase its vote share. Japan has consistently provided over one-third of the funding for the Asian Development Fund, but voting shares are determined by subscriptions to the Ordinary Capital Resources (OCR), where Japan and the United States have maintained an equal share since the bank's founding. Japan, therefore, waged a long campaign for a Special Capital Increase in its share of OCR contributions, entitling Tokyo to a larger share of the vote. The campaign triggered opposition from the United States and some Asian member nations, resulting in a compromise increase in both Japan's and America's share. That is, Japan did not attain preeminence in vote shares but acquiesced to the status quo of U.S.-Japanese vote-share parity. However, that Japan attempted to abandon its status as coequal partner of the United States in favor of preeminence is a significant departure from its traditional policy approach.

Japan also found the ADB useful to pursue its policy goals in Asia. Tokyo increasingly focused on the potential role of the bank in contributing to the reconstruction of Cambodia, on the resumption of lending to Vietnam (halted after Hanoi's 1979 invasion of Cambodia), on bolstering the Filipino government of Cory Aquino after the 1986 fall of Ferdinand Marcos and on the changing status of India to borrower status in the ADB.[12] These policies paralleled Japanese bilateral efforts outside the ADB to support Cambodian reconstruction, induce Vietnam to withdraw from Cambodia and focus on its domestic economy, channel more than $1 billion worth of aid to Manila through the Multilateral Aid Initiative with the United States, and improve relations with the subcontinent through prime ministerial (Nakasone Yasuhiro and Kaifu Toshiki) visits to the region.

Japan's China policy was more complicated. Tokyo initiated aid to Beijing in 1979, and China became the largest recipient of bilateral Japanese ODA in the 1980s. Japan responded to overtures from China in the early 1980s on ADB membership by strongly supporting ADB President Fujioka Masao's efforts to bring Beijing into the bank without ousting Taiwan. Fujioka's memoirs mention the frequent high-level consultations with Japanese Finance and Foreign Ministry officials during his shuttle diplomacy.[13] Fujioka consistently stopped in Tokyo on his way to and from Beijing and Taipei, at one point even requesting that a Foreign Ministry China specialist be seconded to the ADB.[14]

China joined the ADB in 1986. However, in the wake of China's massacre of students in Tiananmen Square in June 1989, Western donors initiated aid sanctions against China, and Japan followed suit by suspending a $5.6 billion bilateral aid package. Japan initially followed the lead of others in the ADB as well, especially the United States, in supporting the cessation of loans to China.

Japan's actions outside the bank, however, tell a different story. After Tiananmen, Japan almost immediately initiated a campaign to soften sanctions on China. At the July 1989 Paris summit, Tokyo successfully obtained compromise wording in the joint communiqué less harsh than originally intended.[15] Following the summit, Japan argued that sanctions had induced a favorable, if partial and still inadequate, response from China, including permission for dissident Fang Lizhi and his wife (who had taken refuge in the American Embassy) to depart the country. Japan consistently argued that China must not be isolated from the world community, and that continued deprivation of aid and economic stagnation would aid the hard-liners. According to Minister of International Trade and Industry Muto Kabun, "What we are concerned about at this moment is that we do nothing that might weaken the group trying to democratize."[16]

Japan's position was forcefully articulated at the July 1990 Houston summit, when Japan unexpectedly placed the resumption of aid to China prominently on the agenda. Houston symbolized the first time in summit history that Japan participated in an international agenda-setting and rule-making role through the pursuit of its own China policy. Japan had already decided to resume the $5.6 billion aid package before the summit and sought understanding from its allies. Prime Minister Kaifu attained the tacit agreement of President George Bush in a meeting prior to the summit and obtained the tacit understanding of hesitant Europeans during the summit.

Following Houston, Japan approved yen loans to China in October totaling $270 million. The Japanese did not approve the $890 million requested by the Chinese, but the aid sanctions were lifted.[17] In December Japan unilaterally approved $35 million for a hospital and resumed cultural exchanges.[18] And in November the

ADB, with Japanese support, approved a $50 million agricultural loan and a $480,000 technical assistant grant to Beijing. At the April 1991 Board of Director's meeting, Tokyo urged the full-scale resumption of ADB loans to China and announced its support for allowing Beijing to borrow from the soft-loan window, the Asian Development Fund (the ADB had restricted China's borrowings to the OCR).[19] This call was followed with an issue of $145 million in bonds on the Tokyo market, the first since Tiananmen, in June. The ADB once again reflected Japan's bilateral Asia policy.

Another objective of Japanese ADB political activism was to dampen a strengthened politicization of American policy toward the bank. The Reagan administration took office in 1981 and immediately signaled a shift in its MDB policy, expressing its intention to downplay its contributions to international financial organizations.[20] On the other hand, the administration took a high-profile policy stance within the bank, hammering away at an ideological commitment to private-sector lending, graduating borrowers, Basic Human Needs, and policy dialogue. This policy line hit the ADB especially hard in the mid-1980s because the policy was pushed by a young, hard-hitting, abrasive American executive director.

The strong ideological justification for American policy positions bothered the Japanese greatly. They believed the approach naïve and overly rigid, ignoring the diversity among Asian nations and their development stages and patterns. For example, they found it difficult to support an across-the-board application of the emphasis on private-sector support, especially in countries lacking a significant or strong private-sector. Others basically questioned the U.S. development strategy, pointedly noting that Asia "is not Latin America. . . Latin America followed U.S. [development] philosophy, and it has become the world's baggage [*sekai no nimotsu*]."[21]

The Japanese were also hesitant in the application of conditionality to ADB loans and policy dialogue, which exerted pressure on recipient nations to follow bank policy dictates as a condition for loans. They prefer to avoid conditionality and policy dialogue in bilateral aid as well, citing opposition to interference in domestic affairs and respect for Asian sensitivity toward Japanese presence and influence. In the ADB, the rationale for softening conditionality is the preference for the "Asian way" of policy consultation and consensus rather than policy dictation based on political criteria.

The Japanese were also concerned by the ensuing personality as well as policy clash between the American director and President Fujioka, who also possessed a strong personality and policy convictions. These clashes began to affect the internal morale and operations of the bank, which forced the Japanese to greater involvement and decisiveness.

The Japanese response to American assertiveness took the form of (1) an increased financial commitment to the bank, leading to the desire for greater vote strength, while accepting American policy positions in principle; (2) a personnel policy designed both to placate the United States by selecting a new, less confrontational president and to raise its voice on the Board of Directors by dispatching of a new type of executive director—Finance Ministry officials who began to speak out on policy issues and counter some of the perceived excesses of the American director and policy; and (3) an inclination to side with Asian members against perceived American excesses, provided that Japan's positions did not provoke serious friction with the United States.[22]

Japan has exhibited greater self-confidence and a clearer direction in the bank. It engages in political activism to pursue its national interests in Asia, to preserve tranquility in the bank and both to support and to moderate America's political and ideological agenda. At a minimum, the ADB provides a nonpolitical facade for the increased politicization of Japan's ADB and Asia policy.

The European Bank for Reconstruction and Development

While one can detect agenda-setting initiatives in Japan's policies toward the ADB (and the Houston summit), Tokyo adopted a decidedly more low-key, supportive approach on East European issues, befitting its peripheral role in the EBRD's founding process. However, Japan's participation in EBRD negotiations thrust it into the most explicitly political role of any of its MDB relations.

The Japanese are apparently pursuing closer ties with the Europe through the use of three multilateral channels:

—The Conference on Security and Cooperation in Europe (CSCE). All European nations (plus the Vatican and with the exception of Albania) and the United States and Canada created CSCE in Helsinki in 1975. With the collapse of the East European bloc and the Warsaw Pact, some voices are advocating a new security arrangement centered on CSCE rather than on NATO.[23] Japan has voiced a wish to become an observer at CSCE gatherings, with officials expressing concern that Europeans are soliciting Japanese financial contributions for East European reconstruction without soliciting Japanese views.[24]

—The European Community. Japanese interest takes the form of concern over European unification in 1992 and its expressed interest in forging closer and deeper relations with Europe as part of a general process of forging a new international order rooted in a U.S.-Europe-Japan trilateral foundation.[25]

—The European Bank for the Reconstruction and Development (EBRD). The EBRD represents a potential new channel to shore up Japan's relations with European nations through participation in the reforms sweeping East Europe. Japan announced its decision to join in December of 1989 and is one of forty-two member nations and institutions (i.e., forty nation-states plus the European Investment Bank and the European Commission).

The EBRD is a French inspiration, attributed to Jacques Attali, financial adviser to Francois Mitterrand. Mitterrand proposed the formation of the bank at the EC meeting in Strasbourg in December of 1989. The EBRD currently has a French president (Attali), a headquarters located in London, capitalization totaling $12 billion, prospective customers (East European countries[26] and the newly created republics of the former Soviet Union), and priority sectors (60 percent private and 40 percent public sector lending). The bank opened its doors for business in May 1991.

Specifically, bank founders agreed upon an American contribution of 10 percent of total capital, followed by Britain, France, Italy, Germany, and Japan at 8.5175 percent each (approximately $1 billion each), and East Europe at 7.45 percent. The founders had also envisioned a contribution of 6 percent from a still united Soviet Union. West Europe's total share totals 51 percent, East Europe 12.4 percent and nonregional members 24.7 percent. At the April 1991 inaugural meeting, Finance Minister Hashimoto Ryūtarō pledged an additional $6.3 million for a Japan-Europe Cooperation Fund to be set up within the EBRD to support project-finding efforts and human resources development.[27]

Japan's aid to East Europe is shaped by a multilateral framework established at the 1989 Paris summit, which came to an agreement on aid to Poland and Hungary, and at the G-24 meeting prior to the Houston summit, at which agreement was reached to provide aid to the other East and Central European nations.[28] Prime Minister Kaifu journeyed to West and East Europe in January 1990 (West Germany, Britain, France, Italy, Poland, Hungary) and pledged financial, technical and food assistance to Hungary and Poland, totaling nearly $2 billion,[29] and has since pledged further aid to other East European nations (Czechoslovakia, Bulgaria, Yugoslavia) that began to dissolve in late 1991 and early 1992.

Japan's major concern in the negotiations that resulted in the signing of the May 1990 EBRD accord focused on aid to Gorbachev's Soviet Union, a preview of the Japanese position at the July Houston summit. During negotiations, the Japanese followed the American lead in opposing Soviet aid, supporting Washington's aid preconditions: arms cuts and reduction in Soviet aid to Cuba, items later reiterated at Houston. Japan focused especially on the massive amounts required by the Soviets, fearing diminution of aid available for East Europe (and Third World nations).

Japan's concern about Soviet aid surfaced forcefully at the Houston summit following the signing of the EBRD Charter. The French and West Germans in particular pressured summit participants to approve massive aid to the Soviet Union (estimated at $15–20 billion at the time). While the United States expressed hestitation, Japan expressed adamant opposition.[30] Its opposition took the form of support for U.S. insistence on the need for Soviet implementation of economic and political reforms and reduction of military spending and aid to Cuba. But Japan especially emphasized doubts about Soviet "management, technique, and know-how."[31] Foreign Minister Nakayama Taro insisted that aid to the Soviet Union "would be no more than money down the drain." And Japan added its own strong concern over the unsettled Northern Territories issue, muted during EBRD negotiations. Japan managed for the first time to get summit participants openly to endorse Japan's claim to the Kurile islands in the joint communique.

Ultimately, primarily because of American pressure and despite Japanese opposition, bank founders compromised on aid to the USSR: The Soviets would be allowed to borrow, but only up to the amount equivalent to their contribution for the first three years. A change in borrowing status after three years would require the support of 85 percent of Board of Director votes, which would give the United States (10 percent) and Japan (8.5 percent) combined a veto.

Japanese hesitation on Soviet aid survived the 1991 dissolution of the Soviet Union into Russia, under Boris Yeltsin, and the Commonwealth of Independent States. In fact, the growing instability and uncertainty resulting from decentralization reinforced Japan's lack of confidence in Russian management capabilities. Japan did pledge $2.6 billion in credits and humanitarian aid, but this figure amounts to only 3 percent of total pledges by Western donors, and Japan has been extremely slow in distributing this aid. Tokyo insisted that it had nearly reached its limits on aid at the forty-seven nation conference on Commonwealth aid coordination hosted by the United States in January 1992.[33]

Japan places great significance on participation in East European reform as a prime example of its fulfillment of an international responsibility. A Foreign Ministry official is quoted as saying, "We hope future historians will say Mr. Kaifu's trip to West Berlin and East and West Europe was our first move in meeting the real challenge of our global role."[34]

Notably, while Japan downplays its political objectives in the ADB and Asia, Kaifu stressed Japan's commitment to a political role in East Europe: "I am convinced that Japan. . . as a leading member of the industrialized democracies is expected to play a major role not only economically but also politically." Japan, he added, is "ready to positively support democratization of Eastern Europe and help them bring about a new order."[35]

Of course, Japan has little choice but to play a political role if it wishes to join the EBRD. The EBRD is the first multilateral development bank to explicitly state and require adherence to political-ideological principles and policies. The bank's creation is "a political decision of the first order. . . to construct a joint destiny for Europe," according to its first president.[36] Specifically, the bank's recipient nations must (1) adhere to the rule of law, (2) respect human rights, (3) introduce a multiparty political system, (4) hold free and fair elections, and (5) develop market-oriented economies.[37]

Japanese participation thus requires a departure from their policies toward other MDBs because of the explicitly political objectives of the institution. The appeal for Japan of MDBs is the ostensibly nonpolitical nature of loan decisions. MDBs are, in fact, highly political institutions that often make decisions based on the political agendas of their donor members, but the Japanese prefer this to remain implicit. The facade of the nonpolitical nature of MDBs is shattered in the EBRD, which explicitly links aid to internal reforms: democratization, political pluralism, market economy, and human rights. Thus Kaifu in Europe specified an a priori political condition for Japanese assistance: "Democracy, freedom and a market economy must be the framework for *any country* offered assistance"[38]—a condition never before applied explicitly to any Japanese Third World bilateral loan or grant, or to any multilateral subscription or contribution.

Japan's use of political criteria for supporting aid to East Europe and for opposing aid to the Soviet Union/Commonwealth goes against the grain of the traditional diplomacy of separating politics from economics. To some extent, the EBRD seems to constitute the most visible break from a basic assumption of the Yoshida diplomacy.

Multilateral Diplomacy: Assessment

As we move from the ADB to the EBRD, the politicization of Japan's multilateral diplomacy becomes increasingly more explicit—politicization under a nonpolitical umbrella in the ADB and the formal, explicit incorporation of political principles and conditions in the EBRD. What clues to understanding Japan's multilateral diplomacy emerge from this look at these two multilateral institutions?

1. Japan's venture into international politics will take it into new arenas, requiring greater knowledge, clarity, and integration of policy objectives and marshaling of diplomatic tools. But Japan's adjustment to this policy thrust has not been smooth, exposing contradictions in policy implementation.

Prime Minister Kaifu's statement that democracy, freedom, and a market economy must serve as the framework for economic aid policy undermines a fundamental characteristic of Japan's ODA policy since its inception in the 1950s. The Japanese have consistently downplayed, denied, or camouflaged political-strategic aid objectives, professing adherence to noninterference in a nation's domestic affairs and even citing this principle as the most attractive feature to recipient nations. How are we to assess East European aid— an exception to the rule or a basic revision of aid policy principles and objectives?

There are some suggestions that politicization may become the rule. The 1991 white paper on aid advocates the inclusion of political dialogue and ideological criteria in making loan decisions,[39] and in April, Kaifu suggested that aid policy take into account the recipient nation's military spending, arms sales and nuclear weapons policies.[40] The criticism of Japan's economic support for Saddam Hussein's Iraq prior to the 1991 U.S.-UN military action triggered the call for political criteria and conditionality. However, if Japan does adopt overt political and ideological criteria in its aid policy, the foundation and model for the policy will be found in East Europe. Such a significant change would reflect what one might call the "East Europeanization" of Japan's overall aid policy. It is by no means clear at present whether Japan will decide to follow this course, but the open advocacy of the option is significant given the aversion in Japan to overt politicization of aid policy.

On multilateral aid in particular, the Japanese argue that multilateral institutions are, by nature, nonpolitical, and thus Japan does not pursue political objectives through MDBs. And yet the EBRD is unique in that it is the first MDB that explicitly justifies the political objectives of its loans. In fact, political criteria are written into its charter, and aid will be denied unless recipients can demonstrate a commitment to democratization, economic liberalization, and human rights. This is the type of conditionality that Japanese multilateral aid policy has officially rejected, accounting for the hesitancy in the ADB on policy dialogue and conditionality. If Japan devises a general political rationale for aid through the European Bank, how can it deny its relevance for the Asian (or any other) multilateral development bank?[41]

On aid to China, in the ADB Japan initially supported the cessation of bank loans after Tiananmen and continued to support the American position against resumption, based largely on human rights criteria. However, in West Europe and at Houston, Kaifu presented arguments that could justify a reversal of the ADB's loan freeze as well as the lifting of bilateral aid sanctions, including domestic political and economic ramifications and some human rights progress.

On aid to Russia and the Commonwealth of Independent States, a question might be asked why Japan would support aid to a totalitarian, brutal, insular regime in Beijing whose commitment to democratization is, at best, questionable, while denying it to a Commonwealth currently making historic efforts to liberalize and democratize its politics and economy, an effort that has tremendous implications for a new world order. This rationale also lies at the heart of the justification for massive and rapid aid to East Europe. If East Europe should be encouraged on the road to democratization, market economies, pluralism, and human rights, why shouldn't the same rationale justify aid to the Commonwealth and continued abstinence on aid to China? Why should the Russians be punished for efforts in line with Western interests and the Chinese rewarded for authoritarian obstinence?

Our cases starkly expose the politicization of diplomacy in the absence of deep-seated political principles that guide overall Japanese diplomacy. Japan's pragmatism has sheltered it from having to devise rationales that could be applied consistently to all regions. The problem is now coming home to roost. We are thus treated to the spectacle of high-level Japanese officials attempting to apply a political aid policy formula designed for East Europe to its aid policy toward China. Ironically, in the 1980s, Japanese aid officials had pointed to China as the prime evidence that Japanese aid policy was nonpolitical. But now, Japanese are insisting on democratic political, free-market economic, and human rights reforms as a precondition for aid. "I strongly expect China to make more efforts to continue reforms and open-door policies," Kaifu told Sun Pinghua, chairperson of the China-Japan Friendship Association. On another occasion, he told Chinese representatives that they must stop jamming the Voice of America and institute educational reforms as well as promote democratization. Kaifu also dispatched high-level Foreign Ministry officials and Liberal Democratic party politicians to convey the same message to China.[42] In the past, the Japanese would have clearly hesitated in presenting political demands as a precondition for its economic aid—especially to China.

2. Despite the rhetoric of political leadership in East Europe, Japan remains tied to Asia. Of all MDBs, Japan is most active in the ADB. It is intimately involved in the rule-making, agenda-setting, and operational aspects of the bank's functions. It made an attempt at preeminence in the 1980s, and the ADB serves as a convenient conduit for its active Asia policy. Japanese policy makers consistently cite a deep emotional as well as policy commitment to the ADB, a commitment lacking in relations with other MDBs.

In EBRD negotiations and at Houston, Japan's concern for Asia was always close to policy makers' minds. At Houston, Japan made clear that it saw itself as a voice for developing nations, especially those in the Asian Pacific region, against the overconcentration on East European and Soviet issues.[43] It was through Japan's efforts that the summit communiqué recognized political and human rights advances in Asia and not just Europe, specifically in Mongolia, Nepal, and the Philippines, and even an acknowledgment of some improvements in China. On issues that Japan pursued actively, other than a wish to keep Asia on the global agenda, these were all close to home: neighboring China and the Northern Territories.

Even in EBRD negotiations, Asia is an underlying concern. The Japanese do fear some slippage of aid from the Third World to East Europe. Japan took pains to assure Asians that this would not happen in Tokyo: As a Foreign Ministry official asserted, "To live up to world expectations, Japan will boost assistance to Europe, Latin America and the Middle East. Some Asian nations seem to fear they will get a thinner slice of the aid pie because of this, but the fact is that the pie will surely grow."[44] In other words, Japan will discharge its global responsibilities without sacrificing Asia.

In fact, during his European trip, Kaifu justified Japan's participation in East European affairs in part on its importance for Asia: "The moves toward reform in East Europe will affect not only the European scene but the basic structure of the current international order as well and thus will have a significant impact on the stabilization of the Asia-Pacific situation."[45] After his return from Houston, he reiterated, "By not just extending funds, Japan's positive cooperation in ways such as personnel, technology and cultural exchanges will directly contribute to peace and stability not only in Europe, but also in Asia, the Pacific region and the world."[46]

Japan reiterated its commitment to the ADB and the Asian region at the April 1991 ADB Board meeting. Finance Minister Hashimoto announced Japan's intention to increase financial contributions to the ADB, pledging not to neglect Asia after Japan's pledges to the EBRD, which would open its doors for business in May, and the Inter-American Development Bank, which had met for the first time in Japan in April.[47]

3. Beyond Asia, Japanese diplomacy seems to be played out increasingly in a multilateral, and especially a trilateral, framework. Japan hesitates on making unilateral moves. In the ADB, Japan stepped back from its attempt at preeminence through an increase in vote shares when confronted by U.S. and some Asian resistence. On the other hand, Japan's attempt at preeminence can also be interpreted as an effort to move beyond the bilateral U.S.-Japanese partnership in the bank.

On China, Japan had been testing the waters in Europe and the United States since the 1989 Paris summit, when Japan succeeded in forestalling joint sanctions against Beijing.[48] During his January 1990 visit to Europe, Kaifu suggested to West German Chancellor Helmut Kohl that the West should not isolate China and he specifically suggested a trilateral framework for the resumption of aid to Beijing.[49] Kaifu acquired President George Bush's tacit understanding for resumption of aid just prior to the Houston summit.

On East European aid, Japan has fashioned its aid programs within the context of the trilaterally fashioned Paris summit and G-24 framework for East European assistance, and Japan's policy toward the Russian states clearly reveals efforts to place issues in a multilateral context. Japan lifted the Northern Territories issue from the bilateral to the multilateral level in Houston. In early December 1990, the Japanese reversed their official policy on Soviet aid, dropping the a priori condition of a settlement of the Northern Territories issue. However, Japan's aid package at that time totalled only $20 million for medical assistance to victims of the Chernobyl nuclear accident, $7.7 million for emergency food and medical supplies, and $100 million in Export Import Bank credits for emergency food relief. Notably, the Japanese stressed the humanitarian nature of this aid and packaged some of it as multilateral rather than bilateral (through the World Health Organization and Red Cross).[50]

What Japan apparently envisions is a role that entails serving as Asia's representative to trilateral partners and as the trilateral coalition's representative in Asia. This implies a Japanese version of global burden sharing or division of labor, with Japan taking responsibility for Asia and other trilateral members taking responsibility for "their" regions. As a Foreign Ministry official states, "The top priority Japan gives to Asia will n⸍ ⸍er change. Japan is an Asian country and best placed to help fellow Asians among the G-7. France is mostly helping its former African colonies, and half of U.S. aid goes to Egypt and Israel."[51] If we follow this logic, Britain would take responsibility for their Commonwealth nations, France and especially Germany will take the lead in East Europe (and for Russian aid), and the United States can take charge of Latin America (e.g., regional stability, debt relief, and the war on drugs).

Kaifu's strong stand on China thus becomes understandable as an effort to serve as an intermediary between China and the West. While representing China in the ADB, at Houston, and in Europe, Japan carried the trilateral message to Beijing: Japan "will communicate to the Chinese the opinion around the world that China must proceed with reform. . . . As a member of the Asian community, we will do our best to promote cooperation with China."[52]

And if Japan does envision a trilateral management of international affairs, its involvement in distant East Europe becomes even more understandable. Greater involvement in European political affairs would strengthen what Japan feels to be the weak link in its trilateral relationship. There is no question that the Japanese-U.S. link, despite its friction, constitutes the strongest of the three legs of the trilateral relationship. The active participation in the EBRD can serve as one means of strengthening that Japan-Europe leg.

4. Japan's relations with the United States in multilateral forums reveal a complex picture of supporter and challenger but not free rider, to use Inoguchi's terminology.[53] Japan remains basically wedded to an American policy framework. It shows few signs of moving toward a pax Nipponica. However, Japanese policies increasingly reflect greater independence; policies are not simply dictated in Washington.

In the ADB, Japan's relations with Washington pose a difficult balancing act. Tokyo's activities reveal shifts between equal partner (the traditional relationship during the first decade and a half), mild challenger (especially over vote shares and moderating some U.S. positions in the 1980s), and supporter (especially on issues since the Special Capital Increase, the departure of President Fujioka, and the advent of the Bush administration).

In EBRD negotiations (and at Houston), Japan's opposition to Soviet aid originated in Tokyo. Japan's position often seems more hardline than the American opposition, which has shown signs of softening since Houston. Japan made it clear that the only condition under which it would support Soviet aid is the threat of Japanese isolation resulting from standing alone on the issue against all other G-7 nations. Although Japan echoed American arguments, its own national interests dictated policy, namely, the Northern Territories, the fear of overextension of donor nation resources in a Soviet quagmire (i.e., a general feeling that the Soviets may be unable to effectively manage their economic reforms and foreign aid), and concerns about continued Soviet military strength and presence in the Asia Pacific region, including Vietnam.

Japan is now responding to the need of a newly formed Russian Commonwealth States for aid, but it is the last, and the most unenthusiastic, among the Western donors to do so. Gorbachev left Japan in April 1991 without any commitment of Japanese economic aid,[54] and Tokyo adamantly opposed Gorbachev's participation in the 1991 London summit. Kaifu refused to consider large-scale aid and insisted that Gorbachev be invited separately from the summit and refrain from discussing economic aid.[55] And the new Miyazawa cabinet has yet to announce any new initiative in Commonwealth aid. To the contrary, Japan continues to exhibit greater hesitation than any of the prospective donors, including the United States.[56]

On aid to East Europe, the Japanese proved more enthusiastic initially than a United States that was concerned with its own financial difficulties. Kaifu's initiative responded primarily to European requests for Japanese involvement, and to requests from East European nations themselves, especially Poland. A Foreign Ministry official insists, "This time, we made the decision to come to East Europe on our own, including the aid packages."[57] And friction has flared already between Japan and the United States. Tokyo bitterly opposed Washington's forgiveness of Poland's (and Egypt's) debt in April 1991, and even threatened to cancel aid previously pledged by Kaifu. The issue involved differences of opinion concerning the most effective debt-resolution strategy, and the best political strategy for encouraging internal reforms.[58] This clash reflects the evolution of a Japanese development and debt strategy, pursued in the ADB and World Bank, one that reflects some differences with U.S. approaches.

Tokyo realized full well that it would receive considerable criticism from the U.S. Congress and much of the world on its resumption of Chinese aid. The Japanese have been stung by European criticism of the unwillingness of Japan to support greater liberalization in the Soviet Union while pushing for aid to a brutal Chinese government, and by American criticism of a perceived rush to Chinese markets while ignoring human rights violations. To placate critics, the Japanese have engaged in high-level attempts at persuading China to improve its human rights record, and aid distribution seems moderated by concern over concrete human rights advances in China. Japan has also untied its aid to Beijing. But Japan persisted on its own policy course and has taken special pains to stress the independent nature of its China policy. Prime Minister Uno justified Japan's soft response toward sanctions on China, in part, by stating that Japan cannot blindly follow U.S. policy.[59]

In sum, U.S.-Japanese relations have grown increasingly complex within (and without) multilateral forums, revealing an emerging role somewhere between dutiful supporter and mild challenger.

Conclusion

The recent activism and politicization of ADB and EBRD policies reflect changes in Japan's overall MDB policy during the 1980s. Tokyo's activities are less low key and more high profile, and it has not avoided the kind of politicial maneuvering it would have shunned in the 1960s and 1970s. In MDB policy, at least, Japan has taken a small but significant step away from the value-neutral, "separation of politics from economics" approach of the Yoshida Doctrine. Tokyo's policy is showing signs of increased involvement, breadth, and complexity. However, two questions remain unanswered: Why do we see this activism in MDBs in particular, and what does Japan ultimately seek from this new activism?

There are numerous explanations for MDB activism, including MDB policy as a reflection of a general diplomatic activism. But MDBs are more than just a reflection of overall foreign policy activism. They are also a reason for that activism; the form is also the cause. MDBs encourage and induce Japan toward proactivism, making initiative taking more inviting and easier. As these case studies show, MDBs provide an inviting forum for activism in numerous ways:

—MDBs allow policy articulation and serve as conduits for national policies. The ADB serves as Japan's sounding board and policy tool for its Asia policy and debt strategy, while the EBRD forms a new component in its policy toward Europe.

—MDBs legitimize controversial policies, helping Japan to share the risks and the blame. The ADB provided a nonpolitical cloak and the Houston summit a multilateral cover for the controversial resumption of aid to China, while the EBRD can soften domestic criticism of aid to the states of the former Soviet Union in the absence of a settlement of the Northern Territories issue.

—MDBs allow Japan to fulfill international responsibilities as a nonmilitary power. Neither the ADB nor EBRD requires Japan to contribute military aid. They require only financial assistance, personnel, technical assistance, and moral support.

—MDBs enhance national resources. Japan may be the largest creditor nation, but it is still plagued by large national budget deficits. The ADB and EBRD can, therefore, pool member nations' resouces and provide more bang for the buck/yen.

—MDBs compensate for Japan's diplomatic shortcomings. Japan may be an Asian nation, but the ADB fills the many gaps in policy makers' knowledge about Asian development problems. And Japanese remain fairly uninformed about East European languages, cultures, and economic and social conditions. The EBRD can help fill this gap.

—MDBs allow globalization without sacrificing Asia. Through a global division of labor and burden sharing, Japan can remain the predominant supporter of Asia's bank while playing a subordinate but supportive role in Europe, thus fulfilling both international as well as regional responsibilities.

—MDBs allow greater independence within an American policy framework. Both case studies reveal that Japan remains basically supportive of, but not necessarily subordinate to, American policy interests. Japan seems increasingly willing to follow its own course, whether challenging the U.S. through a vote share increase in the ADB or through moving ahead of Washington in opposing Russian aid and favoring Chinese aid.

—MDBs enhance national prestige. The ADB and EBRD have a demonstration effect, where Japan can demonstrate that it is a good regional and world citizen. There is no question that MDBs in general are attractive to Japan because of their ability to heighten the nation's stature.

The question remains: For what purpose? What is Japan attempting to accomplish through political activism in these multilateral organizations? We know the method and form to be multilateral, but what is the "big picture"? The following composite picture of Japanese themes and objectives emerges from our case studies.

Japan fears the flux and instability that have arisen from the momentous changes in the world community during the 1980s and early 1990s, triggered by a perceived decline of pax Americana, the demise of the pax Sovietica bloc, and the threat of Third World insolvency and conflict. Japan perceives these changes in the international environment more as potential dangers than opportunities. However, Japan does not possess an alternative answer to the flux in world affairs. It lacks its own vision of a new order. Therefore, Japan works toward the maintenance of stability in the absence of a new post–Cold War order.

Specifically, Japan seems to work on the basic assumption that national stability forms the basis for regional stability, which in turn contributes to global stability. National stability depends on economic development and growth, which brings about political and social stability. Thus, assistance to foster successful economic reforms in unstable countries is essential. This assumption underlies Tokyo's strong feelings on aid to China and East Europe, designed to foster the domestic stability which serves as the prerequisite for regional and, in an interdependent world, global stability.

In the absence of a new world order, the most effective manner of fostering global stability involves a trilateral collective management coalition comprised of the advanced industrialized nations and the utilization of existing (and, if appropriate, new) multilateral institutions. Trilateralism is made necessary by American economic and military decline and made possible by the rise of Asia, led by Japan, and West Europe, led by Germany. Together, they can forge a working relationship in which Europe and Japan will basically shore up America's decreased ability to be the world's policeman and banker and cushion the disintegration of the Soviets' ability to play a similar role in its East European bloc. Trilateralism in the 1990s is, therefore, a response to the decline of the two superpowers and the resurgence of the two new middle powers, Japan and West Europe.

As for multilateral organizations, many of them did serve as the pillars of the postwar world order. In the current system, these permanent or semipermanent institutions serve as relatively stable anchors amid the flux. In the future, they may serve as the building blocks for trilateralism and a new "post–Cold War" world order since they are in the vortex of current efforts to fashion a possible new order, albeit in piecemeal fashion. These institutions have become basic pillars of an emerging international order, whether MDB efforts in debt strategy, GATT efforts to restructure the international trading system, or the resurgence of the UN peacekeeping role. Japan can thus take a lead role in bolstering the financial foundation of these institutions and their operations, compensating for the unwillingness or inability of U.S. and European donors to increase their contributions because of "aid fatigue." This would entail a larger voice in the management of these agencies, commensurate with Japan's financial contributions. The Japanese have stepped up their contributions to these organizations and are attempting to increase their presence and weight in MDBs, including the ADB.

How would trilateralism and multilateralism work? The Japanese seem to envision a functional and regional burden sharing and division of labor. Functionally, the United States would continue to focus especially on the security dimension globally, while West Europe and Japan would play a support role in their regions and globally, with Japan's contribution limited to self-defense, support for American troops in Japan, and a commitment to nonmilitary support roles and resources outside national territory. The United States would continue to take the lead in international economic issues, although here West Europe and Japan would play more of an equal partner role, occasionally taking selective initiatives. Japan considers itself extremely well-situated to play these roles, given its nonmilitary national strengths (economic, financial, technological, and human resources), especially in the field of economic aid. Japan's aid policy was understandably the centerpiece of its diplomatic efforts in our case studies.

Regionally, Japan would take the lead in providing economic assistance to Asia, with the United States and Europe in a support capacity. Tokyo can increase its involvement in other Third World regions by assuming, in turn, a support role for trilateral partners in "their" regions—the United States in Latin America, France in Africa, Britain in the Commonwealth nations. West Europe, with American support, can be expected to take the initiative in support of the reform efforts in Russian states, with Japan providing only lukewarm support. In East and Central Europe, the United States and Japan can play a joint support role for West Europe's "takeover" of responsibility from the Soviets for the region's democratization and liberalization process. The addition of East Europe and possibly the Commonwealth of Independent States to its foreign aid policy roster represents a significant expansion of Japan's concept of great power regional responsibilities.

Multilateral organizations are an extension of Japan's regional burden-sharing approach to international responsibilities. Since Japan considers its global political reach limited beyond Asia, its growing weight in multilateral institutions provides opportunities to participate indirectly and directly in a global agenda-setting and rule-making role. They compensate for its lack of knowledge, confidence, and experience in the international politics of non-Asian corners of the world, and they supplement Japan's nonmilitary diplomatic resources.

If these institutions play a central role in Japan's effort to globalize its diplomacy through agenda-setting and rule-making efforts, then the critical questions remain: What is on Japan's political agenda, and what political rules does it want to make? Unfortunately, the ultimate objectives of Japan's politicized multilateral diplomacy remain unclear, other than stability and enhancement of national prestige. It is true that Japanese diplomacy has increasingly sounded political and ideological themes. Yet judging from these case studies, the incorporation and integration of these themes in Japan's foreign policy are still suspect. The Japanese voice these concerns loudly in East Europe, where their influence is weakest and most indirect, and remain relatively silent in the ADB, where their influence is considerable and direct. They appear extremely lenient toward neighboring China, where these principles are struggling, with great difficulty, to take hold and survive. On the other hand, they seem cold and unsupportive toward republics of the former Soviet Union currently struggling, with great difficulty, to move in this direction. All of this yields a picture of Japanese political activism in the absence of a strong commitment to basic political principles.

Japan seems caught between its preference for the comfortable world of pax Americana and fear of the uncertain post–Cold War world ahead. Neither now appears stable, propelling Japan into a difficult adjustment period, a challenging rite of passage. The new diplomatic activism, and its policy inconsistencies, reflect Japan's attempt to cope with the momentous changes in the international system, and MDB policy is one component of this effort to match a newly emerging world with a new diplomacy. MDB policy thus reflects the flux, ambiguities, and inconsistencies characteristic of a world and policy yet to be stabilized. On the other hand, multilateral organizations provide the Japanese with an opportunity to experiment with and learn from greater diplomatic activism and politicization. And if, as most observers assert, the Japanese have much to learn, they need to start somewhere. Perhaps multilateral development banks like the ADB and EBRD is that somewhere.

Notes

1.   For a taste of this debate in English, see Kenneth B. Pyle, "Japan, the World, and the Twenty-first Century," in Takeshi Inoguchi and Daniel I. Okimoto, eds., *The Political Economy of Japan.* Vol. 2: *The Changing International Context* (Stanford: Stanford

University Press, 1988); Yasusuke Murakami and Yutaka Kosai, *Japan in the Global Community: Its Role and Contribution On the Eve of the 21st Century* (Tokyo: Tokyo University Press, 1986); and Takeshi Inoguchi, "Four Japanese Scenarios for the Future," *International Affairs* 65 (Winter 1988/89): 15–28. For some recent Japanese sources, see Amaya Naohiro, *Saraba chonin kokka* (Tokyo: PHP Kenkyujo, 1990) and *Nihon wa doko e iku no ka* (Tokyo: PHP Kenkyujo, 1988); Inoguchi Kuniko, *Posuto-Haken shisutemu to Nihon no sentaku* (Tokyo: Chikuma Shobo, 1987); Suzuki Masatoshi, *Saiken koku Nihon no yukue* (Tokyo: Chuo Keizai Sha, 1988); Watanabe Shoichi, *Nihon no seiki no yomikata* (Tokyo: PHP Kenkyujo, 1989); Takeda Tatsuo, *Nihon no gaiko; Sekkyoku gaiko no joken* (Tokyo: Simul Shuppankai, 1990); Sangyosho Tsusho, *Nihon no sentaku; 'Nyu gurobarizumu' e no koken to 'shin-sangyo bunka kokka' no sentaku* (Tokyo: Tsusho Sangyo Chosakai, 1988); Yashichi Ohata and Sadao Tamura, *Nihon no kokusai tekio-ryoku* (Tokyo: Yuhikaku, 1989).

2. She was appointed in December 1990. See *New York Times*, December 20, 1990.

3. Sadako Ogata, "Shifting Power Relations in Multilateral Development Banks," *The Journal of International Studies* (January 1989): 19.

4. Horiuchi Toshihiro, *Sekai keizai o doo kaeru ka; Nihon no kokusai kinyu senryaku* (Tokyo: TBS Buritanika, 1988), pp. 241–45.

5. Ryokichi Hirono, "Japan's Leadership Role in Multilateral Development Institutions," in Shafiqul Islam ed., *Yen For Development; Japanese Foreign Aid and the Politics of Burden-Sharing* (New York: Council on Foreign Relations, 1991), p. 172.

6. Tadashi Saito, "Japan's Role in Multilateral Financial Organizations," *JEI Report* (February 22, 1991), p. 1.

7. For Japan-ADB relations from the founding process to 1982, see Dennis T. Yasutomo, *Japan and the Asian Development Bank* (New York: Praeger Special Studies, 1983). General studies of the ADB's founding and early years include Po-Wen Huang, Jr., *The Asian Development Bank: Diplomacy and Development in Asia* (New York: Vantage Press, 1975); R. Krishnamurti, *ADB —The Seeding Days* (Manila: ADB Printing Section, 1977); Watanabe Takeshi, *Ajia kaigin sosai nikki* (Tokyo: Nihon Keizai Shimbunsha, 1973). For a recent study critical of Japan's influence over ADB agricultural policy, see Robert Wihtol, *Asian Development Bank and Rural Development* (New York: St. Martin's Press, 1988).

8. For a more detailed study of the evolution of activism in Japan's ADB policy in the 1980s, see Dennis T. Yasutomo, "Japan and the Asian Development Bank: Multilateral Aid Policy in Transition," in Bruce Koppel and Robert M. Orr, Jr., eds., *Power and Politics in Japan's Aid Policy* (forthcoming). For a general overview of developments in the ADB in the 1980s, see the study commissioned by the bank by Dick Wilson, *A Bank for Half the World; The Story of the Asian Development Bank, 1966–1986* (Manila: Asian Development Bank, 1987).

9. For a discussion of these debt plans, see Terutomo Ozawa, *Recycling Japan's Surpluses for Developing Countries* (Paris: OECD, 1989); Hiroshi Okuma, "Japan in the World: The Capital Recycling Programme," *Trocaire Development Review 1988*: 69–83; and Ministry of Foreign Affairs, *Japan's Official Development Assistance 1989* (Tokyo: Association for Promotion of International Cooperation, 1990), p. 43.

10. See Yasutomo, "Multilateral Aid Policy," for details on Japan's debt relief policy.

11. From Okurasho, Kokusai Kinyu Kyoku, "Dai-22-kai Ajia kaihatsu ginko (ADB) nenji sokai supesharu shotai chosokkai haifu shiryo," May 1989; *Asian Development Bank Annual Report, 1988;* and "ADB Invites Students to Apply for Scholarships," *ADB News Release,* April 3, 1989.

12. See Yasutomo, "Multilateral Aid Policy."

13. See Fujioka Masao, *Ajia kaigin sosai nikki: Manira e no sato-gaeri* (Tokyo: Toyo Keizai Shimposha, 1986).

14. Interviews with Foreign Ministry officials, June–July, 1990.

15. Matsuura Koichiro, *Enjo gaiko no saizensen de kangaeta koto* (Tokyo: Kokusai Kyoryoku Suishin Kyokai, 1990), p. 234.

16. Joe MacDonald, "Muto Says Relations Should Be Based on Cooperation in International Aid," Associated Press, December 7, 1990.

17. *JEI Report*, October 19, 1990, p. 11.

18. See K. V. Kesavan, "Japan and the Tiananmen Square Incident," *Asian Survey*, 30 (July 1990), 671–77.

19. *JEI Report*, May 3, 1991, p. 10.

20. United States, Department of the Treasury, United States, *Participation in the Multilateral Banks in the 1980s* (Washington, D.C.: U.S. Government Printing Office, 1982).

21. Ministry of Finance official, August 1989.

22. For a detailed treatment of the U.S.-Japanese relationship in the ADB in the late 1980s and into 1990, see Yasutomo, "Multilateral Aid Policy."

23. See Craig R. Whitney, "The Legacy of Helsinki," *New York Times,* November 19, 1990.

24. See *Asahi shimbun,* May 23 and July 1, 1990, for comments from Japanese officials.

25. See Takekazu Kuriyama, "New Directions For Japanese Foreign Policy in the Changing World of the 1990s; Making Active Contributions to the Creation of a New International Order" (mimeo, n.d.).

26. East and West Germany were unified in October of 1990, and, therefore, "East Germany" will not borrow from the EBRD.

27. *JEI Report,* April 26, 1991, pp. 10–12.

28. The exception was Romania, which had engaged in a brutal suppression of political protestors.

29. For details of Kaifu's aid package to Poland and Hungary, see Barbara Wanner, "Japan's Relations With the 'Soviet Bloc,' " *JEI Report,* January 19, 1990.

30. See Jerry Norton, "Japan Flexes Muscles at G-7 Summit," Reuters, July 11, 1990, and "Land of Harmony Sounds Different Note at G-7," Reuters, July 8, 1990.

31. Mark O'Neil, "Japan Reluctant to Join Soviet Aid Package," Reuters, July 3, 1990.

32. *Japan Times,* July 21, 1990.

33. See Thomas L. Friedman, "Bush to Press Congress to approve $645 Million for

Ex-Soviet Lands," *New York Times,* January 23, 1992, and "Ex-Soviet Lands to Get Swift Aid," *New York Times,* January 24, 1992.

34. Eugene Moosa, "Japan Takes Timid First Step in Global Role," Reuters, January 17, 1990.

35. Eugene Moosa, "Kaifu Says Japan Should Play Political Role," Reuters, January 9, 1990.

36. "East and West Meet To Sign Statutes of New Development Bank," Reuters, May 29, 1990.

37. Stephen Jukes, "West Flexes Economic Muscle to Force Changes in Eastern Europe," Reuters, July 17, 1990.

38. Tom Minehart, "Japan Will Be Strong Actor on New World Stage," Associated Press, February 6, 1990. Emphasis added.

39. See *Japan Times Weekly,* April 15–24, 1990.

40. Kyodo News Service, April 16, 1991.

41. For a discussion of some other problems posed by Japanese participation in the EBRD, see Tanaka Yoshiaki, "To-O Enjo de Tamesareru Nihon no Enjo Gaiko," *Ekonomisuto,* February 20, 1990, pp. 50–53. Tanaka mentions the need to shift aid policy focus from the Third World to East Europe, the geographical expansion of aid, and technical problems (e.g., the high per capita income of East European nations relative to developing nations).

42. See Tom Minehart, "Japan Will Be Strong Actor on New World Stage," Associated Press, February 6, 1990; Mark O'Neil, "Japan Differs with Summit Partners on China," Reuters, July 5, 1990; and "Japanese Official Arrives in China to Resume Lending," Reuters, July 16, 1990.

43. Jerry Norton, "Japan Sees Itself As A Balancing Voice at G-7," Reuters, July 5, 1990.

44. Masaru Sato, "Japan Says Aid to East Europe Won't Be at Asia's Expense," Reuters, July 6, 1990.

45. Ferdinand Protzman, "$1 Billion Plan for Poland and Hungary," *New York Times,* January 10, 1990.

46. "Prime Minister Kaifu Leaves on European Tour," Associated Press, August 1, 1990.

47. *JEI Report,* May 3, 1991, p. 9.

48. See Kesavan, "Tiananmen Square," pp. 669–81.

49. Eugene Moosa, "Japan's Aid to East Europe is Global Responsibility," Reuter, January 9, 1990; and Barbara Wanner, "Japan's Relationship With the 'Soviet Bloc,' " *JEI Report,* January 19, 1990, p. 4.

50. *New York Times,* December 5, 1990, and *Japan Times Weekly,* December 24–30, 1990.

51. Masaru Sato, "Japan Says Aid to East Europe Won't Be at Asia's Expense," Reuter, July 6, 1990.

52. David Briscoe, "Japan Will Lend to China, Push Reforms," Associated Press, November 9, 1990.

53. Takashi Inoguchi, "Japan's Images and Options: Not a Challenger, But a Supporter," *The Journal of Japanese Studies* 12 (Winter 1986): 95–119.

54. *New York Times*, April 22, 1991, and *Japan Times Weekly,* April 29–May 5, 1991.

55. *Japan Times Weekly,* June 1–23, 1991.

56. Germany has pledged 57 percent of total aid pledges, with other Europeans pledging over 21 percent. The United States has pledged 6.5 percent. See *New York Times*, January 23, 1992. The Bush administration hosted the January 1992 aid coordination conference in Washington, D.C., with Europeans viewing it "as a gimmick, basically designed to allow the United States to take credit for leading the global aid effort for the commonwealth without having to spend any more of its own money." See *New York Times*, January 24, 1992.

57. Eugene Moosa, "Japan Takes Timid First Step in Global Role," Reuters, January 17, 1990.

58. *New York Times*, April 14, 1991.

59. Kesavan, "Tiananmen Square," p. 672.

Chapter 16
Japan's UN Diplomacy:
Sources of Passivism and Activism

Yasuhiro Ueki

In the ever-shifting dynamics of world politics, the United Nations, as the only global political institution, has weathered a variety of stormy challenges for nearly five decades. For Japan, the United Nations has been a source of its own legitimacy in the community of nations, which had been lost in the aftermath of World War II. This legitimacy was accorded in 1956 when Japan was admitted to the world body after several earlier attempts had been prevented by the Soviet veto in the Security Council. Japan then set out to enhance its international status through the United Nations by supporting its goals and principles. Yet it did so without clearly defining the objectives and strategies of its UN diplomacy. Japan's postwar foreign policy framework, often referred to as the Yoshida doctrine, which relied heavily on the United States for security, maintained minimum self-defense capabilities, and pursued economic gains, was too successful to discard. Contrary to the official pronouncement of "UN centrism" or "UN-centered diplomacy," Japanese diplomacy has been far from UN centric. Japan's attitude toward the United Nations has been ambivalent and pragmatic, generally consistent with its minimalist approach to the conduct of foreign policy and the pursuit of national interests.

Japan's economic success, however, has begun to undermine this long-sustained foreign policy framework and has created expectations both in and out of Japan for a larger but still undefined international role and responsibility "commensurate with Japan's economic power." At the same time, the United Nations itself has grown in importance and usefulness, following the significant changes in East-West relations in the late 1980s. Support for a strengthened United Nations has become identical, in the eyes of many Japanese, with Japan's increased international role and responsibilities. Japan thus has begun to contribute more actively to the UN's peacekeeping and peacemaking activities by providing both financial support and personnel. This emerging political activism, however, has been tempered by several constraints. Foremost among them is Japan's extreme wariness toward the use of force and involvement in realpolitik, which often manifests itself in the domestic political, legal, and constitutional debate. This wariness derives in large part from the legacy of its past militarism and the "constitutional pacifism" of the postwar era. Political activism and moves to strengthen military itself are also viewed with suspicion by its Asian neighbors. Other constraints include Japan's mixed identity as Western and Asian and the inadequacy of universal values upon which Japan can structure its UN diplomacy in a coherent manner; constraints of the alliance structure that often create a dichotomy of dependence and autonomy; the fact that Japan is not a permanent member of the UN Security Council; and the limitations of the United Nations itself.

After briefly reviewing the characteristics of Japan's approach to the United Nations, this chapter looks into the sources of passivism and activism in Japan's UN diplomacy and examines the ongoing friction between these two imperatives as a measure of Japan's political realism. Japan's attempts to break out of the self-imposed constraints and to play a more activist role in international affairs by identifying its activism with the resurgent United Nations are examined in some detail in the light of recent developments.

UN Centrism?

There were strong elements of idealism in Japan's initial attitude toward the United Nations, even though they never altered the basic orientation of Japanese foreign policy. The official pronouncement of UN centrism, coined soon after Japan was admitted to the United Nations, epitomized this idealism.

In his opening address to the Parliament on February 4, 1957, Foreign Minister Kishi Nobusuke stated that the basic policy of Japanese diplomacy should be to contribute to world peace and prosperity, "centered around the United Nations," Kishi added that Japan should collaborate with other democracies, while maintaining its position as a member of Asia.[1] These three policies were to constitute the basic principles of Japanese diplomacy.

Right after Japan was admitted to the United Nations, there was a high degree of enthusiasm and support for the organization. The world body had enjoyed high esteem among the population, which longed for Japan to be accepted again as a legitimate member of the international community. UN membership symbolized the recovery of this legitimacy in the eyes of the world. Japan therefore had to uphold this international recognition through its UN diplomacy. There was also a strong idealistic sentiment that Japan's security should be protected by the United Nations so as not to repeat the past militarism. A strong United Nations, disarmament, and accommodation of the aspirations for self-determination were viewed as desirable for world peace and stability, which in turn was seen as necessary to help Japan devote its energies to economic growth with minimal defense and involvement in realpolitik.

UN centrism, however, was never clearly defined. It was not meant to make the United Nations the central focus or arena of Japanese diplomacy, nor was it meant to structure Japanese diplomacy on the basis of the views and actions taken by the United Nations. It meant nothing more than the generality that Japan should conduct its diplomacy in line with the objectives and principles of the United Nations, which are basically identical with those of the Japanese Constitution. By stressing UN centrism, the Japanese government at that time wanted to deflect domestic criticism that it leaned too one-sidedly toward the United States, compromising its independent foreign policy.[2] The United Nations was also used to justify the 1951 U.S.-Japanese security treaty, which was presented as a temporary arrangement until such time that the United Nations could provide Japan with the necessary security protection through its collective security system.[3] There was strong domestic opposition to the security link with the United States because of provisions of the Japanese Constitution that renounce war as a means of settling international disputes, prohibit the existence of armed forces, and reject the right of collective defense. The government justified the security treaty in terms of the right of self-defense as far as Japan alone was concerned.

Soon, it became clear that UN centrism was untenable even at the rhetorical level. Even when the expression was coined, Japanese officials stressed that the United Nations had not succeeded in providing for collective security despite its lofty goals, and that Japan's priority relationships with the Western democracies therefore were fully justified.[4] The idea of UN centrism also was logically inconsistent in that the United Nations was by design a forum to discuss divisive issues and intractable problems. How could Japan follow the UN-centered policy when the United Nations itself was often marked by differences between East and West or the West and developing countries on political, disarmament, economic, decolonization, and human rights issues? The United Nations itself was divided and could be successful in reconciling those divisive issues only in limited circumstances. Consequently, Japan's national, bilateral, and regional interests had to take precedence over undefined multilateral interests. By 1961, Japan was openly stating that its primary policy goal was to maintain its status as a member of the Western democracies.[5]

UN centrism was thus relegated to occasionally used rhetoric but it was never quite dead. It came back in the official jargon late in 1990 when, following the Persian Gulf crisis, the United Nations became the center of attention in world politics. The Japanese government again stressed the "UN-centered" orientation of Japanese diplomacy to buttress Japan's tangible support for the collective action authorized by the United Nations against Iraq. With the United Nations still enjoying popular esteem and support among the Japanese people, expression of strong support for the organization thus became a political asset. Yet the Japanese government was more concerned about how to cope with bilateral pressure from the United States than it was with bolstering its diplomacy through the United Nations. The predominance of bilateral concerns warped the national debate.

Unlike the 1950s when the government used UN centrism essentially as a way to justify its minimalist foreign and security policy, in a sense to shield Japan from realpolitik with idealism, this time it attempted to use UN centrism to bring Japan out of its self-imposed constraints to face the realpolitik of the outside world. It was, however, caught in the web of constitutional pacifism and could not fully overcome the enormous hesitation Japanese still felt toward facing the reality of world politics.

Japan's Mixed Identity

The fact that Japan is located in Asia and yet aligned with the West has given rise to Japan's mixed identity at the United Nations This is both an asset and a liability for Japan.

Japan's mixed identity is reflected in the UN's electoral process. Member states are elected from regional groupings to the various committees of the General Assembly, to the Economic and Social Council and its subsidiary commissions, as well as to the Security Council for its nonpermanent seats. The principle of geographical distribution is designed to give balanced representation to all regions and to prevent the domination of numerically overwhelming regions or group of countries. Japan is elected from the Asian group because of its location, even though it considers itself part of the West.

Given its unique position in Asia, Japan has desired to play a moderating role between opposing forces at the United Nations. In his speech to the UN General Assembly on December 18, 1956, when Japan was admitted to the body, Foreign Minister Shigemitsu Mamoru stated that Japan, whose politics, economy, and culture had been influenced by both the American-European and Asian civilizations over the past century, could become a "bridge" between East and West.[6] In this case, East was meant the developing countries of Asia and Africa. East and West were later replaced by North and South.

In some cases, Japan did find itself able to play a useful role in a middle position. For instance, when Laos brought to the United Nations a complaint about military incursions from Vietnam in 1959, the Security Council, in response to a suggestion of the United States supported by the United Kingdom and France, set up a subcommittee to investigate the complaint. The Soviet Union opposed this fact-finding mission, creating the possibility of a East-West showdown, but the Soviet move was overridden on procedural grounds. Japan was at that time a nonpermanent member of the Security Council and was asked to head the four-country subcommittee, which subsequently submitted its findings to the Council. This helped defuse the potential conflict between Vietnam and Laos and even a larger conflict between East and West.[7]

Japan's mixed identity, however, was soon found to be a mixed blessing. It often became a liability for Japan when issues were divisive. For instance, when the

Soviet Union presented a draft declaration on decolonization in 1960, the developing countries of Asia and Africa formulated their own text in which they demanded an immediate and unconditional granting of independence to colonial countries and peoples. Such a radical demand was not acceptable to Western colonial powers, which preferred a more gradual process of decolonization. Japan had felt special sympathy for demands for decolonization. Japan had been the only Asian country that successfully resisted the Western colonial powers, and it also embarked on its own unrestrained colonial expansion, which had led it into the Pacific War and final defeat. From its own experience Japan understood the force of nationalism and wished to support the moves for decolonization in a manner in which the aspiration for self-determination would not turn into an aggressive nationalism. For this reason, Japan joined the drafting committee, and attempted to soften the radical language contained in the draft text of the declaration and forge a compromise acceptable to both the West and the developing countries. Its efforts were not successful, however. The balance of power in the General Assembly had shifted in favor of developing countries. Japan in the end did not cosponsor the General Assembly resolution on the declaration proposed by the developing countries, even though it voted for the resolution.[8]

Human rights are another area where Japan often has found itself in an awkward position. Human rights constitute a pillar of democracy in the West, whereas they are often perceived as a threat to the regimes in power in nondemocratic countries and where they are hence ignored or suppressed. The tension created by these opposing positions on human rights acutely manifests itself in the United Nations where the accused often accuses the accuser of interference in domestic affairs. Japan in general upholds the concept and principles of human rights, but its approach to specific human rights issues has been selective and country-specific.[9] This is particularly true in Asia, where Japan feels that it better understands the situation in which many of its Asian neighbors find themselves with regard to human rights. Japan is also extremely sensitive to the potential accusation of domestic interference by Asian countries in case Japan takes an accusatory stance similar to the Western countries on human rights against them. Japanese criticism of other Asian countries because of their human rights policies provokes suspicion of Japanese motives and leads to fears of a revival of prewar Japanese expansionism. It also can affect Japan's self-perception that it represents the interests of Asian countries before the Western nations. Thus, Japan often gives priority to maintaining good political relations with other Asian nations over the protection of individual human rights. This is reflected in Japanese voting behavior in the human rights area. In many contentious cases it simply abstains.[10]

The difficulty of coming down on one side or another of an issue because of Japan's mixed identity also can be seen in cases involving South Africa's apartheid, Middle East and Palestinian questions since the oil shock of 1973, and the

North-South confrontation of the 1970s over the debate for a new international economic order. Japan's mixed identity often leads to the "politics of abstention."

Dichotomy of Dependence and Autonomy

Japan is often torn between a sense of dependence on the Western democracies, particularly the United States, and a desire for autonomy. The United Nations is one forum where all issues can be brought in and debated. Therefore, this dichotomy frequently manifests itself there.

In the area of security and disarmament, for instance, Japan's dependence on the United States for its own security makes it hard for it to disagree with the United States on fundamental security and disarmament questions. Japan's security policy is based on the U.S.-Japan Security Treaty, the implicit U.S. nuclear umbrella and a minimum-level self-defense capability. Japan is aware that its security rests on an overall East-West balance of power and on nuclear deterrence. Consequently, on disarmament issues Japan tends to vote affirmative at the United Nations when the United States votes affirmative; it tends to abstain when the United States votes negative.[11]

On the other hand, Japan has a special sense of mission, as the only country against which nuclear weapons were used, to appeal for nuclear disarmament. Japan's three nonnuclear principles—not to possess, not to manufacture, and not to introduce nuclear weapons into Japan—as well as its acceptance of the nuclear nonproliferation treaty are a reflection of this sentiment. The "Peace Constitution," which renounces war as a means of settling international disputes, is another basis from which to promote disarmament. Given the domestic and external constraints on Japan's military power, a general reduction in conventional arms is also viewed as enhancing the security of Japan. These factors provide Japan with an opportunity to pursue a more autonomous disarmament policy. This is manifest in Japan's active support for a comprehensive nuclear test ban and its vote against an arms race in outer space, which stray from the U.S. position. In 1984, for instance, the Japanese foreign minister proposed a step-by-step approach to a comprehensive nuclear test ban at the Conference on Disarmament, a multilateral negotiating body serviced by the United Nations. The proposal was aimed at gradually reducing the threshold of nuclear test explosions under effective verification, eventually leading to zero.[12] Japan was eager to assist in improving the verification mechanisms.

The ambivalent position in which Japan often finds itself on disarmament issues at the United Nations sometimes leads to inconsistent attitudes. In 1961, for example, Japan voted for the declaration on nonuse of nuclear weapons on moral grounds. From the following year, however, Japan has either abstained or voted against similar resolutions on this question, stressing the importance of nuclear deterrence.[13] In this case, Japan's innate desire to ban nuclear weapons was tempered by considerations of realpolitik. Japan's lack of military power and its security dependence on the United States limit the extent to which Japan can maneuver or show its own autonomous position on disarmament issues at the United Nations.

A similar dichotomy can be seen in other political as well as economic areas, but a more subtle case appeared in the mid-1980s when Japan proposed the establishment of an expert group to review the administrative and financial efficiency of the United Nations.[14] At that time, U.S. support for the United Nations was at an all-time low. The Japanese proposal was an offshoot of the domestic attempt to reform the administrative functioning of its own government bureaucracy. But given the harsh U.S. criticism of the United Nation and the resultant withholding of its financial contributions, Japan's action was timely and aimed at preserving the viability of the United Nations, which was being jeopardized by its serious financial crisis.

Japan's eagerness to reform the United Nations, however, met a cool response from the developing countries because any attempt to reduce the activities of the organization was perceived as a scheme to reduce its contribution to their development and hence their influence there. The United States initially did not make active efforts to reform the United Nations, thus putting Japan at the forefront of the reform movement and giving an impression that Japan was acting as a pawn of the United States. Japan took pains to dispel this impression and stressed its intention to strengthen the United Nations through reform. The United States was more interested in regaining fiscal and hence political control of the budgetary process of the body, which had fallen into the hands of the developing countries. Strengthening the United Nations was not to the liking of the United States; regaining political influence was. Thus there were major differences in the American and Japanese approaches to the reform issue.

Nevertheless, Japan did share some goals with the United States and other major financial contributors. One major goal was to streamline the UN bureaucracy by preventing uncontrolled bloating of the budget and personnel. Another was to introduce a consensus rule to budget making. A timeframe was introduced for the implementation of the reform. A 15 percent personnel cut was agreed upon. There were some differences among the Western, Eastern, and developing countries on the consensus budget making, but a common understanding on the need for consensus in the main budget-making body was reached. Thus, the major goals were met. It should be noted, however, that behind the success lay the threat as well as the actual withholding of U.S. contributions, which created a serious financial crisis for the United Nations as well as a sense of urgency. Japan did not follow the U.S. lead for budgetary and political reasons. It did not wish to be seen as a UN basher behind the United States when none of the Western countries resorted to such forcible means and the developing countries were critical of the U.S. tactics. Nonetheless, Japan did rely on the U.S.

threat to push through the reform, thereby demonstrating the limited political maneuverability of Japanese multilateral diplomacy at the United Nations.

Emerging Political Activism at the United Nations

The impetus for getting out of the closed circuit of the postwar foreign policy framework appeared in the mid-1980s when Japan began to participate gradually in agenda setting in international affairs, primarily through the summits of the Western democracies. There was a gradual realization that with the relative decline of the United States, Japan must play a more active international role, particularly in the economic area, to preserve a system that had been beneficial to Japan. Moreover, though the idea of translating economic power into the tools of raw power politics is still resisted in Japan, since such outright use of power evokes the memories of the past militarism, Japan began to recognize that the reality of world politics demands Japan's involvement. No economic power had been able to remain aloof from the dynamics of world politics in the past, and Japanese slowly came to accept the fact that their economic power had an unavoidable political dimension. There was also some incipient sense of nationalism and a national sense of pride.

Japan's emerging activism coincided with the changes taking place in East-West relations, which helped boost the role of the United Nations in resolving regional conflicts. The United Nations came out of the serious political and financial crisis of the mid-1980s and began scoring some successes, starting with the Geneva Accords over Afghanistan in May 1988, which were the culmination of several years of negotiation through the United Nations. This was followed by an end to the Iran-Iraq War, which came about with the assistance of the UN secretary-general in August 1988 on the basis of a Security Council resolution adopted the previous month. Namibia and others were to follow.

The United Nations in a sense provides a convenient cover under which Japan can justify its more assertive political role and which helps quiet the lingering domestic opposition to Japan getting involved in real politique. It also helps dispel fears of its Asian neighbors about Japan's assertive political behavior. Thus, Japan found a marriage of convenience with the United Nations.

Japan's active political involvement in the United Nations in the 1980s began out of self-interest and somewhat fortuitously. During the Iran-Iraq War, Japan, as a country friendly to both Iran and Iraq, attempted to assist the UN's efforts to end the war.[15] As early as August 1983, Japan sent its Foreign Minister to both countries, seeking an early resolution of the war. In the following year, it urged a ban on the use of chemical weapons and safe navigation in the gulf.

When the Iran-Iraq War escalated into a "tanker war" in the gulf in the mid-1980s, seriously threatening the shipping and safety of crews, Japan faced pressure to contribute to keeping the sea lanes open since Japan was the single largest beneficiary of open sea lanes in the area. Japan depends on oil from the Middle East, which comes through the gulf, for about 70 percent of its oil consumption. Prime Minister Nakasone Yasuhiro even floated the idea of sending Japanese minesweepers to the gulf to assist the fleet sent by the United States and some other Western countries, arguing that this was permissible under the Japanese Constitution.[16] He later retracted the proposal in the face of stiff domestic opposition to anything involving sending Japanese armed forces overseas. In the end, as the price for Japanese contribution, Japan decided to contribute $20 million to the UN's good offices mission in Afghanistan and later as seed money to set up the UN Military Observer Group in Afghanistan and Pakistan (UNMOGAP) to monitor the implementation of the Geneva Accords on Afghanistan. The rest was to be used for other UN peacekeeping activities.

The next move came in mid-1988 when the Japanese government decided to second a middle-level Foreign Ministry official to UNMOGAP based in Kabur and Islamabad. The government's decision to pick a Foreign Ministry official rather than some other person in or out of the government was clearly intended to show its political nature. Soon afterward, the government seconded another Foreign Ministry official to the UN Iran-Iraq Military Observer Group (UNIIMOG) which was established to monitor the ceasefire between Iran and Iraq. By this time, "not only money but also sweat" became the emerging consensus for international contribution in Japan.

Namibia was the next opportunity to expand Japan's political role through the United Nations. This time, the operation involved large-scale electoral supervision, the first such activity of the United Nations, along with the traditional type of peacekeeping. The UN Transition Assistance Group (UNTAG) began its operation in April 1989. The Japanese government seconded twenty-seven electoral supervisors, many of whom were selected from local governments and had some electoral supervisory experience in their localities. All the non-Foreign Ministry officials were seconded to the Foreign Ministry, which had the mandate to send its people overseas for diplomatic functions. In this way, the government could skirt any potential legal or political problems. The successful Namibia mission was followed by much smaller-scale electoral observer missions in Nicaragua and Haiti in 1989–90.

Throughout these well-publicized test cases, the government was extremely nervous about the well-being of the Japanese personnel. Any loss of life might have created negative domestic repercussions, preventing similar political participation in UN activities in the future. "Money and sweat were all right but not blood" was still the mentality of the Japanese toward Japan's political involvement in the international arena, even through the United Nations.

Gulf Crisis and UN Peace Cooperation Corps

The dispatch of civilian personnel to UN peacemaking and electoral missions did not create serious domestic political or legal problems. However, a more contentious case appeared with the gulf crisis in August 1990. It provoked a national debate on Japan's role and responsibilities in the post–Cold War world and through it a debate on Japan's relationship with the United Nations and its collective security system. The debate exposed several severe constraints in expanding Japan's activism through the United Nations, while also spawning a possibility of more active participation in UN peacekeeping operations.

The gulf crisis provoked by the Iraqi invasion of Kuwait on August 2, 1990, precipitated a massive military buildup by a multinational coalition led by the United States and joined by Arab and other forces in the gulf region. In response to the Iraqi actions, the UN Security Council adopted a series of twelve binding resolutions, which included the condemnation of the Iraqi actions, a demand for immediate and unconditional withdrawal of Iraqi forces from Kuwait, economic sanctions, a demand for immediate release of foreign detainees/hostages, implicit sanction for the use of force to enforce economic sanctions, reparations, an air embargo, and eventually an authorization to use force. The crisis tested Japan's political readiness to implement the binding resolutions of the United Nations, legal limits under the Japanese Constitution for sending military personnel, transport, and equipment for this purpose, as well as key political relations with the United States.

The world reaction to Iraq's invasion and occupation of Kuwait revolved around the UN Security Council. The United States immediately deployed its military forces by claiming the right of collective defense under article 51 of the UN Charter. Other states, including some Arab states, followed suit, thereby constituting multinational forces. Not being a member of the Security Council, Japan was in no position to participate in the decision making or agenda setting of the council. Substantive agreements were initially hammered out among the five permanent members of the council before they were submitted to the other nonpermanent council members. Japan probably would not have been able to influence the course of the Security Council even if it had been a council member. Nevertheless, the fact that Japan was not a member made the issue seem not as immediate for Japan as otherwise.

The sense of urgency of the matter rather came from the United States. Even though Japan swiftly condemned the Iraqi actions, following the lead of the United States and the European Community, its verbal condemnation was not accompanied by more forcible actions, except the freezing of Kuwaiti assets in Japan. The United States, by contrast, immediately imposed a total ban on imports and exports with Iraq and with occupied Kuwait. It issued a joint communiqué with the Soviet Union on August 3, appealing to other countries to join them by taking punitive measures against Iraq.

Japan was first planning to wait for the UN Security Council to recommend punitive measures before taking its own.[17] However, U.S. pressure on Japan mounted quickly, first with a letter from U.S. congressional members on August 3 and then a personal phone call from President Bush to Prime Minister Kaifu Toshiki on August 4 seeking Japanese cooperation against Iraq. In this case, Japan looked to the European Community for its lead as it was in a similar position as a major importer of oil from the gulf region. The EC decided to impose economic sanctions on August 4. The following day Japan announced a ban on trade including oil, suspension of loans, investment, and other commercial deals, as well as a freeze on economic cooperation projects.

U.S. pressure continued through formal and informal channels, prodding Japan to provide more tangible support to the multinational forces, some form of direct assistance to the defense of the gulf states, and additional financial support to pay for the expenses of the American forces in Japan as well as to purchase U.S.-made advanced weaponry, particularly AWACS.[18] Thus, bilateral concerns became as much a preoccupation for Japan as the central issue of how to respond to an aggression through the United Nations. The confusion over the nature of the multinational forces, as opposed to the more clearly defined UN peacekeeping forces, compounded the difficulty of explaining to the Japanese people what the Japanese contribution to the multinational efforts against Iraq was about. The government's attempt to cloak Japan's contribution to the multinational forces, which was akin to exercising the right of collective defense, in a U.N. mantle of collective security was another source of confusion.

The ensuing debate centered around financial, nonmilitary, and noncombatant military contributions. The financial issue was essentially the question of how much to pay. Prime Minister Kaifu pledged on August 29 to contribute a total of $1 billion, some being used to charter flights for displaced persons, some for the multinational forces, and some for the "front-line" states suffering adverse economic consequences.[19] This amount was clearly not enough to satisfy the United States, which continued to mass troops in the gulf area. With U.S. prodding, Japan pledged an additional $3 billion on September 14. Of this amount, $1 billion was to be used to finance the multinational forces and $2 billion for economic assistance to the front-line states.

Japan's nonmilitary contribution, which was announced on August 29, involved transport of food, water, and medicine as well as sending of up to 100 medical experts. Questions were raised in Japan whether the transport of troops and war materiel could be allowed. The government was quick to deny any intention to send troops or war materiel since they could be considered direct participation in war. Even the transport of nonmilitary materiel became an issue when the union representing ship crews initially refused to go to a potential war zone. The government also found it difficult to find doctors who were willing to serve in a conflict area. Nevertheless, the nonmilitary contribution was in the end considered the minimum Japan could do to assist the multinational efforts.

The question of a military contribution raised longstanding constitutional, legal, and political questions. Article 9 of the Japanese Constitution renounces war as well as use or threat of use of force as a means of settling international disputes. Armed forces are prohibited for this reason, and the right of belligerency disavowed. The government interprets the article as permitting Japan the right of self-defense, and therefore the right to have "self-defense" forces, but not the right of collective defense. However, the multinational forces were deployed by exercising the right of collective defense, under the UN Charter. Moreover, the Self-Defense Forces (SDF) Act restricts the permissible range of actions the forces can take. It allows only forcible actions to defend against external aggression, mobilization in case of large-scale internal civil disorder, and disaster relief activities. It has no provisions which allow the dispatch of forces overseas.

The government first considered enacting a new law that would permit a nonmilitary contribution without getting involved in this longstanding constitutional and other legal debate. Prime Minister Kaifu announced on August 29 his intention to enact "UN Peace Cooperation Bill" within the confines of the constitution. This set the tone of debate. By stressing "within the confines of the constitution," the government imposed on itself the outer limits of its contribution. And yet, it soon became clear that the large part of the gulf operation would be military-related, requiring the know-how of the military.

The proposed bill, which was made public on September 27, attempted to kill two birds with one stone, that is, to respond to the immediate need to assist the multinational forces as well as provide for more general involvement in UN peacekeeping activities.[20] The bill provided for the establishment of a UN Peace Cooperation Corps that would assist the United Nations as well as UN member or other states in the maintenance of international peace and security on the basis of UN resolutions or to "ensure effective implementation of UN resolutions". The corps would participate in the observation of ceasefires, guidance or supervision of administration of a transitional government, electoral supervision, and the management, transport, communications, maintenance and repair of equipment, medical and health care relief activities, and postwar recovery. Logistical support was intended for the multinational forces. The question of military involvement was left ambiguous for further debate as there was a serious difference of views on this matter in and out of the government.

The debate over SDF participation centered around several issues: outright dispatch of the SDF including minesweepers, the issue of command authority, the status of SDF personnel, and whether SDF personnel could carry small arms. The idea of dispatching armed SDF forces overseas, which was advocated by some conservative politicians of the ruling Liberal Democratic party, was discarded in the face of strong opposition in and out of government as well as of some fears expressed by Asian neighbors. Nevertheless, the Defense Agency and the SDF attempted to retain their command authority for effective participation in logistical or nonmilitary duties. This was resisted by the Foreign Ministry in particular, which feared losing civilian control. After a hard-fought battle, the command authority was placed under the prime minister alone. Some compromises were also reached within the government and the LDP on other issues, allowing movements of SDF personnel as "units," permitting SDF personnel to retain their original status even though they would engage themselves only in the duties of the new Corps, and allowing them to carry small arms for defensive purposes.

These propositions were hard to sell, however. The ruling LDP controlled only the Lower House of the Diet but not the Upper House. It required the approval of both Houses for the proposed bill to be enacted into a law. Among the opposition parties, the Democratic Socialist party supported the dispatch of the SDF as part of the new corps. The Komeito (Clean Government party) initially accepted nonmilitary duties of the SDF personnel. Both the Socialist party and the Communist party strongly opposed any participation of active duty SDF personnel in the corps. The Komeito, which was considered holding a swing vote in the Upper House, gradually hardened its position as there appeared some future possibilities of the SDF getting involved in the use of force even within the framework of the United Nations, and began opposing the proposed corps mainly composed of the SDF. Even some leading members of the ruling LDP began suggesting some changes in the proposed bill.

Meanwhile, as the UN Security Council adopted a series of resolutions against Iraq, there appeared a possibility of creating a UN force. Even though a number of ambiguities remained in creating such a force under the enforcement provisions of the UN Charter, the urgency of the crisis certainly made it plausible. This raised another testy question for Japan as to whether it should or how it could participate in UN enforcement actions.

Fearful of possible isolation and international criticisms for not being able to contribute enough in such an event, the Foreign Ministry tried a new line of thought on this issue by introducing the concept of collective security, as opposed to collective defense. It argued that in the event a UN force was created for the maintenance of international peace and security, it would be within the limits of the Japanese Constitution for the SDF to join such a force even if use of force was envisaged in its operation. The goal of the UN force would be identical with the goal of the Japanese Constitution.[21] The government's interpretation of the constitution in this matter up to then had been that while the constitution did not necessarily exclude the possibility of SDF participation in the UN's peacekeeping activities as long as they did not entail use of force, the SDF Act did not have any provisions allowing the SDF to engage themselves in such activities. The Foreign Ministry's line of thought went beyond this interpretation.

The Legal Bureau of the cabinet, however, expressed serious reservations about the Foreign Ministry's view. Citing the constitutional limits under article 9, it argued that the SDF could not be dispatched overseas even for the UN's collective security actions if the SDF were to be engaged in the use of force.[22] Prime Minister Kaifu initially supported the collective security argument but soon backed away from this position, sensing strong opposition to involvement in forcible actions even under UN authority.

Thus, it became clear by the end of October that the UN Peace Cooperation Bill had no chance of passage through the Diet. The bill was formally abandoned on November 8. Again fearful of international criticism for not doing anything to contribute to maintaining international peace through the United Nations, the major political parties immediately sought an alternative to the bill. The LDP, DSP, and Komeito agreed to introduce a new bill with a view to establishing a new organization able to participate in the UN's peacekeeping operations. The Socialist party supported participation in unarmed UN observer missions but opposed armed, however lightly armed, UN peacekeeping operations.

Once war broke out after the January 15, 1991, deadline, the main issue for Japan shifted to the question of how to raise the $9 billion requested by the United States to support the initial allied offensive. Another issue, which was raised even before the war, was possible dispatch of SDF aircraft to Jordan to help transport refugees and displaced persons. This question was again mired in the political and legal debate. SDF could not be mobilized even for humanitarian purposes as long as they had to go out of the self-contained boundary. When the war ended in early March, participation in the UN's possible peacekeeping operation in the gulf was again debated, only to face the same old questions, particularly the role of the SDF.

Japan stood idly when the Iraqi troops suppressed the antigovernment Kurds in the north and Shiites in the south, which provoked another international intervention, in part through the United Nations, on humanitarian grounds.

Toward limited Participation in UN Peacekeeping Operations

It was this inability to respond swiftly to the calls for more active role in the maintenance of peace and humanitarian assistance that led to further soul-searching on Japan's own place in the world. This was evident when the opposition parties, particularly the Socialist party, were set back in the local elections in April. By this time, the public mood had shifted to favor a more activist role for Japan. Support for Japanese participation in the UN's peacekeeping operations grew considerably. Against this background, the government decided at the request of Saudi Arabia to dispatch mine sweepers to the Persian Gulf.[23] Externally, Japan carefully sought understanding of its Asian neighbors that this undertaking was purely peaceful in intent, and not military. Domestically, Japan portrayed it as a postwar undertaking called for the safety of navigation through the passage vital to Japan.

Another major move was the laying of a more concrete political and legal foundation for Japanese participation in the UN's peacekeeping operations as well as in humanitarian interventions. The government submitted to the extraordinary session of the Diet in September 1991 legislation that would enable such participation, albeit on a limited scale.[24] The key aspect of the bill was SDF participation—the most contentious point that derailed the previous bill. This time around, SDF participation was basically supported by the Komeito and the Social Democratic party, the two smaller opposition parties that held the swing vote in the Upper House. The Socialist party and the Communist party, holding the view that the UN's peacekeeping operations may use force, remained opposed to dispatching the SDF even for these operations.

The government put several safeguards in the peacekeeping bill to allay the fear of possible militarism by the name of peacekeeping. The consent of the parties to the conflict was required. Once the consent disappeared or a ceasefire broke down, the Japanese peacekeeping units would be withdrawn. The type of equipment to be used in peacekeeping operations would be determined by the UN secretary-general. The prime minister would be obliged to report to the Diet when decision was made to participate in peacekeeping or humanitarian operations, or when changes were made in those operations, when those operations were completed. Only small firearms would be allowed to carry, and they would be used only in self-defense.

The role of the Diet in the safeguard process remained the most controversial. The government and most of the LDP members favored the reporting requirement, whereas the Democratic Socialists and some within LDP preferred the right of the Diet to approve or disapprove Japanese peacekeeping participation.

Consensus was thus not obtainable by the end of the extraordinary session of the Diet in October. Subsequently, the differences seemed to be narrowing. The LDP and the Komeito favored the right of the Diet to approve or disapprove "continuation" of Japanese participation in peacekeeping after two years of operation. The Democratic Socialists favored the Diet to approve or disapprove the dispatch of peacekeeping units post facto after six months. Despite the initial optimism, however, those differences did not narrow further.

With Miyazawa Kiichi, long exposed to foreign affairs, now replacing Kaifu as prime minister, the government and LDP hastened the passage of the legislation and decided to go ahead with their version of the peacekeeping bill in the resumed extraordinary session toward the end of 1991. This motion alienated the opposition parties, including the Democratic Socialists, and led to a wrangling in the Diet. The bill was passed forcibly in the Lower House. But the hard-nosed tactic of the government and LDP created a serious apprehension among the public about their intentions behind the peacekeeping rhetoric. Fearful of further backlash, the Komeito began wavering its support of the bill, which still had to pass the opposition-dominated Upper House. The loss of confidence in the bill even by the Komeito led to the demise of the bill in December.

Increasing public support for Japanese participation in UN peacekeeping operations was mired in technical arguments and political maneuvering, which revived a deep-seated apprehension about the military, whatever its role might be. It took another half a year finally to pass a new peacekeeping legislation. It contained a number of safeguards to obtain the support of the Democratic Socialists and the Komeito, including the requirement to obtain from the parties to a conflict their consent to Japanese deployment, the right to withdraw once a ceasefire is broken down, and the use of force only in self-defense. However, it met stiff resistance, particularly from the Socialists. It took considerable difficulty to overcome their parliamentary filibustering. Only then was it possible to send civilian police and military personnel to UN peacekeeping operations like the one in Cambodia.

Japan's response to the gulf crisis, the war, and its aftermath has well demonstrated some of the heavy constraints that Japan faces in dealing with realpolitik. Behind the constitutional and legal arguments against the dispatch of the SDF is the extreme wariness many Japanese feel toward getting involved in armed conflict or conflict situation. Japan's past memories and the worries of the Asian neighbors are often evoked to justify their wariness. There is also residual anxiety even among government leaders about a resurgent military. Another domestic political factor relates to the polarity of power in the Diet. The ruling LDP enjoys a majority in the Lower House, but lost its majority in the Upper House in the 1989 elections. The proposed U.N. Peace Cooperation Corps, the financial package for the gulf war, and the new peacekeeping legislation, for instance, had to pass both House to be enacted into laws. This makes the government's parliamentary maneuvering a necessity, creating an additional burden for Japan.

One positive fallout of the gulf crisis and its aftermath has been that the political value of support for the United Nations has markedly increased. The crisis created a national debate on Japan's role in the implementation of the UN resolutions as well as Japan's possible participation in the peacekeeping operations of the United Nations. The concept of UN centrism was brought back to life in an attempt to break the political and sociopsychological barrier of constitutional pacifism. The strict legal approach to the gulf crisis was politically untenable. Even though the first attempt did not succeed, the subsequent debate offered a chance to prepare the legal and political ground to increase Japan's further contribution to the United Nations, particularly its peacekeeping operations, and through it Japan's political and diplomatic status. The third attempt finally broke the logjam.

Aspiration for Greater Status: The Case of Cambodia

Despite the present domestic constraints, Japan continues to aspire to greater political status. Even though it has not yet come to grips with what it wants to do with such enhanced status, Japan views the United Nations as an appropriate conduit through which to seek a greater political role for itself.

One diplomatic activity Japan has been pursuing in an attempt to translate its aspiration into a tangible accomplishment through the United Nations involves Cambodia. Japan sees itself playing a useful role in helping solve this conflict for several reasons. First, the United Nations has become a key player in the conflict because the permanent members of the Security Council have found that their interests converge on the desire for a settlement. Cambodia, therefore, may be a case in which Japan can exercise an activist UN-centric diplomacy relatively free of domestic constraints. Second, the settlement of the Cambodian conflict will require substantial financial contributions which Japan is able to provide. This applies not only to Cambodia but also to Vietnam, an indirect party to the conflict and a country deeply in need of economic assistance. Japan is willing to respond to such needs but does not want to be simply forced to pay the bill without any say in the process. Japan also recognizes that the perception that Japan's contribution is indispensable is itself a source of political influence.

Third, Japan is one of a few countries whose hands are "clean" in Cambodia, and as such, it may be in a position to offer compromise proposals. Finally, Cambodia is in Asia, a region where Japan, as an Asian power, feels particular responsibility for contributing to maintaining peace and stability.

The movement toward a settlement of the Cambodian issue started when the major backers of the parties to the conflict, China on one hand and the Soviet Union and Vietnam on the other, began to seek an end to the conflict. The United States and some other countries also showed an active interest in bringing about a political settlement. Two formal tracks of negotiations were opened. One was the Paris Conference on Cambodia, which was first held in January 1990, cochaired by France, a former colonial power in Cambodia, and Indonesia, which maintained relatively good relations with Vietnam. Another was with the permanent members of the UN Security Council, who began to draft a comprehensive peace plan.

Japan became involved directly in the negotiating process when the Paris Conference deadlocked over several key issues, particularly the question of a ceasefire and the composition of a Supreme National Council (SNC), which was to play a central role in the transition phase. In collaboration with Thailand, which began to seek a role of its own in the Cambodian peace process by developing ties with the Hen Samrin government in Phnom Penh and with Vietnam. Japan invited the four Cambodian factions to Tokyo in June 1990 to sign a formal agreement for a ceasefire that Thailand had helped work out. This in effect opened another track of negotiations. The ceasefire agreement was symbolic in that there was no monitoring mechanism. As far as the composition of the SNC was concerned, the Hen Samrin side wanted equal representation by the two sides on the council, while the three anti–Hen Samrin factions initially wanted equal representation by all factions. In the initialed memorandum for a ceasefire that the four factions brought with them to Tokyo, the three anti–Hen Samrin factions agreed to equal representation (six representatives each) while welcoming a member to be chosen as its chairman, an implicit reference to Prince Norodom Sihanouk. Even though the Pol Pot faction hardened its position on the representation issue in Tokyo and in the end refused to join the agreement, Japan managed to have the memorandum signed by two sides.

In August 1990, the permanent members of the Security Council presented a comprehensive peace plan on Cambodia, giving the United Nations an "enhanced" role in the transition period.[25] The Supreme National Council was established in September, but in its first meeting in late December 1990 it deadlocked over such issues as the extent of UN authority in the transition period, the demobilization of armed forces, and reference to genocide during the Pol Pot regime, even though they accepted the basic framework of the Security Council peace plan. Japan saw another opportunity to get involved and offered a new proposal to the two sides in February 1991 to complement the comprehensive peace plan of the permanent five. It suggested in essence to strengthen the verification role of the UN's peacekeeping forces in each stage of demobilization and to establish a mechanism in the United Nations for the protection of human rights in Cambodia that would help prevent another genocidelike situation.[26]

Japan followed up its action through further diplomatic and ministerial contacts with China, Vietnam, and the four Cambodian factions. However, China and Vietnam, desiring accelerated rapprochement between themselves, pressured the Cambodian factions for further compromise. Consequently, agreement was reached on 70 percent reduction in armed forces at the SNC meeting in Pataya, Thailand, in August. Another deadlock was resolved on the electoral mechanism in the New York negotiations in September, paving the way to the Paris Conference on October 23 to sign the final agreement on Cambodia. Japan played an important part in it, but essentially remained on the sidelines. What facilitated further Japanese involvement in Cambodia was the appointment of a senior Japanese official to head the UN transitional Authority in Cambodia (UNTAC) and the adoption of a long-awaited peacekeeping legislation in June 1992. The appointment of Akashi Yasushi as the special representative of the UN secretary general highlighted Japan's tangible role and strong interest in furthering the political process in Cambodia. Following the enactment of a new peacekeeping legislation, Japan sent military observers and a logistical unit, along with civilian police, to Cambodia. Japan also hosted in June 1992 an international conference on Cambodian reconstruction. When the UNTAC operation ran into difficulty in obtaining the necessary cooperation from the Khmer Rouge, Japan, together with Thailand, attempted to persuade the Khmer Rouge to abide by the Paris Accords and rejoin the political process. While Japan's political influence in the Cambodian issue has been supplementary, UN involvement and commitment to the final settlement of the Cambodian issue has helped Japan get involved in the political process and hope to enhance its political status in Asia and the United Nations in the long run.

Permanent Membership of the Security Council

Japan's desire for greater political status also lies behind its desire for a permanent seat on the Security Council. That goal is all the stronger now that Japan is a major economic power and the second largest financial contributor to the United Nations. At present, Japan must run for a nonpermanent seat without any guarantee that it will win. The nonpermanent seats are not renewable consecutively. Lately, Japan runs about every five years. Once in 1978, Japan lost the election to Bangladesh, one of the poorest countries in Asia, causing a domestic uproar.[27]

Permanent membership in the Security Council brings with it several tangible benefits. Permanent members do not have to run for their seats. With their veto power, they can influence the selection of the secretary-general and occupy several top key posts. They can veto UN actions detrimental to their own political and security interests. They enjoy membership in many committees and subcommittees. They can influence UN decisions in many ways, even though their influence is not absolute. In this sense, the permanent membership is a symbol of political influence.

Japan's desire for a permanent seat is hard to realize, however. The UN Charter would have to be amended, which requires support of two-thirds of the member states, including the five permanent members of the Security Council. Such a move would inevitably invite other countries to apply for a similar status. It would also raise other questions, particularly the right of veto itself, culminating in wholesale moves for the amendment of the Charter, thereby making the Charter amendment impracticable.

One idea being promoted by some in and out of the Japanese government is to create additional permanent seats without veto power. Japan, Germany, India, Nigeria, Brazil, and Egypt are mentioned as possible candidates, taking into account the customary UN principle of geographical distribution. Italy is also interested in attaining a permanent seat. The Security Council had been expanded once in 1965 from the original twelve to fifteen, and the Charter amended accordingly.

Though not implausible, this approach may not be acceptable at this point for several reasons. Several countries who have rivalry with some of the countries mentioned as possible candidates or those countries that feel left out despite their comparable abilities may also attempt to obtain the permanent status. Too large an expansion of the Security Council membership would make the council less efficient and is hence not practicable. The permanent members have begun to form their own group in resolving conflicts. This trend began early in 1988 following the aboutface of the Soviet attitude toward the United Nations. This led to Security Council resolution 598 on ending the Iran-Iraq War and their collaborative actions on Cambodia. The gulf crisis solidified the permanent five. They therefore seem to feel that this system of decision making is functioning for now and that a new mechanism is not necessary. A serious question for Japan is whether Japan can be an effective permanent member of the council without the capability to enforce actions in the event of an aggression. The main function of the Security Council is to maintain international peace and security. Its duties may entail forcible actions, as is outlined in chapter 7 of the UN Charter. At present, Japan is not willing to use force except for the defense of Japan. Even the new peacekeeping legislation is not adequate to answer the question since it specifically prohibits the military personnel to use force or threaten use of force in carrying out their duties. The new legislation allows use of small firearms only in self-defense.

In the long run, however, Japan's permanent membership with or without veto power cannot be ruled out. With Germany unified and given the prospect for an European integration, the political map of Europe is likely to change, and with it, the question of separate permanent seats of the United Kingdom and France. If in fact the European Community emerges as a single political entity, with Germany in it, and hence gives up one permanent seat, Japan will have a perfect justification to seek a legitimate status in the Security Council. This may be a long shot, however.

A more immediate possibility emerged when the Soviet Union broke up toward the end of 1991. The legitimacy of the permanent seat of the Soviet Union was called into question. This uncertainty was answered when the eleven independent republics of the former Soviet Union agreed in Alma Ata to let the Russian Federation take over the Soviet seat. This position was not challenged by other member states of the United Nations. Japan did see a chance to raise the question of membership of the Security Council, including the permanent membership, but in the end it did not find it opportune to pursue it at this time because of the legality of the Russian succession and of the political and legal difficulties involved in hastily amending the Charter to accommodate the Japanese aspiration. Nevertheless, Japan is likely to raise the question, together with other aspirants, in the subsequent debate on the strengthening of the United Nations and in the process leading to the fiftieth anniversary of the United Nations in 1995.

It should be noted in this connection that the Japanese government feels strongly that the so-called enemy state clauses contained in the UN Charter be removed. Specifically, these refer to articles 107 and 53. Article 107 states: "Nothing in the present Charter shall invalidate or preclude action, in relation to any state which during the Second World War has been an enemy of any signatory to the present Charter, taken or authorized as a result of that war by the Governments having responsibility for such action." One significance the Japanese government attaches to this article is that Russia, the legal successor to the Soviet Union, might use it to justify their rule of the disputed Northern Islands, which occurred as a result of the Second World War. In fact, the former Soviet Union was reported to have referred to this article in bilateral negotiations in 1989 to justify the Soviet position on this issue.[28]

Article 53 authorizes enforcement action against former enemy states taken under regional arrangements or by regional agencies without the authorization of the Security Council. Even though this article has no practical meaning and is considered "dead," it still leaves room legally for military action against Japan without the UN authorization.

A more psychological aspect of this issue is that being implicitly branded an "enemy," even though this is qualified by "during the Second World War," Japan feels that it is still treated like a second-class citizen in the UN Charter. Moreover, Japan feels it helpful to have the enemy state provisions removed if it is to seek a permanent seat on the Security Council. Although these provisions do not themselves prevent Japan from pursuing such a status, they are obviously illogical and irritating to a country that is trying to enhance its role and position in the organization.

Conclusion

Over nearly a half century, the role of the United Nations for Japan has shifted from a source of legitimacy in the community of nations and a world body in which to enhance its international status to a spring board from which to persuade domestic skeptics to break out of the self-imposed constraints and to seek a more activist role in international affairs.

The gulf crisis and its aftermath provoked this change, even though the change was gradually forthcoming with the dwindling Cold War and the increasing role of the United Nations in regional conflict resolution.

The attempt to grow out of the successful and yet untenable, in the long run, foreign policy framework has met strong resistance, however. Behind this resistance is the lingering national psychology stemming from the legacy of the past. It shuns overt realpolitik and anything smacking of war or the use of force, even though in reality realpolitik considerations have been at the basis of Japanese foreign policy ever since Japan regained independence.

Constitutional, legal, and political constraints have compounded Japan's anguish. The constitution is viewed almost as sacred. The legal base for expanding Japanese contribution beyond financial and personnel is still in the making. The wartime generation, which still dominates the domestic scene in Japan, remains extremely nervous about getting involved in power politics. The lack of a majority in the Upper House is a political burden for the LDP-led government.

201100000000000000000

00

In light of these domestic constraints, Japan has been urging the United Nations to strengthen its preconflict prevention functions, particularly the use of the secretary-general's good offices and fact-finding missions of the Security Council. On some occasions, Japan did actively support these functions by getting indirectly involved in a conflict situation, such as the Iran-Iraq War, and by providing extrabudgetary money. However, this type of indirect contribution alone is not sufficient to raise Japan's political status at the United Nations. Cambodia finally offered Japan some room to get involved in the agenda-setting and negotiating processes.

Japan's mixed identity, sense of dependence and lack of coherent strategy also accentuate its passivity in UN diplomacy. As a latecomer to international politics and sapped by its militaristic past, Japan still lacks a strong internal driving force for activism in multilateral diplomacy. Japan is too preoccupied with its immediate surroundings and immediate interests to create a strategic multilateral diplomatic framework of its own. Furthermore, Japan views itself as part of a supporting cast for the international order created and maintained by the United States. The relative decline of the United States has only reinforced this perception.[29]

Nevertheless, Japan has recognized its enormous stake and responsibility in the maintenance of a peaceful and stable world. It has revived UN centrism to convince the skeptics in and out of Japan of an increasingly active role Japan should undertake in international affairs. This has so far been successful only half way. Japan's military participation in UN peacekeeping operations is being accepted domestically and by its Asian neighbors. However, Japan has skirted larger and more fundamental issues of realpolitik, such as collective security and enforcement actions to deal with aggression under chapter 7 of the UN Charter. Japan's "look at thy neighbor" attitude in this area has limited its ability and influence in UN diplomacy.

Japan's imperative for activism, particularly through the United Nations, has not yet overcome the resilient passivism still manifest in its domestic and external behavior. Ultimately, Japan's passivism and activism in its UN diplomacy are both reflections of the degree of its political realism, and this political realism, at the moment, is still in the making.

Notes

1. Toshinori Yoshikawa, "Kokuren ni okeru Nihon no Kihon Shisei," in *Kokusai seiji,* (Tokyo: Yuhikaku,1964), p. 10.
2. Shizuo Saito, *Kokusai rengo ron josetsu* (Tokyo: Shin-yudo, 1977), p. 58.
3. Gaimusho, *Waga gaiko no kinkyo* (Tokyo: Okurasho Insatsukyoku, 1958), 2 :171.
4. Ibid., 2:173.
5. See Ibid., 1961, vol.5.
6. See Shigemitsu's speech, General Assembly document A/PV.623.

7. Tamio Amou, *Takokukan gaiko ron*, (Tokyo: PMC Shuppan, 1990), pp. 439–41.

8. Ibid., p.205; Yasushi Akashi, *Kokuren biru no madokara* (From the windows of the United Nations)(Tokyo: Simul Press, 1984), pp. 208–9.

9. Sadako Ogata, *Kokuren karano shiten*, (Tokyo: Asahi Evening News, 1980), p. 113.

10. See, for example, Japan's voting behavior in the Third Committee in the forty-sixth session of the General Assembly in 1991. Of the eight recorded votes on human rights issues excluding cases relating to Iraq, Japan abstained in five and voted against in two. This contrasts with the United States, which voted against in six and abstained in one, and with India, which voted for all eight. The voting behavior of the ASEAN countries was similar to that of India.

11. See, for example, Japan's voting behavior in the First Committee, which deals with disarmament issues, in the same General Assembly session.

12. For the proposal, see *Waga gaiko no kinkyo,* 1985, vol. 29.

13. Akisato Sakurakawa, "Nihon no gunshuku gaiko," in *Kokusai seiji*, 1985,80:71–72.

14. For the general background and proceedings of the expert group, see Shizuo Saito, "Kokusai kikan ni taisuru Nihon no seisaku to kadai," in *Kokusai mondai*, no. 324 (1989):35–38.

15. Japan defined its diplomatic activities as aimed at creating an atmosphere for a peaceful resolution of the war and not at an outright mediation. See *Waga gaiko no kinkyo,* 1984, 28:46.

16. This point was reaffirmed during the gulf crisis in 1990. See Yasuhiro Nakasone, "Waga taikenteki yuji kodo ron," *Bungei shunju*, (October 1990):114.

17. *Yomiuri shimbun*, August 7, 1990. It also reported that the Ministry of International Trade and Industry advised Prime Minister Kaifu not to ban oil import hastily, but that the prime minister was leaning toward imposing such a ban. The Foreign Ministry favored a ban.

18. Ibid., August 19, 1990.

19. For further details, see ibid., August 30, 1990.

20. For the full text of the bill, see ibid., September 28, 1990.

21. Ibid., October 16, 1990.

22. They also cited Japan's letter of application for a UN membership submitted on June 16, 1951, in which Japan pledged to carry out its duties under the UN Charter "by all means at its disposal." They interpreted this phrase as meaning means permitted under the Constitution and hence no use of force.

23. Six mine-sweeping vessels were dispatched on April 26. They operated in the Persian Gulf from June to September, destroying a total of thirty-four mines, and came back to Japan on October 30.

24. For the full text of the proposed bill, see *Yomiuri shimbun*, September 9, 1991. A companion legislation was submitted to amend the 1987 Bill for Dispatch of International Emergency Assistance Corps in order to allow SDF participation in emergency assistance activities overseas. This did not create a serious controversy and was generally accepted by all the parties.

25. For the full text, see Security Council document S/21689, August 31, 1990.

26. *Asahi shimbun*, March 12, 1991.

27. For the background, see Sadako Ogata, *Kokuren karano shiten*, pp. 31–33.

28. Tamio Amou also refers to the Soviet reference to the "enemy" clause. Together with his view of this issue, see *Takokukan gaiko ron*, pp. 194–5.

29. Kuriyama Takakazu , deputy foreign minister, points out that Japanese diplomacy had been "reactive" (*'ukemi'*) under the international order supported by the United States. Now that Japan has become an important member of the advanced democracies, hence a part of this order, Japan cannot remain reactive to the order. *Gaiko Forum*, Tokyo (May 1990):16.

Index

Abe Isao, 75–76
Abe Shintaro, 23, 156*n.34*, 283, 291–92
Accession Ceremony, 76–77, 79, 81, 82–84
ADB. *See* Asian Development Bank
Advanced thermal reactor (ATR), 182
AEC. *See* Atomic Energy Commission
Afghanistan, 250, 311, 354, 355
Agency for Natural Resources and Energy
  (ANRE), 189
Agricultural issues
  fand burden sharing, 241
  decline in workers, 124–25
  foreign economic policy, 108, 112, 113, 119,
    126–27, 129
  and nuclear energy, 195
  politics and the yen, 139, 141, 143, 144
  Soviet Union, 291
  trade restrictions, 101, 117, 204
Aid programs. *See* Foreign aid; Official
  development assistance
Airline industry, 121, 322*n.25*
Akashi Yasushi, 364
Akihito, Emperor, 64, 65, 66–67, 82, 84–85,
  88–89*nn.74, 75*, 264
Akishino, Prince, 64
All-Asian Security Forum, 311, 312
All-Japan Seamen's Union, 22
Amaterasu omikami (sun goddess), 78, 82
America bashing, 251, 255
"American Challange, The" (Servan-Schreiber),
  173
Anglo-Dutch Wars (1652–54; 1665–67;
  1672–78), 224–25
ANRE. *See* Agency for Natural Resources and
  Energy
Antinuclear movement, 182, 192–94, 198
See also Nuclear weapons, nonnuclear principles
Aoki Masahiko, 163
Armacost, Michael, 20, 40*n.38*
Arms control. *See* Antinuclear movement;
  Nuclear weapons
Arms issues. *See* Military issues; Nuclear
  weapons
Asahi Glass (co.), 116
ASEAN (Association of Southeast Asian
  Nations), 103
Asian Collective Security System, 311
Asian Development Bank (ADB), 260*n.28*,
  325–30, 333–42

Aspin, Les, 33, 42*n.55*
Association of Agricultural Cooperatives. *See*
  Nokyo
Atomic energy. *See* Nuclear energy
Atomic Energy Basic law, 187
Atomic Energy Bureau, 189
Atomic Energy Commission (AEC), 185, 190
ATR. *See* Advanced thermal reactor
Attali, Jacques, 331
Australia, 213
Automobile industry
  foreign economic policy, 109, 115, 116
  multinational corporations, 160–64, 167–68,
    175
  political games, 53, 60*n.9*, 61*nn.15, 17*
Aviation. *See* Airline industry

Baker, James, 146, 151, 221
Balanced budget principle, 110
Baldrige, Malcolm, 102, 146
Bandung principles, 322*n.18*
Bangladesh, 365
Banking and finance
  foreign policy, 204
  loans to China, 320*n.3*, 328
  multilateralism, 324–33
  multinational corporations, 160–61, 174
  politics and the yen, 138–39, 147, 158*nn.61,
    63*, 159*n.76*
  and U.S.-Japanese alliance, 220
  See also Currency issues; Ministry of Finance
Bank of Japan, 105, 113, 152
Battel Memorial Institute, 163
Baucus, Max, 145
Bentsen, Lloyd, 223
Berlin Wall, 252
Board of Rituals, 62
Bonn summit (1985), 249
Bradley, Bill, 145
Brazil, 365
Bretton-Woods System, 110, 114, 115
Brezhnev, Leonid, 280, 281, 282, 289
Brzezinski, Zbigniew, 282
Buddhism, 78, 79
Bulgaria, 65
Burden sharing, 235–57
  1950s, 237–44
  1960s and 70s, 244–47
  1980s, 247–52

371

United States *(continued)*
  as Japanese ally. *See* United States-Japanese
    alliance
  and Japanese diplomacy, 3, 5, 15, 16, 36,
    38n.6, 99
  Japanese emperor visits, 65
  and Japanese yen, 139, 144, 145–46, 150–51,
    153
  and Korea, 264, 267, 272–73, 316–17
  military games, 46–48
  multilateralism, 325, 327, 329–30, 331, 337,
    338, 341, 346n.56
  multinational corporations, 160–76
  nuclear energy, 182, 196, 197
  Persian Gulf crisis, 16–17, 19–24, 26, 29,
    40n.38, 356–57
  and South Korea, 86n.20
  and Soviet Union, 48, 233, 277–78, 280, 287,
    294–95, 309, 310
  trade games, 48–54, 60n.9
  and United Nations, 353, 354, 360
United States Congress
  and Japanese alliance, 220, 222–23, 228
  and Japanese culture, 55
  and Japanese yen, 139, 145–46, 151
  Persian Gulf crisis, 20, 24
  trade issues, 51, 57–58
United States-Japanese alliance, 218–33
  burden sharing, 236–57
  current debate, 221–30
  future scenarios, 230–33
  Nakasone position, 92–93, 100–102
  recent events, 219–21
  Yoshida strategy, 92, 218–19
United States-Japan Security Treaty, 205, 206,
    216–17n.6, 222, 223, 236, 237–38, 243,
    244, 245, 256, 275, 277, 279, 292, 349,
    352
United States-Japan Systems Science and
    Technology Forum, 250
United States-Japan Trade Council, 48
Universities, 53
Uno (prime minister), 254, 338
Uno Sosuke (foreign minister), 285
Usami Takeshi, 74
Ushiba Nobuhiko, 249
USSR. *See* Commonwealth of Independent
    States; Russian Federation; Soviet Union
U.S. Strategic Defense Initiative. *See* SDI
    program
Utilities, 147–48, 181, 183–84
  See also Nuclear energy

Value-added tax, 129

Vietnam, 45, 209, 242, 248, 327, 338, 350, 363,
    364
Vietnam War, 244, 245, 246, 247, 260n.33, 311
Vladivostok Doctrine (1986), 311

Watanabe Akiyuki, 86n.20
Weisman, Steven, 80
Whaling industry, 241
Wholesale industry, 140, 155n.13
Wilson, Joe, 166, 173
Wood industry, 141
Workers
  demographics, 124–25, 144
  immigrant, 97, 105, 118
  Japanese, 111, 115
  multinational, 174
  nuclear energy, 183, 192, 195
  unions and strikes, 125–26, 136n.62
World Bank Group, 324, 325, 326

Xerox: American Samurai (Jacobsen), 165
Xerox Corporation, 165–67, 170, 172–73

Yakovlev, Aleksandr, 287, 293
Yalta Agreement (1945), 275, 280, 294
Yamaguchi Toshio, 122
Yamaichi brokerage house, 121
Yamamoto Satoru, 75
Yamamura Kōzō, 114
Yamamura Shinjirō, 147
Yanagisawa Hukuo, 155n.18
Yanayev, Gennady, 289, 313
Yano Tōru, 64, 68, 70
Yasujima Hisashi, 75
Yayoi period, 77
Yeltsin, Boris, 298, 332
Yen. *See* Currency issues
Yen-Dollar Talks (1984), 145
Yeutter, Clayton, 151
Yoshida Doctrine, 218–19, 275–76, 277, 290,
    293–94, 323, 339, 347
Yoshida Shigeru, 3, 92, 93, 99, 219, 275, 276
  and burden sharing, 239–40, 241, 242, 243,
    244
Yoshihara Hideki, 113
Yukawa Morio, 75

Zaire, 15
Zenchu (Central Union of Agricultural
    Cooperatives), 127
Zhao Ziyang, 303, 316
Zhen Shuyuan, 318
Zhou Enlai, 240, 281

STUDIES OF THE EAST ASIAN INSTITUTE
Selected Titles

The Fateful Choice: Japan's Advance into Southeast Asia, edited by James W. Morley. New York: Columbia University Press, 1980.

State and Diplomacy in Early Modern Japan, by Ronald Toby. Princeton: Princeton University Press, 1983 (hc); Stanford: Stanford University Press, 1991 (pb).

The Manner of Giving: Strategic Aid and Japanese Foreign Policy, by Dennis T. Yasutomo. New York: Free Press, 1986.

The Japanese Way of Politics, by Gerald L. Curtis. New York: Columbia University Press, 1988.

Aftermath of War: Americans and the Remaking of Japan, 1945-1952, by Howard B. Schonberger. Kent, OH: Kent State University Press, 1989.

Neighborhood Tokyo, by Theodore C. Bestor. Stanford: Stanford University Press, 1989.

Education in Japan, by Richard Rubinger and Edward Beauchamp. New York: Garland Publishing, Inc., 1989.

Financial Politics in Contemporary Japan, by Frances Rosenbluth. Ithaca: Cornell University Press, 1989.

Competitive Ties: Subcontracting in the Japanese Automotive Industry, by Michael Smitka. New York: Columbia University Press, 1991.

Explaining Economic Policy Failure: Japan and the 1969-1971 International Monetary Crisis, by Robert Angel. New York: Columbia University Press, 1991.

Driven by Growth: Political Change in the Asia-Pacific Region, edited by James W. Morley. Armonk, NY: M. E. Sharpe, 1992.

Social Mobility in Contemporary Japan, by Hiroshi Ishida. Stanford: Stanford University Press, 1993.

Japan's Foreign Policy after the Cold War: Coping with Change, Gerald L. Curtis, ed. Armonk, NY: M.E. Sharpe, 1993.

For Product Safety Concerns and Information please contact our EU
representative GPSR@taylorandfrancis.com
Taylor & Francis Verlag GmbH, Kaufingerstraße 24, 80331 München, Germany

www.ingramcontent.com/pod-product-compliance
Ingram Content Group UK Ltd.
Pitfield, Milton Keynes, MK11 3LW, UK
UKHW021427080625
459435UK00011B/187